Of the Times and Seasons
and the Delay of the Return of Christ

Kevin Straub

World rights reserved. This book or any portion thereof may not be copied or reproduced in any form or manner whatever, except as provided by law, without the written permission of the publisher, except by a reviewer who may quote brief passages in a review.

The author assumes full responsibility for the accuracy of all facts and quotations as cited in this book. The opinions expressed in this book are the author's personal views and interpretations, and do not necessarily reflect those of the publisher.

This book is provided with the understanding that the publisher is not engaged in giving spiritual, legal, medical, or other professional advice. If authoritative advice is needed, the reader should seek the counsel of a competent professional.

Unless otherwise indicated, all Scripture quotations are taken from the King James Version. Italics indicate words added in the translation that are not in the original text. Other versions used are: *God's Word Translation* (GWT). GOD'S WORD is a copyrighted work of God's Word to the Nations. Quotations are used by permission. Copyright 1995 by God's Word to the Nations. All rights reserved. *The Living Bible* (TLB). Copyright ©1971 by Tyndale House Publishers, Wheaton, Illinois 60187. All rights reserved. *Holy Bible, New Living Translation*, copyright © 1996, 2004, 2015 by Tyndale House Foundation. Used by permission of Tyndale House Publishers Inc., Carol Stream, Illinois 60188. All rights reserved. The *New King James Version*® (NKJV), copyright © 1982 by Thomas Nelson. Used by permission. All rights reserved. *The American Standard Version* (ASV), published in 1901 by Thomas Nelson & Sons. The Holy Bible, English Standard Version (ESV). Copyright © 2001 by Crossway, a publishing ministry of Good News Publishers. All rights reserved. The English *Revised Version* (RV), 1881–85.

Copyright © 2017 TEACH Services, Inc.
       © 2017 Kevin Straub for 4th Angel Publications

ISBN-13: 978-1-4796-0741-9 (Paperback)
ISBN-13: 978-1-4796-0742-6 (ePub)
ISBN-13: 978-1-4796-0743-3 (Mobi)
Library of Congress Control Number: 2017910206

Straub, Kevin, 1961
Compiler of *As He Is: Issues in the "Character of God" Controversy* (2012)

Published by

Acknowledgments and Thanks

The Spirit of God, Guide to All Truth.

My wife, Nicola, God has brought you to the world for such a time as this. I couldn't have done this without you.

Mom and Dad, ever generously supportive.

Elder Demetrius Leach, apostle of Christ, a bright light in this world.

Dr. Elliot O. Douglin, preacher of truth.

Dr. Herbert E. Douglass, valued source of counsel and encouragement; I wish we had had more years with you.

Ron Duffield, author of one of today's most important books, "The Return of the Latter Rain," my friend in the quest for true history.

All the Reformers, Truthers and Whistleblowers whose courageous research and reporting is the foundation of Section II.

Friends who contributed time and means to this project—you know who you are—may God richly reward each one.

Preface

In this book, you will ...

- Be invited to double earnestness in personal preparation for the Day of the Lord.

- Consider the prophetic parable of Joel 1:2–4, which uncannily corresponds to forty-year generations of Adventism from 1844 into the 21st century.

- Revisit the story of the 1888 message and of Elders Jones and Waggoner, the "first call" messengers to the Advent people. You will understand the impact this story has had upon every generation as it is woven into the tapestry of Adventist history.

- Discover what God intended for the educational and medical work of the Seventh-day Adventist Church and where the church deviated from the pattern.

- Meet Elders Wieland and Short, the "second call" messengers to the movement, who lit a fire in Adventism as they came to comprehend the depth and breadth of the 1888 message of righteousness by faith and realized that contemporary Adventism was preaching an evangelical knockoff of the message instead.

- Follow the development of the "great divide" in Adventism over historical and theological issues, as the Wieland and Short claims were denied and as high level meetings between Adventist officials and Calvinist theologians quietly took place.

- Carefully examine the development of the return to the latter rain as it swells to the loud cry of the third angel in the context of a detailed analysis of the differences between the "professed," "militant," and "true" (purified) churches of the remnant.

About the Author

Kevin Straub is a graduate of the Seventh-day Adventist educational system, with an education degree, minors in English and Religion, and a specialization in Outward Pursuits. He taught for several years in the Seventh-day Adventist school system as well as the public sector. An avid reader and student of the Bible and the Spirit of Prophecy, he has been actively engaged in promoting the truths of the three angels' messages and the fourth Angel of Revelation 18 through both speaking and writing. As a Bible worker, He and his wife are regularly involved with short-term independent international ministry tours. The Straubs currently live in Saskatchewan, where they raise horses and maintain gardens and a large greenhouse while continuing their ministry of sharing Bible truth.

Table of Contents

Section I: The Generation of the Restoration and the Midnight Watch

Introduction 17

1. Cyclical History 19

    The Principle of Time Cycles 19

    Time and Judgment 20

    The Flow of History Relative to God's People 20

    The Knowledge of God's Purposes Given to His People . 21

    The Knowledge of the Chosen Generation 21

    The Forty-Year Generation 22

    Time Cycles of Four 22

    Seeds of apostasy in division 23

    The Generational Cycle in Joel 24

    Ancient Israel Establishes a Monarchy and Reaps a Divided Kingdom 24

    The Initial Four Generations in the Ancient Israelite Monarchy 25

        Saul reigned forty years 25

        David reigned forty years 25

        Solomon reigned forty years 25

    The Lesson for Our Time 25

    Of the Times and Seasons 26

    Modern Israel Called 26

    No Time Prophecy Beyond 1844 27

    The Four Generations of Modern (Spiritual) Israel . . 27

    Promise of Restoration 28

    Restoration Comes after the Fourth Generation 28

    Hosea's Prophecy: "Days" Equal Generations 28

    View One: Offence in the Second Generation; the "Fourth Angel View" 30

    View Two: Offence in the First Generation—the "Laodicean View" 32

    The Outcome is the Same 33

    The Revival is the Latter Rain Outpouring 33

2. Following On to Know the LORD 35

    Seeing Him As He Is 35

    The Beginning of the Loud Cry 36

The Advance of the Loud Cry Reveals God's Character	36
God's People Must Advance in Knowledge and Experience	37
The Great Final Issue—Is It about Correct Days or Correct Character?	38
Claims of New Light	38
God's Character is the Light of His Glory	39
The message is a loud cry, and it begins in the house of God	40
It is the last message of mercy for the world.	40
The light of His glory is the last message	40
The Experiential Knowledge of God Brings Christ Back to Take Us Home	41
The Final Generation Will Be Fully Recovered from Error	41
We are the Final Generation	42

3. The Watches . . . 43

Four Generations Equal One Historical Cycle, Eaten Up!	43
Restoration after Four Generations	43
Introducing the Watches	44
Establishing the Watch as a Decade of Time	44
Watch and Pray	45
Hastening His Coming	45
Which Watch Shall It Be?	46
The 1335 Days and the "Blessed Hope"	46
Watch and Be Sober	47
Waiting for the Lord's Return from the Wedding	48
An Apparent Delay	49
First, Second or Third Watch	50
The Midnight Watch and the Loud Cry	50
Do We Know the Time? The 1906 Pathology Need Not Be Ours	51

4. Last Generation Typology in Gideon . . . 53

Tearing Down the Altar of Ba'al	53
The Called, Chosen and Faithful	54
Going Down to the Enemy Camp	54
Visions and Dreams	54
Trumpets, Empty Pitchers, Lamps	56
The Beginning of the Second Watch and the Changing of the Guard	56
War Commences Under Sunday Legislation and the Rise of the Loud Cry	60
Self-Destruction of the Enemy	60

Section II: The Devoured Generations

Introduction . . . 65

5. The Palmerworm . . . 69

The Oracles of God . . . 69

Worshipping at Satan's Throne . . . 71

Moving Forward with the Oracles of God, or "the Truth as It Is in Jesus" . . . 73

It Was to Be a Short Work . . . 74

A Delay! Why? . . . 74

Occupy Until I Come . . . 75

Anatomy of a disappointment . . . 75

The development of self-preservation and worldliness . . . 77

How then shall we be occupied? . . . 79

The Laodicean Third Angel's Message . . . 80

A Critical Spiritual Pathology: The LLC Virus . . . 82

The twin prongs of modern Laodiceanism . . . 84

6. The Locust . . . 86

The 1888 Message . . . 86

The Righteousness of Christ is Made Manifest
in Obedience to All the Commandments of God . . . 86

The Cure for the Lukewarm
Laodicean Condition . . . 89

What Did We Do With This "Most Precious Message?" . . . 90

Modern Times: Adventism's Point Man for Subverting A. T. Jones? . . . 92

Spiritual Death, Pretension, and Impenitence . . . 95

Who Will Constitute the Remnant? . . . 95

Organizational Apostasy in the Second Generation:
Organization as God's Permissive Will . . . 98

Human Organization Irrelevant Under Final Movements . . . 99

What Church is about to Fall? . . . 100

The 1888 Message's Rejection of Light and Kingly Rule . . . 101

God Calls for a Change, 1901 . . . 104

The King is in There Still . . . 104

No Change Was Made . . . 104

The 1903 General Conference . . . 105

Mrs. White Decries Centralization in 1904 106
God Still Called for a Change in 1907 107
What about Our Day? 108
Deeper Offense 108
To Those Assembled in the General Conference of 1913 109
Satan's Supposition and Re-organization 111
What Might Have Been 112
What Will Be 113
The Blueprint for the Medical Work—Fact or Myth? 113
A "Losing Battle" at Battle Creek; Restarting at Loma Linda 115
Blueprint Concepts after which the Medical Work is to be Patterned 115
The Loma Linda College of Medical Evangelists and the Day of Opportunity . . . 116
Pressure Test and Crisis 119
The Relation of Loma Linda to Medical Institutions 127
God's People Spoil Their History 131
The 1919 Bible and History Teachers Conference
and the Entrenchment of the "Conservative/Liberal" Divide 136
Early History of Ecumenical Aspirations in the Seventh-day Adventist Church . . 140
The American Sentinel's ecumenical aspirations *140*
Ballenger's ecumenical aspirations *140*
The first wrong step toward ecumenism approved in 1926 . . . . *141*
The Foreign Missions Conference 143
Concluding Thought on the Generational Midpoint: Adventism in the Balances . . 143

7. The Cankerworm 144

Roots of the "Acceptance Myth" in the Late 1920s 144
Man's Rules—The Development of a Church Manual 150
Establishment of the Ivory Towers 151
Again, it is seen that man assumes the higher authority *152*
Secular Accreditation in Adventist Education 154
The backstory *158*
Coming Back to the 1935 Fall Council: "The Drift" Identified 159
George Knight Weighs In on Accreditation 162
Inroads to the Evangelical Counterfeit Gospel Laid in—Wieland Recounts . . . 165
Who was E. Stanley Jones? *167*
Voicing concerns to D. E. Rebok, Wieland is expelled from the seminary. *167*
Vandeman recommends E. Stanley Jones in the February 1950 Ministry *168*

Wieland does not keep quiet. 169
A former GC president warns of encroaching mysticism 169
1950 General Conference Session, San Francisco, CA 170
A lifetime defined by a moment 172
The September interview begets the "1888 Re-Examined" manuscript 173

The Tectonic 1950s: Evangelical Conferences of 1955–57
and the Birth of Evangelical Adventism 174
The conferences 177

A Bird's-Eye View of the History of the Evangelical Conferences 178

The Main Issues of Doctrinal Concern 179
Issues regarding the atonement 180
Issues regarding the nature of Christ 185

Moore Offers a Middle Ground Resolution to the Nature of Christ Conflict . . . 187

The Misleading Heading 188

The Vicarious Bearing of Human Nature in Questions on Doctrine 188

The Myth of Overwhelming Support for Questions on Doctrine 190

The Publishing of Questions on Doctrine and the Pilate Effect 191

In Summation of the Questions on Doctrine Saga 192

1888 Re-visited: Another Call to Bring in Everlasting Righteousness 192

"We Have No Need" 195

The Two Calls of Matthew 22, a Parabolic Dual Prophecy 198

Ecumenism in the Third Generation 203

Concluding Material for the Third Generation 206

8. The Caterpillar 209

The Beginning of the Loud Cry Begins Again 210

Continuing Developments Regarding 1888 in Answer
to the Wieland and Short "Second Call": the Myths 214
The Protestant doctrine re-emphasis myth 220
Sidebar discussion on the true advance of the Reformation 222
Further thoughts on the Protestant doctrine and acceptance myth shell-game . . . 223
The "confessions" myth 225

Securing the Destiny of the Movement in its Fourth Generation 227

The Strange Claim: Those Mystical Missing Affidavits 229

"An Explicit Confession ... Due the Church" 232
Sidebar discussion: concerning "denominational" and "corporate" repentance—
are these terms synonymous? 234

Would We Also Stone Stephen?
Movement of Destiny Makes Clear Statements of Rejection 236
    What was the publication and re-publication of
    Froom's Movement of Destiny but this very thing? 237

1973–1974 Annual Councils; 1976 General Conference Meeting at Palmdale . . . 237

Fireless Torches: "Minneapolis II," the 1988 Centennial Celebration. 238

George Knight Strikes Again: Angry Saints (1989) 241

The Message That Just Won't Go Away; 1995–2000:
The "Primacy of the Gospel Committee" Report Maintains the Stance 243

Enter Desmond Ford; A Fourth Generation Storm Surge 246

The 1976 Biblical Research Institute Meeting in Australia 248

The Brinsmead Factor 249

Palmdale 250

Meanwhile, Back in Australia. 252

The Protestant Duo: Geoffrey Paxton and Robert Brinsmead 252

Glacier View 256

Brinsmead Follows the Theology to its Logical Conclusion 260

Winding Back to the Annual Council of 1973 261

Financial Mismanagement and Malfeasance in the Church:
The David Dennis Disclosures 263
    Davenport 263
    Harris Pine Mills 264
    Adventist Health System debt problem compounded by exorbitant salaries for executives. . 265
    Shooting the watchdog 267
    Consolidating power 268
    ADRA 268
    The worthy student fund and Christian Education donation "irregularities" . . . 269
    The recommendation to axe the unions 270
    Cronyism and rewards programs. 270
    The parsonage exclusion violations 271
    The take-down 272
    Dennis litigates 274
    The crash landing of a career churchman 277
    The end of the road in the Dennis lawsuit 278

Kingly Rule Solidifies Further: Utrecht Consolidation of Power 1995 280

Walter Martin Again 283

Ecumenism Ascending: Faces to the Rising Sun 284

    The Apostate Bloom 302

        Species: The bloom of worldly entertainment methodologies
        in celebrationism, music, theatrics 303

        Further doctrinal ramifications 312

        Species: the bloom of Babylonian church-growth paradigms—
        CGM, Purpose-Driven Church, and the felt-needs focus 312

        Bill Hybels' "Willow Creek," a market-driven, new-paradigm church model . . . 314

        Sidebar discussion: What is spiritualism? 315

        "America's Pastor," Rick Warren, Saddleback, and the Purpose-Driven movement . . . 319

        Species: The bloom of spiritualism—the train to perdition has a station in Adventism:
        The spiritual formation, contemplative spirituality,
        and the emerging church (EC) phenomenon 322

        Emerging Adventism 329

        Thoughts on the Omega 331

        Spiritual Formation officially set loose on Adventism
        in the latter part of the Fourth Generation 333

        What about Spiritual Directorship? 333

        More about Derek Morris 336

        Species: The bloom of Neuro-Linguistic Programming and Seventh-day Adventism . . . 339

        Relation of NLP to Spiritual Formation 343

    Concluding Thoughts Regarding the Fourth Generation 344

9. Adventism Today 346

    The Explosion of Contemplative and Mystic Spirituality in Adventism 346

    The "Protestantization" of Adventism Nurtured by Questions on Doctrine . . 348

    Where is This All Going, and Where Has the True Church Gone? 351

        The second shaking 353

    The True Church in the Bible and the Spirit of Prophecy 361

    The Church Militant 362

        The first shaking 363

    The Professed Church 365

    True Organization 369

    Where Then Shall We Go? 370

Section I
The Generation of the Restoration and the Midnight Watch

Watchman, what of the night?
Watchman, what of the night?
The watchman said,
The morning cometh, and also the night:
if ye will inquire, inquire ye:
return, come.

(Isaiah 21:11, 12)

Arise,
cry out in the night:
in the beginning of the watches
pour out thine heart like water before the face of the Lord:
lift up thy hands toward him for the life of thy young children,
that faint for hunger in the top of every street.

(Lamentations 2:19)

Introduction

At this time in history, we are challenged to find within the churches those who will sound the trumpet in clear tones and proclaim the three angels' messages. It is high time that we gain a deeper understanding of the last-day message so that we may be prepared to proclaim it. Sadly, many are asleep, even as most of the organized church is asleep. Is there none who will sound the cry?

It was not the scholarly theologians who had an understanding of this truth [*of the everlasting gospel of Revelation 14*], and engaged in its proclamation. Had these been faithful watchmen, diligently and prayerfully searching the Scriptures, **they would have known the time of night; the prophecies would have opened to them the events about to take place**. But they did not occupy this position, and the message was given by humbler men. Said Jesus: "Walk while ye have the light, lest darkness come upon you." John 12:35. Those who turn away from the light which God has given, or who neglect to seek it when it is within their reach, are left in darkness. But the Saviour declares: "He that followeth Me shall not walk in darkness, but shall have the light of life." John 8:12. Whoever is with singleness of purpose seeking to do God's will, earnestly heeding the light already given, will receive greater light; to that soul some star of heavenly radiance will be sent to guide him into all truth. (*The Great Controversy*, p. 312)

Joel 2 calls for the sounding of an alarm in Zion. Herein we have our mandate to declare the time of the emergence of a people great and strong in the day of the Lord, who run as mighty horsemen with a message of God's glory for all peoples. This is the time of the creation and rise of the 144,000 remnant elect of God. This is the generation of the restoration, when in the time of the latter rain, God's people—His true church, represented by the wheat, will rise up from the generations that have been devoured by the destroying pests.

Section I details the concept of the cycle of four, forty-year generations with the dividing of each generation into four periods called "watches." It begins with a consideration of the restoration that is to take place in the "fifth" generation of Adventism (which, as we will discover, is the "first" generation of a new set of time cycles). The majority of **Section II** examines the first four generations, according to the mandate given in Joel 1:2-4.

Some might wonder why our study covers the generation of the restoration before the previous four generations of the degradation. We start here because humans are most interested in themselves. We love to talk about ourselves. Thus, we will begin with the generation in which we live—the final generation. As probation is about to close and Jesus is about to come, there is an urgency that drives our interest in the current generation.

We believe that we are in that time of history. We see the fulfilling signs all around, and this study serves as one more piece of evidence that we are in the very last few minutes before midnight, when time runs out. After the close of probation, we will have already fixed our decision for eternity (Rev. 22:11, 12). This is what makes our generation the most important one. If we never got to the rest of the story to find out how things got to where they are today, we would have covered that which is most important. It is crucial that we know where we are in prophetic history and that we act accordingly, earnestly preparing our souls for the soon-coming "day of the Lord" (1 Thess. 5:2; 2 Peter 3:10).

Delaying to prepare and wandering from our purpose have constantly marred our history. Nonetheless, the Lord could not and cannot come without a people to come for. His rhetorical question about the time before His return is, "Will I find faith on the earth?" Thankfully, the answer is "Yes, praise the Lord, He will!" As it is written: "Here is the patience of the saints: here *are* they that keep the commandments of God, and the faith of Jesus" (Rev. 14:12). We are living in the time in which the 144,000 saints are finally made manifest, when the preparation of the final generation of living saints comes to maturity in the "full corn in the ear" (Mark 4:28, 29).

The message of Jesus' coming was proclaimed over four biblical generations ago, in the era leading up to 1844. He was to come to His temple to prepare a people for the physical redemption at the literal second advent. All things were to have been fulfilled early in that first generation. Yet, four generations have passed. We are now in "overtime"—in an additional generation beyond the first four. How did this delay occur? It was not of God's design, but it is a natural consequence of a "falling away" among the professed Advent people.

It should be noted that the goal of this book—particularly in **Section II**—is not to bash the Seventh-day Adventist Church, though I will readily admit that the history this book recounts will likely not be easy to read. As a third generation Seventh-day Adventist, I have marveled at the shipwreck of the church raised up to be "the remnant." It has never been easy to be a trailblazer, and calling attention to sad chapters in the church's history requires a willingness to bear the cross of being labeled an enemy of the faith, a heretic, a wolf or infiltrator, a smiter, and an accuser of the brethren.

Nonetheless, I humbly present the following exposition of prophecy out of love for the Advent people, for the truth that they were given to develop and proclaim, and for the Savior who gave Himself for His church and called it into being.

May God's Spirit be with you as you thoughtfully read.

CHAPTER 1.

Cyclical History

The Generation Concept in Ancient and Modern Israel

The Principle of Time Cycles

Human history follows a cyclical pattern of human behavior in the outworking of the principles of sowing and reaping, of cause and effect. Future events cast their shadows before; past events are anticipatory of what will take place in the future. Generations come and go; yet, there is a consistency of human response to the basic issues of the great controversy. The principle of cyclic time is particularly relevant with regard to religious history and the antagonism of the carnal heart toward the purposes of God in advancing the reformation.

> The work of God in the earth presents, from age to age, a striking similarity in every great reformation or religious movement. The principles of God's dealing with men are ever the same. **The important movements of the present have their parallel in those of the past**, and the experience of the church in former ages has lessons of great value for our own time. (*The Great Controversy*, p. 343, emphasis added)

It is most certainly true that "history repeats itself" (*Signs of the Times*, Nov. 8, 1899). Additionally, as the issues at stake are repeated in the six millennia of historical cycles in the great controversy on this planet, they grow more pronounced and widespread. Each time the conflict between right and wrong—between truth and error—is repeated, it grows more and more intense as it accelerates toward its inevitable climax.

The cycles of nature and the cycles of history hold some similarity. The wise man Solomon gave great thought to these matters and recorded, in Ecclesiastes 1, some of his reflections on the cycles of nature and history. Notice his conclusion:

> The thing that hath been, it *is that* which shall be; and that which is done *is* that which shall be done: and *there is* no new *thing* under the sun. (Eccles. 1:9)

Solomon explained this mystery further in chapter 3:

> That which hath been is now; and that which is to be hath already been; and God requireth that which is past. (Eccles. 3:15)

The *Living Bible* renders it this way:

> Whatever is, has been long ago; and whatever is going to be has been before; God brings to pass again what was in the past and disappeared.

However, Solomon did not stop there. He described two very important basic principles, which have always driven the cycles of history. These are: "the curse causeless shall not come" (Prov. 26:2), which is the principle of cause and effect, and "to every purpose there is *time and judgment*" (Eccles. 8:5, 6), which is the principle "time will tell."

Time and Judgment

Time and judgment are essential elements in everything. The element of time has to do with the sowing, and the results are observed in an assessment, or judgment, of the outcome. If you plant corn seeds, in time the results that come will be judged by the fruit of that plant, which will be corn. This is why we say, "Time will tell," for it always does.

> As the bird by wandering, as the swallow by flying, so the curse causeless shall not come. (Prov. 26:2)

The curse is the result of the action of the agent and not the result of any arbitrary decree meted out by God.

> Whoso keepeth the commandment shall feel no evil thing: and a wise man's heart discerneth both time and judgment. Because to every purpose there is time and judgment, therefore the misery of man is great upon him. (Eccles. 8:5, 6)

These same principles are also expressed in the New Testament:

> Be not deceived; God is not mocked: for whatsoever a man soweth, that shall he also reap. For he that soweth to his flesh shall of the flesh reap corruption; but he that soweth to the Spirit shall of the Spirit reap life everlasting. And let us not be weary in well doing: for in due season we shall reap, if we faint not. (Gal. 6:7–9)

> Let no man say when he is tempted, I am tempted of God: for God cannot be tempted with evil, neither tempteth he any man: but every man is tempted, when he is drawn away of his own lust, and enticed. Then when lust hath conceived, it bringeth forth sin: and sin, when it is finished, bringeth forth death. Do not err, my beloved brethren. Every good gift and every perfect gift is from above, and cometh down from the Father of lights, with whom is no variableness, neither shadow of turning. (James 1:13–17)

So, misery comes upon man because of what a man has sown. Time will pass, and judgment will come.

The present is a time of overwhelming interest to all living. Rulers and statesmen, men who occupy positions of trust and authority, thinking men and women of all classes, have their attention fixed upon the events taking place about us. They are watching the relations that exist among the nations. They observe the intensity that is taking possession of every earthly element, and they recognize that something great and decisive is about to take place–that the world is on the verge of a stupendous crisis. (*Prophets and Kings*, p. 537)

The world is watching intently for something to happen, but they do not know what it will be. We know, for we have the sure Word of God to guide us, or, at least, we *should know*, for we have been given the oracles of God and are privy to the revelations given through these inspired channels. We have no excuse for not searching into these things and advancing in knowledge and understanding.

> The Bible, and the Bible only, gives a correct view of these things. Here are revealed the great final scenes in the history of our world, events that already are casting their shadows before, the sound of their approach causing the earth to tremble and men's hearts to fail them for fear. (*Prophets and Kings*, p. 537)

Great events are about to occur, and God's people are living as though they have another lifetime.

The Flow of History Relative to God's People

Let us now apply these principles to the study of God's dealing with His people and their response to His grace. God, in His wisdom, knows the events of the future even before they come to pass. He understands the cycles of history and has seen them before they occur. That which causes men to fear has already been solved in the mind of the great "I Am." God is never in a hurry. When we are running out of time, God has eternity!

> But like the stars in the vast circuit of their appointed path, God's purposes know no haste and no delay. (*The Desire of Ages*, p. 32)

Our God has heaven and earth at His command, and He knows just what we need. We can see only a little way before us; "but all things are naked and opened unto the eyes of Him with whom we have to do." Hebrews 4:13. Above the distractions of the earth He sits enthroned; all things are open to His divine survey; and from His great and calm eternity He orders that which His providence sees best. (*Testimonies for the Church*, vol. 8, pp. 272, 273)

Behold, the former things are come to pass, and new things do I declare: before they spring forth I tell you of them. (Isa. 42:9)

And the LORD said, Shall I hide from Abraham that thing which I do. (Gen. 18:17)

Surely the Lord GOD will do nothing, but he revealeth his secret unto his servants the prophets. (Amos 3:7)

Let us not miss the significance of this. We do not need to flounder in the darkness. God reveals to His people what is about to take place! He knows the future, and He desires to inform His servants what is to come so that they can cooperate with Him in His work of saving souls. Thus has it always been. God told Daniel when the time of the seventy weeks would be finished so that He could pray intelligently for the fulfilling of the heavenly Father's will.

As we are guided by the Holy Spirit in the study of the prophecies in God's Word, He gives us the vision to go forth and prophesy, as we find in the following words written of old:

The secret of the LORD *is* with them that fear him; and he will shew them his covenant. (Ps. 25:14)

The Knowledge of God's Purposes Given to His People

From the greatest to the smallest, God's people are given to know the ways of the Lord.

Shew me thy ways, O LORD; teach me thy paths. (Ps. 25:4)

All the paths of the LORD *are* mercy and truth unto such as keep his covenant and his testimonies. (Ps. 25:10)

If any man will do his will, he shall know of the doctrine … (John 7:17)

And they shall not teach every man his neighbour, and every man his brother, saying, Know the Lord: for all shall know me, from the least to the greatest. (Heb. 8:11)

God communicates His plans for us. He shows them to us for the purpose of restoring us to righteousness.

I will make a man more precious than fine gold; even a man than the golden wedge of Ophir. (Isa. 13:12)

Arise, shine; for thy light is come, and the glory of the LORD is risen upon thee. For, behold, the darkness shall cover the earth, and gross darkness the people: but the LORD shall arise upon thee, and his glory shall be seen upon thee. And the Gentiles shall come to thy light, and kings to the brightness of thy rising. (Isa. 60:1–3)

The Knowledge of the Chosen Generation

The Lord wants us to know the generation in which we are living, and He wants us to understand that we are a chosen generation whose purpose is to perform His will on earth, as Peter declared:

But ye *are* a **chosen generation**, a royal priesthood, an holy nation, a peculiar people; that ye should shew forth the praises of him who hath called you out of darkness into his marvelous light. (1 Peter 2:9, emphasis added)

This calling is ours. Looking down through the generations, God saw the final generation that will be purified and prepared to stand in the sight of heaven as a spotless bride. It is likely that our generation is the one that God saw from the days of eternity ushering in the second coming of Christ. It may well be that our generation provides the elect who will live to see the end of all things. What a privilege! *In our small slot in time, we can be the ones God foresaw making the difference!* He desires that it be so.

Who hath wrought and done *it*, calling the generations from the beginning? I the LORD, the first, and with the last; I *am* he. (Isa. 41:4)

This final generation is called out of darkness into God's marvelous light (1 Peter 2:9). We recognize ourselves to be the final generation because of the rapidly fulfilling signs, which are the "beginning of sorrows" predicted by Jesus (Matt. 24:8). We are witnessing the formation of the political-religious tyranny that will escalate into the crisis of the "mark of the beast." We are enjoying advances in the understanding of God's character, which were prophesied to come in the message of the fourth angel of Revelation 18:1, who comes down from heaven having great power to lighten the earth with His glory. So, while we said, "It may well be that our generation provides the elect who will live to see the end of all things," we really mean that we are that chosen generation that God will make more precious than gold. This generation is extremely important to the closing up of the great controversy.

> Who hath wrought and done *it*, calling the generations from the beginning? I the LORD, the first, and with the last; I *am* he. The isles saw *it*, and feared; the ends of the earth were afraid, drew near, and came. (Isa. 41:4, 5)

God knows which will be the last cycle and the last generation, and He has revealed these things in His Word. Because He knows these things and reveals His secrets to His servants, He is now revealing to us that we are the last generation. As we understand the "watches" within the generations, we will see that He has pointed out which of these is mostly likely to be the last. May the precious words of Christ be ours, and may we be the ones who fulfill them.

> Now learn a parable of the fig tree; When his branch is yet tender, and putteth forth leaves, **ye know** that summer *is* nigh: so likewise ye, **when ye shall see all these things**, know that it is near, *even* at the doors. Verily I say unto you, **This generation shall not pass, till all these things be fulfilled**. (Matt. 24:32–34, emphasis added)

Notice that Christ is talking about that generation that would be looking for His return. He was answering the disciples' two-part question—

> Tell us, when shall these things be? and what *shall be* the sign of thy coming, and of the end of the world? (Matt. 24:3)

Jesus revealed that, through the events to take place, His followers would know which generation would "not pass." He is not going to allow the last generation to come without revealing which one it is! To make such an identification does not require time setting, for Jesus declared that His followers would know the *generation* when these things would occur. He declared: "When ye shall see all these things, **know** …"

The Forty-Year Generation

The Scriptures reveal that the time period required for the maturation of the choice and direction of any generation following the Flood is forty years, or one functional generation. Notice that this is not a *biological* generation but a *functional* one. *Sociologically it has to do with the maturation and fixedness of the choice and customs of the people as a whole.* We see the functional generation illustrated in Scripture:

> And your children shall wander in the wilderness forty years, and bear your whoredoms, until your carcases be wasted in the wilderness. **After the number of the days in which ye searched the land,** even **forty days, each day for a year, shall ye bear your iniquities,** even **forty years**, and ye shall know my breach of promise. (Num. 14:33, 34, emphasis added)

> Wherefore (as the Holy Ghost saith, To day if ye will hear his voice, Harden not your hearts, as in the provocation, in the day of temptation in the wilderness: when your fathers tempted me, proved me, and saw my works **forty years**. Wherefore I was grieved with that **generation**, and said, They do alway err in *their* heart; and they have not known my ways. (Heb. 3:7–10)

Time Cycles of Four

That it takes four generations to make up one complete cycle of sowing and reaping is confirmed by God Himself in Exodus 20:5—

> for I the LORD thy God am a jealous God, visiting the iniquity of the fathers upon the children unto the third and **fourth generation** of them that hate me.

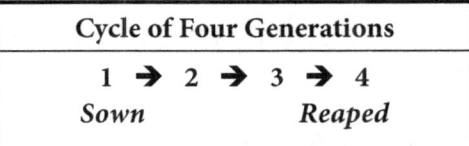

Israel clamored for a king so they could be like the other nations. God told Samuel that, in so asking, they had not rejected Samuel, but they had rejected God. At their insistence, God gave them the first king, Saul. This was actually a manifestation of wrath, as we can read in Hosea 13:11, for the seeds of apostasy sown will yield their sure harvest. We will consider this more later.

The Cycle of Four in Israel's Choice for Monarchy			
1	**2**	**3**	**4**
Saul →	David →	Solomon →	Jeroboam/Rehoboam
40 yrs.	40 yrs.	40 yrs.	*Harvest reaped*
Seeds of apostasy division			*in*
sown in kingly rule			*and war*

This cycle of four is seen in the history of world empires after the Flood. The prophecies of Daniel predicted and history has confirmed that there would be only four world-ruling empires. The iniquity sown in the first empire, *Babylon*, developed through the second, *Medo-Persia*, and into the third, *Greece*, resulting in the complete collapse of imperial unity by the time that the fourth empire, *Rome*, had ended.

The Cycle of Four in the History of Empires—Daniel, Chapters 2, 7, 8			
1	**2**	**3**	**4**
Babylon →	Medo-Persia →	Greece →	Rome
Seeds of iniquity		*Harvest reaped in the*	
sown in pride	→	*fall of the world empire*	

The prophet Daniel foretold that, after the collapse of the Roman Empire, any attempt to produce political unity in a world empire would be doomed to failure. Read Daniel 2:40–43 and notice the completeness of the disunity: *"… but they shall not cleave one to another …"* (Dan. 2:43).

This cycle of four is also seen in the history of Christianity from apostolic times to the times of the great Roman Catholic apostasy, as we see in Revelation, chapter 2, and Second Thessalonians, chapter 2:

The Cycle of Four in the History of Christianity			
1	**2**	**3**	**4**
Ephesus →	Smyrna →	Pergamos →	Thyatira
31–100 AD	100–321 AD	321–538 AD	538–1600 AD
Mystery of iniquity →	*Continued growth of* →	*Harvest reaped*	
sown (2 Thess. 2:7)	*the mystery of iniquity*	*in the development of the papacy (2 Thess. 2:3)*	

The seeds of the "falling away" (2 Thess. 2:3), which were sown in the Ephesus period, developed slowly at first because persecution kept the church pure. After Constantine's conversion and his Sunday legislation (AD 321), ongoing compromise further developed the apostasy until its fruition in the full "falling away" under papal ascendancy, which dominated Europe for more than a thousand years!

The Generational Cycle in Joel

The prophet Joel, in Joel 1:1–3, explains that it takes four generations to make up one complete cycle of sowing and reaping. That is, it takes 160 years to complete a historical cycle.

> The word of the LORD that came to Joel the son of Pethuel. Hear this, ye old men, and give ear, all ye inhabitants of the land. Hath this been in your days, or even in the days of your fathers? Tell **ye your children** of it, and *let* your children *tell* **their children**, and their children **another generation**. (Joel 1:1–3, emphasis added)

The four-generation concept for a historical cycle is found in this passage, in that the first generation is addressed as "ye"; the second as "your children"; the third as "their children"; and the fourth as "their children another generation."

One Cycle of Four Generations

First	Second	Third	Fourth
"Ye"	"your children"	"their children"	"another **generation**"
Palmerworm	Locust	Cankerworm	Caterpillar

Going on to the fourth verse, we see that these are four deepening levels of erosion, or degradation, within a cycle of the sowing to sin.

> That which the **palmerworm** hath left hath the **locust** eaten; and that which the locust hath left hath the **cankerworm** eaten; and that which the cankerworm hath left hath the **caterpillar** eaten. (Joel 1:4, emphasis added)

Note the parallel that can be drawn:

- "ye," devoured by the palmerworm
- "your children," devoured by the locust
- "their children," devoured by the cankerworm
- "their children another generation," devoured by the caterpillar

Again, the concept is that *four biblical generations equal one cycle of sowing and reaping.*

Ancient Israel Establishes a Monarchy and Reaps a Divided Kingdom

In the fourth generation, the kingdom split as the result of the generations of degradation, which began when the people rejected God for a human king to rule over them.

> Then all the elders of Israel gathered themselves together, and came to Samuel unto Ramah, and said unto him, Behold, thou art old, and thy sons walk not in thy ways: now make us a king to judge us like all the nations. (1 Sam. 8:4, 5)

> And ye have this day rejected your God, who himself saved you out of all your adversities and your tribulations; and ye have said unto him, *Nay*, but set a king over us. Now therefore present yourselves before the LORD by your tribes, and by your thousands. (1 Sam. 10:19)

After Solomon's reign, the kingdom of ancient Israel was divided as a result of the sowing of the seeds of discord and sin in asking for a king and rejecting God as their head. Solomon's son Rehoboam put an excessive taxation on the people, and Jeroboam came up against Rehoboam causing the kingdom to split into two separate kingdoms with ten tribes in the north, under Jeroboam, and two tribes in the south under Rehoboam. Judgment came in the fourth generation.

The Initial Four Generations in the Ancient Israelite Monarchy

Saul reigned forty years

Saul reigned because of the people's apostasy. They rejected God and wanted a human king to rule over them.

> And afterward they desired a king: and God gave unto them Saul the son of Cis, a man of the tribe of Benjamin, **by the space of forty years.** (Acts 13:21, emphasis added)

So this was the first generation in the apostasy.

David reigned forty years

The second functional generation after the apostasy came under David.

> And the days that David reigned over Israel were **forty years**: seven years reigned he in Hebron, and thirty and three years reigned he in Jerusalem. (1 Kings 2:11, emphasis added)

Under David there was no great movement of repentance or ushering in of everlasting righteousness. Hebrews 4:7 says: "Again, he limiteth a certain day, saying in David, To day, after so long a time; as it is said, To day if ye will hear his voice, harden not your hearts." Yet, repentance did not come, as we well know. There were other days of opportunity in salvation history that arose after David, and all of them were failures. We are still in this world, and, even to this day, we have not entered God's rest. Yet, today is the day—this will be the generation that seizes the moment!

> David was greatly tried in his day in seeing men pouring contempt upon God's law. Men threw off restraint, and depravity was the result. The law of God had become a dead letter to those whom God had created. Men refused to receive the holy precepts as the rule of their life. Wickedness was so great that David feared lest God's forbearance should cease, and he sent up a heart-felt prayer to heaven, saying, "It is time for thee, Lord, to work: for they have made void thy law. Therefore I love thy commandments above gold; yea, above fine gold." (Ellen G. White, Ms. 105, 1894, in *Seventh-day Adventist Bible Commentary*, vol. 3, p. 1152)

Solomon reigned forty years

The third generation followed along into further degradation.

> And the time that Solomon reigned in Jerusalem over all Israel was **forty years**. (1 Kings 11:42, emphasis added)

> The marks of Solomon's apostasy lived ages after him. In the days of Christ, the worshipers in the temple could look, just opposite them, upon the Mount of Offense, and be reminded that the builder of their rich and glorious temple, the most renowned of all kings, had separated himself from God, and reared altars to heathen idols; that the mightiest ruler on earth had failed in ruling his own spirit. Solomon went down to death a repentant man; but his repentance and tears could not efface from the Mount of Offense the signs of his miserable departure from God. Ruined walls and broken pillars bore silent witness for a thousand years to the apostasy of the greatest king that ever sat upon an earthly throne. (Ellen G. White, *Health Reformer*, May 1, 1878, in *Seventh-day Adventist Bible Commentary*, vol. 2, p. 1032)

The Lesson for Our Time

In all of these things, we are not only establishing the principle of a forty-year biblical generation, but we are showing parallels between ancient and modern spiritual Israel—the people of God in the world who have the "oracles of God"—and how the history of the ancient may be a type of the modern. The concept that history will be repeated is not only a key to greater understanding of our times but a reality that should inculcate a sense of consternation within us.

> Now all these things happened unto them for ensamples: and they are written for our admonition, upon whom the ends of the world are come. (1 Cor. 10:11)

This blighted fig tree with its pretentious branches is to repeat its lesson in every age to the close of this earth's history.... If the spirit of Satan entered unto unsanctified hearts in the days of Christ to counterwork the requirements of God in that generation, it will surely enter into the professed Christian churches in [our day]. History will repeat itself.... (Ms. 32, 1898, in *Christ Triumphant*, p. 256)

Today Christ comes to his people, hungering to find in them the fruits of righteousness. But many, many, have nothing but leaves to offer him. They have left their first love, and upon them has fallen spiritual blindness, hardness of heart, stubbornness of mind. They pray to God, and present Bible truth to the people; for they are in the habit of doing so; but they have lost that which would make their service acceptable. How blind they are! how defective their service! Boastingly they say, "I am rich, and increased with goods, and have need of nothing." But God says to them, "Thou art wretched, and miserable, and poor, and blind, and naked! I counsel thee to buy of me gold tried in the fire, that thou mayest be rich; and white raiment, that thou mayest be clothed, and that the shame of thy nakedness do not appear; and anoint thine eyes with eyesalve, that thou mayest see."

Will God's people accept this reproof? Let them beware of remaining in their present condition; for time is fast passing, and the work that ought to be done is not done. (*Review and Herald*, June 9, 1903)

The judgment pronounced upon the barren fig-tree not only symbolizes the sentence passed upon the Jews, but is also applicable to the professed Christians of our time, who have become formal, selfish, boasting and hypocritical. (*The Spirit of Prophecy*, vol. 3, p. 19)

Of the Times and Seasons

The times and seasons are given for us to know. Sadly, this is often denied in the repetition of common sayings in the popular pulpit such as "God has a timetable"; "Since His purposes know no haste and no delay [*The Desire of Ages*, p. 32], He will come back when He is ready"; "We don't know why there is a delay; but Jesus said the times and seasons are *not* for us to know" (Acts 1:7)—though Paul said that God's people would be well enough informed that that day would not overtake us as a thief (1 Thess. 5:1–5); or, "Our job is to 'occupy until He comes' " (Luke 19:13), which translates into patiently waiting while we live out our lives producing and acquiring goods.

Jesus' disciples wanted to know if He would, at that time, establish the kingdom. Of course, they were still stuck in their thinking, with an earthly geo-political power in view and their Lord and Master on the throne. Jesus told them, in their particular paradigm of thought, that it is not for us to know the times and the seasons. It was as if He were saying, "We're not even going there."

Just before leaving His disciples, Christ once more plainly stated the nature of His kingdom. He recalled to their remembrance things He had previously told them regarding it. He declared that it was not His purpose to establish in this world a temporal kingdom. He was not appointed to reign as an earthly monarch on David's throne. When the disciples asked Him, "Lord, wilt Thou at this time restore again the kingdom to Israel?" He answered, "It is not for you to know the times or the seasons, which the Father hath put in His own power." Acts 1:6, 7. It was not necessary for them to see farther into the future than the revelations He had made enabled them to see. Their work was to proclaim the gospel message. (*Acts of the Apostles*, p. 30)

However, when we read Paul, we realize that we cannot compare Jesus' words to the disciples with His words to us. Paul wrote the Thessalonians that the knowledge of the times and seasons are not going to be hidden or to be a surprise (1 Thess. 5). The children of the day *will* know. In Matthew 24, Jesus gave the signs that would be manifest in the time of the final generation. He gave us the command to *watch*. *That* generation *will* have the understanding of the times and seasons, though they will not know the day and hour of His return.

The "times and seasons" that define the *day and hour* of the second coming are *not* for us to know now. The "times and seasons" that specify a timeframe for the *nearness of the end* and call for the urgency of preparation *are* for us to know, as we shall see in the further unfolding of this study.

Modern Israel Called

As 1844 approached, God initiated a wonderful work of revival in the earth through the proclamation of the first angel's message in the context of the belief in the imminent second coming of Christ.

In the United States of America, William Miller, at first, and others, later on, were called to present the message of the imminent return of Christ and the prophecies of Daniel and the Revelation. Miller entered upon his work in 1831, and, by 1840, the revival known as the "Great Advent Awakening" swelled to greater levels of Spirit-anointed intensity.

Miller and his associates misunderstood the event that was to occur at the end of the 2300 years of Daniel 8:14. They thought that Christ would return on October 22, 1844. However, the prophecy foretold not the second coming of Christ to earth but the coming of Christ to the most holy place in the heavenly sanctuary to commence the final phase of His high priestly ministration. This is well-known history, understood by most Seventh-day Adventists today.

Since the time of the 1844 movement of Christ into a new phase of ministry, He has been waiting for His remnant church to be harvest-ripe and ready for His second coming. Yet, there has been a long delay! Why is this? This is a very important question and one that remains unanswered, and it is even swept under the rug by teachers and preachers standing in Seventh-day Adventist pulpits.

No Time Prophecy Beyond 1844

This message of the midnight watch that we are developing is not a time prophecy. We are not attempting to show any reckoning of specific dates or timelines for the close of probation or the second coming. The study we are making in this book establishes that we can be reasonably certain of the *timeframe* for these events, due to the focus of Scripture on the symbol of the "midnight watch," which we will later explore regarding its meaning and dating. According to the Spirit of Prophecy, there is no definite time fulfillment after 1844.

> I plainly stated at the Jackson camp meeting to these fanatical parties that they were doing the work of the adversary of souls; they were in darkness. They claimed to have great light that probation would close in October, 1884. I there stated in public that the Lord had been pleased to show me that there would be no definite time in the message given of God since 1844. ("An Exposure of Fanaticism and Wickedness," PH030, p. 9, in *Selected Messages*, bk. 2, p. 73)

> Our position has been one of waiting and watching, with no time-proclamation to intervene between the close of the prophetic periods in 1844 and the time of our Lord's coming. (Lt. 38, 1888, in *Manuscript Releases*, vol. 10, p. 270)

> The people will not have another message upon definite time. After this period of time [Rev. 10:4–6], reaching from 1842 to 1844, there can be no definite tracing of the prophetic time. The longest reckoning reaches to the autumn of 1844. (Ms. 59, 1900, in *Last Day Events*, pp. 34, 35)

Having said this, it behooves us not to overbalance and also to take in the following warning:

> But if that evil servant shall say in his heart, My lord tarrieth; and shall begin to beat his fellow-servants, and shall eat and drink with the drunken; the lord of that servant shall come in a day when he expecteth not, and in an hour when he knoweth not, and shall cut him asunder, and appoint his portion with the hypocrites: there shall be the weeping and the gnashing of teeth. (Matt. 24:48–51, ASV)

In **Section II** of this book, we will apply the principles of the cycle of four generations, mentioned in the prophecy of Joel 1, to Adventist history, and we will see a parallel degradation, or slide into entrenched Laodicean lukewarmness. This is a sensitive subject for many members and workers in the denomination. On the other hand, there are many faithful and concerned "Daniels" in modern spiritual Israel who recognize that much has gone wrong and that we have a urgent need of revival and reformation through the Holy Spirit's arrival in latter rain power. We need an experience that we have never had in all of our history, save in that which was seen in the Millerite movement prior to the great disappointment.

Before we get to that discussion, however, we need to show the breakdown of the four functional generations of modern spiritual Israel, which is the movement that began with the preaching of the Great Advent Awakening message of the Millerite movement and later formed into the Seventh-day Adventist organization.

The Four Generations of Modern (Spiritual) Israel

Each is a forty-year period, using October 22 as the starting and ending date:

- Generation 1: 1844–1884
- Generation 2: 1884–1924
- Generation 3: 1924–1964
- Generation 4: 1964–2004

Altogether, these four functional forty-year generations make up one cycle of time for sowing and reaping, totally 160 years. The progression of the resulting degenerative lukewarmness is symbolized in the book of Joel as the work of devouring pests (Joel 1:3, 4).

Some may have already been wondering how we can prove that it is not a matter of speculation to start this time cycle at 1844. We will point out the support for the generational cycle of four when we examine the "watches" that divide each generation into four parts, or decades, each corresponding to the four biblical watches of the night. In doing so, we will also be showing that there is a cycle that started in 1844.

Promise of Restoration

Remember that the four generations of sowing to Laodicean lukewarmness, or "the flesh," only results in the degradation of the expected harvest by the palmerworm, the locust, the cankerworm, and the caterpillar.

> But this *is* a people robbed and spoiled; *they are* all of them snared in holes, and they are hid in prison houses: they are for a prey, and none delivereth; for a spoil, and none saith, Restore. (Isa. 42:22)

> I will go *and* return to my place, till they acknowledge their offence, and seek my face: in their affliction they will seek me early. (Hosea 5:15)

The people have been mugged and left bleeding on the side of the road. There has been a great offence committed. In His merciful kindness, God has promised that He will not leave His people in this degenerate state, though they have sinned against Him. With the balm of Gilead, He will certainly return to them and heal them of their backsliding. Notice, however, that with respect to free choice, He cannot return to them with healing until they acknowledge their offence and seek Him by responding to His overtures of mercy. We will return to the matter of the "offence" later as we are here only setting the table for the meal to come.

Restoration Comes after the Fourth Generation

> And I will restore to you the years that the locust hath eaten, the cankerworm, and the caterpillar, and the palmerworm, my great army which I sent among you. And ye shall eat in plenty, and be satisfied, and praise the name of the LORD your God, that hath dealt wondrously with you: and my people shall never be ashamed. And ye shall know that I *am* in the midst of Israel, and *that* I *am* the LORD your God, and none else: and my people shall never be ashamed. (Joel 2:25–27)

The word of the Lord is restored:

> And it shall come to pass afterward, *that* I will pour out my spirit upon all flesh; and your sons and your daughters shall prophesy, your old men shall dream dreams, your young men shall see visions: And also upon the servants and upon the handmaids in those days will I pour out my spirit. And I will shew wonders in the heavens and in the earth, blood, and fire, and pillars of smoke. The sun shall be turned into darkness, and the moon into blood, before the great and the terrible day of the LORD come. And it shall come to pass, *that* whosoever shall call on the name of the LORD shall be delivered: for in mount Zion and in Jerusalem shall be deliverance, as the LORD hath said, and in the remnant whom the LORD shall call. (Joel 2:28–32)

So, after four generations, a new cycle begins, and, more importantly, in the first generation of this new cycle, the restoration comes!

Hosea's Prophecy: "Days" Equal Generations

Now we come back to the "offence" and an interesting time prophecy set within the context of the latter rain:

> I will go *and* return to my place, till they acknowledge **their offence**, and seek my face: in their affliction they will seek me early. Come, and let us return unto the LORD: for he hath torn, and he will heal us; he hath smitten, and he will bind us up. **After two days** will he revive us: **in the third day** he will raise us up, and we shall live in his sight. Then shall we know, *if* we follow on to know the LORD: his going forth is prepared as the morning; and he shall come unto us as the rain, as the latter *and* former rain unto the earth. (Hosea 5:15; 6:1–3, emphasis added)

Pertaining to this study topic, there are *two views* regarding the nature of the "offence" and the assignment of the three days in these verses. These involve a little technical discussion, as will follow. Nonetheless, we should first establish a biblical connection between "days" and "generations." Let us review Joel's statement:

Hear this, ye old men, and give ear, all ye inhabitants of the land. Hath this been in your days, or even in the days of your fathers? Tell ye your children of it, and *let* your children *tell* their children, and their children another generation. (Joel 1:2, 3)

Adventists would be naturally prone to use the day-for-a-year principle in interpreting Bible prophecy. However, in this case, the application is post-1844, beyond which date there is to be no more reckoning of prophetic time. As we noted above, Ellen White stated that, after the "passing of the time" in the close of the 2300 days, there were to be no more time prophecies. Thus, we must look for another meaning of the "days" in Hosea's prophecy. We find the key in other Scriptures as the terms "days" and "generations" appear in parallel to one another:

Remember the **days of old**, consider the **years of many generations**: ask thy father, and he will show thee; thy elders, and they will tell thee. (Deut. 32:7, emphasis added)

Awake, awake, put on strength, O arm of the LORD; awake, as in the **ancient days**, in the **generations of old**.... (Isa. 51:9, emphasis added)

Often when recounting a former time, people will use the expression, "back in my day," or "back in the day when …" They could just as easily say, "back in my generation" or "back in the generation when …"

Finally, consider that, conceptually, the "days" in Hosea's prophecy are representations of acceptable times when God would have worked for the people. Each generation represents a new opportunity for getting back on track—a new "day of opportunity"—which is represented as such in the Bible in the fourth chapter of Hebrews:

Seeing therefore it remaineth that some must enter therein, and they to whom it was first preached entered not in because of unbelief: Again, he limiteth a certain day, saying in David, To day, after so long a time; as it is said, To day if ye will hear his voice, harden not your hearts. For if Jesus had given them rest, then would he not afterward have spoken of another day. There remaineth therefore a rest to the people of God. (Heb. 4:6–9)

Returning to the book of Joel and its context of the latter-day four generations and subsequent restoration, we read about the call and awakening of the people of God after generations of darkness:

Blow ye the trumpet in Zion, and sound an alarm in my holy mountain: let all the inhabitants of the land tremble: for the day of the LORD cometh, for *it is* nigh at hand; a day of darkness and of gloominess, a day of clouds and of thick darkness, as the morning spread upon the mountains: a great people and a strong; there hath not been ever the like, neither shall be any more after it, *even* to the years of many generations. (Joel 2:1, 2)

Therefore the redeemed of the LORD shall return, and come with singing unto Zion; and everlasting joy *shall be* upon their head: they shall obtain gladness and joy; *and* sorrow and mourning shall flee away. (Isa. 51:11)

Early in the "third day"—the fourth generation (1964–2004)—came earnest seeking for the knowledge and truth of the message to heal the people's lukewarm Laodicean condition (Rev. 3:14–21). That message has been identified in the Spirit of Prophecy as the beginning of the latter rain of the Holy Spirit. At that time, the work of Robert J. Wieland and Donald K. Short brought the message back to the people's attention. These were the "second call" messengers and revivalists who appealed, in the 1950s, for the church to return to the message of 1888, which came through the "first call" messengers and revivalists, A. T. Jones and E. J. Waggoner.

There were many independent groups that formed as the light of true Seventh-day Adventist history came to the forefront via the Wieland and Short manuscript, "A Warning and Its Reception." Thus, began the process of the return of the Latter Rain, which was spurned from the 1888 era until the time of the *second watch* of the *first generation* of the *new time cycle* that began in 2004.

> **View *One*: Offence in the *Second* Generation**
>
> **Offence in Rejecting Righteousness by Faith Message Arising in the Second Generation (1888)**
>
> Generation 1, 1844–1884
> Day 1. Generation 2, 1884–1924 - OFFENCE
> Day 2. Generation 3, 1924–1964
> Day 3. Generation 4, 1964–2004 - REVIVAL
>
> Using inclusive reckoning, "Day 1" parallels the crucifixion of Christ in the rejection of the 1888 message; "Day 2" continues in rejection and apostasy; "Day 3" sees the resurgence of the 1888 message.
>
> *"After two days will he revive us: in the third day he will raise us up, and we shall live in his sight" (Hosea 6:2).*

View One: Offence in the Second Generation; the "Fourth Angel View"

One train of thought we may identify as the "Fourth Angel View" since it pertains to the proclamation of the message of the fourth angel, which is "the beginning of the loud cry" (A. G. Daniells, *Christ Our Righteousness*, p. 62). This book takes this view as the most favorable. In this view, we will find that *the offence occurred in the second generation*, when God, in 1888, sent a "most precious message" to the Adventist people through His messengers Jones and Waggoner (Lt. 57, 1895, in *The Ellen G. White 1888 Materials*, pp. 1336, 1337). The message was not generally received, though there were local revivals throughout the next few years. Students of this history have recognized that there has been a determined official rejection of the men and the message from that time until the present. (The reader will find a detailed study of this rejection in **Section II** of this book, "The Devoured Generations.")

The "Fourth Angel View" employs *inclusive reckoning*, typical of the Hebrew method of accounting time, in which a part of a day or a year can stand for the whole, indicating that the *second generation* would be the *first "day"* of the prophecy. That generation belongs to the forty years spanning from 1884 to 1924. The "offence" would have taken place partway into that first day, yet it stands as the first day as a whole. We compare this reckoning of time to the reckoning of the crucifixion of Christ. The offence of the crucifixion would have been the first day, the preparation day—our Friday—and the resurrection on the third day, or first day of the week—our Sunday, and the total time was called "three days and three nights," though it was not a full 72 hours (Luke 23:54; 24:1, 21; Matt. 12:40).

In Isaiah 8:14, Jesus is called a "stone of stumbling" and a "rock of offence" to Israel. The ancient people of God were so offended by Him that they crucified Him. We find the modern parallel in the 1888 era, which is considered a crucifixion event, as Christ was rejected in the person of the Holy Spirit. This is an important point, so we will back it by three witnesses.

Men professing godliness have despised Christ in the person of his messengers. Like the Jews, they reject God's message. The Jews asked regarding Christ, "Who is this? Is not this Joseph's son?" He was not the Christ that the Jews had looked for. So today the agencies that God sends are not what men have looked for. (*Review and Herald*, Aug. 17, 1897, in *The Ellen G. White 1888 Materials*, p. 1651, emphasis added)

When I purposed to leave Minneapolis, the angel of the Lord stood by me and said: "Not so; God has a work for you to do in this place. The people are acting over the rebellion of Korah, Dathan, and Abiram.… **It is not you they are despising, but the messengers and the message I send to My people.** They have shown contempt for the word of the Lord. Satan has blinded their eyes and perverted their judgment; and unless every soul shall repent of this their sin, this unsanctified independence that is **doing insult to the Spirit of God**, they will walk in darkness.… They have obscured their spiritual eyesight. **They would not that God would manifest His Spirit and His power**; for they have a spirit of mockery and disgust at My word.…" (Lt. 2a, 1892, in *The Ellen G. White 1888 Materials*, p. 1067, emphasis added)

Those who **resisted the Spirit of God at Minneapolis** … pronounced in their heart and soul and words that this manifestation of the Holy Spirit was fanaticism and delusion. They stood like a rock, the waves of mercy flowing upon and around them, but beaten back by their hard and wicked hearts, which resisted the Holy Spirit's working. Had this been received, it would have made them wise unto salvation; holier men, prepared to do the work of God with sanctified ability. But **all the universe of heaven witnessed the disgraceful treatment of Jesus Christ, represented by the Holy Spirit. Had Christ been before them, they would have treated him in a manner similar to that in which the Jews treated Christ**. (Lt. 6, 1896, in *The Ellen G. White 1888 Materials*, pp. 1478, 1479, emphasis added)

So disturbed by the spirit of the opposition she witnessed, Ellen White was on the verge of leaving the meeting.

> Thus it was in the betrayal, trial, and crucifixion of Jesus—all this had passed before me point by point. The Satanic spirit took control and moved with power upon the human hearts that had been opened to doubts and to bitterness, wrath and hatred. All this was prevailing in that meeting. I decided to leave the meeting, leave Minneapolis ... (Letter 14, 1889, in *The Ellen G. White 1888 Materials*, p. 310)

Yet, Mrs. White then informs us that Jesus came to her and said: "It is not you they are despising, but the messengers and the message I send to My people. They have shown contempt for the word of the Lord" (Lt. 2a, 1892, in *The Ellen G. White 1888 Materials*, p. 1067). That it was Christ that was then rejected, a parallel action to His rejection and crucifixion by the Jews in AD 31, is a matter of immense gravity.

> Sarcastic remarks were passed from one to another, ridiculing their brethren A. T. Jones, E. J. Waggoner, and Willie C. White, and myself.... (Lt. 85, 1889, in *The Ellen G. White 1888 Materials*, p. 277)

> Said my guide, "This is written in the books as against Jesus Christ.... This spirit bears no more the semblance to the Spirit of truth and righteousness than the spirit that actuated the Jews to form a confederacy to doubt, to criticize and become spies upon Christ, the world's Redeemer.... there was a confederacy formed to allow of no change of ideas on any point or position they had received any more than did the Jews." (Lt. 85, 1889, in *The Ellen G. White 1888 Materials*, p. 278)

Some have claimed that leading rejecters of the 1888 message later repented and set things right, but this is historical myth. (**Section II** deals with the history of their rejection.) The state of affairs from that time forward has never been made right by denominational authorities in any kind of official capacity. The call for corporate repentance has been held in contempt. Officials have demanded that those making the call for repentance retract their call and apologize for misleading the people.

So it is that the Lord has not been able to finish the work in His people because of their impenitence. As a consequence, the Lord would "return to His place" (Hosea 5:15).

The *second day*, which was the *third generation* in the generational time cycle since the end of the 2300 days, spanning from 1924 to 1964, saw the leadership receive a re-introduction by Wieland and Short of Jones and Waggoner's message with the history of the rejection of that message by church leadership of the previous generation. Such was another opportunity lost. Yet, when the documentation of the proceedings came into the people's hands, many took hold of the message independently—in spite of the distractions, obfuscation and confusion foisted upon the church through the rejection of light, the compromises with Babylon, and the Laodiceanism. This is documented in the section of this book, "The Devoured Generations."

On the "third day," which was the same period as the *fourth generation* in the time cycle that lasted from 1964 to 2004, many voices and independent movements arose to proclaim the messages of true righteousness by faith and of the covenants *as proclaimed in 1888*, along with an advanced understanding of the light of the knowledge of the glory of the character of God, shining in the face of Jesus Christ (2 Cor. 4:6). In so doing, they fulfilled Hosea 6:3, which brings into view the rise of the character of God message, connecting the advance in the knowledge of God with the latter rain.

To summarize in chart form the progression under the "Fourth Angel View," we note that the prophecy of Hosea reveals that the fourth angel has to come twice before his mission is successfully accomplished:

- *First Day* (1888–1893) a specific period of emphasis under Jones and Waggoner within the second generation of Adventism (1884–1924), the fourth angel's first appearance.

- The *fourth angel returns to his place* to await the repentance of the Advent people (Hosea 5:15).

- *Second Day* (1950–1962) a specific period of emphasis under Wieland and Short within the third generation of Adventism (1924–1964), calling for the acceptance of the light of 1888 and repentance for rejection of the history, the fourth angel's second appearance (Hosea 6:1, 2), when the majority rejected him again.

- *Third Day* fourth generation of Adventism (1964–2004) and beyond, when God raises up His people who now live in His sight in the true message.

- The *latter rain falls*, the power of God comes on those who follow on to know the Lord; Hosea 6:3 predicts the rise of the character of God message (see *Fundamentals of Christian Education*, p. 444; *Christ's Object Lessons*, pp. 414–416).

- *Then comes the end.*

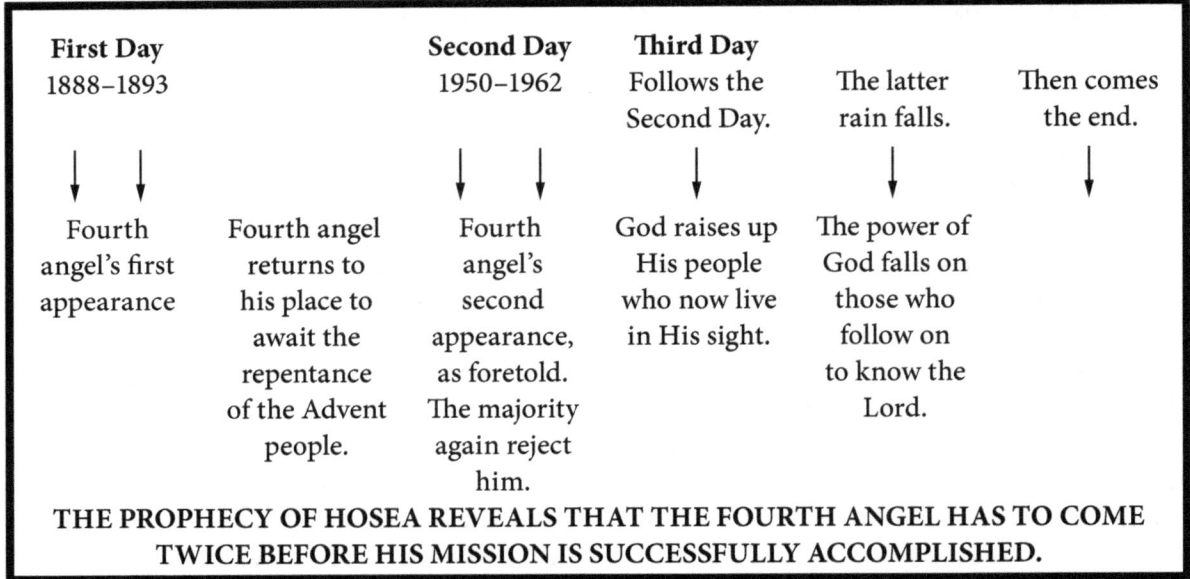

THE PROPHECY OF HOSEA REVEALS THAT THE FOURTH ANGEL HAS TO COME TWICE BEFORE HIS MISSION IS SUCCESSFULLY ACCOMPLISHED.

*This view is held by Dr. Elliot O. Douglin and can be found in the book, *The Harvest Principle and the Generation Concept in the Proclamation of the Acceptable Year of the LORD*. It is also the view held by Fred T. Wright in *The Seven Angels*, chapter 13, "The Fourth Angel Returns."

View *Two*: Offence in the *First* Generation

Offence in Laodiceanism
Arising in the First Generation (1859)

Generation 1, 1844–1884 - OFFENCE
Day 1. Generation 2, 1884–1924
Day 2. Generation 3, 1924–1964
Day 3. Generation 4, 1964–2004 - REVIVAL

The Offence is the backsliding to Laodicean lukewarm condition, by 1859, in the first generation. "Days 1 and 2" are the resulting decline into apostasy; "Day 3" is the fourth generation resurgence of the 1888 message.

"After two days will he revive us: in the third day he will raise us up, and we shall live in his sight" (Hosea 6:2).

View Two: Offence in the First Generation— the "Laodicean View"

A second approach to this subject, held by other Bible students, is that *the offence occurred in the first generation*, as God's people sank into Laodicean lukewarmness, and, by the testimony of the prophet regarding the gross spiritual declension of the Advent people, they earned the title of Laodicean by 1859 (*Testimonies for the Church*, vol. 1, p. 186), the date most often given by researchers. However, there is evidence of this being the case as early as 1852 (*Review and Herald*, June 10, 1852).

This view bypasses the Hebrew reckoning of time, discounting the first-generation "day of offence" in the prophecy of Hosea 6:2, interpreting it as being precursory to the three days. Therefore, the phrase "after two days" would be reckoned as generations two (1884–1924) and three (1924–1964), and the third day would be reckoned as the fourth generation in the time cycle (1964–2004). In other words, in this view the first generation—the generation of offence—does not line up with any day mentioned in Hosea 6:2. The second and third generations of apostasy are equated with the "after two days" in the text, and the fourth generation of apostasy is equated with the "third day" of the text. There is no particular linkage to the ministry of the fourth angel in this schema. The revival of the third day, in the fourth generation, would be the healing of the Laodicean condition, which is accomplished through the embracing of the fullness of the true gospel of the 1888 "beginning of the latter rain" and "loud cry" message, which is the righteousness by faith message proclaimed by Jones and Waggoner.

The Outcome is the Same

Both views come to the same conclusion, following the typology of ancient Israel's offence in rejecting God.

In the *first view* of the *offence in the second generation* of modern Israel, it is the rejection of the latter rain message, which is the rejection of the Holy Spirit and, therefore, the rejection of Christ. In this is a crucifixion event that parallels ancient Israel. In the *second view* of the *offence in the first generation*, we find that, in both ancient and modern Israel, the spiritual decline was the result of looking to humanity for leadership and strength. In so doing, the first generation rejected God and demanded a king, then followed three more generations with the end result of a divided kingdom.

Whichever view one favors, the outcome is the same. The fourth generation of Adventism was a great shaking period—a period of intensifying lukewarmness and even apostasy amongst many in leadership and the millions of followers—*while it was also a time of increased knowledge and acceptance of the message and its increasing glory by many in the Seventh-day Adventist world*, that is, those who were anxious not to lose sight of the true message of righteousness by faith as the latter rain message and as "the third angel's message in verity" (*Review and Herald*, April 1, 1890). God's purposes were fulfilled in all of this in *raising up a final generation* to receive the latter rain outpouring of the Holy Spirit, as discussed under the "Fourth Angel View."

It could be argued that the passing of the fourth generation (1964–2004) and the beginning of another generation would nullify this interpretation of Hosea's prophecy. Yet, there is no reason that it must move right through to the consummation in the third day. The prophecy says that the people will arise in the third day, and, if they follow on in the knowledge of God, He will bring the latter rain for the finishing of the work.

So, the awareness raised and the agitation fomented in the fourth generation resulted in a new groundwork being laid in the formation of many independent groups and publications. This raising of the final generation of restoration is the work of God that is expected to swell in the first generation of this new cycle (2004–2044) to complete the work of the restoration of the kingdom through the proclamation of the loud cry message under the added power of the fourth angel.

The Revival is the Latter Rain Outpouring

Hosea 6:3 unmistakably sets the context for revival as that of the outpouring of the latter rain:

Then shall we know, *if* we follow on to know the LORD: his going forth is prepared as the morning; and **he shall come unto us as the rain, as the latter and former rain** unto the earth. (Hosea 6:3)

The inspired counsel turns to Hosea 6:3 in discussing the latter rain. Notice that, in this context, there is a message about following on—or progressing—in the knowledge of the Lord. We will come back to this. Yet, first we want to draw attention to the point the counsel made regarding the prophecy in Joel.

The work will be similar to that of the Day of Pentecost. As the "former rain" was given, in the outpouring of the Holy Spirit at the opening of the gospel, to cause the upspringing of the precious seed, so the "latter rain" will be given at its close for the ripening of the harvest. "Then shall we know, if we follow on to know the Lord; His going forth is prepared as the morning; and He shall come unto us as the rain, as the latter and former rain unto the earth." Hosea 6:3. (*The Great Controversy*, p. 611)

The exposition in *The Great Controversy* continues with quotations from Joel 2 and Acts 2. In Acts 2, Peter quoted from Joel 2:16–21. Where was it that we read about the restoration from the years that the insects had eaten? *In Joel, chapter 2*. The connection is clear! The prophecy applies to *our day* and *the flow of history through the generations of Adventism*. God saw all of this, and the prophets wrote as they were moved by the Holy Spirit.

"Be glad then, ye children of Zion, and rejoice in the Lord your God: for He hath given you the former rain moderately, and **He will cause to come down for you the rain, the former rain, and the latter rain.**" Joel 2:23. "**In the last days, saith God, I will pour out of My Spirit upon all flesh.**" "And it shall come to pass, that whosoever shall call on the name of the Lord shall be saved." Acts 2:17, 21.

The great work of the gospel is not to close with less manifestation of the power of God than marked its opening. The prophecies which were fulfilled in the outpouring of the former rain at the opening of the gospel, are again to be fulfilled in the latter rain at its close. **Here are "the times of refreshing" to which the apostle Peter looked forward** when he said: "Repent ye therefore, and be converted, that your sins may be blotted out [*in the Investigative Judgment*], when the times of refreshing shall come from the presence of the Lord; and He shall send Jesus." Acts 3:19, 20. (*The Great Controversy*, pp. 611, 612, emphasis added)

What did we just say? That there is a biblical and Spirit of Prophecy linkage between Hosea's prophecy regarding the offence and revival in the third day and Joel's prophecy regarding the generations of degeneration and apostasy and the restoration in the time of the latter rain in our day. (Several Spirit of Prophecy statements apply Hosea's prophecy to our day; see Ms. 101, 1901, par. 41; Ms. 106, 1902, par. 26; Ms. 76, 1905, par. 15; and Lt. 50, 1907, par. 26.)

It is very exciting to understand that the story of the generations fulfils prophecy in that it causes the people to understand what has happened in history to bring about confession and true repentance that they might now follow on to know the Lord!

CHAPTER 2.

Following On to Know the LORD

We will continue from where we left off in the previous segment, exploring the role of the final generation of the people of God, who are reformers and restorers of God's truth.

> **Then shall we know,** if **we follow on to know the LORD**: his going forth is prepared as the morning; and he shall come unto us as the rain, as the latter *and* former rain unto the earth. (Hosea 6:3, emphasis added)

Seeing Him As He Is

It is following on to know the LORD that will bring the restoration. Knowing the Lord means intimate biblical knowledge that produces fullness of experience. We must know who He is, know His true character, and *experience* Christ in the life through the transformation of heart and mind that we may be able to present Him to the world *as He is*.

> Beloved, now are we the sons of God, and it doth not yet appear what we shall be: but we know that, when he shall appear, we shall be like him; for **we shall see him** as he is.
>
> And **every man that hath this hope in him purifieth himself**, even as he is pure. (1 John 3:2, 3, emphasis added)

We will *see* Him as He is, enabling us to *tell* others who He is. More importantly, we will *be* as He is, enabling us to *demonstrate* to others convincingly who He is, showing the righteousness of God. The "most precious message," which was given by A. T. Jones and E. J. Waggoner in the 1888 session at Minneapolis and heartily endorsed by Ellen White, is the beginning of the latter rain, and it is the message of righteousness by the faith of Christ. We will validate this conclusion as we continue.

Following on to know the Lord will effect in us the fullness of the righteousness of Christ through complete transformation of character with true obedience from the heart and not from fear of punishment or hope of reward. This is the purification of God's church. It takes place in the hearts of *individuals* who enter into the fullness of an abiding relationship with Christ, the Head of His church. (This is not to confuse "denomination" with "church," for they are not synonymous in this context.)

As this becomes the experience of the final generation, the way is open for advancement into all the light that God would have us shine into the world, not only preparing us for the harvest but also bringing the whole world to decision.

The truth of Christ and His Righteousness makes manifest the *true* character of God as we see Him "as He is." It is a marvelous thing to consider that the *true* work of God and the *true* view of God will be what *will shake the church as it shakes the world* until the pronouncement is made: Let the righteous be righteous still, and let the unrighteous be unrighteous still; come, ye blessed of my Father, inherit the kingdom prepared for you; Ephraim is joined to his idols,

The Beginning of the Loud Cry

Remember, the 1888 message was the beginning of the latter rain. Here is a passage that confirms it:

> Let every one who claims to believe that the Lord is soon coming, search the Scriptures as never before; for Satan is determined to try every device possible to keep souls in darkness, and blind the mind to the perils of the times in which we are living. Let every believer take up his Bible with earnest prayer, that he may be enlightened by the holy Spirit as to **what is truth, that he may know more of God and of Jesus Christ** whom he has sent. Search for the truth as for hidden treasures, and disappoint the enemy. **The time of test is just upon us, for the loud cry of the third angel has already begun in the revelation of the righteousness of Christ, the sin-pardoning Redeemer. This is the beginning of the light of the angel whose glory shall fill the whole earth.… If you would stand through the time of trouble, you must know Christ, and appropriate the gift of His righteousness**, which He imputes to the repentant sinner. (*Review and Herald*, Nov. 22, 1892, emphasis added)

As we move through this section, keep fixed in mind the linkage between the knowledge of God and the glory of the fourth angel.

The Advance of the Loud Cry Reveals God's Character

The study of the "most precious message" of our sin-pardoning Savior will produce a greater understanding of righteousness, for we will see more of who God is in the character of Jesus.

> If we would develop Christian characters, **we must study the character of Christ**, that we may come into full union with him. (*Review and Herald*, Dec. 12, 1878, art. B, emphasis added)

> We cannot by searching find out God. But **He has revealed Himself in the character of Christ, who is the brightness of the Father's glory**, and the express image of His person. **If we desire a knowledge of God, we must be Christlike.…**
>
> **He who does not seek each day to be more like Christ, cannot know the character of God.** Living a pure life through faith in Christ as a personal Saviour brings the believer into **a clearer, higher conception of God. No man whose character is not noble and Christlike can set forth God in a correct light**. He may preach Christ, but he does not show his hearers that Christ is an abiding guest in his heart.… (Ms. 133, 1899, in *This Day with God*, p. 272, emphasis added)

This "clearer, higher conception of God" is what we must now have. Have you recently been hearing references to the "character of God" with increasing frequency? What is the "character of God"? Have we not always had the right view of it? What is this "clearer, higher" picture of God? We cannot plumb the depths of it right now, yet it is available to you. Have you been praying for the latter rain? It is now here!

The latter rain is in the *preaching and receiving* of the living message, and it is even now in the process of swelling to its loud cry. (See the book, *As He Is: Issues in the 'Character of God' Controversy*, by 4th Angel Publications).

Does this sound like a bold claim? Are we really to expect such developments? Yes, we are! Inspiration declares that there is to come a time when new light of truth is to come to view. Because of this declaration, every new group that develops pulls out the quotations regarding "new light" to support their particular message, even though very few even hint as to what the "new light" will be. Yet, we find one reference that indicates that the "new light" will be with regard to "the character and attributes of God" (Ms. 22, 1895, in *Fundamentals of Christian Education*, p. 444).

The reformation is to advance until the end.

> The Reformation did not, as many suppose, end with Luther. It is to be continued to the close of this world's history. Luther had a great work to do in reflecting to others the light which God had permitted to shine upon him; yet he did not receive all the light which was to be given to the world. **From that time to this, new light has been continually shining** upon the Scriptures, and **new truths have been constantly unfolding.** (*The Great Controversy*, pp. 148, 149, emphasis added)

So, do we want to be *conformers*, or do we want to be *reformers*? Let us not be conformed to the character and ways of this world. If we become transformed through the renewing of our minds, we will be a part of those who are again wielding the torch of reformation in the world.

We must not think, "Well, we have all the truth, we understand the main pillars of our faith, and we may rest on this knowledge." **The truth is an advancing truth, and we must walk in the increasing light.** (*Review and Herald,* March 25, 1890, emphasis added)

If we think that we have all that we need to take us right on through and that we are not to receive greater revelations and unfolding of truth as time goes on, then we are of that class that receives the rebuke of Jesus, and we need to be thoroughly aroused regarding our condition and receive the remedy for it. Maintaining the truth that we have been given does not preclude receiving new light.

It is a fact that we have the truth, and we must hold with tenacity to the positions that cannot be shaken; but **we must not look with suspicion upon any new light which God may send**, and say, Really, we cannot see that we need any more light than the old truth [*historic Adventism*] which we have hitherto received, and in which we are settled. **While we hold to this position, the testimony of the True Witness applies to our cases its rebuke**, "And knowest not that thou art wretched, and miserable, and poor, and blind, and naked." Those who feel rich and increased with goods and in need of nothing, are in a condition of blindness as to their true condition before God, and they know it not. (*Review and Herald,* Aug. 7, 1894, emphasis added)

God's People Must Advance in Knowledge and Experience

We who have been blessed with the oracles of God bear responsibility to advance in light. This does not mean waiting for conference leaders, university professors, or the personnel of the Biblical Research Institute to do it for us. We have our Bibles! We have the Spirit of Prophecy. We have access to the Holy Spirit. The history of the three angels' movement is ours. Do we know it? Do we study how to advance it?

Upon every individual who has had the light of present truth devolves the duty of **developing that truth** on a higher scale than it has hitherto been developed. (*Review and Herald,* Sept. 21, 1897, emphasis added)

It is seen most clearly today by many diligent students of the Word of God, and we are now proclaiming to you that *the knowledge of God's character is the special emphasis of truth for ripening the harvest.* Without the correct understanding of the character of God, no one will be prepared for the crisis ahead. Also, it is apparent that even God's church has not come far enough out of the darkness to give the right message. However, this situation will change and *is changing* at the level of the heart and mind in both mainstream and independent spheres of influence.

So it will be in the great final conflict of the controversy between righteousness and sin. While **new life and light and power are descending from on high upon the disciples of Christ**, a new life is springing up from beneath, and energizing the agencies of Satan. Intensity is taking possession of every earthly element. With a subtlety gained through centuries of conflict, the prince of evil works under a disguise. He appears clothed as an angel of light, and multitudes are "giving heed to seducing spirits, and doctrines of devils." 1 Timothy 4:1. (*The Desire of Ages,* p. 257, emphasis added)

Without a more advanced understanding of His character, it will not be reproduced in us. Up until the final generation, God's people have not come far enough in their understanding and knowledge or in revival and reformation to make manifest His character as He truly is, thereby ending the controversy. This statement is painfully self-evident because we are still here and Christ is still waiting to return from the wedding. "**When the character of Christ shall be perfectly reproduced in His people, then He will come to claim them as His own**" (*Christ's Object Lessons,* p. 69, emphasis added).

Christ and His righteousness is the theme of the last-day remnant. We see it as the subject that must swallow up all others (*The Ellen G. White 1888 Materials,* p. 765). Christ's dominion cannot be secured forever to the joy of all creation until we see for ourselves His divine righteousness in all His dealings with the rebellion of men and angels—from the beginning of the great controversy to its end—and proclaim it to the world in word and in deed.

As we continue, please bear in mind that our discussion in these few pages is not intended to be an in-depth study of the present truth message of the character of God. We are rather pointing to some of the main ideas about the subject, while encouraging the readers to seek out this message from other sources and study it carefully.

The Great Final Issue—
Is It about Correct Days or Correct Character?

In the context of "the great and final conflict," we should understand that this advanced message regarding the character of God is the central issue that comes to the forefront. The issue of Sabbath vs. Sunday is *the mechanism* that will cause the final conflict to surface as the world system, controlled by Satan, imposes upon the conscience the requirement of bowing to human supremacy in matters of worship. They will command all the world to bow down to the figure claiming to be Jesus Christ through adherence to Sunday observance:

> Satan ... will come personating Jesus Christ, working mighty miracles; and men will fall down and worship him as Jesus Christ. **We shall be commanded to worship this being,** whom the world will glorify as Christ. (*Review and Herald*, Dec. 18, 1888, art. A, emphasis added)

> ... in his assumed character of Christ, he claims to have changed the Sabbath to Sunday, and **commands all to hallow the day which he has blessed.** (*The Great Controversy*, 1888, p. 624, emphasis added)

The issues of *freedom* and *liberty of conscience* will overshadow the matter of which day is the right day to observe the Sabbath commandment. This is where *the principles* of the true Sabbath and its Lord are contrasted with the false sabbath and *its* lord. Then, the character and attributes of both will be seen as they truly are. The contest will be between the power of "might" (force) vs. the power of "right" (love and freedom). *The conflict is really about the character of the two systems and their creators*:

> Jesus Christ is the Restorer. Satan, the apostate, is the destroyer. **Here is the conflict** between the Prince of life and the prince of this world, the power of darkness.... (Lt. 34, 1896, in *Christ Triumphant*, p. 247, emphasis added)

It is ever our desire to impress upon our brothers and sisters the gravity of this knowledge and its implementation in our life and character. We must know God as He truly is if we are to have His character reproduced in us. Those who fail in this regard will not stand in the final crisis. It is that serious!

At every revival of God's work the prince of evil is aroused to more intense activity; he is now putting forth his utmost efforts for a final struggle against Christ and His followers. The last great delusion is soon to open before us. Antichrist is to perform his marvelous works in our sight.... Those who endeavor to obey all the commandments of God will be opposed and derided. They can stand only in God. **In order to endure the trial before them, they must understand the will of God as revealed in His word; they can honor Him only as they have a right conception of His character, government, and purposes, and act in accordance with them.** None but those who have fortified the mind with the truths of the Bible will stand through the last great conflict. (*The Great Controversy*, pp. 593, 594, emphasis added)

Claims of New Light

There is something here in the message regarding God's character that we have missed or even misunderstood. We believed that we had it right when apparently we had it wrong. We thought that because we repudiated eternal hellfire that we had the right understanding of the character of God. Yet, I would assert, that that is not it. There are "new views" to come that go beyond what we have traditionally taught. Consider the following general inspired statements:

> **There is no excuse for anyone in taking the position that there is no more truth to be revealed, and that all our expositions of Scripture are without an error.** The fact that certain doctrines have been held as truth for many years by our people, is not a proof that our ideas are infallible. Age will not make error into truth, and truth can afford to be fair. No true doctrine will lose anything by close investigation. (*Counsels to Writers and Editors*, p. 35, emphasis added)

> **We have many lessons to learn, and many, many to unlearn.** God and Heaven alone are infallible. Those who think that they will never have to give up a cherished view, never have occasion to change an opinion, will be disappointed. As long as we hold to our own ideas and opinions with determined persistency, we cannot have the unity for which Christ prayed. (*Review and Herald*, July 26, 1892, in *Christian Experience and Teaching of Ellen G. White*, p. 203, emphasis added)

> **Different periods in the history of the church have each been marked by the development of some special**

truth, adapted to the necessities of God's people at that time. Every new truth has made its way against hatred and opposition; those who were blessed with its light were tempted and tried. The Lord gives a special truth for the people in an emergency. Who dare refuse to publish it? He commands His servants to present **the last invitation of mercy to the world** [which is a "revelation of His character," *Christ's Object Lessons*, p. 416]. They cannot remain silent, except at the peril of their souls. Christ's ambassadors have nothing to do with consequences. They must perform their duty, and leave results with God. (*The Great Controversy*, pp. 609, 610, emphasis added)

Those who lived in past generations were accountable for the light which was permitted to shine upon them. Their minds were exercised in regard to different points of Scripture which tested them. But they did not understand the truths which we do. **They were not responsible for the light which they did not have.** They had the Bible, as we have; but **the time for the unfolding of special truth in relation to the closing scenes of this earth's history is during the last generations that shall live upon the earth.**

Special truths have been adapted to the conditions of the generations as they have existed. **The present truth, which is a test to the people of this generation, was not a test to the people of generations far back.** If the light which now shines upon us in regard to the Sabbath of the fourth commandment had been given to the generations in the past, God would have held them accountable for that light. (*Testimonies for the Church*, vol. 2, pp. 692, 693, emphasis added)

There are many claims to "new light" today. Groups are claiming that their light is *the* final generation light. All are contenders for authentication as that which pertains to the outpouring of the latter rain. Gusting winds are bringing in aberrant doctrines like tumbleweed, such as:

- returning to the observance of the typical feast days;

- the "lunar sabbath," with its re-ordering of the calendar to follow the cycles of the moon to give us the supposed proper days to keep the Sabbath;

- mind-numbing wrangling over the nature of the Godhead and its Three: the Father, the Son, and the Holy Spirit;

- the so-called "2520 prophecy."

Various "new light" theories, such as those mentioned above, are being promoted, and their champions support them from hefty compilations of inspired statements, leaving us to ask, "How are we to determine what 'new light' is valid? Will the real 'new light' please stand up?"

The Scriptures clearly define that which is valid. In addition, we are thankful for the definitive guiding light that the Lord has provided through the gift of prophecy, for it is most assuredly a beacon built upon the Rock of Christ to light our way and guide us safely into the heavenly harbor, keeping us from running aground on the rocks of error and making shipwreck of our faith.

At no period of time has man learned all that can be learned of the word of God. There are yet new views of truth to be seen, and much to be understood of the character and attributes of God,—**his benevolence, his mercy, his long forbearance, his example of perfect obedience. "And the Word was made flesh, and dwelt among us, (and** we beheld *his glory*, the glory as of the only begotten of the Father,) **full of grace and truth." This is a most valuable study, taxing the intellect, and giving strength to the mental ability. After diligently searching the word,** hidden treasures are discovered, **and** the lover of truth breaks out in triumph.... (Ms. 22, 1895, in *Special Testimonies on Education*, 1897; p. 147, emphasis added)

Looking at the testimony above, I have to ask teachers and students of Adventist history some pointed questions: "Can you identify anything in our progress in biblical study over the generations and in our calling to advance the reformation that would fulfill this prophecy? Is there anything we could call a 'new view' of the character and glory of God that we could definitively identify as a discovery of hidden treasures—something that has caused us to 'break out in triumph'?"

God's Character is the Light of His Glory

The new views to come to God's people have to do with the light on His character, and this light is to be a message proclaimed with a loud voice. God's people have not brought this particular message out in the past in the fine detail and particular emphasis that is being revealed today or that will be revealed through the final movements. During this time, the followers of the true Christ will be shining with the glory of God as they give the "loud cry" message. His glory is His character (see *Amazing* Grace, p. 322).

> He causes "the light to shine out of darkness." 2 Corinthians 4:6. When "the earth was without form, and void, and darkness was upon the face of the deep," "the Spirit of God moved upon the face of the waters. And God said, Let there be light; and there was light." Genesis 1:2, 3. So in the night of spiritual darkness, God's word goes forth, "Let there be light." To His people He says, **"Arise, shine; for thy light is come, and the glory of the Lord is risen upon thee."** Isaiah 60:1.
>
> "Behold," says the Scripture, "the darkness shall cover the earth, and gross darkness the people; but the Lord shall arise upon thee, and His glory shall be seen upon thee." Isaiah 60:2.
>
> It is the **darkness of misapprehension of God that is enshrouding the world.** Men are **losing their knowledge of His character.** It has been misunderstood and misinterpreted. At this time a message from God is to be proclaimed, **a message** illuminating **in its influence and saving in its power. His character is to be made known.** Into the darkness of the world is to be shed the light of His glory, the light of His goodness, mercy, and truth. (*Christ's Object Lessons*, p. 415, emphasis added)

Although we are not actually getting into the advanced and distinctive features of the message of God's character in this study, the very fact that there is agitation regarding this message is evidence that, even now, we are going into the time of final crisis. Even though some would consider us to have false light, the prophetic word of God declares that this is the subject of the final message. The message regarding the character of God is, in fact, designated the last message of mercy to be given to the world.

The message is a loud cry, and it begins in the house of God

For the Lord's people to give the final message to the world with clarity and strength, they must first understand the message.

> This is the work outlined by the prophet Isaiah in the words, "O Jerusalem, that bringest good tidings, **lift up thy voice with strength**; lift it up, be not afraid; **say unto the cities of Judah, Behold your God!** Behold, the Lord God will come with strong hand, and His arm shall rule for Him; behold, His reward is with Him, and His work before Him." Isaiah 40:9, 10. (*Christ's Object Lessons*, p. 415, emphasis added)

It is the last message of mercy for the world.

> Those who wait for the Bridegroom's coming are to say to the people, "Behold your God." The **last rays of merciful light**, the **last message of mercy** to be given to the world, **is a revelation of His character** of love. The children of God are to **manifest His glory**. In their own life and character they are to reveal what the grace of God has done for them. (*Christ's Object Lessons*, pp. 415, 416, emphasis added)

The light of His glory is the last message

The glorious fourth angel of Revelation 18 appears to give added power, impetus and light to the third angel's message. This is the messenger of the latter rain. A great power attends the message of this angel and it brings down the kingdom of Satan.

> And after these things I saw another angel come down from heaven, having great power; and **the earth was lightened with his glory.** (Rev. 18:1, emphasis added)

What is the glory of God?

> **The glory of God is His character.**... This character was revealed in the life of Christ. (*That I Might Know Him*, p. 131, emphasis added)

As it was in Him, so too will it be revealed in us. We read in Isaiah 60:1, 2, as we saw in *Christ's Object Lessons* above—the glory of the LORD *upon us* will dispel the darkness. Again, what is the darkness?

> It is the **darkness of misapprehension of God** that is enshrouding the world. Men are losing their **knowledge of His character.** It has been misunderstood and misinterpreted. (*Christ's Object Lessons*, p. 415, emphasis added)

Again, what is the glory of God?

> **The glory of the Lord is his character** that was revealed to Moses; but how different is the representation of himself from that made by Satan, the father of lies! (*Signs of the Times*, June 27, 1895, emphasis added)

It is a global message to bring the light of God to the forefront:

> For the earth shall be filled with the **knowledge of the glory of the LORD**, as the waters cover the sea. (Hab. 2:14, emphasis added)

How is this glory to fill the earth? The Lord through Isaiah says that it arises in His people, and here again, Paul confirms it in the New Testament:

> For God, who commanded the light to shine out of darkness, **hath shined in our hearts**, to *give* **the light of the knowledge of the glory of God in the face of Jesus Christ**. But **we have this treasure in earthen vessels**, that the excellency of the power may be of God, and not of us. (2 Cor. 4:6, 7, emphasis added)

One more time, to fix it fast in our minds and to give a third reference, let us ask: What is the glory of God in the face of Jesus Christ?

> **The glory of Christ is his character**, and his character is an expression of the law of God. (*Signs of the Times*, Dec. 12, 1895, emphasis added)

This revelation is all to awaken and prepare us and the world for the closing of the great controversy and the return of Christ. We must arouse at this time and not be like the five foolish virgins, for they were the ones who have neglected this most important study. We read that "the class represented by the foolish virgins have been content with a superficial work. They do not know God. They have not studied His character ..." (*Christ's Object Lessons*, p. 411).

The Experiential Knowledge of God Brings Christ Back to Take Us Home

The message of Christ's righteousness and the knowledge of God's true character produce a translation ready church.

> Awake to righteousness, and sin not; for **some have not the knowledge of God**: I speak *this* to your shame. (1 Cor. 15:34, emphasis added)

"When the fruit is brought forth, immediately he putteth in the sickle, because the harvest is come." [Mark 4:29.] Christ is waiting with longing desire for the manifestation of Himself in His church. **When the character of Christ shall be perfectly reproduced in His people, then He will come to claim them as His own.**

It is the privilege of every Christian **not only to look for but to hasten** the coming of our Lord Jesus Christ, (2 Peter 3:12, margin). Were all who profess His name **bearing fruit to His glory**, how quickly the whole world would be sown with the seed of the gospel. Quickly the last great harvest would be ripened, and Christ would come to gather the precious grain. (*Christ's Object Lessons*, p. 69, emphasis added)

The Final Generation Will Be Fully Recovered from Error

Before this time, God winked at ignorance. However, in the final showdown, there is no room for erroneous views about God. In fact, *any* misconceptions or false teachings will be the downfall of professed Christians. Erroneous belief leads to erroneous actions. It is my contention that, if we believe God will destroy His enemies by proactive measure, by wielding personal force, then we will have nothing better to behold than a destroying God. By beholding, we are conformed into the same image. Our minds, characters and personalities are shaped by the images and philosophies to which we expose them.

We have been in error with regard to the character of God. The "new views" that have come to light at this time are showing it to be so. It is time to recover from this error so that we can embrace the present truth message that will prevent us from embracing the errors that will ripen the wicked into readiness for the harvest of destruction. Following on to know the Lord *as He is* will bring the righteous into harvest readiness unto the kingdom of God. In all of this, the great controversy will catapult forward to its conclusion.

> **At the time of the loud cry of the third angel those who have been** in any measure **blinded by the enemy, who have not** fully recovered **themselves from the snare of Satan, will be in peril**, because **it will be difficult for them to** discern **the light** from heaven, and they will be inclined to accept falsehood. **Their erroneous experience will color their thoughts, their decisions, their propositions, their counsels. The evidences that God has given will be no evidence to those who have blinded their eyes by choosing darkness rather than light**. After rejecting light, they will originate theories which they will call "light," but which the Lord calls, "Sparks of their own kindling," [Isa. 50:11] by which

they will direct their steps.... (*Review and Herald*, Dec. 13, 1892, emphasis added)

The reformation is completed in the last generation time of judgment, when God's people obtain the discernment that comes from the correct view of His character.

> Then they that feared the LORD spake often one to another: and the LORD hearkened, and heard *it*, and **a book of remembrance was written** before him for them that feared the LORD, and that **thought upon his name**. [*NOTE: His name equals His character; see Ms. 21, 1891; Youth's Instructor, Dec. 15, 1892.*] And they shall be mine, saith the LORD of hosts, **in that day when I make up my jewels**; and I will spare them, as a man spareth his own son that serveth him. **Then shall ye return, and discern** between the righteous and the wicked, between him that serveth God and him that serveth him not. (Mal. 3:16–18, emphasis added)

We are the Final Generation

Remember how we saw in the second chapter of Joel that there would be a restoration of the years eaten by the devouring pests. The knowledge of the Lord would be coming up in the fourth generation amongst God's faithful ones amidst a general spiritual declension. The faithful would, in fact, follow on to know the Lord in all His glory. In this very same chapter of Joel, verse 23, the context is the time of the latter rain.

We His people today are in a most privileged position, for the latter rain has begun, and it is now coming upon us in preparation for the final events. Joel says that we therefore should be glad for this.

> Be glad then, ye children of Zion, and rejoice in the LORD your God: for he hath given you the former rain moderately, and he will cause to come down for you the rain, the former rain, and the latter rain in the first *month*. (Joel 2:23)

So, the revival and reformation comes up in the fourth generation (1964–2004), and it will continue and culminate in the actual restoration in the first generation of a new cycle (2004–2043). However, we should not expect the restoration of righteousness in His people and the return of Christ to come during the end of that first generation of the new cycle. Romans 9:28 sets the restoration as occurring *early*, for the Lord "will finish the work, and cut *it* short in righteousness: because a short work will the Lord make upon the earth" (Rom. 9:28). Let us not forget what Hosea says:

> I will go *and* return to my place, till they acknowledge their offence, and seek my face: in their affliction they will seek me early. (Hosea 5:15)

> Then shall we know, *if* we follow on to know the LORD: his going forth is prepared as the morning; and he shall come unto us as the rain, as the latter *and* former rain unto the earth. (Hosea 6:3)

Coming into the time of the restoration, the glory of the Lord rises upon His people. They will seek Him early even as the dark night of woe settles down upon the world. The manifestation of Christ in His people will be a demonstration of the righteousness of God.

> With my soul have I desired thee in the night; yea, with my spirit within me will I seek thee early: for when thy judgments *are* in the earth, the inhabitants of the world will learn righteousness. (Isa. 26:9)

CHAPTER 3.

The Watches

Four Generations Equal One Historical Cycle, Eaten Up!

Tell ye your children of it, and let **your children** tell **their children, and their children another generation**. That which the palmerworm hath left hath the locust eaten; and that which the locust hath left hath the cankerworm eaten; and that which the cankerworm hath left hath the caterpillar eaten. (Joel 1:3, 4)

Four generations of Adventism have been eaten up. When we look at the Seventh-day Adventist Church, we do not generally see pure Adventism any more. It has been *eaten up*! How did that happen? It was through invitations, flirtations, and infiltrations. The man of sin has found his way in through open doors. Adventist leaders have attempted to meld the evangelical gospel of first-apartment mainstream Babylon with the distinctive Seventh-day Adventist message, creating a theological quagmire. The spiritualism of New Age doctrine, under various guises such as Spiritual Formation and Contemplative Spirituality, has been given a hearing in some Adventist educational institutions and in many of the churches. Many practices of the world are in the church, and the church is in the world, not converting the world but being converted by the world.

Why has the logo been drastically changed? Many believe that this was not an innocent upgrade of graphical

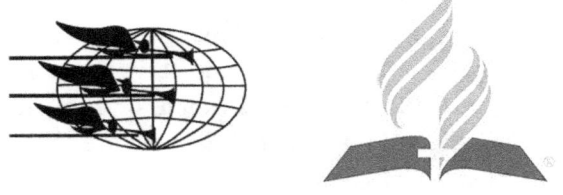

Past and current Seventh-day Adventist Church logos

representation. What was dropped out of the logo? Where are the three angels? Let the reader reflect on how many Seventh-day Adventist churches they see today with a graphic representation of the three angels anywhere on or in the building.

However, God has promised that restoration will come, and you and I can be a part of it.

Restoration after Four Generations

And I will restore to you the years that the locust hath eaten, the cankerworm, and the caterpillar, and the palmerworm, my great army which I sent among you. (Joel 2:25)

What a promise! God is speaking to those of us who are living in the fifth generation, the first generation of a new cycle. The promise is for you and for me. Our opportunity is here. What are we going to do with it?

Introducing the Watches

A generation is a night of waiting and watching. In the time of Christ, there were the four watches of the night. Thus, we can apply four watches to each generation, as we see demonstrated in the following New Testament narrative:

> Watch ye therefore: for ye know not when the master of the house cometh, at **even**, or at **midnight**, or at the **cockcrowing**, or in the **morning**: Lest coming suddenly he find you sleeping. And what I say unto you I say unto all, Watch. (Mark 13:35–37, emphasis added)

Now, we have learned that we are going to have restoration in Generation One, according to the Word of the Lord. The question is, "Which watch will it be? In which ten-year period in Generation One will these great developments transpire?"

> Blessed *are* those servants, whom the lord when he cometh shall find watching: verily I say unto you, that he shall gird himself, and make them to sit down to meat, and will come forth and serve them. And if he shall come **in the second watch**, or come **in the third watch**, and find *them* so, blessed are those servants. (Luke 12:37, 38)

Ellen White applied the concept of the watches to those awaiting Christ's return:

> A company was presented before me in contrast to the one described. They were waiting and watching. Their eyes were directed heavenward, and the words of their Master were upon their lips: "What I say unto you I say unto all, Watch." "Watch ye therefore: for ye know not when the Master of the house cometh, at even, or at midnight, or at the cockcrowing, or in the morning: lest coming suddenly He find you sleeping." [Mark 13:35, 36.] The Lord intimates a delay before the morning finally dawns. But He would not have them give way to weariness, nor relax their earnest watchfulness, because the morning does not open upon them as soon as they expected. **The waiting ones were represented to me as looking upward. They were encouraging one another by repeating these words: "The first and second watches are past. We are in the third watch, waiting and watching for the Master's return.** There remains but a little period of watching now." I saw some becoming weary; their eyes were directed downward, and they were engrossed with earthly things, and were unfaithful in watching. They were saying: **"In the first watch we expected our Master, but were disappointed. We thought surely He would come in the second watch, but that passed, and He came not. We may be again disappointed. We need not be so particular. He may not come in the following watch. We are in the third watch, and now we think it best to lay up our treasure on the earth, that we may be secure against want."** Many were sleeping, stupefied with the cares of this life and allured by the deceitfulness of riches from their waiting, watching position. (*Testimonies for the Church*, vol. 2, p. 192, emphasis added)

Establishing the Watch as a Decade of Time

> I saw that **watch after watch was in the past**. Because of this, should there be a lack of vigilance? Oh, no! There is the greater necessity of unceasing watchfulness, for **now the moments are fewer than before the passing of the first watch**. Now the period of waiting is necessarily shorter than at first. If we watched with unabated vigilance then, **how much more need of double watchfulness in the second watch. The passing of the second watch has brought us to the third**, and now it is inexcusable to abate our watchfulness. The third watch calls for threefold earnestness. **To become impatient now would be to lose all our earnest, persevering watching heretofore.** The long night of gloom is trying; but the morning is deferred in mercy, because if the Master should come, so many would be found unready.... (*Testimonies for the Church*, vol. 2, pp. 193, 194, emphasis added)

Here we may confirm that in 1868 the Advent believers were in the *third* watch of the first generation. *We should also note that all of this is inspired confirmation of the truth of the generation concept as a forty-year duration.*

Something here that is important to tuck in the memory is that Mrs. White does not mention a quadrupled intensity of watching in the fourth watch, only that to become impatient in the third "would be to lose" all the earnest watching of the previous watches. This does suggest that the cycle of four in sowing and reaping persists, even within a biblical generation.

We should now see the testimony of the Lord as designating time segments of decade-long watches within forty-year generations. Earlier we have shown four generations as a cycle of sowing and reaping, or of "time and judgment."

Watch and Pray

We have the admonition to watch and pray. What does it mean to watch? Does it mean studying prophecy and seeing how close we are to the end so that we can quickly get ready? Is it some kind of sensationalism based on time excitement? Not at all. That would be a false watching. True watching it is the sober-minded expectation of a sojourner in this world who eschews the spirit of the world and chooses to reject the pursuit of pleasure and gain.

> God's unwillingness to have His people perish has been the reason for so long delay. But the coming of the morning to the faithful, and of the night to the unfaithful, is right upon us. **By waiting and watching, God's people are to manifest their peculiar character, their separation from the world. By our watching position we are to show that we are truly strangers and pilgrims upon the earth.** The difference between those who love the world and those who love Christ is so plain as to be unmistakable. While worldlings are all earnestness and ambition to secure earthly treasure, God's people are not conformed to the world, but show by their earnest, watching, waiting position that they are transformed; that their home is not in this world, but that they are seeking a better country, even a heavenly. (*Testimonies for the Church*, vol. 2, p. 194)

> Arise, cry out in the night: in the beginning of the watches pour out thine heart like water before the face of the Lord: lift up thy hands toward him for the life of thy young children, that faint for hunger in the top of every street. (Lam. 2:19)

As we come into the true attitude of watchfulness, we will do the work of hastening the coming of Christ.

Hastening His Coming

> But, beloved, be not ignorant of this one thing, that one day *is* with the Lord as a thousand years, and a thousand years as one day. The Lord is not slack concerning his promise, as some men count slackness; but is longsuffering to us-ward, not willing that any should perish, but that all should come to repentance. (2 Peter 3:8, 9)

He has promised to come quickly, but He wants every man to have a part with Him in the great inheritance. He is not going to come in a way that would surprise us. He is going to let us know when He is coming. Why is that? It is because He wants us to understand so that we can cooperate with Him in prayer and action. Daniel understood by the prophecy of Jeremiah that Israel would be in captivity in Babylon for 70 years, and he says that, when he understood this, he went and prayed. God had prophesied, declaring that, after seventy years, Jeremiah should go pray (Jer. 29). Understanding where we are in the cycle, generation, and watch helps us pray intelligently for the coming of the Lord because we know that we are in the generation of restoration. Knowing the times helps us to be instant and purposeful in our watching and praying.

In First Thessalonians, chapter 5, Paul declares that we are not in darkness that the day of the Lord should overtake us if we are awake and watching. Likewise, Peter refers to the suddenness of Christ's coming.

> But the day of the Lord will come as a thief in the night; in the which the heavens shall pass away with a great noise, and the elements shall melt with fervent heat, the earth also and the works that are therein shall be burned up. (2 Peter 3:10)

Peter says that the day of the Lord will not come as a thief in the night for those who are watching and fully attired in the righteousness of Christ.

> *Seeing* then *that* all these things shall be dissolved, what manner *of persons* ought ye to be in *all* holy conversation and godliness. **Looking for and hasting** unto the coming of the day of God, wherein the heavens being on fire shall be dissolved, and the elements shall melt with fervent heat? (2 Peter 3:11, 12, emphasis added)

Not only are we to be looking for his coming, but we are to be actually "hasting unto" it. If we can *delay* His coming by failing to come into working order with God, it stands to reason that we can also shorten the time of waiting. We do so by full surrender to Him, allowing Him to do that which He wants to do in us. Not only does the phrase "hasting unto" mean "speeding on" or "urging on," it also means "studying" and "awaiting eagerly."

> Nevertheless we, according to his promise, look for new heavens and a new earth, wherein dwelleth righteousness. (2 Peter 3:13)

We thank God for the promise of His return, and today we are especially thankful that He does not leave us in the dark. In Amos 3:7, God tells us that He reveals His plans to the prophets. Does God have prophets today? Prophesying means proclaiming the word of the Lord. Every one who proclaims God's word is a prophet of the Lord. God is revealing to us His plans, which have been kept secret, so that we can pass them on to others with intelligent prayers, cooperating with Him in bringing about His will in the earth and putting an end to the reign of sin.

What a privilege has been given to us as a people that we can know who we are, where we are in time, and what we ought to be doing! Let us not squander the privilege.

Which Watch Shall It Be?
Again, we would remind the reader that we are not prophesying a specific date for the second coming, for the close of probation, or for any other event, based on day-for-year timelines. We believe and teach that no man knows the day or the hour of His return until it is announced by the voice of God just before Jesus returns (Ellen Harmon, *The Day-Star*, Jan. 24, 1846, in *Life Sketches*, p. 65).

So, while we urge caution on the one side, we know from our studies that Jesus told us that we would know when He is even at the doors. We know that we can confidently state that we are given to know the generation of His return as a matter of revealed truth and that it is to be proclaimed at the correct time as "present truth" in that it will have been given only to the generation to which it pertains.

Moreover, we are also to understand that He wants us to have a more refined understanding of the time as we look at the ten-year periods called "watches."

Is this not exciting to ponder? Indeed it is, and it will create its own stir and excitement. Were we warned about stir and excitement? Not without qualification. What we were warned about is having an agitation of this kind in which "principle does not control," for this places the excitement upon "a wrong basis."

> We want not to move the people's passions to get up a stir, **where feelings are moved and principle does not control**. I feel that we need to be guarded on every side, because Satan is at work to do his uttermost to insinuate his arts and devices that shall be a power to do harm. Anything that will make a stir, **create an excitement on a wrong basis**, is to be dreaded, for the reaction will surely come. (Lt. 34, 1887, in *Last Day Events*, p. 35)

The Spirit of God would have us lay down the teaching of true Righteousness by Faith and the advance of the reformation in the light on the true character of God as the foundation for this message, that we might see Him aright and know Him as He truly is, for the world *and the church* have been under gross darkness. We are told: "There are yet new views of truth to be seen, and much to be understood of the character and attributes of God" (Ms. 22, 1895, in *Special Testimonies on Education*, p. 147).

In the time of the latter rain, we can expect a breaking forth of the light of the glory of God in such a way that it will make an impact in the world like never before— including in the day of Christ—for it will precipitate the crisis described as "the time of trouble such as never was."

The 1335 Days and the "Blessed Hope"
In some of the historical expositions of the timelines, we learn that, in AD 508, the French Emperor Clovis put in place the foundation for the Holy Roman Empire. When we add the 1335 days of Daniel to AD 508, we come to 1843, the time of the first disappointment in the experience of those at the time of the Great Advent Awakening.

> **Blessed** *is* he that **waiteth**, and cometh to the thousand three hundred and five and thirty days. (Dan. 12:12, emphasis added)

There is a blessing pronounced upon those who come to that time, and James admonishes us to be patient as we wait for the rains that bring the harvest to readiness.

> Be **patient** therefore, brethren, unto the coming of the Lord. Behold, the husbandman **waiteth** for the **precious fruit** of the earth, and hath long patience for it, **until he receive the early and latter rain**. (James 5:7, emphasis added)

Patiently waiting is bound up in the concept of the *blessed hope of Christ's return*, though the understanding of "the blessed hope" was misplaced in viewing it as Christ's coming back to the earth when the hope is in looking for *the transformation of our character* into His image, so we can reflect the glory of God to the world and prepare our generation for harvest as a result of experiencing both the early and latter rain outpourings in our lives. The natural consequence of this hope is that it brings with it the return of Christ, and it is realized through the movement of Christ into His role in the most holy place of the heavenly sanctuary—the then misunderstood event that transpired in 1844. The advanced understanding of the gospel, as God's people came out of Reformation darkness, supplied the necessary ingredients to move forward into God's purposes for His people, that the great controversy might come to a close.

> **For the grace of God that bringeth salvation** hath appeared to all men. (Titus 2:11, emphasis added)

The grace of God brings salvation in that we are both forgiven and cleansed from all unrighteousness. This is faith *that works.*

> Teaching us that, denying ungodliness and worldly lusts, we should live **soberly, righteously, and godly**, in this present world; looking for that **blessed hope**, and the **glorious appearing** of the great God and our Saviour Jesus Christ. (Titus 2:12, 13, emphasis added)

> For we through the Spirit **wait** for the **hope of righteousness by faith**. (Gal. 5:5, emphasis added)

The people of God were to be watching and waiting for the movement of Christ. Though they were disappointed, they later came to understand that Christ *was* indeed returning to the earth but could only do so through the most holy place of heaven. It is in the heavenly most holy place that He can prepare a people to cooperate with Him in *bringing the world to repentance and judgment.*

The Lord's final revelation of Himself through the 144,000 would be the method He would use to accomplish this. This revelation is our reason for being; it is our purpose. God purposed that we should be the final generation showing forth His praises. As the Lord raises up His church to fulfill her commission, the intensity of Satanic hatred that brought Jesus to the cross will again be aroused, and the final events will rapidly unfold. It is a sad fact that it was the people that had the oracles of God who crucified Him. (Let the reader understand.)

Watch and Be Sober

As we have received the light of what Jesus is doing and have entered the time of preparation for His return, we are admonished to keep watching, as children of the light. At this time, even as we study the message, we are already linked with the fourth angel of Revelation 18:1. He is coming in to give added power and impetus to the messages of the three angels. There is increased light on the glory of God, which is His character.

> Ye are all the **children of light**, and the children of the day: we are not of the night, nor of darkness. Therefore let us not sleep, as do others; **but let us watch and be sober**. For they that sleep **sleep in the night**; and they that be drunken are drunken in the night. (1 Thess. 5:5–7, emphasis added)

We are to maintain our sobriety in watching. In Matthew 25, we see that Christ has depicted the people of God as sleeping virgins. Notice that, in this context, sleeping is equated with drunkenness. It is saying that we have become intoxicated with the cares of this life and earthly pursuits, and our religion has become adulterated with the wine of Babylon. One does not have to go very far in studying institutionalized religion to recognize that this is so.

Even though we are in the night of watching and waiting, we are not of the night. Rather, we are of the day. We are of the kingdom of Christ, and we already dwell in the light of the day of God, as, by faith, we await the time when all things are to be made new, even as our hearts and minds are now being made new by the work of the atonement.

> But let us, **who are of the day, be sober**, putting on the breastplate of faith and love; and for an helmet, the **hope of salvation**. For **God hath not appointed us to wrath**, but to **obtain salvation** by our Lord Jesus Christ. (1 Thess. 5:8, 9, emphasis added)

Our salvation is a hope that is in motion. The work is not static but dynamic, as we choose to look to Him and our choice to reflect His image becomes fixed, or sealed, by the Holy Spirit. Again, it is the *blessed hope of a saving work of transformation* made manifest in lives that are disciplined after Christ, which come to be "a series of uninterrupted victories" (*The Desire of Ages*, p. 679). This saving work is not merely from past sin but from any desire to continue in it, as He works to fit us for the eternal glory of His presence.

The 144,000 are a class that follows Jesus wherever He goes, and they are students of God's Word and of history. They have followed Him in the sanctuary and know the work that He is doing there. As they keep their eyes fixed upon Him, they will surely receive more and more light, *obtaining salvation* as they continue in fellowship and witness, seeing the day approaching.

Waiting for the Lord's Return from the Wedding

What should the people of God be watching and waiting for? Most of God's expectant people are waiting for the second coming, or the so-called "rapture." Yet, there is another return that they should be waiting for. And what return is that?

They should be waiting and watching for Him to *return from the wedding*. What does that mean? Is not the return from the wedding the same thing as His coming to the earth? When you are traveling, you are watching the signs as you go along—especially the closer you get to your destination. It is the same for those who are waiting for the coming of the Lord. They also will be provided with signposts in their pilgrim journey.

> Let your loins be girded about, and *your* lights burning; and ye yourselves like unto men that **wait for their lord**, when he will **return from the wedding**; that **when he cometh and knocketh**, they may open unto him immediately. (Luke 12:35, 36, emphasis added)

This return is *from the wedding*—not to the earth. God's people in 1844 followed Him into the wedding, and they did so by faith. Now God's people must follow Him as He is doing a work in heaven while they wait for Him to return from the wedding. The coming of the Bridegroom from the wedding is associated with His *knocking*. We can see this in Revelation 3 where Jesus says that He stands at the door and *knocks*.

So this is all associated with our having a deep and fixed relationship with Him to the degree that our minds are settled with Him. This would be in reference to the closing of human probation because, logically, the coming of Christ from the wedding would mean that He has married His bride and, thus, all choices have been fixed. We will consider the evidence for this in a moment.

> Blessed *are* those servants, whom the lord when he cometh shall find **watching**: verily I say unto you, that he shall gird himself, and make them to sit down to meat, and will come forth and serve them. And if he shall come in the **second watch**, or come in the **third watch**, and find *them* so, blessed are those servants. (Luke 12:37, 38, emphasis added)

Notice how He introduces the watches. In saying, "Blessed are those … whom the lord when he cometh shall find watching," He refers to the first watch. Yet, then He moves on to the possibility of His finding them in the second or third watch. This means that He wants to come in the first, but if not then, He looks to the second or the third. There is no mention of a fourth watch, as we noted earlier in the statement from *Testimonies*, volume 2. Jesus says:

> And this know, that if the goodman of the house had known what hour the thief would come, he would have watched, and not have suffered his house to be broken through. Be ye therefore ready also: for the Son of man cometh at an hour when ye think not. (Luke 12:39, 40)

We will not know the day, nor will we know the hour, yet we are definitely told to have care to discern the watches. We have seen the time cycles. We have seen the generations. Now we are to consider the watches. Which watch will it be? The Lord's answer does not contain any idle words. We are to tap into the meaning of every word that proceeds from the mouth of God and live by them. The Lord gave His servant a view of the wedding.

> I saw the Father rise from the throne, and in a flaming chariot go into the holy of holies within the veil, and sit down. Then Jesus rose up from the throne, and the most of those who were bowed down arose with Him.… Then He raised His right arm, and we heard His lovely voice saying, "**Wait here**; I am going to My Father to receive the kingdom; keep your garments spotless, and in a little while **I will return from the wedding** and receive you to Myself." (*Early Writings*, p. 55, emphasis added)

The waiting ones are here instructed to wait for him to *return from the wedding*.

> Jesus has left us word: "Watch ye therefore: for ye know not when the Master of the house cometh, at even, or at midnight, or at the cockcrowing, or in the morning: lest coming suddenly He find you sleeping. And what I say unto you I say unto all, Watch." We are waiting and watching for the return of the Master, who is to bring the morning, lest coming suddenly He find us sleeping. (*Testimonies for the Church*, vol. 2, p. 190, emphasis added)

He does not want to surprise us, nor does He want us to be sleeping. He wants us awake, watching, and aware of what it is that He is doing and what He is about to do.

The statement continues:

> What time is here referred to? **Not to the revelation of Christ in the clouds of heaven to find a people asleep. No; but to His return from His ministration in the most holy place of the heavenly sanctuary**, when He lays off His priestly attire and clothes Himself with garments of vengeance, and when the mandate goes forth: "He that is unjust, let him be unjust still: and he which is filthy, let him be filthy still: and he that is righteous, let him be righteous still; and he that is holy, let him be holy still." [Rev 22:11.] (*Testimonies for the Church*, vol. 2, pp. 190, 191, emphasis added)

The return of Christ from His ministration in the most holy place clearly designates *the closing of probation*. Jesus wants us to be aware of the imminence of this particular event. He is pleading with us not to miss it. If we see it looming large on the horizon, we may be moved to understand the gospel properly, to make sure we are in the true gospel, and to make sure that we are serious about being found in Him. We will study fervently the science of coming into complete union with Christ so that our relationship with Him may become solidified and that we may become forever sealed into it. This is not something to delay or trifle with in any case, for we do not know either the day or the hour when our life shall end.

An Apparent Delay

The Lord's first preference was that His servants would have been ready in the first watch of that first generation, yet they were not. He would have prepared that generation quickly in the first-watch period of 1844–1854 to receive Him. The children of Israel, leaving Egypt and receiving the oracles of God, were to move immediately from there and go into the Promised Land. From Mt. Sinai to Kadesh-Barnea was only an eleven-day journey. Likewise, in the experience of modern spiritual Israel, God wanted His people to proclaim the three angels' messages in that they had received from Him the oracles of the law with the Sabbath, the Sanctuary, and the Spirit of Prophecy. If they had kept in step with their heavenly Commander, they would have completed their work in the world and would have moved into the heavenly Canaan.

> The history of ancient Israel is a striking illustration of the past experience of the Adventist body. God led His people in the advent movement, even as He led the children of Israel from Egypt. In the great disappointment their faith was tested as was that of the Hebrews at the Red Sea. Had they still trusted to the guiding hand that had been with them in their past experience, they would have seen the salvation of God. If all who had labored unitedly in the work in 1844, had received the third angel's message and proclaimed it in the power of the Holy Spirit, the Lord would have wrought mightily with their efforts. A flood of light would have been shed upon the world. Years ago the inhabitants of the earth would have been warned, the closing work completed, and Christ would have come for the redemption of His people.
>
> It was not the will of God that Israel should wander forty years in the wilderness; He desired to lead them directly to the land of Canaan and establish them there, a holy, happy people. But "they could not enter in because of unbelief." Hebrews 3:19. Because of their backsliding and apostasy they perished in the desert, and others were raised up to enter the Promised Land. In like manner, it was not the will of God that the coming of Christ should be so long delayed and His people should remain so many years in this world of sin and sorrow. But unbelief separated them from God. As they refused to do the work which He had appointed them, others were raised up to proclaim the message. In mercy to the world, Jesus delays His coming, that sinners may have an opportunity to hear the warning and find in Him a shelter before the wrath of God shall be poured out. (*The Great Controversy*, pp. 457, 458)

By the time the material in volume 2 of the *Testimonies* was being released in individual testimonies (June 1868 to May 1871, though containing earlier testimonies), God's people were in the third watch of that first generation. However, He did not return from the wedding in that first generation. They went into a backslidden condition, and they would not recover throughout that entire generation.

Early in the second generation (1884–1894), the Lord tried to bring them up in righteousness. Yet, here too, they failed to thrive. What happened in this first watch of the second generation? Four years into it, He sent the cure for their backsliding in the 1888 message.

> The Lord in His great mercy sent a most precious message to His people through Elders Waggoner and Jones. This message was to bring more prominently before the world the uplifted Saviour, the sacrifice for

the sins of the whole world. It presented justification through faith in the Surety; it invited the people to receive the righteousness of Christ, which is made manifest in obedience to all the commandments of God. Many had lost sight of Jesus. They needed to have their eyes directed to His divine person, His merits, and His changeless love for the human family. All power is given into His hands, that He may dispense rich gifts unto men, imparting the priceless gift of His own righteousness to the helpless human agent. This is the message that God commanded to be given to the world. It is the third angel's message, which is to be proclaimed with a loud voice, and attended with the outpouring of His Spirit in a large measure. (Lt. 57, 1895, in *The Ellen G. White 1888 Materials*, p. 1336)

It would have been His desire that the people get on board quickly and hasten His coming in the first watch of that era.

> The Spirit of God has been present in power among His people, but it could not be bestowed upon them, because they did not open their hearts to receive it....
>
> The Lord designed that the messages of warning and instruction given through the Spirit to His people should go everywhere. But the influence that grew out of the resistance of light and truth at Minneapolis tended to make of no effect the light God had given to His people through the Testimonies....
>
> If every soldier of Christ had done his duty, if every watchman on the walls of Zion had given the trumpet a certain sound, the world might ere this have heard the message of warning. But the work is years behind. What account will be rendered to God for thus retarding the work? (Lt. 77, 1893, in *The Ellen G. White 1888 Materials*, p. 1129)

First, Second or Third Watch
In Luke 12, Jesus makes no mention of a return in the fourth watch. This is significant. It suggests that, if God's people are not ready in the first three watches of any given generation, they will not likely be ready in the fourth. When it comes to the fourth watch, there is a fixedness of choice in that generation according to the cycle of four in sowing and reaping. That whole last watch will have to pass, and then He will have to start again, seeking to revive them to righteousness and the hope of glory.

Though the first watch is His preferred time for coming, human nature procrastinates. Because He mentioned the second and third watches, it would seem that this is the time to keep one's eye on.

As we apply the watches to the church's history, we recognize that we have entered the first generation of a new cycle. Since 2004, we have been in a new time cycle of sowing and reaping, and, once again, Jesus would have had His preference of coming in the "first watch." However, as with every previous generation, the first watch has passed. For us, it passed in the year 2014. We are now into the second watch, of which the prophet has stated that we have need of taking a position of "double watchfulness" (*Testimonies*, vol. 2, p. 193). Will we take our place at this time? God is desirous that we should thrill with this very message and lay down all our worldly burdens and look to Him, the author and finisher of our faith, believing His promise that He will cut the work short in righteousness and see the great controversy come quickly to its close.

Again, we should realize that we are in a *new time cycle* and that we are in the *first generation* of that cycle. The *first watch* has now past, and we are in the *second watch—the midnight watch*. We are seeing tremendous events in the world, rapid movements of historic magnitude. Is it possible that we will rise to the challenge in the short time left in this watch? Oh, let it not be the third, when the times will call for "threefold earnestness."

The Midnight Watch and the Loud Cry
We are in the second watch of this generation of restoration, which we see depicted in Joel 2. Can it be that He will return from the wedding in this midnight watch? What does the Word of God have to say on this matter?

> And at **midnight** there was **a cry** made, Behold, the bridegroom cometh; go ye out to meet him. (Matt. 25:6, emphasis added)

When does the midnight watch begin? It begins when the evening watch has passed, and the evening watch has passed. The evening watch was from 2004 to 2014. The second watch, the midnight watch, is from 2014 to 2024.

> **Watch** therefore, for ye know neither **the day nor the hour** wherein the Son of man cometh. (Matt. 25:13, emphasis added)

Jesus has assured us that we are not now given to know the day or the hour. However, we have been given to know the time cycle, the generation, and even the very watch in which He will return from the wedding.

Jesus said that at midnight there was a cry made. What is that cry?

> O Zion, that bringest **good tidings**, get thee up into the high mountain; O Jerusalem, that bringest good tidings, **lift up thy voice with strength**; lift *it* up, be not afraid; say unto the cities of Judah, **Behold your God**! (Isa. 40:9, emphasis added)

The good tidings is the gospel; the gospel is the good news. And what does it mean to lift up the voice with strength? It means giving the *loud cry*! And what is the message in the context of the midnight cry? To see God as He truly is, declaring, "Behold your God!" Thus, the message regarding the character of God is the message of the loud cry, the equivalent of "Behold, the Bridegroom cometh." These proclamations refer to the same message. Those who are waiting for the second coming of Christ must be living and proclaiming the message of God's character. As we proclaim the message of God's character, we are also proclaiming, "Behold, the Bridegroom cometh." This is the proclamation of the brightness of His coming, which is working out the destruction of those who reject it.

> **Those who wait for the Bridegroom's coming are to say to the people, "Behold your God."** The last rays of merciful light, the last message of mercy to be given to the world, is **a revelation of His character of love**. The children of God are to manifest His glory. In their own life and character they are to reveal what the grace of God has done for them. (*Christ's Object Lessons*, pp. 415, 416, emphasis added)

So those who are proclaiming this message are doing the work of the fourth angel and are engaging directly in the ministry that occurs under the outpouring of the latter rain. Therefore, it is imperative that we understand and live out the character of God that we may participate in giving this last message of mercy.

Do We Know the Time?
The 1906 Pathology Need Not Be Ours

The purpose in diligently watching is that we may identify where we are in earth's history and know the time of our visitation and not be found sleeping. We must watch more earnestly than those of former times, such as those in 1906:

> This is what has been presented to me—that we are asleep, and do not know the time of our visitation.... (Lt. 54, 1906, to Brother and Sister Farnsworth, in *Manuscript Releases*, vol. 21, p. 438)

This is the pathology of Seventh-day Adventists today. We are asleep. We are therefore drunk and not watching or waiting, nor looking for the return of the Master from the wedding. The minds of the people are focused largely upon the things of the world, and they are asleep to the eternal realities that are even now breaking upon us. The statement finishes with the following possibility:

> But if we humble ourselves before God, and seek Him with the whole heart, He will be found of us. (Lt. 54, 1906)

This is the generation that the Lord has indicated for His people. Though we do not have a dated time prophecy as did Daniel, we have a time frame reference and know where we are in it.

> And **I will restore to you the years** that the locust hath eaten, the cankerworm, and the caterpillar, and the palmerworm, my great army which I sent among you. (Joel 2:25, emphasis added)

We have looked at biblical indicators of the launching of the final sequences of the "loud cry" and the closing of probation early within the second watch.

> And at **midnight** there was **a cry** made, Behold, the bridegroom cometh; go ye out to meet him. (Matt. 25:6, emphasis added)

> So Gideon, and the hundred men that *were* with him, came unto the outside of the camp **in the beginning of the middle watch**; and **they had but newly set the watch**: and they blew the trumpets, and brake the pitchers that *were* in their hands. (Judges 7:19, emphasis added) (See chapter 4 on the last generation typology in the story of Gideon.)

God is not going to tell His people to watch without giving them instructions on what to watch for or without a time frame for the final movements. As trouble bears down upon the world, the people of God will need hope and courage to stand up under the hardship and privation that they are called upon to endure. God will not make their wait unbearable. He reveals to them the future.

> Behold, the former things are come to pass, and new things do I declare: before they spring forth I tell you of them. (Isa. 42:9)

> Surely the Lord GOD will do nothing, but he revealeth his secret unto his servants the prophets. (Amos 3:7)

> We are living in the last days. Soon Christ is coming for his people to take them to the mansions he is preparing for them. But nothing that defiles can enter those mansions. Heaven is pure and holy, and those who pass through the gates of the city of God must here be clothed with inward and outward purity.... (*Review and Herald*, June 10, 1902, art. B)

Let us have our lamps trimmed and our garments on as we burn the midnight oil.

CHAPTER 4.
Last Generation Typology in Gideon

Tearing Down the Altar of Ba'al

Now we are going to look at the Gideon story as a *type*. That is to say, we want to understand the typology of Gideon's battle to see the symbolism it contains pertaining to the final generation as an *antitype*. We will discover that it gives us clues about which watch of the night we should expect to bring in the beginning of the final war on earth. In our overall study, we have narrowed this expectation down to the time cycle, the generation, and even the watch.

The people of Israel were in bondage to the Midianites. Idolatry was rampant throughout Israel and even in Gideon's own house. God told Gideon that he was to act against idolatry by pulling down the altar of Ba'al from his father's house and by cutting down the grove adjacent to it. With modern idolatry in our midst, how are we to come against it today?

We are told that, when we have the wrong concept of God, we are as much worshipers of Ba'al as were the ancient Israelite idolaters. The testimony we have on this states:

> No outward shrines may be visible, there may be no image for the eye to rest upon, yet we may be practicing idolatry. It is as easy to make an idol of cherished ideas or objects as to fashion gods of wood or stone. **Thousands have a false conception of God and His attributes. They are as verily serving a false god as were the servants of Baal.** Are we worshiping the true God as He is revealed in His word, in Christ, in nature, or are we adoring some philosophical idol enshrined in His place? God is a God of truth. Justice and mercy are the attributes of His throne. He is a God of love, of pity and tender compassion. Thus He is represented in His Son, our Saviour. He is a God of patience and long-suffering. If such is the being whom we adore and to whose character we are seeking to assimilate, we are worshiping the true God. (*Testimonies for the Church*, vol. 5, pp. 173, 174, emphasis added)

We are to pull down all such idolatry through the power of Christ! We need the Spirit of Christ in us to teach and preach Christ as the express image of the Father and as our Righteousness, pulling down false altars.

After pulling down the altar and before going to battle, God wanted Gideon to build an altar and sacrifice a bullock to Him (Judges 6:25, 26). Like Gideon, before we can enter the coming battle with our end-time foes, we must rid our homes, our lives, and our churches of idolatry. We should not expect such a cleansing within the church at large, though God has promised that there will be an emergence of a restored people whose knowledge of God is manifest in their life and character. They will look like Jesus because He lives continually in them.

The Called, Chosen and Faithful

When Gideon made the call, 32,000 responded. Yet, that was too many. God did not want them to rely upon military might or great numbers for their salvation. Therefore, God told Gideon to send home the fearful, and 22,000 left for home while 10,000 remained. Thus, only one third of the *called* were *chosen*.

Nonetheless, God said that there were still too many. Even though everyone in that group would have an interest in God's work, they did not understand His ways, and that would cause problems. Those who came out of *the called* were *chosen*, yet God wanted to go even further. He made a further call for those who would move by faith alone. The resulting final group were the *faithful*. Because this is a parallel to what will exist at the end of the world, Jesus asked if He would find faith in the earth when He comes, for faith is what is required. Many are called; few are chosen; even fewer will be faithful. The remnant-elect have the testimony of Jesus.

As the final test, Gideon took this band of ten thousand down to a body of water and determined by the manner in which they drank who would be faithful to their calling. Three hundred of the men scooped the water in their hand and lapped it up like a dog; the rest went down on their knees, face down. Those in the smaller group were the only ones who kept their eyes on the horizon as they drank from their hands. The vast majority were more interested in self-gratification—with their eyes seeing only their own reflection. It is critical that we understand that our motivation in the end cannot be merely our own salvation. The cause for which we live and die must be that of the vindication of God's character. Only He can make this a reality in us, for the examination of our experience in faith may prove it to be based upon the hope of heaven rather than upon concern for speaking well of our God in the great controversy.

While we may think it an honor to be called and found advancing further among the chosen, our consecration must go deeper if we are to be found among the faithful. The faithful go into the heat of the battle, not with the carnal sword, but with the Word of God.

> John in the Revelation writes of the unity of those living on the earth to make void the law of God: "These have one mind, and shall give their power and strength unto the beast. These shall make war with the Lamb, and the Lamb shall overcome them: for he is Lord of lords, and King of kings: and they that are with Him are **called**, and **chosen**, and **faithful**" (Revelation 17:13, 14).… (Ms. 7a, 1896, in *Manuscript Releases*, vol. 8, p. 344, emphasis added)

These are the ones that went forward and blew the trumpet of the Loud Cry with lamps covered by earthen vessels and the sword of the Lord in their hands. When God first made the call, 32,000 responded. However, the group of 300 men who finally went to battle with Gideon was less than one in one hundred, that is, less than one percent. It will be the same in modern Israel.

> And they overcame him by the blood of the Lamb, and by the word of their testimony; and they loved not their lives unto the death. (Rev. 12:11)

Like Gideon's 300, these soldiers of the cross are not interested in themselves. They do not love their own lives but are all for God and for His cause in the earth and in the universe.

Going Down to the Enemy Camp

> And the LORD said unto Gideon, By the three hundred men that lapped will I save you, and deliver the Midianites into thine hand: and let all the *other* people go every man unto his place. So the people took victuals in their hand, and their trumpets: and he sent all *the rest of* Israel every man unto his tent, and retained those three hundred men: and the host of Midian was beneath him in the valley. And it came to pass the same night, that the LORD said unto him, Arise, get thee down unto the host; for I have delivered it into thine hand. But if thou fear to go down, go thou with Phurah thy servant down to the host: And thou shalt hear what they say; and afterward shall thine hands be strengthened to go down unto the host. Then went he down with Phurah his servant unto the outside of the armed men that *were* in the host. (Judges 7:7–11)

They were instructed to go down and hear what the enemy was saying. Observing the enemy is part of watching. To be observant of the movements in the world—in the enemy camp—is included in what it means to be watchful.

Visions and Dreams

The story of Gideon is a parallel to the last generation of the faithful. Just as visions and dreams were involved in the story of Gideon and his men, so too will the end-time remnant experience the guidance of visions and dreams.

> And the Midianites and the Amalekites and all the children of the east lay along in the valley like grasshoppers for multitude; and their camels *were* without number, as the sand by the sea side for multitude. And when Gideon was come, behold, *there was* a man that told a **dream** unto his fellow, and said, Behold, I dreamed a dream, and, lo, a cake of barley bread tumbled into the host of Midian, and came unto a tent, and smote it that it fell, and overturned it, that the tent lay along. And his fellow answered and said, This *is* nothing else save the sword of Gideon the son of Joash, a man of Israel: *for* into his hand hath God delivered Midian, and all the host. And it was *so*, when Gideon heard the telling of **the dream, and the interpretation thereof**, that he worshipped, and returned into the host of Israel, and said, Arise; for the LORD hath delivered into your hand the host of Midian. (Judges 7:12–15, emphasis added)

It is interesting to discover that Gideon received a message from the enemy camp while the enemy was oblivious that they were transmitting any message to God's people. The watchers of today are aware of these types of information as preparations for the great battle are even now underway. Gideon's awareness of happenings in the enemy camp informed him that it was time for the battle to begin. So too should the enemy's movements tell us that we should be ready for warfare.

The main enemy who will begin the final war, as we have been taught in prophecy, is the Papacy. Acting through the instrument of the United States of America, the Papacy will exert her craft and cunning to achieve her designs in sitting atop the New World Order. The United States will stand as the enemy of God's people in that they will set up the image to the beast, and then all the world will come together in similar fashion. We see the movements in progress now, even as the enemy is oblivious to the fact that their actions are actually against the God of heaven in fulfillment of the prophecies.

As we come into the end times, the Lord has promised to speak to his servants and reveal all things to them in various ways, even if by dream or vision.

> And it shall come to pass afterward, *that* I will pour out my spirit upon all flesh; and your sons and your daughters shall prophesy, your old men shall dream dreams, your young men shall see visions: And also upon the servants and upon the handmaids in those days will I pour out my spirit. (Joel 2:28, 29)

However, we must be extremely careful to seek first the kingdom of God as taught in the Word of God and in Jesus Christ rather than to seek after the supernatural. Why is that? Satan is now saying:

> We must work by **signs and wonders** to blind their eyes to the truth, and **lead** them to lay aside reason and the fear of God and **follow custom and tradition.** (*Testimonies to Ministers*, p. 472, emphasis added)

Satan is going to use signs, wonders, miracles, dreams, and visions to deceive God's people and everyone in the world that he may derail the messages of warning and obscure the truths that are being presented to the world in the last work in history. This does not mean, however, that signs and wonders will not be associated with the true work of God, for they will be. Nonetheless, we must remember that the foundation of the last message is the word of God as given in the Scriptures and through the testimony of Jesus' life and ministry. These will be the test of authenticity of anything of a "supernatural" character. Signs are to follow the believers; believers are not to follow the signs.

> **Mighty miracles are wrought, the sick are healed, and signs and wonders follow the believers.** God is in the work, and every saint, fearless of consequences, follows the convictions of his own conscience, and unites with those who are keeping all the commandments of God; and they sound abroad the third message with power. **I saw that the third message would close with power and strength far exceeding the midnight cry.** (*Spiritual Gifts*, vol. 1, p. 195, emphasis added)

As an aside, the midnight cry spoken of here is that which was manifest in the early Advent preaching of the Millerite movement, which, unbeknownst to most at the time, heralded the entry of Christ into the second apartment phase of ministry in the most holy place and the time of judgment. That was one aspect of the "early rain" showers of blessing. However, there is a counterpart to this in the loud cry of the final movement, when Christ *leaves the most holy place* and probation closes. This is also the midnight cry, or the loud cry, which goes forth under fourth angel power. It is attended by the *latter rain* shower of blessing, calling the people to receive the righteousness of Christ and to behold their God, seeing His character as it truly is.

> I saw the **latter rain** was coming as [*suddenly as*] **the midnight cry**, and with ten times the power. (Ms. 4, 1852, in *Spalding and Magan Collection*, p. 4)

Under this topic, we must not leave out the importance of revelation by watching events. God will reveal matters by visions and dreams, in accordance with the sure word of prophecy that we have in the Bible. He will also speak to the sober-minded watchers through what is taking place around them, giving them a right interpretation of events.

> Those who place themselves under God's control, to be led and guided by him, will **catch the steady trend of the events** ordained by him to take place. Inspired with the spirit of him who gave his life for the life of the world, they will no longer stand still in impotency, pointing to what they cannot do. Putting on the armor of heaven, they will go forth into the warfare, willing to do and dare for God, knowing that his omnipotence will supply their need. (*Review and Herald*, Aug. 5, 1902, emphasis added)

Trumpets, Empty Pitchers, Lamps

Now, we see some very interesting implements of war that are in the arsenal of Gideon's army.

> And he divided the three hundred men *into* three companies, and he put a **trumpet** in every man's hand, with **empty pitchers**, and **lamps** within the pitchers. And he said unto them, Look on me, and do likewise: and, behold, when I come to the outside of the camp, it shall be *that*, as I do, so shall ye do. (Judges 7:16, 17, emphasis added)

What are the trumpets to signify?

> And if ye go to war in your land against the enemy that oppresseth you, then ye shall **blow an alarm with the trumpets**; and ye shall be remembered before the LORD your God, and ye shall be saved from your enemies. (Num. 10:9, emphasis added)

The blowing of the trumpets is the sounding of an alarm. This is a symbol of the sounding of the last message of warning. It is the loud cry, which goes forth to the whole world.

God's warriors also have lamps in their pitchers. The empty pitchers are our hearts. The lamp is the word.

> Thy **word** have I **hid in mine heart**, that I might not sin against thee. Thy **word** *is* a **lamp** unto my feet, and a light unto my path. (Ps. 119:11, 105, emphasis added)

> I delight to do thy will, O my God: yea, thy **law** is **within my heart**. (Ps. 40:8, emphasis added)

God's character, which is His glory, will be manifest in the final generation of the remnant elect.

> For God, who commanded **the light to shine out of darkness, hath shined in our hearts**, to *give* **the light of the knowledge of the glory of God** in the face of Jesus Christ. But **we have this treasure in earthen vessels**, that the excellency of the power may be of God, and not of us. (2 Cor. 4:6, 7, emphasis added)

This light is to fill the whole earth as the message goes out in latter rain power.

> For the earth shall be filled with the **knowledge of the glory of the LORD**, as the waters cover the sea. (Hab. 2:14 emphasis added)

What does the latter-day army have to do to let the light shine? They have to first be empty, so they can be filled with the light of God from His Word, and then they have to be broken so that the light can shine forth. They have to be broken on the Rock who is Christ, having nothing in themselves to bring to God except the righteousness of Christ alone. The light of the knowledge of the character of God is that which is to shine in strength and clarity.

> And after these things I saw another angel come down from heaven, having great power; and **the earth was lightened with his glory.** (Rev. 18:1)

The Beginning of the Second Watch and the Changing of the Guard

When in the watch will the loud cry messengers do their work? We are now in the second watch, the midnight watch. We return to the account of Gideon.

> When I blow with a trumpet, I and all that *are* with me, then blow ye the trumpets also on every side of all the camp, and say, *The sword* of the LORD, and of Gideon. So Gideon, and the hundred men that *were* with him, came unto the outside of the camp **in the beginning of the middle watch; and they had but newly set the watch**: and they blew the trumpets, and brake the pitchers that *were* in their hands. (Judges 7:18, 19, emphasis added)

This account points to the time frame being early in the midnight watch, which, in our time, translates into the early part of the 2014–2024 period. Notice the wording in *God's Word Translation*:

> Gideon and his 100 men came to the edge of the camp. It was the beginning of the **midnight watch** just at the **change of the guards**. They blew their rams' horns and smashed the jars they were holding in their hands. (Judges 7:19, GWT, emphasis added)

How does this apply to us? The breaking of the pitchers and the blowing of the trumpets occurred in the beginning of the middle watch. This is when the loud cry goes forth in full strength. The blowing of the trumpet is the last warning to the world of imminent and certain judgment, which will come as the result of separating from God's righteousness embodied in His law of love, honoring Him through ceasing labor on the seventh-day Sabbath. The breaking of the pitchers represents the last message of mercy to be given in the light of God's character of love.

They had newly set the watch. As soon as the *guard was changed*, the battle began.

In applying typology to events in the enemy camp, we should be looking for the meaning of the "changing of the guard." Who, or what, is *the guard*? We know that the principles of the United States Constitution protect individual liberty of conscience and other rights and freedoms. These rights have been seriously eroded, and God foretold that the nation would eventually repudiate every principle of the Constitution. This would seem at first glance to be an obvious place to find the changing of the guard. However, a serious obstacle to such a conclusion arises when we realize that the changing of the guard took place *in the enemy camp*, for the guard was protecting the *enemy*. The Constitution of the United States of America has protected *the people* by guarding the principles of freedom and not *the enemy* and his objective of exerting his will and power over the people in all things, even to the denial of religious freedom. Therefore, *we must look for a change to take place in that which has protected the interests of the enemy*. So what is it that has guarded the interests of the enemy?

We must also be clear on *who is the enemy*. The enemy in the great controversy is Satan. On this earth, the theater of the conflict, Satan is working through the beast system, whose visible representative is the "man of sin," the papacy. The final scenes of conflict will be opened up in the United States of America, where the people, through their government, will make "an image to the beast" both politically and religiously. So, the question can be further refined as we ask, "What is it that has served to guard the interests of the papacy in the United States?"

Careful attention to the movements taking place reveals that the United States of America, in both their religious and political aspects, have been rapidly fomenting a religious-political unity, following the suggestions of the papacy and turning over their political will to the agenda of the papacy and of the mainstream "Protestant" Christian element, which is itself being shaped by the papacy. This is taking place obviously and openly, *though it was not always so*.

There has been a change. Students of American history will understand that, since the inception of the nation and the formation of its Constitution, the influence of secret societies has run in the background, like a virus in a computer program set to act by a predetermined trigger event. It is outside the scope of this discussion to detail this influence, but many are aware that a Jesuit-controlled "shadow government" has been in operation, serving an interest higher than the people and the Constitution of the United States and that this "shadow government," or "deep state," is, in fact, *an enemy* of both.

The papal power received a deadly blow in 1798 and, as a leopard watching its prey, has had to bide its time until it could again rise to the ascendancy and assert its authority over the whole planet. During this "downtime," it has had to operate in "stealth mode." The prophecy gives us a hint of this when it says:

> And through his policy also he shall cause **craft** to prosper in his hand; and he shall magnify *himself* in his heart, and by peace shall destroy many: he shall also stand up against the Prince of princes; but he shall be broken without hand (Dan. 8:25, emphasis added)

It is probably no coincidence that the word "craft" appears here as an indicator of the agency by which "his policy" would be carried out. Freemasonry is also called "The Craft" or "Craft Freemasonry." Freemasonry is a global phenomenon, having members from all sectors of society, especially business and finance, religion, and politics, though not excluding education, healthcare, law, and entertainment. Masonic influence is widespread and powerful, and it incorporates other secret institutions that operate in the world. There is much evidence showing that Masonry is linked with Catholicism, and is even a creation of it and Jesuitism, in particular. (One can begin to further pursue this subject by viewing "America's Secret Beginnings," a PSTV documentary series that, although not exposing the papal connections, did an excellent job documenting the fact that a secret society cabal has been operating in the American government since its inception.)

The secret society system was established to serve the interests of the papacy. It operated below the radar in the realm of the "conspiracy theorists." Those who have an interest in studying and talking about these things are relegated, in the mainstream Jesuit-controlled media and educational systems, to the realm of those who wear "tinfoil hats" to shield their brains from the electronic mind-control beams of extra-terrestrial aliens! In other words, they are derided as "kooks" and "cranks." Yet, the idea of a conspiracy against the inhabitants of earth by a Luciferian power is not an idea that should be denigrated by anyone claiming to be of God. The Bible talks about a very real last-day confederacy of three entities symbolized as the dragon (Satan or spiritualism), the beast (the papal system), and the false prophet (apostate Protestantism). The Spirit of Prophecy names Lucifer as the great conspirator: "For thousands of years this *chief of conspiracy* has palmed off falsehood for truth" (*The Great Controversy*, p. 670, emphasis added).

No longer is it a secret that this establishment, which serves the interests of the papacy, exerts powerful influence in government. Now it has come out into the open.

In the fall of 2015, the United States government invited the papacy to give a formal address to its leaders. Prior to this papal address in Congress in September 2015, the Vatican sent a delegation to hold meetings with government leaders. At the same time, a group of Adventists organized a protest on their own initiative, traveling to Washington, DC, to counter the address of the papacy in Congress and promote the third angel's message. Spokesman for the group Don Frost asked the Catholic delegates what was the purpose of their meeting. He explained:

> Catholics and these Catholic priests were being drawn to our demonstration because we really looked like people that were there to support the papal visit. They would get up to where we were, and they saw we had some tables out. They would look on the tables, and they would see *The Great Controversy* and they would be like, "Oh!" And I said, "What exactly are you guys doing in there?" They said, "We're here with the 'advance team' from the Vatican, and we're here to train the US Senate on what specifically the pope's climate change agenda is about and educate them as to what we are trying to achieve."
>
> That's when I said to them, "You know, I read the pope's climate change encyclical and I notice that the pope mentions the Sabbath in the encyclical, and he talks about animals having a day of rest, and I'm 'putting two and two together' and it looks to me like the pope wants to have a 'Sabbath rest' for the land—a Sabbath rest for the environment—and it seems to me like the pope wants to have a worldwide Sunday law put in place and through this … Sabbath rest for the environment that the whole world would shut down their businesses and factories and everything one day a week, and, thus, you'd be able to lower greenhouse emissions."
>
> And he looked at me and said, **"That's exactly what this is about."** With that, they just turned on their heels and walked away. (Don Frost, video interview with Daniel Biggs, "D. C. Evangelism," YouTube, http://1ref.us/ht, starting 14:00, published Feb. 19, 2016, accessed 10/14/16, edited for grammar and clarity)

Through personal inquiry, this author has verified that there were others, along with Mr. Frost, who heard this statement by the Vatican representative. As we are examining the typology of the Gideon story, we may recognize in the activity of Don Frost and his assistants an example of antitypical Gideon and Phurah sneaking down into the camp to gather information.

Many saw the unprecedented papal address to the United States government in September 2015 as a sign that the papacy is now openly wielding great influence in the United States. The papacy went so far as to give orders regarding how the papal visit would be conducted and even had control over the flow of information for the event. The issuance of press passes was controlled by the Vatican and not by the United States.

The change from stealth mode to open manifestation of papal influence is now solidifying before our very eyes. *This is the changing of the guard.*

Perhaps even more telling than the verbal admission of the Vatican delegate regarding the nature of their business is the order of events surrounding the papal address to Congress. Here is portrayed in physical movements an astonishing reality that something very significant is taking place. Mr. Frost discussed this in his February 19, 2016 "**HEAL TH**eir Land" ministry video report:

> Well, what happens here is that the pope comes to Washington, flies into Andrews Air Force base, meets with the president at the White House. They have a parade for him; he goes to Congress … delivers his speech, and then goes out on to the west front of the United States Capitol building, facing the Washington Monument, which is an obelisk, and addresses the American people.
>
> As we were there … realizing what was going on, we were like, "Wow, we've made an image to the Papacy," because, the U. S. Capitol building architecturally looks like St. Peter's at the Vatican—even down to the detail … that St. Peter's has an obelisk … in front.… And the United States Capitol building, which is architecturally similar to St. Peter's, also has an obelisk in front.
>
> … Every four years we have an election, and, on the years when we elect a new president, there is a tradition here in America that the new leader meets with the president at the White House and then … travels to Capitol Hill, where he meets with Congress at an event they usually call the "Prayer Breakfast." … Then after the meeting with Congress takes place, he then walks on to the west front of the Capitol, takes the oath of office by the Chief Justice of the Supreme Court and then speaks to the American people as the president, for the first time.
>
> As we were there, we were thinking about this whole thing, and we saw later a clip from then-Speaker of the House, John Boehner, saying that the Pope had requested that he was going to speak to the American people. As we saw all … that was taking place, [we understood that] it was all choreographed. Obviously, it wasn't the pope that was the new president, but the … [staging], from one place to another, was exactly the way it is to the new coming president—first meet with the president of the United States, then meet with Congress, then go out onto the west front of the Capitol building, facing the obelisk, and address the American people for the first time.
>
> The only difference is this: When you are at the Vatican, and they elect a new pope, … the special color smoke comes out of this little pipe, and then the new pope comes out of this … balcony door, and he addresses the waiting masses in front of the obelisk. This happens every time there is a new pope. After the pope addressed Congress, we had thought that he was going to come out and address the American people at that platform area where the president takes the oath of office, but that's not what happened. There's a balcony that's on the west side of the Capitol building with a door, and the pope came out of that door just like at the Vatican … balcony, and he addressed the people from this balcony *above* where the president normally speaks to the American people.
>
> I've never seen any foreign leader or even a president, that I know of, address the American people from such an elevated position. So, it was just like … the choreography as if the Pope were at St. Peter's, I mean, everything was in detail, like "Hey, here's the new leader," so to speak. (Don Frost, video interview with Daniel Biggs, "D. C. Evangelism," YouTube, http://1ref.us/ht, starting 26:10, edited for grammar and clarity)

So, the "choreography" that Bro. Frost described is strikingly similar in *both* how a newly elected pope comes out at St. Peter's *and* the course a newly elected president of the United States takes to assume office in the White House. Herein we have an enacted melding of church and state fixed visually in the minds of the American people and the world. Yet, we see one chilling modification: the pope is represented to the American people as a higher figure than any United States president. Again, this haughty power will presume to sit as king of kings.

This visit has also been seen as a fulfillment of the early approach of the Roman armies and the signal that it is time to flee the cities.

> As the approach of the Roman armies was a sign to the disciples of the impending destruction of Jerusalem, so may this apostasy be a sign to us that the limit of God's forbearance is reached, that the measure of our nation's iniquity is full, and that the angel of mercy is about to take her flight, never to return.

The people of God will then be plunged into those scenes of affliction and distress which prophets have described as the time of Jacob's trouble. (*Testimonies for the Church*, vol. 5, p. 451)

We are now in the beginning of the second watch. We are not looking for the second coming of Christ to earth, but, rather, for the coming of the bridegroom from the wedding. This points to the pending close of probation and the time of trouble such as never was during the outpouring of the seven last plagues.

In the second watch, we are expecting America to advance serious legislation that will eventually impinge upon the freedom of conscience of America's citizens. In this study, we are not in any fashion setting a date for Christ's return. We have no biblical mandate or foundation for any such thing, but we have some watching to do, and it has to do with "keeping our garments" while we keep our attention fixed also upon time and events, without the setting of specific dates.

War Commences Under Sunday Legislation and the Rise of the Loud Cry

It is under the "national apostasy" of Sunday legislation that the battle lines are drawn.

> There are true Christians in every church, not excepting the Roman Catholic communion. None are condemned until they have had the light and have seen the obligation of the fourth commandment. But when the decree shall go forth enforcing the counterfeit sabbath, and **the loud cry of "the third angel" shall warn men against the worship of the beast and his image, the line will be clearly drawn between the false and the true**. Then those who still continue in transgression will receive the mark of the beast.
>
> With rapid steps we are approaching this period. When Protestant churches shall unite with the secular power in sustaining a false religion, for opposing which their ancestors endured the fiercest persecution, then will the papal Sabbath be enforced by the combined authority of church and State. **There will be a national apostasy, which will end only in national ruin.** (*Signs of the Times,* Nov. 8, 1899, emphasis added)

How do these events relate to our study of Gideon's battle? In that narrative, the breaking of the pitchers and the spreading of light occurred with a loud cry.

> And the three companies blew the trumpets, and brake the pitchers, and held the lamps in their left hands, and the trumpets in their right hands to blow *withal*: and **they cried, The sword of the LORD, and of Gideon**. And they stood every man in his place round about the camp: and **all the host ran, and cried, and fled**. (Judges 7:20, 21)

Who do the three companies of Gideon's army represent? They must all be people who have the true message of the third angel. They must be part of the church militant within the three segments of Adventism.

- They will come from the mainstream—the wise virgins who have been waking up and following on to know the Lord.

- They will be found in the "supporting ministries" of "independent Adventism."

- They will also be found in the ranks of the various true independent churches and movements that work without any ties to the mainstream.

The loud cry is given by God's people who "stand in their place" as Sunday rest is enforced first upon business and secular labor, and then, as these laws gradually become more stringent, they will be formulated to come against those who keep the seventh-day Sabbath. The drama plays out through the close of probation and the falling of the seven last plagues, ending with the complete self-destruction of Babylon.

Self-Destruction of the Enemy

> And the three hundred blew the trumpets, and **the LORD set every man's sword against his fellow, even throughout all the host**: and the host fled ... (Judges 7:22)

Notice that, when the loud cry of Gideon went forth, the enemy became confused and turned upon one another. God's people were not involved in the slaying of the enemy. God's people have nothing to do with internecine warfare. Consider the inspired testimony:

> A noise shall come even to the ends of the earth; for the LORD hath a controversy with the nations, he will plead with all flesh; he will give them that are wicked to the sword. (Jer. 25:31)

And the sixth angel poured out his vial upon the great river Euphrates; and the water thereof was dried up, that the way of the kings of the east might be prepared. (Rev. 16:12)

And the ten horns which thou sawest upon the beast, these shall hate the whore, and shall make her desolate and naked, and shall eat her flesh, and burn her with fire. (Rev. 17:16)

For her sins have reached unto heaven, and God hath remembered her iniquities. Reward her even as she rewarded you, and double unto her double according to her works: in the cup which she hath filled fill to her double. How much she hath glorified herself, and lived deliciously, so much torment and sorrow give her: for she saith in her heart, I sit a queen, and am no widow, and shall see no sorrow. Therefore shall her plagues come in one day, death, and mourning, and famine; and she shall be utterly burned with fire: for strong *is* the Lord God who judgeth her. (Rev. 18:5–8)

The people see that they have been deluded. They accuse one another of having led them to destruction; but all unite in heaping their bitterest condemnation upon the ministers. Unfaithful pastors have prophesied smooth things; they have led their hearers to make void the law of God and to persecute those who would keep it holy. Now, in their despair, these teachers confess before the world their work of deception. The multitudes are filled with fury. "We are lost!" they cry, "and you are the cause of our ruin;" and they turn upon the false shepherds. The very ones that once admired them most will pronounce the most dreadful curses upon them. The very hands that once crowned them with laurels will be raised for their destruction. The swords which were to slay God's people are now employed to destroy their enemies. Everywhere there is strife and bloodshed. (*The Great Controversy*, pp. 655, 656)

As the plagues are unleashed and the angels of God have no more jurisdiction over the wicked, Satan is allowed to have full control of the earth. At that time, there will be strife and bloodshed over the earth on a greater scale than has ever been seen in history. With the sixth plague, all of Babylon's support is withdrawn and the eighteenth chapter of Revelation reveals the kind of great conflagration that will then be ignited. At the seventh plague and the coming of Christ, the wicked will war amongst themselves, even as the elements of nature are devastating the earth and men.

In the mad strife of their own fierce passions, and by the awful outpouring of God's unmingled wrath, fall the wicked inhabitants of the earth—priests, rulers, and people, rich and poor, high and low. "And the slain of the Lord shall be at that day from one end of the earth even unto the other end of the earth: they shall not be lamented, neither gathered, nor buried." Jeremiah 25:33.

At the coming of Christ the wicked are blotted from the face of the whole earth—consumed with the spirit of his mouth, and destroyed by the brightness of his glory. Christ takes his people to the City of God, and the earth is emptied of its inhabitants. "Behold, the Lord maketh the earth empty, and maketh it waste, and turneth it upside down, and scattereth abroad the inhabitants thereof." "The land shall be utterly emptied, and utterly spoiled; for the Lord hath spoken this word." "Because they have transgressed the laws, changed the ordinance, broken the everlasting covenant. Therefore hath the curse devoured the earth, and they that dwell therein are desolate: therefore the inhabitants of the earth are burned." Isaiah 24:1, 3, 5, 6. (*The Great Controversy*, p. 657)

"He which testifieth these things saith, Surely I come quickly. Amen. Even so, come, Lord Jesus" (Rev. 22:20).

Section II
The Devoured Generations

Tell ye your children of it,
and let your children tell their children,
and their children another generation.
That which the palmerworm hath left hath the locust eaten;
and that which the locust hath left hath the cankerworm eaten;
and that which the cankerworm hath left hath the caterpillar eaten.

(Joel 1:3, 4)

Declare this in the house of Jacob, and publish it in Judah …
this people hath a revolting and a rebellious heart;
they are revolted and gone.
The prophets prophesy falsely,
and the priests bear rule by their means;
and my people love to have it so:
and what will ye do in the end thereof?

(Jeremiah 5:20, 23, 31)

Introduction

There will be messages borne; and those who have rejected the messages God has sent, will hear **most startling declarations**. The Holy Spirit will invest the announcement with a sanctity and solemnity which will appear terrible in the ears of those who have heard the pleadings of infinite love, and have not responded to the offers of pardon and forgiveness. **Injured and insulted Deity will speak, proclaiming the sins that have been hidden**. As the priests and rulers, full of indignation and terror, sought refuge in flight at the last scene of the cleansing of the temple, so will it be in the work for these last days. (Lt. 56, 1896, in *The Ellen G. White 1888 Materials*, p. 1490, emphasis added)

In **Section I**, we examined the generation of the restoration, which is the first generation of a new time cycle. What happened during the preceding four generations that required there being a new and final generation for restoration? That is a story that every Adventist needs to consider. In recounting it, we are providing what could be called an "unauthorized" biography of the Adventist movement and organization, or, to put it more colorfully, "Adventism Unplugged."

Before we begin the review of this history, let us state what this section is *not*: it is not an apologetic for Adventism. In other words, it is not an attempt to justify present-day Adventism as a prophetic movement and the last manifestation of the Reformation and the trustees of the oracles of God (which, I must hasten to affirm, is the definition of *true Adventism*). The author assumes that readers know that the reason for the existence of the Advent movement is twofold: (1) to prepare a people for translation so they can counter Satan's claims in the great controversy and (2) to provide a vehicle through which the last message of mercy, or the "third angel's message," will be given to the world under the direction of God alone before the closing up of human probation and Christ's return.

As outlined in the introduction to **Section I**, the author wishes to re-emphasize that this exposition of history is not produced with any desire to merely air "dirty laundry" or to "tear down the church." Neither does he desire to be viewed as conducting a "ministry of rebuke." The rebuke comes, however, in the accurate relation of history.

It is for the love of the church that this expository material is provided for study. Nonetheless, when speaking of the true church, it is the view of this writer that we are speaking of a people that profess the third angel's message without respect to affiliation with an earthly corporate structure. Professors of the message may be found: (1) in the denominational structure which is owned and operated by the corporation known as the General Conference of Seventh-day Adventists, (2) in the self-supporting ministries which are also known as "supporting ministries" to that structure, and (3) in the various truly independent circles, having no functional ties to the General Conference entity nor to the supporting ministries and having varying organizational structures of their own. We do not hold that the members of the end-time "church militant" are qualified by affiliation with the legal denominational entity for this would necessarily make individual registration on the books of an earthly religious system a factor with regard to salvation. All of this is more thoroughly examined at the end of **Section II**.

So, what is this section of the book? It is the sad tale of the devoured generations, as brought to view in Joel 1:2–4, with its injunction to *tell* the story. It is a story told with a purpose in mind. Adventists are almost entirely devoid of understanding of the true history, which is a history of devouring pestilence. The truth has been ignored and denied; it has been papered over with a "new order of books" that have been part of Satan's plan to take the church off-track, as revealed to Ellen White. Some of the new books are theologically aberrant; others tell historical tales. Both categories of books work to turn the mainstream church into an offshoot.

> **Recognizing in our history a clear call to "repent" is for the good of modern Israel as well as for the vindication of our Lord.** There is therefore no need of apologizing for proclaiming His call as found in His Word and as illustrated in our history. "As many as I love," He says, "I rebuke and chasten." Such "chastening" does not require the personal services of another living prophet to take the place of Ellen G. White. [*We still have her in her writings and the clear history is there presented.*] **All that is required is to know the full, unvarnished, whole truth of our denominational history.** Honest hearts will immediately respond. (Robert J. Wieland and Donald K. Short, *An Explicit Confession ... Due the Church*, p. 39, emphasis added)

There is a fundamental problem in institutional Adventism. In fact, it is a problem in all human institutions. That problem is the reliance of human beings upon the power and direction of humanity. In the world, this is all that is possible, for humankind is in a state of separation from God. So the kingdoms of this world, while represented in Scripture as set up and taken down by God, are not truly His design or doing. Statements that they are, are written in the language of His permissive will, which is in reality a state of divine wrath. It is what we obtain as a function of the carnal mind, as God allows us to follow our own choices (see Hosea 13:11). I often speak of this trust in humanity and the machinery of the church as "churchianity" and of those who subscribe to it as "churchians"—a term closely related to another term that has been coined—"sheeple," which denotes blind followers of men and their governing systems. My late friend and sometime mentor and "elder statesman in Adventism," Dr. Herbert Douglass, heard me use this term and one time lamented to me that "churchianity is the bane of the church." He was one of the very few men of authority in Adventism who would even speak of these things directly. Here is the flavor of the open address to the church that he was presenting in his last years:

> For hundreds of years, "Potemkin" has signified something that appears elaborate and impressive but in actual fact lacks substance. It is part of Russian literature wherein Russian plutocrats, especially Potemkin, did amazing things to impress a King, Queen or Czar. Potemkin had in fact directed the building of faux fortresses and settlements, and the grand tours solidified his power. So, "Potemkin village" has come to mean any hollow or false construction, physical or figurative, meant to hide an undesirable or potentially damaging situation....
>
> It seems that our Lord's description of the Laodicean church is best labeled as a "Potemkin Village" [Rev. 3:5–8 quoted] ... (Herbert E. Douglass, keynote address from Battle Creek presentation, summer 2012, sermon notes sent to Kevin Straub, Aug. 15, 2012)

The drifting into the Laodicean malady in the first generation and the subsequent loss of our message due to the second generation rejection of the cure for the illness is largely a story of the development of kingly rule in the church. This reliance upon the "arm of flesh" brought in all manner of corruption in its train. What has happened can euphemistically be described as "degenerative," but the hard reality is that it is best described by the A-word—**a**postasy. The alpha of apostasy came in the second generation, at Battle Creek, and our prophet trembled for what was coming in the omega of apostasy.

It is considered heresy to suggest that the denomination is in apostasy. Yet, we have been told that it was coming. Are we to look around us in the institutional church, observe all that is taking place, and with a straight face and sincere tone speak of the omega as something yet to come? Apparently so, for the people today are in such a deep hypnotic stupor that no one seems to realize that the church is in the throes of the advanced stages of the outworking of the omega. The only way to break the fetters of the mind that produce the "churchian" state is to educate people regarding the church's true history.

History molds both a nation and its people. It has been said that it does not matter who writes a nation's laws, but that **it is of utmost importance who writes its history**. A nation's history largely molds and shapes the philosophy, experience, and development of future generations. The laws of a nation and even the interpretation of its constitution are but reflections of its collective thinking and philosophy. In the same way, **the history of a movement or church molds and shapes it.**

> If we do not forthrightly present the history of the 1888 General Conference session and its aftermath, we as a denomination **perpetuate the sin committed at Minneapolis in 1888**. By doing so, we join our spiritual forefathers and virtually crucify Christ anew in the person of the Holy Spirit. (Arnold Valentin Wallenkampf, *What Every Adventist Should Know About 1888*, p. 75, emphasis added)

> The impulse to obscure dark facts comes from the need to preserve the integrity of the self.… It is easier to go along with the silent agreements and keep unpleasant facts quiet and make it hard to rock the boat. But **societies can be sunk by the weight of buried ugliness.… Truths must be told if we are to find our way out**. (Daniel Goleman, *Vital Lies, Simple Truths: The Psychology of Self-Deception and Shared Illusions* [1985], pp. 239–248, quoted in Elaine Giddings, "The Other Truth," *Adventist Review*, March 13, 1986, p. 23, emphasis added)

> He who controls the past controls the future. Lukewarmness and spiritual weakness are a consequence of misinterpreting history. (Robert J. Wieland and Donald K. Short, *1888 Re-Examined*, p. 201. This book references the online edition, available at http://1ref.us/hu, accessed 11/10/16)

This is also a work for any who are already bowed down with the tears of sighing and crying for the abominations done in the midst (Ezek. 9:4). It is the observation of this writer that almost every man and woman with the hope of restoration—whether in the mainstream or in the self-supporting "independent" ministries (who do not accept tithes) and even in some of the truly independent ministries (who do accept tithes)—is looking to the healing of the *denomination*. This belief is as though the "purification of God's church" is some sort of purge of the false shepherds and their followers, leaving the organization with its current structure of governance to continue working under the common order and sail on through to the heavenly harbor as the "church triumphant."

So, while this rendering of events may call for adjustments in the thinking of those who are of a "historic" or "reform" mindset with regard to one's relation to institutional Adventism or the General Conference, it is very much a "cry aloud and spare not" endeavor. It is not the intent or even the hope of this account to bring about any calls for the reform of the structure. That day is past. It is not the salvation of an organization that is to be effected. This was actually never heaven's intent. God is interested at the level of individuals, and it is individuals that make up the church, not legal registrations in the books of men through compliance with lists of regulations and requirements. Accordingly, we present this historical corrective with the desire of freeing many from the shackles of "churchianity," fully realizing that many of the leaders and laity alike will rise up against it. Yet, that is not our concern. *The mandate we have is to publish and to do so unflinchingly and without respect to persons.*

> When men standing in the position of leaders and teachers work under the power of spiritualistic ideas and sophistries [*and all apostasy falls into this category*], shall we keep silent, for fear of injuring their influence, while souls are being beguiled? Satan will use every advantage that he can obtain to cause souls to become beclouded and perplexed in regard to the work of the church, in regard to the word of God, and in regard to the words of warning which He has given through the testimonies of His Spirit, to guard His little flock from the subtleties of the enemy.

> When men stand out in defiance against the counsel of God, they are warring against God. Is it right for those connected with such ones to treat them as if they were in perfect harmony with them, making no difference between him that serveth God and him that serveth him not? Though they be ministers or medical missionaries, they have dishonored Christ before the forces of the loyal and the disloyal. Open rebuke is necessary, to prevent others from being ensnared.

> To believe that evil must not be condemned because this would condemn those who practise the

evil, is to act in favor of falsehood....

The enmity that God has put in our hearts against deceptive practises, must be kept alive, because these practises endanger the souls of those who do not hate them....

It should now be clearly understood that we are not really helping those who are determined to do evil, when we show them respect, and keep our words of reproof for those with whom the disaffected one is at enmity. A grave mistake has been and is being made in this matter. Shall the servants of Jehovah, into whose heart He puts enmity against every evil work, be assailed as not being right when they call evil evil, and good good? Those who feel so very peaceable in regard to the works of the men who are spoiling the faith of the people of God, are guided by a delusive sentiment.

There is to be a constant conflict between good and evil. Those who are enlightened by the Holy Spirit's power are to strive with every power of their being to snatch the prey from the seductive influences of men who refuse to obey the word of God, whether they be in high places or in low. Christ's property is not to pass out of His control into the control of the children of darkness.

If this matter were rightly understood and closely guarded, God's servants would feel a continual burden of responsibility to counterwork the efforts of the men who do not know what they are about, because they are enchanted by the delusive allurements of Satan. When God's people are fully awake to the danger of the hour, and work fully on Christ's side, there will be seen a sharp contrast between their course and that of those who are saying, "Good Lord, and good devil," [*mixing truth with error*] and we shall see much firmer and more decided work done to counterwork the schemes of satanic agencies. (Ms. 72, 1904, in *Special Testimonies* B02, pp. 9–11)

CHAPTER 5.

The Palmerworm

The First Generation of Adventism, 1844–1884

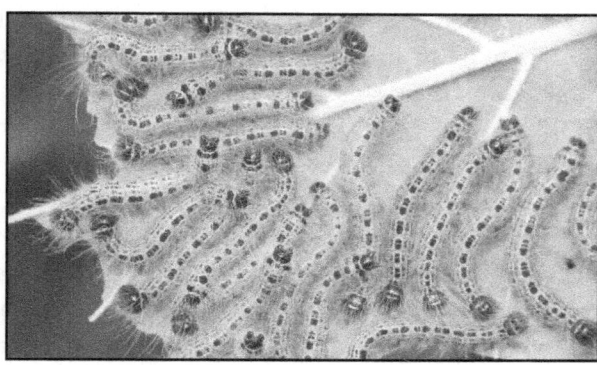

The first generation of the third angel's movement was the forty-year period from 1844 to 1884. On October 22, 1844, Christ's change of ministry into the most holy place in the heavenly sanctuary signaled God's intention to finish the work in that first generation!

The date is extremely important in that it is the end of the 2300-day prophecy of Daniel 8:14. It is the pivotal event that begins the closing sequence of events of earth's sinful history.

As, in fact, Christ made a transition in His ministry in the heavenly sanctuary from the first apartment, or the holy place, into the second apartment, the most holy place, the Millerites were preaching correctly with regard to *Christ's movement, or His "coming."* However, they had the event in error, since they held that He would at that time be coming to the earth to cleanse the earth. Christ did come, but the question is: "Where did He come *to* when it is obvious that He did not come to the earth?" The coming of Christ was "to the Ancient of Days."

> I saw in the night visions, and, behold, *one* like **the Son of man came with the clouds of heaven, and came to the Ancient of days,** and they brought him near before him. (Dan. 7:13, emphasis added)

This was the inauguration of the judgment.

> A fiery stream issued and came forth from before him: thousand thousands ministered unto him, and ten thousand times ten thousand stood before him: **the judgment was set, and the books were opened.** (Dan. 7:10, emphasis added)

The destination of His "coming" is part of "Adventism 101," of which most readers of this study already possess a fair understanding and acceptance. All Seventh-day Adventists should understand that this "judgment hour message" is the fundamental reason for the existence of the Seventh-day Adventist church and that it is this message that sets them apart from the rest of Christianity, which is today identified in prophecy as "fallen Babylon."

The Oracles of God

So, although the Lord would have desired to come at that time and the early Adventists were expecting it, they were not ready. Just as the Israelites, who came up out of Egypt and were newly baptized in the Red Sea into an experience with God, were still not ready to go straight into the Promised Land, so too were the Advent people unprepared for the Lord's return to earth. There was yet something they had to receive. After modern Israel's calling from Egypt, they first had to go to Sinai, to receive the oracles of God. Again, the oracles are: the sanctuary, the law with an emphasis on the Sabbath, and the Spirit of Prophecy (think of "the three S's."[1] During the 1888-era of modern Israel, it was said:

> Light flashed from the oracles of God in relation to the law and the gospel, in relation to the fact that Christ is our righteousness, which seemed to souls who were hungry for truth, as light too precious to be received. (*Review and Herald*, July 23, 1889, in *Selected Messages*, bk. 1, p. 355)

God instructed ancient Israel to build a sanctuary so that He could dwell among them and teach them the way that He wanted to dwell in their hearts by faith in the Lamb of God who would come to take away their sins. God's way is in the sanctuary (Ps. 77:13).

An "oracle" is something that speaks with divine authority. The Scriptures identify the Most Holy Place as "the oracle" (see 1 Kings 6:16; 8:6, 8; 2 Chron. 5:7). It is necessary for God's people to understand, believe, and live out the principles of the law that is kept in the sanctuary, for God's people are identified as keeping the commandments of God and having the faith of Jesus (Rev. 14:12).

The Sabbath is embedded in the very heart of the law to remind us of God who created us and saved us and rested on the seventh day from His work on the occasions of our creation and our redemption. Sabbath rest is much more than ceasing from ordinary labor on a day. It is a symbol of ceasing from our own works to solve our problems and gain salvation. True Sabbath rest is trusting God to perform His good work of righteousness in us (Rom. 8:4; Eph. 2:10), transforming our heart and character so that we can keep all His commandments out of gratitude and love and respect for who He is, according to the principles of love.

This is why it is essential that we keep the preamble to the Ten Commandments intact with the commandments whenever we discuss, teach, or experience commandment keeping. Otherwise we will not maintain the proper relation between faith and works. The Ten Commandments in Exodus begin with the preamble:

> And God spake all these words, saying, I *am* the LORD thy God, which have brought thee out of the land of Egypt, out of the house of bondage. Thou shalt have no other gods before me. (Exod. 20:1–3)

In Deuteronomy 5, Moses paraphrased the words that God spoke at Sinai:

> I *am* the LORD thy God, which brought thee out of the land of Egypt, from the house of bondage. Thou shalt have none other gods before me. (Deut. 5:6, 7)

Egyptian bondage is a symbol of the darkness and hopelessness of the experience of sin, the condition into which every human has been subjected through the fall. Sin is defined as "the transgression of the law" (1 John 3:4), and the work of redemption restores us to keepers of the law. Sinners cannot do this by sheer force of will. Keeping the law is not mere outward compliance. The true works must stem from an inner change based upon righteous motivation. This only God can give. Sinners cannot say, "I will deliver myself out of the bondage of sin." The carnal mind is not subject to the law of God, and it is an impossibility for it to become so (Rom. 8:7). So it is that God does not give us the commandments until He informs us who it is that is going to bring us into conformity. That is why the first thing He does is to identify Himself as the One who brings us out of bondage, and that is why we can have no other gods besides Him. It has been said that "it is all about the first commandment" and this is true. *The first commandment is the basis for all commandment-keeping because God has to do it!*

They—and we—needed to enter into true Sabbath rest to understand and practice *resting in God*. The Sabbath teaches absolute rest in God. This is what is meant by "proclaiming the Sabbath more fully"—something the end-time generation will do in the sight of men that will be the end of all dependence on humanity. You cannot be obedient to God—you cannot keep the commandments of God—unless you are resting in God. John 14:15 says, "If you love me, keep my commandments." 1 John 5:2 adds: "By this we know that we love the children of God, when we love God, and keep his commandments." Love is expressed in obedience to God. Yet, as we have already said, the unregenerate mind is incapable of obeying God. The heart is desperately wicked of itself. To write the law upon our hearts and teach us the true meaning of Sabbath-keeping in the new covenant experience, as pertaining to total dependence upon God as our Creator, Provider, Protector, Burden-Bearer, Problem-Solver, and Plan-Maker, God's people needed then and God's people need now the ministration of Christ in the sanctuary.

Last of all, the Spirit of Prophecy was committed to both them and us. God's people will keep the commandments of God because they possess the faith of Jesus which produces the testimony of Jesus. In one sense, this testimony is a life lived as a true witness to the character of God, and we know that God's law is a transcript of His character (*The Great Controversy*, p. 434).

The testimony of Jesus is also identified as the "spirit of prophecy," as we can understand from reading Revelation 12:17; 14:12; 19:10; and 22:8, 9. The "spirit of prophecy" is not to be thought of solely as visions, dreams, and the foretelling of the future, although these elements can and do certainly follow the believers. The Spirit of prophecy is the Holy Spirit's guidance in understanding the Word of God; it is the lesser light of inspiration that leads to the greater light of Jesus, the Son of God, who is the Truth and who is revealed in Scripture, which is also the greater light. In a specific administrative sense, God's ancient people received the Word of God through Moses and the prophets. God's modern Israel also received guidance through Moses and the prophets, with the addition of the New Testament apostles. Modern Israel, as the endtime Israel of God, to whom was given the final message of the three angels, received all the Scriptures with the addition of the ministry of Ellen White.

The Millerites, who were the vanguard of the Reformation in their day, needed *all* of the "oracles of God." Modern Seventh-day Adventists, who are to continue advancing the Reformation, desperately need all of God's oracles as well. The experiences of ancient Israel parallel those of modern spiritual Israel. Today's generation of God's people all need to know where Christ is and what He is doing. They also need the leading of the testimony of Jesus—the spirit of prophecy—to find and keep the Sabbath as the heart of the law. Where is the law kept but in the most holy place in the sanctuary? Mainstream Christianity today remains focused on the first apartment. However, since 1844, Christ has been in the second apartment. So, whom would they be following?

Worshipping at Satan's Throne

To answer that question, we need to take a little side-trip to consider an early revelation about Jesus' movements in heaven and how those who belong to Him followed Him. In 1846, Mrs. White saw a representation of these things. Her description is in *Early Writings* and other publications. However, only one of these publications contains the last sentence to which I would like to draw your attention:

> I saw a throne, and on it sat the Father and his Son Jesus Christ. I gazed on Jesus' countenance and admired his lovely person. The Fathers person I could not behold for a cloud of glorious light covered him.... Before the throne was the Advent people, the Church, and the world. I saw a company bowed down before the throne, deeply interested while most of them stood up disinterested and careless.... Then I saw an exceeding bright light come from the Father to the Son and from the Son it waved over the people before the throne. But few would receive this great light. Many came out from under it and immediately resisted it. Others were careless and did not cherish the light and it moved off from them. Some cherished it and went and bowed down before the throne with the little praying company. This company all received the light, and rejoiced in it as their countenances shone with its glory. Then **I saw the Father rise from the throne and in a flaming chariot go into the Holy of Holies** within the vail, and did sit. There I saw thrones which I had not seen before. Then Jesus rose up from the throne, and most of those who were bowed down rose up with him.... **Those who rose up when Jesus did, kept their eyes fixed on him as he left the throne, and led them out a little way, then he raised his right arm and we heard his lovely voice saying, wait ye, I am going to my Father to receive the Kingdom. Keep your garments spotless and in a little while I will return from the wedding, and receive you to myself.** And I saw a cloudy chariot with wheels like flaming fire. Angels were all about the chariot as it came where Jesus was; he stepped into it and **was borne to the Holiest where the Father sat**.... And I saw **those who rose up with Jesus send up their faith to Jesus in the Holiest, and praying, Father give us thy spirit. Then Jesus would breathe on them the Holy Ghost**. In the breath was light, power and much love, joy and peace. **Then I turned to look at the company who were still bowed before the throne. They did not know that Jesus had left it. Satan appeared to be by the throne trying to carry on the work of God.** I saw them look up to the throne and pray, My Father give us thy spirit. Then **Satan would breathe on them an unholy influence**. In it there was light and much power, but no sweet love, joy and peace. **Satan's object was to keep them deceived and to draw back and deceive God's children. I saw one after another leave the company who were praying to Jesus in the Holiest, go and join those before the throne and they at once received the unholy influence of Satan.** (*The Day-Star*, March 14, 1846, emphasis added)

The 144,000 final generation of the remnant elect, the virgins and firstfruits who will be translated alive at His coming, are those who "follow the Lamb whithersoever He goeth" (Rev. 14:4). It is very important that they are found going into the second apartment because that is where Jesus is! He is there to do the special work of preparing His final generation to be the spotless Bride who will reflect the Father's character completely as He does. They can only do this as they become one with Him. That is why this is represented as a wedding. "The bride" are those who have gone into the wedding. They are now to wait and "watch" for Him to "return from the wedding" (that is, leave the most holy place at the close of probation), keeping their garments as they wait (Mark 13:37, Luke 21:36, Rev. 16:15).

Now, we must know and understand that those who remained behind, prostrate before the first apartment throne, are those who did not follow on to know where Jesus went or the work that he commenced to do. These rejected the first angel's message and became fallen Babylon, as preached in the second angel's message. (This information is well documented in other works available to the student of Reformation and Adventist history.) We should have it clear in mind that those in the current religious environment claiming *Christ* are worshipping at *Satan's* throne! The usurper has taken up residence in a pseudo first-apartment ministry. It is a "pseudo" ministry because the work Satan is doing is, of course, not truly a first-apartment ministry; it is pretense only. He is only posing as Jesus, a deception that he will carry right through until he makes an actual appearance on the earth, as the real Jesus will leave the sanctuary and appear above the earth. The point of the vision is that Satan has successfully captured the mainstream Christian world under the guise of being in the place that Jesus left. The power and light that the Christian world receives there is a *dark* power and a *dark* light (yes, there can be "dark light"—see Luke 11:35).

What we must really stop to consider carefully, however, is the identity of those who are brought into focus in the last sentence in the statement: "I saw one after another leave the company who were praying to Jesus in the Holiest, go and join those before the throne and they at once received the unholy influence of Satan" (*The Day-Star*). At first glance, we might think that we are looking at the great disappointment and its aftermath in which most of those caught up in the excitement of the expectation of Christ's return to earth at that time subsequently abandoned the movement. Yet, we must question this conclusion because the second apartment ministry was not understood until after the great disappointment was understood. The truth of the cleansing of the sanctuary was only established after subsequent study. The terrible upheaval of spirit and mind endured by those who went through that experience was resolved by understanding what actually took place. Those who fell out did so immediately. They did not go into the second apartment at any time, as described in the *Day-Star* statement. Those who went into the second apartment were those who came through the experience and afterwards understood what it was that actually took place.

This is the light that came on October 23, 1844, after a small group of believers knelt to pray in the barn at Hiram Edson's homestead. Having their confidence in God reassured in their troubled minds and knowing that He would reveal what went wrong, they set out to encourage others to remain steadfast in the Lord. As Hiram Edson and O. R. L. Crosier were walking through a corn field, light flashed into Edson's mind:

> "I was stopped about midway of the field. Heaven seemed open to my view, and I saw distinctly and clearly, that instead of our High Priest *coming out* of the Most Holy of the heavenly sanctuary to come to this earth [*on October 22*], … that he for the first time *entered* on that day the second apartment of the sanctuary; and that *he had work to perform* in the Most Holy before coming to this earth." (C. Mervyn Maxwell, *Tell It to the World: The Story of Seventh-day Adventists*, p. 49)

The "little flock" that kept moving forward after this development were the people of the third angel's message who later became the Seventh-day Adventists. Ellen White's comment is that many of these, *who went in to the second apartment with Christ*, would later "leave the company who were praying to Jesus in the Holiest, go and join those before the throne" which Satan took up in the first apartment which Jesus has left. This is a way of representing the fall of Babylon and the official change of leaders in the various Protestant churches of the day. The message is clear. Many who had followed on to embrace the third angel's message would afterwards turn back to join with those who refused the message.

In the context of the generations eaten up by the devourer, this is a highly significant statement, for it points out that, from the early beginnings of the movement, "one after another" would draw back into the first apartment. As we move forward in this study, we will find that this is exactly what has happened. Adventism today is in serious trouble theologically—especially since certain high level conferences in the 1950s with first-apartment evangelicals. Fundamental shifts in our doctrine began to show up in church publications; we started sending our people to non-Seventh-day Adventist universities for post-graduate work; the skepticism of "higher criticism" in biblical exegesis entered the denomination, among other things. The result has been the fracturing of Adventism and the springing up of independent ministries among those who wish to adhere to the fundamentals of the original movement.

We now leave our sidebar question and answer and come back to the main thread. We will later consider other elements of the apostasy of modern Israel.

Moving Forward with the Oracles of God, or "the Truth as It Is in Jesus"

At this point in history, our focus should be on the next movement of the Savior—the impending transition. Jesus is still in the second apartment, the most holy place. However, He is getting ready to leave it, and He will soon *return from the wedding*. The event for which we should be in solemn preparation is not the second coming in the clouds of glory but the *close of probation*. Mainstream Adventism today emphasizes the second coming but does not talk about the close of probation. It is no longer popular because it gets into the subject of the character perfection of the final generation, of living in the sight of God without a mediator for ongoing sinning. This is why, in order to avoid speaking about the work of final cleansing, we have seen the dismantling of fundamental Adventist teaching regarding the cleansing of the sanctuary and the atonement. We have opened the door to "making mistakes" (i.e. sinning) until Jesus comes. We have denigrated the reality of living in His sight as a spotless bride by relegating such a concept to the realm of "perfectionism" and "legalism." We often hear the insinuation that those who would teach and strive to be among the 144,000 are operating under a paradigm of works, of achieving their status with God in the strength of the flesh. Nothing could be further from the truth. This insinuation is a straw man argument that is set up to deflect the discussion from the real issues at stake.

Our work is truly pressing and short because an alarmingly sizeable cross-section of modern Adventists are so far behind Him that they no longer know where He is and what He is doing. Try asking ten people in your church to give a short talk on the three angels' messages and what they signify. Then ask them what the other angel of Revelation 18:1 is all about. Alternately, ask them what "final atonement" means! When I raised the subject of final atonement in a Sabbath School class, one church elder told me, "Thou thinkest too much!" I heard a sermon preached in a Seventh-day Adventist church in which the main point was to show that the scapegoat of the Day of Atonement service was a symbol of Christ. This is "Babylonian" teaching. Immediately following, in the parking lot of the church, I asked the head elder if what he heard from the pulpit that morning was okay with him. He was hesitant and then unsure as he told me that it seemed that something was not right about what was preached, and he said he would have to go home and check the books. Really? I am in my fifties, and this man is of my father's generation. Why would he be confused? How can we forget that easily? This is what happens when we no longer study the Bible and the Spirit of Prophecy for ourselves but, rather, rely upon the leaders trained in seminaries under professors who have drunk of the deep waters of Babylonian wells. Many think that reading the weekly lesson from the denominationally published quarterly is personal Bible study when it is only more reliance upon leaders and professors.

God's distinctive message, designed to prepare the way for the Advent of Christ and taught through the lessons of the sanctuary, has gone by the wayside. This is true of both Israels. Ancient Israel lost sight of the true meaning of the Lamb. They relied upon their system, with its priests, scribes and rulers, and all its sacrifices and ceremonies. This kept them all busy as they waited for their national deliverer. Modern Israel has also lost sight of Jesus. The third angel's message was to be presented as the everlasting gospel, including pardon and cleansing, forgiveness and power to keep the commandments. (See *The Ellen G. White 1888 Materials*, p. 1336.) However, now the distinctive image of the three angels has disappeared from the denomination's logo, and that same image has all but disappeared from the classes and pulpits of modern official Adventism.

Indeed, as we study salvation history, we find many parallels between ancient and modern Israel. As ancient Israel had a prophet to lead them, namely Moses, so also has God given modern Israel a prophet, namely Ellen G. White, to guide them in their journey. The Israelites came through the Red Sea and, three days later, came to the place called Marah, where the water was "bitter" (Exod. 15:23). They had a "bittersweet" experience, for, in that place, the water was healed and made "sweet" for them (Exod. 15:25). So also did the Millerite movement have a bittersweet experience as they looked for the second coming of Christ to the earth, but they were deeply disappointed in their unrealized expectation. Yet, they later found it to be a sweet experience when they realized what had actually happened. Christ had moved from the first apartment to the second apartment in His ministration. They then studied Hebrews 8 and 9 and came to a proper understanding and resolution of the crisis of their disappointment.

So, here they received an understanding of the sanctuary and the law, and, two years later, they received an understanding of the Sabbath. It was soon after the "passing of time," or the great disappointment of 1844, that Ellen Harmon received her first vision, the messenger of the Lord was raised up, and the Advent believers received the oracles of God.

> What advantage then hath the Jew? [*Or the Seventh-day Adventist?*] … Much every way: chiefly, because that unto them were committed the oracles of God. (Rom. 3:1, 2)

This is the setting in which the final generation was formed and equipped to enter God's rest. God could now enter His loving work of bringing His people into perfection of character, finish the work on the earth, and bring us home.

It Was to Be a Short Work
Jesus wanted to come very early in the experience, but it was not to be. Having received the oracles of God, the Advent believers were to continue on until they entered the Promised Land. Unfortunately, instead of following on to know the Lord, they started focusing on doctrinal messages and lost sight of Christ, the Originator of the messages. They lost their spiritual fervor and took on the Laodicean condition. Israel came out of Egypt, traveled straight to Sinai and then to Kadesh, an eleven-day journey that took them forty years! The same thing happened within Seventh-day Adventism. Shortly after 1844, possessing the oracles of God, they were to move right into the experience in which Christ could come for them. Yet, through unbelief, they have wandered in the wilderness ever since, having done even worse than ancient Israel. How many years have we been in the world since 1844? It has been multiple periods of forty years!

The first generation in the third angel's movement was the period of 1844–1884. It was God's intention to finish the work in that first generation. The prophet to the final generation expected the Lord's return earlier rather than later in that generation. In 1856, she wrote:

> I was shown the company present at the Conference. Said the angel: "Some food for worms, some subjects of the seven last plagues, **some will be alive and remain upon the earth to be translated at the coming of Jesus.**" (*Testimonies for the Church*, vol. 1, pp. 131, 132, emphasis added)

What she saw here in vision was a company of Adventists in her day with the angel's designation of three destinies: some would pass away, some would receive the mark of the beast, and some would see Jesus come without dying! The last two destinies did not happen for this group. Why? The answer is one that is not well understood by mainstream Christians and that gets them in trouble with interpretation of prophecy. It is this: All of God's promises are based upon condition of obedience.

In 1872, Ellen White wrote:

> Because time is short, we should work with diligence and double energy. Our children may never enter college. (*Testimonies for the Church*, vol. 3, p. 159)

Then, in 1876, she wrote:

> It is really not wise to have children now. Time is short, the perils of the last days are upon us, and the little children will be largely swept off before this. (Lt. 48, 1876, in *This Day with God*, p. 140)

These statements indicate that God had intended to finish the work in that first generation.

A Delay! Why?
In 1883, as the first generation period drew to its close, Sister White wrote:

> **Had Adventists, after the great disappointment in 1844, held fast their faith** and followed on unitedly in the opening providence of God, receiving the message of the third angel and in the power of the Holy Spirit proclaiming it to the world, they would have seen the salvation of God, the Lord would have wrought mightily with their efforts, the work would have been completed, and **Christ would have come ere this** to receive His people to their reward. (Ms. 4, 1883, in *Evangelism*, p. 695, emphasis added)

We must ever emphasize the point that Christ's coming is dependent upon the fidelity of His people. He will not just show up one morning—"ready or not!" We have to be saying, "Come, Lord Jesus!" This does not mean just saying words; it means calling Him by the life we live and by His Spirit's renewal of our minds.

> It was not the will of God that the coming of Christ should be thus delayed.... For forty years did unbelief, murmuring, and rebellion shut out ancient Israel from the land of Canaan. **The same sins have delayed the entrance of modern Israel into the heavenly Canaan. In neither case were the promises of God at fault. It is the unbelief, the worldliness, unconsecration, and strife among the Lord's professed people that have kept us in this world** of sin and sorrow so many years. (*Evangelism*, p. 696, emphasis added)

The seeds of Laodicean lukewarmness were sown early in that first generation. Writing in the mid-1850s, the servant of the Lord penned the following solemn warning:

> Dear Brethren and Sisters: The Lord has shown me in vision some things concerning the church in its present lukewarm state, which I will relate to you. The church was presented before me in vision. **Said the angel to the church: "Jesus speaks to thee, 'Be zealous and repent.'"** This work, I saw, should be taken hold of in earnest. **There is something to repent of. Worldly-mindedness, selfishness, and covetousness** have been eating out the spirituality and life of God's people. (*Testimonies for the Church*, vol. 1, p. 141)

In the aftermath of the great disappointment, there was a reason why covetousness and "worldly-mindedness" developed amongst God's people.

Occupy Until I Come

The great disappointment struck deep into the Adventist soul. Many did not plant crops or put up hay for their animals. It was a bitter, hard winter for general survival, in addition to the ridicule they faced from unbelievers and those in the other churches. An unspoken attitude developed in the subconscious psyche: "Never again." So it is today that, in general, the typical Adventist is nearly as engrossed in establishing a "comfortable" life as is any other sector of society. A fundamental problem of Seventh-day Adventists is apparent in the development of an erroneous understanding of the words, "Occupy until I come."

Anatomy of a disappointment

There is more to this than meets the eye. In all that transpired, we can see that, had the disappointment been prevented, there may have been a much better outcome for the movement on the whole.

It is said that God's "hand covered a mistake in the reckoning of the prophetic periods" and that "God designed that His people should meet with a disappointment" (*Early Writings*, p. 235). These words have been grossly misunderstood, as if to say that God deliberately set them up for all that happened. This is *language* that is used in the same way as when Exodus says that God "hardened" Pharaoh's heart (Exod. 10:1) or that He put "a lying spirit in the mouth of all his [Ahab's] prophets" (1 Kings 22:22). In inspired language, God is said to *do* that which He *allows*. By trying to prevent calamity or trying to save, He is said to have *caused* the ruin, as if He had done it personally. We can see the principle also stated in terms of presenting the saving news of the gospel:

> Let ministers and people remember that **gospel truth ruins if it does not save**. The soul that refuses to listen to the invitations of mercy from day to day can soon listen to the most urgent appeals without an emotion stirring his soul. (*Testimonies for the Church*, vol. 5, p. 134, emphasis added)

This is always the principle by which destruction occurs. This is a wonderful theme of study that greatly enriches our understanding of God, our experience of Him and our relationship with Him forever. However, it is the subject of other books, such as *As He Is: Issues in the 'Character of God' Controversy*.

In the case of the disciples' disappointment in Christ's crucifixion, we know that Jesus did all that He could to let them know what was going to happen, but their preconceived ideas caused them to refuse even His direct statements that He was going to be crucified at Jerusalem. In the same way, God tried to send messages to the advent believers that would have prevented their misunderstanding. Before any messages were sent through Ellen White, two other messengers were selected to bring messages to the people. The first, a mulatto man named William Foy, was given three visions. As a side note, Ellen White recalled in 1912 that Foy had *four* visions and that they had been published, though she misplaced her copy ("William Foy – A Statement by E. G. White," DF 231, available at http://1ref.us/k5, accessed July 11, 2017). However, there is no record of a fourth vision.

In the second vision, in particular, on February 4, 1842, Foy saw a mighty angel with a silver trumpet in hand, descending *three steps*. After a time of traveling and preaching, he received a third vision sometime in 1844, prior to the time of the disappointment in which he was shown a pathway to the heavenly city, involving three steps, or platforms, on which the people of God would travel. Writing years later in 1858, Ellen White would also see the three steps:

> I saw a company who stood well guarded and firm, and would give no countenance to those who would unsettle the established faith of the body. God looked upon them with approbation. **I was shown three steps—one, two and three—the first, second and third angels' messages.** Said the angel, Woe to him who shall move a block, or stir a pin in these messages. The true understanding of these messages is of vital importance. The destiny of souls hangs upon the manner in which they are received. (*Spiritual Gifts*, vol. 1, pp. 168, 169, emphasis added)

Significantly, in Foy's second vision, scene 6, Jesus, as a mighty angel, "stood with his right foot placed before him, as though walking; and his object appeared to be to reach the earth. But three steps remained for him to take" (William Foy, *Christian Experience*, p. 18). Foy heard a voice in this scene saying, "The sixth angel hath not yet done sounding" (Rev. 9:13, 14), which Delbert Baker commented upon, saying:

> This angel is vitally important because, looking back from our vantage point, we recognize that he was the one who held the key to an understanding of the judgment-hour message; he also held the light that might have enabled the people to avoid the Great Disappointment.... we can see graphically how God sought to protect His people against the Disappointment by sending a message that pointed to the Bible and the needed light. (Delbert W. Baker, *The Unknown Prophet*, pp. 108–110)

Baker is correct in his comments. The visions would have made it clear that there were events to transpire before Christ's return to earth. He described how the Advent people were so focused on the first angel's declaration of the judgment and so full of expectation:

> Unfortunately, that is all they saw. The brightness and glory of the first angel so filled their eyes that they but faintly perceived the second angel, and the third not at all. (Baker, p. 118)

J. N. Loughborough recorded that Foy could not understand the vision of the three platforms due to his belief in the imminent coming of Christ and that, shortly thereafter, he "ceased public work" (T. Housel Jemison, *A Prophet Among You*, p. 486, citing *The Great Second Advent Movement*, pp. 146, 147). Historical research, however, has proven conclusively that "Foy lived until 1893, almost 50 more years, and that he continued to pastor, preach, and hold revivals up to the time of his death" (Baker, p. 130). In the aftermath of the Great Disappointment, the various Millerite splinter groups held a conference, seeking unity. One of their agreed resolutions was to oppose all claims of "special illumination," effectively placing "Foy and Ellen White outside the main remnant of the Millerite movement" (Baker, p. 131).

Foy heard Ellen White later relate her first visions, and he called out, during her talk, that this was exactly what he had seen. He was so animated and jubilant in his expressions that he then became self-aware, apologized profusely for his outburst, and left the meeting. The main body of Adventist believers lost contact with him. However, history has been unkind to him and has made it seem as though he went out refusing God as a lost man when this is unsubstantiated.

> William Foy's role was not the same as that later filled by Ellen White. The two people stood at different foci of history, confronted with different circumstances and challenges. William Foy was a spokesman for God, largely to the Advent movement in the pre-Disappointment period. He was a herald and mouthpiece to the early Adventists, assuring them of God's personal interest, motivating them to greater revival and reformation, and bringing timely truths that would, if understood, spare His people the Great Disappointment or at least prepare them for it. Foy received a limited number of visions. He never suggested that his prophetic role was to extend past 1844, or that he was to receive more visions.
>
> Here is where a misleading generalization is often made: that if Foy is accepted as a genuine prophet to the Advent movement (pre-Seventh-day Adventist), having received legitimate visions from God, he must also be a prophet to the Seventh-day Adventist movement as well. This belief, though understandable, is unsupported. (Baker, pp. 147, 148)

Then there was another man, Hazen Foss (whose brother was married to Ellen White's older sister Mary), who, only a few weeks before the time of the expected advent, also received a vision on the journey of the Advent people to the city of God with the accompanying dangers. Soon after the Great Disappointment, he was instructed to tell his vision to the people. His vision "corroborated that of William Foy, thus increasing the effectiveness of his message." Like Foy, Foss "was shown a vision of 'three steps by which the people of God were to come fully upon the pathway to the Holy City.'" (Baker, p. 137). Loughborough stated that Foss, "being a firm believer in the Lord's coming 'in a few more days' (as they then sang), the part of the vision relating to the three steps onto the pathway was to him unexplainable; and being naturally of a proud spirit, he shrunk from the cross, and refused to relate it" (*The Great Second Advent Movement*, p. 187). Ellen White (then Ellen Harmon) would receive her first vision in Portland, Maine, right after his decision. He was at first warned that trial and persecution would come to him for taking up the work. In his refusal, he also declared that he had been deceived in regard to the advent message. The vision was later repeated, and this time the Lord told him that, if he should refuse to go forward, the calling would be extended to another—"one of the weakest of the Lord's children" (*The Great Second Advent Movement*, p. 182). Ellen White related a third-party report that Foss had lost the Spirit of God in that he himself related how he had heard a voice at the time of his refusal, pronouncing the judgment, "You have grieved away the Spirit of the Lord" (Lt. 37, 1890, cited in T. Housel Jemison, *A Prophet Among You*, p. 487). Foss was seized with fear at what he had done and told the Lord he would go. He later tried to reinstate himself by recounting the vision in a meeting and could not. In great distress, he declared himself a lost man. About three months later, he spoke with Miss Harmon and told her to be faithful, for she would now get the crown that he might have had. As for himself, he told her that "he would be henceforth as one dead to spiritual things" (Lt. 37, 1890, in Jemison, p. 489). Having lost the temperament of a man with Christian graces, he lived for another fifty-some years, passing away without Christ.

The point of relating these most interesting stories, of course, is to underscore that God had tried to warn the people ahead of time that there were *three steps* before He would come. This would have informed them that there was a problem with the teaching of His coming to earth on October 22, 1844 and would have led them to study out the truth of the matter. In the case of Hazen Foss, it was certainly far too late to prevent the Great Disappointment, but would have certainly helped them to deal with the aftermath.

> … immediately before the Great Disappointment would have been an opportune time to establish a new spokesman for the Lord. Not only would he have offered prophetic guidance, but he also would have been in position to offer much-needed encouragement to God's people in the post Disappointment period. (Baker, p. 140)

Even so, on the first day after the Great Disappointment, the Lord in His mercy revealed to Hiram Edson what had just happened, though Edson was not called into prophetic office.

> One of the serious blockages in the minds of the Millerites was the idea that they had the final message. Therefore, they saw only one angel where they should have seen three at least. (See *The Great Controversy*, 353.) Had this shortcoming been corrected, they would have looked for the appearance of the other two heavenly messengers and the messages and movements they represented. They would have realized that the Saviour could not have come in October, 1844, for there were still other prophecies to be fulfilled before the advent. (Fred T. Wright, *The Seven Angels*, p. 125)

So it is that preconceptions can lead to errors that are not without far-reaching and serious consequences. What happened in the early Advent history set the people up for failure. They would not go forward to the Second Coming of Christ in their generation. Instead, they would succumb to the disease of the lukewarmness of the Laodicean condition.

The development of self-preservation and worldliness

The cleansing that took place in the aftermath weeded out those who were in it for fear of being lost or for hope of eternal riches. Yet, this did not make everything all right. There were deep and lasting consequences to what had happened. The blow the church received at that time has much to do with the steady drift into apostasy suffered by the movement in subsequent generations.

There developed a formalism and reliance on possessing doctrinal truth, while the blessing of the gospel faded away and self-interest took the place of sacrifice for the cause. In 1855, Ellen White had a vision, which she described:

> I saw that the Spirit of the Lord has been dying away from the church. The servants of the Lord have trusted too much to the strength of argument, and have not had that firm reliance upon God which they should have....
>
> I saw that many in different places, East and West, were adding farm to farm, and land to land, and house to house, and they make the cause of God their excuse, saying they do this that they may help the cause. They shackle themselves so that they can be of but little benefit to the cause. Some buy a piece of land, and labor with all their might to pay for it. Their time is so occupied that they can spare but little time to pray, and serve God, and gain strength from Him to overcome their besetments. They are in debt, and when the cause needs their help they cannot assist; for they must get free from debt first. But as soon as they are free from debt they are farther from helping the cause than before; for they again involve themselves by adding to their property. They flatter themselves that this course is right, that they will use the avails in the cause, when they are actually laying up treasure here. They love the truth in word, but not in work. They love the cause just as much as their works show. They love the world more and the cause of God less; the attraction to earth grows stronger and the attraction to heaven weaker. Their heart is with their treasure. By their example they say to those around them that they are intending to stay here, that this world is their home. Said the angel: "Thou art thy brother's keeper."
>
> Many have indulged in needless expense, merely to gratify the feelings, the taste, and the eye, when the cause needed the very means thus used, and when some of the servants of God were poorly clothed and were crippled in their labor for lack of means. Said the angel: "Their time to do will soon be past. Their works show that self is their idol, and to it they sacrifice." Self must first be gratified; their feeling is: "Am I my brother's keeper?" Warning after warning many have received, but heeded not. Self is the main object, and to it everything must bow.
>
> I saw that the church has nearly lost the spirit of self-denial and sacrifice; they make self and self-interest first, and then they do for the cause what they think they can as well as not. Such a sacrifice, I saw, is lame, and not accepted of God. All should be interested to do their utmost to advance the cause. I saw that those who have no property, but have strength of body, are accountable to God for their strength. They should be diligent in business and fervent in spirit; they should not leave those that have possessions to do all the sacrificing. I saw that they can sacrifice, and that it is their duty to do so, as well as those who have property. But often those that have no possessions do not realize that they can deny themselves in many ways, can lay out less upon their bodies, and to gratify their tastes and appetites, and find much to spare for the cause, and thus lay up a treasure in heaven. I saw that there is loveliness and beauty in the truth; but take away the power of God, and it is powerless. (*Testimonies for the Church*, vol. 1, pp. 113–115)

From this sorry condition, the church has never recovered. In 1890, Ellen White related how she saw the "state of the Laodicean Church as never before," showing the true condition of their spiritual destitution (*Review and Herald*, Aug. 26, 1890). Fred T. Wright comments:

> The Lord sent Elders Waggoner and Jones to bring the church out of the Laodicean condition and back to the third angel's message in verity, the living, powerful, saving gospel of Jesus Christ. But the effort failed. The majority of the members remained where they were. Since then the one message which would cure the malady has been kept out of the church. The sickness of lukewarm Laodiceanism to which the church succumbed by 1859, has never been cured, nor is there any hope that, in the Seventh-day Adventist organization, it ever will be.
>
> This tragedy is the worst result ever to develop from the error taught in 1844, and demonstrates that the effects of erroneous teachings and practices are far more deadly and far reaching than is usually supposed. Recall, for instance, the consequences which developed when Paul, during his final visit to Jerusalem, allowed the church leaders to become his problem-solvers in God's place. This led to his arrest, his premature death, the accelerated apostasy in the church, the excessive extension of time, and the awesome development of the papacy.
>
> The depth of the wound inflicted on the 1844 movement by the great disappointment is not measured merely by the numbers who were shaken out. The problem goes much deeper than that. Those who were shaken out no longer influenced or directed the

course the church would take, but those who remained, bearing the mental and spiritual scars inflicted upon them, did decide the destiny of the church.

An indication of the problem is revealed in the particular iniquities which beset the Advent believers as they descended into Laodiceanism. Repeatedly in those early testimonies, the Lord named selfishness and covetousness as the sins which separated them from God, and invited the devil's presence. (Wright, *The Seven Angels*, p. 133)

The danger of God's people for a few years past has been the love of the world. Out of this have sprung the sins of selfishness and covetousness. The more they get of this world, the more they set their affections on it; and still they reach out for more. (*Testimonies for the Church*, vol. 1, p. 141)

Why were the sins of selfishness and covetousness named as the specific besetments of believers during this time? Why were they fixated upon material gain and earthly security?

There is a very valid reason for this. They had passed through a harrowing experience in the great disappointment which had affected them very deeply. They were never the same again, because they were unable to emerge from the ordeal with their trust in God undamaged. (*The Seven Angels*, p. 134)

The faith of the majority was damaged beyond repair. These left the truth never to return. No longer a part of the movement, their reaction had no effect on its future history. But the survivors were the ones who did. Even though they still retained faith in the truth and accepted the light which showed where they had been mistaken, they were still wounded. Although they might not dare to give utterance to the thought, yet, deep down where it really counts, they felt that God had deceived them, that He had used them, and that they had been betrayed. They did not understand the beautiful truths we now cherish on God's perfect and righteous character. They had never been shown that God is a righteous God who keeps all His own laws, that He is the truth and never deceives anyone, that He does not destroy, and that His love is truly infinite and contains not the slightest trace of selfishness....

Because they did not know God in this light, they felt that they could not trust Him unconditionally. Therefore, they turned to their own works to establish their own security. They labored with a diligence and intensity worthy of better aims, to add farm to farm, land to land, and house to house. They acted as if this earth were their heaven. It was a natural reaction, which, because of the very magnitude of their disappointment, became an obsession. Hence, covetousness and selfishness were the natural fruit of these unfortunate and unnecessary developments. (*The Seven Angels*, pp. 135–137)

How then shall we be occupied?

We have seen that the people carried out their occupation by settling into the pursuit of worldly gain. It is no different today. At the individual level, most of those who call themselves the "remnant people" are fully occupied in worldly pursuits of careers, family, wealth, status, possessions, homes, and lands, so that they must necessarily be entirely engaged with these earthly goals while being far from fully occupied with fulfilling their commission to go into all the world, giving the message from the oracles of God that was committed to them, the final generation of modern spiritual Israel.

On the denominational level, that which calls itself the "remnant church" has occupied itself building massive structures in the world—hospitals, educational institutions, communications networks, humanitarian organizations, non-governmental organizational institutions. In addition, offices and programs have been set up for the purpose of interfacing with Babylonian religious systems, and their existence is justified as activity that brings people into the third angel's message, the truth as it is in Jesus. Leaders and laity alike glory in their ability to achieve greatness in so many areas of human achievement and in their massive evangelistic programs, yet they are no closer to being ready for Jesus to come than were those of the first generation after 1844.

So what of the matter? How are we to occupy? How are we to live?

As a matter of fact, Jesus' injunction to "Occupy till I come" is diametrically opposed to the idea of laying up material comforts and possessions here:

God has left us in charge of His goods in His absence. Each steward has his own special **work to do for the advancement of God's kingdom**. No one is excused. The Lord bids us all, "Occupy till I come." By His own wisdom He has given us **direction for the use of His gifts**. The talents of speech, memory, influence, property, are to **accumulate for the glory of God and the advancement of His kingdom**. He will bless **the right use of His gifts.**

We claim to be Christians, waiting for the second appearing of our Lord in the clouds of heaven. Then what shall we do with our time, our understanding, **our possessions, which are not ours,** but are entrusted to us to test our honesty? Let us bring them to Jesus. Let us **use our treasures for the advancement of His cause.** Thus we shall obey the injunction, "**Lay not up for yourselves treasures upon earth**, where moth and rust doth corrupt, and where thieves break through and steal: but lay up for yourselves treasures in heaven, where neither moth nor rust doth corrupt, and where thieves do not break through nor steal: for **where your treasure is, there will your heart be also**." [Matt. 6:19–21] (*Review and Herald,* April 9, 1901, republished in *Counsels on Stewardship,* pp. 116, 117, emphasis added)

We are not saying that we must forsake all earthly responsibility and work. It is true that we are not to give ourselves up to "idle contemplation," living as in a "religious dream" in abandonment of life's duties. We are told that we are to engage in business, in sowing and reaping, and in grinding at the mill (Ms. 26, 1901, in *Last Day Events,* p. 76). Yet, though we are going to be engaged in business, God will examine how we have conducted ourselves in it.

The Master has given directions, "**Occupy till I come.**" He is the great proprietor, and has a right to investigate every transaction, and approve or condemn; he has a right to rebuke, to encourage, to counsel, or to expel. The Lord's work requires careful thought and the highest intellect. **He will not inquire how successful you have been in gathering means to hoard, or that you may excel your neighbors in property, and gather attention to yourself while excluding God from your hearts and homes.** He will inquire, **What have you done to advance my cause** with the talents I lent you? What have you done for me in the person of the poor, the afflicted, the orphan, and the fatherless? I was sick, poor, hungry, and destitute of clothing; what did you do for me with my intrusted [*sic*] means? **How was the** time **I lent you employed? How did you use your** pen, **your** voice, **your** money, **your** influence? I made you the depositary of a precious trust by opening before you the thrilling truths heralding my second coming. What have you done with the light and knowledge I gave you to make men wise unto salvation? (*Signs of the Times,* Nov. 20, 1884, emphasis added)

The Laodicean Third Angel's Message

In that first generation, the third angel's message was lost even while that which was staunchly proclaimed to be the third angel's message continued to be preached. In fact, originally the message was not even accurately articulated within its proper setting of the cleansing of the sanctuary. It could not have been, for they did not have light on that subject yet. That is to say that the message of the first angel was not seen so much then as the true everlasting gospel as it was in 1888. Prior to 1888, the message of the gospel was understood as being the same as that preached in Reformation Protestantism. The standard gospel of that time was preached in the setting of an urgent emphasis regarding the imminent second advent of Christ to the earth. William Miller also taught the non-immortality of the soul and the annihilation of the wicked after the judgment. These teachings were later adjusted and also augmented by the sanctuary message and the Sabbath, with the addition of further distinctive doctrines such as the Spirit of Prophecy and the millennium. The second and third angels were presented as historicist prophecy, identifying the man of sin and the beast system with all the attending warnings about how to avoid receiving the mark of the beast by becoming a Seventh-day Adventist and keeping all of the Ten Commandments! While all of these are rightly a part of the package known by traditional and historic Adventists as "the third angel's message," as a mere stand-alone set of doctrines, they do not reflect the "everlasting gospel" message of the first angel.

This is not to say that they did not have the third angel's message in *experience*. The little band were earnestly waiting to meet Jesus in 1844 and following on the upward path of light, despite the large number of other believers who abandoned them after the great disappointment in 1844. Moreover, they *did* have the experience of the gospel, though they did not have it in the clarity of expression or with the biblical foundation in advance of the Reformation gospel of justification by faith as inherited from their Protestant fathers. To explore this subject, we will consider information taken from Fred T. Wright's *The Destiny of a Movement,* chapter 17, "More on the Real Issues at Minneapolis."

By late 1844, the Adventists had been given the first, second, and third angel's messages which came to be known in combined form as the third angel's message. But it was not very long before they lost the message, though they did not know they had.

Subsequently, they preached the laws and doctrines of the message under the title belonging to the message itself which is, in verity, justification by faith, or the everlasting gospel. Thus, the mighty unifying power contained in the real third angel's message was lost to them, permitting the continuation and development of divisive theories among them. (Wright, *The Destiny of a Movement*, p. 253; available at http://1ref.us/hv)

These "divisive theories" would have to do with "the eternal verities" that were previously defined by Wright.

During the first forty-four years, the positions of the Advent believers are divided into two classifications known as the "Testing Truths" and the "Eternal Verities".

The "Testing Truths" of the Advent faith were the special doctrines of the Advent message: the Sabbath, the Sanctuary, Non-immortality, the Spirit of Prophecy, the Three Angels' Messages, Prophecies, and the Imminent Advent. It is correctly argued that belief in these positions was mandatory if one was to remain within the fellowship of the Adventist Church.

The "Eternal Verities" covered such subjects of the everlasting gospel as the Deity of Christ, the Trinity, Sinlessness of Christ, the Holy Spirit, and the Atonement in Relation to the Cross. What one believed in these areas was optional; one's position on the deity of Christ for instance could be quite the opposite from that of a brother without incurring the risk of church discipline. (*The Destiny of a Movement*, p. 237)

So, they lost the message that they thought they already had but did not.

In order to correct the fault, the third angel's message had to be reintroduced to them. Let it be stressed that it was not a call to a re-emphasis of something they had held all along but had allowed to become second place after prophecy and doctrine. Nor was it merely a restatement of what had been taught back in the 1840's. It was a presentation of the third angel's message with a scope and glory never before announced among the advent people. It was a message sent from God through His chosen servants which is the message to be given to the world and which is designated the third angel's message. (*The Destiny of a Movement*, pp. 253, 254)

That "most precious message" to come by Jones and Waggoner in 1888 would present a message called by inspiration "the third angel's message," which is "justification through faith in the Surety" with an invitation for "the people to receive the righteousness of Christ." It needed to be experienced in a way that they had not previously done. The fullness of experience of obedience was lacking, for their religion was essentially legalistic in nature. They needed to hold the commandments in proper relation to the gospel, showing how the true gospel of Christ's *imputed* righteousness brings His *imparted* righteousness to the "helpless human agent" (see *Testimonies to Ministers*, pp. 91, 92).

When they heard it, many Adventists were puzzled. They had never listened to such teachings before and questioned the place for them in Adventism, the movement commissioned to teach nothing but the third angel's message. They were assured by the Lord that they were hearing the third angel's message in verity, even though the message as they had been taught it, was quite different from this. (*The Destiny of a Movement*, p. 254)

Church members wrote to Ellen White asking whether what they were hearing was the third angel's message, and she responded emphatically, "It **is** the third angel's message—in verity!" (*Review and Herald*, April 1, 1890, emphasis and punctuation added). Then she went on to explain that it was the glory message of the fourth angel of Revelation 18.

All of this is not to claim that they did not previously have the third angel's message in verity. What Miller, Fitch, Litch, Edson, Crosier, the Whites, Bates, and others preached *was* the right message, and the message they proclaimed under the name of "the third angel's message" did come by heaven's grace and it was attested to by the Spirit of Prophecy. Yet, the message of present truth was not understood in all its connections and in its fullness. The early experience of the fledgling movement faded in time and was supplanted by another concept—that the third angel's message consisted solely in doctrine and prophecy.

Waggoner himself emphasized that the gospel is the third angel's message, not that the warning against receiving the mark of the beast was the gospel but that the warning of the third angel and the pronounce of the second were the necessary follow-up to the preaching of the everlasting gospel in the first angel, for the first angel would necessarily continue to sound in the proclamation of all of the angels' messages.

> Mark it, the first angel proclaims the everlasting gospel; the second proclaims the fall of every one who does not obey that gospel; and the third proclaims the punishment that will follow that fall, and come upon those who do not obey. So the third is all in the first,—the everlasting gospel. Yes, that everlasting gospel carries with it all truth. It is the power of God. That everlasting gospel, remember, is all summed up in one thing,—Jesus Christ and him crucified, and of course risen again. We have nothing else in this world to proclaim to the people, whether we be preachers, Bible workers, colporters [sic], or canvassers, or simply people who in the humble sphere of their own home let the light shine. All that any of us can carry to the world is Jesus Christ and him crucified. (E. J. Waggoner, *General Conference Daily Bulletin*, March 25, 1891, p. 240)

The next paragraph of Waggoner's discourse reveals what the thinking of the general membership had become since the first generation of God's Advent people:

> Says one, That is taking an extreme view; are we going to throw away all the doctrines we have preached,—the state of the dead, the Sabbath, and the law, and the punishment of the wicked? Throw them away?—No; by no means. Preach them in season and out of season; but, nevertheless, preach nothing but Christ Jesus and him crucified. For if you preach those things without preaching Christ and him crucified, they are shorn of their power, for Paul says that Christ sent him to preach the gospel, not with words of man's wisdom, lest the preaching of the cross of Christ should be made of none effect. The preaching of the cross, and that alone, is the power of God. (Waggoner, p. 240)

Wright continued in his commentary:

> The tragedy is that when the gospel's light and power go out of the message, the people do not know it. They then continue to preach the doctrines without the gospel, believing that there has been no change from the original. (*The Destiny of a Movement*, p. 257)

The tragedy was really about losing the *first love* of the Philadelphian experience, including love for God seen through brotherly love. Ellen White described what happened in the early Christian church:

> But gradually a change came. The believers began to look for defects in others. Dwelling upon mistakes, giving place to unkind criticism, they lost sight of the Saviour and His love. They became more strict in regard to outward ceremonies, more particular about the theory than the practice of the faith. In their zeal to condemn others, they overlooked their own errors. They lost the brotherly love that Christ had enjoined, and, saddest of all, they were unconscious of their loss. They did not realize that happiness and joy were going out of their lives and that, having shut the love of God out of their hearts, they would soon walk in darkness. (*The Acts of the Apostles*, p. 548)

The more we study with objective eyes, the more we realize that the experience of God's people runs in repetitive cycles. Their experience is our experience. That is why Ellen White began sounding alarms not long after the great disappointment, as we find in her 1855 statement, "I saw that the Spirit of the Lord has been dying away from the church" (*Testimonies for the Church*, vol. 1, p. 113). She went on to outline how that believers were engrossed in adding house to house and land to land and that the loss of a sacrificial spirit for the cause would shut out the presence of God. The work could never be finished without His Spirit.

A Critical Spiritual Pathology: The LLC Virus

So it was that the critical spiritual pathology in the Laodicean Lukewarm Condition (LLC) resulted from the absence of the gospel as a vital, living experience. The Lord sent warning after warning to the church in that first generation. Not that no one responded to the message but that the church as a whole did not allow the message to prepare it for the harvest.

> We are fully sustained in our positions by an overwhelming amount of plain Scriptural testimony. But we are very much wanting in Bible humility, patience, faith, love, self-denial, watchfulness, and the spirit of sacrifice. We need to cultivate Bible holiness. Sin prevails among the people of God. The plain message of rebuke to the Laodiceans is not received. Many cling to their doubts and their darling sins while they are

in so great a deception as to talk and feel that they are in need of nothing.

They think the testimony of the Spirit of God in reproof is uncalled for or that it does not mean them. Such are in the greatest need of the grace of God and spiritual discernment that they may discover their deficiency in spiritual knowledge. **They lack almost every qualification necessary to perfect Christian character.** They have not a practical knowledge of Bible truth, which leads to lowliness of life and a conformity of their will to the will of Christ. They are not living in obedience to all God's requirements. (*Testimonies for the Church*, vol. 3, pp. 253, 254, emphasis added)

I was shown that the testimony to the Laodiceans applies to God's people at the present time [1859], and the reason it has not accomplished a greater work is because of the hardness of their hearts. But God has given the message time to do its work. The heart must be purified from sins which have so long shut out Jesus. This fearful message will do its work. When it was first presented, it led to close examination of heart. Sins were confessed, and the people of God were stirred everywhere. Nearly all believed that this message would end in the loud cry of the third angel. But as they failed to see the powerful work accomplished in a short time, many lost the effect of the message. I saw that this message would not accomplish its work in a few short months. It is designed to arouse the people of God, to discover to them their backslidings, and to lead to zealous repentance, that they may be favored with the presence of Jesus, and be fitted for the loud cry of the third angel. As this message affected the heart, it led to deep humility before God. Angels were sent in every direction to prepare unbelieving hearts for the truth. The cause of God began to rise, and His people were acquainted with their position. If the counsel of the True Witness had been fully heeded, God would have wrought for His people in greater power. (*Testimonies for the Church*, vol. 1, p. 186, emphasis added)

The evidences for the fact of the first generation's falling away could fill an entire book, but we will end this section with this revealing passage penned in 1882, just as the first generation of Adventism was drawing to a close.

I have been shown that **the spirit of the world is fast leavening the church.** You are **following the same path as did ancient Israel.** There is **the same falling away from your holy calling as God's peculiar people**. You are having **fellowship with the unfruitful works of darkness.** Your **concord with unbelievers** has provoked the Lord's displeasure. You know not the things that belong to your peace, and they are fast being hid from your eyes. Your **neglect to follow the light** will place you in a **more unfavorable position than the Jews** upon whom Christ pronounced a woe.

I have been shown that **unbelief in the testimonies** has been steadily increasing as the people **backslide from God**. It is **all through our ranks**, all over the field. But few know what our churches are to experience. I saw that **at present we are under divine forbearance**, but no one can say how long this will continue. No one knows how great the mercy that has been exercised toward us. But few are heartily devoted to God. There are **only a few** who, like the stars in a tempestuous night, **shine here and there among the clouds.**

Many who complacently listen to the truths from God's word are **dead spiritually, while they profess to live**. For years they have come and gone in our congregations, but they seem only less and less sensible of the value of revealed truth. They **do not hunger and thirst after righteousness**. They have no relish for spiritual or divine things. They **assent to the truth, but are not sanctified** through it. Neither the word of God nor the testimonies of His Spirit make any lasting impression upon them. Just according to the light, the privileges, and opportunities which they have slighted will be their condemnation. **Many who preach the truth to others are themselves cherishing iniquity**. The entreaties of the Spirit of God, like divine melody, the promises of His word so rich and abundant, its threatenings against idolatry and disobedience—all are powerless to melt the world-hardened heart.

Many of our people are lukewarm. They occupy the position of Meroz, neither for nor against, neither cold nor hot. They **hear the words of Christ, but do them not**. If they remain in this state, He will reject them with abhorrence. Many of those who have had great light, great opportunities, and every spiritual advantage **praise Christ and the world with the same breath**. They **bow themselves before God and mammon**. They **make merry with the children of the world**, and yet claim to be blessed with the children of God. They wish to have Christ as their Saviour, but **will not bear the cross and wear His yoke.** May the Lord have mercy upon you; for if you go on in this way, nothing but evil can be prophesied concerning you. (*Testimonies for the Church*, vol. 5, pp. 75–77)

What an indictment! Notice the phrase, "at present we are under divine forbearance." This is the same as being under God's "permissive will." God was permitting them to continue as an organization under grace in spite of their condition. The question that is ever in view as we examine these things is: "When did this state of affairs finally undergo remediation?"

The twin prongs of modern Laodiceanism

So how does Laodiceanism present in contemporary Adventism? Is it the same today? Well, that is one of those "yes" and "no" questions. It depends upon what segment of Adventism one is addressing.

Going back to historic, conservative Adventism, we find the notable Seventh-day Adventist pioneer J. N. Andrews releasing a book that was representative of Adventist thinking in that day and progressed through no less than five editions. *The Three Messages of Revelation 14:6–12, Particularly the Third Angel's Message and Two-Horned Beast* (1877) was clearly presented as the message of the third angel, as we can see by its title. Wright says that "its claim [of] being a true statement of the third angel's message, was, as far as we know, never challenged" (*The Destiny of a Movement*, p. 260). As such, we might expect to find within its pages a study of justification by faith in verity in relation to the two-horned beast, as per its title. However—

> there is not a single page in the book devoted to this topic. Instead, the material covers prophetic developments in the rise of the Advent people and of the two-horned beast pictured in Revelation 13. Thus the Adventists had come to call something which was not the third angel's message, by that name....
>
> This is why, when the real message of the third angel was brought by God's appointed messengers in 1888, the church could not recognize it as such. They compared what those men had to teach with what they had always regarded as being the third angel's message and they correctly recognized that they were not the same.
>
> This imposed upon them the necessity of making a specific choice between what they regarded as being the real message to which they fondly referred as being the old landmarks, and what the True Witness told them was the message in verity. The lapse into the Laodicean condition in 1858 or thereabouts, was not a temporary one. It settled into a fearful permanence so that by 1888, they were in a state of even worse spiritual poverty. (*The Destiny of a Movement*, pp. 261, 262)

So, the real concern for this period was that "doctrines and prophecies" were posing as the three angels' message. In our time, those who view doctrines and prophecies as the three angels' message exist within the conservative element of mainstream Adventism and also within supporting ministries and independent ministries. Yet, there is another group that began developing in earnest in the third generation, hardening in the fourth generation into the "divided kingdom" as did ancient Israel after Solomon. That faction came to be known as liberal Adventism, and today it can generally be regarded theologically as mainstream Adventism within the general membership of the churches, particularly in the larger ones in more heavily populated regions. Here we find that secular accreditation, ecumenism, and the historical revisionism of leading men have been major contributors to a version of pre-Adventist justification by faith known as Protestant Reformationism—a belief that had existed before the addition of light regarding Christ's movement into the most holy place in the heavenly sanctuary in 1844. The development of the sanctuary truth was an advancement in the reformation, and it had vital meaning for the experience of God's people. Without it, the development of the final generation probation cannot close and Christ cannot come.

We have asked: How is it with today's Advent people? When we read about ancient Israel, we cluck our tongues. Surely we would not do as *they* did! Yet, bringing this closer to home, we read about the first generation of Adventism and the prophet and *Heaven's* diagnosis of the *Laodicean Lukewarm Condition (LLC)*. Will we cluck our tongues at our forefathers? Will we shake our heads at their disgrace? Are we in a more favorable position than were they? Is there any validity at all to setting up in our minds an "us vs. them" dichotomy? If so, what basis do we have for doing so? We cannot point to our own repudiation of worldliness in all its forms. We have not repudiated our secular pursuits, institutional operations, and ecumenical ideation and alliances. We cannot claim greater consecration or obedience to the Lord. Rather, the popular pulpit engages in veiled self-praise as leaders point to material blessings as confirmation of God's gifts and pleasure in us. Especially at camp-meetings do we hear leaders praising the Lord, the church and themselves for all the accomplishments of recent times! This is not just a contemporary phenomenon. History warns us of the dangers of judging God's favor by our material blessings.

As Solomon continued to conform to the customs of the world, his pride greatly increased. And **the worldly prosperity that attended his apostasy, was regarded by him as a token of God's favor.** So fully had he yielded himself to evil influences, that his spiritual discernment was well-nigh destroyed. He could not see the terrible losses that were sustained by the nation spiritually because he brought into the kingdom an abundance of the gold of Ophir and the silver of Tarshish.

Today there exists the same danger of mistaking prosperity for the favor of heaven. The prosperity that often for a time attends those who turn from a plain "Thus saith the Lord" to follow a way of their own choosing, is not an assurance of divine approval. Men many interpret it thus, but it is no sign that God's prospering hand is with them. (*Review and Herald*, Jan. 18, 1906, emphasis added)

Summing up what we have just described, we find that modern Laodiceanism expresses itself in different ways. There is a misappropriation of the content of the central message and experience of the third angel's message. This can take different forms, depending on which portion of the Adventist spectrum we are analyzing—whether it is the conservative or the liberal side of the divide. Within the mainstream, there is rampant laxity and worldliness, which has compromised the distinctiveness of the Seventh-day Adventist message. The liberal element has run the ship onto the rocks through shifts in doctrine, ecumenism, and disregard of the testimonies. In the conservative element within the mainstream and in much of the independent Adventist world, we may often find an intellectual knowledge of the truth with a tendency toward legalism, along with a tendency to emphasize the third angel's message as doctrines and prophecies over the real calling of the message as it is in the gospel: to behold the righteousness of Christ and become what He is.

We have come to the close of our overview of the first generation. Regardless of where we might think we are today, what we have established so far is that, when Generation One of the first cycle ended, the church was not ready. Christ had not come—even though it would have been His preference:

The history of ancient Israel is a striking illustration of the past experience of the Adventist body. God led His people in the advent movement, even as He led the children of Israel from Egypt. In the great disappointment their faith was tested as was that of the Hebrews at the Red Sea. Had they still trusted to the guiding hand that had been with them in their past experience, they would have seen the salvation of God. **If all who had labored unitedly in the work in 1844, had received the third angel's message** and proclaimed it in the power of the Holy Spirit, the Lord would have wrought mightily with their efforts. A flood of light would have been shed upon the world. Years ago the inhabitants of the earth would have been warned, the closing work completed, and **Christ would have come for the redemption of His people**.

It was not the will of God that Israel should wander forty years in the wilderness; He desired to lead them directly to the land of Canaan and establish them there, a holy, happy people. But "they could not enter in because of unbelief." Hebrews 3:19. Because of their backsliding and apostasy they perished in the desert, and others were raised up to enter the Promised Land. In like manner, it was not the will of God that the coming of Christ should be so long delayed and His people should remain so many years in this world of sin and sorrow. But **unbelief separated them from God. As they refused to do the work which He had appointed them**, others were raised up to proclaim the message. In mercy to the world, **Jesus delays His coming**, that sinners may have an opportunity to hear the warning and find in Him a shelter before the wrath of God shall be poured out. (*The Great Controversy*, pp. 457, 458, emphasis added)

Had Adventists, after the great disappointment in 1844, held fast their faith and followed on unitedly in the opening providence of God, **receiving the message of the third angel and in the power of the Holy Spirit proclaiming it to the world**, they would have seen the salvation of God, the Lord would have wrought mightily with their efforts, the **work would have been completed, and Christ would have come** ere this to receive His people to their reward. But in the period of doubt and uncertainty that followed the disappointment, many of the advent believers yielded their faith.... Thus the work was hindered, and the world was left in darkness. **Had the whole Adventist body united upon the commandments of God and the faith of Jesus, how widely different would have been our history!** (*Evangelism*, pp. 695, 696, emphasis added)

CHAPTER 6.

The Locust

The Second Generation of Adventism, 1884–1924

The second generation of the third angel's movement of Seventh-day Adventism was the period from 1884 to 1924.

At the start of that generation, the time had arrived for God to pour out a special blessing of grace, light, and truth through a message that was to bring the people out of the Laodicean state so that they could be prepared for heaven. This "most precious message," sent early in the period of generation two, was to crown all the warnings that He had been sending throughout the period of generation one. This took place in the autumn of 1888 at the Minneapolis General Conference Session.

In this chapter, we will call attention to an inspired statement that is often used to arrest the attention of Adventists and help them question *why* it is that the "*most* precious message" committed to Adventism is all but extinct in our churches, *why* it is that we do not know about it, and *why* our people today are so unfamiliar with the names and teachings of Jones and Waggoner:

The 1888 Message

The Lord in His great mercy sent a most precious message to His people through Elders Waggoner and Jones. **This message was to bring more prominently before the world the uplifted Saviour**, the sacrifice for the sins of the whole world. It presented **justification through faith in the Surety**; it invited the people to **receive the righteousness of Christ, which is made manifest in obedience to all the commandments of God. Many had lost sight of Jesus.** (Lt. 57, 1895, to O. A. Olsen, in *Testimonies to Ministers*, pp. 91, 92, emphasis added)

It is extremely important that we understanding this message because it is what empowers us to work in hastening Christ's return.

Looking at the first part of this statement, we might well ask how it is possible that the church could have rejected it. Surely the Seventh-day Adventist ministry brings the uplifted Savior before the world. Surely Christ is presented in the church as the Surety for salvation from sin by justification through faith. Yet, the fact is that Jesus was lost from sight, and He has remained lost from sight throughout the generations. Otherwise, Christ's work would have been finished and He would have returned by now. There is hardly a greater testimony to the assertion that the message has been rejected.

What about receiving His righteousness? Could there be a problem with our experience regarding "obedience to all the commandments of God?"

The Righteousness of Christ is Made Manifest in Obedience to All the Commandments of God

As we examine all of the theological wrangling that goes on with regard to the gospel message, we come to the issues of obedience, sin, and perfection. Perhaps we think that preaching the seventh-day Sabbath and attending church and not turning on the television until sundown on Sabbath means that we are obeying all the commandments of God? Is that righteousness? What about all the ways in which Seventh-day Adventists have disobeyed the counsel of God in Scripture and the messages to the final generation through Ellen White? We can go down the list and find many requirements we choose not to do. Take *sports*, for instance. Let's be real about this. At the mention of the topic, many of our people will bristle with indignation at the suggestion that we have carried on with sports far beyond that which is healthy. Yet, seriously, what did the LORD—not Ellen White—tell His people on the matter?

> I do not condemn the simple exercise of playing ball; but this, even in its simplicity, may be overdone.
>
> I shrink always from the almost sure result which follows in the wake of these amusements. It leads to an outlay of means that should be expended in bringing the light of truth to souls that are perishing out of Christ. The amusements and expenditures of means for self-pleasing, which lead on step by step to self-glorifying, and the educating in these games for pleasure produce a love and passion for such things that is not favorable to the perfection of Christian character.
>
> The way that they have been conducted at the college does not bear the impress of heaven. It does not strengthen the intellect. It does not refine and purify the character. There are threads leading out through the habits and customs and worldly practices, and the actors become so engrossed and infatuated that they are pronounced in heaven lovers of pleasure more than lovers of God. In the place of the intellect becoming strengthened to do better work as students, to be better qualified as Christians to perform the Christian duties, the exercise in these games is filling their brains with thoughts that distract the mind from their studies....
>
> Is the eye single to the glory of God in these games? I know that this is not so. There is a losing sight of God's way and His purpose. The employment of intelligent beings, in probationary time, is superseding God's revealed will and substituting for it the speculations and inventions of the human agent, with Satan by his side to imbue with his spirit.... The Lord God of heaven protests against the burning passion cultivated for supremacy in the games that are so engrossing. (Lt. 17a, 1893, in *The Adventist Home*, pp. 499, 500)

After observing the actual practice of Adventist schools at all levels, it is fair to ask whether we are obedient or insubordinate to God's counsel. And this is just one example. There is an alarming number of other issues that require scrutiny, though we will not discuss them here. The issue is about whether we believe the gospel and have Jesus, and whether our eyes need to be re-directed to Him. *The gospel produces obedience to all the commandments of God!*

Without launching into a grand treatise on this subject, let me summarize my belief that the heart of the gospel is Jesus, who is eternal God, coming to earth in human sinful flesh, subject to temptation through the pull of the flesh, yet also possessing the divine mind, which did not yield to the flesh. He relied on the Father for power through the Spirit to sustain Him. By His meritorious life, death, and resurrection and His subsequent acceptance by the Father, He was able to bestow upon us that same Spirit for the regeneration of our minds while in fallen, sinful flesh so that we might be kept from falling into sin. Righteousness by faith is forgiveness, cleansing, and power to walk as He walked through submission to God and a willingness to die to self.

Thus it is that, amongst the brethren, we come down every time to friction over this issue of living without sin. The careless will ask every time, "Well, are you without sin?" Don't make that mistake, for that is the wrong question. Instead, ask, "Are you in Christ?" If you are in Christ, you are a *new creation*, and in Him, there is no sin. Therefore, when I am in Him, I am without sin. And, yes, that means that neither my flesh nor my mind will be acting out in any sin because, by my choice, my operating system will be *His* mind. So, if we want to ask a pertinent question, we need to ask if we have chosen for Christ to live in us and if self is crucified with Him (Gal. 2:20). If the answer is, "yes," but our works do not correspond, then we will know that there is a problem, according to passages such as Luke 6:46, 1 John 3:9, John 10:27, and Zechariah 6:15.

> That which God required of Adam before his fall was perfect obedience to His law. God requires now what He required of Adam, perfect obedience, righteousness without a flaw, without shortcoming in His sight. God help us to render to Him all His law requires. We cannot do this without that faith that brings Christ's righteousness into daily practice. (Lt. 55, 1886, to G. I. Butler and S. N. Haskell, in *Manuscript Releases*, vol. 12, p. 325)

The mind of the flesh hates the thought of actually putting sin away. Yet, what exactly do we overcome, in Christ's strength, if it is not sin? We cannot read the Bible or the Spirit of Prophecy without coming away with the solid truth that the work of God is not only to cast our past sin into the depths of the sea but to draw us to Christ and enable us to choose Him that He may live in us and work His works in us to the glory of God. What starts in the mind and heart is carried out in the body. It is not mere "accounting" in the heavenly "books of record" but a genuine and active *living witness* to the power of God to raise us up to righteousness in all our ways, now and forever. We do not wait until glorification at Christ's second coming to gain the victory over the world, the flesh, and the devil. We do not even wait for the time of the latter rain to empower us for victory. That is the work of the early rain. The latter rain is to add impetus to what has already been accomplished in us; it is to move the message forward quickly. We cannot wait until another time to be cleansed from sin. *Now* is the day of salvation.

Let us come back to that well-known passage about the "precious message" and hear its appeal to receive the message brought by Waggoner and Jones, noting that the message is given a certain identification that should make us sit up straight with our eyes wide open:

> **They needed to have their eyes directed to His divine person, His merits,** and His changeless love for the human family. **All power** is given into His hands, that He may **dispense rich gifts unto men, imparting** the priceless gift of His own righteousness to the helpless human agent. **This is the message that God commanded to be given to the world. It is the third angel's message, which is to be proclaimed with a loud voice, and attended with the outpouring of His Spirit in a large measure.** (Lt. 57, 1895, in *Testimonies to Ministers*, p. 92, emphasis added)

What a declaration! What was it that was given in 1888? It was a message of both imputed and imparted righteousness. *This was the loud cry message!* What marks the giving of that message? *The outpouring of the latter rain Holy Spirit*! Why do Seventh-day Adventists organize global movements to seek the Holy Spirit, why do we groan and pray with great fervency for the Spirit's moving, when directly in front of us is the remedy that we need? If the 1888 message is the answer to all our prayers, then why should we not get off our knees and take hold of the divine answer and run with it, praying as we go?

Ponder how the Jews looked for the Messiah to come, and yet, when He came, rejected Him and, to this day, are still looking for the Messiah. Do I need to spell out the parallel? Let there be no mistake—Seventh-day Adventists have been looking for the *loud cry*; we have been anticipating the *latter rain* for generations. The latter rain has come, but, as a whole, we rejected it and are still looking for it.

That is the reason we have problems. It should be no mystery to us why the Church is like this. "The curse causeless shall not come" (Prov. 26:2). We can trace the reasons that things are as they are. The path that ancient Israel trod is the same as that which modern Israel now treads. Both rejected the message and the messengers who point to Jesus.

When rebellion was running high at the 1888 session at Minneapolis, the prophet was about to pack her bags and leave, but JESUS came directly to her with a message:

> When I purposed to leave Minneapolis, the angel of the Lord stood by me and said: "Not so; God has a work for you to do in this place. **The people are acting over the rebellion of Korah, Dathan, and Abiram**. I have placed you in your proper position, which those who are not in the light will not acknowledge; they will not heed your testimony; but I will be with you; My grace and power shall sustain you. **It is not you they are despising, but the messengers and the message I send to My people. They have shown contempt for the word of the Lord**. Satan has blinded their eyes and perverted their judgment; and unless every soul shall repent of this their sin, this **unsanctified independence that is doing insult to the Spirit of God**, they will walk in darkness. **I will remove the candlestick out of his place except they repent** and be converted, that I should heal them. They have obscured their spiritual eyesight. They would not that God would manifest His Spirit and His power; for **they have a spirit of mockery and disgust at My word**. Lightness, trifling, jesting, and joking are daily practiced. They have not set their hearts to seek Me. They walk in the sparks of their own kindling, and **unless they repent they shall lie down in sorrow**. Thus saith the Lord: Stand at your post of duty; for I am with thee, and will not leave thee nor forsake thee." These words from God I have not dared to disregard. (Lt. 2a, 1892, in *The Ellen G. White 1888 Materials*, p. 1067, emphasis added)

If we take nothing more from this study, we should ask ourselves this: Do we truly want the latter rain outpouring of the Holy Spirit?

This is what prepares the way of the Lord. It not only brings us to harvest readiness, but it is the power and driving force for the proclamation—both *in word* and *in living testimony*—of the last message of mercy to the world. That last message will bring all people to their final position with regard to God and His law. If we want all of this, what is it that we need? It is the 1888 message, which is the fourth angel, and the angel is Christ! Appropriated, that message brings the power of the Holy Spirit for victory. We need to go back where we got off track and find our way back onto the right path again. Only then can we arrive at the intended destination. *We must study to comprehend the message that was given there by the messengers Jones and Waggoner and make it our own experience.* It is true that knowledge is power, but here we must exercise caution, for head knowledge avails nothing if we choose not to put it into practice.

The Cure for the Lukewarm Laodicean Condition

The 1888 message is the cure not only for Laodicean lukewarmness but it is also the means of staying out of both of the "gospel ditches," which are generally defined as "conservative" and "liberal." (Experience has shown that the Laodicean condition can arise out of either experience.) Back in the time of the message in second generation Adventism, the issue was tending more toward the ditch of dry law keeping, or legalism. Today, the issue is tending more toward the ditch of cheap grace and antinomianism, operating through once-saved-always-saved, name-it-and-claim-it religion. That is why modern proponents of the 1888 message may tend to stress the obedience part of the message to counteract "cheap grace."

It may seem strange to say it, but genuine salvation by grace through faith is a works program! It is a program that works because it is the merits of Christ at work. His works are always pure and always perfect righteousness. His perfect works are efficacious for believers. Through the eye of personal faith, beholding continually the righteousness of Christ, obedience is bestowed upon the children of God, fitting them for eternal life. It is the merits of His works that grant all penitent souls an entrance into heaven.

Study the following teaching of the Spirit to understand how this works. Looking to Jesus, our sins are removed from our lives today, in reality. We no longer continue in them, and by grace, we are saved from sin and death.

The uplifted Saviour is to appear in **His efficacious work** as the Lamb slain, sitting upon the throne, **to dispense the priceless covenant blessings**, the **benefits He died to purchase** for every soul who should believe on Him. John could not express that love in words; it was too deep, too broad; he calls upon the human family to behold it.

Christ is pleading for the church in the heavenly courts above, pleading for those for whom He paid the redemption price of His own lifeblood. Centuries, ages, can never diminish the **efficacy of this atoning sacrifice**. The message of the gospel of His grace was to be given to the church in clear and distinct lines, that the world should no longer say that Seventh-day Adventists talk the law, the law, but do not teach or believe Christ.

The **efficacy** of the blood of Christ was to be presented to the people with **freshness and power**, that their **faith might lay hold upon its merits**. As the high priest sprinkled the warm blood upon the mercy seat, while the fragrant cloud of incense ascended before God, so while we confess our sins and plead the **efficacy** of Christ's atoning blood, our prayers are to ascend to heaven, fragrant with the merits of our Saviour's character.

Notwithstanding our unworthiness, we are ever to bear in mind that there is One that can take away sin and save the sinner. Every sin acknowledged before God with a contrite heart, He will <u>remove.</u> This faith is the life of the church. As the serpent was lifted up in the wilderness by Moses, and all that had been bitten by the fiery serpents were bidden to look and live, so also the Son of man must be lifted up, that "whosoever believeth in Him should not perish, but have everlasting life."

Unless he makes it his **life business** to **behold the uplifted Saviour**, and **by faith to accept the merits** which it is his privilege to claim, the sinner can no more be saved than Peter could walk upon the water unless he kept his eyes fixed steadily upon Jesus.

Now, it has been Satan's determined purpose to eclipse the view of Jesus and lead **men to look to man**, and **trust to man**, and be educated to **expect help from man**. For years the church has been **looking to man** and **expecting much from man**, but not looking to Jesus, in whom our hopes of eternal life are centered. Therefore God gave to His servants a testimony that presented **the truth as it is in Jesus, which is the third angel's message**, in clear, distinct lines.... (*Testimonies to Ministers*, pp. 92, 93, emphasis added)

If you still aren't convinced, then spend some time reading the book *Faith and Works*, and it will come perfectly clear. Notice the following statement:

> We have reason for ceaseless gratitude to God that Christ, **by His perfect obedience**, has won back the heaven that Adam lost through disobedience…Jesus regained heaven for man by bearing the test that Adam failed to endure; for He **obeyed the law perfectly**, and all who have a right conception of the plan of redemption will see that they **cannot be saved while in transgression of God's holy precepts**. They **must cease to transgress the law and lay hold on the promises of God that are available for us through the merits of Christ**.
>
> From the pulpits of today the words are uttered: "Believe, only believe. Have faith in Christ; you have nothing to do with the old law, only trust in Christ." How different is this from the words of the apostle who declares that faith without works is dead. He says, "But be ye doers of the word, and not hearers only, deceiving your own selves" (James 1:22). **We must have that faith that works** by love and purifies the soul. Many seek to substitute a superficial faith for uprightness of life and think through this to obtain salvation.
>
> **The Lord requires** at this time just what He required of Adam in Eden—**perfect obedience to the law of God. We must have righteousness without a flaw, without a blemish.** God gave His Son to die for the world, but He did not die to repeal the law which was holy and just and good. The sacrifice of Christ on Calvary is an unanswerable argument showing the immutability of the law. Its penalty was felt by the Son of God in behalf of guilty man, that **through His merits the sinner might obtain the virtue of His spotless character by faith in His name**.
>
> The sinner was provided with a second opportunity to keep the law of God in the strength of his divine Redeemer.…
>
> Satan … has claimed that the death of Christ made obedience to the law unnecessary and permitted the sinner to come into favor with a holy God without forsaking his sin. He has declared that the Old Testament standard was lowered in the gospel and that men can come to Christ, **not to be saved from their sins but in their sins**. (*Signs of the Times*, May 19, 1890, in *Faith and Works*, pp. 88–90)

So, we have the cure. Modern Israel, who were given the oracles of God after 1844, went into the lukewarm Laodicean condition by 1859. Nonetheless, God sent us the cure in the 1888 message, which is also known as the "Laodicean Message," or the "Counsel of the True Witness to the Laodiceans." It was given to take the Laodicean character out of the remnant people.

What Did We Do With This "Most Precious Message?"

You will hear many highly educated teachers and writers in Adventism proclaiming boldly that the message has *now been accepted*. This is simply not true. *It was not accepted then and it has not been accepted to this day.* Those of us who are engaged in the work of spreading the message of the fourth angel have seen and experienced this first-hand. We were warned outright by church leadership not to bring Jones and Waggoner into one local Seventh-day Adventist church. Had their message ever been accepted, then, to this day, there would have been a completely different environment in the church and in the world. The loud cry would be going forth under latter rain power and Christ would have come! That the message was rejected and not allowed to work is a fact acknowledged in 1893 by the pen of inspiration:

> The Spirit of God has been present in power among His people, but it could not be bestowed upon them, because they did not open their hearts to receive it.…
>
> The Lord designed that the messages of warning and instruction given through the Spirit to His people should go everywhere. But the influence that grew out of the resistance of light and truth at Minneapolis tended to make of no effect the light God had given to His people through the Testimonies.…
>
> If every soldier of Christ had done his duty, if every watchman on the walls of Zion had given the trumpet a certain sound, the world might ere this have heard the message of warning. But the work is years behind. What account will be rendered to God for thus retarding the work? (Lt. 77, 1893, in *The Ellen G. White 1888 Materials*, pp. 1129, 1130)

This gracious message was not allowed to do its intended work. Notice the interesting point that she made. Even five years after the 1888 conference, the work of finishing up the proclamation of the message to the world was delayed. Even then the church was "years behind." What would she say to the church today, almost one hundred and thirty years later?

Of course, there were individuals who accepted the

message when it was first given, but the church in general—and the leadership in particular—did not respond in the way that Heaven intended. Even though some of the leaders repented and confessed in the years following 1888, the messages did not produce a harvest-ripe remnant church in the second generation period.

We read the following solemn warning issued a few years after 1888 (April 11, 1895), which is worth penitent consideration even today, for we are still engaged in the same work.

> I would speak in warning to those who have stood for years resisting light and cherishing the spirit of opposition. **How long will you hate and despise the messengers of God's righteousness?** [*She is here speaking of Jones and Waggoner.*] **God has given them His message.** They bear the word of the Lord. There is salvation for you, but only through the merits of Jesus Christ. The grace of the Holy Spirit has been offered you again and again. Light and power from on high have been shed abundantly in the midst of you. Here was evidence, that all might discern whom the Lord recognized as His servants. But there are those who despised the men and the message they bore. They have taunted them with being fanatics, extremists, and enthusiasts. **Let me prophesy unto you: Unless you speedily humble your hearts before God, and confess your sins, which are many, you will, when it is too late, see that you have been fighting against God.** Through the conviction of the Holy Spirit, **no longer unto reformation and pardon**, you will see that these men whom you have spoken against have been as signs in the world, as witnesses for God. Then you would give the whole world if you could redeem the past, and be just such zealous men, moved by the Spirit of God to lift your voice in solemn warning to the world; and, like them, to be in principle firm as a rock.... (Lt. 57, 1895, to O. A. Olsen, in *Testimonies to Ministers*, pp. 96, 97, emphasis added)

Here she was pleading with the leadership. They despised the men who brought *God's message*. She faithfully and continuously implored them with words from the Lord which said, in effect: *Stop spurning the men and the message; you are on your way to grieving the Holy Spirit.*

> Your turning things upside down is known of the Lord. **Go on a little longer as you have gone, in rejection of the light from heaven, and you are lost.** "The man that shall be unclean, and shall not purify himself, that soul shall be cut off from among the congregation." [Num. 19:20.]
>
> I have no smooth message to bear to those who have been so long as **false guideposts**, pointing the wrong way. **If you reject Christ's delegated messengers, you reject Christ**. Neglect this great salvation, kept before you for years, despise this **glorious offer of justification through the blood of Christ and sanctification through the cleansing power of the Holy Spirit**, and there remaineth no more sacrifice for sins, but a certain fearful looking for of judgment and fiery indignation. [Heb. 10:26, 27.] (Lt. 57, 1895, to O. A. Olsen, in *Testimonies to Ministers*, pp. 97, 98, emphasis added)

The words that follow serve to bring this matter home. What happened on that occasion was as serious as it gets for God's people. It is not a stretch to say that the leadership of the Seventh-day Adventist Church at that time were very nearly guilty—if not actually guilty—of a crucifixion event.

> On many occasions the Holy Spirit did work, but those who resisted the Spirit of God at Minneapolis were waiting for a chance to travel over the same ground again, because their spirit was the same. Afterward, when they had evidence heaped upon evidence, some were convicted, but those who were not softened and subdued by the Holy Spirit's working, put their own interpretation upon every manifestation of the grace of God, and they have lost much. They pronounced in their heart and soul and words that this manifestation of the Holy Spirit was fanaticism and delusion. They stood like a rock, the waves of mercy flowing upon and around them, but beaten back by their hard and wicked hearts, which resisted the Holy Spirit's working. Had this been received, it would have made them wise unto salvation; holier men, prepared to do the work of God with sanctified ability. But **all the universe of heaven witnessed the disgraceful treatment of Jesus Christ, represented by the Holy Spirit. Had Christ been before them, they would have treated him in a manner similar to that in which the Jews treated Christ.** (Lt. 6, 1896, in *The Ellen G. White 1888 Materials*, pp. 1478, 1479, emphasis added)

We must take heed, for what was written still applies—"If you reject Christ's delegated messengers, you reject Christ" (Lt. 57, 1895, to O. A. Olsen, in *Testimonies to Ministers*, p. 97). Today, the same work goes on as church leaders cast shadows on the messengers of 1888. When the names of Jones and Waggoner are mentioned in the mainstream churches today, the most noteworthy detail pointed out about them, rather than considering their message, is often that they apostatized from the church. Calling this to the people's attention, the aim of the enemy of souls has been to poison the well for those who do not study for themselves. Sadly, it is a successful ploy, for the dark work of character assassination is effective. Saul Alinsky wrote "Rules for Radicals," a manifesto for political subversives. The last of his rules is: "Pick the target, freeze it, personalize it, and polarize it" (Alinsky, *Rules for Radicals*, p. 130). This means to—

> Cut off the support network and isolate the target from sympathy. Go after people and not institutions. (This is cruel, but very effective. Direct, personalized criticism and ridicule works.)" (Glenn Beck, http://1ref.us/hw)

Modern Times: Adventism's Point Man for Subverting A. T. Jones?

In current Adventism, there is one scholar who has written several books on the subject of 1888 and A. T. Jones, whose stated purpose has been to emphasize Jones's flawed nature. Responding to a questioner, the scholar said:

> I will have to confess ... that I must have failed to communicate effectively. I was doing my best to demonstrate that Jones was aberrant from beginning to end. In the late 1880s and early 1890s this is demonstrated by his harshness and failure to demonstrate Christian courtesy, his extreme use of language that seemingly led some toward the holy flesh excitement, his extremes in nearly every area of religious liberty, his support of Anna Rice in 1893 and 1894, and so on. The point that I was attempting to communicate was that throughout Jones's "hero" period, he was beset by serious character traits, in spite of Ellen White's endorsement of him. (George Knight, *Adventist Currents*, April 1988, p. 43)

It is true that A. T. Jones did receive counsel from the Lord with regard to his manner. The counsel said:

> In the past you have presented the truth in a fierce way, using it as if it were a scourge. This has not glorified the Lord. You have given the people the rich treasures of God's Word, but your manner has been so condemnatory that they have turned from them. You have not taught the truth in the way that Christ taught it. You present it in a way that mars its influence.... (Lt. 164, 1902, in *Manuscript Releases*, vol. 21, p. 95)

Coming from a military background, Jones was at times overbearing, and for this, he was admonished. Yet, his forcefulness was praised under other circumstances. It is always important to consider the context of a counsel and avoid generalizations.

> Let not those who have neglected to receive light and truth take advantage of the mistake of their brethren, and put forth their finger, and speak words of vanity, because the chosen of God have been too ardent in their ideas, and have carried certain matters in too strong a manner. We have need of these ardent elements; for our work is not a passive work; our work is aggressive. (Lt. 27, 1894, to S. N. Haskell, in *The Ellen G. White 1888 Materials*, pp. 1246, 1247)

Jones's aggressive nature did not serve him well at that time, and it is a legacy that hinders his work to this day. Great stock has been taken of this fact in the overall denominational campaign to turn minds away from the man and the message. However, we no longer have to deal with *the man* or any of his rough edges that were at times manifest. We have only *the message*, which the Lord has declared to be from Him. In a more recent publication, George Knight turned to not so subtly attacking the message:

> **The problem** [*of pantheistic tendencies*] showed up in his public presentations ... in early 1902 and in his *Consecrated Way to Christian Perfection*. (George Knight, *A. T. Jones: Point Man on Adventism's Charismatic Frontier*, p. 242, emphasis added)

Pacific Press published *Consecrated Way to Christian Perfection* in 1905. If there is any pantheism in it, we would like someone to point it out. *The Consecrated Way* is also included in the Ellen G. White Estate publication of the 2008 Comprehensive Research Edition of the Ellen G. White Writings CD-ROM. Of his later written works, it is said that this book "is possibly the best presentation of the essence of the message of Jones in 1888" (Publisher's Preface, *The Consecrated Way to Christian Perfection*, republished by *Truth for the Final Generation*, 2007, p. 5).

Knight went on to say:

> To put it mildly, the Adventist air was quite heavy with ideas that one could interpret as pantheistic in the late nineties and early 1900s. Some of them undoubtedly grew out of **exaggerated and overly literalized views of the indwelling Christ**. The concept of the indwelling power of Christ was inherent in the 1888 message, but when pushed too far it **easily** crosses the border into pantheism. It was certainly so in the case of Waggoner …
>
> It is **probably no accident** that the three foremost ministerial proponents of righteousness by faith in the 1890s—Jones, Waggoner, and Prescott—**all got entangled in pantheistic language and sentiments**. (George Knight, *A. T. Jones: Point Man on Adventism's Charismatic Frontier*, p. 242, emphasis added)

This seems to be a tactical ploy, for the picture that Knight's brush paints is seen to be, upon investigation, largely unfounded. For instance, he makes no attempt to give any example of an "exaggerated and overly literalized" depiction by Jones of the indwelling Christ. While Knight claimed that Jones "does not appear to have been a pantheist in the same sense as Kellogg and Waggoner" and that he did not abandon "the traditional Adventist teaching on the sanctuary and its cleansing," Knight asserted that he must be confused along pantheistic lines because he was somehow errant in his use of "language and symbolism" regarding "the indwelling of God in the living human temple and the cleansing of the body temple with the doctrine of the heavenly sanctuary and its cleansing" (Knight, *A. T. Jones*, pp. 239–241). The appraisal is highly subjective, conjectural and unsubstantiated.

A thorough study of Ellen White's writings can provide examples that could be used to make the claim that she did the very same thing. Yet, we do not insinuate that she was ever tending toward pantheism.

In the book in question, Jones is not mixed up with pantheistic thought. The teaching is plain for all who will read it as it is instead of gaining an understanding of what it says from someone else's interpretation. Read *The Consecrated Way* and discover what it says for yourself. In it, Jones speaks of God's personal presence dwelling in "individual lives" (p. 52, *Truth For the Final Generation* edition) that He may "reform and make holy the lives of His people" (p. 55) by "dwelling in their hearts" (p. 56).

Jones's teaching is always based upon the Scriptures, and his description of the cleansing of the soul temple concerns the cleansing of the conscience of the guilt of past and present sin "that in the life and works of the believer in Jesus sin shall have no place" (pp. 59, 60). Jones talks about "Christ fully formed … within each believer" (p. 85) and about "God alone manifest in the flesh of each believer in Jesus." For these descriptions, some might imagine him to be a pantheist. Yet, there is nothing in statements like these that is not also given in the inspired statements of Ellen White. We see, for example, statements like the following:

> You need **Christ formed within** you the hope of glory.… (*Testimonies for the Church*, vol. 2, p. 543, emphasis added)

> … if **Christ** is not **formed within**, if you have not the mind of Christ, and do not practice the words of Christ; … you will never reach heaven. (*Review and Herald*, July 22, 1890, emphasis added)

> Transformation of character is the testimony to the world of an **indwelling Christ**. (*Prophets and Kings*, p. 233, emphasis added)

> Man, made for **the dwelling-place of God**, became the habitation of dragons. (*Review and Herald*, Oct. 22, 1895, emphasis added)

The same type of thoughts can be found in Scripture:

> And what agreement hath the temple of God with idols? for ye are the temple of the living God; as God hath said, I will dwell in them, and walk in *them*; and I will be their God, and they shall be my people. (2 Cor. 6:16)

> In whom ye also are builded together for an habitation of God through the Spirit. (Eph. 2:22)

Jones's teaching is focused on the sanctuary cleansing work of believers putting away sin from their hearts and lives. It crosses no line into pantheism whatsoever. If—as Knight's concern would tend to suggest—there is any relation drawn in *The Consecrated Way* between the physical cleansing of the body temple and the indwelling of God, it is not apparent to this writer, even though one could see where it might be found in the Spirit of

Prophecy writings, with regard to providing a fit vessel with healthy blood to feed the organs and the mind and give mental clarity for receiving and understanding the Word of God through study and being so finely tuned that one will be able to hear the subtle impress of the Holy Spirit's guidance.

Let no one at any time steer you away from studying the 1888-era writings of Jones and Waggoner by casting aspersions upon the men and their message because they later "went into apostasy." Actually, the inspired pen makes the point that their later troubles came about because of the terrible manner in which they were treated.

> It is quite possible that Elder Jones or Elder Waggoner may be overthrown by the temptations of the enemy; but if they should be, **this would not prove that they had had no message from God**, or that the work that they had done was all a mistake. But should this happen, **how many would take this position, and enter into a fatal delusion because they are not under the control of the Spirit of God.** They walk in the sparks of their own kindling, and cannot distinguish between the fire they have kindled, and the light which God has given, and **they walk in blindness as did the Jews.** (Lt. 24, 1892, p. 5, to Uriah Smith, in *Manuscript Releases*, vol. 1, p. 143, emphasis added)

> I have no smooth message to bear to those who have been so long as false guideposts, pointing the wrong way. **If you reject Christ's delegated messengers, you reject Christ**.... (*Testimonies to Ministers*, p. 97, emphasis added)

The message that made them God's anointed at that time is still the message of anointed men, whether or not they held true to their calling. The positive testimonies by the pen of Ellen White, with regard to the men and message, are decided and clear. To repudiate the messengers is to reject the Spirit of Prophecy, which is the testimony of Jesus. There is no other way to honestly assess the matter. The undermining of the message has gone on for a very long time. Leaders who have known better have stood by and watched it happen. They have set the course for later leaders who acted similarly, turning a blind eye to deepening apostasy. Those few who have not been so easily taken in by the herd mentality, who have picked up the torch and brought the message back to the attention of the people, have experienced the same sort of treatment as the original messengers. A stern warning is given to those who would do this baleful work:

> Satan has gained marked advantage ... because the people of God have not guarded the outposts. The very men whose labors God has signified that He would accept if they were fully consecrated have been the ones to be deceived, to fail in their duties, and **to prove a terrible burden and discouragement, instead of the help and blessing that they should have been.** These **men who have been trusted to keep the fort have well-nigh betrayed it into the hands of the enemy.** They have opened the gates to a wily foe, who has sought to destroy them.
>
> **Men of experience have seen stealthy hands slipping the bolts that Satan might enter;** yet they have held their peace with apparent indifference as to the results. (*Testimonies for the Church*, vol. 4, p. 211, emphasis added)

Passing the buck, current leaders who are asleep at their own post of duty serve their time in reliance upon the poor judgment of their fathers.

> Some have been glad to see this, as it seemed an extenuation of their past neglect, which made it a necessity to call for others to fill the posts of responsibility that they had abused or neglected. This lack of watchfulness on the part of these newer incumbents seemed to excuse the former for their own want of faithfulness, as it showed that others were fully as derelict in duty. These persons do not realize that God holds them responsible for every advantage gained by the foe who is admitted to the fort. **The desolation and ruin following lie at the door of the unfaithful sentinels, who, by their neglect, become agents in the hands of the adversary to win souls to destruction.**... (*Testimonies for the Church*, vol. 4, pp. 211, 212, emphasis added)

This is where the discussion of "corporate repentance" could logically come in. Do we expect that the entire administrative body will ever repent? No. "Are we hoping to see the whole church revived? That time will never come" (*Review and Herald*, March 22, 1887, in *Selected Messages*, bk. 1, p. 122). What this means is that, *as honest individuals* coming to recognize what took place, we will repent for what our fathers have done because we too have been asleep at the helm. This means that we will choose to do differently than they have done.

We will shake off the fog of slumber, take up our post of duty and stand for the right, even though we may suffer the same burden of discouragement at the hands of the brethren as did they.

Spiritual Death, Pretension, and Impenitence

Spiritual death has come upon the people that should be manifesting life and zeal, purity and consecration, by the most earnest devotion to the cause of truth. The **facts** concerning the **real condition** of the **professed people of God**, speak more loudly than their profession, and make it evident that some power has **cut the cable that anchored them to the Eternal Rock**, and that they are **drifting away to sea, without chart or compass**. (*Review and Herald*, July 24, 1888, emphasis added)

The church is like the unproductive tree which, receiving the dew and rain and sunshine, should have produced an abundance of fruit, but on which the divine search discovers **nothing but leaves**. Solemn thought for our churches! solemn, indeed, for every individual! Marvelous is the patience and forbearance of God; but "except thou repent," it will be exhausted; **the churches, our institutions, will go from weakness to weakness, from cold formality to deadness, while they are saying, "I am rich, and increased with goods, and have need of nothing."** The True Witness says, "And knowest not that thou art wretched, and miserable, and poor, and blind, and naked." **Will they ever see clearly their condition?** (*Review and Herald*, Dec. 23, 1890, art. B, emphasis added)

What hope is there? As we look around today at the state of the people and the continued alliances with the world at every level, how can we rejoice in the hope of repentance, revival, and reformation without any indication that they are taking place at the visible corporate level? Can we lift our hands in victory for the people and the arrival of the long overdue great outpouring of the latter rain upon the church? Is it not claimed today that 1888 was a victory for the truth and that the message of 1888 is being taught today in the denomination? Such conclusions are mockery, for, if they were true, would not the outpouring of the latter rain be upon us?

Is there a remnant of God who are following on to know the Lord? Where are they? Listen—

Who Will Constitute the Remnant?

There is neither hope in Sardis nor Laodicea. **Out of these conditions must the victors come into that of Philadelphia**—brotherly love.... He has **no promise to Laodicea as a whole [corporately] ... but the individual who opens the heart's door and lets Christ in,** who comes into that wonderful communion with the divine Lord, will by that very process come into the condition of brotherly love [Philadelphia]. **They will constitute the remnant** who keep the word of His patience, against whom He has no condemnation, who are ready for translation.... (Milton C. Wilcox, *Signs of the Times*, Jan. 17, 1911, p. 7, emphasis added)

But the counsel of the True Witness does not represent those who are lukewarm as in a hopeless case. There is yet a chance to remedy their state, and the Laodicean message is full of encouragement; for the backslidden church may yet buy the gold of faith and love, may yet have the white robe of the righteousness of Christ, that the shame of their nakedness need not appear.... (*Review and Herald*, Aug. 28, 1894)

There is no such thing as a "remnant within the remnant." There can only be one remnant—those who let Jesus come in. The church is not composed of an earthly registry but of a heavenly one. There is no salvation by denomination, and the opposite is also true—there is no damnation inherent in the act of leaving a *denomination*. The ship of our salvation is Christ!

The final remnant elect will heed the call as well as give the call of the fourth angel whose glory fills all the earth. Those who give the loud cry message will not be visible groups along human organizational lines; they will be individuals in the mainstream church and in supporting and independent Seventh-day Adventist groups. The loud cry is given by those who have "the third angel's message in verity," "the truth as it is in Jesus." Not all who call themselves Israel qualify as such.

One may ask, "Where is the proof that the members of the invisible church reside in the visible church? Are there any members of the visible Seventh-day Adventist organization who are a part of the invisible church?"

We may not find a direct statement, in so many words, that some members of the visible church are members of the invisible and some are not. However, we can show that this principle is true by examining the light we have on the Lord's assessment of those who are in the

```
┌─────────────────────────────┐   ┌─────────────────────────────┐
│   MODERN ISRAEL—            │   │   SPIRITUAL BABYLON         │
│   CLAIMANTS TO ADVENTISM    │   │   & ENDTIME BEAST SYSTEM    │
│   AND 3RD ANGEL'S MESSAGE   │   │   RELIGIOUS AND SECULAR WORLD│
│   Many shaken out           │   │   Many come in              │
│   Repository of the sacred oracles— │ Have not the sacred oracles │
│   *Law with the Sabbath     │   │   3rd angel's message under loud cry │
│   *Sanctuary Truth          │   │   brings many to spiritual Israel │
│   *Spirit of Prophecy       │   │   the rest take mark of the beast. │
└─────────────────────────────┘   └─────────────────────────────┘
```

**ENDTIME REMNANT—
PRESENTLY INVISIBLE OR INACTIVE; FUTURE VISIBLE**
<u>Faithful</u> Souls in the SdA Denomination
<u>Faithful</u> Souls in Supporting and Independent SdA
<u>Called-Out Faithful</u> in Babylon and End-time Beast System
THE SANCTIFIED ROYAL FAMILY (19MR 176)

---

visible church. The Lord's teaching reveals the principle that profession of a name—visibility—is not what He desires:

> Not every one that saith unto me, Lord, Lord, shall enter into the kingdom of heaven; but he that doeth the will of my Father which is in heaven. Many will say to me in that day, Lord, Lord, have we not prophesied in thy name? and in thy name have cast out devils? and in thy name done many wonderful works? And then will I profess unto them, I never knew you: depart from me, ye that work iniquity. (Matt. 7:21–23)

> And in that day seven women shall take hold of one man, saying, We will eat our own bread, and wear our own apparel: only let us be called by thy name, to take away our reproach. In that day shall the branch of the LORD be beautiful and glorious, and the fruit of the earth *shall be* excellent and comely for them that are escaped of Israel. (Isa. 4:1, 2)

The truth is that, of the numbers present in the visible church, there are many who will be lost. This is the key to understanding that *visibility* avails nothing. The *visible* church is the *nominal* church. Here are some examples of this:

There are men in the ranks of Sabbathkeepers who are holding fast their earthly treasures, considering them of greater value than the souls of men. Will such have the "Well done" spoken to them? No; never. **The irrevocable sentence, "Depart," will fall upon their startled senses. Christ has no use for them.** They have been slothful servants, hoarding the means God has given them, while their fellow men have perished in darkness and error. (*Review and Herald, March 14, 1878*, in *Counsels on Stewardship*, p. 123, emphasis added)

In the broad road all are occupied with their persons, their dress, and the pleasures in the way. They **indulge freely in hilarity and glee**, and think not of their journey's end, of the certain destruction at the end of the path. Every day they approach nearer their destruction; yet they madly rush on faster and faster. Oh, how dreadful this looked to me!

I saw **many traveling in this broad road who had the words written upon them: "Dead to the world. The end of all things is at hand. Be ye also ready." They looked just like all the vain ones** around them, except a shade of sadness which I noticed upon their countenances. **Their conversation was just like that of the gay, thoughtless ones around them; but they would occasionally point with great satisfaction to the letters on their garments, calling for the others** to have the same upon theirs. They were in the broad way, yet they professed to be of the number who were traveling the narrow way. Those around them would say: "There is no distinction between us. We are alike; we dress, and talk, and act alike."

Then I was pointed back to the years 1843 and 1844. There was a spirit of consecration then that there is not now. **What has come over the professed peculiar people of God?** I saw the conformity to the world, the unwillingness to suffer for the truth's sake. I saw a great lack of submission to the will of God....

I saw that many who profess to believe the truth for these last days, think it strange that the children of Israel murmured as they journeyed; that after the wonderful dealings of God with them, they should be so ungrateful as to forget what He had done for them. **Said the angel, "Ye have done worse than they."** (*Testimonies for the Church*, vol. 1, pp. 128, 129, emphasis added)

Then I was shown **a company who were howling in agony.** On their garments was written in large characters, "Thou art weighed in the balance, and found wanting." I asked who this company were. The angel said, "These are they who **once kept the Sabbath, and have given it up.**" I heard them cry with a loud voice, **"We have believed in Thy coming, and taught it with energy."** And while they were speaking, their eyes would fall upon their garments and see the writing, and then they would wail aloud. I saw that they had drunk of the deep waters, and fouled the residue with their feet,—trodden the Sabbath underfoot,— and that was why **they were weighed in the balance and found wanting.** (*Christian Experience and Teachings of Ellen G. White*, p. 101, emphasis added, first published in Broadside2, Jan. 31, 1849)

Those who have had opportunities to hear and receive the truth and who have united with the Seventh-day Adventist church, calling themselves the commandment-keeping people of God, and yet possess no more vitality and consecration to God than do the nominal churches, will receive of the plagues of God just as verily as the churches who oppose the law of God. **Only those that are sanctified through the truth will compose the royal family in the heavenly mansions** Christ has gone to prepare for those that love Him and keep His commandments. (Lt. 35, 1898, in *Manuscript Releases*, vol. 19, p. 176, emphasis added)

It always comes back to the question, "What is the true church?" Can the true body of Christ incorporate members who are unfaithful? What concord hath Christ with Belial? The answer to the "true church" question can never point ultimately to a visible church but only to an invisible one:

The church on earth, composed of those who are faithful and loyal to God, is the "true tabernacle," whereof the Redeemer is the minister. God, and not man, pitched this tabernacle on a high, elevated platform. This tabernacle is Christ's body, and from north, south, east, and west, He gathers those who shall help to compose it. (Ms. 142, 1899, in *Signs of the Times*, Feb. 14, 1900)

Many of those in the visible church have early growth failure and will not receive or discern the latter rain.

Many have in a great measure failed to receive the former rain. They have not obtained all the benefits that God has thus provided for them. They expect that the lack will be supplied by the latter rain. When the richest abundance of grace shall be bestowed, they intend to open their hearts to receive it. They are making a terrible mistake.... Unless we are daily advancing in the exemplification of the active Christian virtues, we **shall not recognize the manifestations of the Holy Spirit in the latter rain. It may be falling on hearts all around us, but we shall not discern or receive it.** (*Review and Herald*, March 2, 1897, in *Testimonies to Ministers and Gospel Workers*, p. 507, emphasis added)

Among leadership in the visible church, there are unsanctified ministers; these will miss out on the outpouring of the latter rain, for they will seek to control the work of the Spirit. The implication is clear: these leaders are part of the visible church. However, they are not part of the invisible church.

There are fearful woes for **those who preach the truth, but are not sanctified by it**, and also for those who consent to receive and maintain the unsanctified to minister to them in word and doctrine. I am alarmed for the people of God who profess to believe solemn, important truth, for I know that many of them are not converted nor sanctified through it. Men can hear and acknowledge the whole truth, and yet know nothing of the power of godliness. **All who preach the truth will not themselves be saved by it.** Said the angel: "Be ye clean, that bear the vessels of the Lord." (*Testimonies for the Church*, vol. 1, pp. 261, 262, emphasis added)

The Lord does not ask permission of those in responsible positions when he wishes to use certain ones as his agents for the promulgation of truth. But he will use whom he will use. **He will pass by men who have not followed his counsel**, men who feel capable and sufficient to work in their own wisdom; **and he will use others who are thought by these supposedly wise ones to be wholly incompetent.** Many who have some talent think that they are necessary to the cause of God. Let them beware lest they stretch themselves beyond their measure, and the Lord shall leave them to their own ways, to be filled with their own doings. None are to exercise their human authority to bind minds and souls of their fellow-men. They are not to devise and put in practice methods and plans to bring every individual under their jurisdiction. (*Review and Herald*, July 23, 1895, emphasis added)

Unless … [certain church workers] are aroused to a sense of their duty, they will not recognize the work of God when the loud cry of the third angel shall be heard. When light goes forth to lighten the earth, instead of coming up to the help of the Lord, they will want to bind about His work to meet their narrow ideas. Let me tell you that the Lord will work in this last work in a manner very much out of the common order of things, and in a way that will be contrary to any human planning. There will be those among us who **will always want to control the work of God, to dictate even what movements shall be made when the work goes forward under the direction of the angel who joins the third angel in the message to be given to the world.** God will use ways and means by which it will be seen that He is taking the reins in His own hands. The workers will be surprised by the simple means that He will use to bring about and perfect His work of righteousness. (*Testimonies to Ministers*, p. 300, emphasis added)

There is to be in the churches a wonderful manifestation of the power of God, but it will not move upon those who have not humbled themselves before the Lord, and opened the door of the heart by confession and repentance. **In the manifestation of that power which lightens the earth with the glory of God, they will see only something which in their blindness they think dangerous**, something which will arouse their fears, and they **will brace themselves to resist it.** Because the Lord does not work according to their ideas and expectations, they will oppose the work. "Why," they say, "should not we know the Spirit of God, when we have been in the work for so many years?" Because **they did not respond to the messages**, the warnings, and entreaties of the Lord, but **persistently said, "I am rich and increased in goods, and have need of nothing." Talent, long experience, will not make men channels of light**, unless they place themselves under the bright beams of the Sun of Righteousness, and are called and chosen and prepared by the endowment of the Holy Spirit.… (*Review and Herald*, Dec. 23, 1890, art. B, emphasis added)

It does not matter that a person is a certificate-holding member or even an influential leader. What the Lord requires is that a person be called, chosen, and prepared by the endowment of the Holy Spirit. Such preparation does not come from humans or any of human organizations but directly from the Father, in the name of Christ.

Organizational Apostasy in the Second Generation: Organization as God's Permissive Will

The General Conference Director of Auditing in the years 1976–1994, stated:

> It's time for Adventism to turn from its hierarchical style of administration, modeled on the Roman Catholic, and seriously consider a more simplified method of leadership. (David Dennis, *Fatal Accounts*, p. viii)

We would not be giving proper coverage if we did not discuss the organization and reorganization of the denomination and whether or not the church upheld the counsels of the Lord in the structuring of the work.

It would be exceeding the purposes of this book to launch into a detailed study of the formation of the denomination in 1863. Yet, we should make some quick comments. Remember that Adventists from this period had descended into the lukewarm Laodicean state. As such we cannot expect that they would hold together very well in any *theocratic* or *Holy Spirit-governed* body.

It is the position of this book that every type of human organization is under a paradigm of God's "accommodative" or "permissive" will. By this is meant that the organization operates under divine forbearance. When any human organization bypasses God, there must be some sort of creature governance to prevent complete chaos and dissolution. To this end, the Scriptures declare the powers of earth to be "ordained of God" and "God's ministers" (Rom. 13:1, 6). They have been established according to man's choice, and God grants man that which he has chosen, even though the results can be terrible. At the same time, even a wicked ruler is better than the anarchy of no ruler (1 Peter 2:18). In the world, we are to be subject to the civil powers (Titus 3:1).

In the church, it is not God's will that we should have any "keepers" or controllers of authority. Jesus said unequivocally:

> Ye know that the princes of the Gentiles exercise dominion over them, and they that are great exercise authority upon them. But it shall not be so among you: but whosoever will be great among you, let him be your minister. (Matt. 20:25, 26)

Modern ecclesiology has drifted far from the early church system. Bible translation has taken a certain direction in word choice, and this has fostered Christianity's general concepts of authority in church governance. There is also the contour of Christian history in what is known as the "Constantinian shift" with Christendom's adoption of the paradigms of human governance into the governance of the church. This type of governance is what we would call the "common order." All of this has brought politics, law enforcement, militarism and the notion of the "just war" into Christendom. These are certainly big concepts to unload without explanation, but we must leave it with students to research them on their own. We live in the information age, and a key word search online will launch the researcher into helpful material.

Keep in mind what happened when Israel clamored for a king. God had warned them against asking for a king, desiring that they would consider the ramifications of such a request (1 Sam. 8). Yet, even though it was not His will, He chose for them Saul, their first king, who was to be "the Lord's anointed" (1 Sam. 9:15–17; 24:10). When the will of God gives over to human will, it is still often represented as God's doing, but God's accommodative will is actually a form of His wrath. Hosea makes this plain:

> O Israel, thou hast destroyed thyself; but in me *is* thine help. I will be thy king: where *is* any other that may save thee in all thy cities? and thy judges of whom thou saidst, Give me a king and princes? I gave thee a king in mine anger, and took *him* away in my wrath. The iniquity of Ephraim *is* bound up; his sin *is* hid. (Hosea 13:9–12)

Today the establishment mindset is so firmly entrenched in the hierarchical arrangement—deeming "church authority" as that which is vested in ecclesiastical office—that one gets the sense that it is as much an article of faith as any other of the pillars of doctrine. This is why leadership can boldly assert:

> **The local [Seventh-day Adventist] church becomes the "port of entry" to the kingdom of God**. (North American Division Officers, *Adventist Review*, Oct. 1, 1992, p. 23, emphasis added)

We prefer to think that Jesus was more accurate on this point when He said that He was "the way" and that no man can approach the Father except through Him (John 14:6). *Jesus* is the port of entry into the kingdom of God.

Human Organization Irrelevant Under Final Movements

If God's people had gone forward in righteousness in the 1888 era, the Lord by His Spirit would have taken the helm, and the work would have been finished. The closing up of God's work on earth will not be completed under the auspices of human committees and programs. We can be confident of this by one simple fact of logic if nothing else. That fact is that, when the mark of the beast crisis comes down, there can be no seventh-day Sabbath organization functioning within the legal frameworks of nations. They will be outlawed unless they sell out to the system. Thus, from that standpoint alone, we must deem the hierarchical order of church governance as unessential in broadcasting the loud cry. *The establishment of the common order of human machinery is not in place for the finishing of the work. It exists until human beings get out of the way and let God control the work.*

> Unless those who can help in [advancing the work of God] are aroused to a sense of their duty, they will not recognize the work of God when the loud cry of the third angel shall be heard. When light goes forth

to lighten the earth, instead of coming up to the help of the Lord, they will want to bind about His work to meet their narrow ideas. Let me tell you that **the Lord will work in this last work in a manner very much out of the common order of things, and in a way that will be contrary to any human planning.** There will be those among us who will always want to control the work of God, to dictate even what movements shall be made when the work goes forward under the direction of the angel who joins the third angel in the message to be given to the world. **God will use ways and means by which it will be seen that He is taking the reins in His own hands. The workers will be surprised** by the simple means that He will use to bring about and perfect His work of righteousness. (*Testimonies to Ministers*, p. 300, emphasis added)

Thus **the message of the third angel will be proclaimed.** As the **time comes for it to be given with greatest power**, the Lord will work through humble instruments, leading the minds of those who consecrate themselves to His service. The **laborers will be qualified rather by the unction of His Spirit than by the training of literary institutions.** Men of faith and prayer will be constrained to go forth with holy zeal, declaring the words which God gives them. The sins of Babylon will be laid open. The fearful results of enforcing the observances of the church by civil authority, the inroads of spiritualism, the stealthy but rapid progress of the papal power—all will be unmasked. (*The Great Controversy*, p. 606, emphasis added)

In the last solemn work **few great men will be engaged.… God will work a work in our day that but few anticipate.** He will raise up and exalt among us **those who are taught rather by the unction of His Spirit than by the outward training** of scientific institutions. (*Testimonies for the Church*, vol. 5 [1882], pp. 80, 82, emphasis added)

What Church is about to Fall?

We find, in the counsel above, a negation of the common cry from the popular pulpit, "The church will appear as about to fall but will not fall," in its effort to convince the laity to hold fast to the conference establishment as the ship of God. There is no way to put this delicately, but the fact is that, when God takes the reins in His own hands, conferences and committees will be irrelevant and if they should continue, they will be nothing but a liability. Another way of saying this is: *Anything that is functioning under human governance after the national Sunday law will be the enemy of God's people.* If we read in context, we will find that the church that appears as about to fall can no longer be the General Conference structure. No such organization keeping the commandments of God and the faith of Jesus could function under the pressure of the Sunday law crisis, which will result in the embargo on buying and selling for God's people and the period of the seven last plagues, which, for God's people, is the time of "Jacob's trouble." It will be a time of utmost extremity when the wicked are about to close in to slay the righteous in the midnight inauguration of the death decree. A day of wrath for the wicked, it will be a day of final deliverance for the church. At this time, the wicked will realize that they have been persecuting the beloved of God. This is when the "voice of God" will be heard and God will turn the captivity of His people. It will also be a time of agonizing realization for those who once held the Sabbath truth but chose to drink of the deep waters and give up the Sabbath (see *Christian Experience and Teaching of Ellen G. White*, pp. 100, 101; *Maranatha*, pp. 264–271).

We are to be ready and waiting for the orders of God. Nations will be stirred to their very center. **Support will be withdrawn** from those who proclaim God's only standard of righteousness, the only sure test of character. **And all who will not bow to the decrees of the national councils and obey the national laws to exalt the sabbath instituted by the man of sin to the disregard of God's holy day, will feel, not the oppressive power of popery alone, but of the Protestant world, the image of the beast.**

Satan will work his miracles to deceive; he will set up his power as supreme. **The church may appear as about to fall, but it does not fall.** It remains, while the sinners in Zion will be sifted out—the chaff separated from the precious wheat. This is a terrible ordeal, but nevertheless it must take place. None but those who have been overcoming by the blood of the Lamb and the word of their testimony will be found with the loyal and true, without spot or stain of sin, without guile in their mouths. We must be divested of our self-righteousness and arrayed in the righteousness of Christ. (Lt. 55, 1886, in *Manuscript Releases*, vol. 12, pp. 324, 325, emphasis added)

(We will discuss this theme in greater detail in the concluding segments of this book.)

The 1888 Message's Rejection of Light and Kingly Rule

In the years following the 1888 General Conference, Ellen White, A. T. Jones and E. J. Waggoner continued to promote the message and continued to meet resistance from leadership. There are denominational historians today who downplay this matter and claim that, while some resisted, others did not, and that there was no such thing as an "official" rejection of the message at a denominational level nor is there such a thing today. As we continue to study history from a wide variety of sources and carefully keep up with the state of affairs in the churches, we are better equipped to decide from the evidence available whether this is so. We will cover the high points of this issue later.

We are studying the history of this issue to get answers to the questions: Has the leadership of the denomination changed? Have humans replaced God within Adventism?

The great sin which has been entering the ranks of Seventh-day Adventists is the sin of exalting man, and placing him where God should be. This was demonstrated at Minneapolis. There are few who will be pleased to meet the record of the transactions of that conference. How long and hard the battle was, before men could be led to see that they were only men, finite, erring men, and that **God was dishonored by men making flesh their arm.** (Lt. 88, 1896, to Brother and Sister Prescott, *The Ellen G. White 1888 Materials*, p. 1619, emphasis added)

In 1890, Ellen White forecast what could be coming if the church did not change its attitude:

If you indulge stubbornness of heart, and through pride and self-righteousness do not confess your faults, you will be left subject to Satan's temptations.... The multitude of deceptions that will prevail in these last days will encircle you, and **you will change leaders, and not know that you have done so.** (*Review and Herald*, Dec. 16, 1890, emphasis added)

If the message had been accepted as God intended, the final movements would have been set in motion, and God would have taken the reins of the work into His own hands. The church would have come out of the paradigm of human control, and God's church would have traversed the earth with the light of the fourth angel in latter rain power under the directive of Christ, the sole Head of the church. There would have been no need to reorganize.

An unwillingness to yield up preconceived opinions, and to accept this truth, lay at the foundation of a large share of the opposition manifested at Minneapolis against the Lord's message through Brethren Waggoner and Jones. By exciting that opposition, **Satan succeeded in shutting away from our people, in a great measure, the special power of the Holy Spirit that God longed to impart to them.** The enemy prevented them from obtaining that efficiency which might have been theirs in carrying the truth to the world, as the apostles proclaimed it after the day of Pentecost. **The light that is to lighten the whole earth with its glory was resisted, and by the action of our own brethren has been in a great degree kept away from the world.** (Lt. 96, 1896, to Uriah Smith, in *The Ellen G. White 1888 Materials*, p. 1575, emphasis added)

The message was given and was then rejected because humans looked to other humans, and those other humans ruled over their fellows.

Now, it has been Satan's determined purpose to eclipse the view of Jesus and lead men to look to man, and trust to man, and be educated to expect help from man. **For years the church has been looking to man and expecting much from man, but not looking to Jesus.... Therefore God gave to His servants a testimony that presented the truth as it is in Jesus, which is the third angel's message**, in clear, distinct lines. (*Testimonies to Ministers*, p. 93, emphasis added)

If our brethren were all laborers together with God, they would not doubt but that the message he has sent us during these last two years is from heaven. **Our young men look to our older brethren, and as they see that they do not accept the message, but treat it as though it were of no consequence, it influences those who are ignorant of the Scriptures to reject the light.** These men who refuse to receive truth, interpose themselves between the people and the light.... (*Review and Herald*, March 18, 1890, emphasis added)

That the leading men did not speak for God is expressed in definite terms. In 1901, the pen of inspiration declared:

> Satan ... keenly observes the backsliding of those who have been placed at the head of the work—the very men who through communications have been informed that they were out of place and in error in representing the voice of the General Conference president as being the voice of God. For many years it has not been thus, and it is not thus now; nor will it ever be thus again, unless there is a thorough reformation. (Ms. 124, 1901, in *Manuscript Releases*, vol. 17, p. 240)

Jones was anxious for such a thorough reformation, but it was not to be, as we shall see. He was blindsided by the overwhelming rejection he received.

> Clearly, Jones thought nothing could hinder the success of the loud cry message in the 1890s.... This is the reason for his driving demands for reformation in his day. He felt a mandate in the years following 1888 which Ellen White repeatedly says was divinely motivated; but he lacked the prophetic gift to see beyond rejection. (The 1888 Message Study Committee, *A. T. Jones: The Man and the Message*, p. 21)

Jones was the principal proponent of the move for organizational reform. He was undoubtedly ahead of his time. In fact, he was ahead of the *Lord's* time. It is a temptation for those who are blessed with great insight to run ahead of God, especially when this is combined with an impetuous and impatient nature. If the message had been accepted as he expected, it would have been the time for his idea of "Christ as the Head of every individual, no man is the head of any man in the church" to go into full effect. However, because the church rejected the message, it was consigned by God to continue operating under human governance. This is the unfortunate situation that still exists in the church today.

It is true that the apostolic church did not have a clearly defined three-pointed pyramid form of organization but it was operating under the early-rain power of Pentecost. The Seventh-day Adventist Church will also largely, if not entirely, lose its three-pointed structure when the Holy Spirit power of the latter rain is poured out. It seems that to deform the church pyramid prematurely is to run ahead of, and contrary to, the Lord. The three-pointed **inverted** pyramid of church organization is compatible with the church militant, while the **amputated** pyramid will function at the time of the formation of the church triumphant. (Vernon Sparks, *Laodicea—Her Authority, Organization, and Destiny: Adventism at the Crossroads*, p. 251, emphasis added)

The "amputated pyramid" which Sparks described is that of having no human office of presidency or chairmanship, i.e., no head but Christ alone. In fact, at the time under consideration, *it is not likely that there will be any pyramid at all*, as the structure of the church will not extend, in human terms, beyond local companies. We will next look at the meaning of the "inverted pyramid."

The General Conference session decided in 1901 that there would be a decentralizing of power by enlarging the executive committee and establishing union conferences. The General Conference would have a chairman rather than a president. However, the real issue of God's concern was not about whether or not to have an official head of the General Conference, but whether the organizational pyramid would have its point at the *top* or at the *bottom*.

The upright pyramid represents papal power, kingly rule, with each successive layer subject to those above. The employment of human organization was an inevitable reality, for hearts had not come into line with the working of the Holy Spirit. It is for this reason that many reform movements consider any human organization with layers of authority to be "organizational apostasy." While it is true that the very establishment of human governmental structures are necessitated because God is removed by varying degrees, this is not the organizational apostasy that we are concerned with in our examination of church history. (Humankind was to have dominion over the earth and the animals, not over each other.) However, the church establishment as a hierarchy—being already a structure under the paradigm of "divine accommodation"—was at least to function in a way that is more reflective of God's ways. The real issue at stake in 1901 was whether or not the church would invert the pyramid and make each *descending* level a "higher authority," with the president at the bottom, for the functioning of the Spirit and the grace of Christ in true servant-leadership fashion, which requires the leadership to not *lord it over* but to *serve under*. The authority of the Lord would be invested in men to equip and empower the next level to do their job more efficiently but never to stand in the role of granting permission to workers or of forbidding workers to service God in any particular way according to their conscience. Human beings were to be left free to follow the Lord's leading within their own fields of influence.

> The conferences were not established to exercise dominion over the ministry, nor over the local churches, but rather to plan and expand the work of God in various regions and areas. Furthermore, the conferences were to act as counselors, not as dictators to the people of God. (Colin and Russell Standish, *Organizational Structure and Apostasy*, p. 13)

So, where would we find the idea of "organizational apostasy" at this time in history except in their not coming into working order as the Lord would have had them do in *inverting the pyramid*.

Researcher Vernon Sparks observed that "the real issue of 1901 was not the issue of church structure but of how the structure was operated." He went on to assert that this "is our problem today—the lack of revival and reformation, the usurpation of power, the tendency to rule rather than to serve" (*Laodicea—Her Authority, Organization, and Destiny*, p. 251).

Therefore, it is not accurate to think that the organizational reformation was merely to consist in not having a president or chairman. As already stated, a layered governance was to be established, with adequate tiers of authority as would properly provide for a distribution of administrative function of the work. The reforms had to do with the size of the work, which would require larger administration, and the problem of kingly rule. They did *not* have to do with the organization's visible head. The debate over the presidency was the concern of the Jones camp, and a reading of "The Necessity of Harmony," written to Magan and Sutherland, July 23, 1904, found in the *Spalding and Magan Collection*, p. 362, shows what the Lord's position was as delivered through Ellen White:

> In this perilous time the Lord has given us men of His choice to stand as the leaders of His people. If these men will keep humble and prayerful, ever making Christ their confident, listening to and obeying his words, the Lord will lead and strengthen them. **God has chosen Elder Daniells to bear responsibilities and has promised to make him capable, by his grace, of doing the work entrusted to him.** The responsibilities of the position he occupies are great, and the tax upon his strength and courage is severe; and the Lord calls upon his people to hold up Elder Daniells' hands, as he strives with all the powers of mind and body to advance the work. The Lord desires every church to offer prayer for him as he bears these heavy responsibilities. Our brethren and sisters should not stand ready to criticize and condemn those who are bearing heavy burdens. Let us refuse to listen to the words of censure spoken regarding the men upon whom rest such weighty responsibilities.
> **I know that Elder Daniells is the right man in the right place.** (pp. 362, 363, emphasis added)

Now, we would caution at this point not to take her statement as sweeping approval of any and every elected official in the structure. Pay careful attention to the qualifying "if" that appears in the following statement:

> Thus today, **if the General Conference President, or any other leader at any level of our church organization**, is communicating and leading into obedience to the full will of Christ as found in the Bible and in the Spirit of Prophecy he is letting Christ directly rule His people through him. The contrary is also true. If anyone by word or example is not communicating all of God's inspired instructions as to how to live and work for the Lord to the people he has placed his wisdom between Christ and His people. They have usurped the authority of Christ in the Rulership of His people and they are doing the work of the great usurper Satan. Thus we can see that the real issue of church organization in 1901 and in 1903 was not whether the General Conference was to have a president but as to whether or not the leadership would be submitted to Christ's directives. (Vernon Sparks, *Laodicea—Her Authority, Organization, and Destiny*, p. 250, emphasis added)

If leaders were of such high fidelity throughout the organization, then there would be rapid movements toward righteousness, the final crisis would envelop the world, and *the organization would dissolve*. In this scenario, the church triumphant would be formed, with Christ as Head over every individual as Jones envisioned, and Christ would come.

The statement that God can directly rule His people through the president could lead some people to put their eyes on a man for guidance, as though he were the voice of God. This would be a papal notion. In *our* thinking, "direct" rule means "no intermediaries." It would be better to say that the man who is in obedience to the full will of Christ is communicating and leading authoritatively, as he stands upon the Word of God, which alone has authority to "rule." Every word that comes through a human being must be tested by the Word of God.

God Calls for a Change, 1901

Ellen White attended a meeting that took place before the General Conference actually assembled in session. There, on April 1, in the library of the college building at Battle Creek, she spoke earnestly to the leaders. The following is a verbatim report of remarks she made. She spoke on General Conference matters and organization, declaring that there must be—

> **an entire new organization**, and to have a committee that shall take in not merely half a dozen, that is to be a **ruling and controlling power**, but it is **to have representatives of those that are placed in responsibility in our educational interests, in our Sanitariums** ... there should be a renovation without any delay. To have this conference pass on and close up as the conferences have done, with the same **manipulating**, with the very same tone, and the same order,—God forbid! ... God calls for a change. (Ms. 43c, 1901, in *Spalding and Magan Collection*, pp. 163, 164, emphasis added)

The King is in There Still

> God means what he says, "**I want a change here.**" Will it be the same thing, going over and over the same ideas, the same committees—and here is the little throne: **the king is in there**, and these others are all secondary, those minds that are so much sharper because they have not been working on this narrow, conceited plane. I feel intensely in this matter. I do not want to talk here but I dare not hold my peace....
>
> We are to be representatives of Jesus Christ; we are to be representatives of his character. We are so to do that we are carrying out the living principles in every line of action everywhere, in every country, everywhere, and in every place that there is anything to do with God's service. **He will not accept common fire.** He wants you to take sacred fire that he kindles on the divine altar, and he wants you to work, and that fire [to work] to **consume all your commonness**.... God wants that these committees that have been handling things for so long **should be relieved of their command** and have a chance for their life, and see if they can not **get out of this rut that they are in,— which I have no hope of their getting out of, because the Spirit of God has been working, and working, and yet the king is there still**. (Ms. 43c, 1901, in *Spalding and Magan Collection*, p. 166, emphasis added)

No Change Was Made

The 1901 General Conference Session did implement sizable changes in the right direction in decentralizing the administration of the work and in reversing the spirit of kingly rule. Mrs. White was in high spirits at the apparent success:

> I was never more astonished in my life than at the turn things have taken at this meeting. This is not our work. God has brought it about. Instruction regarding this was presented to me, but until the sum was worked out at this meeting, I could not comprehend this instruction. God's angels have been walking up and down in this congregation. I want every one of you to remember this, and I want you to remember also that God has said that he will heal the wounds of his people. (*General Conference Bulletin*, April 25, 1901, art. A)

It was soon apparent that her joy had turned to ashes. On August 5, 1902, she wrote John Harvey Kellogg:

> What a wonderful work could have been done for the vast company gathered in Battle Creek at the General Conference of 1901, if the leaders of our work had taken themselves in hand. But **the work that all heaven was waiting to do as soon as men prepared the way, was not done; for the leaders closed and bolted the door against the Spirit's entrance.** There was a stopping short of entire surrender to God. And hearts that might have been purified from all error were strengthened in wrong doing. The doors were barred against the heavenly current that would have swept away all evil. Men left their sins unconfessed. They built themselves up in wrong doing, and said to the Spirit of God, "Go thy way for this time; when I have a more convenient season, I will call for thee." (Lt. 123, 1902, in *Battle Creek Letters*, pp. 55, 56)

Then, just prior to the 1903 General Conference, she expressed her disappointment about the failure of the leaders to implement the changes that were decided upon in 1901:

The **result of the last General Conference [1901] has been the greatest, the most terrible, sorrow of my life. No change was made.** The spirit that should have been brought into the whole work as the result of that meeting was not brought in because men did not receive the testimonies of the Spirit of God. As they went to their several fields of labor, **they did not walk in the light** that the Lord had flashed upon their pathway, but **carried into their work the wrong principles** that had been prevailing in the work at Battle Creek. (Lt. 17, 1903, in *Manuscript Releases*, vol. 13, pp. 122, 123, emphasis added)

The 1903 General Conference

Ellen White addressed the delegates at the 1903 General Conference, saying:

> Brethren and sisters, from the light given me, I know that if the people of God had preserved a living connection with Him, if they had obeyed His Word, they would today be in the heavenly Canaan. (Ms. 10, 1903, in *General Conference Bulletin*, March 30, 1903, p. 9)

Mrs. White preached on Josiah's reign, speaking of the investigation that he made and Israel's subsequent punishment for apostasy. She related Israel's consequences to the calamities that had come upon the church and asked the people to "seek to find out what He means when He sweeps away our sanitarium and our publishing house" (*General Conference Bulletin*, April 1, 1903). Then she related what the Lord showed her "might have been" had they followed Him (covered later in this chapter). Hearts were stirred and confessions were made in testimonies that followed from the floor.

As the business meetings progressed, the delegates decided that control of the institutions should come under the church and be owned by the people. This was not the mind of Kellogg and his supporters, however.

The other major matter of discussion was the new constitution. The "majority report" was issued in support of providing for the election of General Conference officials *by delegates from the church*. The "minority report" came from men who were vested in the institutional interests. These contended that the proposed constitution would undo what had been put place in 1901. They argued that insufficient time had been allotted to test the system by which *the General Conference Committee* would choose the officers of the denomination.

Much ado was made then, as it is made today, about the wisdom of choosing "one man as president of the General Conference." However, this statement has been misunderstood as well as others like it. The points being made were that there needed to be more men brought in to conduct the work and that the field should be divided into other conferences. Mrs. White never actually said there should be no president. The idea that 1903 repudiated what was put in motion in 1901 does not have to do with the change in the constitution; the concerns were along other lines, as discussed earlier. In 1896, she had written the following statement, which was read by A. G. Daniells at the 1903 meeting:

> It is not wise to choose one man as president of the General Conference. The work of the General Conference has extended, and some things have been made unnecessarily complicated. A want of discernment has been shown. There should be a division of the field, or some other plan should be devised to change the present order of things....
>
> The president of the General Conference should have the privilege of deciding who shall stand by his side as counselors. Those who will keep the way of the Lord, who will preserve clear, sharp discernment by cultivating home religion, are safe counselors. Of such a one the Searcher of hearts saith, "I know him, that he will command his children and his household after him, and they shall keep the way of the Lord, to do justice and judgment." Counselors of the character that God chose for Moses are needed by the president of the General Conference. It was his privilege at least to express his preference as to the men who should be his counselors. It was his privilege to discern between him that serveth God and him that serveth Him not. But a strange blindness was upon him. There has been a leavening influence upon human minds, and it has been most painful. For years God has been dishonored.... (*Testimonies to Ministers*, pp. 342, 343)

Mrs. White did not engage in any of the debate on the question of the constitution. Apparently, that was not an issue on her mind, nor did the Lord concern her with it. Later on, in fact, she confirmed Elder A. G. Daniells as God's choice for president. Our position in this book on this matter is that the organization is under the forbearance of God—His "permissive will"—and just as Samuel held up the arms of King Saul, so also did Ellen White support Daniells. (This is not to make Daniells an antitype of Saul.) We should also note in the above text that Mrs. White alluded to Moses having counselors chosen by God to assist him in his work. This should be qualified in that she says elsewhere: "The Lord *permitted Moses to choose for himself* the most faithful and efficient men to share the responsibility with him" (*Patriarchs and Prophets*, p. 380). I have emphasized "permitted" and "Moses choosing for himself," for this was God yielding to human weakness and lack of faith. It was not God's perfect plan, as the same passage makes plain, that "serious evils would eventually result" and "They would never have been chosen had Moses manifested faith ... He was not excusable in indulging, in the slightest degree, the spirit of murmuring that was the curse of Israel" (*Patriarchs and Prophets*, p. 380). Nonetheless, for the time being, it had to be that way.

Author Vernon Sparks has brought a balanced thought to this topic:

> It is true that the 1901 General Conference elected a self-organizing executive committee who elected a chairman rather than a president. It may be that people then also interpreted the above statement to support the idea. The reality was that the Lord apparently did not show Ellen White the details of the recommended organization. The brethren were left to their best judgment in working out the details of how best to comply with the principles given by revelation. Thus their various positions were their various interpretations of what the Lord wanted as communicated by the Spirit of Prophecy. It is to be expected that there would be differences of understanding of what God was requesting. (*Laodicea—Her Authority, Organization, and Destiny*, p. 246)

After the 1903 General Conference in Oakland, for legal reasons, there was to be a final meeting at Battle Creek. At the same time, Dr. Kellogg assembled his forces, which outnumbered the others two to one, for a twelve-day session of the International Medical Missionary and Benevolent Association. It was a battle for the control of the institution. Days before attending the meeting, Ellen White wrote out the counsel she had received from the Lord. In the counsel, she still called for reorganization.

> There must be reorganization. Supreme power must not be vested in a group of men connected with a few large institutions. At the General Conference of 1901 the light was given, Divide the General Conference into union conferences. Let there be fewer responsibilities centered on one place. Let the work of printing our publications be divided.
>
> The principles that apply to the publishing work apply also to the sanitarium work.... Let medical missionary plants be made in many places....
>
> The gospel ministry, medical missionary work, and our publications are God's agencies. One is not to supersede the other. But you have sought to make the medical missionary work the whole body, instead of the arm and hand. (Lt. 55, 1903, in *Spalding and Magan Collection*, p. 303)

Mrs. White wrote pointed counsels to the medical establishment and to Dr. Kellogg. As the meetings progressed, these counsels were apparently accepted, and there was rejoicing over the newfound reconciliation and unity between the Daniells and Kellogg camps, and "neither one was asked to compromise the principles of right for which we felt that we were standing" (letter, A. G. Daniells to W. C. White, April 29, 1903, in *Arthur L. White, Ellen G. White: The Early Elmshaven Years*, p. 269). Alas, however, the reconciliation was not genuine. As Mrs. White was about to record in her diary her heartfelt gratitude to God for the change, her hand was stayed, and the following words came from the Lord: "Write it not. No change for the better has taken place. The doctor is ensnared in a net of specious deception" (Lt. 172, 1903, in *Battle Creek Letters*, p. 72).

Mrs. White Decries Centralization in 1904

Although fires leveled the sanitarium in February 1902 and the publishing house on December 30 of the same year, Kellogg rebuilt the sanitarium in Battle Creek against the counsel of the Lord.

> Notwithstanding frequent counsels to the contrary, men continued to plan for centralization of power, for the binding of many interests under one control. This work was first started in the Review and Herald office. Things were swayed first one way and then another. It was the enemy of our work who prompted the call for the consolidation of the publishing work under one controlling power in Battle Creek.
>
> Then the idea gained favor that the medical missionary work would be greatly advanced if all our medical institutions and other medical missionary interests were bound up under the control of the medical missionary association at Battle Creek.
>
> I was told that I must lift my voice in warning

against this. We were not to be under the control of men who could not control themselves and who were not willing to be amenable to God. We were not to be guided by men who wanted their word to be the controlling power. The development of the desire to control has been very marked, and God sent warning after warning, forbidding confederacies and consolidation. He warned us against binding ourselves to fulfill certain agreements that would be presented by men laboring to control the movements of their brethren. (Ms. 94a, 1903, in *Testimonies for the Church*, vol. 8, pp. 216, 217)

The pen of inspiration declared later on:

The heavenly Teacher inquired: "What stronger delusion can beguile the mind than the pretense that you are building on the right foundation and that God accepts your works, when in reality you are **working out many things according to worldly policy** and are sinning against Jehovah? Oh, it is a great deception, a fascinating delusion, that takes possession of minds when men who have once known the truth, mistake the form of godliness for the spirit and power thereof; when they suppose that they are rich and increased with goods and in need of nothing, while in reality they are in need of everything." (Ms. 32, 1903, in *Testimonies for the Church*, vol. 8, pp. 249, 250, emphasis added)

That they were working according to worldly policy was because they were not under Christ, for they had rejected the 1888 message, which is the "truth as it is in Jesus," as seen in the following paragraph:

Unless there is thorough repentance, unless men humble their hearts by confession and receive the truth as it is in Jesus, they will never enter heaven. When purification shall take place in our ranks, we shall no longer rest at ease, boasting of being rich and increased with goods, in need of nothing. (Ms. 32, 1903, in *Testimonies for the Church*, vol. 8, p. 250)

Colin and Russell Standish observed: "In 1903 the 'upright triangle' of the hierarchical form of organization was given great impetus while the 'inverted triangle' of representationalism was greatly weakened" (*Organizational Structure and Apostasy*, p. 9).

God Still Called for a Change in 1907

Ellen White was still talking about humans controlling God's work in May 1907.

In many cases hard judgment has been measured out when encouragement and commendation should have been given; for the results of the work done have shown that the blessing of God was upon it. Wherever this principle has been brought in, **God wants a change to be made**; for it is contrary to His plan. **When man's mind is allowed to become the controlling power**, both parties are injured—the one who allows himself to be conscience for another, and the one who permits himself to be controlled by human wisdom … for one human voice to be a controlling power is a sad mistake, and this should not continue. (Lt. 186, 1907, May 29, to G. I. Butler, in *Manuscript Releases* 311, p. 40)

She also called attention to high-handed exercise of power in August 1907:

A strange thing has come into our churches. Men who are placed in positions of responsibility that they may be wise helpers to their fellow workers **have come to suppose that they were set as kings and rulers in the churches**, to say to one brother, Do this; to another, Do that; and to another, Be sure to labor in such and such a way. There have been places where the workers have been told that **if they did not follow the instruction of these men of responsibility, their pay from the conference would be withheld**. (*Special Testimonies*, B10, p. 12, August 1907, in *Testimonies to Ministers*, p. 477, emphasis added)

For years there has been a growing tendency for men placed in positions of responsibility to lord it over God's heritage, thus removing from church members their keen sense of the need of divine instruction and an appreciation of the privilege to counsel with God regarding their duty. **This order of things must be changed.** There must be a reform. Men who have not a rich measure of that wisdom which cometh from above should not be called to serve in positions where their influence means so much to church members. (*Special Testimonies*, B10, p. 13, August 1907, in *Testimonies to Ministers*, pp. 477, 478, emphasis added)

What about Our Day?

This same reform is still needed. In a Sabbath sermon dated October 9, 2010, at the Annual Council meeting, Elder Ted Wilson repeated the same ideas that he presented earlier in his inauguration address, "Go Forward." He declared:

> There were two things on God's agenda for 1901: reorganization of the church and the outpouring of the Holy Spirit to enable that structure to finish the work. As a result of Ellen White's pleading, the agenda for that General Conference was set aside and the church structure was reorganized to produce the conference and union structure that we have today. It is a good organizational structure and will serve us well for the future. But God's second agenda item never happened, the outpouring of the Holy Spirit. It is still on His agenda. (Ted Wilson, "Remember Your Name," Sabbath sermon, Oct. 9, 2010, Annual Council Meeting, Silver Spring, Maryland, *Adventists Affirm*, vol. 24, no. 3, available at http://1ref.us/hx, accessed 10/24/16)

The Holy Spirit never came because He was not allowed to come to do His work.

> Unquestionably, had the leadership taken hold of the message of Christ Our Righteousness in 1888, they would have willingly and joyously accepted this decentralized organizational plan. However, with only a few accepting the 1888 message, there was a lack of willingness to go all the way with the reorganization, which was the second part of God's program for preparing His people for the end of time. (*Organizational Structure and Apostasy*, p. 4)

Hearts remained hardened, and, as a result, the hierarchical pyramid remains in place to this day.

> **The Seventh-day Adventist Church follows a model of organizational order in the church which is modified from the orders of Roman Catholicism**, but it retains the same notions of clerical order which separates the members of the Church into two classes—**clergy and laity**. The Bible knows no such bifurcation or division. (D. Douglas Devnich, "President's Perspective," *Canadian Adventist Messenger*, Dec. 1993, p. 2)

Many church members would say that the power in the Seventh-day Adventist Church resides with the president—be it conference, union, or division.... He has authority to decide and act. Although his authority is far less than many imagine, he does have considerable power. It flows from several sources:

1. **A representative constituency elects and empowers him....**

2. **He chairs the executive committee.**

3. **He's the spiritual leader of the community of faith.... He's shepherd, guardian, guide and captain.** (Walter Scragg, "Who Holds the Reins of Power?" [Australasian Union Conference] *Record*, June 23, 1990, p. 4, emphasis added)

In 1985, then-President Neal C. Wilson made a revealing Commission Report to the General Conference Committee regarding the "Role and Function of Denominational Organizations." The Committee voted to "accept the full report." In this report, Wilson verbalized the present and future attitude of Seventh-day Adventist leadership towards the hierarchical organization of the church.

> **The General Conference is the highest authority and the sum of all the parts**, not only philosophically, but also (1) organizationally, (2) legislatively, (3) administratively, (4) judicially, (5) in terms of policy and (6) Church standards. This being the case, it seems that it should be the desire of the conferences, unions, and any other organizations **to do everything possible to weld the whole family together and strengthen the hands of the General Conference....**
>
> It would be folly to do anything or say anything that would in any way weaken the influences and limit the leadership capabilities of the General Conference.... To do anything that would encourage congregational government would be a move in the direction of disintegration, and **the inability to achieve our divine mission....** (*Role and Function of Denominational Organizations—Commission Report*, Oct. 14, 1984, p. 84-385, emphasis added, available at http://1ref.us/hy, accessed 10/24/16)

Deeper Offense

Coming back to our early twentieth-century timeline we find the call still going forth to cease from dependence on man.

In my earlier experiences in the message, I was called to meet this evil. During my labors in Europe and Australia, and more recently at the San Jose camp meeting in 1905, I had to bear my testimony of warning against it, because **souls were being led to look to man for wisdom**, instead of looking to God, who is our wisdom, our sanctification, and our righteousness. And now **the same message has again been given me, more definite and decisive, because there has been a deeper offense to the Spirit of God**. (*Special Testimonies*, B10, p. 13, August 1907, in *Testimonies to Ministers*, p. 478, emphasis added)

I have been shown that **ministers and people are tempted more and more to trust in finite man for wisdom, and to make flesh their arm**. To conference presidents, and men in responsible places, **I bear this message: Break the bands and fetters that have been placed upon God's people**. To you the word is spoken, "**Break every yoke**." Unless you **cease the work of making man amenable to man**, unless you become humble in heart, and yourselves learn the way of the Lord as little children, **the Lord will divorce you from His work**. We are to **treat one another as brethren, as fellow laborers**, as men and women who are, with us, seeking for light and understanding of the way of the Lord, and who are jealous for His glory. (*Special Testimonies*, B10, p. 16, August 1907, in *Testimonies to Ministers*, pp. 480, 481, emphasis added)

To Those Assembled in the General Conference of 1913

The call for reformation continued to sound:

> Men of clear understanding are needed now. God calls upon those who are willing to be controlled by the Holy Spirit to lead out in a work of thorough reformation. I see a crisis before us, and the Lord calls for His laborers to come into line. Every soul should now stand in a position of deeper, truer consecration to God than during the years that have passed.... (*Review and Herald*, May 29, 1913, in *Testimonies to Ministers*, p. 514)

Lest it be thought that all the trouble was centered solely in Battle Creek and the great power grab of the medical work under Dr. Kellogg and company, the exercise of "kingly power" has ever been at issue in the denomination. The proper function of the structure as God intended has never been put into practice. The Standish brothers wrote:

> Of course, the principles outlined for the leadership of the work world-wide were not only meant for the upper echelons of the work, but also for all levels of our work through the conferences and through the church organization. While unions were formed in 1901, these were still significantly under the direction of the General Conference. Later, divisions of the General Conference were established, but they were just that, divisions of the General Conference. The leaders of each division, rather than having full authority to superintend, were seen to be vice-presidents of the General Conference, and therefore lacking the full authority that God wanted in His decentralized system of organization. The light that came to God's people at that time should have reflected upon the total direction of the Seventh-day Adventist Church ever since. (*Organizational Structure and Apostasy*, p. 5)

So the second functional generation later came to its close in 1924, and the church settled squarely into its hierarchical organizational structure after the common order with top-down kingly rule. The question before us today is what are *we* going to do with this message? Remember that this message—the "truth as it is in Jesus"—was the gospel understanding that would have finished the work. Had Seventh-day Adventists embraced this message, they would have gone forward in blazing glory, and Christ would have come. Sadly, they rejected Christ in the person of His messengers and His message and went on, figuratively, to build a magnificent edifice in which great satisfaction has been taken. As President Ted Wilson declared, "It is a good organizational structure and will serve us well for the future."

If any would take issue with our assessment of the General Conference structure as a hierarchical pyramid *with point at the top*, we can assure you that this is not our own private conjecture. In addition to the admission of D. Devnich, cited from the *Canadian Adventist Messenger* of December 1993 above, here are several testimonies to the fact, from official church sources:

> We will have to constantly judge what structures must be removed and what new forms must be developed. This will not be easy.... One reason for our reluctance and resistance is that some of us see change more as a

crisis than an opportunity. Others have so identified structure with policy and **the official hierarchy of the church** that change is often viewed as unfaithfulness. (*Adventist Review*, Oct. 6, 1994, p. 51, emphasis added)

In a court transcript of the Reply Brief for the Seventh-day Adventist Church in the 1975 civil case of Merikay Silver [McLeod], former General Conference President Neal Wilson declared what type of organizational structure the Seventh-day Adventist Church operated under:

> From an ecclesiastical-historical standpoint, there are numerous forms of church organization, which are described variously as Presbyterian (which connotes governance by the priesthood), or episcopal (which connotes governance by the bishops of the church), or papal (which connotes governance by a sole chief bishop), or congregational (which connotes governance by individual local church groups)....
>
> These distinctions are without legal significance. **From a legal standpoint,** ... there are but two sorts of church organization which carry with them **significant legal consequences**: the "congregational", and all others, which in law are called "representative", or "hierarchical".
>
> **The plain and undeniable fact is that the Seventh-day Adventist Church is most assuredly not a "congregational" one** (although it contains elements of congregationalism) **but is clearly of the "representative" or "hierarchical" variety.** (*EEOC vs PPPA and GC*, Civil Case #74-2025 CBR, pp. 3, 4, emphasis added)

Later, in the case of Derek Proctor, a professor at Andrews University, against the General Conference, the pragmatic concerns regarding the gaining of a favorable ruling from the court dictated that a clear statement of the nature of the church structure be established:

> Dr. Derek Proctor's long-running lawsuit with the Seventh-day Adventist Church was finally decided on October 29, 1986. Proctor lost the case, in which he contended that the church in various of its entities conspired illegally to interfere in his book-selling business in violation of antitrust and conspiracy laws. **The major strategy of the General Conference in this case was to convince the court that the Seventh-day Adventist Church is essentially an hierarchical church**, in which the directives and orders of the General Conference have binding authority upon all other entities of the church. The General Conference submitted that, **"next to the Roman Catholic Church, the Adventist Church is the most centralized of all major Christian denominations in this country."** (*Student Movement* [student paper of Andrews University], Nov. 6, 1986, in *Organizational Structure and Apostasy*, p. 19, emphasis added)

These claims of the church's structure being of the "hierarchical variety" can only mean one of two things—either the leaders committed perjury when their lawyers deliberately misrepresented the facts in order to win lawsuits or the church has repudiated divine principles in its organization.

Some have posited that the church council in Acts 15 supports the idea of hierarchical organization. The fact is that we do not know what James' actual role was in relation to organizational position. Moses E. Kellogg wrote:

> The thing nearest to universal authority and headship in the church is the action of a general council. The 15th chapter of the Acts of the Apostles will ever stand as unmistakable evidence that the measure of authority, which primarily belongs to the church as a whole, is, at special times, and for certain definite purposes, vested in a council; that the council may be summoned whenever great questions arise that threaten division in the church, or at regular intervals if necessary, for the consideration of questions which affect the interests of the whole church; and that **the decisions of the councils so convened, are advisory rather than actually obligatory on the church. Stated broadly, actual legislative power is not committed to the church. All actual legislation was done by Christ.**
>
> ... But when a council is disbanded, the general and advisory power vested therein is for the time suspended until the next council; and **there is no provision in the Christian system of church government by which the authority of the general and universal council may be transferred to any one who shall represent the council between its sessions, and thus form a general and continuous head to the church on earth.**... (M. E. Kellogg, *The Supremacy of Peter: or Did Christ Establish a Primacy in the Church?* [1897], pp. 261–263, emphasis added)

Does inspiration concur with this? Mrs. White spoke for the Lord:

> Men whom the Lord calls to important positions in His work are to cultivate a humble dependence upon Him. They are not to seek to embrace too much authority; for **God has not called them to a work of ruling, but to plan and counsel with their fellow laborers.** Every worker alike is to hold himself amenable to the requirements and instructions of God. (*Testimonies for the Church*, vol. 9, p. 270, emphasis added)

God has called us to press together in counsel one to another yet never as a system of leaders ruling over subordinates and subordinates submitting to superiors. This is an illegitimate usurpation of the divine prerogative. Such a system of control and submission interposes itself in the relationship between the Lord and His people.

Satan's Supposition and Re-organization

That there was a re-organization is historical fact. That what we see today is what God intended is standard doctrine from church leadership. Whether calculated as such or not, this is a specious re-writing of history. It is touted that today's structure is the result of divine guidance during those conferences of 1901 and 1903, but there is no mention whatsoever of *inverting* the pyramid or of kingly rule being a problem. Former GC president Robert Folkenberg told Seventh-day Adventists that the plan of organization voted into existence in the 1903 General Conference Session was the product of God's will through Ellen White! This is his 1994 statement:

> Through all the growing pains, and particularly at the 1903 General Conference Session, the Spirit of Prophecy gave practical guidance. **The result is the worldwide church structure of today.** (Robert S. Folkenberg, *We Still Believe*, p. 100)

Let us look at the following 1903 statement made by Ellen White, remembering that "the most terrible sorrow" of her life (Lt. 17, 1903) was that the reforms to be instituted in 1901 were not carried through. We have to wonder if the organized body that identifies itself today as the third angel movement is not the predicted "new organization" that some call "New Movement Adventism." We can see how that, through this "re-organization," the way was paved for later fulfillments of Satan's "supposition."

> The enemy of souls has sought to bring in the supposition that **a great reformation** was to take place among Seventh-day Adventists, and that this reformation would consist in giving up the doctrines which stand as the pillars of our faith, and engaging in **a process of reorganization.** Were this reformation to take place, what would result? The principles of truth that God in His wisdom has given to the remnant church, would be discarded. Our religion would be changed. The fundamental principles that have sustained the work for the last fifty years would be accounted as error. A **new organization** would be established. Books of a new order would be written. A system of intellectual philosophy would be introduced. The founders of this system would go into the cities, and do a wonderful work. The Sabbath of course, would be lightly regarded, as also the God who created it. Nothing would be allowed to stand in the way of **the new movement.** The leaders would teach that virtue is better than vice, but **God being removed,** they would **place their dependence on human power,** which, without God, is worthless. Their **foundation would be built on the sand,** and **storm and tempest would sweep away the structure.** (Lt. 242, 1903, in *Selected Messages*, bk. 1, pp. 204, 205, emphasis added)

Today all has been fulfilled except the sweeping away of the structure as the relentless storm descends. God's church will not fall. However, the *structure of the new movement*, contemporary General Conference Seventh-day Adventism, in its present condition, *will fall.* We must not confuse the two.

Later, we will examine the doctrinal transformations that have contributed to the formation of "new movement" Adventism. That it has happened and is happening is recognized by Seventh-day Adventists in various subcultures, causing some to hold firmly to the established beliefs of the past, some to reject the faith, and others to shift into a new expression of Adventism:

> In summary, since 1970, Adventists have experienced what Johnson describes as "a constant process of struggle and rebirth" in a context so dynamic that many believers have adopted one of three competing stances. Carrying what novelist Morris West might describe as "a heavy load of unexamined certainties," **some have found comfort and security in the nostalgia of reversion. Little short of total escape has**

been adequate for others; an unacceptable level of cognitive dissonance has caused them to reject Adventist teachings and opt for a cultural rather than a theological affiliation, or a different expression of Christianity, or secularism. **A third option, the principal one, has sought the transformation of Adventism.**...

As early as 1999, an astute Adventist systematic theologian observed that Ford was "dismissed from the Adventist ministry in 1980 because of his disagreement with traditional Adventist views" but that "subsequent Adventist thinking in North America seems to have moved closer to his position and further away from that of those who dismissed him." ... (Arthur Patrick, "Contextualizing Recent Tensions in Seventh-day Adventism: 'A Constant Process of Struggle and Rebirth'?" *Journal of Religious History*, vol. 34, no. 3, Sept. 2010, pp. 286, 287, emphasis added)

What Might Have Been

Here is the sad account of what the Lord desired to take place at the time of reorganization:

One day at noon I was writing of the work that might have been done at the last [1901] General Conference if the men in positions of trust had followed the will and way of God. Those who have had great light have not walked in the light. The meeting was closed, and the break was not made. Men did not humble themselves before the Lord as they should have done, and the Holy Spirit was not imparted.

I had written thus far when I lost consciousness, and I seemed to be witnessing a scene in Battle Creek.

We were assembled in the auditorium of the Tabernacle. Prayer was offered, a hymn was sung, and prayer was again offered. Most earnest supplication was made to God. The meeting was marked by the presence of the Holy Spirit....

No one seemed to be too proud to make heartfelt confession, and those who led in this work were the ones who had influence, but had not before had courage to confess their sins.

There was rejoicing such as never before had been heard in the Tabernacle.

Then I aroused from my unconsciousness, and for a while could not think where I was. My pen was still in my hand. The words were spoken to me: "This might have been. All this the Lord was waiting to do for His people. All heaven was waiting to be gracious."

I thought of where we might have been had thorough work been done at the last General Conference, and agony of disappointment came over me as I realized that what I had witnessed was not a reality. (*Testimonies for the Church*, vol. 8, pp. 104–106, Jan. 5, 1903, in *Last Day* Events, pp. 57, 58)

Indeed, had not stubborn hard-heartedness, pride of opinion, self-righteousness and desire for the ascendancy reigned in the characters of men, things would have been much different. We would have been in the kingdom long "ere this."

The time has come for the members of God's church to re-examine the true principles of church organization at the General Conference level and at all other levels of God's work. We have the right doctrines and message, but these alone are not sufficient. We must also have the right way to implement them. **Surely the apostasy within the church today is as much a result of abandoning the counsel of the Lord in organization as of rejecting the message of Christ our Righteousness.** (*Organizational Structure and Apostasy*, p. 9, emphasis added)

Let us, then, remember that our weakness and inefficiency are largely the result of looking to man, of trusting in man to do those things for us that God has promised to do for those who come unto him. We need Jesus, the Rose of Sharon, to beautify the character and make our lives fragrant with good works, so that we shall be a savor of Christ unto God. (*Review and Herald*, Aug. 14, 1894, art. A)

The sad fact is that once a paradigm has been established, the chances for reversal are not good. The dependence on humanity rather than upon the Word of God that was established in earlier generations has shown itself to be the mode of operation today.

Leaders naturally tend to support and approve of those workers who look to them for leadership and counsel, seeing them as loyal and faithful.... Once this situation commences, it is a most difficult process to reverse, for indeed the continuation of the process leads to more and more error as one generation passes the torch of imperfect principles to the following generation. Once we have left the mountaintop of truth, the trend always **progresses downhill**, each generation taking apostasy a little further than the generation before. This is exactly how Satan would have it. (*Organizational Structure and Apostasy*, p. 14)

What Will Be

We cannot leave this history with *what might have been* and *what is today*, without projecting what the Lord says *will be* in the final movements.

> Let me tell you that the Lord will work in this last work in a manner very much out of the common order of things, and in a way that will be contrary to any human planning. There will be those among us who will always want to control the work of God, to dictate even what movements shall be made when the work goes forward under the direction of the angel who joins the third angel in the message to be given to the world. God will use ways and means by which it will be seen that He is taking the reins in His own hands. The workers will be surprised by the simple means that He will use to bring about and perfect His work of righteousness.... (Lt. 85, 1885, in *Testimonies to Ministers*, p. 300)

Later we will again visit this subject of organization as we examine further developments in the fourth generation. Now it is time to turn to another important discussion surrounding the development of the medical missionary paradigm, again comparing what *was to be* with *what is*.

The Blueprint for the Medical Work—Fact or Myth?

The fundamental plan for Seventh-day Adventist medical work is summed up in the following statement:

> I tried to make it plain that the sanitarium physicians and helpers were to cooperate with God in combating disease, not only **through the use of the natural remedial agencies** He has placed within our reach, but also by **encouraging their patients to lay hold on divine strength through obedience to the commandments** of God.
>
> ... Physicians and ministers are to unite in an effort **to lead men and women to obey God's commandments.** They need to **study the intimate relationship existing between obedience and health**.... (*Loma Linda Messages*, pp. 161, 162, emphasis added)

This is the basic "blueprint," or plan, for conducting the church's medical ministry. The foundation of it is twofold: (1) It works with natural healing methods in contrast to the world's standard of allopathic medicine, *i.e.*, pharmacology, radiation, machinery, and surgery; and (2) its overarching purpose is to further the propagation of the everlasting gospel as commissioned to the final generation in the three angels' messages, which is forgiveness for sin plus redemption from the ongoing clutches of the habits of sin.

There is a philosophy today that the blueprint concept is a myth. Why is that?

The reader will realize that, in the course of our account of the Seventh-day Adventist story, numerous references have been made to George R. Knight and his books covering this period of history. Indeed, his teaching is probably one of the greatest influences on the Adventist mind today, and it is supportive of the current educational paradigm in Adventism.

Interestingly, earlier in his ministerial career, this thought leader in the church repeatedly attempted to turn in his credentials because he wanted "out—out of both Adventism and Christianity." He had his credentials returned to him twice, and it wasn't until the third resignation letter, in which he frankly told his employer "what he could do with my credentials," that he considered himself a "literary success" (spoken tongue-in-cheek, of course). For six years after this, he did not read his Bible or pray. He used that time to get a doctorate in philosophy under a Jewish agnostic existentialist who "routinely smashed religion in class." Shortly after this, Knight found himself ready to return to the church, even though, by his own admission, he really does not like Adventists to this day. His account of these events is found on pages 9 and 10 of his book *The Apocalyptic Vision and the Neutering of Adventism*. You will have to read further in his work to get a sense of what these experiences meant to the author. While I do not disagree with everything that he writes, I find that much of what Knight has produced tends to encourage us to feel comfortable with aspects of contemporary institutionalized "liberal," worldly Adventism, which is far from the practice of the principles set forth early on through the inspired pen of Ellen White.

I begin this segment talking about Knight's ideas because, in the opening lines of *Myths in Adventism*, he sets right out to disparage the notion of a divine "blueprint" for educational work. This would apply to any "blueprint" for the medical work as well. The Ellen G.

White Estate does not agree. They publish the revelations from the Lord through her pen under the heading, "Blueprint for SDA Health-Care Institutions" (*Manuscript Releases*, vol. 11, p. 187). Yet, those are the compiler's words, as are Knight's. Knight wrote: "The blueprint myth has usually been thought of in terms of education. It is an extension of the deeply rooted American belief in 'the one best method' of education that will meet the needs of the entire population" (Knight, *Myths in Adventism*, p. 17).

However, we are not dealing with a model that is to apply to "the entire population." The world has to function whatever way it can, subject to its god, according to its paradigms of human law and order, and under its notion of maintaining hierarchies of authority. These are "imposed" upon man by God as the "ordinance of God" (Rom. 13:1, 2, 6) due to man's rejection of His authority and ways. Also, the paradigm of pride and the self-ascribing glory of man in his achievements are that which concerns the general population. Just as in anything of a geo-political nature, Jesus' kingdom does not figure into—nor is it concerned with—how man rules over man in the systems of this world. The Lord Jesus said, "Render therefore unto Caesar the things which are Caesar's" (Matt. 22:21). Our educational system and our healthcare system were not to be like Caesar's. They were to advance the kingdom of God and, in particular, to work to usher in everlasting righteousness through the giving of the third angel's message.

That there were marching orders given in the setting up and conducting of our work in the medical field is plain. Knight is correct in saying that Ellen White never called it a "blueprint," per se. Rather, she called it a "pattern" or a "model." Nonetheless, others in our history have not had a problem seeing it as a blueprint. Here are two of them—the first from the 1935 Autumn Council on accreditation, where many men stood to speak against going forward with accreditation.

> I believe that the entire future of the youth of this denomination is dependent upon maintaining, in the institutions of education, the educational policies of this denomination, right principles and **clinging to the blueprint** God has given to us. (Elder S. A. Ruskjer, Canadian Union Conference President, "The Branson Report," Oct. 28, 1935, available at "Branson Report," http://1ref.us/k2, accessed July 11, 2017)

Almost three decades later, A. W. Spalding, author of the four-volume *Origin and History of Seventh-day Adventists*, wrote the following to a certain General Conference vice president:

> I have had the privilege of long connection with and experience in and out of our schools; and I have, through all this half century and more, been a student of the educational principles and structure and processes which God has given through the instrumentality of Ellen G. White. I have perceived in her writings not merely aphoristic maxims to grace dissertations on religion and learning; but rather a deeply conceived, well integrated system of education, embracing philosophy, range, form, content, method, and above all, spirit. **These writings constitute a blueprint** which, alas, our history shows has been little read, less understood, not at all comprehended.
>
> We need now to begin all over again. Reforms must be entered into with heart and soul and will ... If there is not in some respects an education of an altogether different character from that which has been carried on in some of our schools, we need not to have gone to the expense of purchasing lands and erecting school buildings. (A. W. Spalding, quoted in W. E. Straw, *Rural Sociology and Adventist Education History*, in Vance Ferrell, *The Broken Blueprint*, pp. 348, 349, emphasis added)

On pages 18 and 19 of his book, Knight takes issue with the word, insisting that the idea of a *blueprint* is a rigid set of fundamentals to be followed with exacting detail and that this would only serve to lock in every institution as clones of the original plan. It strikes me that he is subtly painting the general educational reformer and medical missionary as inflexible extremists who do not know how to adapt principles to time, place and circumstance and who are only concerned with the strict application of the "letter" or legal code without regard for the principles. Of course, Ellen White has clearly indicated it has never been in the Lord's mind that there is single one-size-fits-all plan for all institutions. "We cannot mark out a precise line to be followed unconditionally. Circumstances and emergencies will arise for which the Lord must give special instruction" (Ellen White, Lt. 192, 1906, to S. N. Haskell, in *Messenger of the Lord*, p. 360). Knight prefers Mrs. White's words that our schools should follow the "pattern." It is fine to have a preference, whether we use "blueprint" or "pattern" is really immaterial. The real concern in all of this is: "*Have we followed it?* Have we made careful reference to the pattern and modeled our institutions after it?" When we examine what God gave us as principles and guidelines in comparison with what is now followed in "Seventh-day Adventist" institutions, our answer must be an unequivocal, "Definitely *not*."

A "Losing Battle" at Battle Creek; Restarting at Loma Linda

The complete history of the medical work would fill volumes. All we are going to show here, in brief, is that the Lord gave a plan for Seventh-day Adventists to work in the medical lines. Whether one wants to call it a blueprint or not is irrelevant. This study will generally refer to it as such, while the reader is free to interpret it as a "pattern" or a "model." The fact is that we have not followed it, and, therefore, it is yet another area in which the denominational reason for being—to promulgate the third angel's message—has been undermined and eroded. We would even say that the change has been so great as to be essentially—to use Knight's word—*neutered*.

J. H. Kellogg established and presided over the American Medical Missionary College at Battle Creek in 1895. He was successful in his medical career because, at first, he followed all the medical advances of the time *only if they were based upon sound principles as given in the Spirit of Prophecy*. This enabled him to avoid the mistakes and remain ahead of the others. At the turn of the century, however, his pride caused him to look elsewhere as he lost confidence in Ellen White. "The Battle Creek Sanitarium was divorced from denominational control in the year 1907" (Arthur W. Spalding, *The Origin and History of Seventh-day Adventists*, vol. 3, p. 141). By 1908, with legal maneuvering, Kellogg gained control of the Battle Creek Sanitarium and the American Medical College, which were part of the same complex. The medical school went under in 1910 and merged with the Illinois State University (Spalding, p. 149). In 1933, the Sanitarium went under in the collapse of Wall Street. In 1942, the facilities were sold to the United States government and became the Percy Jones Hospital for veterans.

Nonetheless, God had a plan to restart the work that should have been done at Battle Creek. A few years before Kellogg took Battle Creek away from the denomination, the Lord was putting things in place to begin another work at Loma Linda. He showed the place to Ellen White in a night vision in 1901. The property she was shown was located, and a down payment was made on it, May 26, 1905. Mrs. White visited the property on June 12. As she stepped down from the carriage, she said to her son who attended with her, "Willie, I have been here before." She later wrote that it was her desire that this place be a true representation of what God wanted of our health institutions (*The Paulson Collection*, p. 170).

Mrs. White intended that this would be a medical missionary training center and do the work that Battle Creek had failed to do. In a general reading of the Spirit of Prophecy for the principles that are to govern the establishment of the medical work and institutions, we may readily identify fourteen points pertaining to the ill-fated medical "blueprint."

Blueprint Concepts after which the Medical Work is to be Patterned

1. It is to be established in a rural location, and the surrounding land should be secured as well.

2. It is to be non-allopathic, i.e., it does not employ poisonous substances nor other harmful procedures such as radiation. Healing comes from right living, the application of "the eight doctors," the use of harmless healing substances, herbs, and a natural diet. The "eight doctors" are: the proper use of water, fresh air, exercise, sunlight, a proper diet, abstinence from things harmful, and the moderation of things beneficial, proper rest, and trust in God.

3. Natural healing and the law of God. Through proper instruction and the cooperation of the patient, optimum health is to be secured. Teaching obedience to natural law—following the laws of nature in maintaining good health as our duty to the Creator—is part of the everlasting gospel and the God-ordained method of healing.

    The healing of the sick and the ministry of the Word are to go hand in hand. *Just as* patients were to be taught the use of "hygienic measures" (the cleansing of impurities from the body) and "rational treatments" (the use of water, herbs, careful diet, exercise, etc., as opposed to *irrational* allopathic methods that can poison the body with drugs, maim with surgery, and weaken with radiation) to promote healing through obedience to the laws of health, *so also* were they to be linked with healing of soul from the ravages of sin by bringing the patient to Christ, who desires to bestow upon the helpless agent the ability to obey by faith the laws of the Creator. In fact, the laws of health are a part of the very law of God itself.

4. Natural healing and the character of God. The purpose of the health institution is not primarily to be that of a hospital. Rather, it is to stand for the principles of the gospel in all its fullness. Many of the sick, like the paralytic, need first and foremost to receive the forgiveness of their sins.

   Contrarily, the principles of allopathic medicine are rooted in correction of disease through the application of external force, in the form of drugs and surgery. This is contrary to God's nature, for *God does not force. Therefore, allopathic medicine cannot reveal the character of God.*

   Worldly medical practitioners and methods do not heal by the eradication of the root cause nor do they cleanse impurity or correct imbalance in the organism brought about through disobedience to the laws of health. Natural healing comes through the patient's cooperation as he or she recognizes defective habits of living and eradicates disease by changing harmful practices into healthful ones.

   There was never a need for us to copy the world. If the patient is not interested in God's methods, then he may have his symptoms alleviated through the world's systems of pharmaceutical substances, radiation therapies and surgical interventions. This is not to say that there is never a time or place for these healing modalities, but that it is not to be our work, for such modalities are not the right arm of the third angel's message.

5. It must keep the spirit of present truth alive, leading patrons to belief, and must not ever lower the standards.

6. The true health work should never develop into professional and commercial lines. Laboring under the whip of the worldly medical establishment and charging large sums of money for services is not in God's plan.

7. It is not for training "bedside nurses" but "missionary nurses."

8. All our people, to varying degrees, are to become medical missionaries.

9. We would endeavor to blend the schools and sanitariums.

10. The work is most efficiently done by setting up small institutions in many places.

11. The school is to provide regular courses of study in the Bible, the Testimonies, and other necessary lines for every worker connected with the institution.

12. There is to be a program of off-campus missionary projects with canvassers going house to house to invite people to participate in lectures and workshops of small groups on temperance, hygiene and health principles, with cooking schools, home treatments where the third angel's message can be shared, dinners and other occasions to make friends with people of the community and the surrounding towns and villages that they might become acquainted with the work being done.

13. Avoid the use of medical equipment that costs a lot of money and requires experts to operate. Often these cause harm. Teach in lines of proper diet and water treatment, exercise, etc. Radiation (x-ray) therapies are not to be used, for, if used unwisely, these may do great harm. The results of some of these treatments are like the use of stimulants, having a net effect of weakening rather than healing. (It is very common for cancer to return soon after chemotherapy or radiation treatments. Usually the second time the cancer is stronger, and the patient dies.)

14. Do not go into debt.

The Loma Linda College of Medical Evangelists and the Day of Opportunity

John Allen Burden (1862–1942) was an early administrator of the sanitarium. Ellen White was guided to choose him to establish the medical evangelism work in southern California. He was instrumental in the purchase of the properties for the Paradise Valley Sanitarium in 1904 and the Glendale Sanitarium in 1905. Burden was the one who also found Loma Linda, which was a Victorian-styled complex named the "Loma Linda Resort Hotel."

The Sanitarium at Loma Linda opened to patients on October 9, 1905 and was called the "Loma Linda College of Evangelists." The training program for nurses began in January 1906. Enrollees in the training program for medical evangelism were required to have nine years of prior schooling. They would take two years of basic nursing to qualify for registration in the medical evangelism course of study. On December 9, 1909, the college was chartered under a new name, "College of Medical Evangelists" (CME). Now they were authorized by the State of California to grant academic and professional degrees.

There were varying views on the direction the institution should take. Even in the early years there were pressures to depart from the principles that were established for the Adventist medical work and conform more to the world. John Burden wrote a letter in 1908 to Dr. Wells Allen Ruble, MD, who served in the capacity of advisor to the church on the medical work at the General Conference in Takoma Park. Two years later, Ruble would become the president of CME and serve as chair of the Medical Missionary Council, which later became the General Conference Medical Department (1913). Burden's letter to Ruble provides us with insights regarding the overall situation and various views on how deal with the controversy surrounding the establishment of the medical work. Burden was solidly in harmony with moving the work forward on the basis of Spirit of Prophecy principles, and this was his advocacy in his letter to the General Conference. In this letter, Burden informed the church that the way was clear to remain true to the principles upon which the Lord desired to establish the work. He believed *the political and legal landscape to be favorable because, at the time, the state recognized natural treatment methods on an equal basis with drug treatment.*

Here is where we shake our heads and ponder why they did not pick up that ball and run with it. Burden outlined four views of how the work should proceed. The following was his favored view, and he advocated for it, believing that the time was conducive and the way was prepared:

> As **the Legislature of California has opened the way for the students of such a school as the Loma Linda College of Evangelists to be legally recognized to practice sanitarium methods of healing, or rational remedies**, some have felt that it would be wise to have the school chartered under the law that such students as complete the entire three years' course and whose qualifications enable them to pass the State examinations, might be free to work as other recognized physicians; *i.e.*, they hold positions in our institutions and comply with all the requirements of the law.…Otherwise no matter how well-qualified they may be to do the work, they would of necessity have to labor as nurses under the direction of legally qualified physicians.
>
> Our understanding of the testimonies is, that while thousands are to be quickly qualified for thorough medical-evangelistic work, some must qualify to labor as physicians. We have been instructed again and again to make the school as strong as possible for the qualification of nurses and physicians; and **the opening of a way for its recognition; and especially in view of the fact that California heretofore has been one of the most difficult States for medical practitioners to gain recognition in, seemed to us a divine providence, coming as it did the next year after we had started our school.**
>
> The battle was fought by the osteopaths, but **the Legislature then threw the gate wide open** for any school whose requirements for entrance to the medical course were equal to a high school preparation on the ten fundamental branches that underlie medical education. (John Burden to Wells Ruble, April 13, 1908, in *The Broken Blueprint*, p. 159, emphasis added)

Mrs. White wrote two years later:

> **Now while the world is favorable toward the teaching of the health reform principles**, moves should be made to secure for our own physicians the privilege of imparting medical instruction to our young people who would otherwise be led to attend the worldly medical colleges. **The time will come when it will be more difficult than it is now, to arrange for the training of our young people in medical missionary lines.** (Lt. 61, 1910, to J. A. Burden, in *Loma Linda Messages*, pp. 545, 546, emphasis added)

So it is revealed what could have happened if the church had settled its mind to obey the Lord, had refused to run in the allopathic track, and had fought to acquire and maintain legal recognition for natural remedies via the eight laws of health. God was making the way clear, and He would have blessed the church in it. Adventism could have been an outstanding witness to the Lord's perfect law if it had steadfastly pursued the way of obedience, and it would today be a shining beacon of light for the advancement of the third angel's message. They could have been at the head of the health reform work instead of the tail of allopathic medicine (for there are much bigger and more prestigious institutions of allopathic medicine in the world). Think of how many families would have been touched by God through natural healing and the influence His ways would have had throughout every segment of society. It also would have made a huge difference with regard to the treatments sought by our own people instead of heading off to the pharmacy for antihistamines at the sign of our first sniffle.

Between 1912 and 1922, and onward, we gradually complied, step by step, with every requirement placed before us by the AMA's Council on Medical Education. Because of our compliance, the AMA gained a full lock-grip on medical and nursing education. The AMA's hidden objective is simple enough: Require that only those methods of treatment be used which make money for drug and medical appliance manufacturers. And what are they? Things that can be patented. It is a well-known fact that those manufacturers funneled kick-back money to AMA coffers through expensive ads placed in the *Journal of the AMA*. The vast wealth of the drug manufacturers is legendary. (*The Broken Blueprint*, pp. 161, 162)

Burden continued in his letter:

Materia Medica [Latin. "medicinal materials," pertaining to things swallowed, injected or applied topically to the skin, which included herbs in the 19th century, but pertained only to drug medications in the 20th century] and surgery are both thrown out; so that **a good, thorough school of hygiene or rational practice would have no difficulty of being recognized in this state.**

And should our school be recognized here, its students would have a vantage ground from which to secure recognition in other states, the same as osteopaths are being recognized. (John Burden to Wells Ruble, April 13, 1908, in *The Broken Blueprint*, p. 162, emphasis added)

Burden was firmly established upon the counsels for the medical work, understanding that it was to be the "entering wedge" for the third angel's message of obedience to the law of God through enabling faith in Jesus.

Treatment with natural remedies and acceptance of our special truths about the law and the Sabbath go hand in hand. Both teach obedience to the laws of God! But, unfortunately, in the crucial years of 1910 to 1922, our leaders temporized and lost the opportunity. (*The Broken Blueprint*, p. 163)

If Burden had been in charge, things would have been different. Ellen White had not wanted him to turn the institution over to the conference when he did, and he later recognized that doing so was a terrible mistake. Ruble could do nothing more, serving only as an advisor to the General Conference. A. G. Daniells was in charge, and he was not exactly a champion of the health message. His stance regarding our denominational schools was not in line with being separate from the world, and, in 1909, he would reject Ellen White's message to quit eating flesh foods. His careless regard for the health message later caught up with him.

In 1935, worn out with the cares of years, Daniells came to Loma Linda and gave five talks to the faculty and students.

One evening, a medical student found him walking in the hallway. Daniells was weeping. Turning to the young man, in an agony of voice Arthur said, "Obey the Spirit of Prophecy. I didn't and paid the price!"

A few weeks later, Daniells was diagnosed with cancer and entered the Glendale Sanitarium.... He sent out an urgent request that three men come to his room. They were G. A. Roberts, president of the California Conference; Roy Cottrell, former China missionary and currently chaplain at Glendale; and George B. Starr, a close friend of Ellen White in Australia, by that time retired. All three were faithful to the Spirit of Prophecy writings. Elder Daniells asked the three ministers to anoint him for healing.

Stepping outside the room to discuss the matter the three said to one another, "How can we pray for his healing when, for years, he has persistently gone against the Spirit of Prophecy instruction in his diet and so many other ways and has never changed?"

Politely, they refused Daniells' request to anoint him. He got other men to pray for him, and soon after (1935) died. (*The Broken Blueprint*, pp. 343, 344; story related by the medical student to Elder James Lee)

It is always the best course of action to heed God's counsels! Time has proven it again and again. Later on, as we examine the institutional drift into worldly policy and accreditation, we will see that these men understood that their decision put souls in peril, for the third angel's message would lose its force, and the world would overtake both teachers and students. When God's people obeyed His plan, these things would not happen. God is too wise to err! Burden wrote:

It is now evident that this early effort to develop the field work [going into the surrounding areas and doing literature evangelism, Bible meetings in homes and tent meetings] molded the students for the mission field perhaps more than any other one feature of their class work. **Not one of that first class was lost to the work.** When they were graduated they were ready for the foreign fields. Some found their way to India, others to South America. Others dedicated their lives to the work in the homeland.... Thus is demonstrated that the following principles in harmony with God's purpose and plan will result in producing workers after God's order. (John Burden, letter dated June 8, 1906, in *The Broken Blueprint*, pp. 182, 183, emphasis added)

Pressure Test and Crisis

Only a few days after announcement of the closing of the American Medical Missionary College [in Battle Creek], this notice appeared in the church paper:

September 29 [1907] was a red-letter day in the history of our medical missionary work. A new milestone was passed in the opening of the College of Medical Evangelists, our denominational school at Loma Linda, Cal. ["College of Medical Evangelists," *Review and Herald*, Oct. 27, 1910, p. 17]

This marked the formal opening of the medical school. It had been incorporated the year before, and for five years it had been in process of formation and operation as a combined medical and evangelistic training school.... (Spalding, *Origin and History of Seventh-day Adventists*, vol. 3, p. 150)

The closing of the AMMC, mentioned above, must be in reference to the decision of the "stockholders of the Battle Creek Sanitarium ... to decline official denominational ownership and control," precipitating the dropping of the college from the denominational Yearbook in 1907, though it did not completely dissolve until 1910 (*Seventh-day Adventist Encyclopedia* [1985], p. 37).

There was a council meeting held at CME in Loma Linda with General Conference leaders, October 28–31, 1907. On the last day of the meeting, with A. G. Daniells present, Ellen spoke with certainty:

We want a school of the highest order,—a school where the word of God will be regarded as essential, and where obedience to its teachings will be taught. For the carrying forward of such a school, we must have carefully selected educators. Our young people are **not to be wholly dependent on the schools where they are told, "If you wish to complete our course of instruction, you must take this study, or some other study,"**— studies that perhaps would be of **no practical benefit** to those whose only desire is to give to the world **God's message of health and peace**. In the education that many receive there are not only subjects that are **non-essential**, but much that is decidedly **objectionable**. We should endeavor to give instruction that will **prepare students quickly for service** to their fellow-men.

We are to seek for students who will plow deep into the Word of God, and who will conform the life-practice to the truths of the Word. **Let the education given be such as will qualify consecrated young men and young women to go forth in harmony with the great commission** ... (Ms. 151, 1907, in *Loma Linda Messages*, p. 4, emphasis added)

As we continue our study of the complexities of Seventh-day Adventist history, it will be clear to the reader that we persistently emphasize the fundamental principles of the work God intended we perform. We should be clear what our response to God's leading *was to be* when He gave us those principles with clarity through the prophetic gift. Then we will be able to accurately assess what the actual response *has been* in comparison to the instructions of the Lord.

Additionally, we must be careful and honest students of the primary documentation and of the counsels of inspiration so that we may be equipped to compare it with the contemporary lore and recognize and identify it for what it is: *revisionist* history. We would then understand that what was built on man's foundations at that time has not somehow become God's foundations a hundred years later. What was disobedience then has not through age and philosophy become obedience today.

Naturally, today's official reporting of denominational work in various media makes no mention of the work continuing under the paradigm of human wisdom and insubordination to the counsels! Volumes are written that blatantly ignore these realities, such as the last line of chapter 9, "Medical Evangelism," of *Origin and History of Seventh-day Adventists*, vol. 3, in which the author states "physicians and surgeons of great capabilities and consecration have given their service to the building up of this second and far greater Seventh-day Adventist medical college [Loma Linda], which **under the blessing of God has nerved and animated the right arm of the message**" (Spalding, *Origin and History of Seventh-day Adventists*, vol. 3, p. 167, emphasis added). We cannot agree with this statement. *The "right arm" of the third angel's message is the medical missionary ministry which adheres to natural remedies, not to slash, burn and poison techniques of modern "scientific" medicine.*

As this manuscript is being produced, the White Memorial Hospital is celebrating its centennial. The *Adventist Review* reported:

> The hospital proudly bears the name of Ellen G. White as a living memorial to the woman who advocated for the establishment of a medical school and launched the building of hundreds of Adventist hospitals and clinics worldwide. These places, she believed, could offer a unique kind of medical care that attended to both physical and spiritual needs—and could introduce patients to new ideas about healthful living.
>
> Although she died before she could actually visit the hospital, White's son W. C. White was able to tell her that Mrs. Lida Scott had offered to make a liberal gift to CME to establish a students' home and hospital in Los Angeles.
>
> The news so moved her that she trembled with emotion as she replied: " 'I am glad you told me this. **I have been in perplexity about Loma Linda**, and this gives me courage and joy.' After a little further conversation, I knelt down by her side and thanked the God of Israel for His manifold blessings, and **prayed for a continuance of His mercies**. Then Mother offered a very sweet prayer of about a dozen sentences, in which she expressed gratitude, confidence, love, and **entire resignation**" (CMBell Company, "One Hundred Years of Care and Healing," *Adventist Review*, Feb. 28, 2013, p. 18, citing Arthur L. White, *Ellen G. White*, vol. 6, p. 429, emphasis added).

Ellen White was perplexed indeed because they were getting far off track and the demands of the American Medical Association were placing upon them many heavy financial burdens, which had to be borne by reallocating funds that should have been used for mission work. Of course, Mrs. White would have been relieved to hear of Lida Scott's financial support. Scott was the wealthy daughter of Isaac Funk of the publishing company Funk and Wagnalls in New York.

The Lord had been ignored in the building up of the work as it was being conducted. Prayer for mercy was in order! W. C. White was well aware of what was going on. In an earlier meeting, he assured Scott, a new convert, that his mother believed that God would not let this church so fully apostatize that there would be the need for a new organization. He recounted some of the historical cycles of "ambitious men" taking the church "away from right principles" and how God had worked to correct matters and "bring the church back to loyalty" (Arthur L. White, *Ellen G. White*, vol. 6, p. 428). So it was that Scott was brought on board. What could Mrs. White do but resign herself and place matters entirely in the Lord's hands?

The 2013 report from the *Adventist Review* is not a cause for pride but for shame, as what Ellen White actually revealed from the Lord was that—

> The Lord has at no time guided in the large plans that have been laid for buildings in Los Angeles. He has given light as to how we should move, and yet movements have been made that are contrary to the light and instruction given.
>
> The complete plan in regard to the purchase of the Hill Street property was not laid before me till my last visit to Los Angeles. I was then taken to see this property, and as I walked up the hill in front of it, I heard distinctly a voice that I well know. Had this voice said, "This is the right place for God's people to purchase," I should have been greatly astonished. But it said, "Encourage no settlement here of any description. God forbids. My people must get away from such surroundings. This place is as Sodom for wickedness. The place where my institutions are established must be altogether different. Leave the cities, and like Enoch come from your retirement to warn the people of the cities."
>
> The words were spoken: "The divine hand is not guiding in the steps that have been taken in regard to this property. The spiritual vision of men has been darkened. Plans have been made that the Lord has not inspired."
>
> I was afterward instructed that the whole matter was inspired by human wisdom. Men have followed their own wisdom, which is foolishness with God, and which, if they continue to follow it, will lead to results that they do not now see. The spiritual eyesight has been blinded.
>
> I am astonished that our brethren should have thought of purchasing the property on Hill Street…. After I had seen its situation, I knew that I could not

for a moment give my consent to the establishment there of an institution of any kind.

To establish an institution for the advancement of God's work in such a place, would be contrary to the light that God has given regarding this work. Think of the annoyance to which the workers would be subjected in such a location. How long would they, with an immense hotel right beside them, be allowed to keep the Sabbath in peace? For us to establish a sanitarium there would be like Lot going into Sodom. It would be worse, because as far as the outward surroundings of Sodom were concerned, it was like the garden of Eden. But on the Hill Street property there is no spare land, and no opportunity to see the beauties of nature. (Lt. 182, 1902, in *Manuscript Releases*, vol. 1, pp. 250, 251)

Contrary to the light that God had given regarding this work, they forged ahead and—

On Sunday afternoon, April 21, 1918, as a crowd of over 2,000 were assembled for a dedicatory service in an open-air meeting outside the White Memorial Hospital, the largest earthquake in 18 years suddenly shook the city, and even damaged some of the buildings at Loma Linda. (*The Broken Blueprint*, p. 286)

Furthering the discussion of the principles of the work to be accomplished, we read:

If we are to go to the expense of building sanitariums in order that we may work for the salvation of the sick and afflicted, we must plan our work in such a way that those we desire to help **will receive the help they need**. We are to do all in our power for the healing of the body; but we are to **make the healing of the soul of far greater importance. Those who come to our sanitariums as patients are to be shown the way of salvation**, that they may repent and hear the words: Thy sins are forgiven thee; go in peace, and sin no more.

Medical missionary work in Southern California is **not to be carried forward by the establishment of one mammoth institution for the accommodation and entertainment of a promiscuous company of pleasure lovers, who would bring with them their intemperate ideas and practices**. Such an institution would absorb the time and talent of workers who are needed elsewhere. Our capable men are to put forth their efforts in sanitariums established and conducted **for the purpose of preparing minds for the reception of the gospel of Christ.**

We are not to absorb the time and strength of men capable of carrying forward the Lord's work **in the way He has outlined**, in an enterprise **for the accommodation and entertainment of pleasure seekers, whose greatest desire is to gratify self**. To connect workers with such an enterprise would be perilous to their safety. Let us keep our young men and young women from all such dangerous influences. And should our brethren engage in such an enterprise, they would not advance the work of soul saving as they think they would.

Our sanitariums are to be established for one object, the advancement of present truth. And they are to be so conducted that a decided impression in favor of the truth will be made on the minds of those who come to them for treatment. The conduct of the workers, from the head manager to the worker occupying the humblest position, is to tell on the side of truth. The institution is to be pervaded by a spiritual atmosphere. We have a warning message to bear to the world, and our earnestness, our devotion to God's service, is to impress those who come to our sanitariums. (*Testimonies for the Church*, vol. 7, pp. 96, 97)

Here are some observations relating to these statements:

- "Pleasure seekers" are not to be the concern of Adventist health work. In context, Ellen was writing about building and presenting facilities that portray an appearance of wealth after the worldly manner. Such things require extravagant sums to build and maintain. The type of patrons that are attracted by plush interiors and high maintenance grounds are the pleasure loving, worldly persons who are not interested in a change of life but only to "get fixed up" so they can go on living with the same health-destroying habits. These can go to the world's institutions and get what they want; they are not suitable clients for our work, which is to lead to the knowledge of the Saviour.

- We must be clear on the idea represented by the designation "sanitarium." The facilities are to be clean and sanitary. However, our work was not to be that of mere hospitals patterned after the world, which rely on toxifying, polluting drugs, chemotherapy, radiation, and surgery. The use of drugs that poison the system and cause the adverse effects that we see on drug labels are contraindicative to treatment and cure of disease, for, while they may suppress symptoms, they cause further disease, euphemistically called "side effects." Natural methods, or "hygienic measures" cleanse the body of toxins and promote healing from within by rallying the body's own forces to heal itself of the ravages caused by unhealthful practices.

- As we can read consistently throughout the testimonies on the health work, the primary objective was to be the advancement of the kingdom of Christ through the giving of the third angel's message. Our medical schools were to operate in tandem fashion with our evangelistic training schools by giving training in both natural healing methods and Bible evangelism. They were to be "medical missionary factories."

As we pick up again with the Loma Linda story, we will find that full accreditation for CME as a medical school in 1908 would mean coming into full compliance with AMA standards, even though it was possible to gain a partial approval and still stay within the guidelines of the blueprint.

To acquiesce to the counsel of Ellen White and John Burden, a General Conference resolution was passed to restrict Loma Linda to functioning as a special school for the training of medical missionary workers. Under this arrangement, they were able to obtain a state charter and grant various degrees. This was what Burden had desired.

Yet, pressure to gain accreditation was coming from A. G. Daniells and W. W. Prescott along with other college teachers and presidents. As early as 1907, Daniells was pushing for a "full-fledged medical college ... recognized by legal bodies such as the American Medical Association," declaring that it had to have "such recognition to be worth a nickel" (*The Broken Blueprint*, p. 222).

Before them was the example of The American Medical Missionary College. Yet, it did not seem that they could learn from it. In 1909, as the College of Medical Evangelists was being setting itself up to go down the path that veered away from the blueprint, a letter was written to John Burden from Dr. Howard F. Rand, M. D. He was on medical staff at the Battle Creek Sanitarium until Kellogg apostatized. Dr. Rand had intimate knowledge that the reason for the demise of Kellogg's institution was the quest for AMA accreditation. He wrote:

The great difficulty with the American Medical [Missionary College in Battle Creek] was the State told the directors of the college that they **must have certain conditions present** [for AMA recognition]; and, having reached that condition, they **must then have men of standing**.

These men [non-Seventh-day Adventist physicians] gladly gave their services, but they at once said they [the AMMC] must get in the College of Associations [accrediting body] or they would not feel like giving their time to that which did not have the standing of the colleges in the association. The request had to be complied with and in this way; **step by step, they were led into what finally was very deep water.**

We must fight this and endeavor to protect and save men from getting into such a condition that would lead one this way. This is what I am anxious about. (Howard F. Rand, letter to John Burden, Nov. 12, 1909, emphasis added)

Burden fought for the other approach, but was pushed to the side. As time went on, the tides against him grew overwhelmingly strong.

Understanding the movements which were afoot as she traveled to the General Conference Session, Ellen White wrote the teachers at Union College from Washington, DC:

"Be not unequally yoked together with unbelievers: for what fellowship hath righteousness with unrighteousness? [2 Cor. 6:14]" ...

The light has been given me that **tremendous pressure will be brought upon every Seventh-day Adventist with whom the world can get into close connection.**

We need to understand these things. **Those who seek the education that the world esteems so highly are gradually led farther and farther from the principles of truth until they become educated worldlings.** At what a price they have gained their education! They have parted with the Holy Spirit of God. **They have chosen to accept what the world calls knowledge** in the place of the truths which God has committed to men through His ministers and prophets and apostles. And **there are some who, having secured this world education, think that they can introduce it into our schools.** But let me tell you that **you must not take what the world calls the higher education and bring it into our schools and sanitariums and**

churches. I speak to you definitely; this must not be done. ("Instruction to students and teachers of Union College," May 7, 1909, in *Loma Linda Messages*, pp. 405, 406, emphasis added)

This issue was now spoken of as a test that was coming to Seventh-day Adventists. Would we stand firm to the counsels on how we were to conduct our medical work and pass the test, or would we end up teaching and practicing medicine as the world practices it and fail? That same year, Ellen White penned the following counsel to John Burden:

Dear Brother,—

I am instructed to say that in our educational work, **there is to be no compromise in order to meet the world's standards.** God's commandment-keeping people are not to unite with the world, to carry various lines of work according to worldly plans and worldly wisdom.

Our people are now being tested as to whether they will obtain their wisdom from the greatest Teacher the world ever knew, or seek to the god of Ekron. Let us determine that we shall not be tied by so much as a thread to the educational policies of those who do not discern the voice of God, and who will not hearken to His commandments....

Shall we represent before the world that our physicians must follow the pattern of the world, before they can be qualified to act as successful physicians? This is the question that is now testing the faith of some of our brethren. Let not any of our brethren displease the Lord by advocating in their assemblies the idea that we need to obtain from unbelievers a higher education than that specified by the Lord.

The representation of the great Teacher is to be considered an all-sufficient revelation. **Those in our ranks who qualify as physicians are to receive only such education as is in harmony with these divine truths.** Some have advised that students should, after taking some work at Loma Linda, complete their medical education in worldly colleges. But this is not in harmony with the Lord's plan. God is our wisdom, our sanctification and our righteousness. Facilities should be provided at Loma Linda, that the necessary instruction in medical lines may be given by instructors who fear the Lord, and who are in harmony with His plans for the treatment of the sick.

I have not a word to say in favor of the world's ideas of higher education in any school that we shall organize for the training of physicians. There is danger in their attaching themselves to worldly institutions, and working under the ministrations of worldly physicians. Satan is giving his orders to those whom he has led to depart from the faith. I would advise that none of our young people attach themselves to worldly medical institutions in the hope of gaining better success, or stronger influence as physicians. (Lt. 32, 1909, Oct. 11, 1909, in *Loma Linda Messages*, pp. 493, 494, emphasis added)

A few months earlier she made a statement that makes clear what were the foundation principles for the methods of treatment that Seventh-day Adventists were to build upon in contrast to the world. *We need to keep this in mind as we interpret any counsel that may be taken as justifying AMA accreditation and all that goes with it.* Here is what she said:

You may attain success in the education of students as medical missionaries without a medical school that can qualify physicians to compete with the physicians of the world. ("The Loma Linda College of Evangelists," *General Conference Bulletin*, June 4, 1909, p. 308, read before delegates with remarks, June 1, 1909, emphasis added)

The goal we were to achieve was to produce qualified medical practitioners on a different track, not in competition "with the physicians of the world" who did not care about God's laws or the laws of health as espoused in the Adventist message of "health reform." The education we were to receive and give to others was to be "practical," addressing habits of living to get to the root causes of disease. As we continue reviewing her statement, note again the contrast between the practical and the worldly. She makes the distinction crystal clear:

Let the students be given **a practical education.** The less dependent you are upon **worldly methods of education**, the better it will be for the students. **Special instruction should be given in the art of treating the sick without the use of poisonous drugs and in harmony with the light that God has given.** In the treatment of the sick, **poisonous drugs need not be used. Students should come forth from the school without having sacrificed the principles of health reform or their love for God and righteousness.**

The education that meets the world's standard is to be less and less valued by those who are seeking for efficiency in carrying the medical missionary work in connection with the work of the third angel's message. They are to be educated from the standpoint of conscience, and, **as they conscientiously and faithfully follow right methods in their treatment of the sick, these methods will come to be recognized as preferable to the method to which many have become accustomed, which demands the use of poisonous drugs**. (Lt. 90, 1908, to J. A. Burden, in *General Conference Bulletin*, June 4, 1909, emphasis added)

The years of 1909 and 1910 were years of notable agitation and transition. Ellen White attended the biennial session of the Pacific Union Conference, January 25–27, 1910. This was a meeting of grave concern for her. She knew "not only the steps that were being taken in medical education at Loma Linda but also what God would have the school be as an agency in furthering the third angel's message" (Arthur L. White, *Ellen G. White*, vol. 6, p. 270).

There was a fair amount of confusion as to just how to proceed in the program that was to be developed at CME. Some thought her counsels meant that ministers should be trained in medical lines while others thought that the church was to have a school to train physicians. A letter of inquiry was written to Mrs. White seeking guidance. W. C. White went to his mother for her response.

When I called to see how Mother was this morning, and to inquire if she was willing to attend the half-past eight meeting, she began to talk about her interview yesterday afternoon with Elder Evans. Then she inquired about the meetings—how they were progressing. I told her that one of the matters which was delaying the progress of the meeting, was the question which our brethren had submitted to her in writing, about the Loma Linda Medical school. And as the document was lying on her table, I handed it to her, and she read it again. (Interview between E. G. White and W. C. White, Jan. 27, 1910, in *Loma Linda Messages*, p. 489)

Church leaders understood that there was a call to establish a medical school in connection with the sanitarium but were perplexed as to what she meant by the term "a medical school." Willie went on to explain this to his mother—

The question which perplexes many, is this: There are some among our young people who believe they ought to pursue a full line of studies that will enable them to receive diplomas, and take State examinations, and be prepared to meet all the requirements of a legalized physician. Shall the Loma Linda school undertake to furnish them the education they require, notwithstanding the large expense involved, or shall we permit the few who think they must qualify to be regular physicians, to get their education and qualification at the world's best colleges and universities, as they are doing at the present time?

The answer was: "**Whatever education** our young people preparing to be physicians, require, that **we must give**."

Afterward, she took pencil and paper, and wrote out a more complete statement, and sent it to Brother Crisler to be manifolded and placed in the hands of our brethren. (*Loma Linda Messages*, p. 489)

This was her response:

The light given me is, We must **provide that which is essential to qualify our youth** who desire to be physicians, so that they may intelligently fit themselves to be able to stand the examinations required to prove their efficiency as physicians. They should be **taught to treat understandingly the cases of those who are diseased**, so that the door will be closed for any sensible physician to imagine that we are not giving in our school the instruction necessary for properly qualifying young men and young women to do the work of a physician. Continually the students who are graduated are to advance in knowledge, for practice makes perfect.

The medical school at Loma Linda is to be of the highest order, because those who are in that school have the privilege of maintaining a living connection with the wisest of all physicians, from whom there is communicated **knowledge of a superior order**. And for the special preparation of those of our youth who have clear convictions of their duty to obtain a medical education that will enable them to pass the examinations required by law of all who practice as regularly qualified physicians, we are to **supply whatever may be required**, so that these youth need not be compelled to go to medical schools conducted by men not of our faith. Thus we shall close a door that the enemy would be pleased to have left open; and our young men and young women, whose spiritual interests the Lord desires us to safeguard, will not feel compelled to connect with unbelievers in order to obtain a thorough training along medical lines. (Ms. 7, 1910, written Jan. 27, 1910, in *Loma Linda Messages*, p. 496, emphasis added)

Getting into the track of obtaining the necessary rating to attain regular accreditation according to the AMA standard would entail the sacrifice of principles, and this was never to be. As we put together everything we can know about the situation at the time, we understand that they *could have worked on gaining legal recognition from the state for becoming physicians* **in natural medicine**. We must be intelligent about this and realize that the counsel to qualify physicians was not to mean "anything goes." Supplying "whatever education" to the students as may be required to pass exams would have to harmonize with *staying out of the allopathic line of training*. God never changed His mind about that. The following year, this was still the clear message:

Our people should become intelligent in the treatment of sickness without the aid of poisonous drugs. Many should seek to obtain the education that will enable them to combat disease in its various forms by the **most simple methods**. Thousands have gone down to the grave because of the use of poisonous drugs, who might have been restored to health by simple methods of treatment. **Water treatments**, wisely and skillfully given, may be the means of saving many lives. Let diligent study be united with **careful treatments**. Let **prayers of faith** be offered by the bedside of the sick. **Let the sick be encouraged to claim the promises of God for themselves.** (Ms. 15, 1911, in *Medical Ministry,* p. 57, emphasis added)

Many leading men and women of the past and of the present have bought into this the idea that the statement, "whatever education our young people preparing to be physicians, require, that we must give" (*Loma Linda Messages*, p. 489), means the common pharmacological knowledge and so on. However, we were to be attuned to "knowledge of a superior order." The school was to be "of the highest order" not that which the world deems "higher education."

It has been our sad and frustrating experience in reading standard histories published through official channels to find the promotion of this idea and the retelling of the entire history without reference to the realities of the matter as we have presented here. The history has been "white-washed" by quoting selectively to avoid incrimination. On page 280, for instance, of volume 6 of the Ellen White biographies, Arthur L. White footnoted the words, "*whatever may be required,*" from Ellen White's January 28, 1910 statement, saying—

In these words is found the **justification** for accrediting Seventh-day Adventist educational institutions, a point developed in *Counsels to Parents and Teachers* in the statement: "Our larger union conference training schools ... should be placed in the most favorable position for qualifying our youth to meet the entrance requirements specified by state laws regarding medical students."—Page 479. (emphasis added)

Now, "justification" is a word used when speaking in reference to something that is not right. Are we obtaining a license from Ellen White to go against what we know has already been revealed? Contextually, Arthur White's reference above is to "The Medical Student" by Ellen White, October 1, 1909 (see Loma Linda Messages, pp. 428–434). We should not read statements to excuse ourselves in traveling a different path than the one God originally set before the leaders. We should not interpret them for continuing in disobedience. Our medical schools were not to come under the control of worldly men in their fight for recognition, nor adopt the ways of worldly medicine in drug therapy treatments. Leaders became perplexed about how to acquire the professional recognition of which Ellen spoke positively without their leaning on the arm of man. They could only think to achieve it through AMA accreditation.

A theme that is often woven into her counsels on the matter is that, by staying true to the principles and trusting in God and placing God first, the way would be opened not only for recognition but also for validation as having that which is superior.

The light that God has given in medical missionary lines will not cause His people to be regarded as inferior in scientific medical knowledge, but will fit them to stand upon the highest eminence. God would have them stand as a wise and understanding people because of His presence with them....

Let every medical student aim to reach a high standard. Under the discipline of the greatest of all Teachers, our course must ever tend upward to perfection.... Let no one stop to say, "I can not do this." Let him say instead, "God requires me to be perfect, **He expects me to work away from all commonness and cheapness, and to strive after that which is of the highest order.**" (*Loma Linda Messages*, p. 429, emphasis added)

The "commonness" is man's way. The learning of the world is "cheapness." The true "higher learning" is that which comes through the study of the Word of God under the headship of Christ in all things. In this context, the common way is allopathic medicine. Genuine scientific medical knowledge would pertain to that which tends to true healing, not that which the world calls science, "falsely so called," the "profane and vain babblings" spoken of in 1 Timothy 6:20. In seeking accreditation for prep schools, the common education is full of non-essential material that tends away from God. God requires us "to work away from all commonness and cheapness."

So far, so good. Then Mrs. White added:

That knowledge which is termed science should be acquired, while the seeker daily acknowledges that the fear of God is the beginning of wisdom. **Everything that will strengthen the mind, should be cultivated** to the utmost of their power, while at the same time they should seek God for wisdom; for **unless they are guided by the wisdom from above, they will become an easy prey to the deceptive power of Satan.** They will become large in their own eyes, pompous, and self-sufficient. (*Loma Linda Messages*, p. 430, emphasis added)

When she said that the training should include the "knowledge which is *termed* science," does she mean allopathic training—the world's training? Would this be part of that which should be acquired while, at the same time, seeking for the guidance and wisdom of God? Would that which is false science strengthen the mind? Where is the key to this? The text above says, "Everything *that will strengthen the mind* should be cultivated." Therefore, that which does *not* strengthen the mind, that which is *common and cheap*, should *not be cultivated*. If students have to go into the world, let them keep the good and let the rest "go in one ear and out the other." This seems to be what is being counseled. Yet, such a situation is far from ideal, in fact, it is decidedly perilous to souls. Her advice was that "none of our young people attach themselves to worldly medical institutions" (Lt. 132, 1909, in *Medical Ministry*, p. 62).

She was deeply concerned about students leaving to finish their training at worldly institutions, and she optimistically stated that the Lord would open the ways whereby the youth "can be given an education in medical missionary lines without endangering their souls" (Ms. 151, 1905, in *Manuscript Releases*, vol. 1, p. 226). This was her hope. Would the leading men cooperate in faith?

In the medical profession there are many skeptics and atheists who exalt the works of God above the God of Science. **Comparatively few of those who enter worldly medical colleges come out from them pure and unspotted**. They have failed to become elevated, ennobled, sanctified. Material things eclipse the heavenly and eternal. With many, **religious faith and principles are mingled with worldly customs and practices**, and pure and undefiled religion is rare. But **it is the privilege of every student to enter college with the same fixed determined principles that Daniel had when he entered the court of Babylon, and throughout his course, to keep his integrity untarnished** ...

Let not medical students be deceived by the wiles of the devil or by any of his cunning pretexts which so many adopt to beguile and ensnare. Stand firm to principle. At every step inquire, What saith the Lord? Say firmly, I will follow the light. I will respect and honor the Majesty of truth.

Especially should those who are studying medicine in the schools of the world, guard against contamination from the evil influences with which they are constantly surrounded. When their instructors are worldly-wise men, and their fellow students infidels who have no serious thought of God, **even Christians of experience are in danger of being influenced by these irreligious associations. Nevertheless, some have gone through the medical course, and have remained true to principle**.... (*Loma Linda Messages*, pp. 430, 431, emphasis added)

We know that she never condoned such a course as safe or desirable, yet it was still happening. She was simply giving counsel regarding the situation that then existed. Moreover, we have her statement that spells out the remedy to this danger—that qualifying them should be done in-house—and we cited it in Arthur White's "justification" statement above:

It is because of these peculiar temptations that our youth must meet in worldly medical schools, that provision should be made for preparatory and advanced medical training in our own schools, under Christian teachers. **Our larger Union Conference training schools … should be placed in the most favorable position for qualifying our youth to meet the entrance requirements specified by state laws regarding medical students.** The very best teaching talent should be secured, that our schools may be brought up to the proper standard. The youth and those more advanced in years who feel it their duty to fit themselves for work requiring the passing of certain legal tests, should be able to secure at our Union Conference training-schools all that is essential for entrance into a medical college. (*Loma Linda Messages*, p. 431, emphasis added)

How is it to be accomplished? Is it to be done by gaining *accreditation*, which translates to the requirement to "get in line with the world" and "study the things which the world studies"? (Lt. 84, 1909, in *Fundamentals of Christian Education*, p. 534). Is it to be achieved by bringing on board the program of allopathic training when there is strict counsel against the use of drugs? This would be a contradiction. (In our study of the counsels, we have to take all things together and harmonize them, so that one statement does not counter another. True "balancing" means giving statements equal weight so that they support each other within the proper context of their time, place, and circumstance.)

When thrown into the deepest perplexity, what is to prevent us from casting ourselves upon God in our weakness, helplessness, and lack of wisdom?

Prayer will accomplish wonders for those who give themselves to prayer, watching thereunto. God desires us all to be in a waiting hopeful position. What He has promised, He will do; and inasmuch as there are legal requirements making it necessary that medical students shall take a certain preparatory course of study, our colleges should arrange to carry their students to the point of literary and scientific training that is necessary.

And not only should our larger training schools give this preparatory instruction to those who contemplate taking a medical course but we must also do all that is essential for the perfecting of courses of study offered by our Loma Linda College of Medical Evangelists. As pointed out about the time this school was founded, **we must provide that which is essential to qualify our youth who desire to be physicians so that they may intelligently fit themselves to stand the examinations required to prove their efficiency as physicians.** They should be taught to treat understandingly the cases of those who are diseased, so that the door will be closed for any sensible physician to imagine that we are not giving in our school the instruction necessary for properly qualifying young men and young women to do the work of a physician. (*Loma Linda Messages*, p. 431, emphasis added)

Were these things to be accomplished through compromise so that we could point to certain statements as "justification" for our *pragmatism* (a word often used to excuse faithlessness)? Again, one counsel should not cancel another. An intelligent evaluation of "time, place and circumstance" will prevent us from dispensing with common sense and going to silly extremes. Yet, at the same time, it will not lead to discard *principles*, for these are to be maintained across generations, culture, and situations. Adapting to the changing times does not ever make righteousness obsolete; evil never becomes acceptable in achieving a desired end.

At this point, the following discussion between Mrs. White, John Burden, and Willie White serves well to cement in place how the counsels were functioning and what the duty of leadership was with regard to determining how to move forward in securing scientific and legal qualifications without sacrificing the principles already given by the Lord. Ellen White's candid thoughts here are definitive of the Lord's principles and counsel in the entire matter:

The Relation of Loma Linda to Medical Institutions

E. G. White: **We want none of the kind of "higher education" that will put us in a position where the credit must be given, not to the Lord God of Israel, but to the god of Ekron.** The Lord designs that we shall stand as a distinct people, so connected with Him that He can work with us. Let our physicians realize that they are to depend wholly upon the true God.

I felt a heavy burden this morning when I read over a letter that I found in my room, in which a plan was outlined for having medical students take some work at Loma Linda, but to get the finishing touches of their education from some worldly institution. I must state that the light that I have received is that we are to stand as a commandment-keeping people, and this will separate us from the world. The Sabbath is a great distinguishing line. **As God's peculiar people we should not feel that we must acknowledge our dependence upon the transgressors of God's law to give us influence. He will give us advantages that are far above all the advantages we can receive from worldlings.**

J. A. Burden: I know that these thoughts are what you have presented to us before. We do not want to cause you to carry a heavy burden. We simply wanted to be sure that we were moving in right lines. If the Lord gives you light, well and good, we will be glad to receive it, and if not, then we will wait.

E. G. White: If we follow on to know the Lord, we shall know that His going forth is prepared as the morning. **There are some who may not be able to see that here is a test as to whether we shall put our dependence on man, or depend upon God.** Shall we by our course seem to acknowledge that there is a stronger power with the unbelievers than there is with God's own people. **When we take hold upon God, and trust in Him, He will work in our behalf.** But we are to stand distinct and separate from the world.

I feel a decided interest in the work at Loma Linda, and I desire that it shall exert a powerful influence for the truth. **Your success depends upon the blessing of God, not upon the views of men who are opposed to the law of God.** When they see that God blesses us, then people will be led to give consideration to the truths we teach.

We need not tie to men in order to secure influence. We need not think that we must have their experience and their knowledge. Our God is a God of knowledge and understanding, and if we will take our position decidedly on His side, He will give us wisdom. I would that all our people might see the inconsistency of our being God's commandment-keeping people, a peculiar people zealous of good works, and yet feeling that we must copy after the world in order to make our work successful. **Our God is stronger than is any human influence. If we will accept Him as our educator, we will make Him our strength and righteousness, He will work in our behalf.**

These principles [of the world's education and practice] **may result in a condition of things that is not just as we should like them to be. We may like to have** [meet] **certain conditions, that in the end would result in bondage which we do not anticipate.**

Jesus Christ is our Saviour today, and **He is willing to work in our behalf, if we will not put our dependence upon some other power.** If we are sustained by the living God, the superiority of His Power will be manifested in His people. **This is the testimony that I have borne all the way along.**

J. A. Burden: We love to hear the truth over and over again, that we may be sure it is the truth.

E. G. White: You have the Word which tells you that God's commandment-keeping people are to have His special favor, and that they are to be sanctified through obedience to the truth. Shall we unite ourselves with those that are full of error, who have no respect for God's commandments, and shall our students go forth to obtain the finishing touches of their education from them?

W. C. White: What is to be the final outcome? Will all our medical missionaries be simply nurses? Shall we have no more physicians, or shall we have a school in which we can ourselves give the finishing touches? (Interview between Mrs. E. G. White, J. A. Burden, and W. C. White, Sanitarium, Calif., Sept. 20, 1909, *Loma Linda Messages*, pp. 424, 425, emphasis added)

Next follows a very significant statement. We believe that the proper understanding of the nature of the American Medical Association accreditation track meant *confederation* and *alliance with the world*; therefore, it was to be "off the table." Mrs. White said to "do whatever it takes" to prepare students to enter medical training and pass state exams, but this she now qualified:

E. G. White: **Whatever plan you follow, take your position that you will not unite with those that do not respect God's commandments.** (*Loma Linda Messages*, p. 426, emphasis added)

She was not spelling out exactly what plan to follow but was enjoining decision makers to adhere to the principle of not uniting "with those that do not respect God's commandments."

As we shall see, placing themselves under the thumb of the American Medical Association would lock them into dependence upon the world. Again, Ellen White called for honoring God, since it would be God who would open the way for Seventh-day Adventists to have trained physicians.

W. C. White: Does that mean that we are not to have any more physicians, but that our people will work simply as nurses, or does it mean that we shall have a school of our own to educate physicians?

E. G. White: **We shall have a school of our own. But we are not to be dependent upon the world, we must place our dependence upon a power that is higher than all human power. If we honor God, He will honor us.**

J. A. Burden: The governments of earth provide that if we conduct a medical school **we must take a charter from the government. That in itself has nothing to do with how the school is conducted. It is required, however, that certain studies shall be taught. There are ten required subjects. Physiology is one.** It is required that those who labor as physicians shall be proficient in these studies. In starting our sanitariums for the care of the sick, we must secure a charter from the government; our printing office must do the same. **Would the securing of a charter for a medical school, where our students might obtain an education, militate against our dependence upon God?**

E. G. White: **No, I do not see that it would. Only see that you do not exalt men above God. If you can gain force and influence that will make your work more effective without tieing [sic] yourselves to worldly men, that would be right.**

J. A. Burden: That is the vital point, where we have been hanging for three years. **The only thing that we have asked for in this matter is to take advantage of the government provision that would give standing room for our students when they are qualified.** (*Loma Linda Messages*, p. 426)

Here is an allusion to what we showed earlier, that Burden believed that "the Legislature of California has opened the way for the students of such a school as the Loma Linda College of Evangelists to be legally recognized to practice **sanitarium methods** of healing."

E. G. White: I do not see anything wrong in that, as long as you do not in any way lift men above the Lord God of Israel, or throw discredit upon His power.

J. A. Burden: **In planning our course of study, we have tried to follow the light in the Testimonies, and in doing so it has led us away from the requirements of the world. The world will not recognize us as standing with them. We will have to stand distinct, by ourselves.**

E. G. White: **We shall always have to stand distinct. God desires us to be separate.**

J. A. Burden: Now the proposition in this letter was to deviate from that, so that standing as we do, would enable us to stand with them, and to have their advantages. From the instruction that has come, **it has seemed to me from the very first that we were to stand by ourselves in a distinct light, following the light that God has given with reference to physical healing, and that when we do that God will open the way before us, and give us prestige with the people. But if we deviate and connect with these other schools, we would find ourselves being thrown more and more into the very things that they are doing, and our students would be molded after their similitude instead of after the similitude of the truth.**

E. G. White: **That is what I am trying to guard against all the time.** As we read the Bible we see that **God is dishonored when His people go to any worldly power, or put their trust in a worldly power. That is where God's people spoiled their history.** You must arrange the matter the best you can, but that which is presented to me is that you are not to acknowledge any power as above that of our God. Our influence is to be acknowledged of God, because we keep His commandments, and His commandments are not grievous. (*Loma Linda Messages*, pp. 426, 427, emphasis added)

We know by what has been written through inspiration and various discussions that took place in correspondence and meetings that the possibility of being locked into mandatory instruction along lines of allopathic medicine in our schools, *as a means of treating the sick*, was fraught with a high degree of risk. Although the standing counsel is for the student to make God his or her wisdom and guide, the principle that runs counter to this when students are subject to worldly wisdom is that "by beholding we become changed." Additionally, subjecting students to the science and philosophy of allopathic medicine while they are under the tremendous time-pressure of studies and the concerns of daily living is hardly a formula for helping them stay close to God.

Next, Willie White offered some interesting thoughts on how to circumvent the drug issue. Perhaps the Lord could have opened the way to work it out along lines such as he suggested. It is actually rare to find this issue discussed in any official publication of Adventist institutions that have sought worldly qualifications or that are now functioning under them.

> W. C. White: Jesus said at one time, "The scribes and the Pharisees sit in Moses' seat: all therefore whatsoever they bid you observe, that observe and do; but do not ye after their works." [Matt. 23:2, 3] **Now the law says that a man shall not practice medicine unless he has a diploma from a college, and unless he has passed the examination of the state board, and has a certificate. The law would not recognize the diplomas of our physicians unless they have studied some things that we do not think are really essential. For instance, in their preparation they have to study a number of things that we think they might get along without, but we can teach them. We do not have to teach these subjects in their way; we can teach them in our way. When it comes to the study of drugs, they teach how to give them. We teach the dangers of using them, and how to get along without them. In some other schools they teach geology on the evolution basis. We can teach geology and show that evolution is false.** (*Loma Linda Messages*, p. 427, emphasis added)

Again, Mrs. White had no finely tuned instructions on exactly how the objective was to be accomplished. She simply told them to work it out and repeatedly said that *this was a test as to whether they would follow God or go down to the Philistines, the god of Ekron.*

> E. G. White: **Well, you must plan these details yourselves. I have told you what I have received, but these details you will have to work out for yourselves.**

> J. A. Burden: It seems clear to me that **any standing we can lawfully have without compromising, is not out of harmony with God's plan.**

> E. G. White: No, it is not. All I can say is that I have had very distinct light, however, that **there is danger of our limiting the power of the Holy One of Israel.** He is the God of the Universe. **Our influence is dependent upon our carrying out the word of the living God.** We weaken our powers by not placing our dependence upon God, and taking hold of His strength. This is our privilege. (*Loma Linda Messages*, pp. 427, 428 emphasis added)

The contemporary, cultural Adventist takes great pride in our institutions of learning and medical work. I know how it is because I can remember bringing guests to church and swelling with pride as "Mission Spotlight" would play on the screen. I would pray for no distractions, thinking that surely this would impress the non-Adventist seekers, that the visuals of our nice buildings, manicured lawns and equipped institutions, the walls of electronics in our media studios and radio stations, the shining faces of groups of ethnic converts singing praises from all corners of the world, would communicate God's blessing in our *success* and as evidence of our standing as the remnant people. We have thought that developing our institutional work to have the look and professional feel of other institutions gives us status in the eyes of the world, making us appear accomplished and influential. In reality, the pursuit of professionalism has caused us to take on actual worldliness. We are generally oblivious to what God intended for us and how it would look today if we had passed the test that came to us. Instead of still being here in this present world, we could have been basking in the glory of His face, in the everlasting kingdom.

It is true that we are spending a lot of time on the issue of the medical work. There are Adventist educators and leaders who work day and night, in self justification, to bust *what they believe* are myths in Adventism. We also believe that myth busting is a worthy use of our time. However, we have done so by showing that the myth is that we are on course when, in actuality, we have taken a detour in matters of the health and education work, as God laid it out for us, and have gone down to the world, to the god of Ekron, with the only sure result of further worldliness. As we observe the present condition of the church organization that was established under the proclamation of the third angel's message, we will have a more accurate understanding, through a study of the unadorned facts of our history, of how it got that way.

God's People Spoil Their History

And the spoilers came out of the camp of the Philistines ... Now there was no smith found throughout all the land of Israel: for the Philistines said, Lest the Hebrews make *them* swords or spears: but all the Israelites went down to the Philistines, to sharpen every man his share, and his coulter, and his ax, and his mattock. Yet they had a file for the mattocks, and for the coulters, and for the forks, and for the axes, and to sharpen the goads. (1 Sam. 13:17, 19–21)

On April 27, 1910, Mrs. White wrote to John Burden:

It is not necessary that our medical missionaries follow the precise track marked out by medical men of the world. **They do not need to administer drugs to the sick. They do not need to follow the drug medication in order to have influence in their work. The message was given me that if they would consecrate themselves to the Lord, if they would seek to obtain under men ordained of God, a thorough knowledge of their work, the Lord would make them skillful.** Connected with the divine Teacher, they will understand that their dependence is upon God and not upon the professedly wise men of the world. (*Loma Linda Messages*, p. 543, emphasis added)

This was the day of opportunity and the day of decision. It was the time to strike while the iron was hot. Remember that she said at this time, "Now while the world is favorable toward the teaching of the health reform principles, moves should be made to secure for our own physicians the privilege of imparting medical instruction to our young people who would otherwise be led to attend the worldly medical colleges." Then she warned, "The time will come when it will be more difficult than it is now, to arrange for the training of our young people in medical missionary lines" (*Loma Linda Messages*, p. 545, 546, emphasis added).

Dr. Owen S. Parrett, a close friend of John Burden's, who attended Loma Linda from 1907 to 1915 and later worked at Paradise Valley Sanitarium where John Burden had been transferred, was an eyewitness to events of those years. He wrote the following:

My wife recalls, "While we nurses were in training at Loma Linda, Elder Burden would often tell us, You should not desire to become registered nurses in the world's way for a superior ministry of healing. Repeatedly he reminded us that the College of Medical Evangelists was established to provide a superior method of education and a superior method of practice for nurses and physicians, and that our legal recognition was to be for a superior order, unique and separate from the 'regular' training and recognition of the world's medical fraternities. God did not want us to become 'regular' nurses and 'regular' doctors."

... Repeatedly Elder Burden told us medical students, "Sister White tells me that the Lord will give us recognition when we are ready for it." (Owen S. Parrett, M. D., "Recollection of experiences at Loma Linda in 1909," cited in *The Broken Blueprint*, p. 236)

The goal of becoming fully qualified and legally recognized practitioners was not to be understood as becoming "regular doctors," trained in worldly medical practice to be able to return and teach the same to Adventist students. Rather it was to be understood as securing the "privilege of imparting medical instructions to our young people" by means that would not require worldly training and that would give God all the glory. Going down to the "Philistines" for the purpose of adopting their medical pattern meant putting man's ways and wisdom above God.

Ellen White counseled: "We should have in various places, men of extraordinary ability, who have obtained their diplomas in medical schools of the best reputation, who can stand before the world as fully qualified and legally recognized physicians" (*Loma Linda Messages*, p. 545). Daniells misapplied statements like this, assuming that a regular medical college was what Ellen White wanted us to pursue. He could not apply the principles and likely was unable to comprehend them, having his thinking clouded by his own unhealthful practice of the regular use of a flesh diet. In his unwillingness to accept the testimonies on health reform, he was paralyzed both mentally and spiritually, causing him to be unable to make the right decisions. As Ellen White admonished, "Erroneous eating and drinking result in erroneous thinking and acting" (Ms. 37, 1909, in *Counsels on Health*, p. 134).

The inspired statements were never meant to say that the medical work was to become accredited. Ferrell believes that what Ellen White advised was that—

a few of our men, who have extraordinary ability, should attend outside universities and obtain medical (M. D.) degrees, so they can be stationed, here and there, throughout our institutions (and at Loma Linda), so that the world cannot say that none of our men have the highest qualifications. —That is all it says. It does not say that Loma Linda or any other of our schools should obtain institutional accreditation.

In order to initially staff our medical facilities, a few men had to have advanced training. But thereafter, they could train our own students who would become the teachers in our medical schools. (*The Broken Blueprint*, pp. 238, 239)

These selected men were to be "God-fearing men," "wisely chosen," "prudent men" who would adhere faithfully to the principles of the health message (*Loma Linda Messages*, p. 545). In the same manuscript, she continued the mantra, "It is not necessary that our medical missionaries follow the precise track marked out by the medical men of the world. They do not need to administer drug medication in order to have influence in their work." She also wrote: "Some of our medical missionaries have supposed that a medical training according to the plans of the worldly schools is essential to their success.... I would now say, put away such ideas. This is a mistake that should be corrected" (Lt. 61, 1910, in *Loma Linda Messages*, pp. 543, 544). Once again contrasting the world's methods with true health work, she added:

> God's true commandment-keeping people will be instructed by Him. The **true medical missionary** will be wise in the treatment of the sick, **using the remedies that Nature provides**. And then he will look to Christ as the true Healer of disease. The principles of health reform brought into the life of the patient, the use of Nature's remedies, and the cooperation of divine agencies in behalf of the suffering, will bring success. (*Loma Linda Messages*, p. 545, emphasis added)

Are all the doctors and nurses in allopathic medicine today "true medical missionaries?" I understand that this question may step on some toes, yet the only thing to consider is whether we are obeying the truth. Toes will heal.

Another statement that men have taken to erroneous conclusions comes from the 1910 interview that Willie White had with his mother, "Whatever education our young people preparing to be physicians, require, that we must give" (*Loma Linda Messages*, p. 489). Willie White gave a fair explanation of this statement in *The Medical Evangelist* of 1911:

> Our medical missionaries should be given the opportunity to know **the very best things** done by the allopaths [those following the system accredited by the AMA Council on Medical Education], the eclectics, the homeopaths, the osteopaths, and the water-cure doctors; **but none of these systems should be adopted as comprising that which our physicians need to know; nor should the name of any of these systems be adopted as "the sign of our order." Neither are our medical men to give the credit or honor of the results of their labors under God, to any man or group of men, or to any locality, or to any system.** (W. C. White, "Letter to an Osteopath," *The Medical Evangelist*, Oct.-Nov. 1911, p. 132, emphasis added)

Between 1910 and 1922, men operated under their own interpretations of the counsels in accordance with their own desires and sold out to the AMA agenda with the result that, in the 1930s, other Adventist colleges would also insist upon standardization under the world's accrediting bodies. Today all of the church-operated institutions are servants to the dictates of the world's standards, in accordance with unbelievers who know not nor care not for the third angel's message. One must wonder what Jesus would think, were He to walk through our halls, look into the books in our libraries, and peer into our classrooms and treatment rooms. Would He say, "Well done, thou good and faithful servant?" or "Get these things hence!" Would Ellen White recognize even a small percentage of what is taught and practiced today? Would her face light up with affirmation, or would she weep?

When men determine to have their own way, the Lord lets them forge ahead. So, under God's permissive will, the denomination health work today goes along under the rudiments of the world, missing out on much of what He had hoped to do through them. Operating as we are, can the church count on God's special blessing and protection?

John Burden was gradually pushed into the background as men trained in worldly universities steadily took control. Within four years, they were staggering under an immense burden of debt.

Owen S. Parrett, M. D., published his memoirs in 1977. As a first-hand observer of all these things he wrote:

> In the cleavage between the principles of simple health evangelistic training and the complex training of regular AMA doctors, major steps came in the spring of 1910.... Elder Burden desired to see a

special training for Christian physicians, whereas Elder Daniells insisted that an AMA training be given at CME. (*The Broken Blueprint*, p. 245)

Parrett commented on the politics of getting rid of Elder Burden and the loss of financial backers in the process. His memoirs relate Mrs. White's lament:

> She said, "Elder Burden, what are they trying to do to get you out of this institution? ... The Lord sent you here, and your work for this institution is not finished" ... Sr. White suddenly stopped; but added, "These men will yet have to learn their lesson. They think I do not know what is going on, but I know everything that is going on!" (*The Broken Blueprint*, p. 248)

CME was turned over to the General Conference and a board of ten members selected. With this move, Daniells had the power to significantly influence the direction of the college, borrowing money to bring it in line with AMA requirements. There was an authorization for $25,000 for the building of a modest hospital to tend to surgical and critical-care patients. This was going in the wrong direction, for the blueprint called for a treatment and education program involving the use of natural remedies. By contrast, the new hospital was being founded on a critical care patient-in/patient-out pattern as is the protocol for hospitals after the common order. As we have noted, such patients are not interested in lifestyle changes. They simply want to get "patched up" so they can be on their way with a bottle of pills.

In a letter in 1902, Mrs. White related a dream she had concerning surgery:

> Last night I seemed to be in the operating room of a large hospital, to which people were being brought, and instruments were being prepared to cut off their limbs in a big hurry. One came in who seemed to have authority, and said to the physician, "Is it necessary to bring these people into this room?" Looking pityingly at the sufferers, he said, "Never amputate a limb until everything possible has been done to restore it." Examining the limbs which the physicians had been preparing to cut off, he said, "They may be saved. The first work is to use every available means to restore these limbs. What a fearful mistake it would be to amputate a limb that could be saved by patient care. Your conclusions have been too hastily drawn. Put these patients in the best room in the hospital, and give them the very best of care and treatment. Use every means in your power to save them from going through life in a crippled condition, their usefulness damaged for life."
>
> The sufferers were removed to a pleasant room, and faithful helpers cared for them under the speaker's direction; and not a limb had to be sacrificed. (Lt. 162, 1902, in *Spalding and Magan Collection*, pp. 267, 268)

No further comment is required!

September 29, 1910, the College of Medical Evangelists opened its doors as the official denominational medical school. Although one of the principles of establishing God's work was to avoid debt and "not launch out into the work without knowing how much money" would have to be invested (Ms. 93, 1901, in *Medical Ministry*, p. 153), in the bid to come into line with the AMA in the space of four years, the institution was driven into a pit of debt to the tune of $400,000. And that was only the beginning.

In 1912, the quest for accreditation was intense. A year earlier, a representative for the AMA, Dr. Nathan Colwell, paid an informal visit to the institution to see what was happening there. He had a conversation in the office with Burden and President Ruble, and, after learning of the nature of their work there and their goals involving preparation of medical missionaries, informed them that they had no need to pursue accreditation. In spite of this and to the later astonishment of Dr. Colwell, CME pushed to get the rating necessary for accreditation. Colwell noted: "They have gone and done what I told them not to" (W. Frederick Norwood, M. D., *The Vision Bold*, p. 193).

They had also gone and done what the Lord had told them not to, with the sad result of their being left to their own wisdom. Burden's niece, Freeda Rubenstein, in a statement dated September 1973, related the story of Seventh-day Adventist involvement with the AMA:

> When, on several occasions, church leaders came to Sister White for counsel, she objected. When the AMA leaders persisted with their requirements, the brethren came again to Ellen White for counsel. She warned Adventists that if we joined them, we would be forming a confederacy with them and that in no case would we join any worldly confederacy.
>
> Eventually the brethren came back to Sr. White again for counsel; and, after listening to what they had to say, she arose, quietly left their presence, went into her room and shut the door behind her.

Elder Burden said that sometime after one of these meetings, a few church leaders decided to fully conform to the AMA requirement to earn their recognition. (quoted in David Lee, *Stories of the Early College of Medical Evangelists*, pp. 135, 136)

The solemn truth of the matter is this:

I am authorized from God to tell you that not another ray of light through the Testimonies will shine upon your pathway until you make a practical use of the light already given. The Lord has walled you about with light; but you have not appreciated the light; you have trampled upon it. (*Testimonies for the Church*, vol. 5, p. 666)

Even though there was no pressure from accrediting agencies for Seventh-day Adventists to come into line, the Adventists were bending over backwards to achieve the rating they would need to move forward. Adventist history has shown that accreditation is a cruel taskmaster. Its purposes are to serve investors through manipulation of the supply side of supply and demand economics. Ferrell unpacked how this works:

That is why worldly accrediting agencies exist: to devise requirements to limit the number of institutions turning out graduates. As a result, there is a reduced number of training centers, so each can charge a higher tuition and pay higher salaries to their administrators and teachers. Because there are a reduced number of graduates, those who graduate can charge more for their services because they have a degree.

Christ stated His way: "Freely ye have received, freely give" (Matt. 10:8). The way of the world is radically different: Get as much money out of the customer and the employer as you can. In order to do this, the educational world uses accrediting agencies and degrees while workers use professional associations and labor unions. (*The Broken Blueprint*, pp. 269, 270)

The financial demands of seeking accreditation continued to be a black hole for resources. It became cause for trepidation amongst those in decision-making positions. In 1913, it was seen that, in order to continue to satisfy requirements for the ratings that would be needed to gain worldly approval, they would have to add more buildings and equipment. D. E. Robinson reported:

A glance at the minutes of the meeting of the trustees of the College of Medical Evangelists, held in Takoma Park, Washington, D.C., in October, 1913, in connection with the Autumn Council of the General Conference Committee, reveals a feeling of genuine dismay at the seemingly endless streams of money needed for the building program. Emergencies innumerable had been met by the borrowing of more money, and the indebtedness of the institution had been mounting yearly.

Besides this, increasing requirements from the American Medical Association were bringing added perplexities.

… Some were again questioning seriously the "aim of furnishing a complete course for physicians." … "Perhaps," said another, we "made a mistake in going ahead and establishing a full medical school, when we were conducting a medical missionary school successfully." (*Story of Our Health Message*, pp. 392, 393)

There were several days of indecision regarding whether to press on or to go back to a program of medical missionary training. "But, on the evening of the last day of the session, it was hesitantly voted to keep the accreditation attempt going for another two years" (Merlin Neff, *For God and C.M.E.*, p. 172).

In 1914, there was a CME constituency meeting. The March 25 minutes reveal that, once again, John Burden restated that they should be following the plans given by the Lord without any concern for the world's approval. Benjamin Wilkinson, author of *Truth Triumphant* and *Our Authorized Bible Vindicated*, spoke his troubled mind on the "question of standards" and the struggle to meet the expectations of the world. Others voiced similar concerns. C. W. Flaiz presented a special concern that ten thousand dollars in church money collected from offerings were being funneled every year to Loma Linda. In terms of that day, this was an enormous amount of money to be no longer available for foreign missions.

Back in 1905, as Kellogg was set to acquire AMA approval for the American Medical Missionary College in Battle Creek, Ellen White had written:

All this higher education that is being planned will be extinguished; for it is spurious. The more simple the education of our workers, the less connection they have with the men whom God is not leading, the more will be accomplished. Work will be done in the simplicity of true godliness, and the old, old times will be back when, under the Holy Spirit's guidance, thousands were converted in a day. **When the truth in its simplicity is lived in every place, then God will work through His angels as He worked on the day of Pentecost**, and hearts will be changed so decidedly that there will be a manifestation of the influence of genuine truth, as is represented in the descent of the Holy Spirit.

The Holy Spirit never has, and never will in the future, divorce the medical missionary work from the gospel ministry. They can not be divorced. Bound up with Jesus Christ, the ministry of the word and the healing of the sick are one. (Ms. 21, 1906, in *Special Testimonies B07*, pp. 63, 64, emphasis added)

Battle Creek stands as a sad example—the likes of which we shall see again—of a period when "storm and tempest sweep away the structure" and crisis causes catastrophic failure of the machinery. At that time the work can only be done by God's Spirit, and it will be apparent that it is *His* work, for it will be done *His* way!

By 1915, with a minimum "C" rating from the AMA in hand, ongoing pressures had intensified to the point that the institution had to fulfill the demand to build a hospital in Los Angeles in order to achieve full accreditation status. By now, the institution had spent a half million dollars and this would only add to the financial outlay. It would take a minimum of sixty-thousand dollars to begin construction. We have already read what Ellen White had to say about going into Los Angeles—that missionary work was to go out from Loma Linda into Redlands, Los Angeles, and further. Yet, they were not to build anything in these cities, which she likened to Sodom and Gomorrah.

At the Annual Council at Loma Linda in 1915, A. G. Daniells tried to reassure the members assembled to push on in the face of seven more demands from the AMA to earn a "B" rating. There were to be faculty upgrades at the Los Angeles facility opened early in 1913, expanding it to a 200-bed hospital. Then the AMA ruled that the courses at CME were inadequate, the labs were insufficient, *the course in pharmacology was weak*. Besides these, there were registration and student credential issues.

Meanwhile, Ellen White died July 16, 1915 after convalescing for five months after breaking her hip in a fall. In 1916, the foundation was laid for the "Ellen G. White Memorial Hospital" in Los Angeles, which, in our assessment, was named in her honor but was actually a memorial to disobedience.

The original blueprint called for one blueprint medical missionary training school, using "simple methods," at Loma Linda. Through slavish submission to AMA requirements, God's plan was changed into a two-hospital, two-medical school arrangement, specializing in drug medication and surgery. (*The Broken Blueprint*, p. 282)

The whole enterprise had become a colossal money-gulping monster. Merlin Neff explained:

Problems! There was a never-ending stream of them, with the medical school on two campuses. On one occasion President Magan declared, "This whole matter of a divided institution is a very expensive one" (Magan to G. H. Curtis, Dec. 18, 1930). Many of the serious items came in pairs—two faculties, two hospitals, two nurses' training schools, two sets of buildings. (*For God and C. M. E.*, p. 268, in *The Broken Blueprint*, p. 282)

In 1917, the CME received its "B" rating as a special push was made to upgrade and meet requirements so medical students could be exempted from the draft into World War I service. These expenses came on top of all of the fundraising for the new hospital in Los Angeles. After the 1918 flu epidemic, Magan set out to raise another $16,500 to satisfy further demands. Fundraising teams were set up, and there was fierce competition, setting the Loma Linda hilltop on fire. Moreover, it did not end in 1919. Full accreditation was still in the crosshairs. More orders from the AMA had to be filled. They were to locate headquarters in Los Angeles, enlarge the library, renovate the business office, hire more teachers, set up a fully salaried executive committee, centralize all the power in one figurehead, and increase the operating budget for both campuses by 25% (*The Broken Blueprint*, p. 288).

In 1922, they got their "A" rating. More money would have to be spent to maintain it, of course, and that situation has not changed to this day. Loma Linda is kept afloat by a percentage of the World Budget offerings collected in the churches.

All of this was the beginning of serious trouble, which would soon bring harm to the entire denomination. Through this process, we had become the servants of another master—the AMA in Chicago. The next demands to be made were that the medical college could only accept premedical students from accredited premedical programs. Our colleges were not accredited in this way. If they were to align with worldly standards, they too would be subject to all of the demands and subsequent financial burdens of meeting those demands. They would become servants of the world's standards. Furthermore, if one or two colleges became accredited, the others would also want it. These colleges would have to be staffed by teachers with degrees from accredited institutions. Not being able to issue doctoral degrees, students would have to go to outside institutions. This would mean that many students would lose their focus on mission and would become focused on education, career, and status. Accrediting agencies would gain control over libraries and teacher training, and our schools would become secularized. Future leaders of the church would train under men holding degrees from outside universities (for example, former president of the General Conference, Jan Paulsen, received his training at Tubingen, a University in Germany known for its higher criticism and ecumenical focus), and graduates would go into our churches and leaven the congregations with ideas foreign to the third angel's message.

Alas, this projection has become all too true.

Warren Howell, secretary of the General Conference Department of Education from 1918 to 1930 said that we had started down a road that seemingly would tie us "to the tail of a kite, to be carried whither the holder of the string may list—seemingly in the direction of less efficiency to serve the cause of God" (Warren E. Howell, "Separation from the World in Education," *Review and Herald*, July 12, 1923, p. 15).

We pause the story at this point because it has brought us to the end of the second functional generation. There will be more to come in the third generation. Now we need to rewind Adventist history back to the year 1919 and look at another development in the church.

The 1919 Bible and History Teachers Conference and the Entrenchment of the "Conservative/Liberal" Divide

Bert Haloviak wrote: "As the Kellogg-Jones crisis was approaching a peak of intensity, George Butler, former president of the General Conference wrote the then current president, A. G. Daniels, his reaction" ("In the Shadow of the Daily," p. 13).

> It is a terrible, terrible thing! and are we going into the conflict before us ... the great and closing conflict, with two camps wrangling with each other, Arthur? I do not believe it is possible, unless we get this thing fixed up in some way, and union restored, to go on without being terribly crippled for years, and the loss of many souls. (G. I. Butler to A. G. Daniells, April 20, 1905, RG 11, Incoming Letters, 1905-B, in *Messenger of the Lord*, p. 439)

Haloviak continued: "A fundamental element of the wrangling mentioned by Butler concerned conflicting interpretations of the inspiration of the spirit of prophecy" ("In the Shadow of the Daily," p. 13).

We would be remiss in covering this conflict if we did not give some attention to the conference of 1919, which was convened by the General Conference Executive Committee led by A. G. Daniells and held July 1–19, with the teachers' council being held July 20–August 1. This conference occurred at a time that various Bible conferences were taking place within the broader scope of Christianity, giving rise to biblical fundamentalism, which champions the concept of the inerrancy of Scriptures.

This examination of the discussions at the conference is important, for it gives us a better understanding of the Laodicean environment of modern spiritual Israel. The 1919 Bible Conference is recognized as the point at which Adventist theology broke into two camps, being the first time the terms "liberal" and "conservative" were applied to theological positions in Adventism. That we see today a hardened dichotomy of Adventist thought and belief underscores the existence of yet another element of the Laodicean condition. Both sides tend to consider their position as true and faithful, as rich and increased in goods and in need of nothing, when the fact is that both sides, though possessing many valuables, are still missing the fullness of the gold, white raiment, and eyesalve offered by the True Witness to remedy our spiritual condition.

This was the first conference that brought together the most highly educated in the denomination. Two of the denomination's three PhDs were in attendance. Aside from the discussion of various doctrinal matters, a major discussion arose concerning the use of Ellen White's writings. There are contenders for the faith today who point to this conference as one of the major events contributing to the church's slide into apostasy. These are those who are drawn to "the nostalgia of reversion," mentioned by Arthur Patrick, and who hold to the fundamentalist position regarding the inspiration of Ellen White. Adventist historian Michael W. Campbell noted: "These two camps would fragment and overlap through the rest of the twentieth century and continue to impact the church up to the present" ("Book Review. More Than a Prophet: How We Lost and

Found Again Ellen White," *Ministry*, Feb. 2007, p. 29).

The "pioneer position" urged that the writings could not be divided into "inspired" and "uninspired" sections, but seemed to have no real means of dealing with apparent discrepancies. The "new view position," with its emphasis upon context, offered a means of explaining those apparent discrepancies. Each side seemed to have additional concepts that could have been useful to the other. Sufficient opportunity for a dialogue seemed to be present. (Bert Haloviak, "In the Shadow of the 'Daily': Background and Aftermath of the 1919 Bible and History Teacher Conference," unpublished paper presented at Biblical Scholars meeting, Nov. 14, 1979, cited by Herbert E. Douglass, *Messenger of the Lord: The Prophetic Ministry of Ellen G. White*, p. 434)

There were and are a number of concerned watchmen who take what may be an excessively hard view of this conference. It is beyond the scope of this book to discuss in any detail the possible reasons for the positions on the nature of inspiration held by the conference attendees, but it is worth the time of the interested student to delve into their views and compare them with the concept taught in the Bible and Spirit of Prophecy writings. Nor is it the intent of this study to cover the details of the discussions that took place at the conferences. For those interested, the words of Daniells and the other participants are available online. (See "Report of the 1919 Bible Conference," available at http://1ref.us/i0, accessed 12/20/16) What we are concerned with in this study is the upheaval amongst the brethren with regard to the nature of inspiration and its bearing upon unity and moving forward in the light and advance of the Reformation.

There were more than a few men at the time who were adamant that the door to rejection of the Spirit of Prophecy was swung wide open. Here are some of them:

God shows his prophets what will be, and then when circumstances arise, or the prophet has his attention called to it by private letters, he writes what he has seen. It is the same among the people of God to-day who have drifted away from the old landmarks, and who follow their own understanding.... It is thus demonstrated by the Bible alone that Testimonies, letters, symbolic actions, and verbal statements of a prophet are all of the same force.... (Stephen Haskell, "The Crisis," *Review and Herald*, May 10, 1906, pp. 8, 9)

Haskell did not mean to imply that every utterance of a prophet was to be considered divine revelation, but he expressed concern that "the severest conflict ... that the people of God will pass through ... will be over the Testimonies of the spirit of prophecy" (Haskell, p. 9).

Another attendee of the conference and an expert on the writings of Ellen White was Claude E. Holmes (1881–1953). In 1948, he spoke his mind on the matter as a participant in a round-table discussion in Berrien Springs. He talked about "strange and conflicting views of the prophecies" being taught, warning that, "when Bible teachers present views contrary to established positions, students and preachers are encouraged to do the same." He asserted that the 1919 Bible Conference was the door that was opened allowing the new views to be offered to the people (Claude Holmes, Manuscript Proof Read at Round-Table Discussion, Berrien Springs, Michigan, Dec. 18, 1948, RG 11, General Files, 1949–W).

In a 1921 open letter, prior to the 1922 General Conference Session, J. S. Washburn called the 1919 Conference a "Council of Darkness" and a "Diet of Doubts." He later claimed that this letter of his exerted a major influence in neutralizing Daniells' chances of reelection to the office of General Conference president.

There are current critics who concur with the sentiments of these men. Vance Ferrell explained, in a *Waymarks* tract, that the denomination published the 1919 Bible Conference material "in the hope that it would win many historic believers over to ... [a] liberal view of the Spirit of Prophecy," "that this material has been circulated for a number of years by new theology liberals in our church," and that it contains "specious reasoning" (Vance Ferrell, "Analysis of—The 1919 Bible Conference," July 1994, p. 1). Well-known conservatives Russell and Colin Standish wrote: "That infamous Bible Conference, in which high Church administrators expressed doubts concerning aspects of the inspiration of the Spirit of Prophecy, has become a crucial historical event for those who wish to ignore specific Spirit of Prophecy counsels" (Russell R. Standish and Colin D. Standish, *Half a Century of Apostasy*, p. 237).

Our position on the nature of inspiration should be that of the prophet herself, that genuine inspiration works by imbuing the thoughts of the prophet, not by verbatim dictation of the divine mind down to and through the human instrument. Ellen White said that the Bible "is not God's mode of thought and expression" but that of humanity. She said further that "God, *as a writer*, is not represented" in the sacred pages, that "God has not put Himself in words, in logic, in rhetoric, on trial in the Bible," and that *"the writers of the Bible were God's penmen, not His pen"* (Ms. 24, 1886, in *Selected Messages*, bk. 1, p. 21, emphasis added). Of course, the first time this definite statement was published was in Francis M. Wilcox's 1944 work, *The Testimony of Jesus*. Thus, it was not available in 1919. Had they been aware of it at the time, it may have helped them.

An astute researcher of recent times shared with us on the matter:

> The two-day discussion in the Teachers Council on the role and function of Ellen White illuminated how Christians through the centuries, especially since the Reformation, have been in disagreement as to how God speaks through His prophets. One of the Adventist advantages is that Adventists lived very closely to Ellen White throughout her seventy-year ministry. They saw all aspects of her life and work. But even then, some Adventists strongly advocated the verbal inspiration position while others, more keenly aware of the process of revelation/inspiration, maintained the thought-inspiration position. *This fundamental contention lay at the bottom of the discussion in 1919.* (Herbert E. Douglass, *Messenger of the Lord*, pp. 434, 435)

> The Council participants were finding it difficult to see through the dark cloud of verbal inspiration that had enveloped many (perhaps most) of the church's ministers and teachers in 1919. The end result was a church membership, for the most part, that accepted Ellen White's writings without understanding the hermeneutical principles that Mrs. White herself had penned. As elsewhere in Christendom, verbal inspiration led to a sense of infallibility, either in **the words** of the Bible or in Ellen White's writings. Nothing seems to be more unnerving (to the verbal inspirationist) than to be told that Ellen White's words (or certain Biblical words or details) need to be understood in terms of "time, place, and circumstances." To speak in this way awakens insecurity and the cry of "liberalism." (Herbert E. Douglass, *Messenger of the Lord*, p. 437, emphasis added)

Other than her description of inspiration in the Author's Preface of the 1888 Great Controversy, Ellen White's most definitive description of inspiration is in her 1886 manuscript, referenced above:

> **It is not the words of the Bible that are inspired, but the men that were inspired.** Inspiration acts not on the man's words or his expressions but on the man himself, who, under the influence of the Holy Ghost, is imbued with thoughts. But **the words receive the impress of the individual mind. The divine mind is diffused.** The divine mind and will is combined with the human mind and will; thus the utterances of the man are the word of God. (Ms. 24, 1886, written in Europe in April 1886, in *Selected Messages*, bk. 1, p. 21, emphasis added)

Inspiration is the communication of the infallible word of God through human instrumentality. Yet, the actual words and phrases used are not infallible. They are chosen by the human agent. They evidence the mind of God "diffused" through the human mind. The action of diffusion can be understood by recalling how the outside world looks when peering through a frosted or very dirty glass.

That there are two ditches is apparent, and I suspect that even the "modernist" can slide into a ditch because of notions of verbal inspiration. Those on this so-called "liberal" side can end up "picking and choosing" between what is inspired and what is not. Such "cherry picking" often leads people to a complete disregard for the testimonies or the Bible. This is what upsets the traditionalist and reversionist so. Believing that one can identify non-inspiration in one area makes way for disregarding inspiration in the next, and so on. On the "conservative" side, there tends to be a brittle adherence to every word and detail in a verbal sense. Then, when an apparent historical discrepancy or other difficulty becomes evident, the mind of the conservative is thrown into crisis, confusion or denial, no matter how well established the evidence may be.

Bert Haloviak, past director of the General Conference Office of Archives and Statistics, expressed the belief that there was an unfortunate lack of proper communication between the two sides, and the tragedy of—

> the decades that followed the Conference was that each side had elements of truth that were needed by the other. Distrust, however, resulted in one position dismissing the other as "verbal inspirationists," while the second camp considered its opponents to be moving, consciously or unconsciously, toward the destruction of the spirit of prophecy. With that distrust came solidification of positions that rendered more unlikely the needed dialogue. (Bert Haloviak, "In the Shadow of the 'Daily,' " p. 2, available at http://1ref.us/i1, accessed 12/20/16)

Herbert Douglass summarized the conference results:

> But some of those contending for thought inspiration found themselves on the other side of the slippery slope. Though they had a clearer grasp of how God speaks to the minds of prophets, few seemed to possess the inner core of Ellen White's message that provided the theological structure for her global contributions to theology, education, health, mission, etc.
>
> As time passed, some of these otherwise able leaders had nothing to hang on to when they began to separate what was inspired from what was not. When they said that Ellen White could not be trusted in historical and medical matters, or even in administrative and theological issues—where would they stop? If Ellen White could not be considered an authority in these matters, how could she be considered authoritative in others?
>
> We do not know the motivation behind the written or public statements of either verbal- or thought-inspirationists. Generally, however, thought-inspirationists contended for the freedom to interpret Ellen White on the basis of sound hermeneutical principles—**such as the application of time, place, and circumstances. Such sought the principle behind the policy.** (Herbert E. Douglass, *Messenger of the Lord*, p. 440)

At the 1919 conference, Prescott was challenged by an attending General Conference leader to help him understand how to discern between what was authoritative in the writings and that which was not. We are well advised to accept Prescott's position when he said, "I will not attempt to do it, and I advise you not to do it. There is an authority in that gift here, and we must recognize it."

Others who contended against the verbal-inspirationists did not accept, or perhaps did not understand, this larger, more constructive reasoning. The thought would be expressed, for whatever reason, "While I believe [that Ellen White is a prophet of God], I do not believe [that] all she writes and all she says is inspired; in other words, I do not believe in verbal inspiration."

That kind of thinking, if not severely modified, is an open door through which many have walked away from the Adventist Church over the years. Such thinking leads to personal judgment as to what a "prophet" means and to personal judgment as to what is inspired and what is not. This is truly a slippery slope if there is not a prevailing, fundamental message to hold on to.

> At least verbal-inspirationists knew, in their minds, how to hang on to authority—even if it might not have been for the right reasons. Those of this group (and there were many) who remained in the church as strong leaders in administration and evangelism, believed that they were the only ones left who could save the denomination from apostasy. They could point to many who tried to "reinterpret" Ellen White as examples of where such thinking would lead others—men such as the Ballenger brothers (A. F. and E. S.), J. H. Kellogg, A. T. Jones, W. A. Colcord, E. J. Waggoner, L. R. Conradi, and W. W. Fletcher. (Herbert E. Douglass, *Messenger of the Lord*, pp. 440, 441)

All of the high profile leaders who later defected had decided "that the Spirit of prophecy could be divided into 'inspired' and 'uninspired' portions" (Bert Haloviak, "In the Shadow of the 'Daily'," p. 58).

In conclusion, we would say that whatever one might tend to think of the 1919 conference, it must be borne in mind that, although the conference reveals various influences on the denomination through its leaders and teachers, it did not produce any kind of official denominational statement on record with regard to the discussions, which took place in what was a private, closed-session "think-tank" environment. *We believe that the value of their discussion for our study is that it shows that the "slippery slope" on both sides of the high road leads to a ditch, and many have slid to their destruction on either side.*

It is important that we understand the potentially grave consequences of rushing headlong to doctrinal conclusions based upon the research of individuals who hold views regarding the nature of the inspiration of the spirit of prophecy that are located towards the ends of the spectrum and who have *not* sought out the counsel and expertise of the larger community of brothers and sisters of experience.

> It seems relevant that, in most cases, those who began to make such determinations eventually lost confidence in the spirit of prophecy. It also seems relevant that the apostasies sprang from both viewpoints relative to the inspiration of the spirit of prophecy. (Bert Haloviak, "In the Shadow of the 'Daily'," p. 58)

The liberal vs. conservative dichotomy is a discussion of *two ditches* and those who inhabit them. These factions are alive and well in today's churches and organizations, which profess to be part of the third angel's movement.

We have discussed these ditches because they are an indicator of the division in the movement today.

Early History of Ecumenical Aspirations in the Seventh-day Adventist Church

Later in this book we will examine developments in the church regarding her ecumenical tendencies and alliances. Even in the second generation of Adventism, there were early ecumenical flirtations in the denomination. In this segment, we will extract information from Neil C. Livingston's *The Greatest Conspiracy*, Chapter 3, "Early Ecumenical Aspirations," pp. 49–63, which was published from May 1999 through May 2001 by Dr. John Grosboll in his Steps to Life Ministries' *Landmarks* magazine, a historic Adventist publication.

The American Sentinel's ecumenical aspirations

Notice how ecumenical aspirations appeared in the *American Sentinel:* "The first hint of a desire for the acceptance of Seventh-day Adventism by the popular denominations took place in 1890. (MR., No, 1033). Ministers who were in charge of the *American Sentinel* (Seventh-day Adventist religious liberty magazine of the day and forerunner of our current Liberty magazine), met behind closed doors to contemplate dropping the name Seventh-day Adventist from the magazine" (Neil Livingston, *The Greatest Conspiracy*, p. 59). They wanted to gain the favor of the Sunday-keeping churches. However, God kept a step ahead of these men and revealed to Ellen White what they were planning:

> In the night season I was present in several councils, and there I heard words repeated **by influential men** to the effect that if the American Sentinel would drop the words "Seventh-day Adventist" from its columns, and would say nothing about the Sabbath, **the great men of the world would patronize it**; it would become popular; and do a larger work. This looked very pleasing. These men could not see **why we could not affiliate with unbelievers and non-professors** to make the American Sentinel a great success. I saw their countenances brighten, and they began to work on a policy plan to make the Sentinel a popular success. (Ms. 29, 1890, in *Counsels to Writers and Editors*, p. 96, emphasis added)

Because of God's intervention through the prophet, the designs of "the influential men" were thwarted. Livingston went on to examine the course of action in modern Adventism:

Since the living prophet has passed from the scene has the contemporary Church preserved the name "Seventh-day" on its periodicals and institutions? No, it has not! The contemporary Church has dropped the name "Seventh-day" from everything, and simply employs the name "Adventist." Adventist Book Center, Adventist Media Center, Adventist Community Center, etc. Indeed, today many churches and book centers have even dropped the name Adventist, and call themselves simply, Christian Book Center, or Community Worship Center.... The name "Seventh-day" has been dropped from hospitals and clinics. (See, "Portland Adventist Hospital," Portland, Oregon). Indeed, the name Seventh-day has been dropped from the Church's welfare system. Remember when the Church's welfare system was called SAWS, which stood for the title, "Seventh-day Adventist Welfare System?" What is the title of this entity today, friend? ADRA, "Adventist Development and Relief Agency." How about the periodicals? We now have the Adventist Review. What was the name of our Church paper in the days of the pioneers? Advent Review and Sabbath Herald! (Livingston, p. 60)

Ballenger's ecumenical aspirations

Livingston went on to describe Albion Fox Ballenger's role in the pursuit of popular favor.

> There were Ecumenical aspirations in the apostasy of A. F. Ballenger in 1905. In this apostasy, Ballenger introduced new concepts and heresy on the Sanctuary doctrine. The underlying purpose for Ballenger's thesis was Ecumenical! He desired a "new theology" that would be accepted by the main-stream churches of the day, which would make the Seventh-day Adventist Church popular in the religious world.
>
> "How can you accuse Ballenger of Ecumenical motives?" you ask. Because Ellen White places him with the Ecumenical-minded group of men at Salamanca, New York, in 1890 who were proposing to remove the name "Seventh-day Adventist" from the American Sentinel magazine to make it more popular with other Christians. Speaking of the Ballenger apostasy in 1905, Arthur White related the following story:
>
> "At about this time Ellen White met Elder Ballenger in the hallway of the dormitory where she was staying," Arthur White related. "She told Elder Ballenger that he was the minister that the Lord had presented before her in vision in Salamanca, New York, in 1890, as standing with a party who was 'urging that if the Sabbath truth were left out of the American Sentinel, the circulation

of that paper would be largely increased'" (*The Early Elmshaven Years*, vol. 5, 1900–1905, page 408).

"So, we will be nice and will not remind the Sunday-keeping churches that they are in opposition to God's holy law," liberal Adventists erroneously reason. "We'll just remove the offensiveness of the seventh day Sabbath from our periodicals and institutions and emphasize those doctrines that we hold in common with them." (Livingston, pp. 60, 61)

This writer finds it a stark and grave irony that the church today spends hundreds of thousands of tithe dollars in litigation, employing the long arm of the law and the power of the state to enforce a copyright on the name "Seventh-day Adventist." This has been done against ministries who, having found that the church in many ways no longer remains true to its name, have gone on to independently continue to proclaim those distinctive teachings and retain the integrity of the name and the calling that it implies.

The church will blatantly disobey Heaven while persecuting those who wish to obey. This is an amazing state of affairs! The divine counsel on eliminating the name from church publications and institutions was likened to the intervention of Uzzah to keep the ark from falling. Writing in 1890, the Lord's messenger stated:

> **This policy is the first step in a succession of wrong steps.** The principles which have been advocated in the American Sentinel are the very sum and substance of the advocacy of the Sabbath, and when men begin to talk of changing these principles, they are doing a work which it does not belong to them to do. Like Uzzah, they are attempting to steady the ark which belongs to God, and is under His special supervision.... (Ms. 29, 1890, in *Counsels to Writers and Editors*, pp. 96, 97, emphasis added)

Livingston traced these wrong steps:

"This policy is the first step in a succession of wrong steps," Ellen White warned. Why would the "wrong steps" be successful from 1926 onward, and not in 1890 and 1905? The answer is simple. The messenger of the Lord passed from the scene in 1915! Leadership no longer had to answer to a living prophet. What has been the succession of "wrong steps" taken toward Ecumenical policies since these first attempts were made in 1890 and 1905? Sadly, history reveals the answer. (Livingston, *The Greatest Conspiracy*, p. 61)

The first wrong step toward ecumenism approved in 1926

"In the desire to avoid occasion for misunderstanding or friction in the matter of relationship to the work of other societies, the following statement of principles are set forth as a guidance to our workers in mission fields in their contacts with other religious organizations," the General Conference voted in 1926. (General Conference Executive Committee, 1926)

#1. We recognize every agency that lifts up Christ before man **as a part of the divine plan for the evangelization of the world**, and we hold in high esteem the Christian men and women in other communions who are engaged in winning souls to Christ ("Relationship to Other Societies," General Conference Executive Committee, 1926. [emphasis supplied])

Notice that the leadership of the Seventh-day Adventist Church "recognize every agency that lifts up Christ." This would include the Roman Catholic and apostate Protestant churches, evil spirit-filled ... [charismatic] churches. SDA leadership also recognizes these fallen churches of Babylon as "part of the divine plan for the evangelization of the world." (Livingston, p. 61)

How can it be said that these other communions of faith, as fallen Babylon, the hold of "every unclean and hateful bird" and drunken with the "wine of the wrath of her fornication" (Rev. 18:2, 3), are "engaged in winning souls to Christ"? How can it be so when they promote "another Christ" and "another gospel"? In *Early Writings*, we are informed with a certainty that another leader, posing as Christ, leads these other communions.

> And I saw those who rose up with Jesus [*after He relocated to the Most Holy Place ministry in 1844, while the mainstream churches rejected that message and stayed back in the first apartment*] send up their faith to him in the Holiest, and pray—my Father give us thy Spirit. Then Jesus would breathe upon them the Holy Ghost.... Then I turned to look at the company who were still bowed before the throne; they did not know that Jesus had left it.—**Satan appeared to be by the throne, trying to carry on the work of God**. I saw them look up

to the throne and pray, my Father give us thy Spirit; then Satan would breathe upon them an unholy influence ... Satan's object was to keep them deceived, and to draw back and deceive God's children. (*Experience and Views* [1851], p. 43, emphasis added)

There is such a difference between the messages borne by true Adventism and those of the fallen of Babylon that it would seem impossible to have such sentiments as we read in this 1926 church statement. The counsel given is in sharp contradistinction to any kind of ecumenically-trending thought:

Those who engage in the solemn work of bearing the third angel's message, must **move out decidedly**, and in the Spirit and power of God, fearlessly preach the truth, and **let it cut**. They should elevate the standard of truth, and **urge the people to come up to it**. It has been lowered down to meet the people in their condition of darkness and sin. It is the pointed testimony that will bring up the people to decide. A peaceful testimony will not do this.... There is as great a difference in our faith and that of nominal professors, as the heavens are higher than the earth. (*Spiritual Gifts*, vol. 2, pp. 299, 300, emphasis supplied)

Livingston commented:

In these last hours, "God has given to us," Seventh-day Adventists "the special truths for this time to make known to the world." He has not given this message to the Sunday-keeping churches of Babylon. Our commission is to call the people out of Babylon, not to join hands with Babylon! We are not to please the churches of the world by emphasizing doctrines SDA leadership alleges we hold in common with them.

"The world is against us, the popular churches are against us," Ellen White stated, "the laws of the land will soon be against us." (*ibid.*, 5T, p. 236, emphasis supplied).

How can we "recognize" the "popular churches" that are "against us" as being "a part of the divine plan for the evangelization of the world?" Notice also that the contemporary Seventh-day Adventist Church holds "in high esteem the Christian men and women" who teach the false doctrines of the Protestant churches, the churches that the Scripture calls the harlot daughters of Babylon.... (Livingston, p. 62)

Ellen White held up the divine standard:

In our day ... are not religious teachers turning men away from the plain requirements of the word of God? Instead of educating them in obedience to God's law, are they not educating them in transgression? From many of the pulpits of the churches the people are taught that the law of God is not binding upon them. (*Christ's Object Lessons*, p. 305)

The Protestants have accepted the spurious Sabbath, the child of the papacy, and have exalted it above God's holy sanctified day; and our institutions of learning have been established for the express purpose of counteracting the influence of those who do not follow the word of God. (*Review and Herald*, Jan. 9, 1894, in *Fundamentals of Christian Education*, p. 288)

Livingston asked:

Does this sound like Ellen White would approve any idea of ecumenism? But then this action by the General Conference Committee was taken eleven years after her death. How can we "recognize" the Sunday-keeping churches of Babylon as "part of the divine plan for the evangelization of the world" and still be "counteracting the influence" of those churches "who do not follow the word of God?" How can we "recognize" those churches who have "accepted the spurious Sabbath, the child of the papacy, and have exalted it above God's holy sanctified day?"

Ellen White stated that in the Sunday-keeping churches of Babylon "the doctrine is now largely taught that the gospel of Christ has made the law of God of no effect; that by 'believing' we are released from the necessity of being doers of the word." (*Signs of the Times*, February 25, 1897). She stated further that this teaching "is the doctrine of the Nicolaitanes [*sic*], which Christ so unsparingly condemned." (*ibid.*, ST, 2/25/1897, emphasis supplied).

Have the Sunday-keeping churches become more "Adventist" since the death of Ellen White? What was Ellen White's position on the recognition of Sunday-keeping churches of Babylon? Would she agree with the premise that they are "part of the divine plan for the evangelization of the world?" (*General Conference Executive Committee*, 1926). What would she say if she were alive today? She would give the same testimony she gave from the beginning. Truth does not change.

I saw that since Jesus left the holy place of the heavenly sanctuary and entered within the second veil, the churches have been filling up with every unclean and hateful bird. I saw great iniquity and vileness in the churches, yet their members profess to be Christians. Their profession, their prayers, and their exhortations are an abomination in the sight of God. Said the angel, "God will not dwell in their assemblies. Selfishness, fraud, and deceit are practiced by them without the reprovings of conscience. And over all these evil traits they throw the cloak of religion ..." Ellen G. White, *Early Writings*, page 274. (emphasis supplied).

Ellen White's position on the other denominations was that the members of these churches of Babylon "profess to be Christians." The contemporary Seventh-day Adventist Church concurs with these false churches by stating that "we hold in high esteem the Christian men and women in other communions who are engaged in winning souls to Christ." (*ibid.*, *GC Executive Committee*, 1926).

Because we recognize the fallen churches of Babylon, does this mean that they will always love and recognize Seventh-day Adventists as Christian brethren? No, they will not.

"When we reach the standard that the Lord would have us reach," Ellen White warned, "*worldlings will regard Seventh-day Adventists as odd, singular, strait-laced extremists.*" (*Fundamentals of Christian Education*, page 289, emphasis supplied).

We now have the answer to two important questions. (1) Why were the attempted moves toward Ecumenism by "influential men" not successful in 1890 and 1905? (2) Why would the "wrong steps" toward Ecumenism be successful after the year 1926 and onward? Again, the answer is simple.

The messenger of the Lord passed from the scene in 1915—and the written Testimonies of the Lord have been made of non-effect! (Livingston, *The Greatest Conspiracy*, pp. 62, 63)

The Foreign Missions Conference

In an undated paper, Walter R. Beach, Secretary of the General Conference from 1954 to 1970 and father of Bert B. Beach, stated:

In the early years of our overseas expansion particularly at the time of World War I, the brethren felt the need of participating in what was called the Foreign Missions Conference. This, of course, was before the World Council [WCC, formed August 1948] and the National Council [NCC, formed November 1950] organizations. I have not been able to ascertain just when the first contacts were made with the Foreign Mission Conference. The first notation I find in the General Conference Minutes with regard to this organization is in November, 1922. We then were holding membership in the Conference. That year the Committee voted the names of the delegates to attend the Conference, and provided a financial participation in the work of the Conference. (W. R. Beach, in Ferrell, *Seventh-day Adventist/Vatican Ecumenical Involvement*, p. 19, bracketed material in Ferrell's text)

Later, the Foreign Missions Conference (FMC) voted to integrate into the NCC, and, at that time (1950), the General Conference discontinued its membership. However, we should understand that the FMC "was the outgrowth of one of the major ecumenical movements in the 20th century which produced the WCC and its daughter organizations: *Faith and Order* (doctrinal), *Liturgy*, (worship practices), and *Mission* (originally mission work)" (Ferrell, p. 19). For the doctrinal organization, see discussion of B. B. Beach under the fourth generation.

Concluding Thought on the Generational Midpoint: Adventism in the Balances

The second generation of Adventism is the generation that history shows to be when Christ was wounded again in the house of His friends when He was crucified afresh in the person of the Holy Spirit (*The Ellen G. White 1888 Materials*, p. 1478). The call to bring in everlasting righteousness would have finished the work early in this generation except for the stubborn resistance of leading men and of the age-old problem of reliance upon humanity. The first call messengers had come and gone and their message spurned. God would wait for this generation to pass before bringing the denomination back to the same ground. Second call messengers were coming. What would the church do with them? This and many other subjects will be examined under the third generation.

CHAPTER 7.

The Cankerworm

The Third Generation of Adventism, 1924–1964

According to the principle of sowing and reaping (Exodus 20:5), the iniquity of the fathers is visited upon the third and fourth generations.

The seeds of lukewarmness were sown in the first generation. In generation two, there was no ripening response to the 1888–1901 messages of the covenants and righteousness by faith. Nor was there a positive outcome in response to God's idea of organization and the proper function of authority in the denomination (the "inverted pyramid"). This meant that the third and fourth generations would reap the disastrous consequences of the first generation's iniquity!

The third generation in Adventism was the period from 1924 to 1964. Many tumultuous events took place during this period—enough to write an entire book. In fact, many books *have* been written on various aspects of the damages done by the devourer in this period. The church experienced great upset in the 1950s, and we will get there soon enough. Yet, first we would like to return to the 1888 theme and then consider some aspects of Seventh-day Adventist history from the 1930s that have significant bearing on the third generation degradation of the third angel's movement.

Roots of the "Acceptance Myth" in the Late 1920s

The "acceptance myth" came to be widely held in mainstream Adventism. The myth is that the church finally accepted the 1888 message and is teaching it as the true gospel today. This myth is "joined-at-the-hip" with the notion that a newly re-emphasized historical Protestant-Reformation justification-by-faith, thrown in and shaken together with the Sabbath and state of the dead doctrines, was then and is now the "third angel's message in verity." At the same time, the core of Adventism according to the cleansing of the sanctuary message (Dan. 8:14) in all its bearings is marginalized or negated. In the next generation, this marginalization and negation would harden as the doctrinal shift, resulting from the acceptance myth, would become known, ironically, as Adventist "Reformationism." I say "ironically" because the true "reform" in Adventism would be denigrated as heresy when Desmond Ford later taught that the "historic Adventist" view of 1888 should be considered the Omega of apostasy. (See his paper, "The Doctrinal Decline of Dr. E. J. Waggoner: Its Relationship to the Omega Apostasy.") Ron Duffield has pointed out that this concept has been "echoed by others, though not as explicitly" ("Two Rivers of Thought Flowing out of 1888," part 3, slide 66 note). These events tell how evil comes to be called good and good, evil (Isa. 5:20).

Through the mid–20th century especially, numerous books were written on the theme of a supposed great 1888 victory for truth. That historic message that was to be the remedy for Laodiceanism was reworked into something else, something which is, in actual fact, warmed-over

Laodiceanism, served up to make the modern worshipper comfortable with failing to overcome sin and comfortable "playing church." This bland tea was formulated to ensure that all who drink it will studiously avoid the implication that the true history of the church is a story of the rejection of Christ in the Holy Spirit and that the responsibility for the delay of the return of Christ falls upon His own people and particularly upon the leadership. Charges that a heaven-sent message was spurned can now be laughed off, and the crazies who insist upon it can be waved away as a nuisance to the cause.

> The acceptance myth insists, after even a century of delay, that we are "rich and increased with goods" in this matter of accepting and understanding righteousness by faith. Our Lord says that we are "poor." The conflict in view is serious, for the spiritual condition of the world church is affected, as well as His honor.…
>
> Part of the problem is a persistent confusion of thought that appears almost to be willful. As a people we *do accept* the popular Protestant "doctrine" of righteousness by faith just as Protestants profess to believe it. Therefore our apologists insist that this "doctrine" was not rejected in 1888 or thereafter. But this is not the full truth of our history. Our brethren "in a great degree" *did reject* the message which was the beginning of the latter rain and the loud cry. This obvious fact explains the long delay, and nothing else can explain it.
>
> What is the source of this persistent and widespread confusion and misconception? … (*1888 Re-Examined*, p. 198)

To this question we now turn, not in any exhaustive study, but to outline some of the basic events in our story.

A significant source of the acceptance myth, according to Wieland and Short, is found in statements of Ellen White's grandson Arthur L. White, the author of her biography: "The concept that the General Conference, and thus the denomination, rejected the message of righteousness by faith in 1888 is without foundation and was not projected until forty years after … Minneapolis" (*The Lonely Years 1876–1891*, p. 396). It is also in statements of her son W. C. White. The Ellen G. White Estate has been a solid proponent of the acceptance myth, certainly not through the testimony of the documents in its vaults, but through uninspired men who have been in charge of those documents.

> Both Ellen White's son and grandson have rightly enjoyed great esteem in the Seventh-day Adventist Church. They have been utterly sincere in their efforts to educate several generations of our people to believe that the 1888 message was not rejected. We accord to both of them the utmost respect which their unique place in our history warrants. At the same time, we must recognize that Ellen White exercised a still more unique ministry, that of an inspired messenger of the Lord whose ministry is an expression of the testimony of Jesus, the Spirit of Prophecy. Her prophetic gift endowed her with discernment that penetrated beneath the surface. **Even if a thousand eyewitnesses with uninspired judgment contradict the word of an inspired prophet, we must trust that inspired word, for a "thus saith the Lord" is implicit in it.** Ellen White's testimony is so clear and straight-forward that the common man can readily understand it.… (*1888 Re-Examined*, p. 199, emphasis added)

Now, while the principles expressed by Wieland and Short, above, are absolutely correct, it is necessary to understand the context and not go too far in implicating W. C. White for, as we shall see shortly, it was his son, A. L. White, who was involved in attributing to his father a hard stance against the claim of leadership rejection of the 1888 message, even in some way being involved in the confusion regarding the authorship of a certain letter from D. E. Robinson to Taylor G. Bunch (Dec. 30, 1930, DF [Document File] 371). Robinson was a staff member for Ellen White and the Ellen G. White Estate for various periods from 1898 until 1953. The letter came to be mistakenly assigned the authorship of W. C. White and used as a supporting document in historical works by Adventist leaders, including and especially A. L. White. At the time that Wieland wrote about the rejection myth, he would have believed that W. C. White was the author of the letter in question. Thus, he was citing a misattribution of the Robinson to Bunch letter. We will unpack this story as we go forward.

Taylor G. Bunch was a pastor, Bible teacher, and author. Forty years after 1888, Bunch read A. G. Daniells' *Christ our Righteousness* (1926), did his own study of the subject, and produced a pamphlet entitled, *Forty Years in the Wilderness in Type and Antitype* (1928), presenting the parallels between the Seventh-day Adventist Church and the children of Israel in their journey from Egypt to Canaan. The pamphlet was later the basis for the book *Exodus and*

Advent Movements in Type and Antitype (1937). The Ellen G. White Estate took issue with Bunch, denying that there was any such thing as a rejection of 1888.

Bunch was clear on what had taken place and its implications:

> Because of their unbelief manifested in the rejection of the message sent to prepare them for the heavenly Canaan, the Lord had to alter His purpose and turn the Advent people back into the wilderness of sin till they learn the lesson of faith....
>
> It is very evident that the rejection of God's special message in 1888, which resulted in the altering of His purpose to take His people directly into the promised land, marked the beginning of a spiritual retreat toward the world or Egypt....
>
> Like ancient Israel after being turned back from Kadesh-barnea, the Advent movement did not go all the way back to Egypt or the world. But they have gone a long way and there have remained in the Laodicean condition, neither going back into the world nor progressing towards the heavenly Canaan, but wandering about in the wilderness... (Taylor G. Bunch, *Forty Years in the Wilderness: In Type and Antitype*, pp. 15, 17, 18)

> Through the efforts of Satan the glorious message that began in 1888 at the Minneapolis General Conference was made of none effect. It was rejected and despised by many, and while others acknowledged it to be true they failed to take it to heart and enter into the experience of righteousness by faith. This is paramount [sic] to a rejection....
>
> To assent to the truthfulness of a message and not act upon it is equivalent to a rejection. A message that is not accepted is rejected even though it may be acknowledged as the truth. (Taylor G. Bunch, *The Exodus and Advent Movements*, p. 97)

> The message of righteousness by faith was preached with power for more than ten years during which time the Minneapolis crisis was kept before the leaders. This message brought the beginning of the latter rain.... Why did not the latter rain continue to fall? Because the message that brought it ceased to be preached. It was rejected by many and it soon died out of the experience of the Advent people and the loud cry died with it. It can begin again only when the message that brought it then is revived and accepted. (Bunch, p. 107)

> Since "we are repeating the history of that people," we too must get a vision of the past just before our pilgrim journey is ended. Just before the end, the Advent people will review their past history and see it in a new light.... We must study and understand the antitypes of the two Kadesh-Barnea experiences of ancient Israel and profit by the mistakes of our fathers especially during the 1888 crisis. We must acknowledge and confess the mistakes of our fathers and see to it that we do not repeat them and thus further delay the final triumph of the Advent Movement. The history of the past must be reviewed and studied in the light of these mistakes and their consequence in a long delay of the coming of Christ. Such a vision will explain many puzzling questions and will greatly strengthen our faith in the divine leadership of the Advent Movement. (Bunch, p. 168)

Bunch's work was having some effect. A student movement revival sprung up as the message was given during the 1930–1931 school year in the fall and spring weeks of prayer at Pacific Union College. It wasn't long before the Ellen G. White Estate was raising questions regarding his message.

D. E. Robinson, one of the staff at the White Estate, wrote to Bunch, at variance with the Bunch's comparisons of Adventism to ancient Israel. His letter to Bunch was later to become a key document in building the acceptance myth. "This began an era of seeking to free Adventism from charges" that the rejection and resistance from 1888 forward "had brought about a delay in Christ's return" (Ron Duffield, PowerPoint presentation, "Two Rivers of Thought Flowing Out of 1888," part 2, slide 20). Duffield pointed out that D. E. Robinson's response was in an environment of counterattack against what were felt to be false accusations coming out of the Seventh-day Adventist Reform Movement (SDARM), which had migrated to America from Germany. The SDARM highlighted church opposition to and rejection of the message of righteousness. They claimed that this had led to the mainstream church's downfall and its becoming part of Babylon. The originator of "The Shepherd's Rod," Victor Houteff, and others were advancing a similar idea.

> With the above in mind it will better help us understand why there seemed to be such a desire to defend the church against any accusation that all did not go well at Minneapolis.... This would set the stage for the next 20 years of depiction of Adventist history, especially in regard to 1888. (Duffield, part 2, slide 26)

This is not to suggest that the pushback was merely or solely a pendulum effect. However, we will leave analysis aside for now, except to say that it must be a hard pill for any church leader to swallow to think that one's historical peers would have actually retarded the work of God, delaying the return of Christ. It would be humiliating to give credence to a comparison of one's own leadership with that of ancient apostate Israel. It takes a complete attitude of self-distrust, humility, and repentance before God to admit that one had been on the side of the enemy of souls, even though inadvertently.

It is shocking to realize the lengths to which men will go to maintain the status quo and save face. We can expect this in worldly leadership, in politics, and in all things competitive involving the carnal *self*, but that it would occur in the church, where men are to represent the utmost in purity and truth, is truly shameful.

This letter by D. E. Robinson of the White Estate is a case in point. There were three responses to Bunch at the time, which sought to correct his presentation on the 1888 history and its results. These came by D. E. Robinson; by Robinson's father, A. T. Robinson; and by C. C. McReynolds. Through the years 1930–1950 these were the standard stock-in-trade sources for the alternate history regarding 1888. This subject was examined closely in a series of presentations by Ron Duffield in October 2014 at Andrews University. The series was entitled, "Two Rivers of Thought Flowing out of 1888." While the entire study is fascinating, the reader will have to go to Duffield for greater detail. We will be looking at only one of these responses—that of D. E. Robinson.

The D. E. Robinson letter is the most intriguing of the three, since it was later subjected to alterations, either through a chain of circumstances involving human errors or *by design*. In either case, it has been used to give more credibility to the denial of the claims that were forthcoming from the studies and teachings of Elder Bunch. Even in our own day, claims of the general rejection of the message of justification by faith in the 1888 era and the perpetuation of that rejection by the denomination without remedy ever since is still hotly disputed. As Bunch taught, we must never give precedence to the witness of any man over the express declarations of the prophet of God who received revelations straight from the One who sees all and knows all. Ellen White asserted:

> The danger has been presented to me again and again of entertaining, as a people, **false ideas of justification by faith**. I have been shown for years that Satan would work in a special manner to confuse the mind on this point. The law of God has been largely dwelt upon, and has been presented to congregations, almost as destitute of the knowledge of Jesus Christ and His relation to the law as was the offering of Cain. I have been shown that many have been kept from the faith because of the mixed, confused ideas of salvation, because the ministers have worked in a wrong manner to reach hearts The point which has been urged upon my mind for years is the imputed righteousness of Christ. (Ms. 36, 1890, in *The Ellen G. White 1888 Materials*, pp. 810, 811, emphasis added)

> Christ Our Righteousness. I am sorry that so many are doubtful in regard to justification by faith, and that some are standing in opposition to the light that God has given on this subject. (Lt. 134, 1902, in *The Ellen G. White 1888 Materials*, p. 1782)

The church claims that what it teaches today is the 1888 message, which is the good old Protestant-Reformation justification-by-faith, thereby affirming that the denomination accepted the 1888 message. However, this is only a *partial* truth. We do teach justification by faith, as claimed by the leadership of the church. Yet, the imputed righteousness of Christ alone is not the 1888 message. God's elect needed the right teaching on imputed righteousness at that time because they were coming out of the ditch of legalism. However, there is more behind the doctrine of Christ's imputed righteousness than met the eye of the Reformers, and more than has met the eye of the Laodicean church. The message of 1888 also brought the truths of His imparted righteousness.

Not to digress into the theological details, we must get back to our story.

As it occurred, *someone took editorial license with the 1930 letter*, which was written under the E. G. White Estate letterhead by D. E. Robinson. Robinson was only nine years old in 1888, so he apparently constructed his viewpoint on the basis of the recollections of—

- his father, Elder A. T. Robinson (1888 conference delegate, minister, 45 years in service, 26 years as various conference presidencies);

- Elder Cornell C. McReynolds (1888 conference delegate, minister, served as Kansas conference president and various other conference administrative positions at local and union levels);

- and W. C. White (qualifications discussed below).

The identification of his sources come from a slip of paper that was attached to the bottom of the first page of Robinson's letter to Elder Bunch. The typewritten note reads:

> Last Sabbath afternoon, by happy chance, Elder W. C. White, Elder C. McReynolds, **and my father** [A. T. Robinson] were together, and I had the privilege of hearing them give their recollections of the meeting and of what followed. From what I have read, and their story, I should reconstruct that meeting something as follows … (D. E. Robinson to Taylor G. Bunch, Dec. 30, 1930; DF 371, 1433_001.pdf, Ellen G. White Estate, Silver Spring, Maryland, emphasis added)

That letter, bearing D. E. Robinson's signature on the E. G. White Estate letterhead, written to Elder T. G. Bunch on Dec. 30, 1930, together with the attached slip, was to become part of "DF 371," at the Ellen G. White Estate. The document has been designated "D. E. Robinson's Interviews and Memoirs." There is writing in the margin with an arrow and the word "slip," indicating that this paragraph was to be inserted after the third paragraph on the first page.

At some point, this letter was *retyped* and, in the process, separated from the slip containing the added paragraph. Then, being a typewritten reproduction of the original letter (for there were no photocopiers in those days), D. E. Robinson's signature was omitted. The address above the salutation reads:

Elder T. G. Bunch
Loma Linda, Calif.

Dear Brother Bunch,—

Added above the address, in what Tim Poirier, current vice-director of the Ellen G. White Estate, identified as *A. L. White's* handwriting, are the words, "W. C. White to." Thus, the letter was mistakenly identified as "W. C. White to Elder T. G. Bunch" and filed in "DF 331," which is a data file on the topic of justification by faith. This misidentification was used when the Ellen G. White Estate compiled the collection *Manuscripts and Memories of Minneapolis 1888* (see page 333), published by Pacific Press in 1988. Tim Poirier explained how the misidentification came about:

> I was the chief compiler for *Manuscripts and Memories*, and can take the blame for unquestioningly accepting the author credit written at the top of the document, and adding it in brackets after the letter's closing where one would expect the author's name. (That is my handwriting.) The copy in DF 331 was the only version of the letter I was aware of when compiling the collection. (Tim Poirier to Kevin Straub, email Jan. 21, 2016)

There is another file containing the Robinson letter online at the White Estate Digital Research center at http://1ref.us/i2, accessed 10/14/16. This copy is called QA 16-C-1 (formerly QA-274 and also DF 465A). It does not have the cover slip and is a copy of the re-typed version. However, this copy does not have the misidentification "W. C. White to …" Yet, the signature line has in cursive handwriting the initials "D. E. R." Tim Poirier identified this handwriting as that of W. C. White.

Mudding the identification a bit further is the fact that, in the re-typed *original* (DF 331; not the cleaned up version that went into *Manuscripts and Memories*), it appears that, *before* A. L. White wrote "W. C. White to" in the address, someone else had previously written in pencil, in the same spot "A. L. White" and then erased the name, leaving a visible indention underneath the change to W. C. White. Tim Poirier could not corroborate this observation, saying: "I cannot make out that it reads 'A. L. White.' Perhaps it does." Duffield, having examined the original, tends to be more certain about this, saying:

> At that time (1990s) you could see the creasing in the paper even though the lead had been erased to a great degree. Some of this showed up on my copy, which I copied twice, one darker toner than the other, trying to get the underlying writing. But maybe it is all a moot point, my trying to indict the dead because of the years of harassment that A. L. White gave to Wieland and Short, often along with Froom taunting them that if they only had access to all the documents they would see that the message was accepted. (Ron Duffield to Kevin Straub, email Jan. 21, 2016)

In the end of all of this, we have uncertainties about the edits to this letter, yet highly troublesome aspects remain in our minds. First, whoever re-typed Robinson's letter would know who wrote it because it had his signature on it. Yet, we just don't know what happened. All we know is that it *was* re-typed, that the added paragraph was left out or lost from it in the retyping, that it was left unsigned, and that "W. C. White to" was added to the address in A. L. White's handwriting, over an erasure that looks like it could be "A. L. White." Furthermore, we know that this letter has become a primary exhibit in the campaign to produce an "alternate" history of 1888 and its aftermath for the purpose of building a case for a denial of the rejection, by the general leadership, of the 1888 message. It has served to forge what Duffield has called a "chain of inaccuracy" in mainstream works of Seventh-day Adventist history regarding 1888.

Woodrow Whidden and George Knight also make use of it in their books—Whidden's *E. J. Waggoner: From the Physician of Good News to Agent of Division* and Knight's *From 1888 to Apostasy: The Case of A. T. Jones*. It is also referred to in part in "Appendix D" of A. V. Olson's *Thirteen Crisis Years: 1888–1901* (1981), which was the retitling and republishing, by the Ellen G. White Estate, of *Through Crisis to Victory: 1888–1901* (1966), Olson having passed away in 1963. In "Appendix D" (which was written by A. L. White) of the 1981 edition, great stock is made of the author of the letter being W. C. White, whose testimony must necessarily be impeccably stellar due to a list of facts including his relation to Mrs. White in the capacity of *assistant* (it not being at all necessary to mention that she was his *mother*—we all know this already); his service to the church; and of course, his attendance as delegate at the 1888 conference. This appendix devotes two full paragraphs to "look at the credentials of this man who was so very familiar with the General Conference Session of 1888" (A. V. Olson, *1888-1901: 13 Crisis Years*, p. 331). We also find reference to this what is supposed to be W. C. White's letter in Arthur White's 1984 biography, *Ellen G. White, Volume 3, The Lonely Years 1876–1891*, p. 396, item #8, footnote.

Second, we know for a fact that D. E. Robinson wrote the letter, not W. C. White. Not only do we have the letter in DF 371, but this researcher's inquiry to the White Estate confirms it:

> On a **retyped copy** we had in our files it was left unsigned and mistakenly credited to W. C. White in our Manuscripts and Memories of Minneapolis collection. But **the letter was authored by D. E. Robinson**, who also worked in the Elmshaven office at that time. (Tim Poirier, Vice-Director, Ellen G. White Estate, Inc., email to Kevin Straub, January 19, 2016, emphasis added)

If the White Estate knows this, it begs the question, "Why have there not been efforts to correct this mistaken identification, which has ended up in so many published works of Adventist history, producing this 'chain of inaccuracy'?"

What are we to make of these facts? Is there an agenda at work? Looking at any single isolated story, it would be irrational to suggest such a thing. Yet, *multiple* stories detailing historical fabrications and inaccuracies, taken together as an objective history, and the study of how these earlier developments in resistance to the truth gathered momentum and became established history, with author following author in the retelling of fables, we obtain the evidence that a false citadel has been built upon a foundation of rubble. This paradigm of resistance then becomes institutionally entrenched dogma involving everyone from the White Estate, to the BRI, to the publishing houses, to the General Conference. It gets taught in the schools and churches so that the general membership knows none the better (because they trust the machine and they don't much read anything substantial for themselves anymore.) We can safely conclude no less than that the whole matter is systemic, institutional propaganda, an ongoing campaign to uphold the revision of history. I recognize that these are strong words. Yet, this is a serious matter.

Nevertheless, I would add a cautionary note from Ron Duffield, who advised:

> Personally I believe what you have written here is true, and certainly applies to the devil himself and how he has been behind all the twisting of our history. And yet, since none of us can read hearts or motives, and because many of the players over the past 125 years thought they were just protecting the church, or protecting the doctrines of the church, we cannot say assuredly that they all worked together on some well planned out agenda to misrepresent our history.... Adventism has spurned the Holy Spirit away, and all in the name of protecting the institution. (Ron Duffield to Kevin Straub, email Jan. 20, 2016)

The concern is that we ever bear in mind that the blame should go to the devil and our Laodicean condition, from which we must all recover. We must take the Daniel 9 approach and not make this a matter of "us vs. them." We must confess to God, as did Daniel, "We have sinned, we have rebelled against you all these years. Forgive us and our fathers...." This is true corporate repentance.

As you keep reading, you will discover a further examination of 1888 issues in the following segments.

For now, we will turn our attention to other matters concerning the third generation degradation in the General Conference of Seventh-day Adventists, the mainstream of modern spiritual Israel.

Man's Rules—
The Development of a Church Manual

In 1931, the General Conference Committee voted to publish a church manual. The first of these was published the following year.

It has been said that additional rule books and codes are needed when humans don't follow the Word of God. This is true. We develop systems of guidelines and regulations and call them the will of God, claiming God's blessing upon them. The fact is that such rule books are part of God's "permissive will," His accommodation to men when He gives us over to our own way that we have chosen while endeavoring to lead and guide by His Spirit as far as we will allow. Ultimately, if we do not repudiate our own way, it will lead us to decadence and failure, as all human devising must do. At best, the modality of the permissive will preserves God's Word "in the archives," so to speak, until such a generation comes that will return to Him and His ways.

Back in 1883, church leaders decided *not* to have a church manual. This was in keeping with the principle that "the Bible and the Bible alone, is to be our creed, the sole bond of union; all who bow to this Holy Word will be in harmony" (*Review and Herald*, Dec. 15, 1885, art. A, in *Selected Messages*, bk. 1, p. 416). The committee appointed to study the issue commented in their report:

> It is the unanimous judgment of the committee, that it would not be advisable to have a Church Manual.... If we had one, we fear many, especially those commencing to preach, would study it to obtain guidance in religious matters, rather than to seek for it in the Bible, and from the leadings of the Spirit of God, which would tend to their hindrance in genuine religious experience and in knowledge of the mind of the Spirit. (George I. Butler, president, and A. B. Oyen, secretary, "General Conference Proceedings," *Review and Herald*, Nov. 20, 1883, p. 733)

Immediately after that decision, Elder George Butler, General Conference president at that time, wrote:

> The Bible contains our creed and discipline. It thoroughly furnishes the man of God unto all good works. What it has not revealed relative to church organization and management, the duties of officers and ministers, and kindred subjects, should not be strictly defined and drawn out into minute specifications for the sake of uniformity, but rather be left to individual judgment under the guidance of the Holy Spirit. Had it been best to have a book of directions of this sort, the Spirit would doubtless have gone further and left one on record with the stamp of inspiration upon it. (George I. Butler, "No Church Manual," *Review and Herald*, Nov. 27, 1883, p. 745)

Butler continued to argue that the work meets with an array of circumstances and that it is not right to establish a formulaic approach to carry out our duties. "God requires us to study important principles which he reveals in his word," Butler said, "Minute, specific directions tend to weakness, rather than power" (Butler, p. 745). We should not require micro-managing regulations but should rely on the promise of heavenly wisdom to guide us in our course of action. In this way, we will be kept in humility, realizing our need of God for light and counsel rather than leaning on the arm of flesh.

We have seen how, in some places, the results of reliance on the church manual have turned out just as Butler predicted:

> While brethren who have favored a manual have ever contended that such a work was not to be anything like a creed or a discipline, or to have authority to settle disputed points, but was only to be considered as a book containing hints for the help of those of little experience, yet it must be evident that such a work, issued under the auspices of the General Conference, would at once carry with it much weight of authority, and would be consulted by most of our younger ministers. **It would gradually shape and mold the whole body; and those who did not follow it would be considered out of harmony with established principles of church order**.... (Butler, p. 745, emphasis added)

Today, the church manual also incorporates the 28 fundamental beliefs, another work of man that many Seventh-day Adventists believe subordinates the Word of God. In the General Conference Session of 2005, it was voted to accept a three-clause baptismal vow, which may be used instead of the longer thirteen-point vow. The second clause of the three reads:

2. Do you accept the teachings of the Bible as expressed in the Statement of Fundamental Beliefs of the Seventh-day Adventist Church and do you pledge by God's grace to live your life in harmony with these teachings? (*Seventh-day Adventist Church Manual*, 18th edition, p. 47)

This statement is clearly defining Bible teachings as that pertaining to an uninspired human code and asking those desiring to join the body of Christ to do so through submission to that code. Another problem posed here is what happens when the church adjusts the Statement of Beliefs or adds another one? Then we are obligated to accept beliefs not because we have studied and advanced, but because the church has declared a new belief.

The last of the three clauses demonstrates that we are expected to vow absolute loyalty to the denomination:

3. Do you desire to be baptized as a public expression of your belief in Jesus Christ, to be accepted into the fellowship of the Seventh-day Adventist Church, and **to support the Church and its mission as a faithful steward by your personal influence, tithes and offerings, and a life of service?** (*Seventh-day Adventist Church Manual*, p. 47, emphasis added)

It is not merely a vow of one's intent but a promise. After taking these vows, one signs a certificate that affirms commitment to the thirteen-point vow, which states in part:

9. I believe in Church organization. It is my purpose to worship God and to support the Church through my tithes and offerings and by my personal effort and influence. (*Seventh-day Adventist Church Manual*, p. 48)

Supporting the organized structural denomination through tithes, offerings and personal ministry is not only hardened into a signed statement of commitment, but it has become how we have pledged to "worship God." It is plain to see that we are to come into communion with God through "the Church." Further, as we understand the pyramidal system of church hierarchy, with its clearly defined distinction between clergy and laity, we are left to wonder what would prevent us from deeming all of this as but a subtle form of priestcraft?

The Church Manual is a fallible human document, and by no means, should any soul be required to base their faith and practice upon a single line of a human document. Our religion must be based upon the unchanging God and His revealed Word. Changes are made to the church manual every five years. As an example, the 2000 General Conference Session in Toronto saw 800 changes. Ten percent of these were substantial. Another major overhaul of the manual was made in 2010 in Atlanta, which is the revised version in use today.

Establishment of the Ivory Towers

[The] whole history of theologians in the Christian Church is a sorry one indeed. While occasionally godly theologians, such as Paul and Martin Luther, have been mightily used of God to uplift the truth, the major errors of Christendom have originated in the minds of the theologians. (Colin and Russell Standish, *Adventism Challenged*, 2000, p. 126)

In the Autumn Council of 1932, the General Conference Committee voted to establish a school of theology. It was premature and did not harden into reality until 1937, when the denomination opened a temporary location in Takoma Park, Washington, DC, and then moved into a new building in August 1938. "In April, 1942, came authorization to confer the degree of Master of Arts in religion." In 1945, there was in place a program for Bachelor of Divinity degree, and in 1959, the first Master of Theology degree was granted ("Andrews University," *Seventh-day Adventist Encyclopedia* [1985], p. 50).

Today, accreditation for theology degrees is granted by the Association of Theological Schools. One can find a listing of Seventh-day Adventist institutions that are accredited or partially accredited by this non-Seventh-day Adventist authority at the website http://1ref.us/k3, accessed July 11, 2017.

The establishment of a theological seminary is another way that the practices of the fallen churches of Protestantism have been adopted. This has led to a church environment that sees theologians as the ultimate authorities on belief, faith, truth, and practice. Furthermore, the learned "doctors" in things divine are recognized as the way to become authentically educated and trained as pastors, evangelists, and teachers. Should one be gifted in these things by the God of heaven and proceed to exercise said gift in the church without "credentials," he or she would not be recognized within the establishment church, even though the Word of God declares:

When he ascended up on high, he ... gave gifts unto men.... And he gave some, apostles; and some, prophets; and some, evangelists; and some, pastors and teachers; for the perfecting of the saints, for the work of the ministry, for the edifying of the body of Christ.... (Eph. 4:8, 11, 12)

Again, it is seen that man assumes the higher authority

It will be found, upon examination of a sampling of theological works, that there are many references to other theologians. In some instances, one can build an entire chain of references to the source of an idea leading all the way back to one originator of the thought. It just so happened that one or two others repeated the original idea, and then one or two others repeated those others again until a "school of thought" became established. The first author may have been wrong as a result of misquoting Scripture or citing an errant historical reference or simply stating his own opinion, etc. A major problem in theology is the lack of utilization of primary source material, i.e., the Bible and the Spirit of Prophecy. The opinions of men are inappropriately elevated due to the possession of an acceptable degree and pedigree. That is why we hear the expressions, "Says who?" or "Who has believed?" as if someone of adequate training in recognized institutes must originate or endorse a position to make it of any value. To claim the inspiration of the Bible or Spirit of Prophecy as evidence for a teaching is not enough because the "unlearned" cannot be trusted to understand these things aright unless the theologians should interpret or at least endorse them. At minimum, they say, the pastors, evangelists, and teachers who were trained by the theologians should interpret them for us.

As it was in the Dark Ages, so it is today—*the Bible is chained to the church wall.* In all of this, the Protestant ideal of *sola scriptura* is effectively dissolved because the Bible's interpretation is reserved for the men and women in the ivory towers of humanly approved Bible research "think-tanks" and universities. Shall our faith be placed in the human interpreter above the Word of God, which we have in our own hand and in our own language? Ellen White taught that, if we have a teaching, we must submit it to the "brethren of experience" before presenting it publicly.

> There are a thousand temptations in disguise prepared for those who have the light of truth; and the only safety for any of us is in receiving no new doctrine, no new interpretation of the Scriptures, without first submitting it to **brethren of experience**. Lay it before them in a humble, teachable spirit, with earnest prayer; and if they see no light in it, yield to their judgment; for "in the multitude of counselors there is safety." (*Testimonies for the Church*, vol. 5, pp. 291–293)

This is taken to mean the institutionally credentialed. The problem with this interpretation is that we have confused the "brethren of experience" with people possessing academic degrees. These may have little or no practical experience or spiritual maturity. Additionally, they may frequently rely upon systems of theological interpretation that stand above the inspired Word of God alone.

A church leader once admonished me in writing to "stay *above board* in the sense of making your thoughts available for comment among church leaders. The official group dealing with items of this kind would be the Biblical Research Institute and the E G White Estate of course." The sub-text here is that to not submit to the PhDs is to operate outside of righteousness in the hidden rooms down below. To reject the judgment of the learned men of officialdom as the final arbiter of truth is tantamount to spinning out of control as an "independent atom."

Making one's thoughts or studies "available for comment" is entirely appropriate. However, this has nothing to do with staying "above board." From our discussion, it was clear that the comment of the leadership was to be accepted as the final word. In recent history, I came into possession of a communication between certain individuals involved in the securing of an endorsement of the General Conference president on the publication of a certain book about the inroads being made into the church by contemplative spirituality. In that communication, it was stated that the president could not endorse a book without having it first submitted for approval to the Biblical Research Institute.

The result of this shift in reliance upon the theologians is multi-faceted. We have a situation where—

- pastors are trained into the hierarchical mindset; they are no longer trainers of members to dig deep into the Word and become soul-winners; rather, the people are trained to be loyal to the church and to look to the leaders to teach them what to believe and how to teach it;

- there is an oligarchy of the learned powerful who have earned their credentialed authority by sitting at the feet of teachers not of our faith, in the seminaries of the world and who then come back into Seventh-day Adventist institutions to indoctrinate the upcoming generation of youth with the theology of the world;

- experience in the things of God, true humility, piety, and faith in the Word of God is not held in as high esteem as advanced degrees when it comes to placement in high level administration—this is especially true in developing countries;

- committees that steer the church are not perceived as fully informed unless they have the expertise of theologians to advise them;

- the training of youth in our institutions is not focused any longer upon the proclamation of the third angel's message but on becoming a "professional"; the outcome of this is that the true work will be increasingly carried by independent and self-supporting small ministries and institutions;

- the integrity of the lesson quarterlies has become compromised in that the authority of man has been elevated while inspired content has taken a far less significant role than it once had; often non-Seventh-day Adventist authors are quoted—men and women whose own program of study has been heavily influenced by antichrist and occult minds;

- theologians are deemed to be the thinkers, the ones with the keys to proper interpretation, the *authorities*; therefore their pronouncements are truth; however, this is papal and does nothing in reality but keep the laity *from* the truth.

Is it not odd that the theologians are deemed to be the reliable arbiters of truth, yet one cannot find any two of them who would agree with each other on all points? As an example, recall the 1994 book *Who's Got the Truth?* by Martin Weber (then associate editor of *Ministry* magazine). The book examined the gospel teachings of five leading Seventh-day Adventist teachers: Graham Maxwell, George Knight, Jack Sequeira, Ralph Larson, and Morris Venden. Weber, by the way, also has his own version of the gospel. Or for apocalyptic teaching, try comparing LaRondelle, Paulien, Stefanovic, and Hasel. Select a few theologically or doctrinally-rich texts and make a chart, and see if "two walk together."

At the end of the day, we must each trust God and—

Study to show thyself approved unto God, a workman that needeth not to be ashamed, rightly dividing the word of truth. (2 Tim. 2:15)

There is no safety in following men.

Let no plans or methods be adopted in any of our institutions that will bind mind or talent under the control of human judgment; for this is not in God's order.... Satan's methods tend to one end—to make men the slaves of men. (*Testimonies to Ministers*, pp. 360, 361)

Under the showers of the latter rain, the inventions of man, the human machinery, will at times be swept away, the boundary of man's authority will be as broken reeds, and the Holy Spirit will speak through the living, human agent with convincing power.... (Lt. 102, 1894, to J. E. and Emma White, in *The General Conference Bulletin*, Feb. 15, 1895)

We are nearing the close of this earth's history.... There are men who will be taken from the plow, from the vineyard, from various other branches of work, and sent forth by the Lord to give this message to the world. (*Testimonies for the Church*, vol. 7, p. 270)

Now, theology in itself is a neutral term and it means simply the study of God. It is when it degenerates into human speculation and philosophy and "higher criticism" and the learned ones are put on a pedestal that we have a problem. It is in this context that inspiration takes a dim view of theology and theologians.

Many a portion of Scripture which learned men pronounce a mystery, or pass over as unimportant, is full of comfort and instruction to him who has been taught in the school of Christ. **One reason why many theologians have no clearer understanding of God's word is, they close their eyes to truths which they do not wish to practice.** An understanding of Bible truth depends not so much on the power of intellect brought to the search as on the singleness of purpose, the earnest longing after righteousness. (*The Great Controversy*, p. 599, emphasis added)

And **to a large degree theology, as studied and taught, is but a record of human speculation**, serving only to darken "counsel by words without knowledge." Job 38:2. Too often the motive in accumulating these many books is not so much a desire to obtain food for mind and soul, as it is an ambition to become acquainted with philosophers and theologians, a desire to present Christianity to the people in learned terms and propositions. (*Counsels to Parents, Teachers and Students*, p. 380, emphasis added)

It was not the scholarly theologians who had an understanding of this truth, and engaged in its proclamation. Had these been faithful watchmen, diligently and prayerfully searching the Scriptures, they would have known the time of night; the prophecies would have opened to them the events about to take place. But they did not occupy this position, and the message was given by humbler men. Said Jesus: "Walk while ye have the light, lest darkness come upon you." John 12:35. Those who turn away from the light which God has given, or who neglect to seek it when it is within their reach, are left in darkness. But the Saviour declares: "He that followeth Me shall not walk in darkness, but shall have the light of life." John 8:12. Whoever is with singleness of purpose seeking to do God's will, earnestly heeding the light already given, will receive greater light; to that soul some star of heavenly radiance will be sent to guide him into all truth. (*The Great Controversy*, p. 312, emphasis added)

The present generation have trusted their bodies with the doctors and their souls with the ministers. **Do they not pay the minister well for studying the Bible for them, that they need not be to the trouble? and is it not his business to tell them what they must believe, and to settle all doubtful questions of theology without special investigation on their part?** If they are sick, they send for the doctor—believe whatever he may tell, and swallow anything he may prescribe; for do they not pay him a liberal fee, and is it not his business to understand their physical ailments, and what to prescribe to make them well, without their being troubled with the matter? ... (*Counsels on Health*, pp. 37, 38)

As I see libraries filled with ponderous volumes of **historical and theological lore**, I think, Why spend money for that which is not bread?... (*The Ministry of Healing*, p. 441)

We are aware of the counsel of the Lord in which certain well-grounded, spiritually mature men were to be selected to study the theology of the world in non-Seventh-day Adventist institutions as observers so that they would be prepared to "labor for the educated classes, and to meet the prevailing errors of our time," such as was done by the historical Waldenses. These would be infiltrators in Babylon, in a sense. The ministry needed to have more "trained men" but only to "carry forward the work of reformation" and continue in their education while engaged in the work. A caveat to all of this: "They *must* have the word of God abiding in them" (*Testimonies for the Church*, vol. 5, p. 584, emphasis added).

As always, we must not pit inspired statements against each other. Rather, we should harmonize such statements according to time, place and circumstance. Balancing counsels to the "trained men" statement is that we should never "go unbidden to places where the forces of the enemy are strongly entrenched" (*Review and Herald*, April 14, 1904) and that we should be "separate from those who are daily imbibing new errors" because "God is displeased with us when we go to listen to error, without *being obliged to go*; for unless *He sends us* ... He will not keep us" (*Early Writings*, pp. 124, 125, emphasis added).

Returning to our previous discussion, while we believe that the establishment of a church manual and of a theological seminary have laid the foundation for substantial damage to the integrity of the third angel's movement as embodied in historical Adventism, neither of these have been as markedly responsible for the development of apostasy as has the entrance into secular accreditation of Adventist educational programs.

Secular Accreditation in Adventist Education

An "analytical participant in education for over 58 years" and former president of Columbia Union College, which is now Washington Adventist University, Colin Standish stated that he has "come to the firm conclusion that of all the causal factors which opened the floodgate to error into our church, the number one, far above all others, has been the secular accreditation of our schools and colleges" (Standish, *One Disastrous Decision*, p. 47, 32).

> Why would Christian educators imagine such a step—to accept as their standard of God's education the evaluation of worldly educators? How could secular educators guide us rightly in the principles of true Christian education? Did our people believe that God would be pleased by this?

> [Accreditation] … has greatly compromised the training of all our church workers. It has led to the infiltration of deadly heresy into God's chosen church. It has resulted in many professors in our educational institutions being far from the pure truths of God's Word. It has opened the flood gates to vain, time-wasting, worldly entertainment coming amongst our people. (Standish, p. 47)

Secular accreditation has caused a tremendous shift toward the secular. I went to Canadian Union College (which later became "Canadian University College"; and is now called "Burman University"). My first-hand observation and experience is therefore a primary source of support for my understanding and belief on this matter. I could list a number of courses in my program of studies that had no reference to anything of God or the Scriptures but were simply following the world's textbooks. Just one example of this would be the two required courses in Canadian history. It did not fall under the category of "sacred history" in any way. It was merely "history, as commonly studied."

There is a study of history that is not to be condemned. Sacred history was one of the studies in the schools of the prophets. In the record of His dealings with the nations were traced the footsteps of Jehovah. So today we are to consider the dealings of God with the nations of the earth. We are to see in history the fulfillment of prophecy, to study the workings of Providence in the great reformatory movements, and to understand the progress of events in the marshaling of the nations for the final conflict of the great controversy.

Such study will give broad, comprehensive views of life. It will help us to understand something of its relations and dependencies, how wonderfully we are bound together in the great brotherhood of society and nations, and to how great an extent the oppression and degradation of one member means loss to all. **But history, as commonly studied, is concerned with man's achievements, his victories in battle, his success in attaining power and greatness. God's agency in the affairs of men is lost sight of.** Few study the working out of His purpose in the rise and fall of nations. (*Ministry of Healing*, pp. 441, 442, emphasis added)

I won't examine all the courses, and, in fairness, I will say that there were a few classes based on and teachers mindful of the principles of true education, utilizing the Spirit of Prophecy. I would estimate that these classes were roughly ten percent of the whole, and most of these were taught by professors older than my parents.

The college, during those years, was involved in its own bid for accreditation. In one of my courses, it was required reading to study the writings of church historian George Knight, and one of those segments was called "The Accreditation Myth." We will come back to Knight's thoughts on this subject later.

Colin Standish, covering the erosion of Adventist education shows that—

- our institutions are far less mission minded, if at all, and more focused on training youth for worldly career paths;
- the use of secular textbooks is the norm;
- there is a significant loss of spiritual emphasis;
- teachers are chosen by degree qualification; and
- a liberal arts education neglects practical training (Standish, pp. 48–53).

Judging from my own experience, I would say that these statements are true. Before moving forward in this discussion, we should review a few of inspiration's declarations regarding education. I will ask the reader to gain by these readings an idea of how many ways accreditation standards have required the repudiation of these counsels. The quotation from *Ministry of Healing* above, regarding the "study of history that is not to be condemned," should be included in this exercise.

> As a preparation for Christian work many think it essential to acquire an extensive knowledge of historical and theological writings. They suppose that this knowledge will be an aid to them in teaching the gospel. But their laborious study of the opinions of men tends to the enfeebling of their ministry rather than to its strengthening.… (*The Ministry of Healing*, p. 441; *Counsels to Parents, Teachers, and Students*, p. 379)

The Creator of the heavens and the earth, the Source of all wisdom, is second to none. But supposedly great authors, whose works are used as textbooks for study, are received and glorified, though they have no vital connection with God. By such study man has been led into forbidden paths. **Minds have been**

wearied to death through unnecessary work in trying to obtain that which is to them as the knowledge which Adam and Eve disobeyed God in obtaining. (Ms. 22, 1895, in *Counsels to Parents, Teachers, and Students*, p. 444, emphasis added)

At a more recent conference on higher education in 1976 at Andrews University, nuclear physicist and young Earth creationist Robert Gentry, who was among Columbia Union College's science representatives, was staunchly opposed when he gave evidence for and defended the biblical creation model. It is well understood that, in our day, almost four decades since that time, there has been a mammoth problem in the science departments of some Seventh-day Adventist institutions as scientific teachings have, shall we say, *evolved*.

> Only as the higher life is brought to view, as shown in the teachings of Christ, can any learning and instruction rightly be called higher education; and only by the aid of the Holy Spirit can this education be gained. Man's study of the science of nature, unaided by the Holy Spirit, falls short of the precious things Christ desires him to learn from the things of the natural world; for he fails to be instructed in the great and important truths which concern his salvation. (*Counsels to Parents, Teachers, and Students*, p. 375)

> The Bible is not to be tested by men's ideas of science, but science is to be brought to the test of the unerring standard. (*Counsels to Parents, Teachers, and Students*, p. 425)

At that same conference that Gentry attended, one college president asserted that higher learning was not concerned with the spiritual aspect of a student's life. He argued that the student should have been converted by grade eight, or at least by the end of academy, implying that, if the student is not converted, then it is too bad, for it is too late for that now. His proposition was that the function of the college and university is to train the youth to be a success as professionals within society at large.

Here are God's thoughts on what type of advancement is blessed:

> Higher than the highest human thought can reach is God's ideal for His children. Godliness—godlikeness—is the goal to be reached. Before the student there is opened a path of continual progress. He has an object to achieve, a standard to attain, that includes everything good, and pure, and noble. He will advance as fast and as far as possible in every branch of true knowledge. But his efforts will be directed to objects as much higher than mere selfish and temporal interests as the heavens are higher than the earth. (*Education*, pp. 18, 19)

What is true education?

> True education is the inculcation of those ideas that will impress the mind and heart with the knowledge of God the Creator and Jesus Christ the Redeemer. Such an education will renew the mind and transform the character. (*Review and Herald*, Aug. 22, 1912, in *Fundamentals of Christian Education*, p. 543)

What is "higher" education?

> To gain the higher education means to become a partaker of the divine nature. It means to copy the life and character of Christ so that we shall stand on vantage ground as we fight the battles of life. It means to gain daily victories over sin. As we seek for this education, angels of God are our companions; when the enemy comes in like a flood, the Spirit of the Lord lifts up a standard for us against him. (*Counsels to Parents, Teachers, and Students*, p. 388)

> Higher education is an experimental knowledge of the plan of salvation, and this knowledge is secured by earnest and diligent study of the Scriptures. Such an education will renew the mind and transform the character, restoring the image of God in the soul. It will fortify the mind against the deceptive whisperings of the adversary, and enable us to understand the voice of God. It will teach the learner to become a co-worker with Jesus Christ, to dispel the moral darkness about him, and bring light and knowledge to men.... (*Counsels to Parents, Teachers, and Students*, p. 11)

> There should be men and women who are qualified to work in the churches and to train our young people for special lines of work, that souls may be brought to see Jesus. The schools established by us should have in view this object, and not be after the order of the denominational schools established by other churches, or after the order of worldly seminaries

and colleges. They are to be of an altogether higher order, where no phase of infidelity shall be originated, or countenanced. The students are to be educated in practical Christianity, and the Bible must be regarded as the highest, the most important textbook. (*Review and Herald*, Nov. 21, 1893, in *Fundamentals of Christian Education*, p. 231)

Mrs. White has amply revealed that the Lord's intended focus for us in educational lines is not to be upon our earthly needs and wants, nor to be on professions and occupations merely to "make a living" or even to pursue "self-actualization." Rather, it is that we would grow in grace and character, becoming equipped for the work of closing the great controversy in fulfillment of the gospel commission.

> But continue thou in the things which thou hast learned and hast been assured of, knowing of whom thou hast learned *them*; and that from a child thou hast known the holy scriptures, which are able to make thee wise unto salvation through faith which is in Christ Jesus. All scripture *is* given by inspiration of God, and *is* profitable for doctrine, for reproof, for correction, for instruction in righteousness: that the man of God may be perfect, thoroughly furnished unto all good works. (2 Tim. 3:14–17)

> Study to show thyself approved unto God, a workman that needeth not to be ashamed, rightly dividing the word of truth. But shun profane *and* vain babblings: for they will increase unto more ungodliness. (2 Tim. 2:15, 16)

Matthew recorded in chapter 6 of his Gospel those wonderful passages that we have such a hard time believing—how Jesus taught us to trust in God, to consider the lilies of the field that receive all they need from Him, and to never worry about the necessities of life but make it our primary goal to seek first the kingdom of God and then God will address all our temporal concerns.

Let us resume our history lesson on Adventist accreditation.

In 1931, the church governing body at the Autumn Council in Omaha decided to authorize junior and senior colleges to apply for accreditation. Those directing the colleges felt, at the time, that the situation with the medical training was at a critical juncture. The College of Medical Evangelists (which is now Loma Linda University) was coming to the position that it could no longer take in students from the junior and senior colleges unless the colleges were in compliance with the criteria of regionally accredited associations. College officials were urging that the time had come that the training of teachers would also require accreditation.

So the way was then opened and, over the next four years, one of the six senior colleges was partially accredited (Emmanuel Missionary College, now Andrews University), one was fully accredited (Pacific Union College), as was the junior division of Walla Walla College. Difficulties encountered along the way had led to the appointment of a commission at the Spring Council of 1935 to study the entire matter of accreditation. They were to bring a report back in the fall.

The Fall Council of the General Conference met to discuss how to proceed with accreditation. October 30, Elder W. H. Branson gave a speech on the report of the Survey Commission on Education regarding accreditation. I will cite from this report as compiled by Colin Standish in the chapter, "Decision to Seek Accreditation at the 1935 Fall Council," in his book *One Disastrous Decision*.

The commission well understood that the path our colleges were traveling was dangerous. Martin Luther himself had declared what is almost a fundamental of Protestantism: "Every institution in which men are not unceasingly occupied with the word of God must become corrupt" (D'Aubigne cited in *The Great Controversy*, p. 141). Elder Branson related the safeguards that had been recommended at the time of the Council of 1931 in order to "minimize the danger we knew would attend an effort of this sort" (Standish, *One Disastrous Decision*, p. 72).

> We know full well from observation and repeated warnings from the Spirit of Prophecy that by sending our teachers to the universities of the world for advanced degrees, we are exposing them to great danger; **as is evidenced by the number of our men who have already in this way lost their hold upon God**, and realizing that there is great danger to our system of Christian education through the molding influence of these worldly schools on our teachers ... (Standish, p. 72, emphasis added)

Branson went on to say that, in spite of their frank recognition of the dangers, they felt that the pressure to seek accreditation was so great that they had to proceed ahead. To ensure that not too many souls would be lost, they put certain safeguards in place. These consisted in taking special care that the teachers selected to go out to non-Adventist institutions for training be only those who were well grounded in the faith and that they understand the dangers of "being exposed to subtle and almost unconscious influences of infidelity." These individuals would have to "believe with all their hearts the superiority of Christian education" (Standish, p. 73). Now, some may connect this safeguard with Ellen White's suggestion about sending well-grounded individuals to worldly institutions (*Christian Education*, pp. 213, 214). Therefore, it may appear contradictory to suggest that the idea of selecting special individuals for outside training as presented in the 1931 deliberations was unrighteous. Here we must be careful. The motivations in each are not one and the same. Ellen White said that this would be done so that we could labor for the educated and to advance the reformation, *not to meet an accreditation crisis*. The former would be a cause legitimately falling under the category of "God's bidding," whereas the latter would be outside of His protection, the product of man's wisdom to deal with the fallout from man's disobedience.

As we saw in the previous report regarding the history of the medical ministry, it becomes apparent that the main pressure was with regard to the development of an accredited medical work, and it seemed to the leaders that it had come down to a decision between accreditation and shutting down medical training. The third option was not seriously considered: *abandoning allopathic medicine and establishing the medical work along the lines of true health reform.*

The backstory

If I may digress for a moment, we will return to our earlier observation that the denominational medical work today is yet another example of the slide into worldliness. Being plugged into the modern scientific medical wisdom that relies upon treatment of disease itself rather than its causes is part of the world's healthcare system. It is often the case that more harm than benefit is done by utilizing poisonous drugs and invasive techniques, which are in compliance and harmony with the protocols and wisdom of modern research institutes and associations. God's work should have nothing to do with these.

(Please note that this concern is stated with qualification: We should not advise against God's people obtaining life-saving interventions, even if pharmaceuticals or surgery are involved, when the interventions are truly emergency or life-preserving measures. What we are saying is that, if the denomination had followed the blueprint, people would have to go to the world's institutions for these treatments for these treatments are not the right arm of the third angel's message, nor were these the methods we were given to employ.)

Organizations that comprise the modern *Materia Medica*, such as the Institute of Cancer Research and the American Medical Association, "Big Pharma," and the Food and Drug Administration, have all been caught in bed with each other for money according to the cyprian ways of the world. These have served only to establish a technocratic Dark Ages, in which reform is nearly impossible because it would be accurately perceived as a threat to the existence of those who hold tightly to the reins of money and power. These are all connected to high-level political machinery and are part of the Luciferian ruling elites' bid for total control over the conscience of men. This is an important point but a subject for other books. It is readily understood that Satan is "the god of this world" who functions through the highest levels of earthly authorities (2 Cor. 4:4; Eph. 6:12).

The point is that, in various facets of its operation, modern medicine is about the ways of death, and the Adventist medical establishment has not developed along lines that would have established it in righteousness, as a part of the solution.

On its website, Adventist Health lists the cancer treatments it offers: "Radiation Oncology, Chemotherapy, Elekta Infinity Radiation Therapy, Interventional Radiology, and Clinical Trials" ("Cancer care," available at http://1ref.us/i4, accessed 12/20/16). The establishment healthcare system of the church cannot use therapies that the world's system does not allow. If Adventist healthcare and research had taken the opportunity to fight for and hold onto its independence in the early twentieth century, one can only imagine where God would have been able to take it.

For one example of the unconscionably crass and rank iron-handedness of the medical establishment, I suggest you get and watch the DVD documentary "Burzynski," the story of Dr. Stanislaw Burzynski and his antineoplaston treatment. This will be an eye-opening experience. The various factions of establishment medicine are quite willing to kill to keep the power and money within their own borders.

Coming Back to the 1935 Fall Council: "The Drift" Identified

Branson continued to give his report, stating:

> The safeguards that we tried to throw around the policy of accreditation four years ago, when we entered upon this course, have very largely broken down. Therefore, we entered upon a course that we did not plan on, and we know that things have gone further than anticipated.... For instead of a few teachers being selected carefully by college boards as was recommended, teachers who would present outstanding Christian experience, and who have been successful in their Christian work, whose fidelity to the Bible and to the Testimonies is unquestioned, we have found that a large class of very young and immature young people have been finding their way into the universities, believing that it was a highway to appointment in our institutional work. They have not waited to gain these years of Christian experience ... They have not waited to be chosen by some board that would carefully weigh the question of whether or not this or that individual should go to the university. Scores of these young people have been going from the graduating classes of our colleges into the universities ... (Standish, pp. 75, 76)

So it became a byword that the denomination was "drifting." This is a gentle word for neglect of known duty, veering from the established path of righteousness, in another word—*disobedience*.

> Your commission believes, therefore, as a denomination, that we are drifting and that it is entrusted to us at this Autumn Council of 1935 to endeavor to call a halt, to retrace our course, to drive down new stakes, and determine by the help of God that we will rectify anything that is wrong in what we undertook to do four years ago. (Standish, p. 77)

As we shall see shortly, in reality there was no halt called; the forces at play were not to be stopped by any manner of straight talk. Andrew D. Harmon, president of a non-Adventist college, understood very well that the "forces that exterminate institutions have a long drift" as they "move inexorably" toward the destruction of that which lies in their path. In this case, it is the church college. He wrote in an article in *Current History*, December 1930:

> The requirements of standardizing agencies have compelled church colleges to shift their emphasis from morality to scholarship. This has changed the whole mental pattern and modified the spirit of church colleges. They have no developed in recent years along lines that express the urge and soul of vital Christianity. they have given up their natural element of greatest strength, religion, and taken up the tax-supported institution's element of greatest weakness, standardization. (Andrew D. Harmon, quoted by Francis McLellan Wilcox, in "Christian Versus Secular Education: Which Shall We Choose?" *Review and Herald*, Oct. 24, 1935, pp. 3, 4)

The drift of which we speak is further underscored in a report Elder Branson held up in his hand during his presentation to the attendees at the Fall Council. This report came out of one of the accrediting organizations in commendation of what was taking place in one of the denominational schools, serving to highlight for us again that this "drift" was steadily underway:

> The original articles of incorporation in this particular college definitely stated that the college was organized to provide special opportunity for men and women to become acquainted with the mission field and to have education in branches and methods for the same. The school was plainly a part of the missionary program of the church. That ideal has persisted to a considerable extent and has affected the spirit of the curriculum and methods of the college, but a change in emphasis has slowly taken place, and now education as a preparation for various careers and most of all for the art of living is the dominant ideal. (Standish, p. 79)

Here is a clear commendation of the world "because of the fact that we have changed our ideals and are farther away from the idea of training men and women for the mission fields" (Standish, p. 79).

God's purpose for His people is not to liken them to the world. When Balaam came to curse Israel, but God intervened for Balaam to pronounce a blessing instead, here is what Balaam proclaimed:

> How shall I curse, whom God hath not cursed? or how shall I defy, *whom* the LORD hath not defied? For from the top of the rocks I see him, and from the hills I behold him: lo, **the people shall dwell alone,**

and shall not be reckoned among the nations. (Num. 23:8, 9, emphasis added)

In volume 6 of the *Testimonies*, the Lord confirms the drift:

> Though in many respects our institutions of learning have swung into worldly conformity, though step by step they have advanced toward the world, they are prisoners of hope. Fate has not so woven its meshes about their workings that they need to remain helpless and in uncertainty. If they will listen to His voice and follow in His ways, God will correct and enlighten them, and bring them back to their upright position of distinction from the world. (*Testimonies for the Church*, vol. 6, p. 145)

Branson lamented, "Oh, I hope it is still true that we are prisoners of hope! I hope there is a way back to God's plan … I hope God will give us the correction that we need at this time" (*Standish*, p. 81). As we look around us today, can we still claim to be "prisoners of hope" as a denomination? Ellen White counseled, "There is danger that our college will be turned away from its original design.…" God's purpose is that "the study of the Scriptures should have the first place in our system of education" (*Counsels to Parents, Teachers, and Students*, p. 86). In the same book she later told how God revealed that—

> we are in positive danger of bringing into our educational work the customs and fashions that prevail in the schools of the world. If teachers are not guarded, they will place on the necks of their students worldly yokes instead of the yoke of Christ. **The plan of the schools we shall establish in these closing years of the message is to be of an entirely different order from those we have instituted.** (*Counsels to Parents, Teachers, and Students*, p. 532, emphasis added)

Again, did the organizational leadership act upon that hope? Can we see today the results of the reform that was anticipated as taking place?

> We need now to begin over again. Reforms must be entered into with heart and soul and will. Errors may be hoary with age; but age does not make error truth, nor truth error. Altogether too long have the old customs and habits been followed. The Lord would now have every idea that is false put away from teachers and students. We are not at liberty to teach that which shall meet the world's standard or the standard of the church, simply because it is the custom to do so. The lessons which Christ taught are to be the standard. That which the Lord has spoken concerning the instruction to be given in our schools is to be strictly regarded; for if there is not in some respects an education of an altogether different character from that which has been carried on in some of our schools, we need not have gone to the expense of purchasing lands and erecting school buildings. (*Testimonies for the Church*, vol. 6, p. 142)

If the Seventh-day Adventist educational system has turned from its most grievous error, it would no longer be studying what the world studies. Can the accredited denominational institutes of higher learning say today that they have put away the standards of the world or even the standards of the church in favor of the lessons of Christ?

> There is constant danger among our people that those who engage in labor in our schools and sanitariums will entertain the idea that they must get in line with the world, study the things which the world studies, and become familiar with the things that the world becomes familiar with. This is one of the greatest mistakes that could be made. We shall make grave mistakes unless we give special attention to the searching of the word. (Lt. 84, 1909, in *Review and Herald*, Nov. 11, 1909, and *Fundamentals of Christian Education*, p. 534)

This is a very serious matter. Can we look God in the face at the judgment bar in the full knowledge that we understood these things and did nothing?

> The light has been given me that tremendous pressures will be brought upon every Seventh-day Adventist with whom the world can get into close connection. Those who seek the education that the world esteems so highly, are gradually led further and further from the principles of truth until they become educated worldlings. At what a price have they gained their education! They have parted with the Holy Spirit of God. They have chosen to accept what the world calls knowledge in the place of the truths which God has committed to men through His ministers and prophets and apostles. And there are some

who, having secured this worldly education, think that they can introduce it into our schools. But **let me tell you that you must not take what the world calls the higher education and bring it into our schools and sanitariums and churches. We need to understand these things. I speak to you definitely. This must not be done.** (Lt. 84, 1909, in *Fundamentals of Christian Education*, pp. 535, 536, emphasis added)

It is just as one new convert coming into the Seventh-day Adventist Church exclaimed as he observed the situation in the denomination, "You people don't believe your prophet!"

So, at last, Branson stated the conviction of the commission:

It has become a profound conviction with us that we are drifting and that we have departed far from the blueprint that God gave to this people in the matter of establishing and operating our schools. We therefore have been led to the conviction that it is not necessary for this denomination to accredit six senior colleges. We do not believe the pressure we seemed to be under four years ago was all actual…. (Standish, p. 83)

Thus, it was the intent of the commission to call a halt to the drift and to sound the trumpet to the youth who had already gone out to the worldly institutions to come back to the cause of God and gain experience in missionary endeavor. He acknowledged that, in their action of the previous four years, they had gone too far, authorizing "too wide a range to the plan of our institutions seeking for accreditation," and he called upon the leaders to admit the mistake and seek forgiveness and "turn our faces toward the truth and find the way out" (Standish, p. 85). Yet, did they?

In the recommendations set forth by the committee, so clear in their admission of wrong doing and in their convictions to call a halt, two of the senior colleges, "Emmanuel Missionary College and Pacific Union College" were granted authorization "to acquire and maintain accreditation." Walla Walla College was permitted to retain the accreditation already granted it at the junior level, and the four other colleges were permitted to "seek and maintain the accreditation of their junior college sections with regional accrediting associations." The committee also decided that, "if it becomes necessary for our junior colleges to seek accreditation;" "the managing boards" were to "proceed with great caution" (Standish, pp. 86, 87).

The ensuing discussion is fascinating, and you can read it in the book *One Disastrous Decision*. Several voices voiced convictions like the following: "the instruction of the Lord is definite, we have a choice before us, it is in my heart to follow the voice of God" (Watson); "we should eliminate accreditation" (Ruskjer); "I am perplexed by thinking we have saved the cause by eliminating three from accreditation … we will rue this day if we go ahead with this program" (Andreasen); "we have accredited two senior colleges, now we propose to accredit another and that all junior colleges proceed with caution; if this is wrong how can it be right to accredit another" (Rice); and "I don't see any connection between President Watson's speech and the report of the Commission. One says it is wrong and the other says 'We will do it for three schools' … I am going to say 'No'" (Votaw).

Watson further spoke of the medical college as being the primary impetus for accreditation and said that, if this was the entire matter of choice to "continue the medical college or go worldly," then as a leader in the church he would advise discontinuance of the medical work to "keep our principles of true education from being lost to us" (Standish, p. 111). He nailed it right on the head in stating:

It is silly and useless of us to go to the world with any statement that God has given us the principles of true education and then take steps that will lead us to a total ignorance of those principles in the near future. (Standish, p. 111)

The report was passed, in spite of the strong undercurrent of warning. This "was the last time that any restraint was placed upon our colleges regarding accreditation" (Standish, p. 122). The 1935 plan was a total disaster. Within just ten years, the three other senior colleges became accredited and the junior colleges followed along thereafter.

Standish remains a "prisoner of hope," believing that "to abandon accreditation of our educational system would result in the greatest 'earthquake' our church has ever experienced," and yet "it is the only option we have if we are going to bring in everlasting righteousness" (Standish, p. 123). Hopeful writers such as Standish hold tenaciously to the belief that "purification of the church" refers to the transformation of the General Conference denominated structure, even while they make observations and statements such as this. The notion of abandoning accreditation, abandoning our health care system, and more would be laughed to scorn across virtually every boardroom in the denomination. This writer will go on record as saying, "It will never happen."

> But this people hath a revolting and a rebellious heart; they are revolted and gone. (Jer. 5:23)

> Are we hoping to see the whole church revived? That time will never come. (*Review and Herald*, March 22, 1887)

George Knight Weighs In on Accreditation

Now, before leaving this topic, I wrote earlier of my college experience and the assigned reading regarding "The Accreditation Myth" in my education major program. Applying himself to his profession of many years, historian George Knight became a major shaper of Adventist thought. Like the noble Bereans who "received the word with all readiness of mind" (Acts 17:11), we must always remain vigilant and examine the findings of even the most revered of instructors to see if the things he declares are so.

Knight would have us take a dim view of Elder E. A. Sutherland's teaching that the granting of degrees originated in the papacy and that it invites state inspection. However, there is nothing amiss with Sutherland's view.

> Most of the earthly universities of Europe were founded by the pope, and degrees were conferred by his representatives and by virtue of his authority. The custom of awarding degrees spread from Italy to other European states and from Spain, France, and England to the colonies of America. Today degrees are conferred by institutions of learning in all parts of the world.... The title doctor ... was sometimes conferred as an honor by the pope or emperor, and ... after the public exercises had been completed, the chancellor congratulated the candidate and by the authority of the pope awarded the license to teach. The candidate was then invested with the marks of his office. The next sat upon the magisterial chair, a special cap was placed on his head, and he was given a gold ring. (*Encyclopedia of Education*, vol. 3 [1971], p. 26, in *The Broken Blueprint*, pp. 204, 205)

Getting us to conform to the world's standard when, in the scenario of final events the world's standard will come back into line with the papacy, plays into the designs of the beast power for operating an accrediting system with all of its degrees, diplomas, licenses and levies. When the time of crisis comes upon us, we will not be able to partake in the world's trade. The acquisition and granting of qualifications and licenses to practice the various trades and professions in the world is for the purpose of controlling commerce—buying and selling.

So here is where Knight subtly undermines Sutherland's point, when he followed his reference to Sutherland with the comment, "One will search Mrs. White's published works in vain for remarks regarding a prohibition against the granting of degrees" (Knight, pp. 38, 39).

We have shown that the counsel of the Lord on education would preclude going to the world for the accreditation required to attain degree status. We may not find statements against *degrees*, per se, but if we take a principled approach in seeking counsel regarding our institutions and personal conduct, we will find all we need to make righteous decisions. Mrs. White lamented the lack of common sense in the use of her writings. To object that she does not prohibit the granting of degrees is like saying the Bible does not prohibit the use of marijuana, so it must be acceptable.

A crisis in the medical training work developed as the American Medical Association in 1911 gave the lowest possible rating to the new College of Medical Evangelists. It was determined that the situation would require remediation through accreditation of feeder schools and colleges, and college teachers would need graduate degrees from outside schools. We spoke of this earlier as a crisis that had been fomented by the assumption that our medical work needed to be based upon the world's standards. Yet, was it necessary that health reformers submit to the world's standards? One look at governmental dietary guidelines today will tell us that the wisdom of the world is contrary to the counsel of the Lord. This is simple stuff, but somehow it gets complicated in many minds.

So, it was feared that sending teachers out for training would import error back into our institutions and "thereby provide the basis for an educational Babylon in which the faculty members would serve the true and the false together" (Knight, p. 40). Knight reported that several early Adventist educators did indeed defect after receiving graduate degrees, causing notable consternation within the leadership of the church in the 1920s and 1930s and "reinforcing the fears associated with advanced degrees and accreditation" (Knight, p. 40). Yet, their leaving is explained as the result of their being treated with suspicion by the church because the church did not want what they had to offer. That may be the case in those early years, but it is certainly not a primary issue in today's environment, when pluralism is not only tolerated but embraced.

Knight's book brings us back to the debate over accreditation by pitting the two sides against each other, along with the counsels of Ellen White that each side used to bolster its position. On the pro-accreditation side we can place "documentation from Ellen White that logically led to nothing but accreditation" going "back to 1910 when the denomination had faced the problem of the type of medical education to offer at Loma Linda" (Knight, p. 41). As we have said, this was the crux of the matter, for had we taken seriously her counsels regarding the health work, the whole issue of accreditation would have been moot. Knight expands on the matter dealt with in 1910:

> In their concern they placed the matter before Ellen White. Her reply was unequivocal. "We must," she claimed, "provide that which is essential to qualify our youth who desire to be physicians, so that they may intelligently fit themselves to be able to stand the examinations required to prove their efficiency as physicians.... *We are to supply whatever may be required*, so that these youth need not be compelled to go to medical schools conducted by men not of our faith." ... These statements, along with historical developments in professional education, left Adventists with no alternative but to seek accreditation.... (Knight, p. 41)

Knight went on to say that the youth would be protected because the door would be closed to the enemy who would be pleased that the youth "feel compelled to connect with unbelievers in order to obtain a thorough training along medical lines" (*Loma Linda Messages*, 1910, p. 485). Now, in all of this, what would happen to the teachers who, in order to gain accreditation for our schools, would have to go out and train by connecting with unbelievers? Does not the same principle apply to them? I do not find anywhere that things changed so much that we should break this principle that was established from the beginning. She only said that "we must provide that which is essential to qualify our youth who desire to be physicians, so that they may intelligently fit themselves to be able to stand the examinations essential to prove their efficiency as physicians (*Loma Linda Messages*, p. 486). However this was to be accomplished, would it involve contradicting what she wrote in 1909? This was a test to God's people.

> I am instructed to say that in our educational work there is to be no compromise in order to meet the world's standards. God's commandment-keeping people are not to unite with the world, to carry various lines of work according to worldly plans and worldly wisdom.
>
> **Our people are now being tested** as to whether they will obtain their wisdom from the greatest Teacher the world ever knew, or seek to the god of Ekron. Let us determine that we will not be tied by so much as a thread to the educational policies of those who do not discern the voice of God, and who will not hearken to His commandments ...
>
> Shall we represent before the world, that our physicians must follow the pattern of the world before they can be qualified to act as successful physicians? **This is the question that is now testing the faith of some of our brethren**. Let not any of our brethren displease the Lord by advocating in their assemblies the idea that we need to obtain from unbelievers a higher education than that specified by the Lord.
>
> The representation of the great Teacher is to be considered an all-sufficient revelation. Those in our ranks who qualify as physicians are to receive only such education as is in harmony with these divine truths. Some have advised that students should, after taking some work at Loma Linda, complete their medical education in worldly colleges. But this is not in harmony with the Lord's plan. God is our wisdom, our sanctification, and our righteousness. Facilities should be provided at Loma Linda, that the necessary instruction in medical lines may be given by instructors who fear the Lord, and who are in harmony with His plans for the ... treatment of the sick. (*Loma Linda Messages*, pp. 16, 17, emphasis added)

> We cannot submit to regulations if the sacrifice of principle is involved; for this would imperil the soul's salvation.
>
> But whenever we can comply with the law of the land without putting ourselves in a false position, we should do so. Wise laws have been framed in order to safeguard the people against the imposition of unqualified physicians. These laws we should respect, for we are ourselves by them protected from presumptuous pretenders. Should we manifest opposition to these requirements, it would tend to restrict the influence of our medical missionaries.
>
> We must carefully consider what is involved in these matters. If there are conditions to which we

could not subscribe, we should endeavor to have these matters adjusted, so that there would not be strong opposition against our physicians. The Saviour bids us be wise as serpents, and harmless as doves. (*Loma Linda Messages*, pp. 452, 453)

So, when Ellen White said that we are "to supply whatever may be required" to prepare medical students to take their qualifying exams, it would be understood that "whatever" does not mean laying any principle on the altar of sacrifice. Common sense must prevail.

Accreditation was once seen as a great threat to keeping control of our educational institutions. Knight concurred: "One of the greatest fears of Adventist leaders earlier in the century was that regional accreditation would cause Adventist colleges to lose their distinctiveness." He then counters this concern by informing us that accrediting bodies actually help us to ensure that we are maintaining our Christian standards, for we can find wording in the accreditation board statements of purpose that fit this idea. Can we take such things at face value? The reality is, we can also read papal statements upholding principles of religious liberty. When dealing with the systems of Babylon, we must realize that we are dealing with the devil who lurks "in the details."

As we honestly evaluate the entire trend of events and development of Christian education today, even as they are currently unfolding, we can see that these early fears were not unfounded. As this is being written, there is a crisis underway concerning La Sierra University. On February 22, 2013, Michael Peabody, editor of ReligiousLiberty.TV, wrote: "This author is still concerned that the proposed bylaw changes could easily make La Sierra another casualty in the march toward the secularization of academia, and there are a growing number of Seventh-day Adventists who are also extremely concerned because they also love the school and do not want to see it compromised under pressure from an accrediting agency that is overstepping its authority" ("La Sierra University Constituency Non-Meeting/Non-Vote; Legislative Round-up," available at http://1ref.us/i5, accessed 12/6/16).

In another place, Peabody says that the goal of the accrediting body, the Western Association of Schools and Colleges—

in demanding bylaw changes is transparent. There is a perception among the secular world that the education that has been offered by the church is somehow substandard because the church expresses its beliefs through its curriculum. This is not borne out by the facts or consistently high rankings of these institutions but is part of a larger agenda to secularize private parochial education in America....

In other nations, the government has, through a combination of funding and regulation, watered down parochial schools to the point where they barely reflect the spiritual vision of their founders. In the United States, the same is being accomplished by private accrediting agencies. (Michael Peabody, "Accrediting Body Threatens Spiritual Mission of La Sierra University (*UPDATED*)," available at http://1ref.us/i6, accessed 10/27/16)

These things are the results of accreditation.

Knight went on to show how some of the most confirmed non-accreditation brethren capitulated under the pressures of the times. E. A. Sutherland, author of *Living Fountains or Broken Cisterns*, who tells us how the educational system should be set up to comply with the blueprint that God gave us, asserted that the Lord did not change His mind, but that the failure of the people necessitated that He change the plans. Sending some teachers out to obtain degrees so that Madison could meet legal requirements was "simply an adjustment to meet conditions that have been brought upon us because of failure on the part of our denomination to step forward in educational reform years ago" (Knight, p. 43). Again, leaders entertained only two options—"our schools had no real choice but to seek recognition or discontinue a large part of their educational program" (Knight, p. 43).

So here again we come back to the principle of God's "permissive will," under which God permits a "plan B" scenario. This is not because of His intent, but because of human inconstancy, lack of faith, obstinacy, or hard-heartedness. The best of God's men and women can end up running a human program. Yet, so long as this continues, His return will be delayed. God is looking for a people who will pass the tests by remaining faithful to principle, at all costs—even if it looks like it will bring to naught the work of God in the earth. Faithfulness is what He needs from us.

The reality of the situation is that, because of the "occupy until He comes" mentality, allowing for suiting oneself for a comfortable life in this world, many have come to believe that accredited degrees are inescapable as we seek to send our sons and daughters into various professions that require them. The fact is, if we had stayed with the ideal, maintaining a pure vision of God's plan for the work, the work would have been completed a long time ago and we would have had no need for all the complex arrangements of obtaining qualifications in the various lines today. We would not have borne the sad results of absorbing the philosophies, theories, methods, and literature of the world into our educational bosom.

Knight said that "in those days accredited degrees were not the pragmatic necessity that they are today" (Knight, p. 44). "Pragmatic" is the word we use when the compromise of principles is necessary to get things done. To think that we have not been corrupted by these things is to neglect to compare what is with the true standard of the Bible and the Spirit of Prophecy. We are functioning today under God's permissive will, which is divine forbearance. It is an aspect of wrath from which we need to be saved. When God has a people who are in harmony with His perfect will, they will no longer be under forbearance, but will be approved of heaven, filled with the Spirit and the work will be done quickly.

Inroads to the Evangelical Counterfeit Gospel Laid in—Wieland Recounts

[In retelling the following segment of Adventist history, I will be depending largely, by permission, upon the work of Ron Duffield, author of *Return of the Latter Rain*. I will be using his PowerPoint presentation "1950 Re-Examined," derived from "Two Rivers of Thought Flowing out of 1888," which was itself a PowerPoint presentation adapted from a series of talks that he gave to a small group at Andrews University in October 2014. In the latter work, he gleaned pertinent information from two sources: a recorded telephone interview with Robert J. Wieland (Bradley Roy Williams, "Robert J. Wieland Before *1888 Re-Examined*, and Some of His Effect on Adventists," A Report Presented in Partial Fulfillment of the Requirements for the Course CHIS 574, Development of Seventh-day Adventist Theology, Andrews University, Autumn, 1978; Appendix K, "Wieland, Pre-1950," pp. 1–8, transcribed by Williams) and a term paper by Evert Frederick Potgieter (Potgieter, "Another Look at Wieland and Short," A Term Paper Presented in Partial Fulfillment of the Requirements for the Course CHIS 570, History of the Seventh-day Adventists Church, Andrews University, Spring, 1977, p. 1). Additional details in the following segment were derived from a live presentation by Elder Wieland at Southwestern Adventist University, July 2004, "The History of the 1888 Message, Parts 1 and 2," available at http://1ref.us/i7, accessed 11/1/16.

Later we will consider Robert J. Wieland and Donald K. Short's interaction with the church regarding the recounting of 1888 history and the apparent glossing over or rewriting of its true aftermath. We will detail the church's reaction as we study the manuscript that became the book *1888 Re-Examined*, a well-known document in certain Adventist circles. What has not been widely publicized is Wieland and Short's experience leading up to that time.]

As we continually discover, things do not happen in a vacuum. Dark elements are ever working to bring about Satan's designs. Later in Adventist history, particularly in the fourth generation and beyond, we will find strong spiritualistic apostasies developing in the church through a well-camouflaged embrace of Catholic mysticism, known as "spiritual formation" and "the emerging church" movements. What is so surprising to find is how early some of the seeds of this corrupt tree were planted. This goes back to the time when my parents were but children in a generation of Adventism that is now fading from the scene. It is a continual source of amazement for me to note how relatively few church members recognized these creeping philosophies slithering into the church, even though certain things were published that should have alarmed great numbers of the laity. It reveals how little that people actually pay attention to the great controversy as it rages all around them in the very church they consider to be the "remnant of God," the "ship" that is to sail through to the heavenly harbor! People are people, wherever they are—in the world and in the church; they are sleepy, complacent, counting on the faithfulness of leaders to protect their interests, caught up in the love of entertainment and the cares and strivings of temporal life, while evil puts down its roots, largely unchallenged.

Donald K. Short graduated with a Bachelor's degree from Columbia Union College in 1940. In the fall of that year, he left with his family for Africa, where he served as a missionary in Tanganyika. He later served in Kenya, where he would work with Robert Wieland who had first served in Uganda.

Wieland had been a student at Southern Junior College (now Southern Adventist University) and Washington Missionary College (now Washington Adventist University). While studying at the latter institution, he discovered Waggoner's *The Glad Tidings* and was taken by the gospel message presented there. Having known nothing of Jones and Waggoner, the 1888 message, or Ellen White's endorsement of it, Wieland copied large portions of Waggoner's book, which was then out of print. Eventually he took it to Africa, where he was called in 1944 to be Mission Director for the Uganda field in the Southern African Division. Wieland became president of the Uganda field a year and a half later. In 1947 or 1948, Wieland had to meet the challenge of a false revival called "Abalokole," which came into the African churches from the Church of England. This revival is known in history as an African fundamentalist reform movement seeking to renew the Protestant churches in Uganda, Kenya, Tanzania, Rwanda, and Burundi. This East African revival movement has its modern adherents who are referred to as the "Abalokole Abazukuffu," meaning "Awake Born Agains," carrying on their regular services from the Anglican church. The movement was in Wieland's time making its way into the Adventist churches, into which many of the converts from the church of England had come. The movement seemed to carry its participants along in a great revival of gospel joy, having great emphasis on the legal declaration of justification by faith. Wieland went along with it for a short time until he was confronted by senior pastors who were concerned about the rise of immoral conduct amongst those in the movement. After some serious study and counsel with other missionaries, Wieland discovered the concept of agape love in the cross of Christ and confronted the false revival through a presentation of the genuine message of righteousness by faith paralleled with the concept of the cleansing of the sanctuary. He says, "As I preached this to the Africans, the tide turned, the Africans united, we only lost a very small handful of believers because of the Abalokole movement" (Wieland, 1978 telephone interview, cited in Bradley Roy Williams, Appendix K "Wieland, Pre–1950," p. 6).

In 1949, Wieland and Short returned to America on furlough, where they attended the Adventist Theological Seminary on the campus of Washington Missionary College in Takoma Park, working toward their Master's degrees in theology. Wieland was very pleased to enroll in a class that was especially on the subject of righteousness by faith. The teacher of the class spoke of the 1888 General Conference and directed the students to read the literature then available on the subject by authors such as Lewis H. Christian, Arthur W. Spalding, and Norval F. Pease, along with the 1893 *General Conference Bulletin*.

Reading the 1893 *GC Bulletin* was the first dawning upon Wieland's mind that there had been a message from heaven to the church in the 1888 era. This message, he realized, was identified as the beginning of the latter rain. What he had discovered was of monumental importance. Why weren't people talking about it or writing about it?

> As I read ... the 1893 *Bulletin* ... I found clear, strong evidence that the message was not merely a re-emphasis of what Luther and Calvin had taught back in the 16th Century; it was actually the beginning of the latter rain, acceptance would have finished God's work in that generation. All this was just thrilling to me. As I read the message, itself in 1893, my heart was thrilled also and I couldn't help but sense the tremendous difference between that message and what was being taught usually at that time [in 1949]. (Wieland, 1978 telephone interview, p. 8)

What was taught at the time as standard history on the 1888 era came from Spalding's *Captains of the Host* (1949); Christian's *The Fruitage of Spiritual Gifts* (1947); and Pease's master's thesis, "Justification and righteousness by faith in the Seventh-day Adventist church before 1900" (1945)—later to become *By Faith Alone* (Pease, 1962). These all advanced the theory of an "1888 victory," describing the 1888 message as nothing more than a re-affirmation of the 16th-century Reformation gospel. Yet, these were written primarily as a defense to the charges made by Taylor Bunch in the 1930s that there had been a rejection of the message from 1888 onward as well as a response to break-away groups that identified the year 1888 as the time from which the church had become Babylon (i.e., Seventh-day Adventist Reform, Shepherd's Rod, and others). These same denominational books were promoted in the seminary classes in 1949.

A pivotal figure in this discussion is instructor George E. Vandeman, then 33 years of age.

Wieland's heart thrilled as he was personally studying, in the 1893 *GC Bulletin*, the 1888 message of righteousness by faith, which he recognized as more than just 16th-century reformationism. However, he began to sense that the class lessons were promoting evangelical concepts of righteousness by faith along with apparently spiritualistic concepts that were similar to the false Abalokole revival he had dealt with in Africa. Through his direct study of the content of the 1888 message, he could see a sharp contrast between the two gospels presented.

Wieland soon discovered that many of the materials, concepts, and even illustrations presented in the Righteousness by Faith class at the seminary were taken from non-Adventist works, such as:

- Francois Fenelon (1651–1715), a Roman Catholic archbishop, mystic, author of such books as *The Inner Man*, and an active participant in the counter-reformation in France

- Hannah Whitall Smith (1832–1911), a lay speaker in the holiness movement with Quaker and Christian Universalist roots, active in the women's suffrage movement, and author of *The Christian's Secret of a Happy Life* [1875], a very popular book in the genre of Christian mysticism
- Eli Stanley Jones (1884–1973), Methodist Christian missionary to India, theologian and prolific author of over 30 books.

At first, Wieland thought the class was just what was needed to "finish the work." However, he began to realize that something was not right. Then one evening he carefully and prayerfully reviewed all the lessons. In his words:

> I found the same thing that I found in the Abalokole teachings. The Abalokole version of righteousness by faith was the complete detour around the cross. No concept of agape, and no cross for the believer to bear. Then I found that these lessons in the seminary were exactly the same.... There was no concept of the cleansing of the sanctuary.... And I felt deeply impressed, "this is the same thing I had to meet in Uganda." (Wieland 1978 telephone interview, pp. 7, 8)

Then, in the 1950 version of the manuscript *1888 Re-Examined*, Wieland and Short point out that, although the lessons of Vandeman's class "profess to regard the Bible and the Spirit of Prophecy as the shortest distance between two points," assuring students that what was presented is the truth, they "proceed to weave Spirit of Prophecy quotations on a foundation of concept ... indebted to Fenelon," Hannah Whitall Smith, and the basic ideas of E. Stanley Jones (p. 182).

Who was E. Stanley Jones?

Eli Stanley Jones (1884–1973), whose teachings so concerned Wieland and Short as they were promoted in the Adventist seminary, was a Methodist Christian missionary and theologian. He is best known for his interreligious lectures to the educated classes of India, where he spent considerable time with Mohandas K. Gandhi and the Nehru family. He accepted Gandhi's challenge to incorporate a greater respect for the mindset and strengths of Indian culture and religion in mission work. This adaptation of Christianity to Indian mysticism was the subject of his germinal work, *The Christ of the Indian Road* (1925), which sold over a million copies. Jones was a key figure in the re-establishment of the Indian "Ashram," or forest retreat of Hindus as a Christian discipline, which became known as the "Christian Ashram." The Christian Ashram movement, however, had its beginnings under Jesuit influence in the 19th century through ecumenical efforts to meld Christian and Hindu practice.

Not only was this an interreligious bridging with a non-Christian religion, but it is very much also a Christian ecumenical thrust, with a mind to promote "complete equality, the only basis for church union" (E. Stanley Jones, *The Message of Sat Tal Ashram*, p. 3). Jones taught the Christian world that we have a call to not only share our Christian faith but to take in what they have to offer from their own faiths.

> The sharing seems to mean not merely that our Church-life, our civilization and our Christianity, which has been built up round Christ and our creedal and devotional expression of Him, should be added to and supplemented by the non-Christian faiths; but it means that Christ Himself has deficiencies, which are to be supplied by other faiths. It means that Christ is not merely to fulfil the non-Christian faiths, but is to be fulfilled, or completed, by these faiths. (Jones, p. 291)

Other teachings of E. Stanley Jones are quite recognizable as what we today call "New Age" mysticism, God-within-you self-worship—"within, for Another is there" (*The Way to Power and Poise*, p. 113). His teachings are so much blurring of the lines between Christianity and spiritualism, as much as we are told that the "track of truth lies close beside the track of error, and both tracks may seem to be one to minds which are not worked by the Holy Spirit, and which, therefore, are not quick to discern the difference between truth and error" (Lt.. 211, 1903, in *Review and Herald*, Oct. 22, 1903). One will find prayers such as "O Spirit Divine, within me—I fear nothing, not even myself, for Thou art controlling me too.... *I shall love myself in Thee this day*" (*The Way to Power and Poise*, p. 113).

Voicing concerns to D. E. Rebok, Wieland is expelled from the seminary.

Wieland spoke with Elder Vandeman about his concern for the variance between E. Stanley Jones's gospel and the 1888 message. Vandeman assured him that Jones had it right and was a model to follow in Adventist teaching on righteousness by faith. It was December 1949. Elder Wieland turned to the seminary president Denton E. Rebok about his concerns with what was being taught in the school.

I communicated with him quite frankly my concern that the so-called righteousness by faith that was being taught there in the Seminary was not what the Lord had sent to Seventh-day Adventists in the 1888 message; that this was rather a concept borrowed from the popular churches—not the real thing that the Lord wants Adventists to understand. And, of course, I was full of enthusiasm, I was only 33. I had just been caught up on the thrill of the 1888 history and had been immersing myself in the 1893 message. I saw its importance and communicated that to Elder Rebok and I am sure I was very outspoken in my declaration that what was being taught by our workers there in the Seminary was not that message. Well, his reaction was negative—very, very decidedly so. And right quickly he made up his mind that I should leave the Seminary. (Wieland interview, pp. 9, 10)

So it was that Wieland was immediately dismissed from the school. President Rebok told him that he should be spending his furlough gathering seashells at the beach rather than attending seminary. That same day, he personally drove the bewildered Elder Wieland to his apartment to get packed up, for he was not to stay there another day. Before he left the area, however, he finished his study of the 1893 *General Conference Bulletin* and typed out many of its pages on his portable typewriter.

> The more I read the more I copied and the more thrilled I was with the truth of this history, that really the 1888 message was not accepted. If it had been, we'd be in the kingdom by now. This leaped at me from the pages of this 1893 *Bulletin*....
>
> Now this was not generally known or recognized, and as I read [A. W.] Spalding and [L. H.] Christian I found that they had an entirely different view of the significance of the 1888 history. To them, the message had been accepted at least in the end, and all was pretty well. And the blessings of the message were with us. (Wieland interview, p. 11)

Not to be turned aside, Elder Wieland decided that he would go to the Ellen G. White Estate to see what he could find there on the subject of 1888. When he arrived, D. E. Robinson told him that what he was asking for was sensitive subject matter that was not open to the public. After some discussion, Wieland was allowed to look at one of the document files, which he began to copy with permission, using his typewriter.

The next day, however, he returned to find his access denied. This was indeed starting to feel like a cover-up plot to the poor man who had been kicked out of seminary and was now unable as a denominational worker to access Ellen White material! He just could not understand why what Mrs. White had called a "most precious message" was being shrouded in secrecy or why what she had said about the message was contradicted by the teachings of Spalding, Christian, and other Adventist authors.

So as Wieland departed from Takoma Park to travel back to Tennessee and then to Florida, he began contacting retired Adventist pastors who might have known Ellen White and who might have information on 1888, including Ellen White letters regarding the subject. In a short time, he accumulated a sizeable collection of unpublished Ellen G. White material regarding 1888 and its aftermath. The more that Wieland read, the more he realized that his observations from his earlier reading were correct. Something tragic had happened in Adventist history, and the Church was choosing wrongly between a message God sent long ago and an evangelical, mystical message promoted through the writings of men like E. Stanley Jones.

Vandeman recommends E. Stanley Jones in the February 1950 Ministry

Popular evangelist and seminary teacher, George E. Vandeman, whose classes Wieland objected to, earning him dismissal from the institution, wrote a review of E. Stanley Jones's 1949 work, *The Way to Power and Poise*, recommending it to every Seventh-day Adventist worker.

> This most recent volume from the pen of the noted Methodist spokesman and missionary to India promises to have an excellent sale, perhaps larger than the two previous daily reading volumes, *Abundant Living* and *The Way*. We believe that every Seventh-day Adventist worker, who comes close to human problems and deals daily with men and women, will find in this little volume a safe balance in the help given by the mental sciences and the saving provisions of fundamental Christianity. Perhaps the most helpful of these daily reading volumes written by this man was his first, written in 1936, entitled *Victorious Living*. The simplicity with which he illustrates the great truths of righteousness by faith have not been repeated in any of these other volumes.... (George E. Vandeman, "Elective Reviews—Initial January Suggestions. *The Way to Power and Poise*, E. Stanley Jones," *Ministry*, Feb. 1950, p. 8)

If the alpha of apostasy, fomented by Kellogg's *Living Temple*, was not to be read by God's people because of spiritualist ideas in it, so much more would this volume by E. Stanley Jones be identified as fit only for the fires of hell. Why would the church recommend the teachings of this man? Could this be the beginning of the Omega?

After seeing this blurb in *Ministry*, Wieland purchased Jones's book and quickly identified the spiritualistic evangelical admixture in the book as being the same thing he had confronted in the Ugandan Abalokole revival. At the same time, it was coming clear to him that the book would bring serious confusion of the true gospel of righteousness by faith, especially according to his new understanding of the message as it had come to the church in 1888. Jones and Waggoner and E. Stanley Jones were not presenting the same thing! Expressing this discovery and his dismay over it had got him in trouble at the seminary.

> For example, E. Stanley Jones confused telepathic communication with the dead with the reception of the Holy Spirit, and how he was completely opposed to any concept of our bearing the cross or [that] our own self is [to be] crucified. He taught self-love which *Great Controversy* identifies as an earmark of spiritualism.
>
> I was startled and shocked and disturbed that our Ministry magazine should have such a lack of discernment as to commend to our ministers a view of the everlasting gospel that was so much closer to what Ellen White called the Alpha of deadly heresies and doctrines of devils than actually the New Testament concepts of righteousness by faith. (Wieland interview, pp. 17, 16)

Elder Wieland wrote to Elder Vandeman in protest. The latter did not move from his position in that he believed E. Stanley Jones had the true concepts. He asked Elder Wieland if he would kindly keep quiet from now on and not write to him anymore.

Wieland does not keep quiet

Wieland recounted his frustration, "I accordingly wrote to others in the department and got no satisfaction. Finally, I wrote the General Conference president," J. L. McElhany (Wieland interview, p. 16). In due course, as would be expected, Wieland's letter was not well received, though he did receive a letter of acknowledgment from the president. Vandeman, at 33, was already a bright star in Adventism, one of the youngest members to join the Ministerial Association in 1947 as Associate Secretary in the General Conference. As such, very few were willing to question his position on E. Stanley Jones.

> [I questioned whether] Seventh-day Adventists understood and preached righteousness by faith as the Lord gave us the message in 1888, or whether we preached what the popular churches were teaching, which was tinged with spiritualism. The *Ministry* editors were completely unconcerned about it and hostile to any appeal for consideration of the issues. I could sense that the same confusion that afflicted our church in Africa was afflicting our church in North America. It was widely assumed that men like E. Stanley Jones and Billy Graham were preaching genuine righteousness by faith and, if we would just add to what they were preaching certain distinct concepts, such as the Sabbath, we would be able to produce Seventh-day Adventists. It seemed that nothing could be done about it. (Wieland interview, pp. 16, 17)

A former GC president warns of encroaching mysticism

On April 6, 1950, former General Conference president from 1922–1930, W. A. Spicer, ran an editorial article in the *Review and Herald* entitled, "The Spreading Cloud of Mysticism," in which he made reference to the spiritualism that was going around a half century earlier and being offered to Adventists as "a higher view of the third angel's message." He also noted how the Spirit of Prophecy guided us in those times while warning us that the same trouble would come around again and spoke of how historically "some of our people were inclined toward something new and different, and had listened to the books and teachings of men who were 'strangers' to the Advent message."

Spicer studiously avoided mentioning names or books but alluded to E. Stanley Jones's recently published work when he spoke of "a man of India ... a scholar versed in the learning of the East, [who] tells how Hinduism ages ago was pointing the way of peace" and goes on to speak of the "poise" of the mind that brings such peace, suggesting the repetition of an incantation to acquire this poise and peace, "I'm graceful and strong. I'm part of the Supreme Being. I'm harmonious with the Powers. Keep on repeating it" (*Review and Herald*, April 6, 1950, p. 3). Do not miss the point that this is the work that Vandeman was recommending for Seventh-day Adventist leadership to feed upon in his promotion of E. Stanley Jones.

Elder Spicer warned readers that they were at that time being confronted with ancient mysticism adapted to modern context and culture. (We have a name for it today that they were not using back then: The "New Age Movement.")

Obviously the article caught Wieland's attention. Writing to Spicer, he asked if he were referring to the *Ministry* book review and E. Stanley Jones? He also shared the experience that he had at the seminary and his concern about Vandeman's teaching and use of Jones. Spicer wrote back and confirmed that this was exactly what he was writing about and commended Wieland for discerning it as he did and for protesting to the General Conference about it. Spicer informed Wieland that "he regarded E. Stanley Jones as doing about the worst work of any modern religious agent" (Wieland interview, p. 17).

You can hear the tone of mental relief in Wieland's words at his new-found support from a church leader:

But you can imagine the impact that Spicer's letter had on me. Here I was, all alone, standing for what I believed was right against the Seminary, and the *Ministry* magazine and General Conference personnel in the positions that they took. And suddenly an ex-General Conference president takes his stand by my side, emphatically and unequivocally. This, of course, encouraged me. Maybe after all I wasn't completely crazy. Here was somebody else, a former General Conference president, who saw like I did, that two and two makes four. (Wieland interview, p. 18)

Elder Wieland then asked Elder Spicer to join him in open protest, to which the latter agreed but not until after the coming General Conference Session in San Francisco. Then he would write something for the *Review*. This, he did, in an appeal in the November 9, 1950 paper, entitled, "Stand Fast in the Faith," calling out E. Stanley Jones by name and citing from his teachings. He did not veil his intent: "The worst of it is that too much of this miscellaneous literature of unbelief is being read among our own people." He reminded readers that we as a people were introduced to this sophistry in 1903 and that our history should have prepared us to recognize it when it would come around again in the last days and that we have been "repeatedly warned … that these ideas out of the mysticism of the East would reappear."

Researcher and author Ron Duffield noted:

Much has changed in 63 years when one considers the current editorial policy at the *Review*. See: Eric Anderson, "What is a Mystic? Seeking Companionship With Christ," *Adventist Review*, Jan. 10, 2013, pp. 16–20; and, Bill Knott, "Reclaiming the Library," Editorial, *Adventist Review*, March 14, 2013, p. 6, a response written after many letters of concern were sent to the Review in regard to Anderson's article in support of mysticism and the recommending of mystical non-Adventist authors. For more information, see, Ron Duffield, "The Emerging One Project?" PowerPoint presentation number 10, slides 57 to 83, at: http://1ref.us/i8. (PowerPoint "1950 Re-Examined," slide 57 presentation note)

1950 General Conference Session, San Francisco, CA

Donald K. Short and Robert J. Wieland were to be delegates representing the East African Union Mission. Short was continuing his program of studies at the seminary while Wieland spent the months preceding the session collecting more material on the subject of 1888 and its aftermath. The two kept in touch throughout. Wieland told of the burden he felt at the time:

I read deeply into the history of the 1888 era as far as I could go and corresponded with these retired ministers who had known Sister White personally and who expressed concerns to me and convictions. I felt that time was short, World War III could come anytime. We were not ready, we were not giving the trumpet a certain sound and the 1888 message was all but completely unknown to our brethren in the General Conference, our ministers, and to the church at large. It seemed too that genuine righteousness by faith was indeed the third angel's message in verity. I had seen the effect of these concepts on the Africans. I had already had abundant evidence of their effect on the minds of our own church members here in this country, as a result of the various Sabbath sermons I was invited to give here and there [before the General Conference]. I saw that the lay members welcomed the 1888 message concepts whereas ministers seemed not to appreciate them. Genuine justification by faith is a humbling of self. It lays the glory of man in the dust, that of course is unwelcome to the carnal mind. It was abundantly obvious that righteousness by faith always involves controversy. (Wieland interview, pp. 18, 19)

The General Conference pre-session meetings commenced with high desires and expectations that this was a decisive time, that the church was to be preparing earnestly to triumph, and that this should be the most spiritual session ever held. The meetings, however, were conducted by the Ministerial Association, of which George Vandeman was a high ranking official. Would some of these E. Stanley Jones concepts be promoted at this time?

Wieland and Short agreed, as they listened carefully, that they were indeed hearing the same spiritualistic-sounding concepts in the supposed "Christ-centered preaching" of the meetings:

> In the Ministerial pre-session, there was much emphasis on so-called righteousness by faith. I attended all the meetings and listened carefully. I saw that there was no difference in the concepts presented and those being taught by Billy Graham, for example. This was not by any means the third angel's message in verity. (Wieland interview, p. 19)

In his interview, Wieland went on to reiterate how that, in the pre-sessions, the same message was carried forward, "a *kind* of righteousness by faith," as had been promulgated in the theses of the popular books by Adventist ministers Christian, Spalding, and Pease—the teaching that our 1888 message was re-hashed Protestant Reformation gospel. Further, it was as though it was the same message given by the popular evangelicals of that day.

> The general idea was that Seventh-day Adventists are merely a "me too" people echoing the same message with a few doctrinal distinctives thrown in, such as the Sabbath and the health message. Nothing whatsoever related righteousness by faith to the cleansing of the sanctuary or the final atonement that Ellen White speaks of. My heart was deeply stirred. What could I do? (Wieland interview, p. 19)

The Sabbath morning message, however, was a bright spot for Wieland. Elder L. K. Dickson made a rousing call to a fuller personal knowledge of God on the part of every worker, and all came to their feet in a prayer of re-consecration. Elder Dickson also stated that the denomination must come back to 1888 and make a right turn where they had gone wrong. Having studied Wieland, this author knows that, any time there is a glimmer of truth or acknowledgement of accurate history by leadership, the dear Elder would be overjoyed and filled with hope that everything would turn around! So Wieland was impressed. "Maybe somebody was thinking after all," he mused (Wieland interview, p. 20).

On the first day of the conference, the evening session ended with a message from outgoing president James L. McElhany, who spoke about the great dangers being faced in the church—"not from without but from changing emphasis and shifting attitudes from within ..."—dangers which are not present through enemy infiltration but our own thinking, our own "misplaced emphasis, and by our attitudes toward the fundamental ... message." Then, a day of fasting and prayer was called, which was executed the following day, Tuesday, July 11, for the power and Spirit of God in the outpouring of the promised latter rain. For the first time in history, microphones were used in a public address system and delegates came forward to share their testimony in a special devotional service. Wieland was burning to take action, with all he had been experiencing and his discoveries to date. A one minute session at the microphone would not give him time to express his concerns. He determined to do more. Back at his hotel room, he sat at his typewriter and wrote an appeal to the officers of the General Conference, telling of the results of his research and the dangers of a counterfeit coming from Babylon. He spoke of how our people are not equipped to meet the spiritualism coming in "without a clear understanding of the 1888 message, which was practically unknown" (Wieland interview, p. 20). It was a strong letter. Donald Short went over the entire letter at Robert's request, and when he was done, he said, "I will sign that letter, too." In this, he committed the rest of his life to standing shoulder to shoulder with Wieland, forming the team that is now known as "Wieland and Short," which many students of reform believe to be the "second call" messengers to the church.

That letter then had to be retyped to include more than one author! It was written on the very day of fasting and prayer, July 11, 1950, and can be found in the self-published work, *Faith on Trial: A Documentation of 40 Years of Official Dialogue*. In it, Wieland appealed: "We as a people are to seek not to the god of Ekron, but to the God of truth." He told of "great confusion in our ranks," that much of what was thought to be "Christ centered preaching" over the previous days had been "in reality merely anti-Christ centered preaching." He was straight to the point that men "such as E. Stanley Jones, Leslie Weatherhead [Methodist minister, book author, serving as president of the Methodist conference in 1953], Norman Vincent Peal, and Billy Graham are allying themselves with spiritualistic forces, robed in garments of light." He told how that projecting the most winsome of characteristics, they could yet prove to be on the side of the father of lies and that, as Seventh-day Adventists, we ought to have no part "with such a false 'Christ'." The warning was issued that we should not be expecting any crude assault of "apparent, evil, gross … Spiritualism," but that the devil will instead "charm us with specious reasonings, apparently holy." He confidently advised that it would be a simple matter to prove "that the 'Christ' of these modern men is identifiable with the god of modern Spiritualism."

Coming right down to the heart of the matter, he said that it was a sad fact that "no clear distinction whatever has been made between the Christ of Seventh-day Adventism, and this false Christ" and that this situation precluded any possibility of receiving the outpouring sought after in their exercise of fasting and praying. "The most earnest, intercessory, pleading prayers offered unwittingly to Baal will not avail Israel one drop of heaven-sent rain.…" This was strong medicine! Going on to flesh out his words in a treatise of how this modern Spiritualism, proceeding from popular evangelicals, was a species of Baal worship, making a particular point that the ancient Israelites, like their modern counterparts, made a gradual and *unconscious* slide into Baal worship. It wasn't as if they woke up one morning and said, "Today we are going to bow down to an idol god." Wieland further explained that this modern Baal worship was a highly refined Spiritualism, comprised of a "counterfeit species of righteousness by faith" and not the true revival that was to be brought by the message of the men with the heavenly credentials sent to the people in 1888.

Wieland and Short exhorted the GC Committee that they could prove conclusively that this 'Christ' being promoted amongst us, the 'Christ' of modern Babylon, is one and the same with the ancient "Adonis, or Tammuz … the false Messiah of Mithraism, *and the anti-Christ of Romanism*" [emphasis added]. He concluded by saying that there was before the denomination nothing of more urgent attention than this.

What effect would such a bombshell of a letter have? The answer is just ahead.

A lifetime defined by a moment

Little did Wieland and Short realize that Tuesday morning, July 11, 1950, the remainder of their life-long service in the Seventh-day Adventist Church would be driven, guided, influenced and defined by the letter of concern they wrote to the General Conference Committee. Yet, to their deaths, they remained faithful to the conviction that, before we can make it to the heavenly Canaan, we must revisit the truths of the 1888 history and message without equivocation and with a mind to let it accomplish its purpose as intended by heaven.

The conference went on with sermons concerning our great need for seeking the Lord with a new spirit of confession and repentance. Yet, there was no talk about taking that in the specific direction of the denominational failures that have to do with 1888. Then, on the first Sabbath of the session, the new president, W. H. Branson, preached on the theme of receiving the Holy Spirit as a "name it and claim it" proposition—that, through God's forensic declaration, we have been *given it* already. So, *believe it*, and—"voila!"—you *have it*. Elder Branson asked the "Plans Committee" to make an official resolution to get back out into the field with plans for revival meetings in the churches on the topic of receiving the Holy Spirit. The idea was that, under the blessing of the *latter rain that would result*, there would be a promising endeavor to double the membership of the church. (It is shortsighted to think that the latter rain outpouring merely doubles the membership of the church, for it is so much bigger than this. It will do nothing less than finish the great controversy!) In closing, everyone who would claim this promise of the Holy Spirit through faith was asked to stand, and it appeared as though the whole congregation stood to their feet.

Except for Elder Wieland—

People around me must have thought I must be some incorrigible heretic I guess. But I knew the idea was not Biblical and I could not for the sake of impressing people support it.… We were supposed to go out from that 1950 session and finish the work.… Without any repentance for rejecting what the Lord gave as the beginning of the latter rain [in 1888] and no understanding whatever of what that message was, this was a serious situation. For how many decades were we to go on and on like this, never making wrongs right, never really humbling our hearts to accept the message the Lord gave us as the beginning of the latter rain. And here Donald Short and I were about to be put out of the work for expressing our deep concern to the General Conference officers privately. What could we possibly do? (Wieland interview, p. 22)

The session carried on, and no response to their letter was forthcoming. They wrote another letter on July 18,

1950, expressing concern over a rumor they heard that they would not be allowed to return to their African field until the matter was cleared up. They agreed that some follow-up was required for determining whether their conclusions were valid. "This matter is very serious," they declared, "either we are terribly right, or we are terribly wrong." Then they added:

> If the latter is the case, then the fundamental errors of our convictions should be outstandingly apparent to your minds. If the former is the case we would respectfully remind you, dear elders, that to seek to stifle this matter will be a serious tragedy, not for our weak selves, but for yourselves and the church, to whom, under God, you are responsible.

Finally, on Friday, July 22, the last day of the General Conference Session, they received a letter of response from the Associate Secretary, J. I. Robison, written a couple days earlier. The conclusion of the church officers was that Wieland and Short must be having issues regarding their connection to the church and that this would need to be resolved before they could continue serving in their field. As for the charge of Baal worship coming into the church—that was unfathomable. The brethren felt, undoubtedly, that the two elders were going down the same path Satan had traveled before being cast out of heaven. The Holy Spirit was being poured out on the church, and the work was about to be finished. The brethren would not be able to meet until mid-September, and they would then try to settle what would be their future. For the present, returning as missionaries seemed to be out of the question.

So the two men and their wives made the trip back across the nation to Florida, forced into an extended furlough until the fall, while the brethren took their own message of the "latter rain" to the 1950 summer camp-meetings. It was an uneasy time as their very employment was in question. The men reviewed their correspondence and were surprised at their own boldness, even stating as much in yet another letter to the General Conference brethren. However, they held firm to their ground, and Wieland asserted that, "until the positions we have expressed are proven untenable, I cannot be ashamed or regretful that my name is subscribed to those documents" (R. J. Wieland to J. I. Robison, Aug. 3, 1950).

The September interview begets the "1888 Re-Examined" manuscript

On September 13, the conference meeting took place with a small committee. Attending were A. V. Olson, vice president, J. I. Robison, associate secretary, A. L. White, Secretary of the White Estate, an associate from the Ministerial Association (this may have been George Vandeman), and a few others. The two elders were asked to prove their charges, as enumerated in a three-page handout, "Outline of Procedure."

> During the meeting the secretary of the White Estate affirmed positively that the presentation of righteousness by faith at the 1888 General Conference "was accepted." Those who had initially opposed the message made their confessions within five years and the opposition ceased. (Robert J. Wieland and Donald K. Short, *Faith on Trial*, p. 11)

The duo recognized immediately that they could not render instant proof from recall of all that had been studied to date, so they asked for time to write it out. The next day, they made this request in writing. The time was unenthusiastically granted. The next six weeks were spent in the production of the manuscript known then as *1888 Re-Examined*, (1950), and now as *1888 Re-Examined Revised and Updated by the Original Authors. 1888–1988. The story of a century of confrontation between God and His people* (1987).

> The authors knew they must explain themselves as clearly as possible or face dismissal from the ministry. In that sense, the manuscript was written in self-defense, as a follow-up to the original letter of July 11. They voiced their convictions with documentation from Adventist history. Their manuscript in two parts delivered to the Special Committee [in early October] contained some five hundred Ellen White exhibits, and in its finished form ran to 204 pages legal size. It was outlined, written, and typed over a period of six weeks, yet contained far more than the committee had anticipated. (*Faith on Trial*, p. 9)

The first half of the original 1950 manuscript (found in a document compilation entitled *A Warning and its Reception*) dealt with the history of 1888 and the true message of righteousness by faith sent through the two messengers, A. T. Jones and E. J. Waggoner. The manuscript also dealt with (a) the many conflicting views regarding the acceptance or rejection of the message, (b) whether the message was a mere reemphasis of 16th-century Reformation doctrine or the third angel's message in the context of the cleansing of the sanctuary, (c) the treatment of the messengers and Ellen White; (d) the genuineness of the confessions made, (e) whether the loud cry and latter rain had begun, (f) the significance of the 1893 General Conference Session, and (g) why Jones and Waggoner lost their way.

The second half of the manuscript dealt with the alarms Wieland and Short had raised regarding the false Christ, the false Holy Spirit, and Baal worship coming into the church. This condition was seen as the result of not recognizing but discarding true light and of filling the void in the church with the teachings of such men as E. Stanley Jones.

1888 Re-Examined is a marvelous work and a pivotal history, which should be required reading for all who call themselves "Seventh-day Adventist," for—

> If the findings of this essay are correct that the light of the loud cry, as presented at Minneapolis in the teaching of Christ's righteousness, was rejected and spurned by us, it can be seen how inevitably there would be an infatuation with false and counterfeit light. Precisely in proportion as the true, genuine light presented at Minneapolis was undiscerned and misunderstood will the counterfeit light be undiscerned and misunderstood for its true nature. (Wieland and Short, *A Warning and its Reception*, p. 121)

After the turn of the century, Ellen White wrote:

> Unless the church, which is now being leavened with her own backsliding, shall repent and be converted, she will eat of the fruit of her own doing, until she shall abhor herself. (Ms. 32, 1903, in *Testimonies for the Church*, vol. 8, p. 250)

So it was through this complex train of events that the manuscript *1888 Re-Examined* sprang into existence. Neither Robert Wieland nor Donald Short ever dreamed as they headed to America on furlough a year before that they would be drawn into such a controversy over Adventist history and doctrine—a controversy that would define the remainder of their years of ministry and shape their personal lives. Yet, it was unmistakably through God's divine providence that they were introduced for the first time to Adventism's 1888 history in 1949, while confronted at the same time with the inroads of the evangelical counterfeit. Such a contrast helped them see more clearly the subtlety of the counterfeit and the issues at stake, and it laid the very foundation for their warnings to the General Conference. And all of this happened before the beginning of Adventist dialog with evangelicals in 1955, which led to the publication of *Seventh-day Adventists Answer Questions on Doctrine* (generally shortened to *Questions on Doctrine* or *QOD*). It was nearly too late to get this ship turned around, but not entirely. How would the General Conference Committee respond?

There was an official written response of church position and decision in 1951 and again in 1958 (the 1990s saw yet "another kick at the cat," but that will be covered in the fourth generation material). The earlier rejection was much more obscure since the issues were not yet known to the world church and the laity, so it would be the later 1958 rejection that is the most significant.

To not leave our readers in suspense, the General Conference Committee were satisfied that Wieland and Short were safe to return to Africa, although they did not want their approval to convey the idea that they in any way agreed with the pair's claims. They admonished the elders to keep the matter under a lid, saying: "However, we do feel, brethren, that the study of this problem should be confined to the committee to which it is assigned and that the manuscript should not be circulated beyond the circle of this committee" (J. I. Robison to R. J. Wieland and D. K. Short, Oct. 17, 1950, in *Faith on Trial*, p. 73). To do so would be like trying to keep a volcano from erupting! There were even early intimations of legal action for their use of unpublished Ellen White materials, which were later dropped. Such a reaction shows that they had hit upon a matter arousing significant consternation for church leadership and revealing their intent to keep the issue out of the public eye.

We will return later to the recounting of the message of the second call and its reception after we spend some time on another major ground-shifting movement that took place in the denomination in the 1950s. Throw another log on the fire; settle in for a spell. It is going to be a long cold night, and we have another story to tell.

The Tectonic 1950s: Evangelical Conferences of 1955–57 and the Birth of Evangelical Adventism

During the 1950s, a series of high-level dialogues took place between Calvinist evangelicals and Seventh-day Adventists. These were to become the basis for what has been called "the great Adventist theological potluck." The shift of doctrine that came in as a result of these "conversations" over the nature of Christ and the atonement, with all of its implications regarding Adventism's relationship to the sanctuary message and final generation theology, put the foundation in place for later doctrinal architects to further renovate the edifice of Seventh-day Adventism. Dr. Desmond Ford later contributed the materials to further construct an entire wing of Adventism into what has become known as the "new theology."

In 1950, Elders Wieland and Short had come to the church with charges that leaders of the church were promoting a false Christ and bringing in a species of Baal worship. They were insisting that there was a world of difference between the Christ of Seventh-day Adventists, as found in the Bible and in *Steps to Christ*, and the Christ being taught by the evangelical world. Little did they realize that the foundation was already being laid for great changes to come into the church. Unbeknownst to our faithful messengers, an article in the June edition of the evangelical Sunday-worshipping *Eternity* magazine was proving the absolute truth of their assertions.

Researcher Ron Duffield gives us some background in his presentation "1950 Re-Examined," slides 140–147, as follows:

> On November 28, 1949, East Pennsylvania Conference president T. E. Unruh wrote a letter to Dr. Donald Grey Barnhouse commending him for his radio sermons on righteousness by faith based on the book of Romans. At the time, Dr. Barnhouse was a popular Calvinist radio preacher, minister of the Presbyterian Church in Philadelphia, Pennsylvania, author of a number of Evangelical books, and founder and senior editor of the influential *Eternity* magazine. [See Vance Ferrell, "THE BEGINNING OF THE END: DH:101. The Martin-Barnhouse 'Evangelical Conferences' and their aftermath," available at http://1ref.us/i9, accessed 12/16/16.]
>
> Barnhouse was "astonished" that a Seventh-day Adventist minister would write to him, whom he knew denied all the essentials that his teachings sought to reflect from the Bible. He expressed a desire to talk with Unruh but warned him that he believed his views on the work and nature of Christ were absolutely Satanic and dangerous. In his response, Unruh sent Barnhouse a copy of *Steps to Christ*, seeking to affirm "the evangelical character of Adventist doctrine." [See T. E. Unruh, "The Seventh-day Adventist Evangelical Conferences of 1955–1956," *Adventist Heritage*, vol. 4, no. 2, p. 35.] Barnhouse responded with a critique of the book in a June 1950 article published in *Eternity*.

This critique slammed Ellen White as a false prophet and Seventh-day Adventism as a cult.

> Several months ago I had a letter from a man who had been listening to the broadcast of my studies in Romans.... I wrote him that I would like to talk with him and warned him that I believed his teaching to be absolutely Satanic.... My latest word from him is a letter introducing a little book, devotional in nature, which he says represents his personal philosophy of salvation and he asks me to mark portions that are unscriptural. The book is "Steps to Christ," by Ellen G. White, founder of the cult.... (Dr. Donald Grey Barnhouse, "Spiritual Discernment, or How to Read Religious Books," *Eternity*, June 1950, p. 9, available at http://1ref.us/ia, accessed 12/18/16)

Barnhouse adamantly pounded on the theme of the falsity of *Steps to Christ* as "false in all its parts" and, after citing snippets from the first chapter of the book, ended with phrases like "that simply is not true," "There isn't the remotest part of truth in that last sentence," "we can indeed see satanism in this writing." "He did nothing of the kind," etc. (Barnhouse, pp. 9, 42, 44). In one comment, he wrote:

> A great lesson in discernment can now be seen in the next paragraph.... " 'Behold, what manner of love the Father hath bestowed upon us, that we should be called the sons of God.' [1 John 3:1.] What a value this places upon man!"
>   Do you see what is wrong with that? Do you see what is hellishly wrong with that? There is some truth in the statements, but so much satanic error. The first part is true. It is like a worm on a hook from the point of view of the fish. The first bite is all worm, the second bite is all hook. That is the way the Devil works. It is true up to the point where the writer says that John called upon the *world* to behold the love of God. He did nothing of the kind. (Barnhouse, p. 44)

There is no need to quote further from his acidic article or how it led to the actual conferences. Our point here is simply to show that the messengers Wieland and Short, as they were beginning their special calling, were carrying a valid and most serious warning to leadership, and the proof was right before them even at that time of initial warning. History could have turned in another direction had they even a modicum of discernment to heed the warning and steer the church back on course according to the will of God. On this point, Duffield noted:

> Thus, Donald Barnhouse made it clear that the Evangelical Christ, which they presented as from the Bible, was not the same as the Christ found in *Steps to Christ*. This statement made in June 1950, was what Robert Wieland and Donald Short wrote in warning a few weeks later, on July 11, 1950:
>
> It can be proven conclusively that the type of Christian experience preached amongst us to-day is practically the same as that advocated by E. Stanley Jones and others; and that this species of experience is a manifest departure from the truth taught in the Bible and *Steps to Christ* (R. J. Wieland and D. K. Short to "The members of the General Conference Committee," July 11, 1950, in *Faith on Trial*, p. 43)

Is it possible that God was warning the Seventh-day Adventist Church, through Wieland and Short, not to go down the path of Evangelical dialog lest we embrace a different Christ, a different holy spirit, invite Baal worship into our Church? (Duffield, "1950 Re-Examined," slide 147)

This story of the Evangelical Conferences and subsequent publishing of the reference work *Questions on Doctrine* has been covered in a number of books, which have employed the metaphors of great meteorological and geological upheaval and of storm and earthquake. As we cover the story of the ongoing deterioration of Adventism, we agree that it is not an over-dramatization to use such terms in describing this history. In the annotated *Questions on Doctrine*, Knight correctly asserts:

> *Questions on Doctrine* did set forth one problematic change in Adventist theology; a change done in such a way that it alienated various factions of the church theologically. The publication of *Questions on Doctrine* **did more than any other single event in Adventist history to create what appear to be permanently warring factions** within the denomination. (George R. Knight, January 2003, quoted in the third page of the 2003 *Annotated Edition of Questions on Doctrine*, emphasis added)

There was upheaval in the Seventh-day Adventist world and in the evangelical world with explosive reactions taking place between 1956 and 1971 within their respective domains.

For evangelicals, their primary concern was whether or not Adventism could be accepted into evangelical fellowship. But for Adventists, their debate lay with the question of whether or not *Questions on Doctrine* properly represented Adventist beliefs. (Julius Nam, "The *Questions on Doctrine* Saga: Contours and Lessons," p. 1, presented Andrews University, Oct. 25, 2007)

Even while asserting that *Questions on Doctrine* was a rehashing of old heresies, these evangelicals were happy to agree with Andreasen [Seventh-day Adventist critic of the conferences] that the book was a deceptive ploy to present Adventism in a more presentable light. (Nam, p. 5)

As we study the unvarnished history of the devoured generations, we often pause to lament. Looking back along the pathway, we can see so many forks in the road and wonder, "What might have been?" Kenneth Wood, editor of the *Adventist Review* 1966–1982 and Chairman of the Ellen G. White Estate Board of Trustees from 1980 until his death in 2008, gives us a fitting statement to support our introductory thoughts on these conferences of the latter part of the 1950s:

> Much of the theological division of the past fifty years might have been avoided. If the church's leading theologian [M. L. Andreasen] had been invited to participate in the dialogue with the evangelicals, if the writers of *Questions on Doctrine* had understood better how strong was the Calvinist influence on the theology of the evangelicals, if quotations from Ellen White had been presented fairly in the appendix of *QOD* … but why speculate? Today we live with the results, and it is important that we learn whatever lessons may be gleaned from what happened half a century ago.…
>
> Some generation will deal honestly and courageously with the facts … (Kenneth H. Wood, cited in Herbert E. Douglass, *A Fork in the Road*, p. iii)

That generation is ours, but we should not expect this dealing with the facts to come primarily from the professional leaders and teachers or from any who might have a vested interest in the establishment religion. The cost is simply *too high* for *too many* for this to be a realistic hope.

The conferences

During the years 1955 and 1956, there occurred the ill-fated meetings of Adventist leaders Toby E. Unruh, Walter Read, Leroy Edwin Froom, and later Roy Allan Anderson with Sunday-worshipping evangelical leaders Drs. Donald Barnhouse and Walter Martin, which led to the elimination of many Seventh-day Adventist books and the eventual publication of new books—in particular, the controversial *Seventh-day Adventists Answer Questions on Doctrine*. This book, which has done so much to muddy the theological waters of Adventism, was published with no authors' names attached to it, though today it is generally understood that Froom was the principal writer.

The sixteen meetings of the Evangelical Conferences continued over eighteen months at General Conference headquarters in Washington. The whole process was conducted quietly. Even leaders of the church did not know that the meetings were taking place until it was too late.

As these conferences got underway, the key consultants that spoke for the Seventh-day Adventists were Froom and Anderson. Walter Martin would present them with a theological question, and Leroy Froom would respond with a carefully worded reply, which served not only to please Martin but also would often have the effect of compromising or confusing long-established standard Seventh-day Adventist teachings. The answers crafted by Froom would attempt to retain Adventist words and phrases that would make it difficult for members to discern the shift in doctrine that was underway.

I have at times been of the mindset to marvel at my father's generation for dropping the ball of discernment regarding the shift in theology and drift in practice that took place since those conferences. As I have learned and understood more of the history, beginning in the mid-twentieth century, I have found myself frustrated that greater numbers from that generation of laypersons, elders, pastors and teachers did not rise up to meet it. Yet, with continued study of the history I now realize that the process was so insidious, the words were so carefully woven, and the mixture of truth with half-truth so mixed up that it would have been a bewildering undertaking—even for the theologically astute. For most of us, it still is—and we have ready access to the *Ellen G. White 1888 Materials* and the writings of Jones and Waggoner.

Furthermore, as the meetings were taking place, there would have been no way for members to realize what was underway as we can confirm by a study of the history of the time. Researcher Julius Nam has stated as such: "The general membership of the Adventist church remained in the dark as to the details of the conferences and lacked a forum in which to discuss the unfolding events" (cited in Leroy Moore, *Questions on Doctrine Revisited*, p. 219). At the General Conference Session in 1958, the conferences were officially ignored.

I lament that there was not more uprising at the publishing of *Questions on Doctrine*. Even today the general membership is just not that studious. They do not recognize error because they do not read enough of the Bible and Spirit of Prophecy books to recognize truth from error! Most people just go along in their faith program as it is conducted institutionally and do not go into deep analysis, do not probe footnotes and sources, do not question critically, do not take the time to follow what is taking place in the upper echelons of the church, nor do they go wide in their reading. They tend to accept all things from denominationally authorized and credentialed sources as being on the straight and narrow. Their faith and trust in the leaders is so great that, though it is often taught to them in officialdom to "prove all things," they do not see the need to make a concerted effort to actually do so.

So it was that we entered an era of doctrinal compromise and apostasy on the human nature of Christ in the incarnation with confusing terminology on the final atonement in the heavenly sanctuary. We do not normally hear the purity of true Seventh-day Adventism taught in Sabbath School, in the lessons and church papers, or from mainstream pulpits today due to the obfuscation of our message arising largely from what happened in the middle of the 20th century—Generation Three of Adventism.

At the same time, as we experienced a deepening apostasy, we also saw the resurgence of the true messages committed to the movement and the beginnings of the restoration, although it would be taken up by another class besides the mainstream leadership of the denomination.

There are many books and articles covering this controversial subject, and I must leave readers to do their own background reading on it. It is impossible here to give it a full coverage. The Standish team alone has released a six-volume set on this subject, including material related to their attendance of the "Questions on Doctrine 50th Anniversary Conference" at Andrews University, which took place in October 2007. (Look these up at Hartland Publications.) Nonetheless, the Evangelical Conferences and their aftermath were major developments in Adventism. Therefore, it is necessary to provide a minimal substantiation of the overall claim that this story is a highly significant part of the narrative of the great decay of modern spiritual Israel.

Elder Herbert Douglass, who knew the personalities involved and was involved in these events at the very time they were taking place wrote with regard to one of the key players on the Adventist side:

> [Elder Roy Allan] Anderson and I had a father/son relationship. He ate in our home, our children were impressed. In his retirement, especially after his move to Loma Linda, he would call periodically—at least every month. With his famous voice now weak and raspy, he would invariably ask, "Herb, what is happening to our church?" I never did have the courage to suggest that most of the problems he was troubled with started with the publishing of QOD. Elder Anderson died in 1985 at the age of 90—a model preacher and wholesome friend.
>
> But the facts are that our Adventist trio, untrained as theologians, was no match for Martin and Barnhouse, specialists in Calvinistic-Evangelicalism. What made the situation in 1955 even thornier was the deliberate decision to ignore M. L. Andreasen, the senior Adventist theologian for decades. Andreasen had been head of the Systematic Theology department of the Adventist Seminary for years, retiring in 1949. He had written numerous articles and at least 13 books, some of which have never been surpassed. Well-known as an authority on the sanctuary doctrine, he was the author of the section on the book of Hebrews in the Seventh-day Adventist Commentary. (*A Fork in the Road*, p. 27)

A Bird's-Eye View of the History of the Evangelical Conferences

Walter Martin, director of the cult and apologetics department for Zondervan Publishing Company and top authority in America on Christian religious cults, wrote a book entitled *Rise of the Cults* (1955) in which Seventh-day Adventists earned an unfavorable place in his expert analysis. (It would have been far better for the church if we had left things just like they were and trusted God to defend us.) He was later researching for the book, *The Kingdom of the Cults* (1965) and had also been commissioned to write on Adventism for *Eternity* magazine. Believing he should actually dialogue with some Adventist leaders, he turned for advice to Dr. Donald Barnhouse who was the editor of *Eternity* magazine. Barnhouse had been in recent contact with Pastor T. E. Unruh, who, having written a letter of appreciation to Barnhouse regarding a 1949 radio presentation series, would later become one of the Seventh-day Adventist participants in the conferences.

So the meetings were arranged, and Martin came in fully prepared with probing questions to which he expected unequivocal answers. The result of the initial round of exchanges was cause for elation—Adventists had, at long last, been pronounced Christians. Yet, Martin wanted to know why Seventh-day Adventist produced books and materials containing what he considered shocking heresy. The Adventist leaders, admitting their horror, would reply that "correction had begun" (T. E. Unruh cited in Dave Fiedler, *Hindsight*, p. 236). This was the beginning of the dropping of titles from publication and the revision of other books, particularly on issues regarding the nature of Christ and the atonement. A very well known example of this is the 1946 reprinting of *Bible Readings for the Home Circle*. The section entitled "A Sinless life" has been revised.

> No longer did this volume reflect the consistent position held by the denomination over the last ninety-four years. It stood as the bellwether of things to come in muting the heretofore unanimous position of the Adventist Church that Christ had accepted, not the sinless nature of man at his creation, but rather the nature of sinful men whom He sought to save. (Fiedler, *Hindsight*, p. 237)

Furthermore, there was the crowning highlight of the conferences—the publication of the controversial *Questions on Doctrine* (1957). It should be qualified, however, that this volume, for the most part, served well to convey many of the beliefs of Seventh-day Adventists.

> But it did contain serious aberrations of Adventist truth. Perhaps the most noticeable changes concerned the presentation of the Adventist understanding of the nature of Christ and the consequent view on Righteousness by Faith. Further, many believed that the Adventist views of the mark of the beast, Babylon, the Sanctuary, and the Spirit of Prophecy were seriously muted. (Russell and Colin Standish, *Adventism Challenged*, 2000, p. 18)

We will return to the story of the publishing of this book, but let us first have a look at the position that "the Adventist trio"—Froom, Read, and Anderson—had gotten themselves into.

> ... they had the burden of explaining to the Adventist Church why certain books and doctrinal points of the past were to be purged, hoping that church members would understand that their answers to Martin were expressed in ways that Evangelicals could understand.
>
> At that point began the attempt to merge two theological tectonic plates. [Calvinism and Arminianism.] Froom, Read, and Anderson convinced Martin and Barnhouse that the troublesome issues such as the human nature of Christ and the larger view of the atonement were, as Barnhouse wrote, the products of "the lunatic fringe as there are similar wild-eyed irresponsibles in every field of fundamental Christianity." (*A Fork in the Road*, p. 18)

Now, it must be understood that Barnhouse was quoting Froom when he wrote this statement. These were fightin' words to M. L. Andreasen, a leading theologian and authority on these very issues. To find himself thus indirectly leveled with the charge of being a "lunatic" and "irresponsible" was the height of aspersion. It was scandalous! Yet, this indictment would not have only applied to Andreasen. This was the standard position of Adventist leaders down through the generations. A list of distinctive names too long to incorporate here could be given, including personages such as Waggoner and Jones, Francis Nichol, W. H. Branson, Raymond Cottrell, S. N. Haskell, W. W. Prescott., A. G. Daniells, and Ellen G. White.

This led to a bitter and drawn out battle between M. L. Andreasen and the leadership of the church, which resulted in Andreasen's publishing of *Letters to the Churches* and later being stripped of his credentials and, for a time, even his pension. His credentials were not restored until after he had passed away.

When *Questions on Doctrine* was published, Andreasen's "suspicion that the General Conference leaders were emphasizing the place of the cross at the expense of the investigative judgment and its final generation implications was confirmed" (Nam, "*The Questions on Doctrine* Saga," p. 3).

Andreasen believed that this was "more than apostasy." He said, "This is giving up Adventism" (Andreasen, *Letters to the Churches*, p. 64). He referred to what Mrs. White had said with regard to the "alpha of apostasy" when Kellogg was advancing pantheistic ideas: "Do you wonder that when I see the beginning of a work that would remove some of the pillars of our faith, I have something to say? I must obey the command, 'Meet it.'" (Ellen White, *Series B*, no. 2, p. 58, cited in Andreasen, p. 65). "All this", said Andreasen, "was written to meet the apostasy in the alpha period. We are now in the omega period which Sister White said would come, and which would be of a 'startling nature'" (Andreasen, p. 65).

The Main Issues of Doctrinal Concern

There are two main areas of doctrine that are generally associated with the conflict that arose out of the Evangelical Conferences and the publishing of *Questions on Doctrine*. Prior to the conferences, classic Adventism taught:

1. that the atonement of Christ was not completed upon the cross and

2. that He partook of man's fallen nature at incarnation.

The church sought to reassure Seventh-day Adventists that everything was on target and that, in framing answers to the evangelicals, "great care was exercised to do so within our denominationally accepted 'Statement of Beliefs.'" They said that the "answers ... are not in any sense a modification or alteration of what Seventh-day Adventists proclaim to the world as their belief" (R. R. Figuhr, "A Non-Adventist Examines Our Beliefs—The Background of Articles Appearing in Eternity Magazine," *Review and Herald*, Dec. 13, 1956, p. 3).

Yet, this is not entirely true. There were, at best, changes in position for one issue and a change of emphasis and clouding of position for the other. The vast weight of evidence confirms it. Both sides in the conferences were aware of it. For Martin, it was important that the evangelicals should believe that Seventh-day Adventists *were* changing their position; for Anderson, it was important that Seventh-day Adventists should believe that their beliefs were *not* being changed. This got a bit thorny.

Barnhouse had published in the evangelical *Eternity* magazine—

> The position **of the Adventists seems to some of us in certain cases to be a new position**; to them it may be merely the position of the majority group of sane leadership which is determined to put the brakes on any members who seek to hold views divergent from

that of the responsible leadership of the denomination. ("Are Seventh-day Adventists Christians? A New Look at Seventh-day Adventism," *Eternity*, Sept. 1956, p. 7, emphasis added)

Evangelical E. Schuyler English also wrote that he had once believed Adventists to be a heretical non-Christian religion but that his view had changed:

> Investigation that has lasted throughout nearly a year has convinced us that we were mistaken, that **SDA-ism has been undergoing a change** through the past decade, and that there are many brethren in Christ who are within the fold of Adventism. ("Seventh-day Adventism," *Our Hope*, November 1956, p. 271, emphasis added)

Anderson felt he should explain to Martin why, in a December 13 article to be published in the *Review and Herald*, it would be told the readers that there were no changes in doctrine being made in our representations to the evangelicals. He said that it had to be stated as such because there was "a man or two here and there that is inclined to feel that what we are doing is something that will seriously change our position, etc." In this letter to Martin on December 11, 1956, he also stated: "It will serve the best interests of all concerned if we help our own people to know that there is no serious movement to change our belief, but rather to clarify it" (TL, ADF 3773.06c, Ellen G. White Estate, Loma Linda Branch, LLU).

Fifty years later, Ralph Larson would look back on all this and report:

> The "group" at our world headquarters had a very difficult assignment. **They had to produce a double deception, for two different audiences.** They had to prove to the Calvinists that we had changed our doctrines, and at the same time prove to the Adventists that we had not changed our doctrines. ("The Scandal of a Book, Part 4: The Incredible Realities, Part 2," *Our Firm Foundation*, May 2004, p. 15, emphasis added)

Another Adventist researcher, in his doctoral work, wrote:

> In essence, it appears that Adventist leaders such as Anderson were engaged in a double entendre involving the word "clarify." They **assured** fellow **Adventists** that the church was merely **clarifying—i.e., making clear—the traditional** teachings of Adventism. Then, to Barnhouse and **Martin, they asserted that they were in the process of clarifying—i.e., clearing away unorthodox elements** from—Adventist teachings. This shows what an awkward position the Adventist leaders placed themselves in. (Juhyeok [Julius] Nam, "Reactions to the Seventh-day Adventist Evangelical Conferences and *Questions on Doctrine*, 1955–1971," p. 365, emphasis is Nam's)

Issues regarding the atonement

Walter Martin posed the question: "Seventh-day Adventists have frequently been charged with teaching that the atonement was not completed on the cross. Is the charge true?" This is question number 29 in *Questions on Doctrine*. Douglass observed:

> How should the Adventist trio have answered this question? For clarity's sake, they should have replied, "Yes." And then proceeded to explain the larger view of the atonement that a Calvinist would never have thought of. Of course, our Lord's *sacrificial* atonement was completed on the cross, but there is more to be said. The Bible and Ellen White, expanding on the biblical understanding, should have robustly been used to show that the Cross and the heavenly sanctuary are two phases of the Atonement and that the cleansing of the planet from the instigator and consequences of sin completed the Atonement. (*A Fork in the Road*, pp. 62, 63)

Anderson and Froom led Martin to believe that we have always believed that the atonement was completely finished when Christ died on the cross. What we meant by that and what they understood would be two different things.

It is generally believed in the literature discussing the conferences and the publication of *Questions on Doctrine* that great damage was done to the doctrine of the atonement, but a careful examination will find that this claim is somewhat overplayed. This would likely be due to a heavy reliance upon Andreasen, who had valid concerns but overreacted and overstated on other points. It can be seen in the book that language and selective quotations are used to fulfill an agenda. The priestly role is downgraded to a less doctrinally unique "application of the benefits" of that atonement. In the evangelical mind, this feeds into the belief that all that is needful of the believer is to accept the cross. It leads to a disregard for the law of God.

Here is how *Questions on Doctrine* often presents the matter:

> Most decidedly the all-sufficient atoning sacrifice of Jesus our Lord was offered **and completed** on the cross of Calvary. This was done for all mankind ... (*Questions on Doctrine*, p. 350, emphasis added)

Expositor Vance Ferrell wrote:

> **Originally, the word was "atonement." But editors changed it to "atoning sacrifice." Nowhere in QD will you find the word, "atonement," applied to anything done after the cross.** (The phrase, "day of atonement," is mentioned a couple times; but it is repeatedly stated to mean judgment, not atonement.) (*Our Evangelical Earthquake*, p. 192)

One will find in *Questions on Doctrine* a constant downplaying of the priestly phase of the atonement, shifting the wording into an "application of the benefits of the atonement" in such a way as to please the evangelical mind, leaving one hard pressed to find clarity or any emphasis at all upon the overall theme of Christ in the Most Holy Place performing a work there with regard to the cleansing of the final generation remnant to stand in the time after the close of probation with no more mediation for sin. *This subject, the book studiously avoids, for this would not have gotten past Martin or Barnhouse.*

> We believe that the **atonement** provides an all-sufficient, perfect, substitutionary sacrifice for sin, which completely satisfies the justice of God and **fulfills every requirement [for salvation]** ... (*Questions on Doctrine*, pp. 352, 353, emphasis added)

When, therefore, one hears an Adventist say, or reads in Adventist literature—even in the writings of Ellen G. White—that Christ is making atonement now, it should be understood that we mean simply that Christ is now making application of the benefits of the sacrificial atonement He made on the cross ... (*Questions on Doctrine*, pp. 354, 355)

> This sacrifice [on Calvary] was completely efficacious. **It provided complete atonement for all mankind** ... (*Questions on Doctrine*, p. 357, emphasis added)

> Jesus our surety entered the "holy places," and appeared in the presence of God for us. **But it was not with the hope of obtaining something for us at that time, or at some future time. No! He had already obtained it for us on the cross.**... (*Questions on Doctrine*, p. 381, emphasis added)

Clearly, in the typical system it is not taught that the sacrificial atonement was complete and the priestly ministry in the sanctuary was an application of the benefits. In the yearly service, the work inside was called atonement.

> Then shall he kill the goat of the sin offering, that *is* for the people, and bring his blood within the veil, and do with that blood as he did with the blood of the bullock, and sprinkle it upon the mercy seat, and before the mercy seat: and he shall make an atonement for the holy *place*, because of the uncleanness of the children of Israel, and because of their transgressions in all their sins: and so shall he do for the tabernacle of the congregation, that remaineth among them in the midst of their uncleanness. And the bullock *for* the sin offering, and the goat *for* the sin offering, whose blood was brought in to make atonement in the holy *place*, shall *one* carry forth without the camp ... (Lev. 16:15, 16, 27)

Atonement was also made during the daily service.

> And he shall do with the bullock as he did with the bullock for a sin offering, so shall he do with this: and the priest shall make an atonement for them, and it shall be forgiven them.... And he shall burn all his fat upon the altar, as the fat of the sacrifice of peace offerings: and the priest shall make an atonement for him as concerning his sin, and it shall be forgiven him.... And he shall take away all the fat thereof, as the fat is taken away from off the sacrifice of peace offerings; and the priest shall burn *it* upon the altar for a sweet savour unto the LORD; and the priest shall make an atonement for him, and it shall be forgiven him.... And he shall take away all the fat thereof, as the fat of the lamb is taken away from the sacrifice of the peace offerings; and the priest shall burn them upon the altar, according to the offerings made by fire unto the LORD: and the priest shall make an atonement for his sin that he hath committed, and it shall be forgiven him. (Lev. 4:20, 26, 31, 35)

Paul told the Jewish Christians that Christ's atoning acts were ongoing:

> Wherefore he is able also to save them to the uttermost that come unto God by him, seeing he ever liveth to make intercession for them. (Heb. 7:25)

Questions on Doctrine relies upon a heavy use of the phrase, "atoning sacrifice", in such a way as to convey the idea that Christ's death on Calvary was the *only* atonement, often called the "completed atonement", while His ministry in heaven is simply an application of benefit. The implication of this terminology, *assert many conservative Seventh-day Adventist expositors*, is that Christ is ministering ongoing forgiveness, while leaving out the work of purification. We will examine this claim more closely as we proceed.

When one examines "Appendix C" (*Questions on Doctrine*, pp. 661-692), which is a compilation of Ellen White statements on the atonement, it becomes readily apparent that the main focus is on the imputed righteousness of the atoning sacrifice for all humankind. One does not find the clear teaching that is to be found in the Spirit of Prophecy with regard to the cleansing from sin as imparted righteousness, even though there is a carefully selective representation of the writings presented in PART II, the "High-Priestly Application of Atoning Sacrifice," on the sanctuary ministration. This is not to say that there is absolutely *no mention* of the vital nature of the sanctuary service in the overall plan of salvation, as it *is* said on page 682 that Christ's "ministry applies and completes the transaction of the Cross," while quoting only passages that refer to forgiveness and imputation.

In *Questions on Doctrine*, the work of the outer court, which represents the cross, is portrayed in terms of what we today understand as our "objective" salvation. That is to say, it is that aspect of the work of Christ as the New Man, the second Adam, in which He took *corporate humanity* into Himself and redeemed it. Such is the gift that came upon all men. However, there must be an *individual, subjective* application of the atoning sacrifice. The historic position of Adventism also calls this atonement, the Bible calls it atonement, and the Spirit of Prophecy calls it atonement. However, *Questions on Doctrine* strives diligently to steer away from calling it atonement and makes it an easier-to-swallow "application of the benefits of *the* atonement." Christ's work in the sanctuary is referred to always in these terms:

> In this experience Jesus, our High Priest, *applies to us the benefits* of His atoning sacrifice. Our sins are forgiven, we become the children of God by faith in Christ Jesus ... (*Questions on Doctrine*, p. 350)

It is generally claimed that the waters get muddied even further when the concept of the application of the benefits of atonement refers to forgiveness while avoiding cleansing. This has become established doctrine in the anti-*Questions on Doctrine* camp, but it does not exactly bear investigation. Most of the book's commentary speaks about forgiveness and much less is said about cleansing and power from sin, although, to be fair, it *is* described in places, such as page 382: "And in His capacity as High Priest, He gives His people power to overcome sin"; and on page 352 it states that Christ's priestly ministry effects the cleansing of the individual "not only from the guilt but also from the power of sin." When we discuss the matter of the atonement as set forth in *Questions on Doctrine*, we see not so much a denial of our historical position as a shifting emphasis, which is generally understood as having been done to please the evangelicals.

In keeping with the spirit of objectivity, it should also be plainly stated that much ado has been made about the use of the phrase and concept of Christ's "*application of the benefits* of the atonement" rather than Christ's "*making atonement*" with regard to His work in the sanctuary. It appears as though this has been made more of an issue than it ought when the Spirit of Prophecy at times couches the work of atonement in this way:

> The great Sacrifice had been offered and had been accepted, and the Holy Spirit which descended on the day of Pentecost carried the minds of the disciples from the earthly sanctuary to the heavenly, where Jesus had entered by His own blood, to shed upon His disciples **the benefits of His atonement**. (*Early Writings*, p. 259, emphasis added)

> And as the typical cleansing of the earthly was accomplished by the removal of the sins by which it had been polluted, so the actual cleansing of the heavenly is to be accomplished by the removal, or blotting out, of the sins which are there recorded. But before this can be accomplished, there must be an examination of the books of record to determine who, through repentance of sin and faith in Christ, are entitled to **the benefits of His atonement**.... (*The Great Controversy*, pp. 421, 422)

The Spirit of Prophecy freely uses the concepts in an intertwined fashion:

Attended by heavenly angels, our great High Priest enters the holy of holies and there appears in the presence of God to engage in the last acts of His ministration in behalf of man—to perform the work of investigative judgment and **to make an atonement for all who are shown to be entitled to its benefits.** (*The Great Controversy*, p. 480)

All our lives we have been partakers of **His heavenly benefits**, recipients of the blessings of **His priceless atonement.** (Ms. 9, 1883, in *Signs of the Times*, Sept. 27, 1883)

There was indeed a tension between trying to please the evangelicals and referencing the Spirit of Prophecy to show Adventists that they were not attempting to refute important Adventist concepts in their presentation. We can see how the evangelical world came down on Martin as being soft on Adventism by claiming that Adventists were not changing their views and how Adventists came down on Froom and Anderson for selling out Adventism. Neither side was convinced, with both feeling that they had been fed a sales pitch.

The book does seem to distance itself from the fuller understanding and expression of the atonement by speaking of it in terms of something "they" believed, as if "we" no longer believe it.

Some of our earlier Seventh-day Adventist writers, believing that the word "atonement" had a wider meaning than many of their fellow Christians attached to it, expressed themselves as indicating that the atonement was not made on the cross of Calvary, but was made rather by Christ after He entered upon His priestly ministry in heaven. **They** believed fully in the efficacy of the sacrifice of Christ for the salvation of all men, and **they** believed most assuredly that this sacrifice was made once for all and forever, but **they** preferred not to use the word "atonement" as relating *only* to the sacrificial work of Christ at Calvary.... Their concept was that the sacrifice of Jesus *provided* the means of the atonement, and that the atonement itself was made only when the priests *ministered* the sacrificial offering on behalf of the sinner.... (*Questions on Doctrine*, pp. 347, 348, emphasis added)

This really seems to be framing the matter as if to say, "We don't believe it this way anymore." They had to frame it that way for it to pass the Calvinist test. Obviously, "some of our earlier Seventh-day Adventist writers" would have included Ellen White, who said things like:

God had committed to His people a work to be accomplished on earth. The third angel's message was to be given, **the minds of believers were to be directed to the heavenly sanctuary, where Christ had entered to make atonement** for His people.... **The people of God must purify their souls through obedience to the truth, and be prepared to stand without fault before Him at His coming.** (Ms. 4, 1883, in *Evangelism*, p. 695, emphasis added)

Now Christ is in the heavenly sanctuary. And what is He doing? Making atonement for us, cleansing the sanctuary from the sins of the people. Then we must enter by faith into the sanctuary with Him, we must commence the work in the sanctuary of our souls. **We are to cleanse ourselves from all defilement. We must "cleanse ourselves from all filthiness of the flesh and spirit, perfecting holiness in the fear of God."** [2 Cor. 7:1.] Satan will come and tempt you and you will give way to his temptations. What then? Why, come and humble your hearts in confession, and by faith grasp the arm of Christ in the heavenly sanctuary. Believe that Christ will take your confession and hold up His hands before the Father—hands that have been bruised and wounded in our behalf—and **He will make an atonement for all who will come with confession.** (Ms. 8, 1888, in *The Ellen G. White 1888 Materials*, p. 127, emphasis added)

In the final assessment, one cannot fault *Questions on Doctrine*'s position as being strictly in error, as it is clearly stated in the summary of the chapter "Sacrificial Atonement Provided; Sacrificial Atonement Applied," (Question 30):

We feel it to be most important that Christians sense the difference between the atoning act of Christ on the cross as a forever completed sacrifice, and His work in the sanctuary as officiating high priest, **ministering the benefits** of that sacrifice. What He did on the cross was for **all men** (1 John 2:2). What He does in the sanctuary is for those only who **accept** His great salvation.

Both aspects are integral and inseparable phases of God's infinite work of redemption. The one provides the sacrificial offering; the other provides the application of the sacrifice to the repentant soul. The one was made by Christ as victim; the other, by Christ as priest. Both are aspects of God's great redemptive plan for man. (*Questions on Doctrine*, pp. 353, 354)

Perhaps we have a situation in this case of an idea being established in the literature and being given more life than is warranted. That idea can often be traced to one source and then, as it gets quoted, others build upon it and end up quoting each other, until there is an established teaching. Contrarily, if one goes to the original source, the actual documentation would be found to be not quite as has been presented. To a certain extent, this is what has taken place with *Questions on Doctrine*. People who study these issues need to examine the book itself to be satisfied in their own minds.

There is no doubt that the authors of *Questions on Doctrine* avoided the matter of "final atonement," though Ellen White was clear that Christ entered the Most Holy Place in 1844 to make "final atonement" for the blotting of sins, a "final atonement for all who could be benefited by His mediation" (*Early Writings*, p. 253). Classic Adventism teaches a final intercession and a final atonement for all of the righteous, both living and dead, before His ministration closes:

The third angel closes his message thus: "Here is the patience of the saints: here are they that keep the commandments of God, and the faith of Jesus." As he repeated these words, he pointed to the heavenly sanctuary. The minds of all who embrace this message are directed to the most holy place, where Jesus stands before the ark, **making His final intercession** for all those for whom mercy still lingers and for those who have ignorantly broken the law of God. **This atonement is made for the righteous dead as well as for the righteous living**. It includes all who died trusting in Christ, but who, not having received the light upon God's commandments, had sinned ignorantly in transgressing its precepts. (*Early Writings*, p. 254, emphasis added)

The Adventist conferees made efforts to steer away from this by stating: "Adventists do not hold **any** theory of a dual atonement" (p. 390, emphasis added).

We need to make some mention on the matter of final generation theology. There is yet a purpose in the theme of the great controversy for the lapse of time that occurs between the close of probation and the second coming. However, *Questions on Doctrine* does not venture into that territory at all. Rather it sweeps immediately from the close of probation to the return of Christ, avoiding any focus on the group that has come up to full cleansing of sin while still living and that stands during this time without a Mediator. "Having finished His ministry as high priest, our Saviour then returns to the earth in glory …" (*Questions on Doctrine*, p. 444). In other words, there is a careful avoidance of the blotting out of the sins of the final generation of living saints and what the implications of that might be. One can see this by reading the chapter on the investigative judgment, part II, beginning in *Questions on Doctrine* on page 423.

As we draw near the end of this segment, let us consider a complex aspect of the *Questions on Doctrine* controversy that is difficult to encapsulate. We will rely on Herbert E. Douglass for assistance:

[A] … major concern of Andreasen and others looking on from the sidelines was QOD's less than lucid language used to describe the Adventist doctrines of the atonement, sanctuary service (type and antitype), and the investigative judgment.

Froom's February 1957 article in *Ministry* entitled "The Priestly Application of the Atoning Act" was designed to prepare readers for QOD, yet to be published. He continued his typical cherry-picking of Ellen White statements. However, in this article, Froom rightly wrote, on one hand, that the atonement could not be limited to Christ's death on the cross or the investigative judgment in heaven, that the atonement "clearly embraces both—one aspect being incomplete without the other, and each being the indispensable complement of the other." All right, so far!

But, on the other hand, he used unfortunate language to describe that Christ's death provided "a complete, perfect, and final atonement for man's sin" and "a completed act of atonement." Because of these poorly chosen words, Andreasen felt that Froom had swung too closely to the Calvinist viewpoint in over-emphasizing the Cross at the expense of other equally important sanctuary truths. (*A Fork in the Road*, pp. 61, 62)

Douglass believed that "Andreasen's agitation … was overstated on this occasion" (*A Fork in the Road*, p. 62). So did Leroy Moore, in his study of the history, as set forth in his *Questions on Doctrine Revisited*, which is mandatory reading for anyone venturing into this study on the controversy surrounding the Evangelical Conferences, the publishing of *Questions on Doctrine*, and Andreasen's protest. Moore presents evidence to show the unfortunate shift in doctrine regarding the nature of Christ as well as the unfounded nature of some of Andreasen's reactions and claims regarding the content of Anderson and Froom's answers to the evangelicals. One must not rely upon Andreasen's *Letters to the Churches* as the final authority on the controversy. This is where we get the overbalanced assessments such as that given by Vance Ferrell, which declares: "There is **nothing** in QD about power to obey being provided by Jesus to His followers! It is all forgiveness, forgiveness, forgiveness!" (*Our Evangelical* Earthquake, p. 196, emphasis added). This is not an entirely fair report. *Questions on Doctrine* is problematic on the atonement, but we should not make it worse than it is.

Moore accurately observed: "Andreasen cannot recognize our message in language used to communicate with souls who would not even consider our traditional approach" (*Questions on Doctrine* Revisited, p. 101). Moore's magnanimity may be missing important points in that those souls may not be helped to the truth by this back door approach that attempted to make us sound like them or that, if we had not been trying to peddle our distinctive truths in such padded language, the floodgates would not have opened for doctrinal confusion in our own ranks and a future slide into heresy. In other words, history reveals that, ultimately, the linguistic accommodation resulted in harm.

Issues regarding the nature of Christ

Classic Adventism teaches the "postlapsarian" view—that He took the nature of Adam after the fall. The new "prelapsarian" view is that Jesus took the nature of Adam *before* the fall. It is about "sinful nature" versus "sinless nature." That the postlapsarian view was the established Seventh-day Adventist understanding and teaching has not been more thoroughly documented than in Professor Jean R. Zurcher's *Touched with Our Feelings*, a touchstone work on this subject.

Everyone who knows the Spirit of Prophecy on the nature of Christ and who has examined *Questions on Doctrine* knows that there was a selective use of Ellen White's statements with an added heading that was done in such a way as to make her appear to teach the prelapsarian view when such is not the case. We will come back to this after looking briefly at some evidence for the standard position.

A basic Bible text that we appeal to for the teaching that Jesus took our fallen, sinful nature is in the second chapter of Hebrews:

> Forasmuch then as the children are partakers of flesh and blood, he also himself likewise took part of the same; that through death he might destroy him that had the power of death, that is, the devil; and deliver them who through fear of death were all their lifetime subject to bondage. For verily he took not on *him the nature of* angels; but he took on *him* the seed of Abraham. Wherefore in all things it behoved him to be made like unto *his* brethren, that he might be a merciful and faithful high priest in things *pertaining* to God, to make reconciliation for the sins of the people. For in that he himself hath suffered being tempted, he is able to succour them that are tempted. (Heb. 2:14–18)

H. H. Myers wrote:

> Dr. Ralph Larson, in his monumental thesis, *The Word Was Made Flesh*, details some four hundred written statements by Mrs. E. G. White, and approximately eight hundred statements by other SDA writers on Christ's earthly nature. Over a period of one hundred years of SDA writers, Dr. Larson was able to find no statement that Christ received the sinless nature of unfallen Adam, as claimed by Barnhouse. Our leading doctrinal book, *Bible Readings for the Home Circle*, published in the year of Mrs. White's death (1915), had sold by the million. It stated:
>
> > In His humanity, Christ partook of our sinful human nature. If not, then He was not made "like unto His brethren," was not "in all points tempted like as we are," did not overcome as we have to overcome.... The idea that Christ was born of an immaculate or sinless mother, inherited no tendencies to sin, and for this reason did not sin, removes Him from the realm of a fallen world, and from the very place where help is needed. On His human side, Christ inherited just what every child of Adam inherits,—a sinful nature. (*Bible Readings for the Home Circle*, p. 174)

We need not labor long over Ellen White's Christology, as there are many published analyses that will confirm it as will a simple reading of her works such as found in the following article written in 1874. The statement makes it clear what she meant by Jesus' taking our sinful nature, our sinful flesh:

> Christ bore the sins and infirmities of the race as they existed when he came to the earth to help man. In behalf of the race, with the weaknesses of fallen man upon him, he was to stand the temptations of Satan upon all points wherewith man would be assailed. (*Review and Herald*, July 28, 1874)

The new view started coming in during the 1950s. This view introduced the concepts and terminology of the doctrine of original sin and was brought in to please our evangelical critics that we might no longer be guilty of heresy on the nature of Christ.

The standard belief of Christ's fallen nature, in Adventism, was eroded through the idea that the efficacy of His sacrifice lay in his absolute sinlessness—a sinlessness, which could not be attained to while in "sinful flesh." Christ was "that holy thing" (Luke 1:35) and the prince of the world could find nothing in Him (John 14:30). Edward Heppenstall, the chair of systematic theology at the Adventist Theological Seminary, continued popularizing and developing the new view.

The Calvinist soteriology, or study of salvation, rests on the notion of original sin—that we are sinners because Adam sinned, not because we sin personally. Ellen White wrote: "Adam sinned, and the children of Adam share his guilt and its consequences; but Jesus bore the guilt of Adam, and all the children of Adam that will flee to Christ, the second Adam, may escape the penalty of transgression" (*Signs of the Times*, May 19, 1890, in *Faith and Works*, p. 88).

However, in the Calvinist view, Jesus could not have been born as we are or He would not have been sinless, he would have had on him the actual guilt of Adam as all humanity is purported to have in the Calvinistic theological system. He would have been sinful, corrupted, i.e., born a sinner. He therefore could not have been our perfect substitute according to the "forensic justification" or "penal substitution" model of atonement, "wherein, in some way, (1) God's wrath is appeased in the death of Jesus, and (2) the sinner is forgiven by 'faith' that is denuded from any relationship to character change in the process" (*A Fork in the Road*, p. 25). The Calvinist needs to have Christ's sinlessness (and our salvation) secure—and this is legitimate. However, the way of salvation, for the Calvinist, requires that Jesus be "exempt" from all inherited tendencies to sin. This is the same conclusion reached by Catholicism, with the additional interjection of the "immaculate conception" doctrine, by which Jesus was given a sinless nature through the sinlessness of Mary, though we do not know how she would have received it since she was born of sinful parents.

Obviously, Seventh-day Adventists should have great difficulty trying to harmonize their understanding of salvation with their Calvinist friends, no matter how much linguistic gymnastics they could muster. The problem in 1955–1957 was that foggy thinking on the part of the Adventists led them, almost unknowingly, into capitulating to the Evangelicals. Here began fifty years of focus on some kind of objective atonement without equal weight on the subjective aspect of the atonement that would have highlighted our Lord's work as our High Priest. (*A Fork in the Road*, p. 43)

> The Catholic doctrine of the "immaculate conception" is that Mary, the mother of our Lord, was preserved from original sin. If this be true, then Jesus did not partake of man's sinful nature. This belief cuts off the lower rungs of the ladder, and leaves man without a Saviour who can be touched with the feeling of men's infirmities, and who can sympathize with them in their temptations and sufferings.... (William Branson, *Drama of the Ages* [1953], pp. 88, 89)

The implications of the prelapsarian view are that Christ could not be tempted as we are tempted (contra Heb. 4:15), and, therefore, He could not have sinned.

> Yet into the world where Satan claimed dominion God permitted His Son to come, a helpless babe, subject to the weakness of humanity. He permitted Him to meet life's peril in common with every human soul, to fight the battle as every child of humanity must fight it, at the risk of failure and eternal loss. (*The Desire of Ages*, p. 49)

This means, of course, that He could not truly be our example in overcoming. Also, the teaching regarding the final generation of remnant elect living free from sin after the close of probation before Christ comes would be deemed impossible.

The objector feels that the only way to do honor to Christ and to protect Him from all taint of sin is to take the position that He could not sin. But what comfort and assurance of personal victory over sin can we find in a spotless Christ if His freedom from sin as He walked this earth was not truly a victory over temptation but an inability to sin? We would rightly stand in awe of such a Holy Being. But we could not see in Him one who was "made like unto his brethren" "in all things," one who being "tempted like as we are" "is able to succor" us when we are "tempted." (Francis D. Nichol, *Answers to Objections*, p. 393)

Moore Offers a Middle Ground Resolution to the Nature of Christ Conflict

Leroy Moore makes an important contribution to this debate. Moore's approach is ever to put the best construct on the motives of each person, which is commendable, although motives are sometimes revealed through a person's writings or through the testimonies of eyewitnesses. Moore's approach seeks to locate the "poles of truth" that are found on each side of a conflict and determine if there is not a way to bring a harmonious whole out of the situation. In the case of this particular debate over the nature of Christ and the atonement, he sees an age-old conflict still bubbling in the pot:

> The mid–1950s attempt to restore the Minneapolis message [the Wieland and Short manuscript, *1888 Re-Examined*] by again countering undue focus on law resulted in renewing that conflict. The 1888 debate was over the law in Galatians and the covenants, whereas in 1957 it was over Christ's nature and the atonement. But underlying issues were the same. [antinomianism vs. legalism]. Each side needed the other's insights; but neither was listening. Had they humbly listened to each other, QOD atonement principles could have corrected imbalances on both sides. Instead, nature of Christ imbalances and Andreasen's anger and false charges produced a stand-off … Each of apparently contradictory principles regarding Christ's nature that I found in *Desire of Ages* is essential to the integrity of the other. But to defend one, each party undermined its vital counterpart. (Moore, *Questions on Doctrine Revisited*, p. 164)

QOD authors had recovered the concept of atonement at the cross and emphasized the truth of Christ's unfallen, spiritual nature. But in repudiating the "sinful flesh" that He took they destroyed the paradox of truth and triggered intense conflict that can only be resolved by a proper grasp of each element. (Moore, p. 165)

Moore shows how the categorizations of strict "pre-fall" or strict "post-fall" natures are not accurate or helpful and that these categorizations are the root of much conflict. If we take a unity of the poles of truth approach, we will find first that Jesus would be "pre-fall" in the sense that His humanity was never infected with the pull of sin and self-centeredness as are we who are born into with the carnal mind, which is not subject to the law of God (Rom. 8:7) and which we develop and strengthen through indulgence of self, or sinning. Second, we would find Jesus to be "post-fall" in that the human condition into which He was born was degenerated and weakened. His physical humanity was affected by many generations of sin. For Jesus to be truly helpful to us, He had to be the New Head of the race, the New Man. As such, He had to be subject to temptation from birth, able to make choices to render or withhold obedience to the Father, while coming through temptation triumphantly in the same way that we are given to do.

Now, to resolve the dilemma of how Christ could have taken a fallen nature and still remained sinless even from birth, we have to realize that He could not be exactly like we are. That much should be obvious in the first place, for He was also God, having one human parent and one divine. However, we are looking at His human side, so we wonder, "How can it be?" It dawned on Pastor Moore in 1956 as the discussions with Walter Martin were quietly taking place and our men were denying the fallen nature of Christ. This is some valuable commentary, and I will quote a few paragraphs from Leroy Moore's work:

> The solution seemed so obvious I wondered why I didn't see it before…. Unlike any other child of Adam, Jesus surrendered His will to the Father prior to conception, to be fully indwelt and directed by the Spirit:
>
> Wherefore **when He cometh into the world**, he saith, Sacrifice and offering thou wouldst not, but **a body has thou prepared me:** … Then said I, **Lo, I come** (in the volume of the book it is written of me) **to do thy will, O God** (Heb. 10:5, 7, emphasis added).
>
> With a will fully committed to God, the safest time of His life was His infancy, before He could make moral choices. This means that, though just like us in heredity, He was very unlike us in spiritual nature. We enter the world disconnected from God, with a self-centered will enslaved to our emotions. He took sinful nature but remained free, ever directed by

the Spirit (*kata pneuma*). Thus, He never in any way became carnal, by living after the flesh (*kata sarka*).

Great confusion results when we fail to differentiate heredity from spiritual nature, as does Paul as well as Ellen White, whose prolific statements some wrongly see as contradictory. Scores of times she speaks of his "fallen nature"—sometimes even "sinful nature." Yet, she also declares a "sinless nature." The one set of quotes is avoided by those who insist upon a post-fall nature, while the other set is avoided or denied by those who insist upon a post-fall nature.

Christ did not inherit separation. As the second Adam, He came to reverse Adam's declaration of independence and to restore the divinely ordained union by becoming incarnate. Since, via the Holy Spirit, He was ever in complete connection with God from conception to death, He never developed a self-centered, "carnal nature."

Conflict will give way to helpful discussion when, with Paul and Ellen White, we unite both poles of truth and honor the attempts of others to do so, even if expressed differently. As it is, there is no real discussion between the two sides—only rhetoric and invective that destroy Christian experience and undermine confidence, not only in the spirit of prophecy but also in the Scripture itself-with which all Ellen White's testimonies are in full harmony.

QOD authors erred not in seeking to affirm a sinless nature, but in trying to avert the impact of fallen nature statements by evasion and misleading headings. The leaders then erred in passing this new position off as our historic view-even enforcing it as the only valid position, without allowing opportunity for the body to question and discuss the issues in a process that could have produced paradoxical unity. (Moore, pp. 68–70)

The Misleading Heading

"Appendix B" of *Questions on Doctrine*, which was also slipped into volume 7A in the *Seventh-day Adventist Commentary* behind the editors' backs, is a compilation of Ellen White statements with a heading that is not Mrs. White's, which reads: "Took Sinless Human Nature" (*Questions on Doctrine*, p. 650). This compilation used "fragments" and "excerpts contrary to context and ellipses that amounted to scholarly fraud," which have been shown to be far off the mark of careful scholarship (*A Fork in the Road*, p. 54). Yet, Anderson stated in the September 1956 issue of *Ministry* that the section of Ellen White statements supplied in this compilation was—

> as full coverage of this subject as can be found in the writings of Ellen G. White.... As far as we have been able to discover, this compilation fully represents the thinking of the messenger of the Lord on this question. A few other statements have been found, but these are either repetitions or mere verbal variations, and add no new thought. (*A Fork in the Road*, p. 54)

> Obviously if the QOD trio emphasized even slightly the mass of Ellen White quotes that linked our Lord's humanity with fallen mankind, Martin and Barnhouse would have quickly packed their bags and continued their attacks on the Adventists as cultists in their eyes. As Calvinists, they had no other choice. (*A Fork in the Road*, p. 55)

Leroy Moore asserted that the heading "Took Sinless Human Nature" misrepresents all nine quotations. While several of these affirm the sinlessness of our Savior, Moore concluded, "That is not in question. They clearly affirm a sinless nature *in spite of the fallen nature He 'took'!*" He goes on to detail how this takes place through mechanisms such as "carefully selected sentences and italic that are clearly tailored to support the misleading heading" (*Questions on Doctrine Revisited*, p. 61).

The author trio behind *Questions on Doctrine*, in their eagerness to accommodate the evangelicals, tripped over themselves in reading into the expression, "fallen, sinful nature," the "corruptions" that come from sinning. In their desire to assuage Martin and Barnhouse, they allowed these men to take control of the discussion. This should never have been. It remains this writer's assessment that, if our team had been assertive and forthright, the conferences would have ended, and we would have remained a "cult" in the eyes of these leaders from fallen Babylon. Apparently not being an option for our men, they would stop at nothing to achieve their goal of fellowship with the evangelicals.

The Vicarious Bearing of Human Nature in Questions on Doctrine

Questions on Doctrine takes up with the description of Christ's bearing of sinful humanity in a "vicarious" sense, conflating the bearing of our genetic weakness with the bearing of sin throughout His life:

> These weaknesses, frailties, infirmities, failings, are things which we, with our sinful, fallen natures,

have to bear. To us they are natural, inherent, but when He bore them, He took them not as something innately His, but He bore them as our substitute. He bore them in His perfect, sinless nature. Again, we remark, Christ bore all this vicariously, just as vicariously He bore the iniquities of us all. (*Questions on Doctrine*, pp. 59, 60)

Leroy Moore summed it up well:

By vicarious imputation Jesus took our guilt and died our death. He now imputes His perfect righteousness to us, placing it to our account. But He acquired our body genetically, not by imputation! Vicarious imputation involves exchange; He removes our sin and gives us His righteousness. This has nothing to do with taking upon Himself our flesh....

To use either imputed or vicarious for incarnation denies the reality of Christ's humanity and voids both Scripture and spirit of prophecy teaching! ... It is thus a grave error to suggest that the nature literally *imparted* (shared with or united) to His divine person was *vicariously imputed* [sic]. (*Questions on Doctrine Revisited*, p. 76)

So it was that the *Questions on Doctrine* trio taught that it was only in the sense of *vicarious imputation* that Christ took our sinful nature. This, says Herbert Douglass, really lit up Andreasen's "afterburners"! He went on to explain why it is so crucial that we understand this. It is not just a tempest in a teapot.

Though Jesus could vicariously die for our sins, how could His human life of 33 years relate to our salvation vicariously? He made it possible that we will not be punished for our sins—He died *for* us, vicariously. But how could He live as our example vicariously? Does that mean we don't have to live an overcoming life, resisting the tempter at every turn—because He did it for us vicariously? Did He keep the law for us vicariously? Rather, in resisting evil as our Example, He showed us how to "walk as He walked" (1 John 2:6). Although he died for us *vicariously*, He didn't obey for us *vicariously*! Vicariously, He gave us freedom from the "wages of sin." (*A Fork in the Road*, p. 48)

That is because our sin was imputed to Him and He took them in His body in the second death experience, "tasting death for every man."

George Knight also recognized the strange stance taken:

Pages §59–62§ [in *Questions on Doctrine*] set forth the rather curious position that Christ took human nature vicariously in the same way that He bore human sin vicariously. That is, according to *Questions on Doctrine* Christ didn't really take on human infirmities and weaknesses in the incarnation as being innately His, but only in a vicarious or substitutionary sense.

That position is certainly not set forth in the New Testament. Nor was it the one held by Ellen White....

Thus according to Ellen White, at the incarnation, Christ actually, rather than vicariously, took upon Himself "our sinful nature" (*Review and Herald*, Dec. 15, 1896, p. 789).... (George Knight, *Questions on Doctrine*, annotated ed., note 2, p. 56)

There is much confusion in the way the Adventist trio represented Christ's nature, as we see in various places in the book. Another misleading heading placed on a compilation of quotations uses "Bore the Imputed Sin and Guilt of the World" to explain statements that refer to Christ's sinful nature (pp. 655–658). None of the passages quoted under this heading make any kind of reference to "imputed sin and guilt." *Sin was not imputed to Christ until the end of His life, when He went to His cross. If He had borne it earlier, it would have killed Him.*

The simple truth of the paradox is that Jesus, the divine Son of God, holy and sinless in character and mind, took upon Himself the fallen genetic nature of humanity, as it was after four millennia of sin. The presence of the desires and needs of the fleshly nature were ever with Him providing an avenue for temptation. Yet, as A. T. Jones taught, never should we "drag His mind into it" (*General Conference Bulletin*, Feb. 25, 1895, p. 327). Ellen White states clearly:

For four thousand years the race had been decreasing in physical strength, in mental power, and in moral worth; and Christ took upon Him the infirmities of degenerate humanity. Only thus could He rescue man from the lowest depths of his degradation. (*Desire of Ages*, p. 117)

The Myth of Overwhelming Support for Questions on Doctrine

There was a marvelous propaganda campaign surrounding the publication of *Questions on Doctrine* through which it was asserted that 250 denominational leaders had approved the manuscript with wide and glowing acclaim and that no changes in substance whatsoever were called for. It was published as fact, in the *Review and Herald*, that the book was a General Conference project, prepared by top scholars and approved by church leaders all over the world. The real truth of the matter was that there were very few responses that came back when the manuscript was sent out for review by church leaders.

In the editorial in the March 1958 *Ministry*, published half a year after the release of *Questions on Doctrine*, under the title "Unity of Adventist Belief," it was stated in such a way as to give the impression that all of the 250 leaders had responded and had done so with high acclaim. Here are the pertinent passages from that article:

> The manuscript for our recent book *Questions on Doctrine* was sent for appraisal to representatives in all the world field. Some 250 denominational leaders—ministers, Bible teachers, editors, administrators—carefully studied that manuscript before it went to the publishers. And the heartening thing was that, except for minor suggestions, **no change whatsoever in content was called for**. In view of the purpose of this book, and knowing that it would be studied by critical readers, and that **an accurate statement of our beliefs was imperative**, this group of readers was asked to be particularly careful in their examination of the answers given.
>
> It was months before we received all the reports, for as already indicated, these readers were situated in every division of the world field. When the reports came back, the unanimous and enthusiastic acceptance of the content of the manuscript gave remarkable testimony to the unity of belief that characterizes us as a people. Some valuable suggestions were offered, but in no area of doctrine was any major change called for. And that is all the more impressive when we realize that as a denomination we have no "creed" except the Bible, nor have we ever published a systematic theology....
>
> As already stated, from all parts of the world field have come expressions of heartfelt gratitude for the convincing and scholarly answers this book contains. The questions asked are not new; they have challenged us for many decades. Nor are the answers new. However, the way some of the questions were asked called for protracted answers. The unanimous approval of the book from all parts of the world field reveals the unanimity of our denominational beliefs, and a careful reading of *Questions on Doctrine* will reveal that it is in complete accord with the clearest statements of the Spirit of prophecy, which we have had in our libraries for more than half a century. ("Unity of Adventist Belief," *Ministry*, March 1958, p. 28, emphasis added)

Student of the period Leroy Moore brought his research to the table on this issue, in chapter 21 of his *Questions on Doctrine Revisited*, which carries a terrible weight of implication that there was deliberate propagandizing taking place. This is putting it euphemistically, given the facts:

- Only eight replies came back, including a letter from Raymond Cottrell, associate editor of *The Seventh-day Adventist Bible Commentary* series that was underway at the time, explaining that he and his fellow *Review* editor, Don Neufeld, would have no time to finish their review by the deadline but would advance their assessment of the manuscript when they were done. Cottrell's review is included in the eight, although it came in late.

- Only one of the responses came from outside North America (George Keough from Newbold College in England), though there were many copies sent out to the world field.

- No local or union administrator from the North American Division responded.

- The few responses that went beyond a mere complimentary remark came from the General Conference administration or the *Review and Herald* Publishing Association, which were all located within one block of GC headquarters in Washington, DC.

- Not more than half of the responses were real critiques.

- All the responses except one, warned of problems. That one, from Siegfried H. Horn, contained no theological assessment but questioned some historical items, which he said he had no time to verify.

Froom stated, in regard to the call from the world field for an evaluation of the manuscript: "It was sent out to more than 225 Adventist leaders around the world" and "No more eminent or representative group could have been consulted. No more competent group could approve. And that they did." Moore stated: "Froom's false declaration of strong approval is without any defense!" (*Questions on Doctrine Revisited*, p. 216).

The Publishing of Questions on Doctrine and the Pilate Effect

At the time that all of this pre-publication furor was taking place, the Review and Herald office was in the thick of producing the *Seventh-day Adventist Bible Commentary* series. Elder Herbert E. Douglass was working on this project as one of the assistant editors, so he is to us a first-hand witness of what took place. (For those interested in this story, his book *A Fork in the Road* is perhaps the most important book to read of all of the histories on this subject.)

Of all that I have read and studied of this history, one of the things that has astounded and impacted me perhaps more than the actual details of what is in the publication itself is that it was recognized in the publishing office how bad the effect of this book was turning out to be, yet it went forward anyway. It was recognized by many church leaders that "a tornado was yet to come." This one thing that confirms to me that this whole event in Seventh-day Adventist history was indeed a major gathering storm and that what we have today posing as Adventism is the storm as it has burst.

Raymond Cottrell, associate editor of the *Commentary* responded to the request of the Review and Herald's editorial committee to conduct a review of *Questions on Doctrine*. He produced, at last, a sixteen-page breakdown of serious concerns in five areas, including a perceived shift in Adventist theology. Herbert Douglass, working from Julius Nam's research, stated:

> In his closing sentences, Cottrell predicted: "Almost certainly, there will also arise a storm of opposition when our ministry and laity discover the real meaning of the actual terms on which we have achieved rapprochement with Martin and other evangelicals." He said that we should expect "a serious division" among Adventist workers when both QOD and Martin's book were published but that there was still time to "take adequate measures *now* to clear the atmosphere *before* Martin's book is published, and to set forth in [*Questions on Doctrine*] a clear exposition of [Adventism's] true position (Cottrell's emphasis). (*A Fork in the Road*, p. 36, square brackets Douglass')

Leroy Moore devoted chapters 22 to 24 of his book to Cottrell's report. These, contain some of the most fascinating background facts about *Question on Doctrine*'s history.

Francis D. Nichol, editor of the *Review and Herald* wrote to General Conference President R. R. Figuhr, explaining some of his concerns and recognizing the misrepresentations that were taking place.

The process of editing was a struggle:

> So much switching back and forth occurred during the preparation of QD that the editors at the Review, just across the alley from the General Conference building, were deeply concerned They would repeatedly try to correct exaggerations, omissions, and outright mistruths; yet the errors would be placed right back in again. The only main correction they were able to get into QD was that a complete "sacrificial atonement," instead of complete ["]atonement" was made at the cross. But this mingling of truth with error had the effect of causing many who read the statements to consider the errors as possibly true. (Vance Ferrell, *Our Evangelical Earthquake*, pp. 77, 78)

But, consistently, in spite of repeated attempts by the editors at the Review to edit out the problems, Froom and Anderson always won. Ignoring all advice, Froom wrote in the Introduction to QD, these words: "These answers represent the position of our denomination … This volume can be viewed as truly representative" (*Questions on Doctrine*, 1957 edition, p. 8). (*Our Evangelical Earthquake*, p. 78)

Herbert Douglass concurred, saying, "The Adventist trio won out, almost as if keen readers of the manuscript did not count" (*A Fork in the Road*, p. 37). So it finally came down to the wire, and the *Questions on Doctrine* trio informed the Review and Herald editing committee on January 30, 1957, that no more editing would be permitted. The Review and Herald office, therefore, accepted the manuscript on a "text basis." That is, "the publishing house would not be providing any editorial oversight, but simply would serve as a printer and distributor" and therefore "would not be held responsible for its content" (*Our Evangelical Earthquake*, p. 80). Such would not be apparent by merely examining the book, for the inside title page says: "Prepared by a Representative Group of Seventh-day Adventist Leaders, Bible Teachers, and Editors," and it carries the Review and Herald Publishing Association imprimatur. The copyright page says: "Copyright © 1957 by the Review and Herald Publishing Association." (For the past several years, such a copyright has been reserved for books that have undergone editorial review.)

What happened next is stunning:

> That morning in the *Commentary* office, Raymond Cottrell left the room and returned with a towel over his left arm and a basin of water in his right. Then each of us on the *Commentary* staff took turns washing our hands of any more input or responsibility for QOD. We didn't know then the full implications of what we were doing together around that basin! (*A Fork in the Road*, p. 37)

Herbert Douglass went on to explain why the various editors did not publicize their concerns. It was because they never thought the book would fly. They failed to foresee the "push-polling" that would take place by the editors of *Ministry* or the blessing of the General Conference president, along with promotions for the conferences to get the book out to all the workers. The other thing going on was that the new Bible commentary series was coming out, and the Review and Herald did not want to generate any negativity by taking sides on the issues surrounding *Questions on Doctrine*. It was feared that to do so would have a potential impact on the sales of the commentary series. The commentaries would overshadow any impact that *Questions on Doctrine* might have, they thought, as they would forthrightly carry the "classic Adventist understanding of the humanity of Christ and the purpose of the sanctified life in preparing a people to live forever" (*A Fork in the Road*, pp. 38, 39).

In Summation of the Questions on Doctrine Saga

George Knight stated in his "Introduction to the Annotated Edition" of *Questions on Doctrine*:

> Looking back, one can only speculate on the different course of Adventist history *if* Andreasen had been consulted regarding the wording of the Adventist position on the atonement, *if* Froom and his colleagues hadn't been divisive in the handling of issues related to the human nature of Christ, *if* both Froom and Andreasen would have had softer personalities. (*Seventh-day Adventists Answer Questions on Doctrine, Annotated Edition*, p. xxvi)

I would personally speculate, while we are speculating, that, if the Review and Herald had not washed their hands of their responsibility to Seventh-day Adventism, *Questions on Doctrine* never would have seen the light of day, the Evangelical Conferences would have been a bust, and Adventism would have remained on the "outs" with the evangelical mainstream. Anderson and Froom would not have been able to compromise wording to the level of ambiguity that was required to satisfy the Calvinist evangelicals and get it by Seventh-day Adventists.

> In the course of his attack against *Questions on Doctrine*, Andreasen concurred with Martin that the book represented a certain change in Adventist belief. For both, this assertion was central to their arguments, though for widely divergent reasons. Next, anti-Adventist evangelicals and General Conference leaders found themselves agreeing with one another that the book did not represent a change in Adventist theology.... (Julius Nam, "The *Questions on Doctrine* Saga," p. 5)

Nobody really knows what would have happened if the right course had been maintained by the Adventist men. We can certainly understand that the opportunity to share was grossly misappropriated to a level of culpability that can only be qualified as outright *malfeasance*, a word employed by one of Adventism's finest:

> Because of these valiant attempts to reconcile Calvinistic disagreements with an agreeable presentation from the Adventists, major theological issues were misconstrued. No amount of historical analysis will gloss over this theological malfeasance. *Adventists missed the opportunity of the century*! Never had Adventists been given such a platform to cheerfully clarify any misunderstanding with Protestants and to illuminate distinctive doctrines that Adventists think important—but they missed it by a couple of light years. (*A Fork in the Road*, p. 32)

1888 Re-visited: Another Call to Bring in Everlasting Righteousness

It is this distorted understanding of the 1888 message which makes us "modern ancient Israel." (*1888 Re-Examined*, p. 186)

Throughout this recounting of the history of the "second call" to Adventism, we will be citing generously from Wieland and Short's manuscript, *1888 Re-Examined (Revised and Updated)*, which is the primary text in the body of "unauthorized" historical works that exist on this subject and bring to the general readership of Adventism the "dissenting" perspective, or "minority report," for this topic of history. It is appropriate that we use this book, for these were the messengers who brought the second call.

At the same general time that the Evangelical Conferences triggered an earthquake in Adventism, Robert J. Wieland and Donald K. Short, on furlough from mission service in Africa, produced a manuscript that detonated a bomb in Adventism entitled, "1888 Re-Examined." These two developments in the third generation were the catalyst for the divided house of the fourth generation, creating a bloom of independent movements claiming to be returning to historic Adventism, embracing the 1888 message, and going forward in what is known as "reformation" Adventism.

Independent ministries before Wieland and Short were generally self-supporting ministries based upon health work or educational work, which were in symbiotic relationship with the denomination in most respects. However, after the awareness of the 1888 history as Wieland and Short brought to light, along with the denominational Evangelical Conferences with Sunday-keepers Martin and Barnhouse, the independent ministries took on a whole new career, having doctrinal issues with the mainstream. Thus, the fourth generation became a time of great Adventist agitation.

The burden of Elders Wieland and Short was that the denomination as a whole would realize how Christ was crucified afresh by the leadership of the 1888 era, that it would come to the experience of "corporate repentance" in acknowledging the rejection of the message of heaven that came at that time, and that it would enter a new day of opportunity for bringing in everlasting righteousness. The essence of their longing, that we should see the return of the latter rain, is expressed in Ellen White's statement of November 5, 1892, written from her "exile" in Australia:

> Never before have I seen among our people such firm self-complacency and unwillingness to accept and acknowledge light as was manifested at Minneapolis. I have been shown that **not one of the company who cherished the spirit manifested at that meeting would again have clear light to discern the preciousness of the truth sent them from heaven until they humbled their pride and confessed that they were not actuated by the Spirit of God, but that their minds and hearts were filled with prejudice.** The Lord desired to come near to them, to bless them and heal them of their backslidings, but they would not hearken. (Lt. 2a, 1892, in *The Ellen G. White 1888 Materials*, p. 1067, emphasis added)

Over the course of their work, not only did Wieland and Short always believe that Ellen White's counsel applies in principle to contemporary leadership, but they also steadfastly clung to the hope that the contemporary church would ultimately be revived through confession of the 1888-era sin of rejecting the Holy Spirit of Christ. We agree that this specific heartfelt confession alone—and not mere lip service—can bring about the return of the latter rain in the power of the angel that comes in the glory of God. This fourth angel of Revelation 18, verse 1, brings added impetus to "the third angel's message," which is the final proclamation of the righteousness of Christ in the advancing light of the message of the character of God. This proclamation and message is not only a pronouncement, it is a demonstration of the mystery of God, and the completion of God's purpose in Christ, which is to create a new man, combining divinity with humanity that He might be glorified in all. Our conviction at 4th Angel Publications is that corporate repentance is not an institutional repentance but, rather, a heart experience that takes place at the level of each individual involved, for it is individuals who ultimately comprise the church that goes through. It is not a legal denomination that goes through, but the *truth* in a people. Israel cannot be numbered in an earthly registry.

However, it would not be fair to say that Wieland and Short have not published the correct view of corporate repentance. Here is an example of how they describe corporate repentance from their organization, "The 1888 Message Study Committee" (1888 MSC):

> Those who see the need for corporate repentance define it as personally repenting of sins we may not have individually committed but which we could or would have committed but for the grace of Christ.... The sin of 1888 is our sin "but for the grace of Christ," just as the sin of Calvary is likewise ours through our corporate identity "in Adam." (1888 MSC, *A. T. Jones: The Man and the Message*, p. 30)

Coupling this with the belief that the denomination proper would come to this experience, it can only mean that the hope that they held was that the majority of Adventist leadership would come individually to the experience of corporate repentance. It was ever the belief of these reformers that the corporate entity of *the General Conference of Seventh-day Adventists* would see this day of revival and reformation and go on reformed, carrying forward the loud cry of the third angel under latter rain power. This has been also the sentiment of the vast number of independent ministries that have risen up since the 1950s.

Brethren Wieland and Short got their hopes very high in the late 1980s that this was beginning to take place when they elatedly acclaimed the publication by the church of the four-volume series of 1888 documents, *The Ellen G. White 1888 Materials*, and the publication of Arnold Wallenkampf's two books, *What Every Adventist Should Know About 1888* and *What Every Christian Should Know About Justification*. With joy they saw these developments as achieving "a complete historical about-face," a "phenomenal" and "unique dramatic turn-around" a "total reversal of viewpoint" (Short and Wieland, *1988 Re-Examined: One Hundred Years in Retrospect* [1989], p. 36). However, the official publication of one author who advocates for the right side does not constitute a denominational "about face," nor should it be taken to imply even an impending unanimous denominational resolution. Additionally, the publication of *The Ellen G. White 1888 Materials* in four large volumes was done in an almost "passive-aggressive" manner in that it consists of facsimile reproductions that are hard to read and even marked up in some cases with editing and notes. The books come across as a reluctant provision, with the intent that very few should read them. Because of this, one author has pronounced them "disrespectfully" published. (This objection was partially remedied as they became available on CD-ROM and online at http://1ref.us/ib and via the Apple and Microsoft apps.) So then, the facts of the overall attitudes of leadership at that time, in addition to over two decades of post–1988 history make the case that our messengers' excitement was highly overwrought. Sadly, they both passed away after four generations of Adventism without realizing the burning hope of which they were prisoners. That fourth generation is now passed into history, though the same spirit of rebellion lives on.

> They [*the rebel leadership*] were actuated by the same spirit that inspired Korah, Dathan, and Abiram. Those men of Israel were determined to resist all evidence that would prove them to be wrong, and they went on and on in their course of disaffection until many were drawn away to unite with them. (Lt. 2a, 1892, in *The Ellen G. White 1888 Material*, p. 1067)

Returning to Elders Wieland and Short, who first discovered the 1888 message and history in 1938 by reading Waggoner's *The Glad Tidings*, a verse-by-verse study on Galatians. Perceiving that the denomination had largely abandoned Jones and Waggoner and their message and that Christ had been largely lost sight of, they attended the 1950 General Conference Session, which purported to focus on "Christ-centered preaching." Sadly, they became increasingly troubled by the discrepancy between profession and practice as new spiritualist ideas were coming in to fill the void created by ignorance of our history.

> [At that time there were] … no copy machines, no computers as known today, and of course, there were no CD-ROMs to bring our church history and Ellen White's witness to view at the click of a mouse. The Ellen G. White Estate vault was closed to general access and only special approval allowed material to be released. It was in this environment that the private manuscript *1888 Re-examined* was written for the attention of the General Conference Committee and presented to them in 1950.
>
> The contents were serious and far-reaching. It was sensed that more study was required. Therefore the manuscript was placed in the hands of the Defense Literature Committee, which today has come to be known as the Biblical Research Institute.
>
> After more than a year, a reply was received dated December 6, 1951. The brethren said: "We see nothing new in your manuscript.… If you accept this counsel … you will not wish to press your rather critical views nor to circulate them any further."
>
> And so for eight years the manuscript was virtually a clandestine paper surreptitiously copied and passed from friend to friend, around the world. By the year 1958 many of our church members were deeply concerned as to why the document was not accepted by leadership. This situation required an official reply which was provided in a 49-page treatise released in September 1958: "Further Appraisal of the Manuscript '1888 Re-examined'." (D. K. Short, *Let History Speak*, p. 70)

As mentioned earlier, the original form of the 1950 manuscript *1888 Re-Examined* can be found in a 396-page compilation of documents that was published in 1959 under the title *A Warning and its Reception*. The compilation also includes the official church responses. In 1987, the manuscript was republished in a revised and updated edition with additional chapters.

Letting F. T. Wright relate the story from here, we learn:

> By the reply of the leaders, it is evident that they clearly understood the nature of the appeal, and as equally and clearly rejected it.
>
> Wieland and Short virtually let the matter rest there but the Lord did not, for at the same time as the leaders were faced with this question, the Lord so organized events that at the level of the lay people, the message itself began to simultaneously sound again in different lands.
>
> Throughout the world, there were those who had been longing for deliverance from sin, and these eagerly grasped the proffered blessing, but among the leaders in the church, the response was swift and decided. They saw in it something they considered dangerous exactly as had been prophesied they would:
>
> "… In the manifestation of that power which lightens the earth with the glory of God, they will see only something which in their blindness they think dangerous, something which will arouse their fears, and they will brace themselves to resist it. Because the Lord does not work according to their expectations and ideal [original, ideas and expectations], they will oppose the work. 'Why,' they say, 'should not we know the Spirit of God, when we have been in the work so many years?'" *Review and Herald*, December 23, 1890.
>
> They began to apply various forms of pressure in order to keep the light from entering the churches. Anyone who possessed and read the writings of Elders Waggoner and Jones was labelled heretic, schismatic, and dangerous. To be seen talking with this class was to place yourself under suspicion of being one of them. (*Last Day Events*, p. 92)

Now that more than twenty years have passed since Wright published these words, the situation has not really changed. There was, in the official Conference response of 1958, as we shall see, an implied ban placed upon the manuscript of Wieland and Short. Through the years of history, one can find in official publications a rare instance of accurate reflection of the truths of the 1888 history. Yet, the general tenor in the official lines of mainstream communication in the denomination is propaganda, denial, suppression and fear.

In keeping with our theme of the devouring pests, authors Wieland and Short asserted in the preface of the 1987 edition of *1888 Re-Examined*: "The hallmarks of Adventism have become tarnished." Indeed. They astutely conveyed the sad situation that "in a time of exploding human knowledge, we as a people generally still have only a vague concept of what Christ is doing as High Priest in this final Day of Atonement, and scant sympathy with His aims. And what we do not understand we cannot communicate to the world" (*1888 Re-Examined*, p. 4).

"We Have No Need"

So it was that there was an examination of the manuscript and its claims. We have shown already that the men and the message of the "first call" to the marriage in the second generation were rejected. What we will show here is the response of the leading men of the third generation to the "second call" to repent from ongoing rejection and to return to the study, embracing and proclamation of the message.

Much promotion has been given to the church's claim of having accepted the message. A line-up of books by churchmen paints a bright picture as you will find reported in the 2004 publication, *The Harvest Principle and the Generation Concept in: The Proclamation of the Acceptable Year of Our LORD*, by Dr. Elliot O. Douglin:

> In 1950 Pastors Robert Wieland and Donald Short presented a manuscript entitled *1888 Re-examined*. It was a call to (i) study and accept the 1888 message; (ii) express corporate denominational repentance for the sin of rejection in 1888 and (iii) to share the message with the world-wide membership.
>
> Both the **manuscript** and the **call** were not only rejected but, in fact, condemned! This official rejection occurred in 1958. But a number of church members received the manuscript and agitation or "shaking" began. Since then some major books have been published with the blessings of the General Conference leadership, books which ignore, defy, or reject the E. G. White materials on what really happened in 1888. Here is a list:
>
> 1. 1962 *By Faith Alone* by Norval F. Pease

2. 1966 *Through Crisis to Victory 1888–1901* by A. V. Olson [in 1981 retitled more appropriately *Thirteen Crisis Years: 1888–1901*]

3. 1971 *Movement of Destiny* by LeRoy E. Froom

4. 1987 *From 1888 to Apostasy: The Case of A. T. Jones* by George R. Knight

5. 1989 *Angry Saints* by George R. Knight

6. 1994 *The Nature of Christ* by Roy Adams

7. 1998 *A User-friendly Guide to the 1888 Message* by George R. Knight.

All of these books misrepresent the true facts of the history of 1888. Roy Adams' book *The Nature of Christ* is an outright rejection of one of the central truths of the true gospel as presented in 1888, that Christ in the incarnation took on our fallen sinful flesh. George Knight in his books downgrades Jones and the message. Froom's book came with high recommendations by leaders and scholars. It presented 1888 as a victory for the truth. This was a denial of E. G. White's comments that the message was rejected.

In addition to these books which have sought to side step the issues, something else was done. New editions of certain books which are compilations of certain E. G. White writings contained **explanations** by compilers, **explanations** which are used to give a certain biased understanding of the 1888 message and history. For example the 33 page account of the Minneapolis Conference in *Selected Messages Book 3* and a 22 page Historical Foreword in the new edition of *Testimonies To Ministers*.

But scholars and compilers cannot change history. The true history of the 1888 Minneapolis General Conference Session stands written in heaven. The record of the Lord's messenger, Sis White, cannot be altered even by "cover up" or deception! Writing from Australia in [1896] Ellen White penned this solemn warning.

If men would only give up their spirit of resistance to the Holy Spirit, the spirit which has long been leavening their religious experience, God's Spirit would address itself to their hearts. It would convince of sin. What a work! But the Holy Spirit has been insulted and light has been rejected. Is it possible for those who for years have been so blind to see? Is it possible that in this late stage of their resistance their eyes will be anointed? Will the voice of the Spirit of God be distinguished from the deceiving voice of the enemy? ([*The Ellen G. White 1888* Materials], p. 1494).

Moreover, she declared that all the universe witnessed the terrible rejection:

On many occasions the Holy Spirit did work, but those who resisted the Spirit of God at Minneapolis were waiting for a chance to travel over the same ground again, because their spirit was the same afterward, when they had evidence heaped upon evidence, some were convicted, but those who were not softened and subdued by the Holy Spirit's working, put their own interpretation upon every manifestation of the grace of God, and they have lost much. They pronounced in their heart and soul and words that this manifestation of the Holy Spirit was fanaticism and delusion. They stood like a rock, the waves of mercy flowing upon and around them, but beaten back by their hard and wicked hearts, which resisted the Holy Spirit's working. Had this been received, it would have made them wise unto salvation; holier men, prepared to do the work of God with sanctified ability. **But all the universe of heaven witnessed the disgraceful treatment of Jesus Christ, represented by the Holy Spirit. Had Christ been before them, they would have treated him in a manner similar to that in which the Jews treated Christ** ([*The Ellen G. White 1888 Materials*, pp.] 1478, 1479). (Elliot O. Douglin, *The Harvest Principle and the Generation Concept in: The Proclamation of the Acceptable Year of the LORD*, pp. 167–169).

In the above excerpt, Douglin says that the church officially rejected the message in 1958. There was also a written response to the proponents of the message in 1951. I will show both.

Throughout your manuscript [*1888 Re-Examined*] it is evident that you feel the denomination should rectify certain things pertaining to 1888, and then make due acknowledgement and confession of the same....

Then on page 137 you write that "a denominational repentance" is essential before the loud cry can be received.

We do not believe that it is according to God's plan and purpose for the present leadership of the movement to make acknowledgement or confession, either private or public, concerning any of the mistakes made by the leadership of a bygone generation.... **We have no need to go back to 1888; those days are past.**... We need to think in terms of today." (*Letter by the General Conference of Seventh-day Adventists Defense Literature Committee*, [GCDLC] December 4, 1951, pp. 8, 9, in reply to *1888 Re-Examined* by R. J. Wieland and D. K. Short, found in the document compilation, "A Warning and Its Reception" independently published by the Adventist Laymen's Foundation of Arkansas and A. L. Hudson, emphasis added)

However, as a matter of fact, this flies in the face of the inspired command and historical action of God's people. We can never receive the blessing of that message until we have confessed both our own sins *and* the sins of our fathers in rejecting it.

It is just as essential that the people of God in this day should bear in mind how and when they have been tested, and where their faith has failed; where they have imperiled His cause by their unbelief and also by their self-confidence.... As God's people thus review the past, they should see that the Lord is ever repeating His dealings. They should understand the warnings given, and should beware not to repeat their mistakes.... (*Testimonies for the Church*, vol. 7, p. 210)

If they shall confess their iniquity, **and the iniquity of their fathers**, with their trespass which they trespassed against me, and that also they have walked contrary unto me; and *that* I also have walked contrary unto them, and have brought them into the land of their enemies; if then their uncircumcised hearts be humbled, and they then accept of the punishment of their iniquity:

Then will I remember my covenant with Jacob, and also my covenant with Isaac, and also my covenant with Abraham will I remember; and I will remember the land. (Lev. 26:40–42, emphasis added)

When King Hezekiah came to the throne and went to work cleansing the temple and restoring its services, his first act was to make a confession of the sins of his fathers (2 Chron. 29:3–11). The godly Ezra, who led out in a great spiritual revival in Israel during the early days of the restoration, began by a confession of the sins of his fathers (Ezra 9:5–15). Likewise, Nehemiah confessed both his own sins and the sins of his fathers as he viewed the plight of the Israel of his own day, saying, "both I and my father's house have sinned ..." (Neh. 1:6). And let us not forget the confession of the great and true man of God, Daniel: "We have sinned ... neither have we hearkened unto ... the prophets.... O Lord, to us *belongeth* confusion of face," etc. (Dan. 9:5, 6, 8).

How was it, again, that the Seventh-day Adventist churchmen expressed their view on this matter?

We do not believe that it is according to God's plan and purpose for the present leadership of the movement to make acknowledgement or confession, either private or public, concerning any of the mistakes made by the leadership of a bygone generation.... We have no need to go back to 1888; those days are past ... (GCDLC, p. 9)

Regarding the review of the manuscript, we conclude that the committee was a farce, for it was conducted in the same way that governments, militaries and churches carry out investigations, with no intent to subject themselves to independent, objective, and unbiased assessors. A review of the names on the GCDLC will strike the observer as having gross conflict of interest in that these would be highly biased against any favorable assessment of the validity of Wieland and Short's study. For instance, W. E. Read, L. H. Christian, L. E. Froom, J. I. Robison, D. E. Rebok, and A. L. White were some of the very ones who were directly involved in the revising of history and who would be implicated in the charges that the denomination was being led into Baal worship! How could we expect these men to indict themselves of malfeasance? In addition, many of the same members of the various committees who would negatively evaluate the Wieland and Short manuscript over the next several years would also be sitting on the committee to evaluate the manuscript for *Questions on Doctrine*, giving their approval. This is not an insignificant parallel.

In 1958, as the writings of Wieland and Short became available on a worldwide scale, the church gave an even more detailed answer to earnest Bible students. After the leadership's response in 1951, a strong agitation arose in the ranks of Adventism. Their response strongly reaffirmed their stand in opposition to the message of 1888, taking active steps to quiet the agitation and lead the church in the strongest opposition to those who were prepared to study and to spread the message of Waggoner and Jones. I take the following directly from the document itself:

It was thought that the report of seven years ago had closed the matter. The views and conclusions of the two brethren had been dealt with in oral hearing and in written presentation.... any persons referring to, upholding, or even circulating the Wieland and Short manuscript are therefore guilty of improper procedure.... there is no justification for the sweeping charges set forth in the thesis of this manuscript.... the authors of "1888 Re-examined" have produced a manuscript that is detrimental to the church, derogatory to the leaders of the church, and to uninformed individuals who may happen to read it. (*Further Appraisal of the Manuscript "1888 Re-Examined," General Conference, Takoma Park, Washington, DC, Sept. 1958*, pp. 3, 48, 49)

This condemnatory work continues into our day. I myself have spoken with people in different countries who have either been disfellowshipped or commanded to leave or discontinue their teaching for the crime of presenting the message, along with the facts of its rejection by the denominational leaders and the facts of the church's denial of her rejection of the message. Generally any truth-telling or presentation of unvarnished history by individuals in the denominational setting can rapidly saddle them with the titles of "church bashers" and "smiters of the brethren," which not infrequently results in "trial by night" convictions and the execution of disciplinary measures according to the rules of the Church Manual.

The Two Calls of Matthew 22, a Parabolic Dual Prophecy

The twenty-second chapter of Matthew is very important for us to study. It is a parable that does more than teach a principle. It is actually prophetic in nature. Ellen White uses the term "parabolic prophecy" to describe the parable in Zechariah of Joshua and the high priest.

It is not a matter of private interpretation or conjecture that Matthew 22 is a parabolic prophecy, nor is it that the parable of *the two calls to the bidden ones* applies first to the Jews and then to modern spiritual Israel, for it is a dual prophecy.

We take our cue from inspiration before proceeding.

In *The Great Controversy*, Ellen White clearly placed the time setting as that of the investigative judgment, which we know is an application to our specific time-frame upon whom the ends of the world have come. This suggests that the parable is *primarily* addressing modern spiritual Israel, the end-time remnant.

In the parable of Matthew 22 the same figure of the marriage is introduced, and the investigative judgment is clearly represented as taking place before the marriage.... This work of examination of character, of determining who are prepared for the kingdom of God, **is that of the investigative judgment, the closing work in the sanctuary above**. (*The Great Controversy*, p. 428, emphasis added)

Mrs. White based a sermon on Matthew 22, beginning with verses 1–10, in which she said cryptically, "The portion of Scripture presented before us ... is of intense meaning—*much more than I am able to explain. It is of great interest to us, and we should consider it, and let it have due weight upon our minds*" (Ms. 8, 1874, in *Sermons and Talks*, vol. 1, p. 4, emphasis added). Of course, it would be much more than she could then explain, for she could not define what it meant in detail when the first call of 1888 had not yet been given to the denomination, let alone the second call of 1950. I believe that in her mind, all the promises and threats concerning the denomination were held fast in a paradigm of conditionality, as they should have been and as they had also been held with regard to their counterpart, the ancient Israelites.

Let us break this down a little. In this sermon, Ellen White moved from the application concerning the Jews, stepped outside the parable in homiletic fashion, and then applied it to the gospel going to the world with its ultimate rejection. She even included a linkage to Daniel 9:26 (Ms. 8, 1874, in *Sermons and Talks*, vol. 1, p. 5), which is a reference to the fall of Babylon (see Rev. 18). Yet, then she came to the focus of the message, which brought the parable into the present, saying—

The Lord **is** sending His servants, saying unto all who will hear, "Come, make ready for the great marriage supper of the Lamb; He is soon coming to receive all the faithful to the mansions prepared by Him, to partake of the feast which He hath prepared." He **is** sending, and **hath been sending His servants for some thirty years past to say unto His people**, "Come, make ready, put on your wedding garments; clothe yourselves with meekness, humility, and truth, and have yourselves clad in the righteousness of Christ, that you may be able to appear before Him, and enter into the guest chamber with those who shall sit with Me at the wedding of My Son." (*Sermons and Talks*, vol. 1, pp. 5, 6, emphasis added)

She clearly defined the Advent people as "the bidden," saying:

> May **we** heed the invitation given and make **ourselves** ready that **we** may have admittance into the Master's house, **that He say not unto us that none which were bidden shall taste of His supper.** In the parable, those who were bidden heeded not its invitation, but continued excusing themselves, feasting upon the pleasures of this world as the masses do at the present time. (*Sermons and Talks*, vol. 1, p. 6, emphasis added)

Again, she identified it as a message of present truth:

> This same King is sending forth His servants today. He is inviting His guests, saying, "Come, for all things are now ready." (*Sermons and Talks*, vol. 1, p. 6)

> In the 13th chapter of the Acts of the Apostles, 46th verse, we find that if we put God's work from us, [*what is that work, but to accept the invitation, go into the wedding with the garment of His righteousness, the true gospel*] and judge ourselves unworthy of everlasting life, we have no reason to expect an entrance into the kingdom. The 24th verse of the 14th chapter of Luke informs us that "none of those men which were bidden shall taste of my supper."
>
> The great eternal Father has prepared a marriage feast for His Son. **Will we give heed to His servants who have been and are being sent forth to proclaim unto us the solemn invitation?** Or shall we make light of it? (*Sermons and Talks*, vol. 1, p. 8, emphasis added)

Let us now look at the parable itself.

The *making ready* for the marriage is not the marriage itself. It is the preparation for it, and it includes the drawing up of a guest list and the issuing of invitations. We shall see that, in both the history of the Jews and of the Seventh-day Adventists, the making ready for the marriage is a separate item from the two subsequent calls to the wedding.

So the first call is akin to a second invitation; the second call is a third invitation. The reality, however, is that it is not a new invitation but a reminder to respond to the invitation already made. The significance of all of this is that God is not the one who is delaying the consummation. It could have taken place when the invitation was first made. That initial invitation created the group referred to as "the bidden."

Now, what is the marriage? "By the marriage is represented the union of humanity with divinity" (*Christ's Object Lessons*, p. 307). This is what God has always wanted to accomplish. God waited for the church to come out of Babylonian captivity before issuing the invitation to the marriage. This was to set up a new day of opportunity. While in captivity, there was too much in the way. They would never stand up as a church, and they would be crushed. They were not free to develop in righteousness, although there were a few souls that did stand true to God—Daniel and his three Hebrew companions.

The Jewish church demonstrates three historic opportunities which are, again, the invitation and the two calls. The commencement of the prophetic time period in 457 BC represented the invitation to enter into a time to make an end of sin and to bring in everlasting righteousness, etc. (Dan. 9:24). This refers to the 70 weeks (or 490 years) that were cut off from the larger 2300-day prophecy (Dan. 8:14). The invitation was issued first in that they were given the initial "seven weeks" of the seventy weeks to "build Jerusalem … in troublous times" (Dan. 9:25). A further analysis of the "street" and the "wall" to be rebuilt indicates that the return of the town square signifies self-governance and the re-establishment of their worship according to the "wall" of the Ten Commandments, which contains the Sabbath. Let the reader ponder the parallel to this fulfillment as modern spiritual Israel is given the invitation to become a people founded on the restoration of the law of God and true worship. The first call to the marriage feast came when Christ sent out the twelve and then the seventy.

> The call to the feast had been given by Christ's disciples. Our Lord had sent out the twelve and afterward the seventy, proclaiming that the kingdom of God was at hand, and calling upon men to repent and believe the gospel. But the call was not heeded. **Those who are bidden to the feast did not come.** (*Christ's Object Lessons*, p. 308, emphasis added)

The second call to the nation was at Pentecost:

> **The servants were sent out later** to say, "Behold, I have prepared my dinner; my oxen and my fatlings are killed, and all things are ready: come unto the marriage." [Matt. 22:4.] This was the message borne to the Jewish nation after the crucifixion of Christ; but the nation that claimed to be God's peculiar people rejected the gospel brought to them in the power

of the Holy Spirit. Many did this in the most scornful manner. Others were so exasperated by the offer of salvation, the offer of pardon for rejecting the Lord of glory, that they turned upon the bearers of the message. There was "a great persecution." Acts 8:1. Many both of men and women were thrust into prison, and some of the Lord's messengers, as Stephen and James, were put to death. (*Christ's Object Lessons*, p. 308, emphasis added)

When the rejection of the second call was complete, the followers of Christ forever left the synagogue. Physical Israel's day of opportunity was past. The judgment came, and the king sent forth His armies and destroyed the city—a destruction that took place in AD 70 (Matt. 22:7).

With the destruction of the city anchored in time, we "rewind" prophecy to see another kind of call, appearing as a *third* call. This time it was not to the Jews, but to all who would come—from the "highways and hedges." The call would not exclude the Jews, but it was not specifically for the Jewish nation.

How should we understand verse 7, which portrays the wrathful king sending out His armies after the second call and destroying the city? The city was not destroyed until after the call to the Gentiles, which occurs in verses 8–10. Therefore, this is an anticipatory statement of physical destruction. In addition, we can view the "destroying army" in a spiritual sense, which would be the *ongoing message* during a period when probation had already closed for the church of the Jewish nation. Individuals could still respond and leave the city. The synagogues were still functioning. Yet, the institutional church was written off. Its destruction was ensured by its rejection of the message and invitation. When the full time had come and no more individuals would respond, the physical destruction took place. Interestingly, we find in the inspired writings a striking use of how the symbol of the brightness of His coming brings destruction in a comparative application of the second coming to the destruction of the ancient Israelite church:

> Then shall they that obey not the gospel be consumed with the spirit of His mouth and be destroyed with the brightness of His coming. 2 Thessalonians 2:8. **Like Israel of old the wicked destroy themselves;** they fall by their iniquity. By a life of sin, they have placed themselves so out of harmony with God, their natures have become so debased with evil, that the manifestation of His glory is to them a consuming fire. (*The Great Controversy*, p. 37, emphasis added)

It is *the message of mercy spurned* that is represented in the Biblical/Hebraic mode of expression as *that which destroys*:

> Let ministers and people remember that **gospel truth ruins** if it does not save. The soul that refuses to listen to the invitations of mercy from day to day can soon listen to the most urgent appeals without an emotion stirring his soul. (*Testimonies for the Church*, vol. 5, p. 134, emphasis added)

Now we move forward to examine the parable as it applies to Seventh-day Adventism. Coming to the marriage is not a physical act; it is the spiritual work of soul preparation in which sin is put away, for sin is the barrier that prevents the marriage from going forward. The fault lies not with Jesus but with the Bride who is failing to be serious about the betrothal.

> Before He, who is King of Kings and Lord of Lords, can return in the clouds of Heaven, there must be the consummation of the marriage between Christ and His Church. In other words, before the end of probationary time can take place, God must have a church upon this earth, "not having spot or wrinkle or any such thing". Ephesians 5:27. An end must have been made of all sin in every one in this church forever, and everlasting righteousness must have been brought into every one of the members. (Wright, *Last Day Events*, p. 80)

So, God had hoped to consummate the marriage through the Jewish people, but they rejected Him. The first and second calls both failed. The apostolic church went into the wilderness as God waited for the day when He could bring forward another opportunity.

The end of the 1260 years had arrived in 1798. The Protestant reformation opened up a new age of freedom. God again worked toward His purpose to provide a bride for His Son. This day of opportunity came again at the close of the 2300 days in the Great Advent Awakening with the Millerite movement of 1831–1844. The marriage is made, and the invitations are sent.

> God's church on earth was as verily in captivity during this long period of relentless persecution as were the children of Israel held captive in Babylon during the period of the exile. (*Prophets and Kings*, p. 714)

The papal bonds had been broken, the people had religious freedom, and the needed light was shining through to enable them all to make a complete and final end of all sin and sinning. Though not yet consummated, the marriage had been made. (Wright, *Last Day Events*, p. 85)

The guests were bidden through the sounding of the midnight cry, "Behold the Bridegroom cometh; go ye out to meet Him" (Matt. 25:6). (See also Dan. 7:9, 10; Dan. 8:14; Rev. 4, 5; Heb. 1:3, 8:1). "I saw the Father rise from the throne, and in a flaming chariot go into the holy of holies within the veil, and sit down." Why did He do that? This was to go in to make the marriage for His Son. "Then Jesus rose up from the throne … Then He raised His right arm, and we heard His lovely voice saying, 'Wait here; I am going to My Father to receive the kingdom; keep your garments spotless, and in a little while I will return from the wedding and receive you to Myself' " (*Early Writings*, p. 55).

Again, take notice of the movements, plainly defined as going into the most holy place *to the wedding*—to *the marriage*—and we will see that when He leaves that place, it is *the return* from the wedding.

The proclamation, "Behold, the Bridegroom cometh," in the summer of 1844, led thousands to expect the immediate advent of the Lord. At the appointed time **the Bridegroom came**, not to the earth, as the people expected, but to the Ancient of Days in Heaven, **to the marriage**, the reception of His kingdom. "They that were ready went in with Him to the marriage: and the door was shut." They were not to be present in person at the marriage; for it takes place in heaven, while they are upon the earth. The followers of Christ are to "wait for their Lord, **when He will** return from **the wedding**." Luke 12:36. But they are to understand His work, and to follow Him by faith as He goes in before God. It is in this sense that they are said to **go in to the marriage**. (*The Great Controversy*, p. 427, emphasis added)

This going into the wedding in 1844 involves the creation of a people classified as the "bidden ones." These were a people paralleling the historical return of the exiles who were called to rebuild the sanctuary in the days of Ezra and Nehemiah. Both had been in bondage to Babylon, their Babylon was physical and ours is spiritual.

This is the sounding of the seventh angel: "But in the days of the voice of the seventh angel, when he shall begin to sound, the mystery of God should be finished, as he hath declared to his servants the prophets" (Rev. 10:7). What is the mystery of God? "To whom God would make known what *is* the riches of the glory of this mystery among the Gentiles; which is Christ in you, the hope of glory" (Col. 1:27). It is to "present every man perfect in Christ Jesus" (v. 28). The finishing of the mystery of God is the consummation of the marriage.

Nonetheless, it did not happen, as we see in the prophecy and in history. There was a falling away, and a tarrying time came in.

Had Adventists, after the great disappointment in 1844, held fast their faith and followed on unitedly in the opening providence of God, receiving the message of the third angel and in the power of the Holy Spirit proclaiming it to the world, they would have seen the salvation of God, the Lord would have wrought mightily with their efforts, the work would have been completed, and Christ would have come ere this to receive His people to their reward. But in the period of doubt and uncertainty that followed the disappointment, many of the advent believers yielded their faith.… Thus **the work was hindered, and the world was left in darkness**. Had the whole Adventist body united upon the commandments of God and the faith of Jesus, how widely different would have been our history! (Ms. 4, 1883, in *Evangelism*, pp. 695, 696, emphasis added)

Therefore, due to their failure to receive the message of the third angel, which was the invitation to the wedding, there had to come later a special call to Adventists, the bidden ones, to get them to attend the wedding.

In their failure, they had sunk into a state of lukewarmness and legalism. A message and experience was needed to revive and reform them so that the work could go forward as God has always intended. The first call was the presentation of the message of Christ our Righteousness by the men sent of heaven, Elders Jones and Waggoner. This call went out between the years of 1888 and 1893. This call to the marriage is the complete presentation of the gospel, not only showing us that we have a problem with sin but giving counsel regarding the way it is to be dealt with in our lives. If the law is preached without the gospel, the hearer sinks into despair. This was the condition to which Adventism had reached prior to the coming of the call. Search the history books. Search the Spirit of Prophecy. You will not find any such call coming prior to this time. There is much lamenting of the condition of the people but nothing to indicate any special movement to remedy the situation.

The parabolic prophecy states that He "sent out His servants to call those who were invited to the wedding" (Matt. 22:3, NKJV). Compare the following thought from inspiration describing the arrival of His servants with their message in 1888: "The Lord in His great mercy sent a most precious message *to His people* through Elders Waggoner and Jones" (*Testimonies to Ministers*, p. 91, emphasis added).

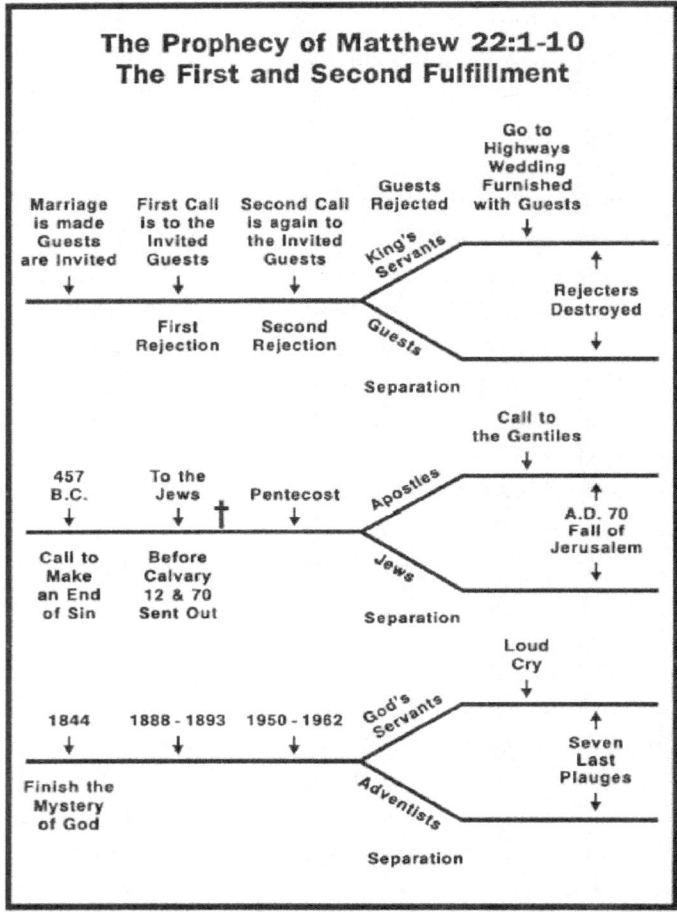

Comparing the two first calls to the ancients and the moderns respectively, we find that God sent the message to *those who were bidden*—the professed people of God. As the twelve disciples were sent out by Christ to the Jewish people, they were instructed to go only to the "lost sheep of the house of Israel" (Matt. 10:6). The disciples were the counterpart to the messengers Jones and Waggoner, whose message was sent to "His people." The later commission to the seventy disciples was to visit both Jews and Gentiles, even as the second call had not yet been issued. In *type* this would also apply to the church of today, which is on a mission to go into the entire world, even while yet being of such an unconverted and wanting Laodicean condition.

This first call was rejected. There is great debate in the church about this, as we have covered in this book. The church claims that the message brought a crisis and the church came through victorious, carrying the message that was received to this day. However, it is clear that the message was not accepted on three basic counts:

- *First, the Bible.* The parabolic prophecy of Matthew 22 declares it by the teaching of the Living Word Himself.

- *Second, the Spirit of Prophecy.* After the 1888 General Conference, the message which came by inspiration to the church states clearly what had happened during those years of 1888–1893, "The prejudices and opinions that prevailed at Minneapolis are not dead by any means" (*Testimonies to Ministers*, p. 467). This clearly indicates that there was no victory for the Lord at Minneapolis. Yet again, "By exciting that opposition [*at Minneapolis*], Satan succeeded in shutting away from our people, in a great measure, the special power of the Holy Spirit.... The light that is to lighten the whole earth with its glory was resisted, and by the action of our own brethren has been in a great degree kept away from the world" (Lt. 96, 1896, to Uriah Smith, in *The Ellen G. White 1888 Materials*, p. 1575).

- *Third, history, the witness of time.* Time always tells. The message, when allowed to run, brings the latter rain and loud cry, and final events play out *and Christ comes*. None of this has happened. If these things are happening at the time of your reading, then the message has, at last, been allowed to work in sufficient strength of numbers, and you are that final generation of living elect.

The failure to heed the first call is not irrevocable. It does not bring the church to the point where it is said, "they which were bidden were not worthy" (Matt. 22:8). The second call must come before this.

Between the years of the first call of 1888–1893 and the mid-twentieth century, the books of Jones and Waggoner and the 1888 message had sunk away to obscurity. Their names were not mentioned, nor were their sermons ever brought to light. This can only be because that is the way the church wanted it. However, at the beginning of the 1950s, when the second call messengers, Wieland and Short, came on the scene, sadly, they too were rejected.

The General Conference of 1962 was seen by some as "the last hope that the church would accept the message. During the previous twelve years, we had seen the light rejected at every level except the General Conference in session" (Wright, *Last Day Events*, p. 92). However, at this conference session, the issue was not addressed in the slightest manner. Truly, the church took it lightly ("made light of it") and went about their business as usual (Matt. 22:5). The conference came and went. The day of opportunity had been wasted again.

So it is necessary that there be another movement in the church of the third angel's message—the church headed by Christ. The church of the fourth angel will give the third angel's message in the power of the latter rain. It will not be "the bidden ones" who give the message. The parabolic prophecy tells us it is so:

> Then saith he to his servants, The wedding is ready, but **they which were bidden were not worthy**.
>
> Go ye therefore into the highways, and as many as ye shall find, bid to the marriage.
>
> So those servants went out into the highways, and gathered together all as many as they found, both bad and good: and the wedding was furnished with guests. (Matt. 22:8–10, emphasis added)

Those whom God is leading and directing are His people, His Church. Who at this time is He leading? Is it the bidden ones who have rejected His call for the second time? Or is it the servants who gave the second call? (Wright, *Last Day Events*, p. 95)

The call to those in the highways and the hedges is the representation of the loud cry given in the power of the latter rain. There is no problem deducing this because of the fact that it is the last message ever to be given. By this means the guests are gathered to the marriage, and, just so soon as they are, the judgment of the living takes place symbolized by the entrance of the King to examine the guests. With this event, human probation ends. While those who are clad in the wedding garment remain in the marriage chamber, those who are dressed in the robe of their own works are expelled and consigned to destruction.

This prophecy would seem to indicate that the gathering in from the highways, which is the going forth of the loud cry, takes place immediately after the rejection of the second call. However, other prophecies such as that of the Ten Virgins and the Shaking show that a period of time elapses between the final rejection by the bidden ones of the second call, and the commencement of the loud cry. During that interval, the Lord prepares the little company for their tremendous work of giving the last message of mercy to a perishing world.

Today we are in that period. (Wright, *Last Day Events*, p. 96)

We will pick up later on more details of the discussion of the second call and its aftermath as it continues into the fourth generation.

Ecumenism in the Third Generation

It is time to continue the discussion of ecumenism as it takes place in the *third* generation by covering certain interesting and key events, though we will find much more on the ecumenical diversion within "the remnant" to discuss when we get to the account of the fourth generation.

> A crucial aspect [*of the formation of the ecumenical connection*] is that Elder Ruben R. Figuhr, the General Conference president who shepherded the entire Evangelical Conferences with his continuing approval, continued on as president until 1966. That provided ten years, from the close of those conferences, for our leaders to lay a solid foundation of friendship with the NCC, WCC, the Evangelicals and, unfortunately, with the Vatican. By that time, the die was cast. We had our men solidly in place at both of them, and we were involved in a number of national councils in Europe and on other continents. (Vance Ferrell, *Seventh-day Adventist/Vatican Ecumenical Involvement: Book One: History*, p. 21)

During the 1950s, the Seventh-day Adventist Church was seen to open up boldly as never before in the establishment of relations with other denominations at the same time that Rome was doing the same.

On January 25, 1959, Pope John XXIII announced to the world that he was convening *Vatican II*—the first General Council since Vatican I in 1869–1870 (the council which approved "papal infallibility").

Vatican II was to have an immense impact, not

only on the Catholic Church, but also on Protestantism. John XXIII tried in every way to be friendly to, what he termed, "our separated brethren." The council, which began October 11, 1962, was to open the door to Vatican representation at the World Council of Churches and "conversations" (formal doctrinal meetings) with other denominations.

John XXIII died on June 3, 1963; the second and third sessions of the Council were held under the sponsorship of Pope Paul VI, who tried to maintain the liberal course marked out by John.

The Protestant world was rocked by the open friendliness they encountered at the Vatican, when they sent their observers and reporters there.... Yet, underlying all the smiles, Rome was unchanging in its basic, apostate doctrines.... (Ferrell, p. 21)

Thousands of copies of *Questions on Doctrine* were sent free of charge to Protestant and Catholic colleges, seminaries, and church offices. Adventist officials Leroy E. Froom, Roy Allan Anderson, and Walter R. Beach (father to Bert B. Beach, GC secretary from 1954–1970, whom we will discuss under the fourth generation) made numerous friendships that resulted in cordial contacts with the National Council of Churches and the World Council of Churches. As the evangelical conferences and the publishing of *Questions on Doctrine* had brought in a new era of compromise with teachings of fundamental Adventist doctrine, it became easy and natural to mix with the Sunday-keeping world of the fallen churches, for now there was found so much in common. The Standish brothers concurred:

The Barnhouse-Martin Dialogue with the General Conference in 1956 opened a floodgate of ecumenism. It led to conversations with the World Council of Churches (WCC) which has drawn us closer and closer in the web of unsanctified ecumenism. (*Half a Century of Apostasy*, p. 31)

Though called "informal," these "conversations" were later formalized as church-authorized and funded annual meetings, as well as by the involvement of the executive committees of the three Adventist Divisions that gave their blessing by their facilitating of the selection of the representatives. This led eventually to the Seventh-day Adventist Church joining the WCC as an "observer" member and the joint-publication of a book by the WCC and the Seventh-day Adventists—*So Much in Common* (to be discussed later under the fourth generation material).

Strange as it may seem, these yearly Consultations are an indirect by-product of Vatican II (1962–1965). In fact, while in Rome in connection with the Vatican Council a WCC staff member and **an Adventist representative** came to the conclusion that an informal meeting of a small group of Seventh-day Adventists with an equal number of representatives from the World Council of Churches would fulfill a useful purpose—Adventists being insufficiently informed regarding the World Council of Churches, and **the WCC staff and church leaders being equally in need of additional and more comprehensive knowledge regarding the Seventh-day Adventist Church**. (Bert B. Beach, *So Much In Common*, p. 98, emphasis added)

"Strange as it may seem ..." said Dr. Beach. Indeed, this ecumenical flame is a strange fire. Of course, the participants always have ways of presenting matters to be able to cultivate a perception of innocence and beneficial purpose. Why would Seventh-day Adventists be eager to give Babylon intelligence on the Lord's work? Does this make sense? Few will raise a flag of warning according to the inspired testimonies to the church. Inevitably, once the church steps onto these slippery slopes, they will soon be sliding at full speed.

The time was when Protestants [Adventists] placed a high value upon the liberty of conscience which had been so dearly purchased. They taught their children to abhor popery and held that to seek harmony with Rome would be disloyalty to God. But how widely different are the sentiments now expressed!

The defenders of the papacy declare that the church has been maligned, and the Protestant [Adventist] world are inclined to accept the statement. Many urge that it is unjust to judge the church of today by the abominations and absurdities that marked her reign during the centuries of ignorance and darkness. They excuse her horrible cruelty as the result of the barbarism of the times and plead that the influence of modern civilization has changed her sentiments. (*The Great Controversy*, p. 563)

Would we be overreaching or did we read in our own opinions in adding "Adventist" in the statement above? Not at all. Seventh-day Adventists had a contingent of four high ranking Adventist officials in attendance at Vatican Council II. Herein the road to Rome was paved.

Among these men was "Uncle Arthur" S. Maxwell, well known for writing the Adventist classic children's series *Bedtime Stories* and *The Bible Stories*. After the session, he gave a glowing report of his proximity to the pope, marking off the distance in paces that he sat from the pope. Speaking of the pope's address at the opening of the final session, Maxwell commented that, "it was a beautiful speech." Then Maxwell asked and then answered his own question, "Do you know what his subject was? Love." Ellen White's reply to this would be that "Her spirit is no less cruel and despotic now than when she crushed out human liberty and slew the saints of the Most High" (*The Great Controversy*, p. 571).

Maxwell was then editor of the *Signs of the Times* and was obviously very excited about his experience as he gave his report at the University Church at Loma Linda, California, entitled, "The Outstretched Hand." His telling of the story reveals a sentiment that is absolutely foreign to the past position of Adventism regarding the papacy. For example, James White wrote: "Where there is not agreement in theory, there can be, in the christian sense, *no real communion of heart and fellowship of feeling*." ("Fifty Unanswerable Arguments," *Review and Herald*, Jan. 14, 1861, p. 53, emphasis added). White said that for believers who close their eyes "to some of the clearest light of the Scriptures," refusing "their most unequivocal testimony," we cannot "extend to him the hand of Christian fellowship" (*Review and Herald*, Jan. 14, 1861, pp. 52, 53, emphasis added).

Here is the first paragraph of Maxwell's report:

First, the friendliness of the welcome. You see, **I've been there several times, that is, to Rome.** Always a sort of an iciness there, but not any more, not any more! And it was evident in so many ways. For instance, in the giving of these press passes, Brother Loewen was there from *Religious Liberty*, Brother Cottrell from the *Review and Herald*, Brother Beach was there from northern Europe, and I was there from the *Signs*, and provided you had a good reason for asking for a pass, you got it. If you were an editor or a correspondent for a real newspaper, they gave the pass, and they gave them to people of all faiths. Here, four Adventists got these passes. I thought you would like to see mine. It's the only document I have which has the crossed keys and the triple crown on it. I have to be careful when I show this. I don't want anybody to think I'm going over to the Church of Rome. But it is a very nice little pass, and it was very valuable. This little pass got me anywhere I wanted to go at the time of the council. (quoted by Neil C. Livingston, *Vatican Council II and Seventh-day Adventists—So Much in Common*, emphasis added)

One must surely wonder why a high ranking Adventist official had been many times to the seat of the Antichrist power, the beast of Revelation 13! In relating the change in attitude toward the Adventists, should we not rather have a healthy measure of consternation than approving applause? Did not the prophet to the end-time people of God warn, "There has been a change; but *the change is not in the Papacy*" (*The Great Controversy*, p. 571, emphasis supplied).

"Catholicism indeed resembles much of the Protestantism that now exists," Ellen White wrote, "because Protestantism has so greatly degenerated since the days of the Reformers." (*ibid.*, GC, p. 571, emphasis supplied). Have we Seventh-day Adventists also "degenerated" to the point that we also are becoming like the Church of Rome? Today one could rephrase Ellen White's statement to read, "Catholicism indeed resembles much of the Adventism that now exists, *because Adventism has so greatly degenerated since the days of the Pioneers.*" (Neil C. Livingston, *The Greatest Conspiracy*, p. 292)

The Roman Church now presents a fair front to the world, covering with apologies her record of horrible cruelties. **She has clothed herself in Christlike garments; but she is unchanged.** Every principle of the papacy that existed in past ages exists today. The doctrines devised in the darkest ages are still held. Let none deceive themselves. The papacy that Protestants are now so ready to honor is the same that ruled the world in the days of the Reformation, when men of God stood up, at the peril of their lives, to expose her iniquity. **She possesses the same pride and arrogant assumption** that lorded it over kings and princes, and claimed the prerogatives of God. **Her spirit is no less cruel and despotic now** than when she crushed out human liberty and slew the saints of the Most High. (*The Great Controversy*, p. 571, emphasis added)

Maxwell's sermon continues with these amazing words:

> Then, another aspect of the friendliness–the way they arranged for the press of the world to have the best seats at the opening ceremony. **I sat closer to the pope than any of the cardinals. I was only forty feet away from him for three or four hours**, and I had the clearest view, just as clear as some of you forty feet away. **The reason I know he was forty feet away–I stepped it out after the service was over**, because I thought, "Nobody will ever believe me, that I sat **so long, so near** to **His Holiness**." But I had a wonderful view, and I saw some most fascinating close-up views which I won't tell you now, but I would tell some of you privately—some very, very interesting little human details, which you see only when you're very close in. (Maxwell, emphasis added)

These words convey a certain attitude of awe and even reverence. We surely must wonder how a high official of the Seventh-day Adventist Church could call the man of sin "His Holiness" or even why he would. Is this not taking part in the blasphemy that is taught by the Roman Church, "The pope is of so great dignity and so exalted that he is not a mere man, but as it were God, and the vicar of God," or "The Pope is not only the vicar of Christ, he is Jesus Christ, hidden under the vail of flesh"? (See original sources at "Papal Claims to Authority," available at http://1ref.us/ic, accessed 10/19/16.)

Reporting on the same event, brothers Russell and Colin Standish related some of Maxwell's "Impressions of Vatican II" sermon, with comments:

> Speaking of the apparent changes he noticed in the Roman Catholic Church, Pastor Maxwell exclaimed:
>> Fascinating! It's a new day, friends. It's a new day! (Maxwell, p. 7).
>
> The level of Dr. Maxwell's imbibed deception may be measured by two statements among many. He was asked, "Is the Catholic Church sincere in this declaration of religious liberty?"
>> Now, my personal view is that they are sincere—they are utterly sincere.... This is a tremendous change that the Roman Catholic Church has embarked upon.... It's an amazing thing that the [Roman Catholic] church has done to set itself alongside Protestants in declaring that every man has the right to choose his own religion and follow the dictates of his own conscience. Whether the church will stay by that forever; **I DON'T KNOW**. (Maxwell, p. 11, emphasis added).
>
> This was a startling admission of ignorance on this matter. Had not Pastor Maxwell read Revelation chapter 13 or *The Great Controversy*? Had Pastor Maxwell lived into the twenty-first century, he would have learned that Pope John Paul II beatified Pope Pius IX who had declared in his diabolical *Syllabus of Errors*, published 8 December, 1864, that:
>> The absurd and erroneous doctrines or ravings in defense of liberty of conscience are a most pestilential error, a pest of all others, most to be dreaded in a state.
>
> Concluding his comments, Pastor Maxwell advised:
>> We must rethink our approach to our Roman Catholic friends. How can we reject an outstretched hand and be Christians? How can we say that they belong to antichrist when they reveal many beautiful Christian attitudes? Does that shock you very much? I hope it does! I just hope it does! ... We can't stamp them with the mark of the beast. What a terrible thing we've been doing to them all through the years. [Maxwell, p. 13]
>
> It has never been the role of Seventh-day Adventists to "stamp" anyone with the mark of the beast. That decision is made by Christ. But Rome IS the antichrist power. (Russell and Colin Standish, *Half a Century of Apostasy*, pp. 35, 36)

Concluding Material for the Third Generation

It is said that the third angel's message is out of date. Yet, that message is what makes us unique! If we do not have that message, we do not have anything special to give, and we might as well disperse into the Babylonian churches!

There was no way that Generation Three could have been ready for the harvest when profound and widespread ignorance of the heaven-sent 1888 message existed throughout the length and breadth of Adventism. Are we today in this same condition? Are we ignorant of the message God sent us? God winks at times of ignorance. Yet, now He commands people everywhere to repent. As individuals, we can change. We can go back and start studying for ourselves. We can start asking the leadership, "Why aren't you proclaiming this message? It is the cure to our problem. Failure to proclaim it is why Jesus has not returned. Why are the people kept in this spiritual disease?"

An unwillingness to yield up preconceived opinions, and to accept this truth, lay at the foundation of a large share of the opposition manifested at Minneapolis against the Lord's message through Brethren Waggoner and Jones. **By exciting that opposition, Satan succeeded in shutting away from our people**, in a great measure, **the special power of the Holy Spirit** that God longed to impart to them. The enemy prevented them from obtaining that efficiency which might have been theirs in carrying the truth to the world, as the apostles proclaimed it after the day of Pentecost. The light that is to lighten the whole earth with its glory was resisted, and **by the action of our own brethren** has been in a great degree **kept away from the world**. (Lt. 96, 1896, to Uriah Smith, in *The Ellen G. White 1888 Materials*, p. 1575, emphasis added)

Notice that it is the power of the Holy Spirit that we need first to "obtain the efficiency" we need to carry the message to the world. It is the power of the Holy Spirit that will finish the work. That work must first be completed in us. Then, the Lord can pour His Spirit into fit vessels for the final movements and not until then. Unless we realize the importance of the message and of teaching our brethren that this work began in 1888, we will not be in line to receive the Spirit's power. Most Adventists do not apprehend that the fourth angel started His work, and then something went wrong. Jesus would have come back in that generation except for the unbelief of His people. Now, we might say that we are glad that this happened because now we too can be included. That is a fair point. Yet, shall we perpetuate unbelief so that we can see another generation of our children and their children? The day of opportunity is today. Let us no longer delay. Once we know the truth, we must impart it clearly to others. We have a responsibility not to perpetuate the delay but to end it.

Ron Duffield, in his book, *Wounded in the House of His Friends: When Will the Aborted Latter Rain Resume?*, described the 1892 camp-meeting revivals, demonstrating that the light of the glory of God in the fourth angel had come. "Ellen White would write to S. N. Haskell one of the most ardent letters she had yet written on the implications of the most precious message of righteousness by faith sent to God's people.... No less than seven times in this single letter Ellen White used present-tense language indicating that the loud cry message of Revelation 18 had already begun, and this could only be possible through the special endowment of the Holy Spirit" (*Wounded in the House of His Friends*, pp. 41, 42). Haskell later wrote a series of articles for the *Review and Herald*, bringing forward the urgency of the times and Ellen White's admonition for the people:

The first movement necessary to fit the people to receive the outpouring of the Spirit of God is to realize that Christ is our personal Saviour, to make to ourselves a personal application of his promises, and to realize that the testimonies of inspiration are addressed to us personally; and in thus making a personal application of the promises of God, we are bringing Christ into the heart, which will fit us to take a part in the closing work; consequently, when our attention is more particularly turned to this phase of the work, and a personal application of the promises is made, it is really the beginning of the loud cry of the third angel's message.... (S. N. Haskell, " 'Watchman, What of the Night?'—No. 3. The Loud Cry," *Review and Herald*, July 26, 1892, p. 474)

In this article, he quoted from Ellen White's personal letter to him:

What more can I say? My heart is filled to overflowing. Only those are fit for this work who are imbued with the Holy Spirit. **The light has come; the light which will lighten the whole earth with its bright rays** has been shining from the throne of God.... I tell you, God is testing us now, just now. The whole earth is to be lightened with the glory of God. That light is shining now, and how hard it is for proud hearts to accept Jesus as their personal Saviour; how hard to **get out of the rut of legal religion**; how hard to grasp the rich, free gift of Christ! ... [Lt. 10, 1892]

Haskell continued:

It is evident, therefore, that none but those who experience this incoming of the Saviour into their hearts will be in a condition to receive and take part in the loud cry which is to be given in the immediate future. **This is really the beginning of it** ... (*Review and Herald*, July 26, 1892, p. 474)

Are we getting this? It is apparent that we have not been realizing the situation we are in. As a people, we profess that we believe in Jesus and have let Him in. Yet, if that were true, we would be in the process of receiving the latter rain and giving the loud cry. Of course, some are. God does have a people. However, those who are giving the loud cry must swell to a greater number. It is happening—by teaching and preaching this message—and the number and the message will expand!

The people need to understand that we are still in "the rut of legal religion." Of course, we do not see this, for we are Laodicean and are rich, increased with goods, and in need of nothing. Yet, Jesus says that we are blind and need our eyesight restored. We believe that we have the gospel and that we have rousing sermons, songs, prayers, and praise sessions. (At least, on occasion.) We preach: "Jesus did it all!" and "Glory to God!" Yet, we still possess neither the power nor the efficiency to finish the work. Of all generations of Adventism, this one believes itself to be the most Christ-centered ever. Grace and justification, righteousness by faith, and "Jesus only" are ever the subjects of discourse in the pulpit and in print and broadcast media. Yet, we are in the rut of legal religion. We are the epitome of churchianity. We believe that we see Jesus, but we do not see Him. We do not understand His character, and we are relying still upon the arm of flesh. Once we know God as He truly is in Jesus, we will receive power from His Spirit, and the work will be finished quickly. We will no longer rely upon human programming and hierarchy. No longer will we follow the common order. Once God's people are submitted and prepared, He will take the reins into His own hands as He has always desired to do, and He will dwell in us fully, bringing the light of Christ to all the world as Divinity flashes through the sinful flesh of humanity as it did in Christ. The world cannot see the revelation of God in Christ until Christ is revealed in us. That is the way it is.

Consequently, over and above any other subject in describing the devouring pests of the four generations, we point to the 1888 message and its rejection as a most pivotal and decisive point of concern to heaven. For, until the message of righteousness by faith comes to fruition in a generation of believers, there can be no closure to the great controversy. Wieland and Short declared, "God cannot vindicate a lukewarm people," and I would add that neither can a lukewarm people vindicate *Him*. Herein lies the main reason for the publication of this book.

In concluding our report on the third generation, let us consider some excerpts from Chapter 12 of Arnold Wallenkampf's book, *What Every Adventist Should Know About 1888*, for some pertinent thoughts that are axiomatic in covering the "unvarnished" history of Seventh-day Adventism:

As present-day ... Seventh-day Adventist[s] ... we are accountable for continued misportrayal of the 1888 General Conference Session and its aftermath.

History molds both a nation and its people. It has been said that it does not matter who writes a nation's laws, but that it is of utmost importance who writes its history. A nation's history largely molds and shapes the philosophy, experience, and development of future generations.... In the same way, the history of a movement or a church molds and shapes it.

If we do not forthrightly present the history of the 1888 General Conference Session and its aftermath, we as a denomination perpetuate the sin committed at Minneapolis in 1888. By doing so, we join our spiritual forefathers and virtually crucify Christ anew in the person of the Holy Spirit. If we pretend that possibly an initial rejection by "some" later turned into a general and enthusiastic acceptance of the glorious message of righteousness by faith by the church at large, we undoubtedly paint too rosy a picture of our church—the Laodicean church.

It is incumbent on us as a people to confess that for a long time we have largely glossed over the virtual rejection of the 1888 message by most of the delegates to the Minneapolis conference in 1888.

God wants all His followers to be truthful and honest. This applies particularly to those who claim to have "the truth"—a true biblical understanding of the gospel.

Lying and falsehood, on the other hand, stem from the great rebel, the father of lies (John 8:44).

So as the sons and daughters of God and lovers of truth, our present responsibility is to tell the truth about the Minneapolis conference of 1888 and its aftermath. There is no virtue in saying that all has been well when this is not so. Further, by continuing to hide the truth about the Minneapolis conference, we become accomplices with the rejecters of the message ... just as the Jews in the days of Jesus became responsible for the sins of their forefathers by perpetuating these sins.

Our faulty presentation of what actually happened at Minneapolis in 1888 and our denominational view that ... [it] marked a great victory in our history have undoubtedly molded our denomination's thinking and concepts. It has helped make us secure in our Laodicean attitude....

CHAPTER 8.

The Caterpillar

The Fourth Generation of Adventism, 1964–2004

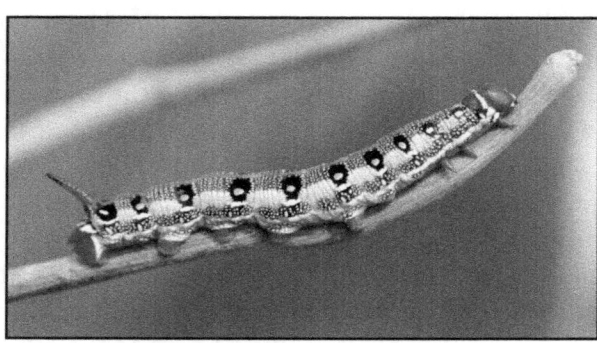

The fourth generation of Adventism, which was from 1964 to 2004, concluded a full cycle of sowing and reaping. The palmerworm, the locust, the cankerworm, and the caterpillar of Joel 1 and 2 have done their baleful work of devouring the message and the people. What a generation the fourth has been! It has seen tremendous events both in Adventism and in the world at large.

Questions on Doctrine's legacy has been a fractured Adventism. Generation Four, coming immediately after those Evangelical Conferences of 1955 and 1956, saw the church become divided into two distinct camps.

Along with the call to repentance of Wieland and Short regarding the denominational rejection of the 1888 message and the concessions to Evangelicalism in the Martin-Barnhouse conferences, we saw the beginning of the disintegration of pre–1950s Adventism, the development of an environment of ongoing controversy, and the formation of a plethora of independent groups all claiming true Adventism. Today we have a church that can be seen in various ways as attempting to hold onto a middle ground but has actually continued losing ground on the slippery slope of liberalism and mainstream Evangelicalism.

Soon the Church was to see the rise of groups defending the old principles of the faith on one hand, and on the other hand the emergence of those who were not content to remain where the authors of *Questions on Doctrine* had ceased. (*Adventism Challenged*, p. 22)

This is yet another example of the parallels between ancient and modern Israel. In **Section I**, we brought out that, after the forty-year reigns of Saul, David, and Solomon, there was a split in the nation. In New Testament times, two infighting factions developed within Israel's leadership—the Pharisees and the Sadducees.

In like manner, in the Fourth Generation of Adventism, we find a split occurring. There were those in the Third Generation who started to study the message of righteousness by faith in Adventism and began the development of two streams of doctrine within the denomination—one called "mainstream" Seventh-day Adventism (evangelical Adventism) and the other called "reform" (historic Adventism). Another general label applied to the two groups would be "conservative" and "liberal." (We are not suggesting that one stream is all right and the other is all wrong.)

We find an ongoing problem, however. Even though many protest groups calling themselves the "reformation" have sprung up in reaction to the rejection of the messages that came in 1888–1893 (first call) and in 1950–1962 (second call), we still see that the Laodicean remedy has not been appropriated or made efficacious. In other words, the same obvious wilderness-wandering status of the mainstream church remains, while the independent movements have not done any better than they, as they build their own houses around their various leaders and remain at odds with the mainstream and with each other. There certainly has been no unified reform among them but only a plethora of "independent atoms." Often the tendency in "reform" is only a pendulum swing that focuses again on the law, on behavior, while not truly entering into the experience of righteousness by faith. The independents believe that they are in the advancing light of the fourth angel. The mainstream also believes itself to be carrying forward this work. Yet, both are still missing elements. As one independent leader put it:

> The reason the message of 1888 failed is that we have never accepted more than half of the message at a time. Adventists of the past preached the law until their preaching was as dry as the hills of Gilboa, but they rejected the other half which gives power to keep the law. In our day many have preached a great deal on what they term faith and justification, but fail to see that the end of true faith is keeping the commandments. (Ron Spear, *Adventism in Crisis*, p. 84)

What can we conclude but that the independents have missed something vital as well? Is it simply that they have become hard-nosed legalists like the Pharisees as many in the "liberal" or "evangelical" camp suggest? While a detailed exploration of this subject is outside the scope of this book, it is clear that there has not been that forward-reaching movement that one would expect if they are truly embracing the light of the glory angel which came in the 1888 era. That message was to be the cure to the Laodicean condition. Yet, the believers are still sick.

The Beginning of the Loud Cry Begins Again

Is true reform alive? As Jesus pondered, "When I return, will I find faith on the earth?" We should all respond with a resounding "YES" because we have read to the end of the book! Jesus comes at that time finding such people of faith, pronouncing, "*He that is righteous, let him be righteous still*" (Rev. 22:11) and He points to them, declaring, "Here are they that keep the commandments and the faith of Jesus" (Rev. 14:12), "Well done, good and faithful servant, thou hast been faithful over a few things ... enter thou into the joy of the Lord" (Matt. 25:23). At some point, these people come onto the scene for the closing of the work in a functionally significant number. They are called the 144,000, a nation of true Israel—people the Lord can use effectively to bring an end to the great controversy by His Spirit in them. They will be a people who embrace the 1888 message. Yet, knowing about that message and appropriating it are two different things. They will have taken it into their bosom, and it will have been their cry day and night as was the cry of Jacob as he clung to the angel, "I will not let thee go, except thou bless me" (Gen. 32:26). As they will have taken the message to heart and opened the door to Jesus, the purpose of the final generation will be demonstrated at last.

Remember that the 1888 era saw what was called only "the beginning" of the light of glory.

> The time of test is just upon us, for the loud cry of the third angel has already **begun** in the revelation of the righteousness of Christ, the sin-pardoning Redeemer. This is **the beginning of the light** of the angel whose glory shall fill the whole earth.... (*Review and Herald*, Nov. 22, 1892, in *Selected Messages*, bk. 1, p. 362, emphasis added)

Recognizing that this was only the beginning, it is clear that there would be more to come. Time and again we have been advised that there would be more light to come.

> If through the grace of Christ His people will become new bottles, He will fill them with the new wine. **God will give additional light**, and old truths will be recovered, and replaced in the framework of truth; and wherever the laborers go, they will triumph.... (*Review and Herald*, Dec. 23, 1890, art. B, emphasis added)

A. T. Jones concurred:

> There will be things to come that will be more surprising than that was to those at Minneapolis,—more surprising than anything we have yet seen. And, brethren, we will be required to receive and preach that truth. But unless you and I have every fiber of that spirit rooted out of our hearts, we will treat that message and the messenger by whom it is sent, as God has declared we have treated this other message. ("The Third Angel's Message-No. 7," *General Conference Daily Bulletin*, Feb. 7, 1893, p. 185)

In their appeal to the church, Wieland and Short also concurred:

> Any reproduction of [the 1888] teachings must therefore be considered as only *the beginning* of the light which is needed ... A sincere acceptance of that self-humbling message would be the necessary preparation for the reception of further light to be

communicated in God's chosen way, in response to the intelligent prayers of His people.... (*An Explicit Confession ... Due the Church*, p. 54)

Many groups have arisen claiming to have that new light. Many of these groups are strong proponents of the 1888 message, as they would have to be to have any credibility. Yet their "light" has often been spurious, unbiblical conjecture. It has been found time and again that these groups also reject the true advance of reformation light when it is presented to them. Thus it is that, as movements, their lights will flicker and fade as the night descends upon the earth. Individuals will make their way, but organized, authoritarian structures of men's devising will be blown away as so much chaff before the winds of the coming hurricane rise to furious intensity. The mainstream will be blown away also, as it is written, "storm and tempest would sweep away the structure" (Lt. 242, 1903, in *Battle Creek Letters*, p. 81).

There is a message that comes out of the advancing light of God's righteous people. It is a new understanding of His character as never before embraced by a movement of God's people with such clarity. A. T. Jones predicted that it would be "more surprising than anything we have yet seen" (*General Conference Daily Bulletin*, Feb. 7, 1893, p. 185). This message has to do with the glory of God and the name of God, which is His character.

The glory of God is His character. While Moses was in the mount, earnestly interceding with God, He prayed, "I beseech Thee, show me Thy glory." In answer God declared "**I will make all My goodness pass before thee, and I will proclaim the name of the Lord before thee**; and will be gracious to whom I will be gracious, and will show mercy on whom I will show mercy." [Exod. 33:19.] (*Signs of the Times*, Sept. 3, 1902, emphasis added)

In every act of life you are to make manifest **the name of God**. This petition calls upon you to **possess His character**. You cannot hallow His name, you cannot represent Him to the world, unless in life and character you represent the very life and character of God. This you can do only through the acceptance of the grace and righteousness of Christ. (*Thoughts from the Mount of Blessing*, p. 107, emphasis added)

Mrs. White clearly pointed to this subject as the advancing light and declared that this is where we should be looking. Heaven has declared through the prophets that the advancing light is a view to a new picture of God:

At no period of time has man learned all that can be learned of the word of God. There are **yet new views of truth to be seen**, and much to be understood **of the character and attributes of God** ... After diligently searching the word, hidden treasures are discovered, and the lover of truth breaks out in triumph ... (Ms. 22, 1895, in *Fundamentals of Christian Education*, p. 444, emphasis added)

Malachi [3:16–18] turns away from the **dark picture which Satan presents** to these professed followers of Jesus Christ, for it is a **libel on the paternal character of God**. Satan has framed this picture for the contemplation of poor, unbelieving, mourning souls, and they have hung it up in memory's hall where they can gaze upon it. But **the Lord has presented another picture** for the contemplation of every believer. "Then they that feared the Lord spake often one to another: and the Lord hearkened ..." [Mal. 3:16]

We are to **seek for precious jewels of truth as for hidden treasure**. We are to have light, that we may diffuse light to others. Those who do this, will be among **that company who think upon the name of the Lord**, and who speak often one to another. They will **study the character of God**, and will become acquainted with their Redeemer. "And this is life eternal, that they might know thee the only true God, and Jesus Christ, whom thou hast sent." [John 17:3.] **Let the character of God be the theme of your thought**; for the Lord Jesus calls the attention of his church to himself, and **would have his people think upon his name**, and impart the knowledge they receive of him to those who are around them. (*Review and Herald*, Sept. 10, 1895, emphasis added)

It is the **darkness of misapprehension of God that is enshrouding the world**. Men are **losing their knowledge of His character**. It has been **misunderstood** and **misinterpreted**. **At this time a message from God is to be proclaimed**, a message illuminating in its influence and saving in its power. His character is to be made known. Into the darkness of the world is to be shed the light of His glory, the light of His goodness, mercy, and truth. (*Christ's Object Lessons*, p. 415, emphasis added)

Mrs. White lamented the darkness on this very point that was upon Seventh-day Adventists:

> At the Kansas meeting my prayer to God was, that the power of the enemy might be broken, and that the people who had been in darkness might open their hearts and minds to the message that God should send them, that they might see **the truth, new to many minds, as old truth in new frame-work. The understanding of the people of God has been blinded; for Satan has misrepresented the character of God.** Our good and gracious Lord **has been presented before the people clothed in the attributes of Satan**, and men and women who have been seeking for truth, have so long **regarded God in a false light** that it is difficult to dispel the cloud that obscures his glory from their view. Many have been living in an atmosphere of doubt, and **it seems almost impossible for them to lay hold on the hope set before them in the gospel of Christ**. (Review and Herald, July 23, 1889, in *The Ellen G. White 1888 Materials*, p. 386, emphasis added)

Ellen White, as does also the Bible, makes many clear key statements about the character of God in relation to His use of violence in the conduct of *His* side of the great controversy. There are defining statements by which we are to interpret the entire body of inspired text with its "language of wrath" that attributes violence to God. These statements show that the proper interpretation of this judgment language of proactive physical force, when it is employed by the divine hand, is to be read as a representation of God's conduct in terms of *doing* that which He *allows*. Statements we hold forth as pivotal in this "new view" of the character of God are for us to study and apply in consistent ways as never before.

While this subject is not to be covered here in any detail, and we recommend the reading of *As He Is: Issues in the 'Character of God' Controversy* by 4th Angel Publications, published by TEACH Services, Inc., we would like to remain on the subject for just a few more quotations for the benefit of the reader who is not already familiar with the content of the "character of God message." As a basic starting point, there needs to be a clarification concerning what the nature of divine wrath is and how it is executed. We begin with the words of the LORD to Moses and several statements through the pen of Ellen White:

> And the LORD said unto Moses, Behold, thou shalt sleep with thy fathers; and this people will rise up, and go a whoring after the gods of the strangers of the land, whither they go *to be* among them, and will forsake me, and break my covenant which I have made with them.
>
> Then my anger shall be kindled against them in that day, and **I will forsake them, and I will hide my face from them**, and they shall be devoured, and many evils and troubles shall befall them; so that they will say in that day, **Are not these evils come upon us, because our God *is* not among us?**
>
> And I will surely hide my face in that day for all the evils which they shall have wrought, in that they are turned unto other gods. (Deut. 31:16–18, emphasis added)

> I was shown that **the judgments of God would not come directly out from the Lord upon them**, but in this way: They place themselves beyond His protection. He warns, corrects, reproves, and points out the only path of safety; then, if those who have been the objects of His special care will follow their own course, independent of the Spirit of God, after repeated warnings, if they choose their own way, then **He does not commission His angels to prevent Satan's decided attacks upon them.** (Lt. 14, 1883, in *Last Day Events*, p. 242, emphasis added)

> **God destroys no man**; but after a time the wicked are given up to the destruction they have wrought for themselves. (*Youth's Instructor*, Nov. 30, 1893)

> This then is the message which we have heard of him, and declare unto you, that **God is light, and in him is no darkness at all.** (1 John 1:5, emphasis added)

> Jesus Christ is the Restorer. Satan, the apostate, is the destroyer. **Here is the conflict** between the Prince of life and the prince of this world … (Lt. 34, 1896, in *Christ Triumphant*, p. 247)

> It is Satan's constant effort to misrepresent the character of God, the nature of sin, and the real issues at stake in the great controversy. (*The Great Controversy*, p. 569)

> Earthly kingdoms rule by the ascendancy of physical power; but **from Christ's kingdom every carnal weapon, every instrument of coercion, is banished.** This kingdom is to uplift and ennoble humanity.

God's church is the court of holy life, filled with varied gifts and endowed with the Holy Spirit. The members are to find their happiness in the happiness of those whom they help and bless. (*Acts of the Apostles*, p. 12, emphasis added)

For the iniquity of his covetousness was I wroth, and **smote him**: I **hid me**, and was wroth, and he went on frowardly in the way of his heart. (Isa. 57:17, emphasis added)

For the trained exegete, note that the statement from Isaiah 57:17 is a chiasm. The center lines of **C**—"*and smote him*" and **C'**—"*I hid me*" are mirror expressions, denoting the same action. This teaches the principle of divine wrath—that the withdrawal of God's presence results in punishment or destruction.

Isa. 57:17 Chiastic Structure

A. For the iniquity of *his covetousness*
  B. Was I *wroth*,
    C. And *smote him:*
    C'. I *hid me,*
  B'. and was *wroth*,
A'. and he went on frowardly in *the way of his heart.*

God does not stand toward the sinner as an executioner of the sentence against transgression; but He leaves the rejectors of His mercy to themselves, to reap that which they have sown. Every ray of light rejected, every warning despised or unheeded, every passion indulged, every transgression of the law of God, is a seed sown which yields its unfailing harvest. The Spirit of God, persistently resisted, is at last withdrawn from the sinner, and then there is left no power to control the evil passions of the soul, and no protection from the malice and enmity of Satan. The destruction of Jerusalem is a fearful and solemn warning to all who are trifling with the offers of divine grace and resisting the pleadings of divine mercy. Never was there given a more decisive testimony to God's hatred of sin and to the certain punishment that will fall upon the guilty. (*The Great Controversy*, p. 36, emphasis added)

Invariably, many questions rise to the surface for the person who has never heard these things before regarding the language of the Bible and what it appears to be saying. A lifetime of the standard teaching of the traditional view of God has been so ingrained in our minds that we have not stopped to consider the glaring contrast between the view of Christ in the Old Testament and the view of Him in the New. We know that He has said that He is the same yesterday, today and forever (Heb. 13:8), so we compartmentalize the *apparently* torturing, arbitrarily vindictive and genocidal God and do not allow ourselves to think about Him. Or we hide behind some vague notion of the sovereignty of a God who can do whatever He wants with His creation, killing almost the entire lot of them if it looks as if His plan is being threatened.

Moses did not think it was a good idea for God to act like this, telling Him, "the Egyptians shall hear *it* ... And they will tell *it* to the inhabitants of this land ... Now *if* thou shalt kill *all* this people ... then the nations which have heard the fame of thee will speak, saying, Because the LORD was not able to bring this people into the land which he sware unto them, therefore he hath slain them in the wilderness" (Num. 14:13–16).

Certainly we have interpreted the wrath, justice, and retribution of Deity after the manner of the pagan view of the gods and the human exercise of wrath, justice, and retribution in a carnal way, missing that James declared: "the wrath of man worketh not the righteousness of God" (James 1:20). Furthermore, we have not truly considered the realities of *saying* we believe in thought (or plenary) inspiration while demonstrating that we are actually clinging to a *verbal* mode of inspiration. The Bible was written according to the Hebrew pattern of thought and expression. Ellen White stated, "It was a maxim among the Jews that a failure to do good, when one had opportunity, was to do evil; to neglect to save life was to kill (*The Desire of Ages*, p. 286). This insight is one of the ways we are given to interpret the language of Scripture regarding God and violence in a new way.

In the fourth generation, this new understanding of God's character came into notice as the Fred Wright movement gained some traction in Australia, the United States, and other places. While that movement fell into disrepute (and this is no cause for disregarding light any more than the later defection of Jones and Waggoner is cause for disregarding the light they brought), there were others who came to the same understanding independently. This trend continues today, as the new view of God's character is coming to light, not only in Adventism, but even among Sunday-keeping Christians. People are taking seriously the concept that, because God is love, He does not punish by the active exercise of physical power. His love is not a sweet, sentimental love, for true love must give freedom—even if that freedom exercised wrongly can bring pain. For God to approach His children seeking their undivided loyalty, respect, and love while threatening that the hand He holds out in friendship will painfully "smite" them should they reject His proposal, completely violates the concept of freedom of choice and non-coercion. Therefore, we conclude that God will "punish" only in the sense that He gives the sinner up to the results of free choice. If left without the interference of grace and mercy, sin actually punishes those who practice it. Ultimately, the soul that clings to sin will go out of existence altogether, for the choice to have sin is the choice to not have God, and only in Him can the soul be sustained. The Bible does not say that the wages of *God* is death, but, rather, that the wages of *sin* is death. God does not pay those wages. By contrast, the gift of *God* is eternal life (Rom. 6:23).

So, while mainstream and independent Adventism largely fail to advance into the fourth angel message of the glory of God, there is a true reformation going on that carries forward to this time and swells into the loud cry in latter rain power, perhaps even as you hold this book in your hands. *This* is the generation of the restoration. The message is going forth to individuals so they can be transformed into the image of God, purified and healed, and so that they can carry the message to the world, bringing about the final events. These will be the final generation servants, arising largely from those in both houses of Seventh-day Adventism. Adventism will go through in the ship called the "Loud Cry of the Third Angel" under the power and by the glory of the Fourth Angel, which is Christ. "And I looked, and behold a white cloud, and upon the cloud *one* sat like unto the Son of man, having on his head a golden crown, and in his hand a sharp sickle" (Rev. 14:14).

Knowing that the 1888 gospel message has the light on God's true character as its natural development, we stand particularly with A. T. Jones, as he brought a significant word on this point at the 1893 General Conference Session:

> We stand pledged to the Lord and before the world that we depend upon God; that He loves His people; that He manifests Himself in behalf of those whose hearts are toward Him. Brethren, there is that fearful word also that touches that very thought, that came to us from Australia [by Ellen G. White]. It is in the testimony entitled, "The Crisis Imminent." What does that say?—"Something great and decisive is to take place, and that right early. If any delay, the character of God and His throne will be compromised." [Ms. 27, 1892.] Brethren, by our careless, indifferent attitude, we are putting God's throne into jeopardy. Why cannot He work? God is ready. Are not God's workmen ready? But if there is any delay, "the character of God and His throne is jeopardized." Is it possible that we are about to risk the honor of God's throne? Brethren, for the Lord's sake and for His throne's sake, let us get out of the way. (*General Conference Bulletin*, Jan. 31, 1893, pp. 73, 74)

There has been a delay in Christ's return, and God's throne has been put in jeopardy. Generations have come and gone while His character has been cast into disrepute as Satan has gleefully carried on in his "constant effort to misrepresent the character of God, the nature of sin, and the real issues at stake in the great controversy" (*The Great Controversy*, p. 569). All the while, the continuing propagation of false information regarding the 1888 message and its reception has fostered an environment of "peace and safety; my Lord delays His coming." Yet, the Lord has not delayed His coming. The *people* have delayed it by their refusal to embrace the gospel as it is in Jesus and the truth about God's character as He is in Christ.

Continuing Developments Regarding 1888 in Answer to the Wieland and Short "Second Call": the Myths

> Whatever the message was, Paul, Luther, and Wesley shared and preached it. (George Knight, *A User-Friendly Guide to the 1888 Message*, p. 86)

While there are many facets to the ongoing death spiral of organized Adventism (see *Review and Herald*, July 24, 1888), which are important to discuss, it is fundamental that we continue the coverage of the church's attitude toward the 1888 message as it came in the first and second calls, for had *this* error been corrected, everything else would have been automatically rectified. The message brings the restoration of all things.

Several myths surrounding the message of 1888 and its history have been inculcated into the collective Adventist mind. This has been effected through various communication channels such as the authorized insertion of statements by the custodians of the writings of Ellen White (such as found in *Selected Messages*, bk. 3, pp. 156–163), through the release of a number of highly promoted new books used in coursework in Adventist schools, through articles in denominational papers, and, of course, through the pulpit. We will discuss these myths because their impact has been the means of keeping the denomination in the sickbed of the Laodicean malady.

The Acceptance/Victory Myth

Much argument and debate has arisen as to whether the church of 1888 did in fact reject the message sent to it. The organization today claims that the message was never totally rejected but that the organization gained a resounding and glorious victory, emerging from the crisis a stronger and more effective church. Among the arguments in support of this view are that it was only a vocal minority that opposed the message, that there was no official meeting or vote taken to reject the message, that later confessions were made accepting the message, that the message was a reintroduction of 16th-century Protestant Reformation justification by faith, which, of course, we have all come to accept, and that, while a large segment did not know what to believe, there was a later shift as a result of great revival meetings.

Even without working through all the evidence of history, it is apparent that the purposes of God were turned aside in three ways:

1. **Prophecy.** In Matthew 22, there is the depiction of the rejection of the two calls by those bidden to the marriage. This not only applies to the Jews, but the pen of inspiration declares that this chapter is "of intense meaning … to us" and that the setting is that of the investigative judgment. This places it squarely in our time.

2. **The Lord's express declaration.** "The prejudices and opinions that prevailed at Minneapolis are not dead by any means …" (Ms. 40a, 1890, in *Testimonies to Ministers*, p. 467). "The light that is to lighten the whole earth with its glory was resisted, and by the action of our own brethren has been in a great degree kept away from the world" (Lt. 96, 1896, in *The Ellen G. White 1888 Materials*, p. 1575).

3. **Time has elapsed with no change.** The unerring witness of time reveals without question that it has never been accepted by the church in a large enough scale to enable the Lord to bestow the Holy Spirit's power for the efficiency of witness that would close the work. If we had kept faith with Jesus, the message would have at that time brought the proclamation of the loud cry. The end would have come or would be now in the process of closing. *We can know that when final events are finally unfolding, the time will have arrived that God has a people who have repented and are advancing in the light.*

In whatever way one may question the channels, methods, and instrumentalities the Lord used to bring the second call to the marriage, the fact is clear that the issues involved in the second call were held before the Church with more than sufficient clarity and pressure as to compel the Church to give an equally clear and definite answer.

And at every official level from the topmost to the lowest, the answer was clear, definite, and unequivocal—the Church had no time for the message.

Of course, the leaders of the denomination claim that they have never rejected the light, and that they truly believe in and earnestly proclaim the Lord our righteousness. True, in an effort to disguise and confuse the issue, she today has set forth another message which she claims is the message of 1888, and then points to her acceptance of *that* as proof that she never rejected the real message. But those who know and have experienced the power of the message of living righteousness sent in 1888 and again today, are not deceived. (Wright, *Last Day Events*, pp. 94, 95)

This also is why we find the relentless suppression of the men and the message, for if it were more readily available through the media of the church, including the pulpit, it would be "game over" because the church would not be able to set forth an imposter and the genuine article all at once. One or the other must be in the ascendancy. Yet, throughout the last three generations, a new order of books has been kept before the people as the standard teaching, and those books have kept coming, as persistent as the wind.

George Knight's 1998 book, *A User-Friendly Guide to the 1888 Message* repeats the same fallacy found in his earlier work, *Angry Saints*. Based on W. C. White's statement, "now that the light had been presented and accepted," Knight claimed that Ellen White, Jones, and Waggoner agreed that the church had largely accepted the message by 1895 (A User-Friendly Guide, p. 147; W. C. White to DAR, Sept. 10, 1895, in *Angry Saints*, p. 37). This conclusion ignores the twelve plus years of statements in *The Ellen G. White 1888 Materials* in which Ellen White used the terms "rejected," "rejection," or "rejecting" more than seventy-five times in relation to the message and the messengers. There is no comparable documentation for the assertion that the church accepted the message, and it is futile to try to prove otherwise.

The question of acceptance or rejection is not merely a "tempest in a teapot." It matters. Confusion about history is not trivial, for failure to grasp the truth about historical events and their effects sets cycles of repetition in motion.

Wieland and Short highlighted the point that we should not be so much concerned about whether *the church* accepted the message but what the *leadership* did with it. "The church never had a fair chance to consider it undistorted and unopposed" (R. J. Wieland and D. K. Short, *1888 Re-Examined*, p. 30). We are told: "Satan succeeded in shutting away *from our people*, in a great measure, the special power of the Holy Spirit that God longed to impart to them.... The light that is to lighten the whole earth with its glory was resisted, and *by the action of our own brethren* has been in a great degree kept away from the world" (Lt. 96, 1896, in *The Ellen G. White 1888 Materials*, p. 1575, emphasis added).

The church's leading men make frequent claims of acceptance of the message—even to the point of calling it the "great Minneapolis revival." The White Estate has shared significantly in the maintenance of this revisionist view. Before we consider a sampling of these claims, we need to recognize that the roots of the acceptance myth were anchored within the second generation.

As Ellen White resided in Australia, having been set aside as a thorn in the flesh of the brethren in America, her son, W. C. White, felt it advantageous to give her a slanted report of the situation since she was so continually burdened with the work of reproving wrongs in the church. It is evident that he did indeed endorse the acceptance view, since he later remonstrated with Taylor G. Bunch over the latter's drawing a typological conclusion from Israel's experience at Kadesh to the rejection of the 1888 message. W. C. White told Bunch that there was no rejection of the message, for he was present and should know. "It is only natural that he would convey the same acceptance view to his son, Arthur L. White, who has served for so many years as secretary of the Ellen G. White Estate" (*1888 Re-Examined*, p. 199).

Thus, one day W. C. White and Elder Prescott took up the mail from America, which included some upbeat reports from the president of the General Conference regarding the high spiritual experiences and successes in America. The men were almost dancing about the room "overjoyed" and "praising the Lord for the good report," only to be brought down to reality the next day when Ellen White read a testimony that she had been writing to those very same men from whom they had received the glowing report. W. C. White related: "She then read me the most far-reaching criticism, the most searching reproof for bringing in wrong plans and principles in their work, that *were ever written to that group of men*" (*Spalding-Magan Collection*, p. 470, cited in *1888 Re-Examined*, p. 200). W. C. White wrote, "This was a great lesson to me," though it was apparently not great enough, for he and his son carried on with the same acceptance story for all of their careers.

Thus, our trust needs to be in the discernment afforded through the gift of prophecy above and beyond all merely human sources. "The gift is not hereditary. It would be only natural for them, as it would be for us, to believe at face value letters from the General Conference president containing such good news. The spirit pervading the church was always up-beat, rejoicing in progress and victories" (*1888 Re-Examined*, p. 200). It is the same today. It is our natural tendency to be "in conflict with 'the testimony of Jesus,' unless specifically enlightened by the Holy Spirit" (*1888 Re-Examined*, p. 200). Mrs. White even wrote of the experience with her son and Prescott, saying she was very troubled by it. Instead of being uplifted, she was "alarmed" (*1888 Re-Examined*, p. 200). One can almost hear her sighs as she penned the words, "If these men cannot see the outcome of affairs, I thought, how hopeless the task of making them see at Battle Creek. The thought struck to my heart like a knife" (Lt. 87a, 1896, in Wieland and Short, p. 200).

Here are various samples of the acceptance theory, as found in the writings of leading men in church publications:

> The General Conference session at Minneapolis, Minnesota, in 1888 is a notable landmark in Seventh-day Adventist history. It was really like crossing a continental divide into a new country. Some smiters of the brethren calling themselves reformers have tried to make out that the session was a defeat; whereas, the truth is that it stands out as a glorious victory and the occasion and the beginning of larger and better things for the advent church.... It introduced a new period in our work—a time of revival and soulsaving.... The Lord gave His people a marvelous victory. It was the beginning of a great spiritual awakening among Adventists. Only those who attended the conference can

understand the spiritual power that was manifest and the victories gained in the struggles and criticism that came in.... The response to these revival appeals was seen in the extended spiritual awakening both here and overseas. They marked the beginning of a strong mission advance and became the dawn of a glorious day for the Adventist church.... Thus the aftereffect of the great Minneapolis revival was the beginning of another era for the advent movement. This blessed period of revival, beginning in 1888, which was so rich in both holiness and mission fruitage, came, above all, as a direct result of the work of the messenger of the Lord through the Spirit of God. (Lewis H. Christian, *The Fruitage of Spiritual Gifts*, pp. 219, 223, 233, 237, 245)

The rank and file of Seventh-day Adventist workers and laity accepted the presentations at Minneapolis and were blessed. Certain leading men there resisted the teaching. (Letter by the General Conference of Seventh-day Adventists Defense Literature Committee, "Further Appraisal of the Manuscript '1888 Re-Examined'," Sept. 1958, p. 11)

It simply is not true historically.... "Some" leading brethren stood in the way of light and blessing. But the ... leaders as a group, never rejected the Bible doctrine of Righteousness by Faith. (Le Roy Edwin Froom, *Movement of Destiny* [1971], p. 266)

So it is correct to say that the [1888] message has been declared, both from the pulpit and through the press, and by the lives of thousands upon thousands of God's dedicated people who have learned the result of spiritual life in Christ.... Adventist pastors and evangelists have announced this vital truth from church pulpits and public platforms, with hearts aflame with love for Christ.... (A. V. Olson, *Through Crisis to Victory*, pp. 233, 237; *Thirteen Crisis Years*, pp. 239, 243)

The concept that the General Conference, and thus the denomination, rejected the message of righteousness by faith in 1888 is without foundation ... Contemporary records yield no suggestion of denominational rejection. There is no E. G. White statement anywhere that says this was so.... (A. L. White, *The Lonely Years*, p. 396)

In all of this, Satan feigns defeat, and leadership cherishes the deception and feeds it to the people. The result has been an infatuation with a false gospel and a false Christ, produced through the spirit of antichrist. Are these words too strong? Ellen White wrote of such, "Your turning things upside down is known of the Lord. Go on a little longer as you have gone, in rejection of the light from heaven, and you are lost" (*Testimonies to Ministers*, p. 96). This was in a letter she wrote to Elder O. A. Olsen (Lt. 57, 1895), which bears the heading "Rejecting the Light." If he had Christ in view, she would not have made such statements.

Wieland and Short said that, if the inspired statements are true, then we had better believe them. They argued further:

If these [acceptance] statements are true, it is hard to understand why Ellen White should be so concerned for a decade and even longer about what she said was continued rejection of the message on the part of "our brethren" at headquarters when so few opposed it. Would the Lord withhold from the entire world church the blessings of the latter rain and the loud cry if **less than ten ministers persisted in opposing it, and they not even leaders**? [A claim made by Froom in *Movement of Destiny*]. (*1888 Re-Examined*, p. 32, emphasis added)

If these claims are accurate, then there were some high ranking "smiters of the brethren" such as A. G. Daniells, former president of the General Conference:

This message of righteousness in Christ should, at the time of its coming, have met with opposition on the part of earnest, well-meaning men in the cause of God! The message has never been received, nor proclaimed, nor given free course as it should have been in order to convey to the church the measureless blessings that were wrapped within it.... The division and conflict which arose among the leaders because of the opposition to the message of righteousness in Christ, produced a very unfavorable reaction. **The rank and file of the people were confused**, and did not know what to do....

Back of the opposition is revealed the shrewd plotting of that master mind of evil ... The very fact of his determination to neutralize the message and its inevitable effects, is evidence of its great value and importance; and how terrible must be the results of any victory of his in defeating it! (A. G. Daniells, *Christ Our Righteousness* [1926], pp. 47, 50, 53, 54, emphasis added)

Daniells said, in 1926: "The rank and file of the people were confused." The General Conference Committee used the same words to say something very different in 1958: "*The rank and file* of Seventh-day Adventist workers and laity accepted the presentations at Minneapolis and *were blessed*" (*A Further Appraisal of the Manuscript "1888 Re-Examined,"* General Conference, September 1958, p. 11, emphasis added). In 1890, Ellen White wrote: "They do not know whether to come and take hold of this precious truth or not" (*Review and Herald*, March 11, 1890). Which do we take—the testimony of the current administration or the testimony of the prophet who exhorted a president of the conference who was also a high ranking church official in the 1888 era? You have your own seat on the jury. You must decide for yourself.

A. T. Jones was as close to the matter as could be, for he was one of the very messengers sent of heaven. What did he say? Preaching at the General Conference Session in 1893, "What did the brethren in that fearful position in which they stood, reject at Minneapolis? They rejected the latter rain—the loud cry—of the third angel's message" (*General Conference Bulletin*, 1893, p. 183). In 1921, he testified:

> I can't now name anyone who accepted the truth at that 1888 meeting openly [besides Ellen White, obviously]. But later many said they were greatly helped by it. One Battle Creek man said at that meeting after one of Dr. Waggoner's meetings: "Now we could say amen to all of that if that is all there were to it. But away down yonder there is still something to come. And this is to lead us to that…. And if we say amen to this we will have to say amen to that, and then we are caught." … There was no such thing, and so they robbed themselves of what their own hearts told them was the truth; and by fighting what they only imagined, they fastened themselves in opposition to what they knew that they should have said amen to. (A. T. Jones, letter to C. E. Holmes, May 12, 1921, cited in *1888 Re-Examined*, p. 35)

I am reminded here again of the attitude expressed by Ellen White: "They will see only something which in their blindness they think dangerous, something which will arouse their fears, and they will brace themselves to resist it" (*Review and Herald*, Dec. 23, 1890, art. B).

In complete harmony with Jones, Ellen White stated in November of 1892:

> Who of those that acted a part in the meeting at Minneapolis have come to the light and received the rich treasures of truth which the Lord sent them from heaven? Who have kept step with the Leader, Jesus Christ? Who have made full confession of their mistaken zeal, their blindness, their jealousies and evil surmisings, their defiance of truth? **Not one** … (Lt. 2a, 1892, in *The Ellen G. White 1888 Materials*, p. 1068, emphasis added)

Notably, she wrote this after most of the "confessions" of men of influence had come in.

Norval Pease, in his book *By Faith Alone*, one of the denominationally approved books touting the acceptance theory, quoted from Jones' May 12, 1921 letter to C. E. Holmes regarding the camp-meeting after 1888:

> Then when campmeeting time came we all three [Mrs. White, Waggoner, and Jones] visited the camp-meetings with the message of righteousness by faith and religious liberty, sometimes all three of us being in the same meeting. This turned the tide with the people, and apparently with most of the leading men. (DF 189, available at http://1ref.us/id, accessed 11/10/16, quoted in Pease, *By Faith Alone*, p. 149)

What Pease failed to do, however, is to quote the next paragraph, which seriously modifies the lines he quoted:

> **But this latter was only apparent, it was never real**, for all the time in the General Conference Committee and amongst others there was a **secret antagonism** always carried on, and **which finally in Daniells, Spicer & Co., gained the day in the denomination**, and gave to the Minneapolis spirit and contention and men **the supremacy** … (A. T. Jones, letter to C. E. Holmes, May 12, 1921, DF 189, available at drc.whiteestate.org/read.php?id=54572, cited in *1888 Re-Examined*, p. 36, omitting "in Daniells, Spicer & Co.," emphasis added)

Now the readers should understand that such a method of writing and displaying out of context "evidence" is not objective, nor is it academically honest or honest in any wise. It is a revision of history, an activity performed for purposes of propaganda. For this reason, the new order of books is heavily promoted and has become the standard reference library stocking the shelves of Adventists of the third and fourth generations. The "rank and file" do not ever think that these volumes, recommended by the church, published by the church and sold at the camp-meetings and book stores of the church, would be filled with a false history. For anyone to come along and suggest that they are would be to heap upon themselves a full measure of scorn and disdain. I am reminded of the story of the long-bearded village street prophet, who came into town in his tattered robe and sandals, carrying a placard, "The bell has fallen from the tower!" They all laughed him to scorn, until he came dragging the bell behind him.

It is needful that we make mention of Ellen White's statements that speak of the positive enthusiasm and acceptance of the message following the 1888 meetings. These statements described the eager embracing of truth at the congregational level in various locales. There is also an instance in which Jones said that the revival meetings "turned the tide with the people." Wieland and Short described it this way:

> However, **there never was an issue or tide to be turned with the people. The problem was entirely with the leaders and the ministry.** The people were ready to accept the light gladly if the leaders should permit it to come to them undistorted and unopposed, or rather, if they should join heartily in presenting it. Many younger ministers were keenly interested. But the continually noncommittal attitude or outright opposition of responsible leaders in Battle Creek and elsewhere quenched the movement. Not only do Ellen White's remarks attest this fact, but the General Conference correspondence in the Archives is also clear. (*1888 Re-Examined*, p. 42)

Rather than provide here a series of testimonies from those archives, we encourage the reader to see the additional note to chapter 4 in Wieland and Short's *1888 Re-Examined*, pp. 45–51 (online version, pp. 49–55; printed version, pp. 45–51) and Ron Duffield's *Return of the Latter Rain*, second edition, pp. 110–172.

Another argument against the rejection of the message is that the claim would fly in the face of the fact that Jones and Waggoner were speaking to congregations, publishing articles and holding office in the church. So, how was the message rejected? In what way was it manifest? The answer is that we find the light of the glory of God countered by opposing teaching, at times by the publication of contradictory articles in the same church paper. In this way, the author of the article stood in between the message and the people, in spite of Ellen White's constant appeals to come into unity on the message of heaven-sent truth. She testified that proof of heaven's blessing on the message came in the results of their work in the revival meetings after 1888 and in the negative response of the leading brethren, "because it was a testimony against them," and they did not come into working order, they "went on in their own spirit, filled with envy, jealousy, and evil surmisings, as did the Jews," opening "their hearts to the enemy of God and man" (*Testimonies to Ministers*, p. 80).

There was a dark undercurrent silently moving, spoken of by Jones as the "secret antagonism," which we can observe in communications such as that of General Conference Secretary, Dan T. Jones:

> I think an Institute in Missouri would be a splendid thing; but I believe an institute **on a quiet plan** will be just as valuable to you as to make a great parade of it and get in … Elder A. T. Jones and E. J. Waggoner. To tell you the truth, **I do not have very much confidence in some of their ways of presenting things**. They try to drive everything before them, and will not admit that their positions can possibly be subject to the least criticism.… In fact, [they] do not dwell upon any other subjects scarcely than those upon which there is a difference of opinion among our leading brethren. **I do not think you want to bring that spirit into the Missouri Conference.** (Letter to N. W. Alee, January 23, 1890, cited in *1888 Re-Examined*, p. 50, emphasis added)

The rejection also tied up God's resources as faithful men and women had to expend their labors countering the resistance:

> The opposition in our own ranks has imposed upon the Lord's messengers a laborious and soul trying task; for they have had to meet difficulties and obstacles **which need not have existed**. While this labor had to be performed among our own people, to make them willing that God should work in the day of his power, the light of the glory of God has not been shining in clear concentrated rays to the world. Thousands who are now in the darkness of error, might have been added to our numbers. **All the time and thought and labor required to counteract the influence of our brethren who oppose the message has been just so much taken from** [the work of warning] **the world of the swift coming judgments of God.**

The Spirit of God has been present in power among his people, but it could not be bestowed upon them, because they did not open their hearts to receive it.

It is not the opposition of the world that we have to fear; but it is the elements that work among ourselves that have hindered the message....

The Lord designed that the messages of warning and instruction given through the Spirit to his people should go everywhere. But the influence that grew out of the resistance of light and truth at Minneapolis, tended to make of no effect the light God had given to his people through the Testimonies. "Great Controversy," Vol. 4 has not had the circulation that it should have had, because some of those who occupy responsible positions were leavened with the spirit that prevailed at Minneapolis, a spirit that clouded the discernment of the people of God. (Lt. 77, 1893, in *General Conference Daily Bulletin*, Feb. 28, 1893, p. 419, emphasis added; "the work of warning" added from Lt. 77, 1893)

This is a leavening that has worked its results to this day.

The later apologists for the "acceptance theory" have failed the people by improperly relating the history of the positive reports of the so-called "revivals." The truth is not a history of glorious acceptance but a story of hope and disappointment. Wieland and Short wrote:

> Earlier statements expressing **prophetic hope** (1889–1890) must be balanced by the **disappointment of the actual subsequent history** which Ellen White was forced to record (1891–97). Every avenue of solid evidence goes in the same direction: her testimony, Jones' testimony, the official archival files, and the obvious import of nearly a century of history. (*1888 Re-Examined*, pp. 44, 45, emphasis added)

This writer does not personally feel comfortable with the notion of "balancing statements," because often this term is used to create an artificial scenario that contradicts Spirit of Prophecy statements. The later record of the actual history of the reaction to the 1888 message reflects a dashed hope that had peaked through in the earlier statements. It is like the person who has contracted a disease experiencing a temporary remission and feeling "much better." Friends and family are relieved and, believing the best, giving praises and testimonies to the goodness of God, only to see the illness quickly reappear, bringing their loved one's rapid demise. A true "balancing statement" is an opportunity and challenge to ferret out principles or historical truths that harmonize all the facts.

The Protestant doctrine re-emphasis myth

It would be very embarrassing to the denomination to give the idea that Adventism rejected the gospel teachings of the great reformers such as Luther and Wesley. So it is that we have slipped into a false view of what the message of 1888 was and is. In recent denominational books, the 1888 message is portrayed as a re-emphasis of the 16th-century Protestant Reformation doctrine of justification by faith as propounded by popular evangelical churches of Christendom.

The woeful result of this portrayal is that it makes us a church of winebibbers. If the Protestant churches accept our teaching of the gospel, then we are surely in big trouble. It cannot be a pure first angel gospel if it gains the acceptance of the churches of fallen Babylon. Our ministers and professors earn their degrees by studying at the feet of non-Seventh-day Adventist PhDs who have no basis for understanding the third angel's message and who have themselves come down through the theological lineage of the denominations that rejected the Advent message under William Miller in the period of "the Great Advent Awakening."

In effect, we have become a denomination whose leadership has been trained by the high priests of fallen Babylon. The Sabbath School lesson quarterlies often contain quotations from these authors and professors—men who have no affiliation with or belief in the third angel's message. What then can the denomination serve up to the people but a failure to advance in the Reformation through a new heaping helping of unbelief, which is nothing less than a modern sophisticated establishment of the high places of Ba'al?

Following is a sampling of the official teachings of the Seventh-day Adventist Church regarding the origin of the 1888 message:

> The greatest event of the eighties in the experience of Seventh-day Adventists was **the recovery, or the restatement and new consciousness, of their faith in the basic doctrine of Christianity.** "Knowing that a man is not justified by the works of the law, but by the faith of Jesus Christ." ...
>
> The last decade of the century saw the church developing, through this gospel, into a company

prepared to fulfill the mission of God.... The church was aroused by the revival message of justification by faith. (A. W. Spalding, *Captains of the Host* [1949], pp. 583, 602, emphasis added)

Some may well ask, **What was this teaching** of righteousness by faith which became the mainspring of the great 1888 Adventist revival, as taught and emphasized by Mrs. White and others? **It was the same doctrine that Luther, Wesley, and many other servants of God had been teaching**.... (Lewis H. Christian, *The Fruitage of Spiritual Gifts*, p. 239, emphasis added)

There were those who accepted **the [1888] emphasis on righteousness by faith**; on the other extreme were those who thought this emphasis threatened the "old landmarks." ... (N. F. Pease, *The Faith That Saves* [1969], p. 45, emphasis added)

This conference really marked a crisis hour in the history of the church, involving the great truth of salvation through faith in Christ alone. It **proved to be the beginning of a re-emphasis of this glorious truth**, which resulted in a spiritual awakening among our people. (M. E. Kern, "The Spirit of Prophecy in the Remnant Church," *Review and Herald*, Aug. 3, 1950, p. 294, emphasis added)

We have not been too well aware of these paralleling spiritual movements-of organizations and **men outside the Advent Movement—having the same general burden and emphasis**, and arising at about the same time. The simultaneous, widespread appearance among men of truth whose time has come for emphasis is characteristic of all enunciations of imperative truth, such as the simultaneous Old and New World Advent Awakening in the years just prior to 1844. The impulse manifestly came from the same Source. And in timing, Righteousness by Faith centered in the year 1888.

For example, the renowned Keswick Conferences of Britain were founded to "promote practical holiness." ... Some fifty men could easily be listed in the closing decades of the nineteenth and the opening decades of the twentieth centuries ... all giving this general emphasis. (Froom, *Movement of Destiny*, pp. 319, 320, emphasis added)

Froom's philosophy would see the Protestant men of the Keswick Conferences as an upward-trending Babylon, recovering from the pronouncement of the second angel. Yet, such a notion flies in the face of the express declaration of the inspired witness of the Bible and the Spirit of Prophecy. There is nothing in the line of prophecy that would indicate any kind of gospel recovery before the message is repeated in Revelation 18:1–3, under the added power of the fourth angel. The declaration there is still: "Babylon is fallen." Also, the clear testimony of Ellen White informs us that fallen Babylon has continued on the same downward trajectory since 1844. Because "they have continued to reject the special truths for this time they have fallen lower and lower" (*The Great Controversy*, p. 389), they will continue to do so until the work of apostasy reaches it culmination in the mark of the beast crisis. In addition, the Spirit of Prophecy informs us that, when the loud cry of the third angel comes, it will include a message exposing additional corruptions that have entered the churches since 1844 (*Spiritual Gifts*, vol. 1, p. 193; *The Great Controversy*, p. 603).

As we comb through these various revisionist books, the obvious inference is that, if the 1888 agitation was actually a re-emphasis of the popular Protestant teaching, then we have much to learn from these other churches if we would only go back to them and, by extension, learn from the modern descendants of the Protestant teachers, whom we once taught as a denomination were "fallen Babylon," a term that has today been relegated to the historical trash heap in the name of political and theological correctness.

These teachers are now deemed the standard by which we may model our teaching of righteousness by faith. This is what we have come to—what could have been the head has become the tail. Moreover, as other denominations are rapidly closing the gap between themselves and the papacy, what does it say for the Adventist denomination? "It is a backsliding church that lessens the distance between itself and the Papacy," even while it is true that "souls like Luther, Cranmer, Ridley, Hooper, and the thousands of noble men who were martyrs for the truth's sake ... are the true Protestants ... [who] stood as faithful sentinels of truth, declaring that Protestantism is incapable of union with Romanism" (*Signs of the Times*, Feb. 19, 1894). Yet, we must realize that they did not have all the light—even on the gospel. We are warned:

The Reformation did not, as many suppose, **end with Luther**. It is to be continued to the close of this world's history. Luther had a great work to do in reflecting to others the light which God had permitted to shine upon him; yet **he did not receive all the light which was to be given to the world**. From that time to this, new light has been continually shining upon the Scriptures, and new truths have been constantly unfolding. (*The Great Controversy*, pp. 148, 149, emphasis added)

The obvious fact that our 1888 gospel message is more than a mere re-emphasis of Protestant doctrine is revealed in Ellen White's insistence that our "most precious message" contains a distinctive and vital element that invites the people "to receive the righteousness of Christ, which is made manifest in obedience to all the commandments of God" (Lt. 57, 1895, in *The Ellen G. White 1888 Materials*, p. 1336). Thus, the message concerns true heart obedience in both spirit and letter and includes entering into God's rest, typified in the seventh-day Sabbath of the fourth commandment, which is *the seal of God* that is enabled by the Holy Spirit *who seals us* into eternal loving obedience.

Sidebar discussion on the true advance of the Reformation

We understand today, as part of the final advance of Reformation light, that the fourth angel glory of God, the righteousness of God, is also revealed in the message of His character, which is love only. We believe that it is appropriate to salt this study of history with a smattering of apology for the advancing light of God's righteousness, i.e., that He never employs violence to get His way or to punish those who refuse Him. These things are always the result of separating from God, never the result of God's direct application of physical force. Love is not love if there is any element of coercion or any threat to freedom of choice involved. If we believe that God Himself will finally create physical liquid fire to rain from the sky upon the heads of His enemies, then we cannot ever hope to portray God's government as being predicated on love. It then would be a government similar to sinful human governments in that it has in it the motivating elements of reward and punishment. This serves to muddy the waters when it comes to loyalty and motivation, for if we are in it to win heaven or avoid hell, then we are wage earners, legalists, serving a fierce employer who offers heaven for compliance and a torturous death for resistance and dissent. There is no way to remove fear from this model. John is clear: "There is no fear in love; but perfect love casteth out fear: because fear hath torment. He that feareth is not made perfect in love" (1 John 4:18). The NIV expresses it wonderfully: "… because fear has to do with punishment."

The threat of punishment is not only fear-based, but it is coercive. Imagine that you go to a doctor and he diagnoses you as having a terminal illness. That puts you under a death sentence. Yet, then he gives you the good news: he has already developed a proprietary cure for your malady. Even better, he charges nothing for the remedy, and it is already prepared and labeled with your name on it. All he asks is that you take it according to his directions. Then, he clears his throat to issue a grave warning: "If you refuse the remedy, change the contents, or change the directions for taking it," he says and then pauses, looking down with sadness, "then for your stubborn refusal I shall have to burn you with fire for some time, until your sentence is complete. Then I will let you die." Is this the picture of God that we have? The traditional theology of God's character is such.

May Heaven help us! And He has! "But the Lord has presented another picture for the contemplation of every believer" (Ms. 32, 1894, in *Review and Herald*, Sept. 10, 1895).

A major element of the final message of mercy is a clear presentation of the great controversy and its central theme of the character of God. We have taught that the controversy is about the law of God, and this is true, if we bear foremost in mind that the law is a transcript of His very character. This includes the commandment, "Thou shalt not kill." For no reason are we to use violence. God also lives by the same "code." This eternal "law" is better described as the basis of existence itself; it is the only foundation upon which life can be manifest and God does not and, in fact, cannot, violate it, for God is not a man that He should lie.

God has no "pleasure" in the death of the wicked. This word in the Hebrew, *chaphets*, indicates that God is *not moved toward*—has *no will of His own* involved—in the fate that they should choose. It is not His doing, from beginning to end. The process of death which they begin during their day of probation and choose to remain in until the end, does not ever involve God, not even in its final days. They go right to the end choosing death.

> And death shall be chosen rather than life by all the residue of them that remain of this evil family, which remain in all the places whither I have driven them, saith the LORD of hosts. (Jer. 8:3)

There is only life in God. Death is not in Him to give. He is "the Father of lights" (James 1:17), and what are those lights? They are symbols of the sustaining power of God that animates every man (see John 1:4, 9). He was that Light (John 1:7, 8), and He was the Life (John 14:6). Remember, the center of the conflict is about separating light from darkness:

> Jesus Christ is the **Restorer**. Satan, the apostate, is the **destroyer**. **Here** is the conflict between the **Prince of life** and the prince of this world, the **power of darkness**.... (Lt. 34, 1896, in *Christ Triumphant*, p. 247, emphasis added)

We cannot take this theme to any further development here, for that would necessitate a detailed discussion of Bible language and stories. However, we would be remiss if we did not identify the genuine advancement of the message as it stands today, in "present truth." The modern evangelical teaching of the gospel is not in a right place to have any view to the advancing light on the character of God because it is rooted in a primitive view of the atonement as blood appeasement of an angry God, a pagan model that God has ever sought to move the minds of people away from.

Further thoughts on the Protestant doctrine and acceptance myth shell-game

For the Seventh-day Adventist Church to teach that the 1888 message is actually a re-introduction of the standard Protestant teaching presents some serious issues to overcome.

One aspect of this is the implication that the testimony of Ellen White regarding the rejection of the message was a rejection of basic Protestantism. This presents a dilemma for the church, for it seemingly makes the denomination non-Protestant. What is it then, some kind of cult? This is what was so studiously avoided in the Martin-Barnhouse conferences. Apparently, escaping the low estimation of evangelical Babylon and shedding the label of "cult" was an objective to be attained at any cost.

Another outcome of the claim of the acceptance theory is that, *if the message was standard Reformation gospel* and Ellen White's testimony is correct that the message was the beginning of the loud cry, the "third angel's message in verity," then the 16th-century Protestant Reformation was also the beginning of the loud cry of the third angel's message.

This myth leaves us with a two-pronged basis for the creation of confusion regarding the testimonies of Ellen White. (This is not to say that the Bible is not sufficient for the establishment of true Protestantism or the light of the third angel's message, for it *is*, but we have in the messenger to the church a critical guide to help us navigate the iceberg infested waters of the final generation. Sent of God for our edification and instruction, the testimonies are not optional.) Therefore, in the setting forth of the acceptance theory, the denomination has cut off the Spirit of Prophecy at the knees, for we could not have rejected the 1888 message *if that message was merely basic Protestantism*. We are Protestants! If we were not, then Ellen White must have been mistaken. Either the acceptance theory has to go, or Ellen White has to go.

In the second place, if the 1888 message is the standard message of the Protestant Reformation, then Ellen White must be mistaken about it being the loud cry because that did not happen in the 16th-century Reformation. It is held to be yet future. Surely the church did *not* reject the beginning of the latter rain of the Holy Spirit! The church still makes concerted efforts and appeals to pray for its outpouring. So, while the church claims to have accepted the 1888 message, *which was the gospel of the reformers*, by that very latter assertion she cannot allow for it to have been the beginning of the glory of God that was to lighten the whole earth. Again, the acceptance theory has to go, or Ellen White has to go. However, a certain subtlety must be maintained in all of this. Often the form taken for the denial that the message was the beginning of the latter rain is *silence*. One will find that revisionist authors and publications studiously avoid informing the people that inspiration makes such declarations. Obviously, airing such information would be quite damaging to their efforts, causing attentive and thinking people to ask too many hard questions!

Is it any wonder why the testimonies are today "made of none effect"?

> Some years ago Louis R. Conradi, our leader in Europe, followed this official idea to its logical end and maintained that Luther preached the third angel's message in the 16th century. Conradi in time left the church. (He had also been an opposer of the message at the 1888 conference.) And we are today losing ministers, members and youth for the same basic reason—they see nothing unique and attractive in our gospel message because these officially endorsed views imply that there is nothing unique about it.
>
> Have our trusted historians unwittingly short-circuited the Seventh-day Adventist movement of

destiny? If so, great damage has been done, for authoritatively published ideas have a great impact on the world church. (*1888 Re-Examined*, pp. 57, 58)

So if the denomination establishes itself as innocent of rejecting the 1888 message yet maintains that that message was the truth of basic Reformation justification by faith, logically implying that it was not the beginning of the loud cry of the third angel's message, then what *is* the third angel's message? This implication sends the church right back to the status quo position of relegating the unique message of Adventism, as a movement carrying the messages of the three angels, to a set of doctrines pertaining to the Sabbath, the state of the dead, etc. Evangelistic efforts today often, in the more conservative churches, still follow the formula of many evenings of doctrinal lectures. While these teachings are basic Bible truths and it *is* necessary to show the change of the Sabbath from the seventh day to the first day, pointing out about the rise of the papacy and the non-biblical doctrines that crept into the church are not what constitute the everlasting gospel. The doctrinal format neglects a deeper approach to imparting light which appeals to principles of God's kingdom and how the principles relate to the doctrines.

On the other hand, the opposite approach taken in Adventism is to steer far wide of the historic position, for it identifies the true nature of the power behind the papacy and apostate Protestantism and runs counter to the desire to be friends with mainstream Christianity and a member of the club of "true Christians." Such reaction avoids any real emphasis on the "landmark" doctrinal approach, which includes the separating call of the teaching of the "mark of the beast" versus the "seal of God," which is so counterintuitive in today's thrust for "unity" in both the world and the church. This leaves only one "safe space" to inhabit, and it has produced within Adventism the evangelical "Jesus did it all" pendulum swing that is devoid of substance and that reflects the cheap-grace, antinomian mindset that fosters an attitude of contempt for the law of God and freely levels the charge of legalism against anyone who points to the keeping of the law as a hallmark of individual justification by grace. The answer to this is not simply to combine the law and the gospel, quoting, "If ye love me, keep my commandments" (John 14:15). The answer is to understand how the message of the gospel and the law fit together in the context of a correct understanding of the character of God, the defining of true love as being grounded in freedom of choice, the nature of sin as separation from the Source of life through the idolatry of self, and the nature of Bible language and of how inspiration works.

The presentation of the 1888 message is not a message to supersede previous truth, but, as the "third angel's message in verity," it is to bring the Reformation light into a fuller understanding and experience in the context of the "time of the end" teaching of Christ's movement into the most holy place of the heavenly sanctuary, where He conducts the unique work of ministering true justification by faith to His followers. At a fundamental level, this faith experience produces a people that behold Him aright. Their characters are formed after His true image. In all of this, the judgment takes place, wherein God recognizes how individuals have judged His character and the dwelling place for His Spirit, which is the human mind, is cleansed of all false ideas about God. Every question of truth and error in the long-standing controversy will then have been made plain. **In the judgment of the universe, God will stand clear of blame** for the existence or continuance of evil. It will be demonstrated that the divine decrees are not accessory to sin. There was no defect in God's government, no cause for disaffection. **When the thoughts of all hearts shall be revealed**, both the loyal and the rebellious will unite in declaring, "Just and true are Thy ways, Thou King of saints. Who shall not fear Thee, O Lord, and glorify Thy name? . . . for Thy judgments are made manifest." Revelation 15:3, 4 (*The Desire of Ages*, p. 58, emphasis added). Thus, they are fitted for the eternal habitation with God. When this message is allowed to do its work, it will produce the 144,000, a generation endowed with the Spirit, "not having spot, or wrinkle, or any such thing," "without fault before the throne of God" (Eph. 5:27; Rev. 14:5). It was God's intent that this message be a catalyst for bringing about the ripening of the harvest of "the firstfruits unto God and to the Lamb" (Rev. 14:4).

We close this segment with the positive word of inspiration:

> Several have written to me, inquiring if the [1888] message of justification by faith is the third angel's message, and I have answered, "It is the third angel's message in verity." The prophet declares, "And after these things I saw another angel come down from heaven, having great power; and the earth was lightened with his glory." [Rev. 18:1.] ... (*Review and Herald*, April 1, 1890)

The loud cry of the third angel has already begun in the revelation of the righteousness of Christ, the sin-pardoning Redeemer. This is the beginning of the light of the angel whose glory shall fill the whole earth.... (*Review and Herald*, Nov. 22, 1892)

The "confessions" myth

Historian A. W. Spalding wrote in 1949:

> Gradually there came the turning and the gathering into the unity of the faith. ... There was both a cutting and a healing power in the messages she [Ellen White] sent, carrying the gospel of righteousness and of good will in Christ, which in general brought the erstwhile estranged brethren together.... (A. W. Spalding, *Captains of the Host*, pp. 598, 599)

This is the general claim that is made in the new order of books. Is it true?

The church leaders and their historians have portrayed a glorious revival that came out of the 1888 experience. This turns out to have been only lip-service with no change of the heart.

> I feel a special interest in the movements and decisions that shall be made at this Conference regarding the things that should have been done years ago, and especially ten years ago, when we were assembled in Conference, and the Spirit and power of God came into our meeting, testifying that God was ready to work for this people if they would come into working order. **The brethren assented to the light God had given**, but there were those connected with our institutions, especially with the Review and Herald office and the [General] Conference, who brought in elements of unbelief, so that the light that was given was not acted upon. It was assented to, **but no special change was made** to bring about such a condition of things that the power of God could be revealed among His people. (Ellen White, *General Conference Bulletin*, April 3, 1901, p. 23, emphasis added)

To assent to a thing and not actually do it, is tantamount to rejection of the truth. The way in which God regards this is shown in the parable of the son who said that he would go but went not. "Words are of no value unless they are accompanied with appropriate deeds. This is the lesson taught in the parable of the two sons." *Christ's Object Lessons*, 272. (*The Destiny of a Movement*, p. 250)

Genuine repentance is rare as diamonds. Esau and King Saul both confessed with tears but never found true restoration borne of genuine contrition. So it was with the post–1888 confessions. The evidences that have been set forth by the church as breathless acclamations of the confessions and repentance of leading men in the years after the 1888 conference need to be examined more closely for what they actually turned out to be—seed that fell into ground that would not sustain them.

Dan T. Jones, who at times held various posts, including Secretary of the General Conference and member of the General Conference Executive Committee, is illustrative of this general phenomenon. In a January 1, 1889 letter to J. W. Watt, he wrote:

> We have had good meetings here ... Bro. A. T. Jones has been doing most of the preaching. I wish you could have heard some of his sermons. He seems altogether different from what he did [*sic*] at Minneapolis. Some of his sermons are as good, I think, as I ever heard. They are all new too. He is original in his preaching and in his practical preaching seems very tender and deeply feels all he says. My estimation of him has raised considerably since I have seen the other side of the man

Yet, he did not follow any of this conviction. Ron Duffield comments:

> Unfortunately, he used his position of authority to influence others in opposition to both Jones and Waggoner. During the Ministerial Institute he was in continual correspondence with other church leaders on the various committees seeking support for his plan of action. (*Return of the Latter Rain*, p. 337)

Dan Jones' story concerns a man determined to pursue his own course, heedless of the testimony of the Spirit. He played a major role in Waggoner's resignation from teaching a course at the ministerial institute of 1890. In one of many letters that he left for posterity to study, he wrote:

> There has never anything happened in my life that has taken me down like this. I have just felt so thoroughly upset by the whole affair that I have hardly known how to act or what to do... . When I saw what the lessons were [the Sabbath School lessons on the covenants written by Waggoner], I decided at once

that I could not teach them; and after studying over the matter some, decided to resign as teacher in the sabbath-school....

I have been worrying and fretting over this thing until it has hurt me worse than a half year's work. (Jones, *Letter to Elder Butler*, Feb. 13, 1890, cited in *1888 Re-Examined*, p. 51)

How astonishing! Here is a high ranking man of the church "worrying and fretting" about the denominational acceptance and proliferation of the message sent by Jesus to prepare the ministers and people for the closing of the work in the earth and His soon return.

A giant in early Adventism, Uriah Smith held tremendous theological and denominational influence. He was one of Adventism's most fluent writers, five times the secretary of the General Conference, holding posts as treasurer and editor of the *Review and Herald*, as well as instructor at the Battle Creek College. Elder Smith's story provides an example of ineffectual confession. It is well-known that Smith was most adamantly and consistently in opposition to the 1888 message. He felt that it was just the basic Protestant teaching of justification by faith and that it was overdone in contrast to what was really important—the law. He thought that "the sanctity of the law of God was being imperiled by the place given to faith and grace" (*Seventh-day Adventist Encyclopedia*, p. 1356). The situation was dire, as Ellen White informed O. A. Olsen by letter:

Elder Smith is ensnared by the enemy and cannot in his present state give the trumpet a certain sound.... yet Elder Smith is placed in positions as teacher to mold and fashion the minds of students when it is a well known fact that he is not standing in the light; he is not working in God's order. He is sowing seeds of unbelief that spring up and bear fruit for some souls to harvest....

Elder Smith will not receive the light God has given to correct him; and he has not a spirit to correct by confession any wrong course he has pursued in the past...

I have been shown that as he now stands Satan has prepared his temptations to close about his soul ... (Lt. 20, 1890, in *The Ellen G. White 1888 Materials*, p. 714)

Wieland and Short reported, "Finally, after the turn of the new year 1891, he made confession to his brethren, and asked the pardon of Mrs. White for his erroneous course" (*1888 Re-Examined*, p. 87). The four volumes of *The Ellen G. White 1888 Materials* record several confessions for Smith. Yet, he went back on them. Independent researcher and author Marilyn M. Campbell says of this:

If his story ended here, we might consider it a victory, but it continues. Events following this "great victory" in early 1891 suggest a profound communications breakdown between Ellen White and Uriah Smith over the definition of "confession" and "repentance." To Ellen these activities included reformation. She supposed that when the brethren repented and confessed it meant they would thereafter take hold of the God-sent message of 1888 and put their whole souls into, first, understanding it and then teaching it for all they were worth. Ellen's articles and letters following Smith's "confession" show he never understood it, therefore, could not teach it. In documents written after Smith's confessions, the four volumes show Ellen's disappointment in Smith's failure to follow through to understand and teach the message. (M. M. Campbell, "The Confessions of 1888," unpublished paper, p. 3)

Over a year later, Ellen White wrote to Smith: "The first position you took in regard to the message and the messenger has been a continual snare to you and a stumbling block.... You have lost a rich and powerful experience, and *that loss, resulting from refusing the precious treasures of truth presented to you, is still your loss*" (Lt. 24, 1892, in *The Ellen G. White 1888 Materials*, pp. 1052, 1053 emphasis added).

We could provide other case studies, but this information can be found in the research of others. As an example, M. M. Campbell compiled all the confessions in the four-volume set of *The Ellen G. White 1888 Materials* and traced the results from the available documentation in those records, along with what Ellen White said about each matter. Her assessment concurs with that of other students of this history:

It's clear that up to and after 1894 Ellen sees no genuine change in the opposing brethren, even though, of those who confessed, most had done so by this time. Only the confessions of Belden and Eldridge came in after this year. The Minneapolis spirit still prevailed. Confessions and repentance had not produced a better spirit by this date.

Wieland and Short listed several points of evidence

that contradict the claim most often made that the majority of leaders who resisted the message later broke down in deep contrition, made a complete work of repentance, and went on to proclaim the righteousness of Christ in power:

> "(1) The confessions were practically extorted by overwhelming, compelling evidence. 'The present evidence of His working is revealed to you, and you are now under obligation to believe,' said Ellen White in 1890 (TM 466). Faith had given away [sic] almost entirely to sight.
>
> "(2) There is evidence that the most prominent and influential confessors subsequently acted contrary to their confessions.
>
> "(3) There was very little frank, open reconciliation that led to brotherly union with A. T. Jones and E. J. Waggoner or acceptance of their message. (Note that it was *after* the confessions that Ellen White was exiled to Australia and Waggoner to Britain)...." (*1888 Re-Examined*, pp. 82, 83)

Paraphrasing point 4, if the leading men had made acceptable confession, the loud cry would have gone forth in latter rain power, and we would not be considering this now.

> "(5) With the exception of W. W. Prescott, there is no evidence that any of the confessors recovered the essence of the 1888 message sufficiently to proclaim it well. (Saul of Tarsus repented so thoroughly that he ever after proclaimed the gospel with power)...." (*1888 Re-Examined*, p. 83).

This last point is readily attested to, even by one of the champions of the acceptance theory, Norval Pease.

> During the nineties the revival centering about this great doctrine was largely the work of the same three people, Mrs. White, E. J. Waggoner, and A. T. Jones. True, there were many harmonizing voices but no Elishas were in evidence by 1900 ready to assume the mantle in case something should happen to the three principal champions of the doctrine. (*By Faith Alone*, p. 164)

To close this segment, we will add just one more contrast of statements. Uriah Smith said in the *Review and Herald* that the message was "going forward everywhere ... increasing in velocity day by day ... with a power that cannot be arrested" and that at that current "rate of progress ... must soon reach its goal" (March 14, 1892). With the authority of heaven, Mrs. White responded in 1893, "The work is years behind. What account will be rendered to God for thus retarding the work?" (Lt. 77, 1893, in *General Conference Bulletin*, Feb. 28, 1893, p. 419). Three years before she had written:

> The prejudices and opinions that prevailed at Minneapolis are not dead by any means; the seeds sown there in some hearts are ready to spring into life and bear a like harvest. The tops have been cut down, but the roots have never been eradicated.... When by thorough confession, you destroy the root of bitterness, you will see light in God's light. Without this thorough work you will never clear your souls....
>
> There has been a departure from God among us, and the zealous work of repentance and return to our first love essential to restoration to God and regeneration of heart has not yet been done.... The true religion, the only religion of the Bible, that teaches forgiveness only through the merits of a crucified and risen Saviour, that advocates righteousness by the faith of the Son of God, has been slighted, spoken against, ridiculed, and rejected. It has been denounced as leading to enthusiasm and fanaticism. But it is the life of Jesus Christ in the soul, it is the active principle of love imparted by the Holy Spirit, that alone will make the soul fruitful unto good works. (Ms. 61, 1890, in *Ellen G. White 1888 Materials*, pp. 954, 955)

Securing the Destiny of the Movement in its Fourth Generation

We could examine many books of the new order in timeline fashion, but that would be a study for an entire volume. However, it is well for us to highlight especially one of these books. A primary propaganda piece, *Movement of Destiny* appeared in print in 1971. This book represents a concerted effort to "lock in" the several myths surrounding the 1888 message and its reception. The volume and its author, Leroy E. Froom, both carry the glowing endorsement of the highest officers in the Seventh-day Adventist Church. Froom was one of the church's most respected and high-ranking scholars. Containing a foreword by *then* General Conference President Robert H. Pierson, the book was published by the official press, the Review and Herald Publishing Association. *Then* Vice President

Neal C. Wilson, also chairman of the guidance committee that oversaw the writing of the book, wrote the preface, describing the commission of the writing of this book since forty years prior. "Not only was the book originally an assignment from the church, but the author had the help of a church-appointed guidance committee ..." (*The Destiny of a Movement*, p. 234). Fifteen hundred free copies were distributed to church leaders in all parts of the globe.

The volume carries a highly significant impact upon the denomination, even as it is still a standard text for the shaping of Adventist minds. How can this be, knowing that the majority of Seventh-day Adventists are scarcely aware of the book? In other words, amongst the grassroots, there may be some awareness of the *title* but not of the book's contents. The general laity does not read that much, and when they actually read, they prefer lighter devotional reading and storybooks rather than books of this sort. However, this is not to say that it has not had a profound influence. The ministerial leaders of the fourth generation have been shaped by its teaching, and this in turn has shaped the laity.

In light of the foregoing, *Movement of Destiny*, a volume having never been recalled or repudiated and still in use, is a true representation of the church's present stance on the 1888 message, of its teaching on the nature of Christ, and of its relationship to the Protestant churches of general Christendom.

It is a special note of irony that the man whom Froom credited with commissioning the writing of this history (*Movement of Destiny*, p. 8) held a view of the reception of the message—and it is the *correct* view—that stands in utter contradistinction to what the book would champion some forty years later.

The message has never been received, nor proclaimed, nor given free course as it should have been in order to convey to the church the measureless blessings that were wrapped within it.... Back of the opposition is revealed the shrewd plotting of that master mind of evil, the enemy of all righteousness. The very fact of his determination to neutralize the message and it inevitable effects, is evidence of its great value and importance; and how terrible must be the results of any victory of his in defeating it! (A. G. Daniells, *Christ our Righteousness*, pp. 47, 53, 54, emphasis added)

Then we come to Froom's appraisal of the message's reception:

The epochal Minneapolis Session stands out like a mountain peak, towering above all other sessions in uniqueness and importance. It was a distinct turning point.... It definitely introduced a new epoch.... 1888 therefore came to mark the beginning of a new note and new day ... **1888 was not a point of defeat but a turn in the tide for ultimate victory.... the 1888 ... battle [was] hard fought and the victory dearly won** ... (Froom, *Movement of Destiny*, pp. 187, 191, emphasis added)

Froom's book discusses the two schools of thought regarding the deity of Christ, which were at odds in the denomination prior to the conference. Uriah Smith held the view that Christ was a created being and Waggoner (along with Jones and E. G. White) held the view of His eternal pre-existence and deity. At the conference, the eternal verity of the deity of Christ won the day, and this is set forth as "the deeper significance of '1888,'" hence the claim that "1888 was not a point of defeat, but a turn in the tide for ultimate victory" (*Movement of Destiny*, p. 187).

Froom has reduced what God did in 1888 to a battle between two contrasting areas of theology. He has made the purpose and intent of that critical and wonderful hour much less than it really was, by presenting it as a time when the Lord desired to clear the church of certain errors to pave the way for ultimate development of the Eternal Verities in fullness of truth. (*The Destiny of a Movement*, p. 243)

Movement of Destiny has produced a very diminished, dimmed, and distorted picture of what really did happen in 1888, and therefore it is a false picture. It has robbed that event of significance and glory. Its real importance has been dismissed in the minds of those who have accepted the arguments propounded by Froom. The evil result is that the average person will sink back into the self-satisfied conclusion that 1888 has nothing for him, as it simply served to correct errors from which he was long since delivered, for, after all, the average modern Adventist has no trouble in believing that Christ was not a created being, but God in fact. (*The Destiny of a Movement*, p. 246)

So it is that, throughout the pages of *Movement of Destiny*, Froom teaches and concludes his examination of the Minneapolis 1888 message as being "Righteousness by Faith in Christ as '*all the fulness of the Godhead*' "

(*Movement of Destiny*, p. 144, cited in *The Destiny of a Movement*, p. 241).

Movement of Destiny is in accord with the previously published *Questions on Doctrine*, vibrating sympathetically with its doctrinal shifts. This would of course be expected, since the books have the same author. The message of 1888 was much more than correcting views on the deity of Christ. Issues regarding the nature of Christ figure in, as well. The message also addressed His humanity. "These messengers of the Lord brought the doctrine that Christ came in the selfsame flesh and blood as the children whom He came to save. It is the teaching that the ladder reached up to the very throne of God and down to the sinful flesh of man.... If men had come presenting only the divinity of Christ, they would have come preaching only God, instead of the saving truth, 'God with us,' which is Christ *in the flesh—the doctrine of Christ*" (Wright, *The Destiny of a Movement*, pp. 268, 269). Thus it was that the messengers came not with a mere message of correcting old error, of a re-emphasis or shift from the law to the gospel, but they came with something that was beyond that which Adventists had ever held before. This is a picture that is steadfastly avoided in *Movement of Destiny* and in other books of the new order. Though Froom faithfully recorded Waggoner's presentation of the deity of Christ, a teaching which harmonized with all of Christendom, he failed to represent Waggoner's teaching on the humanity of Christ. Froom's presentation is misleading in this regard, as it purports to set forth the whole of what Waggoner taught, under the heading "E. J. Waggoner's Actual Message at Minneapolis—No. 1" (*Movement of Destiny*, p. 188).

When Froom sketchily related Waggoner's teaching on the humanity of Christ, he inserted a word that changes the meaning. Instead of reporting accurately that Waggoner taught that Christ became sin for us, *period*, he rather provided a subtle private interpretation that Waggoner meant that Christ became sin for us, *vicariously* (*Movement of Destiny*, p. 197). In this way, the "actual" taking of sin becomes a mystical sympathetic bearing of it. Something cannot be both actual and vicarious. Yet, "vicarious" is needed in order for Adventism to come into line with the fallen churches of modern Evangelicalism, as we have discussed earlier in this book.

The Strange Claim:
Those Mystical Missing Affidavits

It is mind-boggling. The author of *Movement of Destiny* weaves into the book a tremendous claim that there were twenty-six eyewitness attendees at the conference who left for us written affidavits that attest to the leadership's acceptance of the message. Even without being able to see what these witnesses say, right from the start there is an obvious problem in that Wieland and Short stated that, of these twenty-six "participants, observers, or recorders" referred to by Froom, who provided testimony, only *thirteen* of them were actually in attendance. Froom makes sixty-four references to these positive accounts, mentioning one of them fourteen times. Yet, this is the least of his problems. Two chapters, covering thirty-one pages, are dedicated to these alleged affirmations, *but not even once is the reader shown a single sentence from any of them* (*1888 Re-Examined*, p. 175).

> There is not a court or jury in the free world that would accept this kind of inference without evidence. And when supposed evidence so obviously contradicts the testimony of Ellen White, Seventh-day Adventist church members should very earnestly demand that they be permitted to see such evidence. (*1888 Re-Examined*, pp. 176, 177)

Wieland and Short tell of a bizarre round of communications with Froom, prior to the publication of Froom's book:

> Dr. Froom wrote to the present authors on December 4, 1964, before the publication of his *Movement of Destiny*, demanding a retraction of the positions they had taken in *1888 Re-Examined*. We were required to "make a public and published disavowal ... of certain conclusions advanced by you [*that is, that the 1888 leadership rejected the beginning of the latter rain and the loud cry*].... Ere long the full, documented story of the 1888 episode will doubtless be put into print. And unless you have modified your presentation, you may find yourself in a most unenviable position. The contrast will be marked." On April 16, 1965 he wrote to us further: "In my view, you had better act first, and without much delay.... Your contention ... stands out like a sore thumb, conspicuously alone, and in conflict with the virtually unanimous verdict of our scholars.... You have a lot of temerity to contradict the findings of this whole group of men.... I

... feel ... no obligation to share any further evidence with you.... Your unhappy plight makes me think of Elijah's situation.... He sharply disagreed with the historians and the experts in Israel about the situation. He was right, he felt, and they were all wrong. He only was loyally left, and was maligned and persecuted because of his claims and conclusions.... Elijah thus actually defamed and vilified Israel, and gave a misleading and blackening report. He bore an untrue witness, casting aspersion upon Israel and its leadership [Ahab and Jezebel?].... You should cease, retreat, and retract." He claimed that he spoke with the authority of the General Conference behind him, as indeed their unprecedented endorsement of his book soon demonstrated.

One of us replied on May 10, 1965: "To retract on the basis of fear without inspired evidence would hardly ... be the right thing ... to do.... The Lord has never asked a man to do such a thing. In fact, a man can very well ruin his soul by yielding to a pressure of fear and anxiety, and cravenly retracting, without evidence, what he has held in good conscience." On November 10, 1965, the same author wrote to Dr. Froom: "I have repeated my willingness to retract if you will let me see clear evidence from the Spirit of Prophecy. You have categorically refused to let me see such evidence.... It seems strange to me and to others that you should demand I 'retract' while at the same time you deny me evidence which you say you have in unpublished Ellen G. White material that would require of an honest conscience such a retraction.... My prayer is that in the final outcome of this matter [God's] name be honored."

When *Movement of Destiny* appeared in print, the documentary "evidence" was completely absent. (*1888 Re-Examined*, p. 177, fn. 1)

There are, however, extant testimonies of three of Froom's named witnesses, which we can compare with his claims. Wieland and Short quote from them:

I am sorry for anyone at the Conference in Minneapolis in 1888 who does not recognize that there was opposition and rejection of the Message that the Lord sent to His people at that time. It is not too late yet to repent and receive a great blessing. (C. C. McReynolds, DF 189, *Experiences While at the General Conference in Minneapolis, Minn. in 1888*, quoted in *Manuscripts and Memories of Minneapolis*, p. 342)

The writer of this tract, then a young man, was present at that conference meeting [1888], and saw and heard many of the various things that were done and said in opposition to the message then presented.... When Christ was lifted up as the only hope of the church, and of all men, the speakers met a united opposition from nearly all the senior ministers. They tried to put a stop to this teaching by Elders Waggoner and Jones. They wanted the discussion of this subject to cease. (R. T. Nash, *Eyewitness Report of the 1888 General Conference*, in *1888 Re-Examined*, pp. 177, 178)

All the time in the General Conference Committee and amongst others there was a secret antagonism always carried on, and which finally in Daniells, Spicer & Co., gained the day in the denomination, and gave to the Minneapolis spirit and contention and men the supremacy ... (A. T. Jones, letter to Claude Holmes, May 12, 1921, in DF 189, emphasis in original, available at http://1ref.us/id, accessed 10/24/16)

On page 256 of *Movement of Destiny*, we are told in italics, "*There was no denomination-wide, or leadership-wide rejection*, these witnesses insisted. The newly appointed leaders supported it" (C. McReynolds, letter to L. E. Froom, April 25, 1930). It makes sense that, if a writer has a claim to make and has affidavits that contradict his claim, he would avoid citing them. Yet, in the interest of honesty, he should not even make the claim that the people who provided the affidavits support his thesis. On the other hand, it is inconceivable that, if support would be gained by any of those alleged affidavits, would he not do more than merely claim that they exist? Would he not actually *quote them*?

Then there is the astounding claim in the book that sets forth Ellen White as a primary supporter of his thesis.

Beginning on page 221 and continuing for 12 pages, there is an array of isolated words and phrases from Ellen White, again with no source given. Over 100 fragmentary words or phrases and half-sentences leave out vital meaningful portions, omitting contextual information which would give quite a different meaning and would nullify the "victory" theory. Words and phrases from her Minneapolis sermons are surrounded and smothered with the author's interjections, leaving Ellen White's real message indiscernible. (*1888 Re-Examined*, p. 178)

Then, as a veiled reference to the work of Wieland and Short, Froom has the effrontery to indict them in his book for the very work that *Movement of Destiny* is itself engaged in, namely—

REGRETTABLE PLOY OF RECONSTRUCTED HISTORY.—History has sometimes been reconstructed by attempted selectivity—that is, by using out of context or intent such citations as suit an objective—in an attempt to sustain a particular assumption or theory. But such a practice is neither ethical nor honest.... As men of integrity, we must have no part in such manipulation of historical episodes. Servants of the God of truth must ever use quotations, evidence, and lines of argument in such a way as to honor Truth and its Author. (*Movement of Destiny*, pp. 364, 365)

He later takes up two chapters of the book continuing to claim Ellen White as his "peerless witness," yet never quoted her. In the second chapter, he charted a list, year by year, from 1854–1915, set forth as an alleged "Comprehensiveness Profoundly Impressive" essence of her writings, "*each condensed into a single summarizing sentence*" "for the record." In this rendering, we find "a panoramic disclosure ... of the whole counsel of God to the people ... in *Righteousness by Faith*" (*Movement of Destiny*, p. 458). What comes as a surprise, however, is that these summarizing sentences have no connection to the actual titles of the EGW published articles: they "are solely the comments of the author to suit his thesis" (*1888 Re-Examined*, p. 178). This is plainly a vain work of highly dubious value and not befitting the level of scholarship generally claimed for this author. In other words, it is fiction passed off as a true story. (For personal verification of these statements, *Movement of Destiny* can be found online as a free download at http://1ref.us/ie.)

Not to belabor the point, we close with one more of many observations that can be made. Froom sets forth the incoming president, elected in 1888, Elder O. A. Olsen, as the primary determinant of whether the message was accepted or rejected by church leadership (as cited by Wieland and Short in *1888 Re-Examined*, p. 178). Froom wrote:

Now, the record of [O. A.] Olsen's spiritual leadership is clear and loyal.... Olsen seemed to sense the spiritual bearings of the question at issue, and gave quiet but effective leadership to their solution....

The confused philosophy that a man must strive to be good, and to do good-in order to receive the Righteousness of Christ ... was hard for some to yield. Nevertheless, **the years of Olsen's administration saw a real revival and reformation** in application of this prime principle of Christianity—that justification and sanctification come through the reception of Christ into the life, through the operation of the Holy Spirit. And all by grace through faith. **Olsen's tenure of office was a time of awakening from Laodicean self-satisfaction** and self-reliance, a renewal brought about through the growing acceptance of the message of Righteousness by Faith....

So it cannot, with any show of right, be said that Olsen personally rejected or subdued the message of Righteousness by Faith, or led or aided or abetted in such a direction....

Clearly, Olsen did not reject the message of Righteousness by Faith. (*Movement of Destiny*, pp. 359, 361, 363, 364, emphasis added)

A man of Froom's scholarship would surely know what Mrs. White had to say. Though Ellen White did not specifically say that he rejected the light of Minneapolis, she reprimanded him, as a leader, for opposing the light from heaven, for being untrue to his post, and for damaging to the cause of God. Many times as we read this and other books of the new order, we are incredulous and even indignant regarding the discrepancies between the reports in these books and the actual documents of witnesses and inspired testimony. Here is what Mrs. White said about O. A. Olsen in a letter written to A. O. Tait, August 27, 1896:

I feel very sorry for Brother Olsen. I have written him much in regard to the situation. He has written back to me, thanking me for the timely letters, but he **has not acted upon the light given**. The case is a mysterious one. While traveling from place to place he has linked with him as companions men whose spirit and influence should not be sanctioned, and the people who repose confidence in them will be misled. But notwithstanding the light which has been placed before him for years in regard to this matter, **he has ventured on, directly contrary to the light which the Lord has been giving him.** All this confuses his spiritual discernment, and places him in a relation to the general interest, and wholesome, healthy advancement of the work, as **an unfaithful**

watchman. He is pursuing a course which is detrimental to his spiritual discernment, and he is leading other minds to view matters in a perverted light. He has given unmistakable evidence that he does not regard the testimonies which the Lord has seen fit to give His people as worthy of respect or as of sufficient weight to influence his course of action.

I am distressed beyond any words my pen can trace. Unmistakably, **Elder Olsen has acted, as did Aaron, in regard to these men who have been opposed to the work of God ever since the Minneapolis meeting. They have not repented of their course of action in resisting light and evidence.**…

From the light God has been pleased to give me, until the home field shows more healthful heart beats, the fewer long journeys Elder Olsen shall make with his selected helpers, A. R. Henry and Harmon Lindsay, the better it will be for the cause of God. (Lt. 100, 1896, in *The Ellen G. White 1888 Materials*, pp. 1607, 1608, emphasis added)

If it were not for space limitations, we could take up the case of each one of the "big three"—the president, the secretary, and the treasurer—of the *outgoing* (George I. Butler, Uriah Smith, and A. R. Henry) and *incoming* leadership (O. A. Olsen, Dan T. Jones, and Harmon Lindsay) who transitioned in October 1888. Except perhaps for the case of Butler (though no confession is recorded, Ellen White's tone in writing regarded Butler softened), we would find a woeful tale of men whose record seems very dismal in terms of eternal consequences with regard to their attitude and actions surrounding the 1888 message. This other *Reconstructionist accounting* of men is not recounted according to the measuring stick of inspiration: the unerring testimony of heaven.

"An Explicit Confession … Due the Church"

In Froom's book, the church takes a generally high and mighty attitude in its endeavor to deal with a "persisting 'stock' charge that has come to life periodically across the years … to the effect that either the denomination as a whole or at least the leadership of the Movement actually rejected the Righteousness by Faith message of 1888 …" He judged that "this claim had usually come from men of critical bent, sometimes those whose aspirations had been thwarted or who felt that they had not been treated fairly by the leading brethren," charging them with "audaciously" pitting "their personal views and deductions against a score of our most competent, best informed, and loyal leaders, men who had access to *all* the facts, and who have made intensive search for the *full and balanced evidence*, and have not found such an assumption sustained by fact" (*Movement of Destiny*, p. 682).

Movement of Destiny devotes chapter 22 to proving false the "unjustifiable charge of leadership unfaithfulness," without naming Wieland and Short, charging them with unjustly "impeaching the dead," and demanding of them a retraction, saying—

An explicit confession is due the Church today by promulgators of a misleading charge, first of all against the names of the post–1888 leadership, now all sleeping. Moreover, it is likewise due those in the Church today who have been confused and misled by such an allegation. In the ultimate, then, it actually constitutes an impeachment of the dead. That is a gravely serious matter. (*Movement of Destiny*, p. 358)

The authors of *1888 Re-Examined* therefore prepared an official response to the official demand from "Adventism's most noted scholar," entitled "*An Explicit Confession … Due the Church.*" When copies were distributed to General Conference officials, the officials asked that it not be published and called for special meetings to take place. These meetings were held over several years. Wieland and Short wrote: "The officers and the committees considered the Ellen White evidence and were impressed by it, but again urged that *Explicit Confession* not be published. Then after suppressing *Explicit Confession* they republished *Movement of Destiny* with no change in its basic thesis" (*1888 Re-Examined*, p. 181). In the May 1998 "Preface to Facsimile Reprint" of *Explicit Confession*, the authors stated that, while "their 'confession' was not what the General Conference wanted from them, it did spark a serious interest to study the issues" and, after some time of study, the president had made a decision to call for a corporate repentance on the issue of the rejection of the 1888 message. "But the Palmdale Conference of early 1976 led him to reverse his decision and to lend support to the Desmond Ford thesis instead." Really? That is quite an about-face!

So it is that, in *An Explicit Confession … Due the Church*, Wieland and Short again recounted the evidences as given in the testimonies whether or not the premises of *Movement of Destiny* will stand or fall. Many of the stark contrasts are drawn between the two, such as the claim that "the post–1888 leadership 'diligently fostered various Ministerial Institutes in which Righteousness by

Faith was stressed among our ministry [and] fostered the study of the Spirit of Prophecy' and yet in reality exerted an influence that 'spread like the leprosy, until it has tainted and corrupted the whole' ... (Compare *Movement of Destiny*, page 363 with Ellen G. White Letter, May 31 1896.)" (*An Explicit Confession ... Due the Church*, p. 14).

Here is another claim: *Movement of Destiny* states that the majority of the rebels at the 1888 conference made effective confessions over the next decade and that most of these did so within five years, claiming, "Only a small hard core of 'die-hards' continued to reject it" (*Movement of Destiny*, p. 368). Ellen White did not agree in the slightest. She wrote: "The work that will meet the mind of the Spirit of God has not yet begun in Battle Creek. When the work of seeking God with all the heart commences, there will be many confessions made that are now buried. I do not at present feel it my duty to confess for those who ought to make, not a general, but a plain, definite confession, and so cleanse the soul-temple. The evil is not with one man or two. It is the whole that needs the cleansing and setting in order" (Lt. 19a, 1897, in *An Explicit Confession*, p. 15).

Note that some of the testimonies cited by Wieland and Short were not available in the published editions of her writings. (Today we do have them). These messengers reveal that, over a twenty-two year period, the Lord, through "retired ministers and scholars", had placed in their hands "a remarkable collection of unpublished Ellen G. White material that bears directly on the subject matter of this 'confession'" (*An Explicit Confession*, pp. 13, 2). Previous to the publication of *An Explicit Confession*, the authors avoided publishing from these rare materials that had not yet been released by the Ellen G. White Estate, but because *Movement of Destiny* "now says that the 'facts are accessible'" being "neither hidden nor ambiguous," and they are now under obligation to make " 'an explicit confession' publicly," they believe that "the time has fully come to disclose what the Lord's servant has said" (*An Explicit Confession*, p. 13).

Another unpublished document that came into our possession years ago is the original unedited transcript of Ellen G. White's remarks made in the Battle Creek College Library on April 1, 1901, at 2:30 p.m. which presents clear-cut evidence:

When we see that message after message that God has given has been accepted, but no change—just the same as it was before, then we know that there is new blood must be brought into the regular lines.... Not that anyone means to be wrong, or to be wrong; but the principle is wrong, and the principles have become so mixed and so foreign from what God's principles are ... There should be a renovation without any delay.... [Ms. 43c, 1901, in the Spaulding and Magan Collection, p. 163, as reported by J. H. Kellogg] This thing has been acted and reacted for the last fifteen years or more, and God calls for a change.... Our standstill has got to come to an end; but yet every Conference, it is woven after the very same pattern.... Enough has been said; enough has been said over and over and over again, but it does not make any difference; they go right on just the same, professedly accepting it, but they do not make any change. Well, now, that is what burdens me; that is what burdens me.... "You have lost your first love," you have lost it. [Ms. 43a, 1901, as reported by C. C. Crisler]

If we were asked, "Did the post-1888 leadership 'professedly accept' the 1888 message?" we would have to answer 'yes.' But "professedly accepting it" and "not making any change" will never finish God's work, even in a thousand years. It is this "professedly accepting it" which has confused certain sincere denominational historians into assuming that such lip service meant heart-acceptance. Isn't it time now to consider the truth? (*An Explicit Confession*, pp. 15, 16)

So it is that we see Wieland and Short, in their answer to the church's demand to render "an explicit confession," responding by confessing the following seven points (adapted from *An Explicit Confession ... Due the Church*, pp. 36–46):

1. That the truth of the Lord's words in counsel to the Laodiceans is a message directed to the leadership of the church, Revelation 3:17; that Christ is referring here to the denominational pride in their unsullied understanding of the gospel. Leadership explicitly blames the laity for not receiving the message. The book *Crisis to Victory*, by O. A. Olsen, lists how the church has set the teaching forth in so many ways, but "they [*many church members*] have neglected the light that God in His love and mercy has caused to shine upon them. They have failed ..." (see pp. 233–239).

2. The hope that the message will yet do its work and that it will be realized that the Lord is not delaying His coming, but that we have delayed it and the sooner we understand this, the sooner we shall experience the return of the latter rain.

3. The Revelation 3:19 call to repentance is a specific reference to heed the gospel in its fullness as was actually brought to the church in 1888, recognizing the distinction between *that* message and the message which "we proudly assume is 'righteousness by faith' as we practically understand it"—as consisting in "themes and concepts borrowed either from the great Reformers of the sixteenth century or from modern Evangelicals."

4. It is biblical to call for repentance of sins of a past generation (Lev. 26:40, 41; 2 Kings 22:13; Neh. 1:6; Ezek. 16). Christ called for a nation to repent (Matt. 4:17; 11:20; 23:13-27, 29-36). Ninevah represents a type of corporate repentance (Luke 11:29-32; Jonah 3:3-7).

   Ellen White also supported the validity of corporate repentance. She wrote: "Unless we individually repent toward God because of transgression of His law, and exercise faith toward our Lord Jesus Christ, whom the world has rejected, we shall lie under the full condemnation that the action of choosing Barabbas instead of Christ merited," for all who reveal the same unbelief as "manifested by those who put to death the Son of God—would act the same part, were the opportunity granted, as did the Jews and people of the time of Christ" (*Testimonies to Ministers*, p. 38). "Upon all rests the guilt of crucifying the Son of God" (*The Desire of Ages*, p. 745).

   Therefore, corporate repentance is recognizing that as individuals in the present body we share in the guilt of that which has gone before in that we carry on in a system that has not yet recognized its guilt and in so doing continues to carry that guilt though the original players are gone.

   Further, "it is repenting of sin which we may not have actually done, but which we would have committed had we had the opportunity or been under sufficient pressure" ("*An Explicit Confession*," p. 41). "The books of heaven record the sins that would have been committed had there been opportunity" (*Signs of the Times*, July 31, 1901).

   By an extension of these principles, we must recognize that we need to enter into the repentance that is due for the rejection of " 'the beginning of the Latter Rain' at and after 1888" ("*An Explicit Confession*," p. 41), for this the sin of our fathers in which we as individuals may partake through our own individual unbelief—an unbelief not only of the true history of the message, but the very message itself. That rejection is recorded against modern spiritual Israel as a crucifixion event. Theirs was the sin of Laodicean pride. Can we say that we have repented of it?

   The sin of the rejection of the 1888 message was but a modern manifestation of the identical sin that was carried out in the Jews' killing of Christ. "Men professing godliness have despised Christ in the person of His messengers. Like the Jews, they reject God's message" (*Fundamentals of Christian Education*, p. 472). "If you reject Christ's delegated messengers, you reject Christ" (*Testimonies to Ministers*, p. 97).

5. The promise of eventual surrender and corporate repentance [see the sidebar discussion below] will be realized and the work will close.

Sidebar discussion: concerning "denominational" and "corporate" repentance—are these terms synonymous?

While we believe the statement in item 5 as it stands, we differ with the Wieland and Short messengers in a certain respect that is of no minor significance. They ever expressed an unfailing confidence in the General Conference leadership of the denominational Church, with a capital "C," and that *the Lord will honor the principles of organization as embodied in that corporation until the end.* They extrapolated such a conclusion from an allusion to the closing work, in *Testimonies for the Church*, volume 9—a revelation of "a great reformatory movement among God's people," (p. 126) and in the "What Might Have Been" chapter of *Testimonies for the Church*, volume 8, page 104, seeing in these passages and others the realization of a repentance that will begin with the denominational leadership at the General Conference level. As such, it will then work its way down to all the membership in sufficient strength and numbers to actually turn the tide in the denominational church.

We see, rather, the realization of corporate repentance as that which will take place in the body of believers in the third angel's message who have formed up *in sufficient force* and *irrespective of their relation to the legal denomination*. In other words, these individuals will come from various bodies—the mainstream, the independents (supporting and non-supporting), the home churches, and wherever else. It will be *the triumph of the true message, in the invisible body of those that proclaim it as it truly is in Jesus* rather than the triumph of the visible hierarchical structure operating as *a corporate registry in law*, possessing a legal title to a name, logo, real estate, and institutions and as driven by conferences and committees vested with authority conferred by the church organizational system of educational qualifications and votes.

There is confusion in almost every Seventh-day Adventist mind on this point when we do not discern between the organization and the body of Christ. This is because of the tremendous propaganda campaign that has convinced minds that the organization has Jesus as its true Head when they do not realize that the leaders have not actually let Him in, for He is on the outside knocking on the door. That is what He says to this church: "Behold, I am out here knocking. Let me in." The *organization* is not the ship of God. Jesus is the ship of God, and He is the fourth angel, the very embodiment of the message that lives in *the people* who have heard Him knocking on the door and have cleared away the rubbish to let Him in.

This "sufficient force" will be seen in the formation of the body known as the 144,000, who will go forth under latter rain power, bringing the light of the glory of God to the entire planet within the timeframe of their own generation. These are the epitome and climax of the "Movement of Destiny." The whole denominational church, with all its institutions and media organs, even *the majority* of leadership and members, will never be converted. "Are we hoping to see the whole church revived? That time will never come" (*Review and Herald*, March 22, 1887, in *Selected Messages*, bk. 1, p. 122). The bulk of those who make up the final generation church will come in from Babylon, under the power of the loud cry in latter rain.

Therefore, we concur with the second call messengers regarding the relevance of such statements as, "Sometime it [*the full story of post–1888 response*] will be seen in its true bearing, with all the burden of woe that has resulted from it" (Lt. 25b, 1892, in *The Ellen G. White 1888 Materials*, p. 1013), and "There will be great humbling of hearts before God on the part *of every one who remains faithful* and true to the end" (Ellen G. White, sermon at Minneapolis, Ms. 15, 1888, cited in A. V. Olson, *Through Crisis to Victory*, p. 297; *Thirteen Crisis Years*, p. 306, emphasis added). However, we see such statements in a different light. In other words, we would stress that all such statements are referring to the work *of individuals* who, all together, make up the corporate faithful body of the remnant elect and that we cannot look to a visible organization to provide us the prophetic fulfillment of that church "terrible as an army with banners," the purified bride. "This testimony [of the True Witness to the Laodiceans] must work deep repentance; *all who truly receive it will obey it, and be purified*" (*Christian Experience and Teachings of Ellen G. White*, p. 176). This victorious and purified assemblage will be a theocratic movement, working outside of the "common order," as God will be seen to be taking the reins of the work into His own hands (*Testimonies to Ministers*, p. 300). This final church will come into view *outside* of the pale of the directives of committees and conferences, in a time of great flux, as vast numbers—in fact, "the greater part of the followers of Christ" (*The Great Controversy*, p. 382) who are now in Babylon—will come into the message in response to the last call. All the while the leadership of the denomination keep on with the status quo, operating and maintaining the machinery of the institution, creating and administering the various programs of the church, seeking to keep control over the members, and even thinking to be keepers of the very message itself.

> In the manifestation of that power which lightens the earth with the glory of God, they will see only something which in their blindness they think dangerous, something which will arouse their fears, and they will brace themselves to resist it. Because the Lord does not work according to their ideas and expectations, they will oppose the work.... (*Review and Herald*, Dec. 23, 1890)

> There will be those among us who will always want to control the work of God, to dictate even what movements shall be made when the work goes forward under the direction of the angel who joins the third angel in the message to be given to the world. (*Testimonies to Ministers*, p. 299)

All the while that the message has been for years on the rise and will come to a head in the close of probation, there has already been and will continue to be a great apostate exodus, as the shaking "blows away multitudes like dry leaves" (*Testimonies to the Church*, vol. 4, p. 89). In other words, the message has been in progress until the present time, and the purpose of this writing is to add impetus to this work.

Therefore, do not confuse this "exodus" with a flushing out of the supposed "unfaithful" or "sinners" from the denomination. The exodus is spiritual, encompassing the multitudes of those who remain in support of an unrepentant system. Just look at the typology: Who left whom in the destruction of Jerusalem in A. D. 70? Those who were following the Way left those who refused Christ and the message, having to part ways with the synagogues. Where were the tares gathered? Into the *midst of Jerusalem*, the apostate old system! (A type of this can be seen in Ezek. 22:17–31.) There was a godly revival amongst believing Jewish people which took place outside of the auspices of the apostate church. These were the ones who left the city. If the revival had taken place in the city, it would not have been destroyed.

So when we read statements such as, "Standard after standard was left to trail in the dust as company after company from the Lord's army joined the foe and tribe after tribe from the ranks of the enemy united with the commandment-keeping people of God" (*Testimonies to the Church*, vol. 8, p. 41), we cannot interpret the "Lord's army" as the conference churches, but rather as those who keep the commandments of God and the testimony of Jesus.

Students of the true history, such as we have presented in this book, are well aware that for a long time the state of the denomination has been such that the testimonies have been made of none effect (*Testimonies to the Church*, vol. 4, p. 211), and these same students also know that "storm and tempest would sweep away the structure" (Lt. 242, 1903, in *Battle Creek Letters*, p. 81). Now, mark this point of contrast: *For the vast majority of church members*, who do not conduct their independent study, the revelation of the nature of the Omega of apostasy is of "*a most startling nature*" (Lt. 263, 1904, in *Special Testimonies*, B02, p. 16). Why is that?

It is because they have come to realize that the mainstream church, in departing from the message of righteousness by faith of the true third angel's message and in refusing the counsel of the True Witness to the Laodiceans, has itself become an "offshoot." (For the true definition of the term would be "that which is apostate," having "shot off" from the truth.) The lack of such knowledge leaves the majority of members believing the opposite of the truth about the shaking and looking for the wrong thing as they are deceived into a false sense of security from depending upon human leaders to guide them in paths of righteousness instead of Christ. Members must realize that they can be shaken out of *the church* (the true church, not the denominational church) while continuing to sit week after week in the pews of the church and remaining members in good standing.

Returning to the last two of Wieland and Short's points, in their offering of explicit confession, we find them affirming for themselves:

1. There is great need of the church having a most earnest appreciation of the truths that were sent in 1888 as found in the writings of Jones and Waggoner and fully backing the reprinting of the messages contained in their sermons and books.

2. Finally, the authors confess themselves "to be the least and most unworthy of all the Lord's servants," having nothing in themselves to boast. Shying away from Froom's charges of acting out of "sheer stubbornness" (*Movement of Destiny*, p. 686), they insist that what they have come to understand is not by "special inspiration or revelation" but by simply reading the message itself, along with the inspired testimony confirming it to be the beginning of the loud cry of the third angel's message. They say, "What can we do other than tell what we have seen?"

Spoken as true reformers, theirs is the spirit in which this entire study of **Section II**, "The Devoured Generations," is presented.

Would We Also Stone Stephen? Movement of Destiny Makes Clear Statements of Rejection

While the messengers Wieland and Short were certain that the organized institutional denomination is the ship that goes through, they were at the same time clear that there is no unconditional promise. If we tenaciously cling to the organizational paradigm according to their example, we will surely die while waiting, just as did they. "As Judge," they wrote, "God simply cannot and will not clear the guilty, whether it be an individual or a movement. If this is true, it follows that there is before the remnant church a heavy account to settle" (*An Explicit Confession ... Due the Church*, p. 53).

> Our history is as much a part of the great sacred record of the battle between truth and error as is the crossing of the Red Sea by Israel, and their descendants' stoning of Stephen many centuries later.... The question now is, Will we accept our history, or **will we also 'stone Stephen'?**" (R. J. Wieland and D. K. Short, *1888 Re-Examined*, p. 186, emphasis added)

What was the publication and re-publication of Froom's Movement of Destiny but this very thing?

"Away then, with such charges!" proclaims *Movement of Destiny*. This impudent denial is the purpose of Froom's book.

The second call of the messengers Wieland and Short for the church to come to an acknowledgment of the truth of the 1888 rejection of the message in all its bearings, determining to recover the message and make it available to the people through publication and preaching, was flatly denied in official statements in 1951 and 1958. As though this were not enough, the publication of *Movement of Destiny* seems to be the final word on the matter. God's second call to repentance has been given a resounding *"we will not"* in the following words:

> Recurrent harpers ... [and] echoers still persist, maintaining that the leadership of the Movement, at that time, "rejected" the message of Righteousness by Faith, and thereby incurred the continuing disfavor of God.
>
> And along with that assumption and assertion goes a contention that until and unless the *Movement as a whole today*—nearly eighty years later—repents as a body in sackcloth and ashes for the sins of the *"some"* who, back at that fateful time, did definitely reject the Minneapolis Message at and following 1888, the smile and benediction of God will never rest upon the Advent people and Movement, and its message will never be consummated under present conditions.
>
> In other words, such maintain that the Loud Cry and Latter Rain will never be visited upon us until that retroactive penitence requirement is met through some official acknowledgment and action. That is surely a most sobering thought—if true. On this point let us seek out the facts and find the truth concerning such retrospective repentance....
>
> If not true, it constitutes an unjustifiable woe uttered against the Church as a whole today, affirmed some eight decades after the acts of 1888. (*Movement of Destiny*, pp. 357, 358, emphasis by Froom)

He also wrote:

> Is there such a thing as present-day denomination-wide guilt, because of the wrong attitude of the "some" who rejected the Righteousness by Faith message at and following 1888, which must be atoned for by some all-inclusive "corporate" confession of the denomination as a whole before we can receive the unstinted blessing of God?
>
> And God will not hold guiltless those who seek to impugn the men in leadership who personally accepted the message and sought to lead His people forward in harmony therewith.
>
> **Away then, with such charges.**... (*Froom*, pp. 445, 451, emphasis added)

"Away then, with such charges" is a statement of profound repudiation of the counsel of the True Witness to the Laodiceans, who stands at the door, knocking, diagnosing the true condition of the church and calling for repentance. *"Go away!"* is the answer He gets.

1973–1974 Annual Councils; 1976 General Conference Meeting at Palmdale

During these years there were earnest appeals to the world church calling for revival, reformation, and repentance. The claim was made that the 1888 message had aroused the church and that Ellen White recognized it, saying that the loud cry had begun. Wieland and Short quote from the 1973 Appeal:

> In the four years following the historic Minneapolis General Conference, the fresh, compelling emphasis on "righteousness by faith" *had aroused the Adventist Church* in such a way that Ellen White could say that the "loud cry" had begun! (*1888 Re-Examined*, p. 182)

However, this is not accurate. The message did not arouse the church because *church leadership stood in the way*. She would never agree that the church was aroused because she said, in fact, that "Satan succeeded in shutting away from our people, in a great measure, the special power of the Holy Spirit" (Lt. 96, 1896, to Uriah Smith, in *The Ellen G. White 1888 Materials*, p. 1575).

The ignition of the loud cry was not an unqualified spiritual excitement or fervor that began of its own. It had begun by the introduction of an objective *message*. Mrs. White said that "the revelation of the righteousness of Christ ... is the beginning of the light of the angel whose glory shall fill the whole earth" (*Review and Herald*, Nov. 22, 1892). Therefore, any appeal of the church to experience revival and reformation that disregards the need for *repentance* from having rejected the message and that claims that the message was accepted is a spurious appeal that can never generate anything but wrought-up feelings, which eventually fade back to a formal experience that lacks true divine power.

The Annual Councils of 1973 and 1974 were a continuation of the filling of the void with yet another emphasis on the reformation justification by faith, missing the mark as in every other call for revival as is commonly observed throughout the years in the various programs and initiatives of conference campaigns. "Committee appeals have seldom been effective in producing revival or reformation among either the ministry or the laity, because administrative policy can never effect reconciliation with Christ" (R. J. Wieland and D. K. Short, *1888 Re-Examined*, p. 182).

In 1976, the General Conference convened at Palmdale "where certain theologians dominated the discussions and demanded support for their 'Reformationist,' Calvinist views of 'justification by faith.'" They claimed that they were setting forth "a true revival of the 1888 message content, when in fact they were a denial of every basic essential of that 'most precious message'" (*1888 Re-Examined*, p. 183).

Fireless Torches: "Minneapolis II," the 1988 Centennial Celebration

We must consider "Minneapolis II," the church's Centennial Celebration of 1888, held, obviously, in Minneapolis in 1988. A fast moving coverage of this year and its events are given in Wieland and Short's 56-page book, *1988 Re-Examined*, published by the 1888 Message Study Committee.

The Rio de Janeiro Annual Council of 1986 voted to hold a special Centennial commemoration of 1888. The *Review* announced it saying that the 1888 session "was the only General Conference session where Ellen G. White was publicly defied" (Oct. 30, 1988). The stated goals for the commemoration were to "affirm the righteousness by faith doctrine and raise the level of awareness among church members."

At that time, the question was raised, "Could Minneapolis II get the church back on course?" Looking back over the three decades since then, we are well aware what the answer to that question is.

Reading from *1988 Re-Examined*, by the very men who came with the second call to the church:

> In early fall of 1987, a highly recommended new book came from the church presses, [George Knight's] *FROM 1888 TO APOSTASY, The Case of A. T. Jones*. Its thesis became the keynote of the Centennial, setting the stage for a new interpretation of the message and the messengers.
>
> The title suggests that there was something inherently dangerous in the message itself in that it led to "apostasy." The dust jacket asks, "Why did A. T. Jones, often defended by Ellen White, turn against the Adventist Church?" The answer given is, "a fatal flaw in his character." Immediately disturbing questions arise: why did the Lord choose a fatally flawed agent for His special work?
>
> Ellen White often said that he was "the Lord's messenger," "the servant of God,' 'God sent this young man," he was God's "chosen servant," etc. And why would the Lord send a message so potentially lethal that it inclined its bearers toward "apostasy"? Was Ellen White naïve when she supported A. T. Jones so enthusiastically? Must we discount her endorsements of him?
>
> The mystery deepens when we note that Jones was the only Seventh-day Adventist minister in history who shared with his colleague E. J. Waggoner what Ellen White said were "heavenly credentials." ... (*1988 Re-Examined*, p. 6)

A footnote adds:

> In today's climate of church membership standards, Jones would probably remain a member. He never gave up his faith in Christ, always kept the Sabbath, believed all our church doctrines including the sanctuary, never taught pantheism, and was never accused of immorality. His problem: loss of confidence in General Conference leadership. (*1988 Re-Examined*, p. 6, footnote 13)

Short and Wieland noted that, at the time this book against Jones was published, the Lord providentially moved to provide, through the Ellen G. White Estate, a four-volume 1,812-page set, entitled *The Ellen G. White 1888 Materials*.* This set became the basic material for understanding our 1888 history. We can all read this material for ourselves and there should therefore be no need for us to ever regard this history as vague or confusing.

[*Though the printed volumes are hard to read, being facsimile reproductions, with edit marks all over many of the documents, the cleaned-up content is available in electronic format at http://1ref.us/ib and on the *Ellen G. White Writings Comprehensive Research Edition*

CD-ROM. Both sources provide access to Ellen White's writings, including her letter and manuscript files, and the writings of Adventist pioneers.]

Throughout 1988 the church published in its periodicals on an 1888 theme and while a certain amount of truth was let through, the general tenor was denigrating to the messengers and the message they brought. Of the 1,400 pages that were printed on the subject theme that year, Jones and Waggoner were given *one page* each.

At the Minneapolis II session, large pictures of Jones and Waggoner hung over the podium with Ellen White in between, but *not a word* of theirs was spoken during the presentations. The Wieland and Short team were present, and Wieland was given an opportunity to speak, though delivered from the floor and restricted to 30 seconds of time. This is a tremendous comment on the leadership's continued unwillingness to face the music and make a united confession and turn in repentance. Not only were Jones and Waggoner not allowed to speak through their writings, but the living representatives of the men and their message were also shut out. These men have now gone to their rest, and we can hear from them no more except in their writings and electronically recorded sermons and lectures.

The session was a huge disappointment for those who came, hoping to hear the message and hoping that the church leadership would truly commit to moving forward with the message. There was a lot of pageantry and music but very little actual substance. Four evening meetings were given to the general public. There were three panel discussions on "The Fundamentals of our Faith," two forty-five-minute morning devotionals and three one-hour study sessions, two of which were given to George Knight, whose stated purpose for writing his book was to "demonstrate that Jones was aberrant from beginning to end" (*Adventist Currents*, April 1988, p. 43; the examples Knight cited show that he meant *flawed*).

One reviewer of Knight's book, Pastor Wayne Willey, writing in *Spectrum* in 1989, reported that, in reading Knight's book, "it soon became apparent that he had decided to write an 'interpretive' rather than an 'objective' biography" with an obvious agenda to vilify Jones with frequent use of pejorative terms such as "*apostasy, anarchy, extremist,* and *pantheism.*" Moreover, "Jones is painted as such an extremist that the reader may recoil from anything that bears his name or shows even the slightest resemblance to his teachings" ("Knight Falls on Brother A. T. Jones," *Spectrum*, vol. 19, no. 3, Feb. 1989, p. 61). Knight, however, does not give any reason of how such an aberrant individual "could become for 15 years one of the most powerful leaders in Adventism." Willey concluded that, while there is useful information in this book, its reliability and accuracy as a biography is tainted by Knight's polemic intent for writing it.

Some statements of truth were made during the session. Not all leaders were then—nor are they today—on the wrong side, and it would be inaccurate to paint them all with the same brush. The mainstream has gone the wrong way, allowing the wrong individuals to have the major voice, but not every individual subscribes to the majority voice. As we follow the recordings from the session, we become painfully aware that this is a house divided. There were direct contradictions in teachings as presented by official speakers. Here are some comments from the closing statements that show us the confusion:

> Why celebration '88, what does it mean? Are we going to continue to repeat some of those acts of **rebellion** or **apostasy** that we have been guilty of these last 100 years? We can't do much about 1888. That is a matter of historical record. But … we can do something about it from here on. **God forgive us if we don't learn the lesson**. People have said, … "Can't we get finished with the 1888 business? Why do we have so many books this year, so many articles, what's the need for all this? We've got a great job to do. Let's put that behind us." … **There is only one way to put it behind us and that is to learn the lessons of 1888. Unless and until that happens—Lord You had better keep 1888 before us**, and this message.… This church needs a victory.… It's about to happen.… [At the Mt. Carmel experience it was agreed that] the "god" that brings down fire will be really the true God.… [The people shouted,] "The Lord he is God, the Lord He is God." … That's what happened here at this celebration '88. We have acknowledged that the Lord, He is God. The Lord is our righteousness.… The Lord wants to send down fire. It is going to be in response to trust, faith and prayer. (*1988 Re-Examined*, pp. 27, 28)

The authors reported soberly: "This dramatic rehearsal of ancient Israel's experience brought tears of embarrassment to some who were present," while others were in high and jubilant spirits during these "final moments of the celebration" (*1988 Re-Examined*, p. 28).

The fact that they spoke about Carmel with its fire from heaven and shouts of victory is extremely poignant for two reasons. The first is because of what Ellen White had to say about that event:

> The **prejudices and opinions** that prevailed at Minneapolis are **not dead** by any means; the seeds sown there in some hearts are ready to spring into life and bear a like harvest. The tops have been cut down, but **the roots have never been eradicated**, and they **still bear their unholy fruit** to poison the judgment, pervert the perceptions, and blind the understanding of those with whom you connect, **in regard to the message and the messengers**. When, **by thorough confession**, you **destroy the root of bitterness**, you will see light in God's light. (*Testimonies to Ministers*, p. 467, emphasis added)
>
> With many the cry of the heart has been, "**We will not have this man to reign over us.**" **Baal, Baal, is the choice.** The religion of many among us will be **the religion of apostate Israel**, because they love their own way, and forsake the way of the Lord. **The true religion**, the only religion of the Bible, that teaches forgiveness only through the merits of a crucified and risen Saviour, that **advocates righteousness by the faith of the Son of God**, has been **slighted, spoken against, ridiculed, and rejected**. (*Testimonies to Ministers*, pp. 467, 468, emphasis added)

The second reason why appealing to Carmel's fire rang terribly hollow is recounted by authors Wieland and Short, as follows:

> The symbolism at the close left many perplexed. Every segment of church leadership was called to the platform in re-dedication, ... each to receive an embellished brass torch. This was to betoken commitment "to the proclamation of the great truth of righteousness by faith," a dedication to "bear the torch of truth aloft, to declare Christ our righteousness."
>
> The fire department of Minneapolis would never allow actual fire in brass torches in a public auditorium, but nonetheless many felt an uneasy concern, remarking how the symbolism seemed appropriate—**fancy torches, but no fire.** (*1988 Re-Examined*, p. 28, emphasis added)

In the last month of that year, the *Adventist Review* printed this statement, which is set forth here as official admission of the truth of the matter:

> After **squandering a perfect opportunity in 1888 to fully accept and proclaim the message** of righteousness by faith in Christ, **the church hoped this centennial year would be different**, that it would mark the beginning of a renewed emphasis upon preaching and living the heaven-sent message.
>
> Throughout the year, Adventist magazines, books, sermons, camp meetings, Week of Prayer readings, Nairobi Annual Council, and the Minneapolis 1888 Celebration heralded the message of salvation by faith in Christ's righteousness. **Only time will tell whether or not we as a church embraced this truth**, or if we, like our 1888 counterparts, passed by this opportunity, too—rejecting **the message that Ellen White said is "the loud cry"** to revitalize the church and help spread the gospel. (Myron Widmer, "Events That Helped Shape the Adventist Church of Today and Tomorrow," *Adventist Review*, Dec. 29, 1988, p. 8, emphasis added)

These kinds of sentiments do not often find their way into church publications and pulpits, but we are thankful for the few that do. It is absolutely vital that this message make its way forward so that the people can decide.

> If faithful Jews such as those at the Wailing Wall in old Jerusalem could believe that their long-awaited Messiah actually came nearly 2000 years ago and that their ancestors rejected Him, the Jewish nation would be aroused overnight. If the Adventist Church could sense that "the beginning" of the long-awaited latter rain actually came in 1888 and that we "insulted" that presence of the Holy Spirit and treated Him as the Jews treated Christ, this church would be aroused world-wide.... (*1988 Re-Examined*, p. 9)

However, those are big "if's." We believe in pressing on with the message, knowing that we will reach individuals. Institutionally, so long as the denominational press is rolling out publications like Pease's *By Faith Alone* (1962) and *The Faith That Saves* (1969); Olson's *Through Crisis to Victory* (1966), retitled *Thirteen Crisis Years: 1888–1901* (1981); Froom's *Movement of Destiny* (1971); White's *The Lonely Years* (1984); and Knight's *From 1888 to Apostasy: The Case of A. T. Jones* (1987), *Angry Saints* (1989), *A User-Friendly Guide to the 1888 Message* (1998), and *A. T. Jones: Point Man on Adventism's Charismatic Frontier* (2011); Roy Adams' *The Nature of Christ* (1994)—a book which "establishes new low levels of vindictive never before seen in Seventh-day Adventist church publications" (Donald K. Short, *Let History Speak*, p. 76), we know that the Adventist Church is not making any sense of the truth that God was visiting the denomination in 1888. The privilege and joy of carrying the most precious message must therefore fall to others who must also bear the burden of the resistance of those to whom it is primarily addressed.

George Knight Strikes Again: Angry Saints (1989)

As the centennial year ended, another book by Knight was published, apparently to keep up the momentum. *Angry Saints* asserts that the 1888 light was not the beginning of the latter rain and "repeatedly ... denies that the objective 1888 message as brought by Waggoner and Jones is what the church needs" (*1988 Re-Examined*, p. 44). It again stresses the theme that the message was not any Adventist advancement in understanding but was simply an exhortation to get on board with basic Christianity. After nearly forty years had passed since Wieland and Short issued the second call, this book comes as a specific response to their manuscript, *1888 Re-Examined*, "and in particular condemns it" (*1988 Re-Examined*, p. 43). Another stone for Stephen is what this is! Just in case he is not dead yet!

Ostensibly open to instruction by his critics (Knight, p. 12), Knight makes much capital of certain statements of Waggoner for the purpose of forcing him into an evangelical mold of times previous to the third angel's message. Nonetheless, the fact that Waggoner claimed that he was "in harmony with" the reformers does not support the claim that he went no further. We have, in fact, the inspired declaration that the message sent by heaven *was* the loud cry of the third angel. As such, it is advancing light of an advancing reformation and could not be merely what the pre–1844 gospel message would have been. Men may deny that it is so, but they are denying the plain testimony.

Knight's thesis in *Angry Saints* is that Jones and Waggoner's work was to distil the Reformation gospel into an Adventist bottle. Ellen White is said to have implied that this was done by the "combining of the basic Christian truths ... with the distinctive Adventist truths" (such as the seventh-day Sabbath, obviously), and this merger is set forth as the loud cry of the third angel (Knight, p. 112). It is a recurring theme in the book. On page 147 he wrote: "Many at Minneapolis and in the post-1888 period spurned the loud cry that subordinated the distinctive Adventist doctrines to the great truths of evangelical Christianity." Again, he wrote that our "distinctive truths are beautiful, fulfilling, and logical when placed within the context of the great basic truths of evangelical Christianity" (Knight, p. 144). We would ask the question, "What does the idea of 'subordinating' Adventist distinctives to the gospel imply?" Would it not somehow make the "distinctives" such as the Sabbath and the Sanctuary and the State of the Dead less than salvational truths to be heralded under the loud cry? Would it not somehow imply that these truths do not have the gospel bound up inextricably within them? Much discussion could be generated on these points, but we leave the reader to ponder.

We cannot stress the seriousness of what has taken place in all of this. It matters not to the fallen Protestant churches that we keep the seventh-day Sabbath or hold other differing doctrines so long as we subscribe to their view of the gospel. It is when we espouse the gospel as it was truly taught in 1888 that we get into trouble with the greater Christendom, for it is the power to obey all of God's commandments. That is to say, it crucifies the old man, bringing in the righteousness of Christ to produce a victorious life in the flesh we now possess.

The fact is that, in *not* having the truth as it is in Jesus, which includes the impartation of His righteousness for the renewing of our mind so that our thoughts and actions become the same as His thoughts and actions, we do *not* have the gospel. When "the message" is missing, it matters not that one observes the seventh-day Sabbath. Why is that? It is because without Christ doing the works, it becomes a legal form, a work of the law. It is not actually entering into God's Sabbath rest, even though one goes to church on that day or ceases from servile work on that day. Adventists who are taking in this evangelical gospel do not realize that that gospel carries the idea "that Jesus did it all so I don't have to." Yet, the leavening and conditioning is surely taking place. Satan, therefore, as well as our evangelical friends, is pleased with us for joining them in their gospel. Now they call us fully "Christian," and this pleases us. All the while, they are yet thinking it an oddity that we yet retain the form of the seventh-day Sabbath. They simply believe that we are still catching up with them and just need more time. They are probably right. (I speak generally. The opinion that Adventism is a cult is not dead. We have members who believe in the inspiration of Ellen White and who yet teach "historic" Adventism to thank for that!) However, the sad reality is that while the evangelicals believe that they have entered into God's rest while keeping Sunday, they do not realize that they are engaged solely in the works of man. Believing in a weak gospel, they have no power to overcome sin. They are, therefore, doomed to a continual cycle of sinning and repenting. Yet, such is not even genuine repentance; it is a dampening of conscience by a sin-management stratagem. How things do get turned upside-down!

Just today, as I was writing these things, I was also engaged in an online discussion with a former Seventh-day Adventist of over thirty years. He was teaching me that the 1888 message was nothing more than the gospel message of justification by faith taught by the reformers. As we continued our dialogue, it became increasingly clear that this man took this teaching very seriously. Step by step he had come to see things in the same light as other evangelicals, and today he fights against any need for the Sabbath. "Yes, Jesus kept the Sabbath," he said, but "He was born under the law, but I am not. Therefore I am not supposed to do everything Jesus did." "Adventists," he said, "can't see the whole nature of God in the law—in how Christ fulfilled it all." This way of thinking is typical of thousands who have left the Seventh-day Adventist faith and joined the Sunday service churches and fellowships. What does this portend for an entire denomination that refuses to repent?

> If we are merely a church among churches that has joined some distinctive "doctrines" onto "evangelical Christianity" we will never be able to cry "mightily with a strong voice, saying, Babylon the great is fallen, and is become the habitation of devils, and the hold of every foul spirit." If we are but a segment of "evangelical Christianity" we will never with conviction be able to sound the call, "Come out of her, My people." (*1988 Re-Examined*, p. 49)

"Evangelical Christianity" is fallen Babylon. Never should we be seeking to be on one and the same gospel path. To do will result in a *complete* failure to advance in the light of truth. Here are seven points to demonstrate this assertion:

1. Evangelical Christianity teaches that the law of God was done away with at the cross.

2. It vehemently denies that the seventh-day Sabbath is still binding.

3. It does not know that we are certainly in the time of the end, looking for His glorious appearing.

4. It holds the tenet that man has an immortal soul. This obscures the meaning of the cross, for then Christ would not have truly died.

5. It teaches that God will torture His enemies in a most cruel and sadistic manner and for all eternity.

6. It holds out that Jesus was not tempted truly as sinful humans are tempted because, being born in the sinless flesh of Adam before the fall, He could never have sinned.

7. It denies and denigrates the most holy place ministry of Christ as a work of final atonement, not understanding that the "cleansing of the sanctuary … is fundamental to justification by faith in relation to a preparation for Christ's second coming" (*1988 Re-Examined*, p. 49).

Angry Saints continues the myth that we cannot know what the 1888 message was because it was not recorded. He was apparently unaware that it actually *was*. Waggoner's wife was a stenographer, and she took down the presentations. Even Froom tells us as much:

> Waggoner's Studies Recorded In Shorthand.— … we have every reason to believe … [that] the actual studies themselves, given by Waggoner at the Conference, [were] preserved through the shorthand reports taken down by Jessie F. Moser-Waggoner at the time. Here neither the tricks of memory nor the slant of other minds intruded. These transcribed studies were edited by Waggoner himself, then were put into book form—the first of which was published by the Pacific Press in October, 1890. The others appeared later. (*Movement of Destiny*, p. 189)

Furthermore, Waggoner distributed to the delegates a book, *The Gospel in the Book of Galatians*, and, in the following years, Jones, Waggoner and Ellen White traveled the country presenting the message. Many of those sermons are today available, as well as other writings and books, which contain their teachings on the gospel. That we do not know what the message is an assertion that is nothing short of stupefying.

Then Knight makes another odd assertion: "Ellen White did not say that the latter rain had begun with the preaching of Christ's righteousness at Minneapolis" (Knight, *Angry Saints*, p. 126, cited in *1988 Re-Examined*, p. 52). He is mistaken. She *did* say that. Consider her statements:

> Some felt annoyed at **this outpouring**, and their own natural dispositions were manifested. They said, "This is only excitement; it is not the Holy Spirit, not **showers of the latter rain from heaven**." There were hearts full of unbelief, who did not drink in of the Spirit, but who had bitterness in their souls.
>
> On many occasions the Holy Spirit did work; but those who resisted the Spirit of God **at Minneapolis** were waiting for a chance to travel over the same ground again, because their spirit was the same. (Lt. 6, 1896, in *Special Testimonies for Ministers and Workers*, Series A, no. 6, pp. 19, 20, emphasis added)

The time of test is just upon us, for **the loud cry of the third angel has already begun in the revelation of the righteousness of Christ**, the sin-pardoning Redeemer. **This is the beginning of the light of the angel whose glory shall fill the whole earth.** (*Review and Herald*, Nov. 22, 1892)

Knight faults us for making too much of this 1892 statement, downplaying it as obscure and "almost isolated." Yet, it is not. There are many statements that link the 1888 message to the message of that "other" angel of Revelation 18 (the fourth angel), which comes to light the earth with the glory of God. *It is the loud cry* that goes forth in latter rain power. "The loud cry and the latter rain must come together, and when *Angry Saints* agrees that they must come 'simultaneously' it has to contradict and invalidate its own thesis" (*1988 Re-Examined*, p. 52).

So, who are the "angry saints?" They are those "present-day 'Madventists' who ever so sincerely and 'earnestly contend for the faith which was once delivered to the saints.' Their fault is that they believe and promote the 1888 message of Christ's righteousness ..." (*1988 Re-Examined*, p. 54).

On page 152 of his book, George Knight stated that he is "glad 1988 is now gone and past." Yet, the truth that was again evaded in 1988 will not disappear into the past. There are modern messengers who know about all these things, and they are not keeping silent. The written and recorded records are there for us to study. This "confrontation with Christ ... cannot forever be evaded" (*1988 Re-Examined*, p. 56).

The Message That Just Won't Go Away; 1995–2000: The "Primacy of the Gospel Committee" Report Maintains the Stance

There has been another, even a *third* confrontation, of the message of Christ's righteousness, which took place over a five year time period, from 1995 to 2000. The "1888 Message Study Committee" and the "Biblical Research Institute" (BRI), as the "Primacy of the Gospel Committee," (ADCOM-S), appointed May 17, 1994, met to re-examine the question again. If this was not exactly a third call, what should we call it? It turned out to simply be a reaffirmation of the positions of both sides. The Lord will not suffer this light to go out in darkness. It must be preserved, even through further cycles of denial. The results were the same. After meeting eight times, for a total of fifteen days of meetings, the church leadership issued their *Primacy of the Gospel Report*, in which they maintained their position in rejection of any notion that confession and repentance is warranted, while admonishing any ministries to work in harmony with the aims and goals of the church and to submit to the official leadership of the church. Here is their conclusion of the matter:

> We firmly believe that the 1888 Study Committee should discontinue its claims that the true message of righteousness by faith was rejected by the leaders of the Church, that they never genuinely accepted it, and that they have intentionally kept it away from the Church and the world. (Biblical Research Institute, *Primacy of the Gospel Committee Report*, as cited in *Let History Speak*, p. 134)

As pointed out already, and it bears repeating, it is axiomatic that, if the message has not been kept "away from the church and the world," then we should observe and experience a manifest outpouring of the Holy Spirit, the message would be going forth as the "loud cry," and we would be in the throes of disasters and persecutions. If you are reading this book during the time of trouble, you can now observe firsthand what the General Conference Church is doing and see, as was prophesied, God "use ways and means by which it will be seen that he is taking the reins in his own hands" (Lt. 5, 1885, in *Special Testimonies* A06, p. 59). Had it not been kept from the church and the world in the past, these things would be all in the past, and the church would be in the kingdom with Jesus. Heed the words of the prophet:

At the great heart of the work Satan will use his hellish arts to the utmost. He will seek in every possible way to interpose himself between the people and God, and shut away the light that God would have come to His children. (Ms. 18, 1888, in *Review and Herald*, Dec. 24, 1889)

The Lord cannot return until the loud cry has done its work in giving the final warning to the world. In turn, the loud cry can never come until the Lord's people receive from Him the loud cry message both in theory and in actual, living experience. This means that humanity must get out of the way or we will end up left behind. It does *not* mean that the Lord is waiting on the denomination. He is waiting for a people.

Let me tell you that the Lord will work in this last work in a manner very much out of the common order of things, and in a way that will be contrary to any human planning. **There will be those among us who will always want to control the work of God, to dictate even what movements shall be made when the work goes forward under the direction of the angel who joins the third angel in the message to be given to the world.** God will use ways and means by which it will be seen that He is taking the reins in His own hands. The workers will be surprised by the simple means that He will use to bring about and perfect His work of righteousness.... (*Testimonies to Ministers*, p. 300, emphasis added)

The report agrees that it is important to study the Jones and Waggoner message, yet rails against it, saying that the primacy of the Bible is violated because the "scriptural evidence is being examined through the theological understandings of Jones and Waggoner" (D. K. Short, *Let History Speak*, p. 83). Some of the other areas of disagreement are on—

- How to presently apply Ellen White's remarks related to 1888;

- The scope and magnitude of the endorsement she gave to Jones and Waggoner;

- Historical Accuracy—saying: "History must speak for itself, even if it disagrees with Jones and Waggoner's evaluation," but we would wonder if it would perhaps more obviously disagree with "modern interpretations of them and their teachings" (*Let History Speak*, p. 83), such as found in the revisionist history books;

- Corporate Repentance—"The impression should not be given that Ellen White ever called for corporate repentance in respect to events in 1888 or 1893, or that the General Conference administration of O A Olsen took the same position in regard to Jones and Waggoner as the Butler/Smith administration" (*Let History Speak*, p. 83). This would seem to fly in the face of her admonishment: "Unless the church, which is now being leavened with her own backsliding, shall repent and be converted, she will eat of the fruit of her own doing, until she shall abhor herself" (*Testimonies to the Church*, vol. 8, p. 250, from Ms. 32, 1903). This assertion is especially against the counsel of Jesus Himself in Revelation 3:19. Short recounted that Ellen White "pled with the General Conference in session March 12, 1890, to 'fulfill the conditions of repentance and confession' [*The Ellen G. White 1888 Materials*, p. 913]," as well as "similar authoritative calls to the entire church through the church paper as published in the *Review*, August 26, 1890:—'Since the time of Minneapolis meeting, I have seen the state of the Laodicean Church as never before.... Those who realize their need of repentance toward God,... will repent for their resistance of the Spirit of the Lord. They will confess their sin of refusing the light that Heaven has so graciously sent them.' ([*The Ellen G. White 1888 Materials*,] p. 695)" (*Let History Speak*, pp. 50, 53);

- Universal legal justification—"it is confusing to state that everyone is legally saved until they have 'chosen to resist the saving grace of God,' and then turn around and say that one needs faith in order to have saving (rather than legal) justification"

[It is perhaps true that, in every writing and teaching of the 1888 Message Study Committee, the difference between corporate salvation of humanity in Christ relates to His role as the second Adam, which is what grants this life of probation *to every man*. Yet, it is not made effective for the *individual* until individual faith is exercised. In other words, we speak of the difference between "justification of life" (Rom. 5:18) and justification by faith. Nonetheless, just because these distinctions are not made crystal clear in every discussion is no reason to disallow universal legal justification];

- The "in Christ" Motif—"Such a view seems to imply that when a person is born he or she is born legally justified before God"

   [There is again a failure to discern the difference between corporate humanity as being in Christ and the individual being in Christ, relative to the two justifications. There is a failure to discern that the race had been wrested away from the jurisdiction of God through Adam's failure, and, therefore, God was not free to do anything for them until He made them legally His own again. Christ came as the new Head of the race in order to make us legal, to make it possible for God to save us in a righteous manner];

- The Nature of Christ—"The interpretation that Jones and Waggoner gave to the biblical materials on the human nature of Christ is not necessarily supported by Ellen White's full understanding of Christ's human nature";

- Jones and Waggoner and the reformers—"The fuller understanding needs to be framed in terms of relating righteousness by faith to the third angel's message rather than to salvation itself."

   [Though not explained, we are aware from other evidence that the church's position is that the 1888 message is a conflation of the Protestant teaching of justification by faith together with the Adventist distinctives and that the message of righteousness by faith, given by Jones and Waggoner, does not have to do with any advanced understanding of the gospel itself.]

- Independent spirit and separatist activities leads to new organizations—the 1888 MSC carries on its work "without the approval of the acknowledged leaders of the Church.... Many Seventh-day Adventist schismatics initially cut their teeth on 1888-type criticisms";

- The 1888 MSC charges the church with a partial gospel, which is therefore a false gospel—"They are implicitly accusing the Church, or at least the leaders of the Church, of apostasy. We have found such accusations to be groundless as evidenced in the official statements of beliefs of the Church"

   [This is to make the "official statements of the beliefs of the Church" the test of fidelity to gospel truth, and we believe that this is a reversal of the places occupied by man and Christ.] (*Let History Speak*, pp. 83–86).

The BRI's *Primacy of the Gospel Committee's Report* concludes—

We do not question the sincerity of the leaders of the 1888 Study Committee, but we do question the wisdom of the current course of action. **If the committee** [the 1888 MSC, or any who would teach the message] **chooses to continue its work outside the organized Church, we appeal to it to adopt the pattern of what is described as a supportive ministry. Such groups seek places to work where, in harmony with and** under guidance of Church leadership **in that field, they carry out activities that are part of the planned program for that field**. Almost always their efforts are designed to reach out to unbelievers, calling them to Christ and His righteousness, and enlisting them among His remnant people. Supportive ministries promote harmony in both doctrine and relationship with the Church. (*Primacy of the Gospel Committee Report*, as cited in *Let History Speak*, by Donald K. Short, p. 134, emphasis added)

The emphasized type in the above statement serves to fulfill the words of the prophet that they will "want to control the work of God, to dictate even what movements shall be made" when the loud cry fourth angel comes on the scene (*Testimonies to Ministers*, p. 299). In the introduction to **Section II**, we explored the tendency of the carnal mind, especially in churches, to function by the principles of the world, exercising the authority of man over his fellows. This spirit can readily be seen throughout the shameful treatment of the messengers. "And the remnant took his servants, and entreated *them* spitefully, and slew *them*" (Matt. 22:6).

The righteousness of Christ by faith has been ignored by some for it is contrary to their spirit, and their whole life experience. Rule, rule, has been their course of action.... In order to reign and become a power, they employ Satan's methods to justify their own principles. They exalt themselves as men of superior judgment, and they have stood as representatives of God. These are false gods. (Lt. 54, 1895, in *The Ellen G. White 1888 Materials*, pp. 1436, 1437)

Some may yet be reading this book at a time when the world is careening headlong at full speed into troubled times never before experienced in history. If this is the case, then it has a major implication: *the message has been accepted* by the critical mass of people, the 144,000, and final events are earnestly and irrevocably underway. If the corporate denomination is not seen as involved in the acceptance and giving of the message, one can be certain that she has been bypassed in her claim to the title of "remnant church." When these things take place, the true remnant church as a relatively invisible little company is surely doing the work God intended, while the church that *claims* to be engaged in the loud cry of the third angel sees the true workers as a band of fanatics and trouble makers. This is because the mainstream will have come to view matters in "nearly the same light" as the world (*The Great Controversy*, p. 608). It cannot be that those engaged in the true work are the only ones left in the denomination proper while all the false-hearted have been shaken out of it. The logic of this is inescapable, for when the crisis of this storm is approaching and breaking under the Sunday law, the denomination cannot remain faithful to God's commandments and retain her status under law as a registered corporation with the benefits and privileges granted by the authority of the state.

Enter Desmond Ford; A Fourth Generation Storm Surge

Now we rewind the tape on the timeline of the fourth generation to follow another series of events.

Desmond Ford began his education at Avondale with the Standish brothers as classmates, who were conservative men of the church and considered watchmen on the walls through their ministries and the many books they have authored. The Standish brothers are credible witnesses to the Desmond Ford story. Ford interned under George Burnside, the leading evangelist for the Australasian Division. His career as a pastor began in the northern North New South Wales Conference in Australia in the first part of the 1950s. In the mid–50s he returned to Avondale, which was by then accredited, to obtain his Bachelor's degree. At this time, he met Robert Brinsmead, a figure whose story is intertwined with Ford's. Brinsmead had also come to Avondale to study as a ministerial student. After obtaining his Bachelor's, Ford went on under sponsorship to the Theological Seminary at Michigan in the later 1950s, where he came under the influence of Dr. Edward Heppenstall, a "Reformationist theologian." "Graduating with his master's degree he went to the University of Michigan, and in a very short time was awarded a Ph.D. degree in rhetoric" (*Adventism Challenged*, p. 54).

Dr. Ford's effect on the denomination did not occur in a vacuum. The perfect storm was set up from all that had gone before in the tectonic accident of the evangelical conferences (which began in 1956) and in the stormy rejection of the second call of Elders Wieland and Short (1951, 1958), which was a call to return to the true gospel message of 1888. Ford claimed that he was not bringing anything new but that which had already been set forth as truth by leading men of the past such as W. W. Prescott and L. E. Froom.

Indeed, the developments of the 1960s and 1970s would have been inconceivable were it not for the earlier influence of Walter Martin in the 1950s, resulting in the publication of *Seventh-day Adventists Answer Questions on Doctrine*, the downgrading of Ellen White, concessions on the nature of Christ, changes in denominational books, and a distancing from the concept of final atonement in the sanctuary message. Further, the discussion of these developments would not be complete without including some coverage of the 1960s Brinsmead agitation, called the "Sanctuary Awakening Fellowship." Also significant is the publication of Froom's *Movement of Destiny* in 1971, which served to solidify the positions of the earlier *Questions on Doctrine*. Author Dave Fiedler has suggested that the latter book's pages "contained what could easily be classed as some of the most careless, or some of the most dishonest, 'research' that had ever found its way through a Seventh-day Adventist press" (*Hindsight*, p. 243).

Dr. Ford's theology will not be examined here in comprehensive detail, as there are many books and articles that do this, but we may understand, at the outset, the basic departures from standard Seventh-day Adventism, as outlined by H. H. Meyers:

1. *The Nature of Salvation and Righteousness by Faith*

Dr. Ford claimed that obedience to the Decalogue under the power of the Holy Spirit is not possible prior to glorification. He further claimed that sanctification is not part of the gospel message....

2. *The Sanctuary Message*

Dr. Ford claimed that the Atonement was completed at

the cross and that Jesus entered the Most Holy place in AD 31, rather than in 1844. These were the main issues upon which Dr. Ford was later dismissed following the investigations of the Glacier View meetings....

3. *The Age of the Earth*
Dr. Ford taught that creation week occurred thousands of years earlier than the approximately six thousand years testified to in Scripture and the Spirit of Prophecy....

4. *The Infallibility of the Bible*
Dr. Ford taught that there were many errors of fact concerning science, history, genealogies etc. in Scripture, while stating it is free of error in setting forth the path to salvation ... (*With Cloak and Dagger*, p. 140)

In 1960, with the first PhD letters attached to his name, Dr. Desmond Ford was appointed chairman of the theology department at Avondale College in Australia. Later, Colin Standish joined the Avondale education department (1965), where he would eventually become its chairman. The two men were well acquainted. Standish knew Ford's views intimately, having held many discussions with him. Around this time, Elder George Burnside felt the need to visit Avondale to get an understanding of the perceived doctrinal deviations taught by Ford. After these visits, Ford would speak at various meetings with powerful truth, leaving out any controversial issues. This brought criticism to Elder Burnside for perhaps being a man on a witch-hunt. Burnside was Australia's "Andreasen." Later, standing true to his convictions, he was demoted to an assistant position at a lower conference level. This had a dampening effect on other workers. Some even admitted that though they knew the truth, they would keep silent for fear of losing their employment.

It is reported that as the Ford controversy was rising, there seemed to be an issue with the nature of his PhD. He was not deemed a proper theologian, though his dissertation was "A Study of Pauline Epistles as Written Addresses," for which he received his PhD from Michigan University, December 12, 1960. Edward Heppenstall had written a letter of recommendation, August 10, 1959, stating how impressed they were by Ford and that he should go on to a PhD program. This history is set forth from Ford's side as though the obtaining of a second doctorate had nothing to do with any of his efforts (according to information obtained from this writer's direct personal conversation with Eliezer Gonzalez, the Ministerial Director for Ford's international ministry, "Good News Unlimited"). Dr. Gonzalez, a historian, said: "Desmond Ford did not 'want' to get his credentials, he was requested to, and he complied ..." (Facebook conversation, Jan. 29, 2015). However, the Standish brothers report that Desmond himself had—

> **stated** that a number of theologians in the United States would not take his contributions to denominational publications seriously because his doctorate degree was in the area of rhetoric rather than in theology. This circumstance influenced Dr. Ford **to seek approval** to study for a second doctorate, this time in the area of theology. The Australasian Division acceded to **this request**, and Dr. Ford enrolled in the University of Manchester in England to study for the degree **he had requested**. (*Adventism Challenged*, p. 63, emphasis added)

Vance Ferrell concurred with the Standishes, writing:

> And so **he began to press** the Division leadership to pay his way to some prominent university in the world, pointing out the prestige that this would consequently bring to Avondale and to the entire Division. (Tract, "The Origin and Development of the Australasian Controversy," Part One—1950–1970, p. 4, emphasis added)

It was at Manchester University that he studied under theology department chair F. F. Bruce, one of the most prestigious and influential theologians of the Plymouth Brethren Church, purveyor of Jesuit-originated dispensationalist futurism. In 1972, Ford was awarded his second doctorate and returned to Australia to resume his office at Avondale. He would undoubtedly have been most elated with the release of Seventh-day Adventist "new-order" book, *Movement of Destiny*, as it supported his own evangelical views of the gospel.

In 1975, Desmond's second wife, Gillian, wrote a book entitled *The Soteriological Implications of the Human Nature of Christ*, which is entirely in line with Desmond's teaching. It asserted that the traditional view of righteousness by faith and the Seventh-day Adventist view of sanctification was incorrect—even another gospel. "To accept Christ and stress holiness and experience is essentially legalism" (p. 10). "That other gospel says ... Righteousness by faith is both Justification and Sanctification" (p. 9). It was the first time that a significant criticism of Adventist doctrine was published and circulated among Adventists with such wide approval and acceptance.

The 1976 Biblical Research Institute Meeting in Australia

With concern for the strange teachings that were coming forth from the ministerial graduates of Avondale College, ministers and laymen of the Division pressed for a meeting with the leadership. R. R. Frame, president of the Division, agreed to a meeting, but put it in motion through the venue of the Biblical Research Institute (BRI) of Australia where two meetings were eventually held, February 3 and 4, 1976.

> The irony of the situation is, that this institute had been established to examine "new light" and protect the church against the intrusion of heresy. In Ford's case, the BRI had made no attempt to examine his theology. Now the concerned brethren were virtually on trial as they presented the historic Adventist position on doctrines vital to the mission of Seventh-day Adventists. (H. H. Meyers, *With Cloak and Dagger*, p. 14)

So, here we have a strange reversal of protocol in which requirement is made for the men in defense of the standard teachings of Adventism to stand before the Biblical Research Institute, while Dr. Ford and others teaching a new thing were not ever required to make their case before the BRI. Normally, the proper channel for doctrinal change or advancement in the church is that approval must be gained by the General Conference in session. What has been seen in this history is rather a "backdoor" methodology that allows for the introduction of something different into the church via the instructors in the schools training up the next wave of pastors and teachers in the church. This all makes for a de facto, rather than an officially adopted doctrinal change to be allowed to float in the denomination. It puts the practice and teaching of the church at odds with what is on the books.

So, the "Concerned Brethren," the "field men" who upheld the historic position on the sanctuary, presented papers. Dr. Ford's countering replies demonstrated a clear and forceful repudiation of a heavenly dual-apartment sanctuary. The BRI members, consisting of Division officials and various other administrators, made no rebuttal whatsoever to Ford's positions, except for one man, Pastor Raymond Stanley, then Division Ministerial Association Secretary and member of the BRI. He obtained permission to speak and, holding up a copy of the Seventh-day Adventist baptismal certificate, read Article 8, which says:

> Upon His ascension, Christ began His ministry as high priest in the holy place of the heavenly sanctuary, which sanctuary is the antitype of the earthly tabernacle of the former dispensation. A work of investigative judgment began as Christ entered the second phase of His ministry, in the most holy place, foreshadowed in the earthly service by the Day of Atonement. This work of the investigative judgment in the heavenly sanctuary began in 1844, at the close of the 2,300 years, and will end with the close of probation. Hebrews 4:14; 8:1, 2; Leviticus 16:2, 29; Hebrews 9:23, 24; Daniel 8:14; 9:24–27; Revelation 14:6, 7; 22:11.

He went on to say that he could not reconcile this statement with what he had heard from Dr. Ford, and he asked the churchmen to help him solve this quandary.

> The saddest fact of all was that Pastor Stanley's poignant appeal for guidance "went over like a lead balloon." There was dead silence from the members of the B.R.I. Not one of the Division administrators sprang to his feet and voiced support for Pastor Stanley and/or opposition to Dr. Ford. Not one of the college theologians sprang to his feet to do the same. The B.R.I. members seemed like men bewitched. They were as still as statues and as silent as the grave.
>
> Is it any wonder that our Division leaders have lost credibility in the eyes of faithful and loyal ministers and members? Here is a case where our Australasian leaders, in the presence of many witnesses, refused point-blank to declare their loyalty to their own denominational Baptismal Certificate! And yet they-in common with every church member-have solemnly taken Baptismal vows, and thus pledged themselves to observe and defend these precious Articles of our historic faith. (H. H. Meyers, *With Cloak and Dagger*, p. 144)

As we might expect, Ford was exonerated, although on seriously untenable grounds for a Bible-only denomination, in that it was set forth that *he was only teaching what some scholars of the church had already written and taught*. Though the concerned brethren had made powerful presentations from the Bible and Spirit of Prophecy, in three of five areas intended for discussion (the sanctuary, the Spirit of Prophecy, and the age of the earth, not having time to examine prophecy and righteousness by faith), it was found that Dr. Ford's responses lacked the same appeal to the bedrock standard of pioneer Adventism. Far too often Dr. Ford would be heard saying such things as, "Well, I can show you a Seventh-day Adventist who believes the same as I do. If I'm a heretic, so is he!" (Vance Ferrell, Tract: "The Origin and Development of The Australasian Controversy," Part Two—1970-1977, p. 7).

This was surely the first time in denominational history that a new teaching could be established upon something other than the Word of inspiration. Was the church now willing to establish the Bible plus tradition as the foundation of doctrine? "Later, some in the Institute realized the terrible implication of being seen to accept doctrine on the authority of man, so the minutes were amended to add 'the Bible and the Spirit of Prophecy' as a basis for Ford's stand" (H. H. Meyers, *With Cloak and Dagger*, p. 63). However, this put them into another quandary, for surely it would be a futile attempt to show anything but a 6,000-year age of the earth in the Bible and the Spirit of Prophecy.

Meyers stated that "their findings illustrate the tremendous inroads such books as *Questions on Doctrine* and *Movement of Destiny* had made into the thinking of Australasian leadership. They admitted that there had been a 'movement away' from our historic doctrines and then condemned our senior ministers for being unaware of the shift" (*With Cloak and Dagger*, p. 63).

The Brinsmead Factor

Robert Brinsmead's story is interwoven with Ford's. A contemporary of Des Ford, with whom he had actually gone to school and become friends in the mid–1950s at Australian Missionary College in Avondale, he was a champion of the historic view of the nature of Christ in the early 1960s. The Brinsmead movement was largely responsible for the dissemination of the Wieland and Short manuscript, *1888 Re-Examined*. During the 1960s, Brinsmead had studied the 1888 message and accepted it. He was therefore at odds with Ford at that time, but, as he later came into line with the doctrine of original sin, he moved into the new view in the early 1970s, in harmony with the agitation being created by Ford. We will pick up on Brinsmead's doctrinal shift in a later segment.

Brinsmead found a fertile ground for cultivating a following in that the errors that were developing in the Ford controversy were countered by his theology. He was not satisfied with the explanations of how the final generation would be prepared to go through the final movements with no more Mediator in the heavenly sanctuary. So he thought to resolve his questions by asserting that God would, through a special dispensation of grace, bestow an instant character perfection at the time of the close of probation.

The Australian division eventually used Ford to fight against Brinsmead's "Awakening Message" movement. In this combat, Ford taught what he had imbibed while sitting at the feet of Heppenstall—that perfection of character and ceasing from sin was not possible until the second coming and glorification. (Interestingly, behind the scenes, Ford and Brinsmead remained personal friends. Ford's wife developed cancer and Brinsmead's sister moved into their home to administer natural treatments. Over these months the two men had personal conversations and their friendship held intact.)

> This [Awakening] movement attracted many church members, and confused many others. A major contribution to this confusion was that the efforts of those who sought to discredit Brinsmead's teaching were themselves self-contradictory and mutually exclusive. It was argued that Brinsmead put off character perfection until it was too late; and again it was argued that Brinsmead taught perfection too early. Some said that if any had failed of reaching perfection by the time of the final atonement their case was hopeless. Others said that, final atonement or no final atonement, there would be no character perfection this side of glorification. Even those outside Adventist circles have been perplexed as to how the church survived such conflicting viewpoints. (*Hindsight*, p. 242)

For example, on one occasion, as Colin Standish reported, he attended a Brinsmead lecture in Sydney, which was attended by many Adventists, both leaders and lay members. In response, the church held a meeting to counter Brinsmead. They put Elders Frank Basham and Hector Kingston before the people to accomplish their goals. Basham pointed out that Brinsmead was in error because he was preaching victory by supernatural intervention at the sealing time, while the truth was that we can have victory now. Kingston preached that Brinsmead was in error because we would not have victory over sin until the second coming. Herein is the crux of the great divide that had developed in Adventism.

Anglican minister, Geoffrey Paxton, in his research on Seventh-day Adventism, wrote of the confusion of the 1960s.

> In the church's defense of her teaching against the Brinsmead Awakening, the one fountain issued forth material which was mutually exclusive. There are three possibilities open to the interpreter of this phenomenon: (1) It may be that the conflicting nature of the material was not perceived. (2) Perhaps the conflicting nature of the material was perceived, but it was thought that this was a fair price to pay for the removal of the Awakening threat. (3) It may be that the conflicting material was a tacit admission of church leaders that there legitimately existed within the "remnant" church quite different views concerning the core of her confession.... (*The Shaking of Adventism*, pp. 106, 107)

It is a great irony of history that both Brinsmead and the church came to abandon their positions of the early 1960s with regard to the perfection of the final generation. "The concepts first used by Heppenstall to combat the Awakening were eventually persuasive enough that Brinsmead and the majority of his followers capitulated in the early 1970's" (*Hindsight*, p. 243). Colin Standish related a visit he had from Brinsmead in 1969, where the latter informed him that he was going over to the Protestant world. This is exactly what he did, later taking up with Geoffrey Paxton, a Reformed scholar, ordained as an Anglican clergyman, principal of an evangelical college in Brisbane. As they studied together, Brinsmead turned his back on the Spirit of Prophecy in favor of modern (and apostate) Protestantism. Brinsmead kept going down the slippery slope, rejecting the post-Fall nature of Christ, later rejecting also the truth on atonement and the sanctuary, and by 1981 repudiating the Sabbath. The church itself, largely abandoning any teaching of character perfection before glorification, found itself coming into increasing harmony with the evangelical world, built upon the pre-Fall nature of Christ and a completed atonement at the cross (as opposed to a "complete sacrificial atonement" being made at the cross, with an ongoing process of atonement being made in the sanctuary, and "final atonement" being made in the cleansing process in the most holy place—a concept considered by the evangelical world to be theological fiction).

Ford, as well as other Australian students, came into close contact with Dr. Heppenstall at seminary in Michigan, where he completed his Master's degree, undoubtedly having his theology shaped by the latter. Heppenstall was believed to be Bible and Spirit of Prophecy centered, but church leaders apparently did not realize how strongly influenced some of these seminary professors were by "Reformational Theologians" teachers who were grounded in 16th century reform leaders such as Luther and Calvin. So, men like Heppenstall were strong on teaching Calvary and the sacrifice of Christ at the expense of a weakening of interest in the mediatorial work of Christ in the heavenly sanctuary.

It should be understood, regarding Ford's teaching, that he was not bringing forth that which he would have obtained at Avondale or in Australia in the late 1940s and the 1950s. He imported it from America, at the Adventist seminary. It is a wonder to many that the whole Division gave over to these Protestant errors, but it becomes more understandable when we realize that Ford was seen as the great rescuer of the continent from the heresy of Brinsmead.

Palmdale

This underreported yet important historic meeting in Southern California took place April 23–30, 1976. The General Conference, under the presidency of Robert H. Pierson, having received complaints from the Concerned Brethren, formed a representative group and went to Australia, where they met with a delegation from the Australian Division.

The Australian Division stood in the role of kingly authority, deciding that they would be strictly in charge of choosing the eight men to stand for the conference. None of these would be of the Concerned Brethren, of course. A dispute arose in which the Concerned Brethren asked to be able to send but two members at their own expense. It was also suggested by the General Conference President Pierson that this be done. This request was denied, a likely foreshadow that the outcome was a foregone conclusion, in typical "show-hearing" fashion. So, the best that could be done was to prepare a manuscript to send as a silent witness.

Dr. Russell Standish and Dr. Clifford Anderson authored "Conflicting Concepts of Righteousness by Faith in the Seventh-day Adventist Church—Australian Division" and sent it on to the Palmdale meeting. It is reported by Standish that it is not likely that their work had any noticeable effect on the proceedings at Palmdale. However, it did get copied and distributed widely by the laity.

The Palmdale conference ended with the issuance of a consensus statement, which stated at the outset:

> "We agree that when the words RIGHTEOUSNESS and FAITH are connected (by 'of,' 'by,' et cetera) in Scripture, reference is to the experience of justification by faith." (cited in *Adventism Challenged*, p. 123)

Ford came away from this conference excitedly reporting that the church had agreed with him, stating that—

> when the words righteousness and faith are connected, by 'of,' 'by,' etc., Scriptural reference is to justification by faith only. (*Adventism Challenged*, p. 123)

The differences between the statement and *the statement as reported by Ford* reflect the Fordian theology, which is Protestant reformation theology that does not consider the work of sanctification as indivisible from the justification experience. Take notice that the word "experience" is omitted altogether and for extra emphasis, the word "only" is added. This is not saying the same thing. It makes for an entirely objective salvation and the end of it is an antinomian "gospel."

Dr. Ford spread this erroneous report in several documented cases such as a chapel talk at Avondale, May 8, 1976; a letter to Dr. R. Standish, June 7, 1976, and a letter from Dr. Ford, published in the *Review and Herald* in 1976. For the sake of brevity, we will cite only the last of these:

> The Palmdale Group did assent to the fact that in the Pauline writings the term "righteousness" when linked with "faith" by the prepositions, "of" or "by" means justification, and justification **only**. (Desmond Ford, "F.Y.I. Comment—2," *Review and Herald*, Dec. 23, 1976, p. 3, emphasis added)

In addition to the above discussion of weaknesses in the consensus statement of Palmdale, it was found to be somewhat lacking on its treatment of the nature of Christ. It did not actually state error, but fell short of a clear and precise pronouncement of the truth. This is the nature of such statements, which, to employ the metaphor of Elder Herbert Douglass, attempt to merge "colliding tectonic plates" of truth and error.

The Palmdale conference produced a statement intended to clarify the issues. In reality, it clarified nothing.... When the actual wording of the Palmdale statement was made available, rather than the erroneous versions first reported in Australia, it was apparent that the statement did not provide Ford with the unqualified support he had wished. It was, after all, an addition to, rather than a resolution of, the confusion which already existed.

On the question of the nature of Christ, Palmdale did little to settle anything. After describing both the pre-Fall and post-Fall positions, the report of the conference given in the *Review* indicated that "whichever of these views Christians may hold of Christ's humanity, we believe that the central concept is to recognize Jesus as the Saviour of all mankind, and that through His victorious life, lived in human flesh, He provides the link between divinity and humanity."

Here was a clear statement that this point of truth was considered a nonessential. Church members were free to choose between two mutually exclusive views leading to vastly different conclusions ... (*Hindsight*, pp. 245, 246)

In the immediate days and weeks after the Palmdale conference, there was much confusion generated by Ford's skewed reporting, which was only exacerbated by the delay in publishing the statement. Kenneth Wood, editor of the *Review and Herald*, was constrained to make an official report in a series of four editorials, entitled *F.Y.I.*, to set the record straight on what was said in the statement. It served to correct the two defects that we have discussed here.

We would be remiss not to mention that, to the credit of the church, the Wood series asserted that the 1888 era message was the key to the correct view on righteousness by faith, that it had been the time when the loud cry of the third angel had begun, and that the reaction by leadership was such that the glory was withdrawn. It expressed the "desire to benefit from the mistakes of the past so that rebellion, stubbornness, insubordination, suspicion, and envy shall not be found among us" ("Christ Our Righteousness," *Review and Herald*, May 27, 1976, p. 6). Such glimmers of bright truth are not often found any more in official Seventh-day Adventist publications.

The Standish brothers' conclusion on the matter is that—

> Had the Palmdale Statement been as clear on these matters as it undoubtedly should have been, there would have been no need for these explanatory and

follow-up statements in the *Review and Herald;* and the vital six months in which the errors of the *new theology* found fertile ground for propagation based upon these defects would not have gone by. (*Adventism Challenged*, p. 129)

Indeed, had the response to the crisis been more certain, had the Concerned Brethren been given a fair voice, then a clear and definitive statement would have been more likely to ensue. It is rare to find, especially at the present day, such a complete historically correct statement on the 1888 history and crisis ever published in the church press by the official leadership, as the Wood "F.Y.I." series.

Meanwhile, Back in Australia

Ford was enjoying full support by Australian leadership, yet the Concerned Brethren still "persisted in supporting the now-discredited historic Adventism" (H. H. Meyers, *With Cloak and Dagger*, p. 64). The latter were successful in securing a meeting with the new Australasian Division President Keith Parmenter, and other division and union leaders. On March 4, 1977, the meeting was held, where they were advised that this would be the last time that they would be allowed to approach church leadership on this issue. The results:

> In the meeting, Dr. Ford firmly maintained his erroneous position, in spite of clear statements read to him from the Spirit of Prophecy. At the conclusion, the division president and chairman, in ending the meeting, declared himself for Dr. Ford, saying that never before had Dr. Ford stood so high in his estimation as the present. He also stated that he himself had problems in regard to our doctrine of the sanctuary. Then turning his head slightly in the direction of Pastor Burnside, he warned in an intimidatory tone that, if the attacks on Dr. Ford continued, he would have them (the Concerned Brethren) dealt with. (*Adventism Challenged*, p. 212)

Following this threat, issued under kingly power, came other similar acts by "conference presidents and others down the hierarchal line" (H. H. Meyers, *With Cloak and Dagger*, p. 65). Leadership sets the standard.

In July 1977, Ford was transferred from the chairmanship of the Avondale College department to the theology department of Pacific Union College in the United States. It was felt that such a move would ease the tension of schism that had developed in Australia, while it might also help to temper Ford's views by getting him into a bigger fish tank among American theologians. Pastor Cree Sandefur, president of the Pacific Union Conference and chairman of the board at Pacific Union College, spoke of the issues in Australia in a letter to Roy Davies, February 2, 1977:

> That the Pacific Union Conference accepted Dr. Ford primarily to ease the problems in Australia cannot be denied. Speaking of the issues in Australia, Pastor Cree Sandefur wrote: "The Pacific Union has become somewhat involved in the issue, in the light of our invitation to Dr. Ford. We have voted to invite him to the campus at P.U.C. for a two-year term. We think it may be in the interest of the Church in Australia." (*Adventism Challenged*, p. 214)

The American planners of this move may not have realized that "numbers of our American scholars had imbibed the same errors of evangelical Protestantism as had Dr. Ford, and were also stealthily teaching them to their students" (*Adventism Challenged*, p. 213). As such the Americans were an unorganized force waiting to be marshaled to battle. All they needed was a man such as Dr. Ford.

The Protestant Duo:
Geoffrey Paxton and Robert Brinsmead

The Anglican minister, Paxton, mentioned earlier in association with our discussion on Robert Brinsmead, released a book that was published in 1977, entitled *The Shaking of Adventism*. This book was an examination of Adventism's claim to be the vanguard of the Reformation. Yet, Paxton did not believe in an advancing Reformation. His theology was fixed Reformation Protestantism and anything that did not conform to Martin Luther and others of the period would be heretical. Paxton toured the United States calling on Adventism to discard their Catholic beliefs, while holding high the teachings of Desmond Ford and Robert Brinsmead, the pair who had been at theological war in earlier years.

Now that Brinsmead had capitulated in his theology, in the Australasian Division, President Robert Frame, at the Victorian Camp-meeting of 1975, informed the workers that Brinsmead's teaching was now acceptable to the Seventh-day Adventist Church. The down side of this was that Brinsmead went from error to worse error, a trend which would not reverse. Further, now that Brinsmead was acceptable, these two most visible Adventist voices were speaking as one, presenting a formidable obstacle to the truth of standard Adventism of the pre-1950s.

Paxton was a fit with all of these developments. His Reformed theology proclaimed a righteousness by faith that has solely in view the objective gospel of justification of the cross, alleging that it was a *Catholic view* that would weld the work of God in the believer, i.e., *sanctification*, to the concept of righteousness by faith.

A significant aspect of the work done by Paxton in his book is seen in his underscoring that, in fact, great shifts away from standard Adventism were taking place, much to his approval of course:

> Paxton clearly revealed that the leading exponents of the *new theology* have introduced doctrines that are contrary to those of the Seventh-day Adventist Church. He stated: "It is obvious that, while there are some encouraging aspects in Adventism's articulation of the Reformation gospel in the 1960s, the real theological gains of the decade are to be found in the affirmation of original sin and the repudiation of perfection in this life. This significant advance appears in the theology of such men as Edward Heppenstall, Desmond Ford and H. K. LaRondelle." [*The Shaking of Adventism*, p. 119]. (*Adventism Challenged*, pp. 204, 205)

> Perhaps one of Paxton's most telling insights was the observation that the *new theology* breaks down sectarian barriers. "With the coming [to Brinsmead] of the gospel of Paul and the reformers, sectarian mentality began to fade away." [*The Shaking of Adventism*, p. 124.] … This insight is not surprising, since Brinsmead had merely accepted the views of other Protestant churches. The *new theology* had a compelling ecumenism about it, since it had long been the belief held by the fallen Protestant churches. But the truth of the Seventh-day Adventist Church will, by its very nature, build barriers between those true to the Lord and those unwilling to fully follow their Master fully. (*Adventism Challenged*, p. 207)

Going back to the discussion of how the two men came together, we find that after Brinsmead had decided that Adventists weren't receiving him well enough, that he would go to the Protestant world. There he found tremendous success with his writing. His *Present Truth* magazine would become the premier Protestant theological journal in the world, enjoying a circulation to forty thousand clergymen, becoming popularly accepted on the campuses of American theological schools. Adventist distinctive teachings, of course, did not find a place in this journal. It was at this time that Brinsmead came into association with many Protestant ministers.

> Among these was a Queensland Anglican pastor, Geoffrey Paxton, who was principal of a small interdenominational Bible training college. In a short time Paxton had teamed with Brinsmead to present so-called "forums" throughout Australia. At these forums the two speakers presented their concept of the reformed theology to large gatherings of ministers and interested laity. Clearly Brinsmead was now working as much with Protestants as he was working for them—a most dangerous development. (*Adventism Challenged*, p. 73)

Paxton's articles were published regularly in Brinsmead's paper. Through his association with Brinsmead and Ford he planned to work up a thesis for his Master of Arts degree on the topic of the Reformation and contemporary Seventh-day Adventism. This was what was to become his book, *The Shaking of Adventism*. Brinsmead's "Present Truth" organization sponsored his trip to the USA in early 1976 to assist him in his research, where he claimed to have spoken to a significant number of high-level Adventist leaders. He also claimed to have found a marked lack of unanimity in belief amongst them; that the major area of conflict was over the concept of righteousness by faith. We don't need an Anglican minister to point this out to us, though, do we? What else could Adventism possibly demonstrate, having rejected the clear light for almost a century?

> It was quite obvious to both the cursory and careful readers of Paxton's book that much of the material must have been fed to him by persons close to the center of Adventism. It was most unlikely that any non-Adventist could have without this assistance been privy to some of the details presented. Presumably, those assisting Paxton saw him as a useful vehicle for casting doubt upon Adventist doctrine. (*Adventism Challenged*, p. 200)

Ray Martin, a close associate of Brinsmead, himself revealed that the manuscript for Paxton's book was evaluated by Ford, who acted as an advisor, before it went to publication. Furthermore, Brinsmead himself did some of the research. So, when people speak of a Ford-Brinsmead-Paxton triumvirate, it is not simply a loose philosophical association; there is more to it than many would realize.

> A reading of this book left an inescapable impression upon many. The conviction was that Geoffrey Paxton had set himself up to sit in judgment upon the doctrines of the Seventh-day Adventist Church, particularly in respect to righteousness by faith ... (*Adventism Challenged*, p. 200)

Paxton set about his work of evaluating Adventism on the premise that the Protestant Reformation doctrine of righteousness by faith teaches that there is "no perfection until the second advent of Christ," a "radical deviation" from traditional Adventism which Professor Heppenstall taught at the Seminary (*The Shaking of Adventism*, p. 106).

This dangerous thesis, which has its foundation in the religion of Babylon and most other pagan religions and which was introduced into the Christian church by a "converted" pagan—Augustine—in the fifth century of the Christian era, has no foundation in the Bible whatsoever. Despite this fact, Paxton asserted that when Dr. Edward Heppenstall became "the first [Seventh-day Adventist] to openly advocate" ... [*The Shaking of Adventism*, 105] the anti-perfection view, he was making doctrinal progress for the Seventh-day Adventist Church and assisting in fulfilling its claim to be the inheritors of the Reformation. However, in Paxton's view, when "Herbert Douglass ... emerged in the 1970s as the one who is seeking to make the Andreasen-Branson perfectionism dominate in Adventist thinking" (*ibid*. 126), and when, in addition, this theme was taken up by Kenneth Wood, editor of the *Review*, and Robert Pierson, president of the General Conference, they were beating a retreat from the Reformation faith. (*Adventism Challenged*, p. 200)

At the time of the Victorian camp-meetings in 1977, Paxton and Brinsmead were having meetings and drawing in Adventist ministers. Paxton was also presenting his views of Seventh-day Adventism and found, at this time, a good opportunity to attack the Sabbath School lesson quarterly of the second quarter of that year, entitled "Jesus, the Model Man," written by Dr. Herbert E. Douglass, a theologian and historian of the church who taught standard Adventism and whose lessons for that quarter were heavily opposed by the new liberal theology element rising in the church, notably in the United States and Australia. The General Conference, under President Pierson, to its credit, was in support of this lesson quarterly. The Australasian Division was not supportive of it, to put it mildly, and even held a clandestine meeting to strategize upon the subtle methodology to be used by their leading men in continuing to teach the new theology in the Sabbath Schools, in spite of the lesson material that runs contrary to it.

The fact is that that quarterly itself nearly exacerbated all-out revolt by the Division. There were a number of events that could only be described as "intrigue" in the Division. That secret meeting was covertly recorded by an attending new theology man, in disobedience to the demand that what took place there, *stayed* there. Within a half hour that recording was on its way to an associate of Brinsmead, Ray Martin, and from there it went on immediately to Geoffrey Paxton. These are the kinds of shenanigans that develop in the environment of such hatred for the established truths of historic Adventism.

There was a request to publish countering studies to be used supplementally to the Sabbath School quarterly. There was even a push to have the quarterly banned outright. Men in high positions were breaking confidentiality, secreting away correspondence from the office files, in true espionage fashion, feeding them into the "Present Truth" ministry of the Brinsmead organization.

Brinsmead's method of working, however, was to avoid frontally attacking old Adventism in his paper or otherwise. He had adopted a philosophy that the influence he could have on Adventism from the outside would be greater than that he had enjoyed in his earlier years from within. This proved true. His journal was read by thousands of Adventists.

> Quite clearly Brinsmead had no desire to upset the success he was achieving by returning to methods which had proved less successful in earlier years. One serious fact, however, was the growing evidence that Brinsmead continued his attacks vicariously through his Anglican mouthpiece, Geoffrey Paxton. Paxton had no qualms about openly attacking both the Church and its publications. One of Robert Brinsmead's associates, Alan Starkey, stated: "What was presented by Paxton was not his own findings. Bob researched all of this and handed it over to prove that

Adventists were not Protestant, but Catholic." (Letter written by Pastor Mervyn Ball to Dr. R. Standish, dated June 14, 1977). (*Adventism Challenged*, p. 176)

Paxton's method of working surely included frontal assault on Adventism, while claiming to be its friend, but it should be noted that he avoided making any direct attack on either Mrs. White or the sanctuary doctrine. These would have limited his success with Adventists. A reading of his book, however, leaves one with the certain understanding of the tragic fracturing of Adventism that was well entrenched since the 1950s. He gave a basic outline of what he saw as three overall groupings in the church: the liberals, the traditionalists, and the reformationists. He referred to the theologians of Loma Linda University, such as Graham Maxwell and Jack Provonsha as types of the liberal, the general leadership of the General Conference in Washington as traditional, and the Andrews University set as the reformationists. Of course, the last of the three would have been the group which enjoyed Paxton's approval, whose bias unequivocally motivated his entire association with and assessment of Adventism.

Paxton's 1978 tour to the USA was in answer to the increasing invitations to Seventh-day Adventist gatherings. In the spring of that year, he spoke at the Capitol Memorial Church in the Washington, D.C., area; twice at the Rockville, Maryland, church, a few miles from Adventist headquarters in Takoma Park; at Southern Missionary College; in the Loma Linda University Church, packed to capacity (where he followed as the climax of a "week of devotion" with guest speaker Desmond Ford); in the community of Angwin, where Pacific Union College is located; Andrews University; and more.

Russell Standish wrote of his observations at that time, attending three of Paxton's meetings: "His concern is to call the remnant out, and back into Babylon", while "in his meetings openly and frequently refers to himself as a 'Babylonian,' but the only response is one of amusement." He would use "every opportunity to criticize, on any pretext whatever, the General Conference and the Review and Herald," obviously because they were "the only major agencies opposing him and his fellow workers throughout the world field" (Vance Ferrell, Tract: "The Origin and Development of The Australasian Controversy," Part Three—1978–1980, p. 9).

In his choice of title for his book, *The Shaking of Adventism*, Paxton, thinking that he was part of the conducting of a great shaking in Adventism for *his* "truth" of Reformation Protestantism, reveals a truth unbeknownst to him—an inadvertent insight that has also eluded most Seventh-day Adventists. Yes, the shaking was on (and is still on), although the reverse of Paxton's view of it. Not realizing that all of the upheavals that have taken place since the fifties *have been the shaking* already underway in earnest, Adventists have gone on in complacency, unaware of their condition. For what else would it be but the progression of the disease of chronic Laodiceanism?

It is true that the various voices that sound in the church present a formidable barrier to knowing what or whom to believe. Many just give up trying to sort anything out and claim inability and ignorance to know what is truth so that they might excuse themselves for not having a doctrinal stand. Others play the chameleon, following the views of the majority around them or what the leaders are saying.

This attitude has meant that they have had to change their doctrinal beliefs from time to time, but this need has been less disturbing to them than having to defend the truth of God when it has been under attack. For them, the scorn of their peers is more to be avoided than the wrath of God. (*Adventism Challenged*, p. 203)

Ouch!

Coming now to some final commentary on Paxton and his book, we will let Vance Ferrell have a word:

The new theology is continually proclaiming "sola Scriptura" [Scripture alone], as the basis for its teachings when in fact, it is very clear that it is "sola theologica" [theology alone]. Indeed, when Paxton decided to write a book that was to have such an influence on the minds of Seventh-day Adventists, he did so without giving a single text of Scripture as proof! It surely is a sad day when Adventists will permit themselves to be influenced by a book that has no Scriptural validity whatsoever. Paxton's book, like his talks, is full of the words of theologians. (Tract: "The Origin and Development of The Australasian Controversy," Part Two—1970–1977, p. 5)

Though Paxton's theology and, in particular, his faulty understanding of the differences between Protestant and Catholic doctrine stand to nullify most of his general conclusions, his contribution did serve to correctly identify some major problems in the church. He accurately documented the instability of the doctrinal landscape of the Seventh-day Adventist Church of the 1950s through the 1970s.

> Strangely, these doctrinal changes were virtually unrecognized by the vast majority of church members. He also accurately showed that the *new theology* was an innovation and diametrically opposed to the Bible-based Seventh-day Adventist faith. This revelation no doubt alerted a few Seventh-day Adventists to recognize the nature of the *new theology*.
>
> Paxton also clearly demonstrated that the General Conference leadership took a doctrinal position entirely opposed to that of the *new theology*. His implied call for a direct denominational statement on the Church's stand and its reason for rejecting the errors which crept into the Church in the decades of the fifties and sixties merited a positive response.... What is certain is that Paxton's book ... may well have jolted some Seventh-day Adventists out of their apathy....
>
> Since the publication of Paxton's book, there was no longer any excuse to represent one's cowardice as if it were a virtue. Nor did any reason remain to refuse to take an open stand on the side of truth. (*Adventism Challenged*, pp. 207, 208)

Glacier View

It was on Sabbath, October 27, 1979, that Ford decided to "come out" and make public declaration that for thirty years he had not believed in the Adventist teaching on the sanctuary.

> The occasion was an auspicious one. Dr. Ford had been asked to make a presentation before the Associated Students' Forum, in conference at Pacific Union College. Before a packed audience he went farther than he had ever publicly gone before, in declaring his differences with the basic truths of the Sanctuary and the Investigative Judgment. In this lecture, 1844 became nothing more than an opportunity to re-establish the preaching of apostolic times. It was stated in this lecture that we do not have a biblical basis for the day-year interpretation of Bible prophecy; that we do not have substantiation for our positions on Daniel 8:14, or for our linkage between Daniel 8:14 and Leviticus 16; that we are in error on our concept of the ministry of Christ in the Holy Place of the Sanctuary between A. D. 31 and 1844; and that there is no two-apartment Sanctuary in heaven at all. The writings of Ellen White were pitted against each other in such a way as to confuse the hearer, and while Dr. Ford at no time said that he denied the Spirit of Prophecy it was obvious that he no longer had a fundamental faith in the inspiration of these writings. (Vance Ferrell, Tract: "The Origin and Development of The Australasian Controversy," Part Three—1978–1980, p. 12)

This clear sounding of Ford's message got some attention, and, at the end of this year, Ford was given a six month salaried leave of absence from Pacific Union College to go to Washington, DC, for further personal study on his views, where he would prepare a 900-page defense of his theological position. The Ellen G. White Estate archives were opened for him to conduct his research.

This meeting was his undoing because he left himself no room for equivocating. In times previous, he couched his preaching in ways that, when later questioned, he could find an "out" by pointing to other "balancing statements" he had made and thereby set the mind of the questioner at ease. So it was that he had managed to genuinely confuse many people. When people heard that he had not believed in the sanctuary message "for over thirty years, many concluded that Dr. Ford must be one of the most deceptive persons that this Church had ever produced" (*Adventism Challenged*, p. 259). He well knew that he was setting out to change the course of Adventism. He had instructed his students to bide their time in coming out with the new theology until such a day when the tide was sufficiently turned that there would be no further need for discretion.

Some theorize that he chose this time to press boldly for his theology, strategizing that, in the wake of a recent October meeting of leaders in Washington, he might soon be losing his advantage. That meeting was called the "Righteousness by Faith Consultation," attended by the president of the General Conference, six vice presidents, and a delegation of influential conservative men of historic Adventism, including men like Ralph Larson, Robert Wieland, Ron Spear, Colin Standish, Tom Davis, and LeRoy Moore. There was a decided outcome in favor of the old landmarks of the gospel. Ford may have felt also that in coming out boldly, he would consolidate his vast network of support in academia. It didn't happen.

Later on, after the Glacier View meeting in Colorado, August 10–15, 1980, he had his credentials revoked, allegedly because he could not support his positions from the Bible and the Spirit of Prophecy. Yet, it was so much confusion. Those meetings and their results have not pleased anybody. Those who supported Ford's views were upset, of course, while those who supported the positions of the Concerned Brethren from the earlier years of the confrontation with the Biblical Research Institute in Australia were unhappy with the incomplete repudiation of doctrinal error in Ford's system.

At issue was Dr. Ford's teaching on the sanctuary and righteousness by faith, while his "affection for the Roman Catholic invention of original sin and its corollary, a make-believe Saviour who did not inherit our human nature, did not appear to be an issue." This was a situation likely brought about by the influence upon American Adventism by authors such as L. E. Froom, causing them to fail "to see the deadly connection between the heresy of the 'unfallen nature' and righteousness by the kind of faith which does not require obedience" (H. H. Meyers, *With Cloak and Dagger*, p. 66).

> It is possible that history will not deal kindly with the Glacier View meetings. We say this, not because nothing was achieved, but because the key doctrinal issues were not resolved. Evidences of widespread dissatisfaction with the results of these meetings are not hard to find. Naturally, those espousing the *new theology* have spoken out sharply against the dismissal of Dr. Ford, which was a direct consequence of these meetings. These people tended, as we later heard, to welcome the "consensus statement" concerning doctrine, perceiving that it made significant concessions to their views of the Sanctuary. Those supporting the Seventh-day Adventist position were in agreement with the decision to remove Desmond Ford from denominational employment, but expressed grave reservations about, and objections to, the decided trend to accept some of the erroneous positions of Dr. Ford, as if they were the truth of God. (*Adventism Challenged*, p. 264)

Some claim that Ford's firing was politically and not theologically motivated—sheer expediency. Ford's supporters have been heard using the word "scapegoat" (such as the editor of the Australasian *Signs of the Times*). It would not make sense to assert that the real concern was in a way *doctrinal* because history clearly testifies that so much of the standard Seventh-day Adventist position had already been cast aside or obscured by the denomination in all that had transpired in the Evangelical Conferences, the reactions to the second call to God's people through Elders Wieland and Short, along with the general tenor of instruction in the theology departments of major Seventh-day Adventist institutions in America, which were in many cases already sold out to Fordian new theology.

Kenneth Samples, a researcher at Walter Martin's Christian Research Institute, published in their *Christian Research Journal*, an article entitled, "From Controversy to Crisis: An Updated Assessment of Seventh-day Adventism," remarking on the schism in Adventism, stating, "While *Questions on Doctrine* is considered to be the origin of evangelical Adventism, it also fuelled the fire for those who supported Traditional Adventism" (cited in *Hindsight*, p. 251). The defrocking of Ford was particularly disturbing to the evangelicals, for they naturally held him in the highest regard. They believed that the Seventh-day Adventist Church was sending mixed messages and frankly said so.

> While the decisions of the General Conference seem to convey their support of Traditional Adventism, the denomination has denied that it actively sought to eliminate all Evangelical influences [*through the firing or forced resignation of denominational workers*]. Many former Adventist pastors and Bible teachers would vigorously contest this statement. **It would appear that there are still large numbers of Adventists who are of Evangelical persuasion, but certainly not as vocal after Glacier View.** (cited in Fiedler, pp. 251, 252, emphasis in original, bracketed comment by Fiedler)

To the evangelical, traditional Adventism was thought to be "aberrant, confusing, or compromising biblical truth (e.g., their view of justification, the nature of Christ, appealing to an unbiblical authority" (Samples, "From Controversy to Crisis: An Updated Assessment of Seventh-day Adventism," available at http://1ref.us/if, accessed 1/1/17). Unfortunately, we may find that the informed, honest believer in the third angel's message would concur.

The machinery continued to grind out the same product back in Australia. The loyal historic believers expected that the issues would now be settled, only to find that two of their theology lecturers who had attended Glacier View in support of Ford were now commissioned to travel around the Division telling the story of how the decision to let Ford go was fraught with controversy and, in fact, unpopular. It was a campaign of dissent intended to generate sympathy for the cause and to save face for the Australian leadership.

> It was soon perceived by many that Fordism was still alive and well in Australasia. God in His mercy had given the leadership a marvelous opportunity to admit their terrible mistake, to repent and turn the church around in the direction of historic Adventism. But pride and use of "kingly power," the hallmarks of papal-like government re-established in the General Conference in 1903, had now become the norm in the Australasian Division. Elder Figuhr's advice given in Melbourne back in the mid–1950s, regarding the selection of leaders, had long since become common practice. Harmony and unity, a political formula for success, had become paramount. Therefore, no admission of errors of judgment or wrongful action, particularly against loyal watchmen, must ever reach the ears of the laity. All must appear to be well with the Seventh-day Adventist Church. (H. H. Meyers, *With Cloak and Dagger*, p. 68)

The consensus document that came out of Glacier View entitled, "Christ in the Heavenly Sanctuary" (not to be confused with the Palmdale consensus statement), was applauded by Dr. Ford. He felt that he could teach in harmony with it and that it showed a decided shift away from Ellen White's views on the sanctuary. He believed that the church was moving toward his views and would be in complete harmony before too long. This would be in keeping with the advice received from his home division president Keith Parmenter, who pled with him to hold his controversial beliefs "in abeyance and not ... [discuss them] unless at some time in the future they might be found compatible with the positions and beliefs of the Seventh-day Adventist Church" (*Ministry*, October 1980, cited by H. H. Meyers, *With Cloak and Dagger*, p. 66).

It is odd that there could have been forged anything called a "consensus statement," for it was found that Dr. Ford would not concede any points whatsoever to the suggestions of the Committee of the Church.

> It was conceded that Dr. Ford made absolutely no concession with regard to any of his erroneous views, yet he found the consensus statement sufficiently close to his errors to be able to preach under it with comfort. Such a reaction should direct us to re-examine the Glacier View Consensus Statement and rid it of doctrinal error. (*Hindsight*, p. 269)

This consensus document, entitled "Christ in the Heavenly Sanctuary," contains some clever wording designed to be satisfactory to both sides, but, in so doing, it results in a compromise of clearly stated truth.

As Clifford Goldstein has stated, "No attack on the pre-Advent judgment would be complete without the mantra, 'within the veil,' taken from this passage in Hebrews [6:18–20]" (Clifford Goldstein, *Graffiti in the Holy of Holies*, p. 88). One issue very important to discuss is in regard to the interpretation of this text, which states:

> Which hope we have as an anchor to the soul, both sure and steadfast, and which entereth into that within the veil: whither the forerunner is for us entered, even Jesus, made an high priest for ever after the order of Melchisedec. (Heb. 6:19, 20)

Those who have agreed with the apostasy of Albion Ballenger of the early 1900s that Christ ascended directly to the heavenly most holy place were pleased with the consensus document, for it takes the same position in its assessment of the term "within the veil." The document makes concession to Ford's rehash of the old error when it ignores the inspired statements of the Spirit of Prophecy (see *The Great Controversy*, p. 420, cited below) on the matter, in saying—

> There is no intermediate step in our approach to God. Hebrews stresses the fact that our great High Priest is at the very right hand of God (chap. 1:3), in "heaven itself ... in the presence of God" (chap. 9:24). The symbolic language of the Most Holy Place "within the veil" is used to assure us of our full, direct and free access to God (chaps. 6:19, 20; 9:24–28; 10:1–4). ("Consensus Document," *Ministry*, Oct. 1980, p. 17)

The consensus document claims that interpreting Hebrews 6:19, 20 in this way does not mean that we must conclude that Christ was ministering in the second apartment since His ascension in the first century. Even so, we find that the statement engenders confusion in that it apparently acknowledges Ford's theological stance that "within the veil" *technically applies exclusively to the Most Holy Place* while not agreeing with his conclusions. "We acknowledge the insights of Dr. Ford's study of the letter to the Hebrews; however, we do not agree with the theological implications he draws from the term, '*within the veil*'" (*Adventism Challenged*, p. 266). It is claimed that we should understand it only in the sense of teaching that we now have "full, direct and free access to God" (*Adventism Challenged*, p. 266).

All of this sets aside the testimony of inspiration, which has clearly stated:

> The ministry of the priest throughout the year in the first apartment of the sanctuary, **"within the veil" which formed the door and separated the holy place from the outer court**, represents the work of ministration upon which Christ entered at his ascension. (*The Great Controversy*, p. 420, emphasis added)

This is not just something made up by Ellen White, whom we are accused of making our interpreter of the Bible! It is entirely in keeping with the theology of the book of Hebrews, which is making the overall point that—

> instead of the old covenant priesthood and sanctuary, we have the new covenant priesthood and sanctuary, where Jesus is the High Priest ministering in the "true tabernacle," the sanctuary in heaven.... The issue is not which apartment Christ went into, or whether the Day of Atonement ritual (as opposed to the daily sacrifice) had been consummated at Christ's ascension to heaven. That's never addressed anywhere because that's not what Hebrews is about, explicitly or implicitly.... (*Graffiti in the Holy of Holies*, p. 89)

This discussion is necessary to inform us with regard to what is the core of the Ford controversy and of earlier controversies in the history of the Seventh-day Adventist Church, which had never before been allowed to grow and gain such traction as seen from the 1950s onward. So we should take a brief theological side trip to review some critical information on the sanctuary in Hebrews.

A comparison of Numbers, chapter 18, verse 5 with verse 7 shows that "within the veil" can in fact refer to the entire sanctuary.

> And ye shall keep the charge of **the sanctuary**, and the charge of **the altar**: that there be no wrath any more upon the children of Israel. (v. 5)

> Therefore thou and thy sons with thee shall keep your priest's office for every thing **of the altar, and within the veil**; and ye shall serve: I have given your priest's office *unto you* as a service of gift ... (v. 7)

When there are no qualifiers to state that the most holy place is in view, we cannot dogmatically assume that "within the veil" must mean specifically that location.

Also, to study this yet a little further, we would bring to notice that the author of Hebrews makes one specific reference to the earthly Most Holy Place as being behind the "second veil" (9:3), which raises the question as to why, if he meant also to make that specific case in Hebrews 6:19, he did not delineate the veil there also as the *second veil* rather than the generic "within the veil"?

> And after the second veil, the tabernacle which is called the Holiest of all. (Heb. 9:3)

> Which *hope* we have as an anchor of the soul, both sure and stedfast, and which entereth into that within the veil. (Heb. 6:19)

One could argue that these are simply two different expressions for the same thing, but the better answer is that they are not the same thing. Not only would this be because of the overall context and purpose of Hebrews, as already noted, but because of the Greek, *ta hagia* and its variants which occur in the book of Hebrews ten times, meaning, "the holies," or the *general sanctuary*. In Hebrews 9:3, however, the Greek uses *hagia hagiōn*, meaning "holy of holies," a phrase used nowhere else in the New Testament. This particular specification of the Most Holy Place *exclusively*, is important, for in Hebrews 9:25, which may reference the annual entrance of the High Priest into *the sanctuary* (on the Day of Atonement), it is still employing *ta hagia*, or "the holies," and not the Most Holy Place *alone*. In other words, it is not a specific and exclusive reference to the second apartment alone.

> Nor yet that he should offer himself often, as the high priest entereth into the holy place every year with blood of others. (Heb. 9:25)

This is not any surprise, for we find that the High Priest would minister in *both* apartments on the Day of Atonement (see Lev. 16:16–20). The Fordian rendition of this verse aspires to teach that Christ entered into the heavenly most holy place at His ascension and thereby demolish the Adventist position. Yet, in this, it surely fails.

Hebrews 10:19, 20 may also be a puzzle to some, since the King James Version (and other versions) of the passage makes reference to "the holiest."

Having therefore, brethren, boldness to enter into the holiest by the blood of Jesus, by a new and living way, which he hath consecrated for us, through the veil, that is to say, his flesh. (Heb. 10:19, 20)

However, as we have said, the Greek of the Epistle to the Hebrews employs the term "*ta hagia*," meaning literally "the holies," which is a reference to the general sanctuary itself, and not the term "*hagia hagiōn*." The context of the statement is a comparison and contrast between the heavenly and earthly ministries. The passage is saying that we now "have complete and full access to God in the heavenly sanctuary, as opposed to the limited access the old, earthly one offered the believer" (*Graffiti in the Holy of Holies*, p. 97).

Significantly, scholars have pointed out that the author of Hebrews wrote under the influence of the Septuagint (the Greek translation of the Old Testament), which reveals the same pattern of usage. In the Septuagint, *ta hagia* is never used to refer to the Most Holy Place; it refers to the general sanctuary in 106 instances of 109 uses. The remaining three uses are specific references to the "holy things" in the first apartment.

So, while we have not made an exhaustive examination of Hebrews, we have shown enough of the epistle to demonstrate that the detractors cannot stand on the one phrase, "within the veil," which is a rather ambiguous term in and of itself, in order to bring down the Adventist position on the sanctuary.

Coming back to the Glacier View consensus statement, we must emphasize that the effect of such a statement, as is often the case, is that the clear truth is obscured or confounded. Detractors will use such declarations as reasons to reject the inspiration of the Spirit of Prophecy. It is probably not often recognized by well-meaning churchmen that such diplomatic statements cause a ripple effect that swells into a tsunami of destruction. As a later defector from Adventism recognized, "To remove the cleansing of the heavenly sanctuary and the investigative judgment doctrine from SDA theology will bring into question the inspiration and authority of the writings of Ellen G. White and the integrity of the whole Adventist movement" (Dale Ratzlaff, *The Cultic Doctrine of Seventh-day Adventists* [1981], p. 20).

We also recognize that in a system of truth, one cannot move a pillar of teaching without causing damage to others. The work of Christ in the heavenly most holy place is intended by heaven to be a work of cleansing. The sanctuary of the soul is here represented, as that which is to be made a fit place for the indwelling of the Spirit of Christ. Therefore, the truth about the sanctuary is inextricably linked with the truth about the righteousness that is imparted to the believing penitent soul.

Dr. Ford's view of the sanctuary was not formulated without influence upon other doctrines. In particular, it logically necessitated his erroneous view of righteousness by faith. In ignoring this connection, some delegates were blinded to the enormity of the problem they confronted. Some had not sufficiently studied the subject to an extent that they could understand that the Sanctuary message is so much an expression of righteousness by faith, that **it is a rank impossibility for someone to hold the truth on one of these doctrines and be in error on the other**. Yet some at Glacier View harbored the conviction that Dr. Ford's preaching on righteousness by faith had blessed the Church. However, a careful examination of Dr. Ford's teaching on this topic, comparing it with Scripture and the Spirit of Prophecy, reveals that his presentations, **based as they are on the premise that obedience to God's law by a Spirit-filled Christian is not possible**, are incorrect in virtually every detail.... (*Adventism Challenged*, p. 267, emphasis added)

Brinsmead Follows the Theology to its Logical Conclusion

The following words were penned in 1964 as though a prophecy against Robert Brinsmead:

Those who teach that Christ took a superior human nature draw the logical conclusion that it is impossible for the rest of mankind to perfectly obey the law of Jehovah in this life. Those who accept this "new view" of the incarnation, logically take the side of Satan in the great controversy over the law, claiming that God has not made provision for us to obey it perfectly.... Ellen G. White saw that God had three steps to the platform of truth (EW 258). Satan has three steps down from the platform. The first step is the teaching that Christ took the human nature of man as it was before the fall. This leads to the second step—to the teaching that man cannot find grace to obey perfectly the law of God in this life. This will inevitably lead to the third step—giving up the Sabbath. This last step must logically follow the original premise, for if it be conceded that we cannot obey all the law all the time, then there is no point in the

Sabbath being a test question. (Robert Brinsmead, *The Incarnation of Christ, Adam's Human Nature versus Fallen Nature*, pp. 7, 8)

Of course, this is impeccably correct because, if Christ had advantage over us in the struggle against sin, then we must not be concerned about overcoming in our own sphere of experience. The Ten Commandments become something to hang on the wall and point to as something that He kept but that we cannot. Logic demands, therefore, that, as a sign of holiness, the Sabbath commandment cannot merit any particular importance, and, if we should be required to discard it to save our lives and preserve unity with the other Christians and the world, expedience would dictate that that is exactly what we should do. After all, Jesus kept it holy for us because He was holy in a way that we cannot be.

This sequence of descent into error was demonstrated in Brinsmead, to the letter. In the 1970s he switched position on the nature of Christ. He soon was found preaching that full obedience was not possible. In 1980, he publicly proclaimed his abandonment of the Sabbath in his book, *Sabbatarianism Re-Examined*.

> The amazing fact is that the "prophecy" quoted above came from the pen of Robert Brinsmead himself. Thus, with unerring accuracy he had predicted the very road which he was to tread some years later. This prediction surely must be one of the most amazing in recent church history. One can never accuse Robert Brinsmead of being illogical in his beliefs.... In many areas, Desmond Ford has not been as logical as he might have been. His continued support of the Sabbath is one of those areas. The Sabbath, in reality, is absolutely superfluous to his beliefs, since he has accepted the other two steps noted by Brinsmead. Indeed, it is difficult to see how Ford could truly believe in the Sabbath, for he believes in a Sabbath which cannot be kept holy. Such ... is not Sabbath keeping but Saturday keeping. Thus, his defence of the Sabbath is greatly weakened. (*Adventism Challenged*, p. 308)

Winding Back to the Annual Council of 1973

In 1973, General Conference President Elder Robert Pierson initiated a call for revival and reformation, through editorials and articles in the *Adventist Review*. Then, at the Annual Council of the General Conference of the same year, the delegates approved the issuance of an appeal such as had not been made in the lifetimes of the people of that generation. The appeal began by stating:

> "We believe that the return of Jesus has been long delayed, that the reasons for the delay are not wrapped in mysteries, and that the primary consideration before the Seventh-day Adventist Church is to re-order its priorities individually and corporately so that our Lord's return may be hastened." (cited in *Adventism Challenged*, p. 68)

The appeal went on to ask what had happened to the "beginning of earth's final message of warning," which had come in the 1888 era. The church leaders honestly acknowledged the part of leadership without shifting all the blame over to the laity, as had been done in previous times. Quoting poignant material from the Spirit of Prophecy, the document provided a cogent analysis of the situation as it had devolved upon the church. It outlined what yet remains as the standard of commitment and attainment in Christ that must and will be fulfilled before the Christ's return. The message has yet to be appropriated in its fullness, that a "conquering people" will arise "who have learned through experience that all godliness is a result of being sustained by divine power" and that "such people can be [and will be] entrusted with special power because they will use it the way Jesus used power" ("An Earnest Appeal from the Annual Council," *Review and Herald*, Dec. 6, 1973, p. 4, in *Adventism Challenged*, p. 69). This is because they will be like Jesus in all. It was stated that—

> The righteousness of Christ is not a cloak to cover unconfessed and unforsaken sin; it is a principle of life that transforms the character and controls the conduct. Holiness is wholeness for God; it is the entire surrender of heart and life to the indwelling of the principles of heaven. (*The Desire of Ages*, pp. 555, 556, cited in *Adventism Challenged*, p. 69)

Such an analysis, which truly represents God's plan for His people, was far from music in the ears of Brinsmead, Ford and some Seventh-day Adventist theologians. They had absorbed the so-called Reformed Theology and were proclaiming that righteousness by faith included only the objective facts of Calvary, and that it was assuming a Catholic position to include the work of God in the believer (sanctification) as part of righteousness by faith. Indeed, it was from this point that the *new theology* gathered momentum in an effort to counter the plain biblical and Spirit of Prophecy-oriented teachings sponsored by the church leadership. (*Adventism Challenged*, p. 69)

The stand taken at this council was a unanimous declaration which courageously upheld the 1888 Jones and Waggoner message, stating it to be "the heart of the Church's need" (*Adventism Challenged*, p. 69). Highlighted was the need for the members to have a "genuine and complete surrender of the life ... that may well call for revolutionary changes in personal life-styles and in denominational policies and practices" in the face of insubordination to the express will of God; that, as stated in an earlier issue of the church paper, our "institutions may become involved in worthy endeavors in which the world also participates, while neglecting that work which only the church of the remnant can do" ("An Earnest Appeal," *Review and Herald*, Dec. 6, 1973, pp. 4, 5). Admission was made that "counterfeit philosophies" (*Adventism Challenged*, p. 70) were being imported into our system as the wine of Babylon and that the spirituality of the membership comes under continual threat from earthly desires of careers and money.

So, without getting into further detail on areas of apostasy or insubordination, the leadership "fearlessly threw down the gauntlet" in an appeal to rise to the occasion and give themselves to God's claims upon them in truth (*Adventism Challenged*, p. 70).

> There was an eager expectation on the part of some that, following this 1973 challenge, the 1975 General Conference at Vienna would lead to an unprecedented revival of godliness, but tragically this expectation was not to be realized. That it did not happen was largely due to the counterattack on truth mounted by those espousing the *new theology*, and to the apathy of many church members. (*Adventism Challenged*, p. 71)

In 1974, as many young preachers coming out of the educational system were preaching the new theology with unprecedented boldness, General Conference Adventism seemed to be trying to get back on track. Some had felt in those times that things were getting turned around, that there was a recovery taking place. The change in leadership aroused new hope. There was a new administration in the General Conference, and there were also new editors at the *Adventist Review and Ministry* publications. The *Adventist Review* published its "Righteousness by Faith Special," which served to counter the errors that had been coming in, including that which had been fomented by *Questions on Doctrine*. The editorial staff at that time included Kenneth Wood, Herbert E. Douglass, and Donald Neufeld. The tenor of the material being produced was in full favor of General Conference President Robert Pierson, as it confirmed that God's faithful followers could and would be obedient to the law of God in the power of the Holy Spirit rather than a gospel of inevitable continuance in sin while being saved anyway.

The Sabbath School lessons were being written according to the old standards (such as Herb Douglass' quarterly of 1977). The statement of the 1973 Annual Council, the 1979 Righteousness by Faith meetings called by then president Neal Wilson, attended by about 150 church workers, lay people, and six vice presidents, and even the defrocking of Desmond Ford after Glacier View all gave reason for the old school Adventism to hope for revival and restoration. Yet, in the end, as the Standish brothers have observed, "This has subsequently proved to be an all-too-optimistic assessment" (*Adventism Challenged*, p. 199, fn. 2).

Oddly, all of these positive messages and moves took place without addressing the doctrinal shift that had been allowed to take place. We saw this effort to turn things back without really making it clear that "turning back" (repentance) was indeed the nature of the effort.

> However, just as the Church of the 1950s steadfastly refused to acknowledge to its members that a major doctrinal change was being foisted upon them, so, too, there had been a reticence on the part of many to acknowledge, in public, either by writing or by word of mouth, that there was a return toward the Adventist truth in the 1970s. Of course, in private, much has been acknowledged, but public representations have been accompanied by a deafening silence. This fact has caused much confusion in the Church. It is surely time that our brethren in positions of responsibility wrested the initiative from the theologians and from those who would attack our Church and admitted quite plainly that in the last quarter of a century, there have been some quite violent doctrinal movements within our church. (*Adventism Challenged*, p. 203)

We did deny some of our basic truths in the 1950s and 1960s and we must be sufficiently forthright and honest to admit it. We have now [*in the latter 1970s*], under God's mercy, acknowledged truth once more and our people deserve to know why. The steady drift away from truth, which is becoming evident again in the 1980s, will only be halted if such acknowledgments are made. (*Adventism Challenged*, p. 204)

Knowing that, in spite of the attempts made by good men, there was never a resolution to the doctrinal drift, we leave the discussion of the Ford saga and turn our attention to another account in this seemingly relentless reporting of spiritual, organizational, and doctrinal bankruptcies.

This next history lesson is not a "bedtime story." It is not for enjoyment or entertainment. In fact, we understand that it will not be easy to read. Yet, the people need to know these things. It is time.

Financial Mismanagement and Malfeasance in the Church: The David Dennis Disclosures

> In fact, that's what all good auditors are paid to do; we are like canaries in the mine shaft who try to catch fatal accounts before they permeate and affect everybody. I always took that responsibility to heart. (David Dennis, *Fatal Accounts*, p. 108; book available at http://1ref.us/ig, accessed 1/1/17)

> The corruptions of the world always make their way into religious establishments, and once they do, religious authorities lose their credibility. Shortcomings and hypocrisies that would be bad enough in secular politicians are even worse in clerics. (Jon Maecham, "Theocracies Are Doomed. Thank God," *Newsweek*, June 29, 2009, p. 9)

> What the Church did was fundamentally evil and taints us all. (*Fatal Accounts*, p. 105)

> I have been tracking Dennis for years. So sad! Where do you think it will end, if ever? (Herbert E. Douglass to Kevin Straub, email, March 15, 2013)

David Dennis was the Director of Seventh-day Adventist General Conference Auditing from 1976 to 1994. He was a rare breed in that he would actually stand up and give warning to church officials when it was due, as any normal auditor is paid to do. This is a story that has not yet received enough circulation, and we are going to give it considerable weight in this book for the opening of many eyes. In this segment, we are going to follow some basic details of the flow of money and how business was done from the standpoint of a principled number cruncher at the top through the years of his tenure as Chief Auditor. We will also be telling the story of the despicable reactions of church leadership in their bid to keep the truth from seeing the light of day and further misconduct against the professional standing and person of Elder Dennis.

Davenport

When David Dennis came to the General Conference as associate auditor in 1975, he was informed by Ralph Davidson, department head, about the Davenport situation. Davidson told him that there were loans of conference funds taking place that were not in compliance with church policy.

Dr. Donald Davenport was a Seventh-day Adventist church member, son of an Adventist physician and missionary pioneer to China. He started a contracting business to build post offices and lease them to the government and took private loans to fund his venture, promising an exorbitant rate of return of 15–18%. He could not pay the promised rate except by taking in new money, and it quickly developed into a very crooked pyramid scheme. Eventually he was issuing security documents to Adventist institutions that were second, third and fourth mortgages on various personal holdings. Sometimes mortgages were made up on properties that he did not own or that he had sold.

Elder Dennis sent about five hundred pages in total warnings to church officials at various levels in the United States to cease making any loans to Dr. Davenport or recommending that our people make loans. Some members would come to certain of the involved conference officials to put money in trust with the church and would instead be directed to make personal loans to the Davenport scheme. Then Davenport would pay a kickback to the officials, just as any good Ponzi scheme will do. This is how it grows. Yet, the time always comes when it all unravels, and Davenport's operation was no different.

By 1976, people began to notice that loan repayments were falling behind at times, and then, as new money would come in, the arrears would be caught up. That was the beginning of the end. By 1979, things got very bad for Dr. Davenport as the general interest rates were rising in the mainstream investment world, causing the influx of new loans to his operation to dwindle. People began to recall their loans. An Adventist lawyer, Jerry Wiley, began to investigate. *Forbes* magazine published an article in October 1981, citing Wiley's findings. Church leaders scoffed at Wiley, telling him that he was "crying wolf."* Davenport filed for bankruptcy on July 22, 1981, and denominational funds went down the tubes. The losses were reported in the *Washington Post* as follows:

Pacific Union Conference, $939,367.

North Pacific Union, $8,400,000, *plus:*

Montana Conference Association, $186,750;

Upper Columbia Conference Association, $1,600,000;

West Oregon Conference Association, $475,434.

Mid-America Union, Central Union, $213,974;

Kansas Conference Association, $661,335;

Northern Union, $679,118;

South Dakota Conference, $476.443.

Southwestern Union, Southwest Estate Service, $1,500,000.

Southern Union, Carolina Conference Association, $608,503;

Florida Conference Association, $579,448;

Georgia-Cumberland Conference Association, $3,700,000;

Kentucky-Tennessee Conference Association, $173,505.

General Conference: Christian Record, $108,335.

Inter-American Division, $17,328.

Total denominational entities: $20,715,866.

[*As a side note, some might ask why leaders would scoff at Wiley when the bankruptcy filing had already taken place. It is a good question. I can only conclude that this sort of news would be quite troublesome to leaders who were heavily invested with their own money, church money, and the money of church members. They would certainly not be citing the Forbes article in church pulpits and papers and would want to keep a lid on it as much as possible. Additionally, we must understand how the psychological mechanism of denial must surely have come into play in this regard. Humans tend to only believe what they want to believe, hoping that bad news will somehow go away and things will be fine. Therefore, downplaying the matter and scoffing at the naysayers would serve to quiet anyone's fears. Observer Vance Ferrell said that, when the bankruptcy filing took place, there was a "massive cover-up" and a "stalling for time" as a president's commission was created to look into the alleged scandal but was instructed to delay the report back to President Wilson by one year (see http://1ref.us/ih, part two).]

In addition to the loss of church funds, as reported in the *Washington Post*, there were funds that were routed to Davenport via the services of church officials. The amount lost to faithful church members was also more than twenty million dollars, bringing the total damages to over forty million dollars.

> His [Davenport's] Chapter 11 petition lists 31 commercial savings institutions, eight insurance companies, 25 Adventist organizations and at least four dozen church officials.
>
> Parts of the list of creditors read like a Who's Who of Adventist circles. It includes seven officers of the church's world headquarters in Washington, D.C., three regional [union] conference presidents, six local conference presidents, three treasurers, several noted educators, one university president, and a television personality. ("Investment scam embarrassing to Adventists," *Walla Walla Union Bulletin*, Aug. 21, 1981, p. 1)

The fallout from this scandal was of crisis proportions. There are not many church members from that time who will not recall hearing something of the "Davenport affair," or the "Davenport scandal." The General Conference did something it had never before needed to do, in hiring a secular public relations firm, "Hill and Knowlton" to get the church through the storm.

After the bankruptcy, David Dennis was in attendance at an auditors' workshop for Seventh-day Adventist CPAs and was there asked by others why the General Conference Audit Department failed to act in the mounting crisis. He responded that many warnings had been sent, but that the auditors, as they all well knew, did not have any power to make management decisions. The management has to act on the information, which they did not. It is not an auditor problem. The auditor simply keeps an eye on the financial works and makes his reports. Then matters are out of his hands. They understood.

Harris Pine Mills

Harris Pine Mills was a large company that was gifted to the church. In 1953, it was worth 8.5 million dollars and took in almost 5.5 million in profits that year alone. When David Dennis took up his place as head auditor at the General Conference, he wanted to see an audit report on Harris Pine Mills, the largest business enterprise owned by the Seventh-day Adventist Church. Yet, his requests were consistently denied. It continued to grow and amass assets, employing up to 2,700 student workers by 1973. It was thought to be a wonderful business success for the church, but that would not have been known for sure because no audits had been made.

David was a professional and knew how to do his job. This is why he continually pressed to have an audit. He knew that the larger a company became the more danger there would be of its getting into trouble through mismanagement. He was serving the best interests of the church in calling for an audit, which would find problems in time to increase the chances of correcting them. Church policy required a yearly audit. Yet, year after year, no audits were made. It is now known that by the 1980s, there was in fact significant trouble. In 1980, Lance L. Butler came from Australia, where he served as division treasurer, to take over as General Conference treasurer. He joined Elder Dennis in calling for an audit. However, Kenneth H. Emmerson, previous General Conference treasurer, now the CFO of Harris Pine Mills, and Neal C. Wilson, General Conference president, were both adamant that there be no audit of Harris Pine Mills.

At 4:05 p.m., Friday, December 5, 1986, as the Sabbath drew on, bankruptcy proceedings were filed by church officers at a federal courthouse. There were some strange elements to all of the proceedings, and some believe that the company could have been saved. Mrs. Harris, the widow of the couple that had given the company to the church originally, stated that there were enough uncut timber holdings alone to save the company from collapse with other significant assets. The CPA who was appointed by the court to supervise the bankruptcy declared that there were far more assets than indebtedness. The banks reported in the press that they had not been dissatisfied and had not been pressing the company for any reason. It is not known for sure to this day why this company, which was generating $55 million in annual sales, was liquidated in this way. The bankruptcy route that was taken ended up costing the church $13 million in the end. It has been alleged that the church wanted to gain by the process and use the funds to inject into failing entities of the Adventist Health System.

Don Gilbert, the General Conference treasurer at the time of the bankruptcy, told David Dennis personally that, if there had been audits, the problems would have been caught early and there would have been no danger of collapse.

Adventist Health System debt problem compounded by exorbitant salaries for executives

In and around the 1960s the ownership of many of the locally owned Adventist hospitals was shifted over to the unions. This was done by board action and usually without conference constituency approval. In the mid-1970s, hospital executives asked to incorporate hospitals in the southeastern states and the Adventist Health System was born, as Seventh-day Adventist hospitals across the nation wanted to follow the same path and formed a number of subsidiary systems under the "AHS" umbrella. Again, in the mid-1970s and generally by a single committee vote, the ownership and control of these hospitals in the conferences and unions were handed over to the newly founded corporations, which were made subsidiaries of the General Conference. So we see how that the healthcare system was pushed all the way to the top in a centralization process. (However, in the early 1990s, AHS was turned back to the unions as it was feared that a collapse would cause the bankruptcy courts to reach into the treasury of the General Conference for settlement. Pushing it back to the unions would mean that it would be more likely that union and conference assets would be first seized upon.)

In the late 1970s and early 1980s, the executives in charge of these systems "went for broke," literally. Throwing fiscal responsibility to the dogs, debt was piled up beyond recovery in order to expand the AHS empire in a bid to establish an "Adventist presence" in every possible population center (in spite of the fact that most of the workers employed are not Adventists).

As we track the progress of AHS, we find a horrific build-up of debt.

- In late summer of 1983, it passed the 1 billion dollar mark. In contrast to this, ALL of the debt of the rest of the church in North America was less than half a million.

- By spring of 1985, the debt of AHS was up to 1.5 billion.

- August 1986, it was 2 billion.

- By summer of 1988, AHS had a debt ratio more than double that of the average US hospital or hospital system.

- August 1988 saw the first bond default (AHS/Nema).

- Summer of 1989, the Arizona Conference sued AHS/West to try to recoup 11 million in losses from the AHS/West takeover of their hospital.
- August 1989, Imaging Systems, Inc., an AHS subsidiary collapsed, costing the church 92 million dollars.
- August 1989, the total AHS debt load was $2.24 for every dollar in assets.
- November 1990, Adventist Living Centers, an AHS subsidiary, went into default.
- May 1989, the church voted to accept the recommendation of AHS executives to receive a large wage increase.

We need to look at that last point because it is here that the hospital situation really went off the rails. Wednesday, April 5, 1989, AHS leaders stood before the church officers and, with "tear-filled voices," explained how they needed all this extra money. This was a shock to the overseas leaders, as one might well imagine. Yet, these men were actually serious. The non-American leaders were well aware of the news reports of mismanagement and losses and burgeoning debt and of non-payment of bonds and pending bankruptcies, yet here were these poor executives asking for exorbitant wage increases and weaving a tale that somehow this was the answer to the troubles being experienced by AHS!

President Neal Wilson pushed hard in defense of the wage increases. There was heated discussion. Then, there was a decision to table the matter. That evening, heavy pressure was exerted upon world leaders to give in to the demands. The next day the salary increase was passed by a vote of 52–42. Not only were executive wages increased, but all wages in the hospitals were increased to come into line with competitive community rates.

These wage increases for executives were coming to a group of church employees who were already receiving a base rate of four to five times that of other church employees. With the added percentages, that would have brought salaries at that time up to $150,000 per year. By the mid-1990s, this figure ballooned to about $230,000–$250,000 annually, as that vote by church leaders to raise salaries also gave AHS leaders the authority to vote themselves pay raises. As of the 2012 tax year, as reported in the *Orlando Business Journal*, October 9, 2013, the top ten AHS executives received from $1,062,010 to $3,191,124 in remuneration.

Would it have been wrong to reprove all of this? David Dennis was astounded. He wrote a letter to President Neal Wilson to make a heart plea, dated April 17, 1989. We will show some excerpts from that letter.

To me, however, it did seem strange that, after admitting to serious financial failures and mounting debt far beyond accepted norms in the United States, these leaders should now ask for higher pay. Few businessmen could ever accept the assumption that if a manager is ineffective while earning an annual salary of $75,000 he will somehow be successful if his salary is raised to $140,000.

In the annals of the Adventist church history, it is conceivable that Wednesday, April 5, 1989, and the day following, will mark another decision drawing us farther away from basic Seventh-day Adventist principles and from the spirit of democratic leadership....

Perhaps even more trouble to me than the secular arguments advanced to obtain higher wages was the way the recommendation was advanced to a final vote. It seemed to me that the democratic process was not taken very seriously.... I find it hard to understand why a vote was not taken at the conclusion of the day-long discussion on Wednesday. Instead, you recommended and moved that the motion be tabled. Then, late Thursday, the matter was brought back for consideration after much of the opposition had dispersed.... Some leaders who were present concluded that the only purpose for the overnight delay in taking the vote was to permit the political process to take its course....

This is not the first time that delays, tablings, straw votes, and similar strategies have been used in our convocations to push through an unpopular recommendation. While these procedures may bring the desired result, they do not enhance the credibility of church leaders. (David D. Dennis to Elder Neal C. Wilson, President, April 17, 1989)

After writing further on some related issues to strengthen the points he made, David brought up the issue of "lack of disclosure," a euphemism for "cover-up." He talked about the lack of proper information being brought forward from a report on the AHS resulting from "an extremely thorough investigation" by the Financial Review Commission appointed by the General Conference itself, in which David Dennis himself was a member. That report was "direct, incisive" and made "positive recommendations for massive change in the

AHS." He wondered what impact that report would have had upon the vote that took place at the spring meeting. Dennis went on in his letter.

> Only a limited few were aware of the report which provides details of the dangers posed to the church because of the issues of ascending liability, inept management, blurred perception of mission and purpose, political disarray of the present AHS operations, and dangerously high debt.
>
> Unfortunately, in the matter of Review Commissions, church history has not been kind to us. Many of us recall how the Davenport Commission made a report a few years ago. At the sacrifice of considerable time and money, mostly by lay people, decisive actions were recommended. The result at that time, again because of pressures by certain of our union leaders, was to scuttle the report, and the previous GC action was reversed.
>
> Lack of disclosure also has prevailed with regard to the economic devastation created by the AHS North diversification bankruptcy. Even as Director of Auditing for the General Conference I have never been made aware of the facts involved in this debacle. Could it be that the high level leaders of the church, outside the AHS, were personally involved in this scam? Without disclosure we cannot adequately answer such questions. In the business world ... a board chairman would immediately have been placed on administrative leave following such a disaster until the facts could be determined and the degree of his responsibility ascertained....
>
> Clearly, great damage has been done by the action last week.... Why should one small group of church workers be singled out for unreasonably high compensation? Some may differ with me, but I must say I don't believe hospital administrators are in greater need financially than other church employees....
>
> Many of our fellow workers and lay members are frustrated and disheartened. Little wonder that leadership credibility in the church, as in the world, is at an all time low. Little wonder that there is proliferation of independent ministries trying to call the church back to its deeply spiritual mission.... While it is impossible for me to defend the action the Spring Meeting took last week, I can at least appeal to your heart and mine that we turn to the Lord for forgiveness and seek the reformation we must have before the latter rain can be poured out on our church and our people. (David D. Dennis to Elder Neal C. Wilson, President, April 17, 1989)

This letter was a turning point for the career of David Dennis as employee of the General Conference, as far as leadership was concerned, for it was now determined that he had to go.

> When my letter circulated, Wilson demanded that I retract it. I told him that if he could identify any inaccuracies in the letter, I would happily do so. Since he seemed unable to identify any misinformation in my four-page manifesto, I declined to take back anything I had written....
>
> ... Folkenberg and Des Hills, the new chairman of the Nominating Committee, asked me to meet with them. They told me that because of the open letter I had written to Neal Wilson a year earlier, I had not been re-nominated. Folkenberg emphasized the importance of the letter and seemed to be asking me to bow in great tears of repentance. I responded with all honesty that if I had to do it over, I would again write the letter. (David Dennis, *Fatal Accounts*, pp. 44–46)

Fourteen years had he stood true to principle, urging leadership to do what was right. Would a change of leadership finally bring the denomination to its senses?

Shooting the watchdog

Neal C. Wilson was voted out and replaced by Robert Folkenberg as the General Conference president, July 6, 1990. Early in the following week, one of the first things Folkenberg did was to have a little talk with David Dennis and ask him if, in light of the political spot he was in, he would like to resign his position. Elder Dennis replied that this was not in his thinking at all and that his only wish was to stand for a fair democratic vote. Folkenberg assured him that this would be done just so. However, on Wednesday evening of July 11, it was time for the nomination and Folkenberg reneged on his promise. He left David's name off the board and wrote another name, while informing the group that David had committed some kind of "ethical wrong" and they should vote for someone else. So the nominating committee went along with that and voted for the other name. The same evening, David was in another meeting, when he was called out to be informed that, because of his protest letter to Neal Wilson, he was being shut out of the election process.

Thursday morning was the meeting when the names

approved by the nominating committee were presented. The obvious fact that David Dennis' name was absent prompted delegates to rise from their seats and request that the name of the head auditor be referred back to the nominating committee. It was approved. A number of the delegates were not happy at this situation, as it was well-known that there was a political play in progress to get rid of the only whistle-blower in the General Conference. Time was given for the delegates to speak to the matter, and speak they did! They expressed how inappropriate it was to side-line David Dennis when he was only doing what an auditor should rightly do. One elderly worker was quite outspoken, saying, "You're the new president, and the auditor is your watchdog. Do you want it to go on record that you have shot your watchdog?" Another one took the floor, saying, "Are we going to do this again? I thought all the political maneuvering was over, now that we had a new General Conference president." The committee was warned by yet another that, if they did not send David Dennis back to his post as head auditor, it would be a dark message to the workers in responsible positions in the church: If you hold true to righteousness and principle, leadership will oust you.

Thoroughly indignant, the committee cancelled its prior vote and re-elected Dennis as head of the General Conference Auditing Department.

Consolidating power

For over ten years, Neal Wilson worked to concentrate power upwards. When Robert Folkenberg was elected, it was expected that he would work to set matters aright. Back when Wilson was president, it was known that no one dared make a move without his blessing. Nonetheless, there was still the odd time that the Executive Advisory Committee would not go along with his recommendations. However, Folkenberg had a way to fix this. He called his workers together and told them that he wished to delegate. That was a breath of fresh air! So, under his new direction, he set up ADCOM, the Administrative Committee, to carry out the work of running the General Conference. Everything done would have to go through ADCOM approval. However, no sooner was it formed than it was ensured that ADCOM would be a rubberstamp machine. It would vote according to Folkenberg's desires. Yet, there were still departmental workers at headquarters who were elected at the General Conference sessions. Folkenberg was determined to fix this too. The next step was to get the Annual Council to approve a plan whereby the associate departmental leaders would not be elected at the sessions but would be appointed by the president. In October 1994, the request was approved at the Annual Council, to be presented at the 1995 session for final approval. This approval would leave only a few men at the head of the work who would be elected—the departmental heads. It could then be easily arranged by the president that only those who pleased the president would stand to be recommended for those positions.

As for the auditing department? Never again would there be any trouble with whistle blowers.

ADRA

The international service organization for disaster and famine relief established in 1956 was called *Seventh-day Adventist World Service, Inc.* (SAWS). It was registered with US AID of the United States and was eligible to receive surplus foods for distribution to the needy, as well as reimbursements for ocean freight costs. In 1983, it was reorganized under the new name *Adventist Development and Relief Agency International* (ADRA), and it would expand its services to include development and rebuilding projects in addition to supplying food and other materials. Expanded in this way, it would bring in much larger funding from government sources. ADRA went on to become the single most powerful General Conference agency.

It is well known that church involvement with government funding is not innocent, for it invariably implies a two-way deal that relinquishes autonomy for money. The organization must necessarily march to an earthly drummer, not being free to follow God's leading. Governments cannot be offended without risk of losing large sums of funding.

Not only would ADRA be closely linked to governments, but they would also become a full voting member of the largest ecumenical Christian agency, the *Inter-Church Medical Assistance* (IMA), to supply pharmaceuticals to Christian medical establishments of all denominations. *This makes the Seventh-day Adventist denomination a major customer and global distributor for the pharmaceutical companies.*

To be tied to other churches and to governments makes taboo the declaration of our distinctive prophetic messages in Daniel 7 and Revelation 12–14 and the distribution of *The Great Controversy* and proselytizing. Nothing may be done to disturb the entities to which this huge church agency is tied.

Where this story intersects with David Dennis is that the monetary contracts with the various governmental agencies were subject to audits. These would ensure that the money was used exactly according to specifications. As one might imagine, it was a rare contract that was fulfilled without deviations. Ralph Watts, ADRA's director was not one to properly notify governments about these deviations and would therefore be infuriated by the accuracy of Dennis' audit reports. He repeatedly instructed the head auditor to keep the problems out of sight.

There were so many abuses in the ADRA system that sometimes, when malfeasance was discovered, instead of prosecution, the perpetrator would be paid off and quietly dismissed. Why is that? Because he knew too much! One such instance was a worker assigned to oversee the work in Rwanda, James Conran. He was taking goods for distribution to the needy and selling them to personally fund a high lifestyle. The United States government learned of it, and the scandal was covered in the *Wall Street Journal*. He was brought back to America to be "dealt with." What was done? He was given a sum of money and discharged from service!

As anger increased over David's integrity in conducting his job as it should have been performed, it was made clear that new management was required at the Auditing Department. Add ADRA to the list of reasons why the leadership of the General Conference wanted David Dennis *gone*.

The worthy student fund and Christian Education donation "irregularities"

Again, in the course of simply doing his job properly, David Dennis was looking at some problems that arose with regard to numbers on the books and their sources and their destinations. Later on, as it all came out, the problem was made to be in the honest reporting of irregularities rather than the unethical and illegal activities that took place with funds.

In the first case, it was the irregularity of "charitable donations" being given through church channels to set up a "courtesy payroll" for the wives of new General Conference president, Robert Folkenberg, and the new president of the North American Division, Alfred C. McClure. Both men were pleased with the idea. President of the Columbia Union, Ronald Wisbey, who was working on behalf of the donors, thought that this money could be transmitted through the General Conference. Doing it this way would avoid transparency, eliminating the need to set up the payroll accounts through legitimate procedures. So he brought the idea to the new General Conference treasurer, Donald Gilbert. Both Wisbey and Gilbert understood that the General Conference working policy clearly disallowed such funding without approval from the proper committee. Gilbert was afraid of it, so Wisbey decided he would funnel the money through the Columbia Union, a favor for which he would be later rewarded. The money was donated as tax-deductible contributions to the "Worthy Student Fund" of the Columbia Union Conference, and then checks for the wives were written from a payroll account managed by the Columbia Union's treasurer's office which, by the end of 1990 had accrued for the wives a sum of $10,260 each.

In the second case, Wisbey took calls from "secret donors" who wished to know if channels could be worked out to provide a gift to Alfred McClure to purchase a house. Again, it was worked out by Wisbey so that $140,000 would enter in through a donation to "Christian Education" in the Columbia Union. The money was set up as an interest-free loan that McClure and the Columbia Union would use to purchase and co-own the home.

In January 1991, when the General Conference Auditing Department did its routine annual audit of the Columbia Union books, David Dennis discovered these transactions, of course, and he had issues with them. He, along with other staff, let the appropriate men involved know that this report could not be filed unless proper procedures were executed and this involved getting approval from the Columbia Union Executive Committee. Disclosures to the proper constituencies for their approval was a necessity.

A meeting was held in February of 1991 and disclosure was made to an astonished committee of sixty members, half of them lay members. They chose to give their approval after-the-fact.

However, it did not end there. The biennial session of the Columbia Union was coming up in May, at which the General Conference auditor's report would be presented. Wisbey wanted to obscure the fact of the payroll accounts to the wives of Folkenberg and McClure by changing the wording in an appended note on the auditor's report that read "wife of a General Conference officer" and "wife of a North American Division officer" to simply "wives of employees." Perhaps this was because it would not be as likely to draw attention. One has to wonder how much money it cost the church in the time invested in the auditing department, in communications between involved parties, and in all of these meetings involving church executives. Time was surely wasted for reasons of selfish and illicit gain when it should have been spent upon the Lord's business.

An emergency meeting was called a few days before the Columbia Union Constituency Meeting, which would be attended by 400 delegates. David Dennis stood before the leaders and stood firmly for the position that the church must abide by the *Working Policy*.

> Wisbey tried to convince me to modify our audit report, and when this failed, he invited me to meet with a rather large delegation (Church employees, primarily) to hear their reasons why the report should be altered. **The group literally booed me** when I pointed out that this was not an auditors' problem, but a question of Church leaders' integrity, and I quoted Ellen White's statement that our "transactions should be as transparent as the sunlight." (David Dennis, *Fatal Accounts*, p. 49, emphasis added)

The Union Constituency Meeting convened in May 1991, and the anonymous donations were not mentioned from the front, nor were they noticed by any delegates. Here was a collective sigh of relief by leading men who had things to hide. A major hurdle was passed. Was this now going to go away? Not that easily, no.

On June 1, David Dennis' office mailed a copy of that report to the members of the Columbia Union Conference Executive Committee. There was no surprise for them in it. However, while Dennis reminded them that those wives' salaries and the interest free mortgage loan for McClure, which were established by the connivance of the treasurer and three presidents (union, division and General Conference) were a breach of policy, he also made it clear that, if these donors took tax deductions on these monies, the church could very well experience legal problems and serious consequences such as the revocation of tax-exempt status. The implication was that, if this came to further scrutiny by the government, he would not lie to protect them.

The result of this was that they had to tell the General Conference Committee all about it. The meeting to do so was held on June 20, 1991. General Conference Treasurer Don Gilbert introduced the subject, while stating that he wished he could do this entire thing over and would do it differently if he could. Ron Wisbey spoke, putting a certain spin on events that tended to blame the situation on David Dennis, in that the problem obtaining the auditor's report had resulted in having to open up a private matter involving two families to the union executive committee and the union constituency. Neal Wilson, who was on the General Conference Committee, informed the others that, when he was informed about what was happening, he had expressed incredulity that the two leaders receiving such funding should have approved of such a blatant conflict of interest. Wilson was aware that there was a not-so-subtle line of defense being floated that the only problem in the situation was that the auditing department felt it had to open the matter up to a wider audience. Looking directly at Wisbey, he iterated that it was unthinkable that this matter of secret donors would not have come to light without the eye of the auditors picking it up. David Dennis was becoming more of a marked man with each instance of honest execution of his duty.

The recommendation to axe the unions

Dennis undertook to study how to save money for the church. Spending most of his adult life in the investigation of organizational operations and troubleshooting, he was well qualified to make a valid assessment. He was stunned to realize the cost of keeping the union conferences functioning. Between the years of 1986 and 1990 the cost of the unions totaled more than 358 million dollars. In examining them, he found that they actually serve little purpose. He concluded that they are a layer of governance that is redundant and unnecessary. As he discussed his findings with others there were not many who offered any kind of good rationale or reason for keeping them. As he began urging for the closing of the union offices he asked for others to submit an argument justifying the value returned for such an outlay of funds—tithe and offering funds, of course. (As with any governing body, money is obtained from the governed.) As one might imagine, this line of investigation and recommendation was arousing much anger as union officials saw in it the threat to their positions. Freeing up this money would have an enormous impact on the church and would be of benefit in what the economized funds could help accomplish. Yet, it was quickly becoming a "political" issue, for who would be willing to vote himself out of a job?

David's popularity account with leadership went even further into the red.

Cronyism and rewards programs

Legal action was initiated by David Dennis against the General Conference and several of its leaders for several violations of church policy in conflicts of interest. One of the matters that Dennis reported on, found in court documents, was the operation of a business venture known as *Galileo and Associates*. Another name for this venture was *Media for Ministry*.

There was a small video production studio that had been set up by the General Conference in years past, in order to save money spent on outsourcing video production. When Folkenberg took office in 1990, there was a comprehensive equipment upgrade to the studio. Then, in 1992, under the guise of "budget cutting," it was decided to contract out video production. One of Folkenberg's closest friends, Raymond D. Tetz, was to receive the contract for video production, which included a full salary. In addition, the studio he would use would be the General Conference Communications Department studio, newly upgraded. Ray would bill the church for every production. The extra billing is reported to have been in excess of $150,000 a year. In 1994, the General Conference and NAD were billed $158,000 in addition to ADRA and other church entities.

Named defendants in the action included also ADRA board chairman, Kenneth Mittleider. During the discovery process, Dennis asked for a complete accounting of the operation. He wanted to know who all the beneficiaries were and what gratuities were paid out. He was looking to answer why this operation existed as it did—in secrecy and in violation of church policies.

Continuing, Robert Folkenberg hired his brother, Don, outside of the channels of regular approval for employment, to be the financial coordinator for ADRA, 1991–1992. In 1992, Don was made "associate treasurer" of the General Conference where he had the responsibility of handling the funds for *Global Mission*, the new program for outreach which was unveiled shortly after Folkenberg took office. These funds were mainly allocated to projects outside of the United States. David Dennis wanted transparency on the paper trail of those funds, but it proved difficult, for once they left the United States the audit trail was nearly impossible to follow. For example, funds sent to eastern Europe were left unaccounted for. On one occasion, there was a $10,000 donation that was to build a church in a certain Russian town. However, actual investigation proved that there was no record anywhere of the construction of such a church nor did any church leader or worker in that area know of any such project. Where did the money go? There would certainly have been a beneficiary, but nobody knows who.

Dennis continued relentlessly in his quest for proper accounting of funds. He urged that a complete investigation be made of Don Folkenberg's itineraries, especially concerning activities in Switzerland. He wanted to know about Don's prior business deals both for the church and outside of the church, including business operations in Florida.

Then there was Ron Wisbey, president of the Columbia Union. Recalling that Ron was the one who channeled the donations to the wives of General Conference and North American Division presidents, Folkenberg and McClure, as salaries, we find the favor now being returned. A lucrative position was fabricated for him, called *Liaison between the Columbia Union and Adventist Health System*. His salary was that of a hospital administrator or junior executive, reported in the mid-nineties to be around $240,000 a year. This is an obscene level of pay for a man trained only in clerical and pastoral work. Also, this position was created at a time when hospitals were cutting budgets and letting go of nurses, doctors and chaplains. Wisbey's wife also moved on up from office secretary at the General Conference to secretary in the AHS system, for twice the money.

The parsonage exclusion violations

Another area where Dennis would not work to cover up dishonesty had to do with a problem with the reports of "Parsonage Exclusions" on the tax returns of church workers. It is legal, per IRS regulations, for the church to obtain tax write-offs for the housing of licensed and ordained ministers. As per IRS rules, not only is the purchase of a home deducted from taxable income, but so are the cost of furnishings, appliances, fixtures and maintenance. (These housing tax write-offs are now also available to commissioned women ministers.) The church chose to designate other individuals as ministers so the IRS regulations would apply to them. "But gradually, other individuals, who did not properly fit the ministers/priests/rabbis clause, began receiving this church exemption from our leaders. They were given cost-free homes to live in, which could be written off as tax free" (Vance Ferrell, *Collision Course*, p. 38). (A minor point of note here is that tax deductions do not necessarily mean a home is entirely "cost free.")

David Dennis instructed his auditors to flag any illegal exclusions of income. Honesty demanded it. Seventh-day Adventists, of all people, should be completely above board. It is an auditor's responsibility to keep an organization from losing millions of dollars in penalties if infractions are discovered by the government authorities and brought to the law. Rather than thanking Dennis for his faithful work, Tom Mostert, president of the Pacific Union and Al McClure of the NAD put pressure on him to withdraw his reports. Conscientious, Dennis did not wish to participate in anything that might be taken as a cover-up. So, he informed leaders that he would neither withdraw the reports, nor change them.

Then, Mostert attempted a childish tactic and refused to show the books to the auditing department, preventing them from completing their audits. However, it was feared that his actions would be reported to the laity. So, wishing to avoid public scandal, access to the books was restored. These latter actions on Dennis' part generated great animosity against him, and "something had to be done—not to stop the illegalities, but to get rid of anyone honest enough to report it" (*Collision Course*, p. 38).

The take-down

Now the story turned really ugly when leaders employed character assassination to eliminate Dennis' negative reports.

The next General Conference Session would be coming up in Utrecht, Holland, in 1995. By the middle of 1994, there would have been considerable concern that Dennis would be re-elected for another five years. Somehow he must be gotten rid of. How could this be accomplished? The opportunity finally came as the result of a false allegation made in the office of a psychotherapist.

When the Dennis family was stationed in Singapore, an emotionally fragile girl named Elizabeth L. Adels lived in their home, taken in during at a time when it was suspected she was having suicidal ideations. In spite of psychological problems, she kept up a strong relationship with the family after she was no longer in their home. Around the year 1992, she, along with her husband and children, had a happy visit with the Dennis family. However, ongoing family problems and depression plagued her, and she underwent counseling. In those sessions, she underwent "therapeutic" procedures in which thoughts and memories she had never consciously experienced or mentioned before were said to have surfaced. This is done by "talking to the child" (i.e., utilizing the power of suggestion in hypnotic procedures to address the "inner child" of the adult person) in what is called "regressive therapy," and it is a false science that results in the implantation of false memories. In this "recovered memory," it was reported that she had had an affair with Adels in a hotel in 1982. However, this was at a time that David was traveling in company with his wife.

If one is not already aware of this phenomenon, it is readily available information. An education on it may be obtained by going to the *False Memory Syndrome Foundation, Inc.* (FMSF) of Philadelphia, PA, which is today a leading resource to assist those whose reputations and family relationships have been threatened with ruin due to lawsuits containing false allegations of sexual misconduct. Historically, the period between 1993–1999 was the time period when the most recovered memory cases involving families were brought to the courts. By about 1995, over a period of three years, FMSF had on record over 17,000 cases of families destroyed by false-memory implantation techniques. The typical pairing of alleged abuser with alleged victim is that of are a father or a man in a position of authority with a woman in her mid-thirties. Hypnosis is inextricably tied to the false memory problem, *whether its use is formal or disguised*. "Recovered memories" have proven over and over to be unreliable, and professional organizations agree that the only way to distinguish between true and false memories is by external corroboration, as in a fair trial in a court of law, with the presentation of incontrovertible evidence and not hearsay, much less hearsay obtained through trance-state therapies.

Coming back to our story, as soon as word of these allegations came to the General Conference, they were recognized as the golden opportunity needed to get rid of that lone voice of dissent in the auditing department at headquarters. Yet, it had to be done in a way that would not allow Dennis to defend himself.

- Without going first to Dennis, Folkenberg sent lawyer Walter Carson to Ohio to obtain a statement accusing Dennis of a twenty year past sexual misconduct with Adels.

- October 4, 1994, Dennis was called into Carson's office. Mittleider was present. (The chairman of ADRA who, with Ralph Watts, had been angered for years by Dennis' audit reports.) Dennis was shown the affidavit signed by Adels and told he must resign. He refused.

- October 5, David Dennis was called in for another interrogation by Carson and Mittleider. This time they took a different tack. They now tried to accuse him of other things, including improper financial dealings!

- October 9, David was ordered in a third time and bullied around, with threats that the General Conference leaders would destroy him if he would not hand in his resignation.

- October 11, they made a desperate fourth attempt to force his resignation. He was told that the GC now had full documentary proof of all of the allegations. David told them to bring it on. In fits of anger, the leaders demanded that Dennis resign immediately.

Months passed and none of the alleged evidence was brought to light because, of course, it did not exist. There were some false documents produced, which could not prove anything, while Dennis resolutely and consistently maintained total innocence of all charges.

On December 12, an ad hoc disciplinary board was assembled. Before going before this board, Dennis was informed that he would not be allowed an attorney. This is against church guidelines. He was promised that it would be only a non-adversarial fact-finding ecclesiastical exercise. Yet, that was a lie. Walter Carson proceeded to present a seventy-five-minute opening report which sought to indict David of child abuse and adultery and of being a habitual liar with a long history of sexual misconduct. The court reporter who had originally been hired to take the transcript of the meeting was told not to attend and Mittleider's private secretary took the notes instead. When Carson finished, Mittleider took over with more of the same, making the demand that Dennis be immediately relieved of his position.

In the proceedings of the day, it was noted that she had a long history of psychiatric problems and marital infidelities. She had previously made two other rape claims. Also it was reported that she had had a friendly visit to the Dennis home only three years earlier. Then Adels would speak. Under the strong lead of Carson and Mittleider, she made highly unbelievable statements. As she gave her testimony, with a box of tissue and psychological counselor at her side, she contradicted her earlier affidavit by declaring, "upon reflection," that her allegation that … [David Dennis] had groped her in Singapore had been misconstrued in the affidavit." Yet, she did not disavow a separate story involving an alleged motel encounter near her home in Tennessee twelve years earlier. She told those assembled in the room that she had recollected these events while undergoing psychological therapy. David's wife, Charlotte, was brought into the room to testify. Charlotte recounted that she had been with Dennis at the hotel in question during the very times the alleged tryst was supposed to have occurred (*Fatal Accounts*, pp. 3, 4). This was a shock to the prosecutors, for it was new information. Charlotte Dennis described her experience:

> Then came the "Kangaroo Court," with its Gestapo-like proceedings and an ultimatum—that I could either defend David verbally, or sit beside him as a silent witness. The GC brethren would not permit me to do both.
>
> Mittleider, meanwhile, recognized that contrary to plan, David was not going to resign under fire, and Mittleider's anger visibly seethed. I knew as well as David that the affair Beth Adels was describing could never have taken place. Though she said she had met illicitly with my husband in Portland, Tennessee, 12 years before, I distinctly remembered traveling, myself, with David during that time—something the GC officers did not know and Beth in her confused state of mind had forgotten to tell them. In fact, David and I had visited with Beth and her parents in the course of our travels together. I told Mittleider that we had traveled together in the family car, and that we were enjoying the time we had to spend together. David simply would not have had the time or opportunity to do anything like what Beth was describing through psychiatrically induced false memory syndrome.
>
> But as I shared this information at the in-house hearing, Mittleider roughly interrupted me and shouted, "You're lying!" In turn, I told him that I recognized a rigged hearing when I saw one, but even so, I was pledged to tell the absolute truth, as I knew it. (Charlotte Dennis, cited in *Fatal Accounts*, p. 130)

In spite of the obvious malicious and malignant dealing that was underway, amazingly, the disciplinary panel, friends of Mittleider, performed its job and voted a recommendation to terminate Dennis. On December 19 the General Conference Administrative Committee met. Again, Mittleider led out, with Carson at his side, repeating the allegations and urging strenuously for David's dismissal. The next day the full executive committee voted, 39 to 16, to fire David Dennis. At age 56, David was left unemployed, with no health benefits and with the notoriety of alleged sexual misconduct on his name. Notably, one third of these members would not put their rubberstamp on this debacle. [Comment: Lucifer only got one third to his side in the church in heaven; in this story of the church on earth, he is seen to have been twice as successful.]

For years, powerful enemies had been seeking ways to remove me from my position as chief auditor of the worldwide Seventh-day Adventist Church. At last, after many failures, those enemies had succeeded. But paradoxically, I now felt very close to my

Savior. I was bloodied, but unbowed. (David Dennis, *Fatal Accounts*, p. 7)

With glee, the final assassination of the reputation and character of David Dennis was effected through a thorough communications campaign. This would serve to fully stamp out his credibility and cover up all the truth he brought to the light over the years:

- A memo was sent to every department head in the General Conference.

- By personal instruction from the vice-president, Philip Follett, the department heads were to bring in all of their staff, read out the charges and actions against David Dennis, and send them back to work without any discussion.

- An announcement was sent over the CompuServe communication system to tell the world of Seventh-day Adventist workers that Dennis was an adulterer.

- Another announcement was sent over Adventist News Network, the newsletter for Seventh-day Adventist workers.

- Men were sent out in person to have meetings with workers in diverse parts of the world field to further destroy David Dennis.

It was a thorough campaign, which had a chilling effect on workers. This violent take-down was well calculated to put fear into the hearts of workers everywhere. It must be known that one's chances to reach the rewards of retirement are much more readily achieved through compliance and silence. This is how dictatorships function.

In early 1992, Folkenberg imposed an "operating board" over auditing. He appointed Robert J. Kloosterhuis to chair this board and keep control over all auditing operations other than the professional requirements of reporting. The director of auditing would be the only elected auditor at headquarters. All others would serve by appointment. All that was needed was to get a director approved by the president, and the control over finances would be complete.

Dennis litigates

When David Dennis was summarily rebuffed when he had earlier requested of the conference the right to appeal his case to a grievance committee, he finally filed a lawsuit against the conference and against Folkenberg, Mittleider, and Carson, on February 22, 1995. He wanted to have his day in court to tell the story of his being wrongfully accused in order to be taken out of the way due to his dutiful exposure of conference leaders' crooked use of church funds. The conference asked the court to drop the case because of "religious privilege," as they did in the 1970s with the Merikay Silver case, claiming that the church can do whatever it pleases in employer-employee relationships. The conference then began promising church workers that, having all the evidence needed to prove that Dennis' charges against leadership were false, they would provide that evidence as soon as they could. However, at the present, they informed the workers that they were constrained by the proceedings in the case and were not able to share such information as would exonerate the leaders. Of course, that evidence was never presented. They also claimed to have documentation of letters that David had allegedly written to women revealing illicit relationships, as well as evidence of outside business activities. Elder Dennis had previously called for disclosure of this evidence but it was never produced. Yet, these defaming charges continued to be repeated to church workers by certain leaders over the internet and by public speaking.

On June 28, 1995 a letter was written to the General Conference auditing staff. Conference worker, Eric A. Korff, made light of Dennis' charges and informed the staff that they should ignore them. Korff sent copies of his letter to Folkenberg and Kloosterhuis and then went to the session at Utrecht, where he was elected head of the General Conference Auditing Service. It is obvious that this could easily be read as a resounding "good-bye" to any further trouble with whistle-blowers in the auditing department.

The church spent large sums in defending this case, retaining two Washington, DC attorneys. On September 25 papers were filed to dismiss the case against the conference and against Folkenberg. In Folkenberg's paper, attempting to have his own name removed from the case, it was stated:

> Dennis' defamation claim must be dismissed in order to avoid excessive government entanglement with a religious institution. Certainly, litigation of the instant case will subject church personnel and records to subpoenas, discovery, cross-examination, and the full panoply of legal process designed to probe the minds of Church officials in the decision

to terminate Dennis' denominational employment. (Robert Folkenberg, "Memorandum of Points and Authorities," Sept. 25, 1995, p. 6)

At the conclusion of his appeal, he re-emphasized his major concern:

> Dismissal of the defamation claim must be granted in order to protect the Church from having its religious beliefs, concepts of acceptable moral conduct, and system of ecclesiastical government subjected to public scrutiny by a secular finder of fact.
>
> For all of the reasons set forth above, this Court should decline to exercise jurisdiction over the defamation claim and grant this motion to dismiss. ("Memorandum of Points and Authorities," Sept. 25, 1995, pp. 6, 7)

Forbid that the world should have a view to what are the president's and the church's "concepts of acceptable" standards of moral conduct! He reveals that saving his skin is what matters.

> Regardless of when the alleged defamation occurred, all of the allegations against Folkenberg must be dismissed because they strike at the heart of the Seventh-day Adventist Church's religious freedom. ("Memorandum of Points and Authorities," Sept. 25, 1995, pp. 3, 4)

It has been said that, if one substitutes "leadership freedom" for "religious freedom" in the above sentence, it then makes perfect sense.

In all, four motions were filed to have the case thrown out. On January 26, 1996, Judge Turner decided that the case would proceed. Unfortunately, no time limits were set and delays were the name of the game. By now, the conference had three law firms on the case, six attorneys and their staff, whose job was to keep writing petitions for postponement. One firm was employed for Folkenberg and the General Conference, another for Mittleider and Carson, and the third for Elizabeth Adels. All throughout, disinformation was being fed out that the case had been thrown out. This is all the grass roots knew at this time.

At that time it was calculated by expert opinion that it would have cost an estimated 1.5 million, *to that point*, in outside legal fees, not including the costs to church employees in time and travel. Kenneth Mittleider came out of retirement to be paid as a full time worker, along with a number of other church employees, for the sole purpose of working on this case.

Last of all, after six months, the judge gathered together all these attorneys and told them they had until the end of the year and must proceed at that time with the depositions (in which the lawyers examine, in turn, the plaintiff[s] and the defendant[s]). The time came and Dennis, at the insistence of the defendants, was deposed first, including his wife and children. Later, it would become apparent why, as they had no intent to undergo the process for themselves. It took ten days to conduct the deposition of Dennis and his family. The O. J. Simpson case took nine days! Church leaders had a professional video crew in attendance to record everything, in hope that they could find something to use against David. It is estimated that the cost of these ten days of deposition of Dennis and his family was $130,000.

Costs continued to escalate, as further stonewalling tactics were employed. Depositions of the Conference and its leaders were to be conducted next and then would come the discoveries, which allow for cross examination of the records. However, before the depositions of the Conference and its leaders were to proceed, which were to be done in early- to mid-November, petitions were filed in a desperate attempt to stop everything. Again, the "religious freedom" arguments were employed to keep the investigation of conference activities or their treatment of workers. Also, they certainly did not want to come to discoveries and have the evidence examined. They also argued that everything in question was protected as privileged information under the First Amendment. Another problem that was being faced was that Adels would not likely do well in her deposition, which was scheduled for November 7. She was having remorse over charging Dennis with wrongdoing and did not want to testify. The church leaders knew this. Her deposition could be very damaging to their case.

Conference leaders had great fear of what David Dennis might uncover in court. Being the most knowledgeable man of the financial inner workings of the church, he would know what questions to ask. He would also know how to obtain the documents needed. And most importantly, he was willing to stand for the truth, no matter what kind of a crisis it might create for the world church leaders.

In the conference's request to the court to stop the proceedings, as a "motion for summary judgment," and a "motion for protective order to stay discovery," they outlined, in a footnote of the second of two sizeable legal papers totaling fifty pages, all of the documentation that David Dennis would be calling for and *it is apparent that this was going to lay bare a long and dirty laundry list of financial misconduct, which would go on record in the courts and be seen by church members the world over.* This could not be allowed at all costs! The churchmen were terrified at the thought of being so deposed, under oath, and handing over a wide range of incriminating documents. Interestingly, we can read as one of the many concerns of the church:

> Moreover, the Court will then become entangled in doctrinal and Church policy issues such as **the proper use of tithe monies**; the propriety of cash management and investment decisions of the Church; the appropriate pay scale for Church health care workers.... ("Memorandum of Points and Authorities," Sept. 25, 1995, p. 7, emphasis added)

The *Church* is surely most concerned that it does not want the *Court* to become *entangled* in their financial information, concluding at last:

> For the foregoing reasons, the Court should grant this motion and should issue a protective order staying all discovery directed at Church Defendants until after it has considered and resolved the Church Defendants' summary judgment motion. ("Memorandum of Points and Authorities," Sept. 25, 1995, p. 7)

The judge that had previously said no to the church's desire to stop the proceedings was no longer on the case. What would the new judge, James C. Chapin decide? To the chagrin of the church officials, he proved to be reasonable and would not accept the stall tactics, turning down the General Conference motions for summary judgment and protection against discovery. By March 11, 1997, he issued a court order of the schedule to be followed. The church filed a "Motion for Reconsideration," and, on July 25, Chapin rejected that as well. The discovery phase was to be completed by September 15, 1997. The conference did not comply. They simply ignored the court order and made a bold move—an unprecedented move—filing papers on August 25, to get the case into an appeals court before it had even been heard. The appeal would essentially be to reverse Judge Chapin's denial of their Motion for Summary Judgment and his second denial to reconsider the motion. In this action, they stood to gain another twelve to eighteen months of time. It was estimated by a legal authority at that time that the church had by then spent over $2 million on their six outside lawyers, not to mention all the internal costs.

A special trials judge was assigned to the appeals court to deal with the Dennis lawsuit. After this and numerous other strange and mysterious proceedings, which we will not detail here, on December 17, 1999, almost exactly four years after the firing of David Dennis from his eighteen-year post as Director of the General Conference Auditing Service, the presidential wing on the third floor of General Conference headquarters was rejoicing and perhaps even praising God. Over the head of lower court Judge Chapin, the Maryland Court of Special Appeals ruled in their favor! The reason, at stated by Judge Louis A. Becker, was:

> The First Amendment religion clauses preclude a former minister from maintaining a defamation lawsuit against the church based on statements made by church officials regarding his moral fitness.
>
> Indeed, the Constitution bars civil courts from reviewing ecclesiastical governance and disciplinary decisions. (Reported by Vance Ferrell, Waymarks 850, "The Appeals Court Verdict," p. 1)

The reality was that Dennis was not serving in the capacity of an ordained minister, so this was a devious misrepresentation to the court and to the church by the conference.

> ... the GC attempted to demonstrate that the auditor was not really "independent," but was an elected official of the Church. We were stunned as they alleged that it was required that the chief auditor be ordained as a gospel minister! This was absolutely false—I was the first chief auditor in Church history to be ordained.... My ordination was entirely independent of my election as chief auditor. Indeed, my predecessor, Ralph Davidson, served with dignity as the chief auditor for a number of years, without the benefit of ordination. And as of this writing, the current chief auditor ... is not an ordained minister. The Church clearly was willing to risk a conviction of perjury to avoid having to answer my suit in court. (David Dennis, *Fatal Accounts*, p. 87)

This ruling by the special appeals court was a chilling development, as it ran contrary to precedent. It would seem that the church, with impunity and legal immunity, could now brazenly conduct itself any way it saw fit in the protection of self-interests to the potential destruction of its workers.

Now with $5 million dollars of church money spent on outside law firms, we remember how the December issue of the *Adventist Review* printed an article by Folkenberg in which he appealed to the church members to have forbearance and forgiveness toward church leaders and denominational entities when discovered guilty of "error, hypocrisy, incompetence, and mismanagement." Actually, he could have made the list of "indiscretions" quite a bit longer.

February 25, 1999, Dennis' attorney, Richard L. Swick, filed a *Petition for a Writ of Certiorari* with the Maryland Supreme Court. The conference responded in kind, using the same lines of objection as previously had achieved the final victory. Dennis argued that defamation of character is outside the parameters of any immunity the church might obtain on the basis of its doctrines and that to permit this case to stand as it had been left, would be to send a message to all religious organizations that they could ruin their employees at will and not be held accountable to the law. The judges in the Maryland Court agreed and May 14, 1999, overturned the decision of the Court of Special Appeals, effectively remanding the case back to the lower court for Montgomery County to hear.

Ferrell, in his classic style of bringing interesting background information to light, stated:

> It is believed that the Supreme Court recognized that there may have been a political relationship between the Maryland governor and the judges of the Special Appeals Court who had ruled against Dennis. Last August, when the governor was running a close race for re-election, **Robert Folkenberg, a principal defendant in the Dennis case, invited the governor to world headquarters for a special feast in his honor. It is the governor who directly appoints the judges who are on the Special Appeals Court bench**. (Waymarks 893, "Dennis Lawsuit Update June 1999: General Conference Stunned by Decision of Maryland Supreme Court," p. 2, emphasis added)

Yet, this is not evidence of the corruption which David Dennis could prove from other documents, if only the court would compel the Conference to turn them over. We just find it compellingly curious.

Earlier, the conference had trumpeted far and wide that the case had been thrown out. In their report, sent out December 18, 1998, "Dennis Suit Dismissed," they gleefully stated that "The Church has absolute immunity." As we could expect, they did not publish the reversal by the Supreme Court.

All of this was now taking place just as Folkenberg had left the presidency and Jan Paulsen was elected as the new president. Paulsen would not interfere with the lawsuits but let the lawyers carry on as they had been.

The crash landing of a career churchman

Without going into lengthy and complex details, it is noteworthy to insert here a brief account of the terminus of Folkenberg's first-class, high-altitude flight as the president of the Seventh-day Adventist Church.

On Saturday, January 1999, it was reported in the *Los Angeles Times* that there was a lawsuit for fraud filed (received by the conference on Dec. 28, 1998) against Robert Folkenberg for "complicated business dealings" that he had with Sacramento businessman, James Moore, claiming that he had cheated him and a charitable foundation he represented out of eight million dollars involving a major land development project in El Dorado County.

We should note that the *Times* article also reported what we earlier recounted, that Folkenberg "and another top church official had accepted tens of thousands of dollars in the form of salaries for their wives for phantom jobs" and that "the anonymous donations from a wealthy donor were funneled through the church's Worthy Student Fund, intended to be used for charitable scholarships." The *Times* went on to report, with regard to the financial malfeasance, "Folkenberg apologized to the church." The story also ran in the *Washington Post*, placed between news of United States President Bill Clinton's shenanigans with Monica Lewinsky and the illicit liaisons of an errant Baptist minister named Lyon.

The Moore lawsuit was settled out of court on Friday, Feb. 26, 1999. Folkenberg gave his written resignation on January 31 and delivered his resignation speech to the General Conference Executive Committee on March 1, 1999. He stated that a General Conference Corporation insurance policy, which carries an "officers' errors and omissions" provision, played a role in the settlement of the lawsuit. The policy would pay 80% of the legal defense of Folkenberg and of Carson, the defendant church attorney.

So, the fact of this case is that church funds are used to purchase an insurance policy which ends up being called upon to cover church leaders' outside business dealings, should they come into problems arising from "errors" or "omissions." The General Conference Corporation of the Seventh-day Adventists was also named as a defendant in this lawsuit. (This writer has a copy).

The new president, Jan Paulsen, while troubled at the unethical behavior of Adventist leadership, would speak for change, but such was seen as a "less-than-resolute" bid for reformation. No real moves were made in that direction. "But the fact remains that without his nod, Folkenberg could not have stayed on the church payroll" (*Fatal Accounts*, p. 133). Nor could he have "fully rehabilitated himself by reinventing himself as a public evangelist—for which he has a true gift" and gone on to use his political connections to operate a "high profile evangelistic ministry that brings in huge amounts of Adventist dollars each year and disbursed them throughout the world" (*Fatal Accounts*, p. 124). David would later write to Paulsen:

> Folkenberg knows, and I know, and he knows that I know just why he wanted me out of his way! You, as his successor accomplice will never allow disclosure of the total costs of this long legal battle. Certainly, you will never allow a truly independent investigation, such as the earlier promised "blue ribbon group", to report on the facts presented in my original lawsuit. You and I both know that millions in tithes (and other church offerings) were expended just to keep full disclosure out of Court, and from the knowledge of honest church members. (David Dennis to Jan Paulsen, "An Open Letter," Oct. 30, 2001)

The end of the road in the Dennis lawsuit

November 1, 1999, the judge met with eight lawyers. One was David's lawyer. The seven lawyers for the conference did their best to shock and awe the judge with overwhelming and confusing information on the history of the case in an attempt to convince the court that their clients had separation of church and state immunity. The judge recognized what was going on and, cutting through the nonsense, asked where were the documents that the conference claimed it had that would incriminate David Dennis and that they had been ordered to produce in a legal brief, *A Motion to Compel Production of Documents*. The lawyers tried to say that they had not seen that motion. However, Dennis' attorney produced a paper signed by a representative of the opposing team of lawyers, showing that they were in possession of a copy of the *Motion*.

After legal filings brought to a hearing by Judge Chapin on September 18–20, 2001, the judge handed down a partial immunity decision on December 28, 2001, in a paper entitled *Opinion and Order*. The frail and elderly judge ruled that the defendants Mittleider, Carson, and the General Conference would be immune from the defamation claim because the defamatory statements were made in the context of Dennis' termination of employment. Folkenberg and Adels were not named in the *Order*. By then, Adels had moved past her second divorce into an openly lesbian lifestyle. Strangely, on the same date, the judge ordered another hearing to determine if the defamation exceeded the bounds of religious discipline.

So GC lawyers changed tactics and informed the District Court judge, James Chapin, that as internal auditor I served in the capacity of a "highly elected official" of the Church. At this point, the intimidating retinue of attorneys seemed to break the resolve of the frail Chapin, and he agreed to conduct a "trial within a trial" on the issue of whether or not ecclesiastical issues overrode civil law, in my case. (David Dennis, *Fatal Accounts*, p. 86)

The judge passed away a few weeks later.

The glaring fact of this entire matter of the Dennis lawsuit is that, had there been any real evidence against Elder David at all, the General Conference would have welcomed a full trial and saved itself a large sum of money and time, instead of robbing from the resources needed for conducting the mission of preaching the gospel. Costs to the General Conference in legal bills were now well in excess of $7 million.

> Tithe is supposedly used only to compensate those engaged in Gospel ministry and evangelistic outreach, but the Church also allows it to be used to pay for janitorial services of the various conference offices and to subsidize church school teachers' salaries. **And millions in unaccounted-for tithe dollars are invested in prolonged and unproductive lawsuits.** (*Fatal Accounts*, p. 92, emphasis added)

In spite of years in court, and a startling decision in our favor by the highest court in the State of Maryland, we were never able to proceed to a jury trial. **With the help of millions of tithe dollars** the GC repeatedly delayed the judicial process and blocked the discovery phase to keep from us documents we had requested showing to some degree the depth of corruption within the leadership of our church. ("An Open Letter," David Dennis to Jan Paulsen, Oct. 30, 2001, emphasis added)

How does it happen that **the expenditure of millions in tithe dollars for prolonged litigation** is approved? Actually, such approval comes from a very tight circle of administrators. Appropriate committees, such as the General Conference Executive Committee, are never consulted and there is no recorded committee action authorizing massive outlays for litigation. Furthermore, nothing about these vast expenditures in tithe dollars is ever reported in denomination-controlled publications. Decisions of this nature are typically made by only two or three officers, in counsel with highly compensated GC-employed attorneys. They then engage prestigious law firms who, with carte blanche, charge unimaginably large sums.... (*Fatal Accounts*, p. 93, emphasis added)

While we are citing Elder Dennis on the use of the tithes for litigation, it would be well to examine further light from this authority on the use of tithes in the denomination. We must be wise about this. We should not be deceived in any way regarding the appropriation of the monies that are turned over for the Lord's work by members acting in good faith that biblical specifications are followed:

But let's look again at the Church's policy on tithe—an area where as an auditor I have a great deal of experience. Policy specifically prohibits use of tithe for teachers' salaries and capital expenditures. But during the past 25 years, by implementing fund accounting principles, it was disclosed that the Church has been circumventing policy. For example, most funds used for everyday overseas mission work come from tithe, but are not restricted to direct support of the ministry. It poses an embarrassing conundrum, and the policy either needs to be changed or accounting transactions altered. Typically, these matters are ignored as long as possible. But eventually, perhaps, committees will be set up to study the situation and make recommendations. (David Dennis, *Fatal Accounts*, p. 94)

An additional citation is warranted at this point, not of David Dennis, but of a letter of response written by Robert W. Nixon, Associate General Counsel of the General Conference, used in a trademark lawsuit mediation by the "World Intellectual Property Organization Arbitration and Mediation Center, Case No. D2006-0642, between the General Conference and the "Creation 7th-Day-Adventist Church.org" to inform that:

In contradiction to Complainant church's [GC] stated purpose of "the tithing plan", Complainant's church allocated "sacred funds" for prosecuting trademark infringement cases as evidenced by Robert W. Nixon (Associate General Counsel of the General Conference) in his letter dated April 10, 1989: **"Second, you inquired whether tithe is used to pay church litigation. The treasury informs me that all litigation is paid from the annual appropriation made at the Annual Council, and that appropriation comes from tithe."** (WIPO Response, p. 9, available at http://1ref.us/ii, accessed 10/14/16, emphasis added)

At last, David found himself all washed up and was forced to throw in the towel, withdraw the suit. Being told that the appeal could have languished yet for years, he could not go on, for funds were depleted. Jan Paulsen refused a request by church members to have David's allegations investigated by an independent committee and reported back to the church, as had been promised to the church years earlier by Folkenberg when the Dennis suit was being initiated. Paulsen said that such a review would tend to be only a negative step in that it would consume resources of time and money to yield information that is already in the public domain. We should just move past it, forget about it, and get on with the work was the essence of the leader's response.

In 2009, Dennis would write a chilling summation, which provides a prophetic insight that has a direct bearing on what is coming to people in America and the world over, in the name of "ecclesiastical privilege":

It had been Charlotte's and my hope and prayer that the litigation we brought would help bring change in the Church. But the judicial system in America is also broken. I remember the rather personal words of Judge Turner, who first examined my case. He asked the Church attorneys point blank, "If the General Conference had castrated Mr. Dennis for his offenses, would you still try to hide behind First Amendment privilege to avoid paying him damages?"

They answered, "No." But I know that even if the Church had arranged to have me murdered, it still would have argued that it had a First Amendment privilege to do so, in the pursuit of its autonomous practice of religion.

I continue to ask, "How is it possible to commit crimes in the name of religious freedom, without being held accountable? How can an errant Church continue to enjoy tax-exempt status?" These questions apply to all churches.

As things stand today, virtually all [every] Adventist Church employee receives some sort of credential, and by showing these to a court they can turn almost any complaint against them into an "ecclesiastical matter." Yet the Church has the liberty to bring legal actions at any time against anyone it chooses, including its own members. (David Dennis, *Fatal Accounts*, p. 134)

Dave was guilty of no crime other than trying to preserve the fiscal integrity of the Church's accounts. As a faithful servant of the Church, he served it well for nearly 35 years. A great injustice was done him, and he deserves an apology from current Church leadership. Whether an apology comes or not, Dave soldiers on as a faithful servant, active in his local Adventist congregation and in lockstep with his Master, the Lord Jesus Christ. (William H. Shea, M. D., Ph. D., Associate Director (retired), Biblical Research Institute, General Conference of SDA, in *Fatal Accounts*, p. v,)

So we press on. Scars remain from the hurtfulness of those who still feel that they benefit the cause of Adventism by vilifying us. The Church will ultimately believe what it chooses, but the fact remains that no one involved in my destruction has yet sought my forgiveness, though as far as possible I have forgiven them. (David Dennis, *Fatal Accounts*, p. 136)

Charlotte's life and mine revolve around our little Maryland church, between the shadows of the General Conference and the Review & Herald Publishing Association, where I serve as an elder and Charlotte is head deaconess and music coordinator. We give our tithes and offerings, **though not into coffers that could finance litigation or character assassination**. (David Dennis, *Fatal Accounts*, p. 128, emphasis added)

Agreeing with Elder Dennis, I encourage every reader to turn the tithes and offerings over to the men and women who are actually doing the work of the third angel's message in this time of the rise of the fourth angel as it swells to the loud cry or which may even now, at time of reading, be sounding as the loud cry. The storehouse of God is not a den of corruption, it is where the message of Christ's righteousness is sounding.

Kingly Rule Solidifies Further: Utrecht Consolidation of Power 1995

The Adventist Church has grown large, using a hierarchical organizational style with considerable power at the top, consisting of the president, his underlings, and the influential union presidents. Neal Wilson perfected this system, and came to believe that he possessed the kind of administrative genius that deserved a strengthened presidential position. He left this legacy of power to his successor, Robert Folkenberg. (David Dennis, *Fatal Accounts*, p. 67)

As it now is, administration is accountable to administration—a totally unacceptable situation....

It takes no prophetic gift to predict that increased persecution of and strictures upon faithful believers will be the order of the day. (Colin Standish, *Another Journey to Utrecht*, p. 4)

William G. Johnsson, editor of the *Adventist Review*, wrote of General Conference President Robert S. Folkenberg and the changes he brought:

His efforts to reorganize the General Conference headquarters and the church worldwide brought the most far-reaching structural recommendations since 1901.... All change is difficult. The fact of change and the pace of change during the past five years have upset some Adventists.... (William G. Johnsson, "President of Change," *Adventist Review*, July 2, 1995, p. 3)

Vance Ferrell writes in a tract series, "The Utrecht Session," p. 8, regarding what was taking place: "Massive changes were placed before the delegates to enact—which would dramatically change the way the church was governed! What would all these cumulative changes produce? some kind of monster kingship?"

Deceptive maneuvering was employed to bring in far reaching changes that would shift power further upward and especially consolidate power in the hands of one man, the president. Susan Sickler, a member of a commission appointed by the General Conference in 1991 to examine ways of improving church government, reported that they had examined the proposed governing changes and rejected them. Yet, those items were then falsely presented by Robert Folkenberg to the 1994 Annual Council for their approval, as having been "approved" by that commission. These were fifty Church Manual changes and seventy-two Constitution and Bylaws changes. One delegate, Alvin Kibble, commented, "I cannot imagine a constitutional revision of some seventy-two items being suggested to the Constitution of the United States of America! That would represent a rewriting of the Constitution!"

To open up the session, B. B. Beach introduced several non-Adventist dignitaries. One of them, a Catholic Bishop, stood to offer his blessing upon the congregation. Then, Robert Folkenberg got up and gave a flashy multi-media presentation. Even as it was his intent to push through constitutional changes that would give him immense control at world headquarters, assured the people: "We come as more than 2,600 delegates. We have no king. We have no small group of men who rule over us." The General Conference treasurer's office was billed $45,000 for that highly produced sermon.

The changes to come would include but were not limited to:

- Reduce the number of the General Conference committee by nearly one-third

- Executive committee quorum reduced to 15

- Decrease the number of participants in the decision making process at the Annual and Spring Councils, which govern the church between sessions

- Cap the number of delegates at 2,000 instead of 2,650

- Reduce the number of personnel at the division level also

- General Conference departmental leaders no longer have a vote *on* the General Conference committee and barred from being on the committee

- All but General Conference auditors would no longer be elected but appointed by those being audited

- The General Conference president is now to be designated as "First Officer of the General Conference"

- The same power consolidated in the top three of the General Conference—the president, secretary and treasurer—would be given to the three heads of each division; thirty men would run the entire church with absolute authority

- The treasurer and secretary of the General Conference may not bring anything to the General Conference committee until they have first consulted with the president regarding the matter

- Division departmental leaders would be appointed not elected

- Number of laypersons allowed as members of the General Conference committee reduced from 50% to approximately 17%

- Conference/mission presidents will only have voting rights at the councils—when the councils are held within their territory; this skews the vote in favor of North American conference presidents in eight of every ten council meetings

- Session delegates will be chosen by division leadership, instead of by unions. Division officers are closely obligated to the General Conference president for their positions

- Local church boards have greater power at the local level to block membership actions; they may also be able to obtain a two-year term

- Local church members can be disciplined for a longer period of time.

These are just some of the high points. Not listed are actions which did not make it to the General Conference session, which were approved at the 1994 Annual Council, such as the following:

- All officers of higher organizations are automatically *ex officio* members, with full voting rights, of the next lower organization

- Every lower level officer must be approved at the time of his appointment, by the leaders of the next higher level.

There were also parliamentary rule changes. Why this is important is because, by manipulating the rules that govern meetings, a small group of professional committee men can control a large voting constituency, making a de facto oligarchy out of a democracy. The name of the game is the "rules of order." These necessary procedural forms are relatively standardized in the corporate world. However, there are exceptions. The Roman Catholic Church has its own devious set of rules, which it developed in the Dark Ages! Now the Seventh-day Adventist Church has also its own unique set of rules. Two key rule changes look like this:

- All nominations for office or membership on an executive committee—at any level in the church—must be made by a nominating committee. They cannot be made by the delegates, as a whole, or by the membership (or constituency) of the church

- Only one name can be presented to the floor by a nominating committee for each position to be filled.

This is the way that dictators are appointed to office. When only one name is submitted, it is no longer a democratic process—it is a rubberstamp action.

It is important to know how determined was the movement to get changes implemented without arousing equally determined opposition. In the 1995 session, delegate Alvin Kibble happened to be at the microphone at the right time to be able to legally bring a new item on the table when a previous agenda item had just closed. He was concerned about the overall implications of the many changes that were being proposed and voted in, so he moved "that legal counsel provide for this body [*the delegates*] a summation of the total effect of these actions upon the historical privileges and powers of the session when it is seated...." The General Conference in session is the highest authority in the church, and this was a call to determine if the proposed changes would have any corrosive effect on this power. Immediately Chairman K. J. Mittleider said, "I believe your motion would be out of order," when it was actually not. He said that they needed to continue taking things in little bites, "one piece at a time" and that they had not "prepared anyone to give a legal summation." The intent was clear: these men were studiously avoiding any such thing as legal counsel for the delegation! They did not want any "big picture" to be presented nor had they any intent of setting anyone, such as they had not "prepared," to perform such a task. The fact is, Athal Tolhurst was often present on the platform. He was the man who had "crafted" the language of the proposals and was introduced as a man who was "intimately acquainted with how all these policies interact" and that they "touch each other in many ways." So by saying that, they had not prepared anyone for this task means one of three things: (1) he was not previously groomed to make such a presentation in a smart political fashion; (2) he was not the expert that he was represented as being; or (3) there was strong incentive for preventing any such overview to be presented.

Coming back to Chairman Mittleider's side-stepping, Kibble repeated his concern and emphasized, "I believe it would be fair to ask for a legal opinion." Mittleider resolutely responded, "Thank you very much. We're going to proceed ..." and they carried on with other business. The next man at the microphone was Edward Reid, and he made a similar motion but was cut short by Calvin Rock, the Chairman of the Constitution and Bylaws Committee, who started the process of presenting the other matters of the seventy-two proposed changes. The call for an analysis by legal counsel for the education of the delegates by two men, using proper legal procedure, was illegally sidestepped and flat-out refused. As one attendee later stated, "When the delegates attempted to find the bigger picture, they were told, by the various chairmen, to concentrate only on the issues at hand."

As we can see from all of this, in summary, the delegates attending the Utrecht Session were never presented with the full picture. If they had a wider view, they would have been able to more clearly see that a great shift in power and authority had been carefully planned in advance and was being systematically carried out.

Among the mechanisms employed, we find that session business meetings were adjourned early, new items of business were ignored, motions for clarification were ignored, and items sent back to committee for change were at times returned with almost no change.

The changes bestow more power to the higher organizations over the lower. Now also, the General Conference president will have immense power on all levels. Either directly or indirectly through subordinates, he will be able to exercise far more control over subsidiary workers and organizations than any president in the history of the denomination.

Because of the changes, the General Conference will henceforth control the selection of an astonishing seventy-four percent of the total number of delegates to each future session. The General Conference executive committee, which henceforth can meet with a quorum of as few as fifteen members has authority to make drastic decisions and changes in the denomination, yet most of its members are obligated to please the General Conference president.

On the local conference or mission level, the changes not only add union representatives to their business and constituency meetings but division and General Conference representatives are added as well.

The good work accomplished, under the direction of Ellen White, at the 1901 General Conference Session—has effectively been wiped out. We have returned to a "kingly power," the very thing she wanted to eliminate from the church.

Russell Standish, in his summary report, noted:

> No one, *not one*, inquired on any issue that was raised, "Is there a word from the Lord?" One faithful delegate, pointing to the general confusion that was prevailing, pled for a season of prayer for divine guidance. His plea was totally ignored. Had God's wisdom been sought, a large number of items contrary to the plainest testimony of Inspiration would never have appeared upon the agenda. (*Another Journey to Utrecht*, p. 1)

Remember how we quoted earlier that the men in power—

> have been informed that they were out of place and **in error in representing the voice of the General Conference president as being the voice of God. For many years it has not been thus, and it is not thus now; nor will it ever be thus again, unless there is a thorough reformation**. (Ms. 124, 1901, in *Manuscript Releases*, vol. 17, p. 240, emphasis added)

What happened to the "thorough reformation?" Is there anyone that can show where it occurred in Seventh-day Adventist church history?

Walter Martin Again

Switching topics, we rewind again to an earlier point on the fourth generation timeline, to the spring of 1985, when the sixth edition of Walter Martin's *Kingdom of the Cults* was published. Almost 17% of this 544-page book was devoted to Adventism. His careful comments seemed to carry a veiled warning. Remember, this is the man whose opinions had proven to carry so much weight with the Seventh-day Adventist leadership from the start of their interactions with him. Martin wrote:

> I must, for the time being, stand behind my original evaluation of Seventh-day Adventism as presented comprehensively in my first book on the subject and later in this volume. Only events not yet unfolded, but within the knowledge of the Lord Himself, **will determine whether my evaluation will need to be revised in the future**. It is my prayer that the aberrational currents within contemporary Adventism will not prevail and that Adventism will continue to be a Christian and Evangelical, albeit unique, Christian denomination. (*The Kingdom of the Cults*, p. 410, emphasis added)

Martin spoke of the tremendous amount of turbulence seen in the denomination over the previous ten years and of the firings that had taken place because of financial misconduct. He also demonstrated serious concern for the doctrinal schism that had developed (which he had something to do with bringing in) between the evangelical element and "those members and leaders who, because of their emphasis on works-righteousness, legalism, and the prophetic status accorded to founder Ellen G. White, may well move the denomination over time outside of the Evangelical camp and perhaps even into actual cultism" (*The Kingdom of the Cults*, p. 410).

Martin asked Adventists if they still stood behind *Questions on Doctrine* and a letter of reply from the vice-president, W. Richard Lesher, soothed Martin in the affirmative, telling him that in fact, the majority of Seventh-day Adventists are on board that ship. This gave him the assurance needed to state that the "concept taught for more than a century by Seventh-day Adventists—that a work of atonement is going on now in the heavenly sanctuary—'has been repudiated by the Seventh-day Adventist denomination'" (Martin, cited in *Hindsight*, p. 249).

We should understand that supporting *Questions on Doctrine* leaves the Adventist apologist defenseless against the charges of men such as Walter Martin. This was well demonstrated in the examination conducted by Walter Martin of the beliefs of Adventism, on the "John Ankerberg Show," a popular evangelical television talk show, which took place right after the release of Martin's sixth edition of *Kingdom of the Cults*. (At time of writing, this episode of the show is available on the internet, on YouTube, available at http://1ref.us/ij, accessed 12/9/16.) There, Dr. William G. Johnsson, then editor of the *Review*, was mercilessly put on the spot regarding Ellen White, the sanctuary doctrine and the investigative judgment, Desmond Ford, and so on. Later, as questions were opened up from the floor, one identifying himself as an Adventist minister asked of what value was the 1844 message and urged that Adventists should drop it altogether. Such a sentiment underscores the sad fact that few Adventists have a meaningful concept of fundamental Adventism as it is in the third angel's message.

In the winter of 1989, two meetings were held at Loma Linda's Campus Hill Church in which Walter Martin and his associate Ken Samples were invited to speak with Seventh-day Adventists. This was to be Adventism's last encounter with the man. The first meeting invited local Seventh-day Adventist pastors in for dialogue, while the second invited the religion faculty. Martin recounted some items of history from his perspective as the last surviving participant in the dialogues of the 1950s. He spoke that the greatest joy of his life was bringing Adventism into the brotherhood of evangelical Christianity.

Martin related a meeting that was held with some Adventist theologians, Dr. Heppenstall and Dr. Murdoch, in which it was admitted that Christ went into the most holy place at His ascension. Going further, he said, "Now you can read Desmond Ford on this in great detail. He's probably one of your most articulate, and surely one of your most brilliant men I've met on general Adventism and on general theology. I think you'll find that he's done a very commendable job of exegeting [sic] this as well, but that was admitted at that time [in the 1950s]" (*Hindsight*, p. 255).

There were no objections from Seventh-day Adventist leaders to Martin's ongoing assertions against the 1844 doctrine. Martin felt Ford was a modern-day Martin Luther in Adventism, and, if any young ministers would follow suit and take the same stand, that it would be the right thing to do. He went on to explain that he was not against the law and that faith does not negate the law. However, he said that "the only horrible part about it is, you can't keep it" (cited in *Hindsight*, p. 257). Five months later, Martin died of a heart attack.

Martin did not agree with any of the unique teachings of Adventism but was willing to overlook all of them, even admitting to a partially inspired prophet (sometimes she was, sometimes she wasn't), but the two non-negotiables, to keep us from being esteemed a cult were; (1) the finished atonement at the cross and; (2) the sinless human nature of Christ. Satan himself is satisfied for us to adopt these two foundation teachings of Catholicism and Calvinism. The rest will take care of itself.

Ecumenism Ascending: Faces to the Rising Sun

> When those who are uniting with the world, yet claiming great purity, plead for union with those who have ever been the opposers of the cause of truth, we should fear and shun them as decidedly as did Nehemiah. Such counsel is prompted by the enemy of all good. It is the speech of timeservers, and should be resisted as resolutely today as then. Whatever influence would tend to unsettle the faith of God's people in His guiding power, should be steadfastly withstood. (*Prophets and Kings*, p. 660)

> And he brought me into the inner court of the LORD's house, and, behold, at the door of the temple of the LORD, between the porch and the altar, *were* about five and twenty men, with their backs toward the temple of the LORD, and their faces toward the east; and they worshipped the sun toward the east. (Ezek. 8:16)

> And in that day seven women shall take hold of one man, saying, We will eat our own bread, and wear our own apparel: only let us be called by thy name, to take away our reproach. (Isa. 4:1)

Adventist leaders sometimes sit not only as members but as the chairpersons on local ministerial associations, which have been verified as being direct members of national ecumenical councils. It is therefore obvious that by this action, leaders are actively taking part in the overall program and purpose of the World Council of Churches.

The prevailing evangelical and ecumenical spirit that has developed in Seventh-day Adventism, especially since the Evangelical Conferences, has become manifest in so many ways, not only by involvement in the local ecumenical bodies, but in the joint fellowship of pulpit exchanges; joint activities in community services, support in evangelistic outreaches such as Billy Graham Evangelistic Association Crusades, joining up in or hosting ecumenical Easter Sunrise services, signing agreements with other churches, joining national and international bodies with irregular status to avoid the political fallout, etc.

All of the ecumenical trend, this rubbing shoulders and welcoming one another into fellowship and joint worship, is incongruent with the outcome that is prophesied:

When we reach the standard that the Lord would have us reach, worldlings will regard Seventh-day Adventists as odd, singular, strait-laced extremists. (*Fundamentals of Christian Education*, p. 289, emphasis added)

Bear in mind that when we read "worldlings," we read of those in "churches."

We are not to confederate with **worldlings**, lest we become imbued with their spirit, lest our spiritual discernment become confused and we view those who have the truth and bear the message of the Lord from the standpoint of the **professed Christian churches**. (Lt. 86a, 1893, in *Last Day Events*, pp. 84, 85, emphasis added)

From time to time, we are asked whether the Seventh-day Adventist denomination is a member of the World Council of Churches or any of its branches. It is difficult to answer this in brief reply, since our church affiliation with the ecumenical movement is somewhat complicated....

Please understand that many of our leaders probably have been well-meaning in their intentions. However, the end result is not what we are counseled in the Spirit of Prophecy to have. We are playing with ecumenical fire, and it is already damaging us. We should have no part with the daughters of Babylon; doing so requires compromise on our part....

Because of liberalization in the Roman Catholic Church (resulting from Vatican II), in 1966 the Roman Catholic Church sought admission to the WCC on observer status. The same year, only one other denomination also did so: the Seventh-day Adventist Church. Since then, a limited number of others have entered on this basis. Those denominations which do so have some type of official doctrinal bias against full membership, so they enter the organization quietly through a side door—so their members will not be upset....

On the NCC level (remember, "NCC" always refers to the national council in the U.S.), in order to obtain quasi-membership, the General Conference arranged back in the late 1950s for two or three of our workers to be placed as *"personal representatives"* on some of its committees as voting members. These men are generally General Conference staff members or Adventist college or university Bible teachers. This fiction (that they are personally representing themselves) enables the General Conference to have representatives at the NCC ... Replies to inquiries from the NCC indicate that they thereby recognize our denomination as an "associate" or "cooperating" member of the NCC. Our relationship with the WCC also involves "personal representatives." (Vance Ferrell, *Seventh-day Adventist/Vatican Ecumenical Involvement*, pp. 17, 18)

What of the matter of friendship with the world? What is it? James says that it is "enmity with God" (James 4:4). Adventists have traditionally maintained a proper distinction from the Sunday-keeping world, not to be isolationist or exclusive, but to preserve their calling to sound the third angel's message without compromise.

We must be friendly and loving, without attempting to enter into any sort of relationship that would make us *unequally yoked with unbelievers*. For too long now, the idea that the mainstream Christian assembly can be called the body of Christ has been acceptable in the thinking of mainstream Adventism. That the churches became fallen Babylon when they refused to enter into His rest and receive power to obey all of the commandments of God has melted away from the consciousness of the people as leadership has drifted. Those churches fell away in *unbelief* and heaven has a message for the individuals over there: "Come out of her, my people."

It was the preaching of the first, second, and third angels' messages which separated the people of God from the fallen churches.

By the mighty cleaver of truth, the messages of the first, second, and third angels, He has separated them from the churches and from the world to bring them into a sacred nearness to Himself. (*Testimonies for the Church*, vol. 5, p. 455)

If this was the effect of the first three angels, what must the effect be of the mighty angel who fills the *whole* earth with his glory? What must be the effect of this angel who declares in clarion tones the fall of Babylon Will it close the gulf between Adventism and Babylon? *Never!* It can only widen it further! (*The Destiny of a Movement*, pp. 308, 309)

Any connection with infidels and unbelievers which would identify us with them is forbidden by the word. We are to come out from them and be separate. In no case are we to link ourselves with them in their plans or work. (Lt. 95, 1899, in *Fundamentals of Christian Education*, p. 482)

In *Movement of Destiny* (*MOD*), his sequel to *QOD* [*Questions on Doctrine*] for Adventist readership, Froom explained that the "separative" doctrines were a "distinct handicap" of early Adventists. These doctrines made Adventists different and distanced them from evangelicals. (Fernando Canale, "A Close Look at the Adventist Mind," *Perspective Digest*, vol. 17, no. 4, available at http://1ref.us/ik, accessed 12/8/16)

Froom's key role in the Evangelical Conferences demonstrated that was decidedly against any such "distancing." Such has been the general tenor of Seventh-day Adventist leadership since those days with but few words of caution in the church publications or from the high offices and lecture halls of church institutions.

Most independent students of Adventism are aware of former President Neal Wilson's statement in court, minus the italicized part of the statement:

Although it is true that there was a period in the life of the Seventh-day Adventist Church when the denomination took a distinctly anti-Roman Catholic viewpoint, and the term "hierarchy" was used in a pejorative sense to refer to the papal form of church governance, that attitude on the church's part was nothing more than a manifestation of widespread anti-popery among conservative protestant denominations in the early part of this century and the latter part of the last, and which has **now been consigned to the historical trash heap** so far as the Seventh-day Adventist Church is concerned. (EEOC vs PPPA Civ #74-2025 CBR, Reply Brief for Defendants, p. 41, emphasis added)

Let us ever bear in mind the warning:

It is a backsliding church that lessens the distance between itself and the Papacy. (*Signs of the Times*, Feb. 19, 1894)

As the subject of Adventist involvements in the greater Christendom is discussed with leadership, the oft-repeated mantra is that the church must make itself known, as there are so few relative to the population who know who we are. There so much angst over this point that it has conveyed insecurity and inferiority issues.

Why is it so important that the world "knows who *we* are?" This question always strikes me as hearkening back to Babel, where those rebels congregated who sought to build a great city with a tower to make a name for themselves (Gen. 11:4). It is said that the concern is for effective outreach, but the fact is that the mainstream church has shied away from giving the straight messages of angels one, two, and three because they make Adventism stand out as peculiar in doctrine, and, in today's anti-hate speech environment and legislative movements, they are outright *politically incorrect*. What generally trends in Adventist associations with non-Adventists is to focus upon finding commonalities *with them* rather than seeking ways of bringing our distinctive message *to them*.

I have seen that the Seventh-day Adventist Church's methods of "getting known" are not in harmony with inspired counsel and directives. There is constant admonishment to tread ever so carefully when talking about other churches and to always speak positively or remain neutral in speech. These counsels are nothing but a conditioning of minds that will prepare the way for the infiltration of the spirit of antichrist. These sayings are misguided and are a "cloak of false charity" (see *Prophets and Kings*, p. 675, below). We need to be unashamed in our preaching about what is the true church, all the while prefacing our statements with the truth that God's people are yet to be found within all communions that call themselves Christian and even those that are non-Christian. After we have worked with them, however, they must not be allowed to go away feeling comfortable in remaining in these bodies. That is why Adventism was raised up: to *call them out*!

I ever maintain that, if the church would loudly preach the gospel in the context of its historic and troubling distinctives, decrying and exposing the sins and errors of Babylon as depicted by the angel of Revelation 18, it would not be able to continue in the alliances that have been formed with the world and with false Christianity at all levels of church organization.

The world is against us, the popular churches are against us, [this can only be said of *True* Adventism, not today's *Nominal* Adventism] the laws of the land will soon be against us.... God has committed to us the special truths for this time to make known to the world. The last message of mercy is now going forth. We are dealing with men and women who are judgment bound. (*Testimonies for the Church*, vol. 5, p. 236)

Now and ever we are to stand as a distinct and peculiar people, free from all worldly policy, unembarrassed by confederating with those who have not wisdom to discern God's claims so plainly set forth in His law. (Lt. 128, 1902, in *Testimonies for the Church*, vol. 7, pp. 106, 107)

Rather than Adventists getting known by the world, is it not more important that the world knows who *God* is? The preaching of the message of God's character and the living of it in righteousness, under the New Covenant promise, will lighten the whole earth with His glory, by the ministration of the fourth angel. This will be done under the outpouring of the Holy Spirit in the latter rain, which is the power source that drives the final call of the three angels and gets the work done.

Both the indwelling of the living Christ in His people *and* the incontrovertible truths that they preach will arouse the unholy wrath of both worldlings and false Christianity. There will be no "conversations" or "dialogue" or "presenting a united witness to the world of the Savior's love." These kinds of words and phrases are a smokescreen to cover the truth of what is really happening. This leads to a major concern.

Former General Conference president, Jan Paulsen, wrote an article in the June 2007 issue of *Adventist World*, entitled "Telling the World Who We Are." In this article, there are the same old arguments presented to assuage the members' concerns about the church's ecumenism, stating that it is desirable to enter into "dialogues," "conversations," and "cooperative relationships" to "remove misunderstandings and accompanying prejudices." (Would that not be misunderstandings and prejudices, for instance, regarding our believing in some kind of judgment taking place in the heavenly sanctuary at this time or that Christ came in sinful flesh and overcame so that we can live above sin?)

Secondly, it is asserted that there is always "much we can learn" from these thoughtful conversations with others. This is also a well-worn phrase that has never made much sense to me. True Adventism has a complete gospel as no other. All we learn from the others is how to water down the gospel until we are preaching an incomplete gospel or "another gospel" that makes us sound like them.

Dr. Paulsen, in his short article of ten paragraphs, used the word "conversations," or a form of it, no less than fifteen times. He tried very hard to downplay the ecumenism. It brings to mind the typical image of a concerned father admonishing his daughter about spending far too much time on the phone with the bad boy across town and hearing her retort that there is nothing going on, they are friends from school, "just having conversation."

The Ecumenists themselves would not be fooled so easily. They understand that "dialogue" is intended to create "meeting," "mutual understanding, respect and trust," and that it is "a medium of authentic witness" (William E. Swing, *The Coming United Religions*, p. 57).

"Meeting" means "uniting." Do not be tricked by any of this language. "Trust"? Upon what biblical or prophetic basis are we to "trust" Babylon? My understanding is that the great harlot woman of Revelation will ride the beast. I respect God and His word of Truth, while having no respect for error and lies. How is dialogue a "medium of authentic witness?" Is this talking about presenting a unified front to the world, when it is ultimately shown that, as "God" brings us together, we finally have the True Witness? Upon whose platform do we unite? Can we "unite" upon only those points wherein we agree? This is nonsense, for it would not truly be unity, would it? Not while keeping contradictory beliefs in the closet, for they could not be true beliefs if devoid of their corresponding praxis. These baffling words are typical of "ecumenispeak," if I may coin a term, made to sound lofty and important to the common person while bypassing the important questions that a critically thinking person might have.

In the well-known words of Dr. Hans Küng, Roman Catholic Theologian of Germany, ecumenispeak promotes the understanding that there is "no peace among the nations without peace among the religions; no peace among the religions without dialogue between the religions...."

All this "dialogue"—what a "chatty" church ours has become! There is much talk about peace and service to humanity and making a better world through a united presentation of Christian witness. Again, whose platform should we stand upon? Here is a hint: Who is it that lays claim to spiritual "primacy" in the world? Make no mistake—there will be no peace but that which is imposed by the presently coalescing and imminent consolidation of the iron-fisted power of the papacy, in a neo-Pax Romana. It may already be a reality as you are reading this book!

The July 2007 document issued by the old offices (of the Inquisition) of former Pope Benedict XVI at the "Congregation for the Doctrine of the Faith," which restated church teaching on relations with other Christians, shows that Benedict was firmly committed to ecumenical dialogue, and the present Pope Francis is no different.

A Vatican-issued commentary on this document states:

> However, if such dialogue is to be truly constructive, it must involve not just the mutual openness of the participants but also fidelity to the identity of the Catholic faith.... (Congregation for the Doctrine of the Faith, "Commentary on the Document 'Responses to Some Questions Regarding Certain Aspects of the Doctrine on the Church,'" available at http://1ref.us/il, accessed 10/14/16)

Let the point sink in: "dialogue" has one primary objective as far as Rome is concerned, and this is *the ultimate securing of assent to the primacy of the pope*. In his article analyzing the Vatican release of July 10, 2007, Dr. Samuele Bacchiocchi concurred with this point in saying that the pope—

> knows that discussions with other Churches will make no progress on the basis of his exclusivistic claim of the Catholic Church. So the only conclusion that can be drawn is that he has no interest in pursuing ecumenism. The ongoing dialogue that he is promoting with all the major denominations, including the Seventh-day Adventist Church, is designed to persuade other Christians to become Roman Catholics. Evidently this is the pope's approach to other Churches, which is not ecumenism, but proselytism.
>
> Furthermore, the Vatican dialogue with various Protestant Churches is designed to soften their anti-Catholic teachings. This is particularly true of the Seventh-day Adventist Church which has long recognized the prophetic role of the Papacy in leading many Christians into apostasy. Our prophetic calling is to invite people in every nation to come out of the of the Babylonian false worship promoted especially by the papacy. (*ENDTIME ISSUES No. 177*, "Is the Catholic Church the Only True Church?")

The papacy's ecumenism is by its very nature, proselytizing in that it is designed to bring all under the umbrella of the final one world order of the image to the beast to cause all of the world to wonder after the beast. The only foundation for unity other than Christ is to yield to the political-religious power that has established its supremacy in the earth—the papacy. Historically, Adventists have understood this clearly. (See the statement below from *The Seventh-day Adventist Bible Commentary*, vol. 10, pp. 410, 411.)

Let us sharpen our focus a bit by getting back to Jan Paulsen's article. Pastor Paulsen reassured the church: "We do not seek union of any sort—we have not joined the ecumenical movement and will not. Our mission is one that cannot be diluted or restricted by ecumenical alliances." Yet, He immediately he goes on to say: "During the course of a conversation we may explore areas of possible joint endeavor...."

George Orwell says that holding conflicting views in one's mind and believing both is called "doublethink." There is a lot of this going on in this era of *Hegelianism*, or bringing conflicting sides into proximity, shaking them up together and out of the ensuing reactions forming a synthetic view that serves the controlling purposes of the powerful of the earth (who are only puppets of the Archrebel, fallen Lucifer).

It is simply not true to say that we are neither united nor uniting with the world. We will shortly introduce just a few examples out of hundreds that could be given to prove this point and show how the Luciferian agenda, in its particular manifestation of the ecumenical movements of recent decades, has indeed entered Adventism. These things must be exposed to arouse those who would be concerned if only they knew.

> In the work of reform to be carried forward today, there is need of men who, like Ezra and Nehemiah, will not palliate or excuse sin, nor shrink from vindicating the honor of God. Those upon whom rests the burden of this work will not hold their peace when wrong is done, neither will they cover evil with a cloak of false charity. They will remember that God is no respecter of persons, and that severity to a few may prove mercy to many. They will remember also that in the one who rebukes evil the spirit of Christ should ever be revealed. (*Prophets and Kings*, p. 675)

Our prophet told us that our greatest danger would be from inside the church:

> We have far more to fear from within than from without. The hindrances to strength and success are far greater from the church itself than from the world.... how often have the professed advocates of the truth proved the greatest obstacle to its advancement! The unbelief indulged, the doubts expressed, the darkness cherished, encourage the presence of evil angels, and open the way for the accomplishment of Satan's devices. (*Review and Herald*, March 22, 1887)

The work which the church has failed to do in a time of peace and prosperity she will have to do in a terrible crisis under most discouraging, forbidding circumstances. The warnings that worldly conformity has silenced or withheld must be given under the fiercest opposition from enemies of the faith. And at that time the superficial, conservative class, [*this is not speaking about the politically or theologically conservative class but those who tend to edit distinctive and cutting truth out of the message*] whose influence has steadily retarded the progress of the work, will renounce the faith and take their stand with its avowed enemies, toward whom their sympathies have long been tending. These apostates will then manifest the most bitter enmity, doing all in their power to oppress and malign their former brethren and to excite indignation against them.... (*Testimonies for the Church*, vol. 5, p. 463)

Our worst enemies are now among us, speaking smooth things and, unless we are taking up the opportunities and privileges we now have to become educated and grounded in the spirit of truth and in the development of our characters, we shall not stand in the days ahead.

It is time to examine some of the evidences: Are we really "not seeking union of any sort"—have we really "not joined the ecumenical movement", as Paulsen claimed? We will cover some smaller examples and some of the bigger stories alongside, just as a sampling of selections of literally hundreds of items that we could bring in for exposition.

1. Canadian Foodgrains Bank as an ecumenical organization
On page 8 of the 2007 issue of a local Canadian Seventh-day Adventist Church paper, *Red Deer Church News*, was found a local report by ADRA (the Adventist Development and Relief Agency):

Established in 1983, the Canadian Foodgrains Bank is a Canadian based Christian organization that helps provide food and development assistance to people. The Canadian Foodgrains Bank is owned by 13 Canadian Church Agencies, including ADRA Canada.

Being very pleased to announce that the number is now fifteen, as the Catholics and Anglicans have just joined, the report goes on to say:

Member agencies represent evangelical churches, mainline protestant churches, as well as catholic churches, with over 17,000 congregations and parishes connected to this **ecumenical effort** to end hunger in developing countries.

"We're very excited about this," says Rick Fee, Chair of the Board of Directors of Canadian Foodgrains Bank. "**The Foodgrains Bank is truly a unique ecumenical Christian organization**. As Canadians we should be very proud of this **joint Christian witness in the world**. We should never underestimate or down-play the vital role that the Foodgrains Bank is being called to fulfill in today's hungry world. **We celebrate the inclusion of the Anglicans and Catholics as members of this amazing Christian response** to ending hunger." (emphasis added)

Some would not define banding together in humanitarian efforts as "ecumenism." ADRA seems to differ with this sentiment. Furthermore, they define their work as a united "Christian witness in the world." If this isn't an ecumenical sort of idea, then what is it? The stated purpose of presenting a "joint Christian witness" would have to do with propagating the gospel. Yet, this would mean that we need to be working with the same gospel message. That cannot be the third angel's message. We just have to pause and think this out for a minute, and it is not all that difficult to see that we are in deep trouble with this kind of thing. To think that we can join these bodies for the good they do and somehow remain separate from the ongoing ecumenical agenda which ultimately will seek to enlist the powers of civil government to eliminate all dissent is very dangerous. To think that we would not become hampered in our ability to give the loud cry message is to be self-deceived. "Be not deceived: evil communications corrupt good manners" (1 Cor. 15:33).

We must always be sure to emphasize that we are not speaking of individuals in these organizations who do not understand what they are into, any more than low level secret society members understand what they are into. Individuals can be fooled into believing that they are a "Christian" organization, when in reality they are part of a Luciferian enterprise. It's all part of the end-time conglomerate that will seek to stamp out the faithful.

We are not allowed to give our distinctive witness to the world when we are in these alliances. You cannot actively seek to bring people into the third angel's message when working in these groups. Try being a true Adventist witness within these ecumenical bodies and teaching historic Adventism:

- the judgment hour message pertaining to Christ's movement into the Most Holy Place as of 1844 and how that His atoning for sin there is about more than mere forgiveness, but an actual cleansing of it from our present lives, molding our characters like unto His own, in preparation for the last great work of the loud cry of the fourth angel to be given by the final generation, the 144,000

- the ensuing close of probation when there will be no more atonement for sin and characters are sealed for God or marked for destruction

- the Sabbath truth

- the non-immortality of the soul

- the coming persecution under Sunday laws, which we have correctly taught as the implementation of the Mark of the Beast

- the expositions of the man of sin and that apostate's corruptions of the truths of and usurpation of the prerogatives of God

- the expositions regarding the false prophet as post-1844 fallen Protestantism

- the Spirit of Prophecy as manifest in the ministry and writings of Ellen White.

2. The ADRA president took full participation in ecumenical worship service

Not to be particularly singling out ADRA, but we find the president, Charles Sandefur, participating officially on behalf of the Seventh-day Adventist Church in an interfaith prayer and worship service at the Washington National Cathedral on March 16, 2007, as reported by Pastor Ron Spear in *The Eternal Gospel Herald*, vol. 4, no. 10, pp. 6–8. This was "an ecumenical coalition of churches organized" in an event to promote "Christian Peace Witness for Iraq." They were praying, singing, and meditating to beseech God to bring in "lasting peace and unity to this nation and to the rest of the world."

I am wondering if we forgot all about prophecy. The church and its branches of work carry on as if it were never written and somehow it is possible to do something else and bring about another outcome by spurning the heaven-sent counsel. Instead of preaching the message to come out of Babylon, there is an eagerness to foster coziness with the apostates, giving the opening prayers in their services, marching in their candlelit processions, and applauding their speeches.

3. Centura Health Corporation a Joint Venture between Adventists and Catholics

What about the union with the Catholics in Colorado in Seventh-day Adventist health care systems? Centura Health Corporation, the largest health care system in the state of Colorado, operating approximately fourteen hospitals, is jointly owned and operated by Catholic Health Initiatives and Adventist Health Systems, established in 1996. Was it the purpose of God that the "right arm of the message" be grafted to a Roman Catholic body? If "it is a backsliding church that lessens the distance between itself and the Papacy" (*Signs of the Times*, Feb. 19, 1894), then it is a backslidden church which grafts its "right arm" to a Roman Catholic body!

Having looked at the compromise of the health ministry work as God had intended it to be done, we cannot easily be surprised at this turn of events, for if Adventism had stayed true to the blueprint for the medical work, it would have kept the "missionary" part as its primary objective, and it never would have been possible to ally with Catholicism. In reality, therefore, the "right arm" is not grafted into the Catholic body because it has ceased to be deserving of that title. It is no longer actually carrying "the health message" but, rather, doing the medical business after the common order of the world.

It is impossible that the message can have its proper place in a mixed institution. If a patron of such an institution were to receive spiritual guidance, what message would they receive?

> Let not God's people in any of our institutions sign a truce with the enemy of God and man. The duty of the church to the world is not to come down to their ideas and accept their opinions, their suggestions, but to heed the words of Christ through His servant Paul, "Be ye not unequally yoked together with unbelievers...." This means in a special sense marriage with unbelievers, but it covers more ground than this: it means in our instrumentalities ordained of God, in our institutions for health, in our colleges, in our publishing houses.
>
> ... You are not in any case to become contaminated with the spirit or influence of unbelievers. Be afraid of uniting or binding up in bundles with them. Be afraid of communicating the works connected with the Lord's cause to those who have no part with God, or sympathy with those who love the truth of God....

I raise my voice of warning against the mingling in our institutions of the worldly element with those who believe; we have the danger signal to sound. **If in our institutions persons are placed in positions of trust, they are educators. Others are taught to look to these persons for instruction, and in this is a snare to the unwary; their ideas become confused in regard to righteousness and truth.** They hear those persons who have no respect for the truth sneer and speak disparagingly of the truth, which should be held firmly and sacredly as truth. (Ms. 39, 1891, in *Testimonies to Ministers*, pp. 271, 272, emphasis added)

4. The Work of Bert B. Beach

Dr. Beach has been the Seventh-day Adventist Church's foremost liaison to various international religious, ecumenical, and peace conferences and institutes. He contributed to and is listed and described on the back of the *Dictionary of the Ecumenical Movement*, published by the Worldwide Council of Churches in 1991: "Bert B. Beach (Seventh-day Adventist Church) is director of the council of interchurch relations of the General Conference of Seventh-day Adventists, Washington, D.C., USA." Before he retired from the General Conference in 2005, Beach held positions including president of the Adventist Italian Training College in Florence, chair of the History Department at Columbia Union College, director of the Education Department at the General Conference, and Secretary of the Northern Europe-West Africa Division. Beach also served as Director of Public Affairs and Religious Liberty, General Secretary of the General Conference Council on Inter-Church Relations, and Secretary General for the International Religious Liberty Association. For thirty-two years, Beach also served as the Secretary of the Conference of Secretaries of Christian World Communions. At General Conference sessions, he brought in leaders of other churches to join in the proceedings, make addresses, and receive rounds of glowing applause.

His involvement at the WCC was to sit as an "observer" for over twenty years. Much of that time was spent as a senior member of interdenominational committees therein. This arrangement is a way for the General Conference to be represented at the WCC. One of the key committees at the WCC is called the *Faith and Order Commission* (FOC). Beach was a voting member of a smaller committee that served to manage the FOC. The FOC is concerned with the modification of denominational teachings to achieve ecumenical unity. As Secretary of the Annual Conference of Secretaries of the World Confessional Families, he has denied its status as an "organization" because it lacks a constitution and does not receive payment of "dues." Yet, he wrote:

I have been representing our church at this meeting for 9 years now and our involvement consists simply in attending the meeting and participating in the discussions and exchange of information. For the past few years I have served as Secretary of the Conference (this means that I am responsible for preparing the agenda and handling the minutes or report of the Conference). There is no usefulness in giving any publicity to this fact, but I do mention it for your information. (Letter to A. G. Brito, Nov. 15, 1977, in William H. Grotheer, *Steps to Rome*, p. 6)

So, it has officers, an agenda, and minutes but is not an organization. He feels that it will not be well to give publicity to the matter because it is not useful information. As to the relation of the Conference to the WCC, which was much downplayed by Beach, Bishop John Howe stated in a Vatican Radio interview that "we have been able to decide how we shall work together more with the World Council of Churches in understanding the ecumenical role that all of us have" (*Steps to Rome*, p. 14).

As a Seventh-day Adventist, Beach has claimed a decided anti-ecumenical stance. While believing that there are ways in which Seventh-day Adventists should work together with other denominations, he is certain that there are many problems that come with the idea of being a member of ecumenical bodies. He asked, "Would it be wise and honorable [*for Seventh-day Adventists*] to become members of a fellowship of churches, with the intention—imposed by the very *raison d'etre* of the Adventist movement—of witnessing within this fellowship and draw as many as are led to embrace Adventism into the biblical 'remnant', in contrast with the apparently inclusivistic World Council?" Beach implied that it is not wise or honorable. Logic defies any such partnerships. He said also that "membership might have the psychological effect of reducing, for reasons of 'good neighborliness' the vigor and zeal of SDA witness and evangelism. Furthermore, the WCC is pushing for 'joint witness' as much as possible, and this would be hard to harmonize with the distinctive nature of the SDA witness in preparation for the soon coming of Christ." One can read all of this in his 1974 book, *Ecumenism: Boon or Bane?*, in the last chapter entitled, "Seventh-day Adventist Questions Regarding the WCC," published by the church's Review and Herald press. Also, in light of Elder Beach's career, we are surely amazed to read from his book these words:

> Ecumenism is a glittering word in today's religious vocabulary. However, as we face the end of the present age, we will not see a kind of jumbo church representing the people of God, but a persecuted, united remnant having the faith of Jesus and keeping the commandments of God. Prior to the Second Advent "religious jumboism" will lose "all the glitter and the glamour" (see Rev. 18:14). (*Ecumenism: Boon or Bane?*, p. 21)

Medal, pointing to the Sabbath and the Second Coming of Jesus, given to Pope Paul VI by the Seventh-day Adventist representative Bert B. Beach.

What Elder Beach said and did in one context contrasted with what he said and did in another seems to present an enigma. We cannot here go into a detailed study of the man and his work, but suffice a few reports of his activities.

On May 18, 1977, Dr. Beach, as church representative (Secretary of the Northern Europe-West Africa Division), along with other representatives and *leader of* the religious bodies which comprise the Conference of Secretaries of the World Confessional Families (now called Christian World Communions), participated in an audience with Pope Paul VI. The Pope welcomed them as representatives of their churches and sent greetings back through them. Elder W. Duncan Eva, one of the vice presidents of the General Conference, reported that Dr. Beach then presented the pope with a bronze medallion on behalf of the Seventh-day Adventist Church. This was the first time in history that the Seventh-day Adventist Church had ever met with a Catholic Pope.

This medallion was commissioned by the Seventh-day Adventist Church, and it was produced by a company that created similar medallions for many other denominations, after advertising their program to create them, "Great Religions of the World." Yet, only the Seventh-day Adventist Church placed one in the pope's hands.

In a letter dated, March 3, 1978, Elder W. Duncan Eva noted in a very clear manner—"The Northern Europe-West Africa Division Committee authorized Brother Beach's trip to Rome and it understood that the visit to the Pope with representatives of the World Confessional Families was a probability." This "probability" was so sure that the medallion given was "paid for from Departmental expense funds of the Northern Europe-West Africa Division." (cited in *Steps to Rome*, p. 6)

The Yugoslavian Catholic bi-weekly *Glas Koncila* [Voice of the Council] quoted Beach as saying that it was a distinct honor to have had "an audience here in Rome with the Holy Father ["Sveti otac"]" (*Glas Koncila*, June 5, 1977). Beach did not have to refer to the pope as "the Holy Father." What was the necessity of his calling him that?

A very interesting anecdote that would be appropriate to share at this point comes from Russell Standish, who related an interchange with Bert Beach:

> On June 30, 1993, Russell was sitting in the library of the General Conference Office. From opposite directions Dr Beach and Clifford Goldstein, then in the Religious Liberty Department of which Dr Beach was Director, were about to pass in the corridor.
>
> Russell called them both over to him. His purpose was to comment upon the fact that Clifford Goldstein had recently written a defense of Dr Beach's action in presenting that medal to the Pope in 1978, fifteen years earlier.
>
> "Cliff," Russell said, "you just wrote an article supporting Bertie's action in presenting the medal to Paul VI." Before Cliff could speak Dr Beach interjected, "you don't think I was supporting the Roman Catholic Church when I did that, do you?"
>
> Russell candidly replied, "As a matter of fact, Bertie, I do."
>
> "Well," he responded, "the pope gave me a medal. Was he supporting the Seventh-day Adventist Church?"
>
> "Certainly not!" Russell answered with a little emphasis. Dr. Beach, not altogether unexpectedly, accused Russell of patent inconsistency. Looking at the matter from his point of view, no doubt Russell's

answer appeared to possess that defect. But Russell's answer was not based upon logic, but rather Scripture. Our conversation came to an abrupt conclusion when Russell expressed his view. "There is absolutely no inconsistency. Scripture does not declare that all the world wondered after the Seventh-day Adventist Church." (*Half a Century of Apostasy*, pp. 33, 34)

Let it not escape us how diligently Rome pursues her agenda and unabashedly declares it. That Dr. Beach would be unaware of this after all of his experience in ecumenical circles is unthinkable. Yet here is what was published as a news release in the official Vatican newspaper, citing the words of the pope (translated to English):

Dear Brethren in Christ,

We rejoice to be able to receive such an important group today, and welcome you to Peter's See. In you we greet the representatives of a considerable portion of the Christian people, and through you we send our wishes of grace and peace in the Lord to your Confessional Families.

We are happy to express, in your presence, **our common faith in Jesus Christ**, the Son of God, the only Mediator with the Father, the Saviour of the world. Yes, brethren, together with the Apostle Peter, we proclaim that "Neither is there salvation in any other: for there is none other name under heaven given among men, whereby we must be saved." Acts 4:12.

On her part, the Catholic Church is solemnly engaged, through Vatican Council II, in **an ecumenism based on increased fidelity to Christ** the Lord and on heart conversion (see Unitatis Redinte-gratio, 6, 7). At the same time **she is conscious that "nothing would harm the Catholic doctrine and obscure its genuine and precise meaning."** (*ibid.*)

Reinforced by the power of the Word of God, **let us therefore pursue, despite all difficulties, the objective of full unity in Christ and in the Church**. And, with humbleness and love, let us direct our thoughts and our hopes to our Lord Jesus Christ. Glory be given to Him, as well as to the Father and to the Holy Spirit, forever and ever. (Cited in *Steps to Rome*, p. 7, emphasis added)

Thus were the words from the pope to the Seventh-day Adventists. The unity called for "in Christ and the Church" is obviously referring to uniting with the Catholic Church! This is for serious contemplation. Here are more serious words:

It was by departure from the Lord, and alliance with the heathen, that the Jewish church became a harlot ... (*The Great Controversy*, p. 382)

When the leading churches of the United States, uniting upon such points of doctrine as are **held by them in common**, shall influence the state to enforce their decrees and to sustain their institutions, then Protestant America will have formed an image of the Roman hierarchy ... (*Great Controversy*, p. 445, emphasis added)

The book, *So Much in Common*, published by the WCC in 1973, contains "Documents of Interest in the Conversations between the World Council of Churches and the Seventh-day Adventist Church" (*So Much in Common*, p. 1).

One of these "Documents" outlines the history of the "conversations" from their inception in 1965 through 1969. It will be seen that the events which transpired during these years finally led to the meeting of the Conference of Secretaries of the World Confessional Families in Rome, which in turn provided the setting for the audience with Pope Paul VI at which time Dr. B. B. Beach presented the Seventh-day Adventist Church in symbolism [via the bronze medallion] into the hands of the Pope. Further, it was B. B. Beach himself who wrote the history of these "conversations." In fact he co-authored the book [along with Lukas Vischer,

Pope John Paul II greets representative Bert B. Beach (*Adventist Review*, Nov. 8, 2001, p. 10)

Secretary of the World Council of Churches]—So Much in Common! (*Steps to Rome*, p. 3)

So much in common? How could it ever be that Seventh-day Adventists look to Babylon and say these words? It is a sad indictment. It is not true of genuine Adventism, for there is nothing in common after the second angel made its pronouncement in 1844. As the Scriptures say, "And what concord hath Christ with Belial? Or what part hath he that believeth with an infidel? (2 Cor. 6:15).

The very fact that the various bodies had historically rejected the "everlasting gospel" of the first angel is conclusive proof that these have not in fact, followed Christ. They have remained behind, and there it is that Satan has taken up residence pretending to be God (see *Early Writings*, pp. 54–56). Sadly, these fallen ones have endeavored also to "draw back and deceive God's children" (*Early Writings*, p. 56). What is even worse is that God's children have been all too willing and even *eager* to be drawn back. For we read in another publication of this same vision, a little known fact regarding the end of the matter, which was edited out of the *Early Writings* account, retaining the sentence, "I saw one after another leave the company who were praying to Jesus in the Holiest, and go and join those before the throne, and they at once received the unholy influence of Satan" (*Broadside1*, April 6, 1846). All of this is to say that these have another gospel and another "Christ." True Adventism has *nothing* in common with the world. Therefore, to hold that we have "so much in common" is to admit that we have become like the world, so much in common with the great assembly of the churches of Babylon, with the harlot daughters of Rome and even with the Mother herself.

Of all these affairs the *General Conference* has been sure to manipulate perception as to be seen to have nothing to do with the WCC because, although informed of the proceedings, they correctly point out that they took place under the auspices and blessings of the *European Divisional branch offices*. This is a subtlety which is not lost on any who honestly assess the matter because, although the General Conference would not be directly involved, the respective Executive Committees were each "chaired by a Vice President of the General Conference voted to serve as a President over each Division" (*Steps to Rome*, p. 4). The Division heads *are* representatives of the General Conference!

Again, to illustrate the penchant for "side door" entry into ecumenical associations in order to avoid the political repercussions that may come from an aroused laity (questionable though such a speculation may be) we read a statement from R. F. Cottrell, an Associate Editor of the *Review*, April 6, 1967, saying:

> It is with no small measure of regret that SDA's do not find it possible, as an organization, to be more closely associated with others who profess the name of Christ. On the other hand, if the Secretariat on Faith and Order, for instance, were to invite SDA's to appoint someone competent in that area to meet with their group from time to time and represent the SDA point of view, we could accept such an invitation with a clear conscience. (p. 13)

It was only months before such invitation materialized and this side-door entrance was immediately established. Note once again that the Faith and Order Commission is the doctrinal arm of the WCC. Its stated aim is "to proclaim the oneness of the Church of Jesus Christ and to call the churches to the goal of visible unity in one faith and one Eucharistic fellowship, expressed in worship and common life in Christ, in order that the world might believe" (*Faith & Order Paper*, #111, p. viii). "To know this aim, and then request to be a part of this objective is to deny the very uniqueness of Adventism. Evidently, the leadership of the Church did not do its home work well; they did not read the fine print before signing on, or it was a deliberate move to take the Seventh-day Adventist Church into the Ecumenical mainstream" (Grotheer, "Rome's Vision for Church Unity," p. 5)

The WCC Central Committee brought Dr. Earle Hilgert, professor of New Testament and VP for Academic Administration at Andrews University, into the Faith and Order Commission. He later became an ordained Presbyterian minister. His place was later filled by Dr. Raoul F. Dederen, also of Andrews University (the man who would later be involved with proceedings regarding the "Lima Document" on Baptism, Eucharist, and Ministry [BEM]). The Catholics appointed their theologians to the Commission the next year.

So it is that we again see how these relationships are cleverly disguised and how careful wording must be to avoid outright untruth. The Seventh-day Adventist Church can say that it never "appointed" any representative to the WCC Commission on Faith and Order, even while it surely did approve of there being one there, per Cottrell's published statement (fishing for an invite?) and obvious support of the ongoing liaison. The church is very careful to be able to perceive itself as factual and honest when is says, "We are not members of the WCC."

However, its political maneuvering is done in such a way to avoid leaving the impression that the Church is *not* heavily involved in procedural aspects of the conduct of the WCC's work and that it is merely "observational." The manipulation of perception is not promoting untruth? We leave that with the reader to decide.

5. *Welcoming Dr. Robert Schuller*
As another local example of the pervasiveness of the deep ecumenical spirit, we report that the Potomac Conference in the USA, having the largest Adventist Book Center in the world, invited Robert Schuller, presumably for a book signing party. Schuller was then the pastor of the Pentecostal megachurch called "The Crystal Cathedral." Here is the notice:

> Meet in person:
> Robert A. Schuller.
> Associate speaker of
> the *Hour of Power* television broadcast
> and author of the new book
> *Dump Your Hang-Ups.*
>
> Thursday, August 19; 5:00 p.m. to 7:30 p.m.
> Potomac Adventist Book & Health Food Store …
> (*Columbia Union Visitor*, Aug. 15, 1993, p. 15)

6. *Reinder Bruinsma and the Charta Oecumenica*
The following excerpts are taken from Walter Veith's response to Reinder Bruinsma's criticisms published in the *Adventist Review*:

> Reinder Bruinsma was executive secretary of the Trans-European Division from 1995–2001 and succeeded Henk Koning as Union President of the Netherlands Union. Henk Koning was president of the Netherlands Union Conference when he signed the Charta Oecumenica on the 18th of January 2002. Such signing can not be done in a personal capacity, as churches and not individuals are party to the ecumenical movement. Whether Bruinsma was party to the signing or not is not known by me, but by his silence he condoned it and he certainly did not rescind it on becoming Union president himself. Reinder Bruinsma has made his views on relations with the Roman Catholic Church and the traditional view of the Adventist Church, inclusive of the Spirit of Prophecy, very clear even in his doctoral thesis A Historical Analysis of Seventh-day Adventist Attitudes toward Roman Catholicism (University of London, 1993), which was also published by Andrews University Press in 1995 as Adventist Attitudes toward Roman Catholicism 1844–1865.…

Bruinsma [made] … the following statements:

> Although there are many aspects in Roman-Catholic teaching and practice with which Adventists must strongly disagree, honesty demands that they acknowledge that in recent decades, in most places of the world Roman-Catholicism has changed in ways that they must regard as positive. Catholics are now not only allowed to read their Bible but are urged to do so. There is much spirituality in the Roman-Catholic Church of which Protestants can be envious. The Catholic Church has formally accepted the principle of religious freedom. It is not fair to suggest that these and other positive developments in the Roman-Catholic Church are just window dressing and must in fact be watched with suspicion, and be seen as clever tactics to lull other Christians into sleep, while all the time they are just waiting for the fortuitous moment when they will be able to wipe out other Christians, Adventists first and foremost! In their criticism of the Catholic history, Adventists should try to be more balanced than they have often been and should do better than simply offering an extension of the often rather biased and inaccurate picture that many Protestants in past centuries have held of the medieval church. Medieval Christianity also had its positive and beautiful sides! Moreover, Adventists must be willing to acknowledge that modern Catholicism has changed in many ways. It bothers me, in particular, to see how Adventist publications today still refer mainly to nineteenth century sources in their description of Catholic views and intentions. How would Adventists feel if people around them were to base their opinions of Adventism exclusively on sources of more than century ago? Dealing with this issue will, no doubt, be difficult and will take time. Anti-Catholicism is so ingrained in the Adventist world view that change will not come easy, even if the church's administrators and other thought leaders were to agree that a re-orientation would be desirable. But in the meantime, the church could at the very least decide to be less biased in its descriptions of present-day Catholicism.
>
> The present Pope has stated categorically that the ecumenical process is to be regarded as irreversible and

the signing of the Charta Oecumenica by most protestant churches is indicative of the decay which has set in amidst Protestantism. The Charta is an agreement entered into by the Catholic Council of European Bishops' Conference (CCEE) and the Conference of European Churches (CEC), the Protestant alliance of Europe. This document acknowledges apostolic succession, guarantees that there will be no proselytising, and changes the Gospel message from salvation in Christ to a social Gospel of securing human rights for all. Moreover, it advocates a common Eucharist and recognition of all baptismal rites as practiced in the various churches. John Rogers, who had been an associate of Tyndale and Coverdale in the translation of the Scriptures into English, was led to the stake at Smithfield on February 4th, 1555. His crime was the denial of transubstantiation. It is unthinkable that an Adventist could have signed this document. Moreover the very CEC that went into agreement with the Papacy is now campaigning for Sunday legislation in Europe; this comes directly from their own web page, not some obscure source.... [*Veith quotes from Ellen White.*]

We are to give to the people the warnings contained in Revelation. But many workers are engaged in a line of work that is disqualifying them to preach the word and do the very work God has appointed them to do. The truth in regard to the Sabbath of the Lord is to be proclaimed. The seventh-day is to be shown to be the seal of the living God. People are to be shown what they may expect from the papal power. The time has come when the Protestant churches are reaching out to grasp the hand of the power that has made void the law of God ... [Here follows lengthy quotations from Revelation 18 and brief comments.] This is the message Satan would have silenced.... [Lt. 232, 1899, in *Manuscript Releases*, vol. 4, p. 426]

This terrible picture, drawn by John to show how completely the powers of earth will give themselves over to evil, should show those who have received the truth how dangerous it is to link up with secret societies or to join themselves in any way with those who do not keep God's commandments.... [Ms. 135, 1902, in *Manuscript Releases*, vol. 14, p. 152]

This is precisely what the Spirit of Prophecy predicted (conspiracy or no conspiracy), and demonstrates precisely why we should not be involved with those that war against the law of God. If that means exclusivity then so be it, because the directive is not of human devising. Even among the other Protestant churches there are still powerful voices of leaders who stand like the needle to the pole. These bright lights amongst these churches will yet take their stand under the blood stained banner of Prince Emannuel [*sic*]. In 1988, the Free Presbyterian Church of Scotland's Clerk to the Synod, Reverend Donald MacLean's comment in his letter to The Times stated this:

The Ecumenical movement which you praise is the greatest disaster to affect the Christian church this century. It has reduced the professing churches of this country to a collection of bloodless, spineless and boneless organizations, which can hardly raise a whimper on the side of Christ and His Truth. Small wonder that evil progresses as it does, and spiritual darkness becomes more intense as the years go by. You appear to regard a body of professing Christians, of sober conduct, and deep spirituality of mind, as fanatical and bigoted. If this be so then the eminent men of God, such as John Knox in Scotland, John Calvin and Martin Luther on the Continent, and Archbishop Cranmer in England were bigots in their contests with the errors of Popery. We are glad to be in such company.

What an indictment to Adventists who wish to tow [*sic*] the ecumenical line. I have never before discussed our Church's ecumenical relations, but in view of the nature of current circumstances and my duty as evangelist toward those who are contemplating membership in the SDA family, the time has, it seems, come to clarify a few issues. Are we as a Church involved in ecumenical relations? The answer is obviously yes. In Germany the Seventh-day Adventist Church is affiliated with the ACK [German ecumenical body: Arbeitsgemeinshaft Christlicher Kirchen—"Association of Christian Churches"] and there is ample evidence elsewhere that our church is more involved than we might wish to think. Let there be Light Ministries has distributed a booklet entitled The World Council of Churches and the Seventh-day Adventist Church, which saw its first printing in 1996.... (Walter Veith, "Dr Walter Veith replies to criticism by Reinder Bruinsma recently published in Adventist Review," available at http://1ref.us/im, accessed 10/14/16)

7. Ecumenical Television

During the week before Christmas of 1994, the Seventh-day Adventist Church and the National Council of Churches joined together to nationally televise the Christmas Eve Special "A New Noel"! (see *Adventist Review*, Dec. 15, 1994, p. 7). This broadcast was videotaped at a **Sunday church service on December 4 in the Pioneer Memorial Seventh-day Adventist Church at Andrews University**, and Seventh-day Adventist minister Dwight Nelson presented the devotional message (see *Adventist Review*, Dec. 4, 1994, p. 7). It was nationally televised on Christmas Eve (11:30 p.m. Saturday till 12:30 a.m., Sunday) through the ABC-TV network, and the Seventh-day Adventist Church placed a paid advertisement in 14,000,000 copies of the *TV Guide* (see *Adventist Review*, Dec. 15, 1994, p. 7).

The paid advertisement of this event, as well as the televised opening credits for the program, stated:

> The National Council of Churches presents a production of the Seventh-day Adventist Church. (*Adventist Review*, Dec. 15, 1994, p. 7; *TV Guide*, Dec. 24–30, 1994, p. 55, vol. 42, no. 52, issue 2178)

8. Seventh-day Adventist Minister, Booker. T. Rice, welcomes the pope to St. Louis, Missouri

When Pope John Paul II paid an ecumenical visit to St. Louis in January, 1999, representatives of many faiths attended him. The "Dayton Daily News" of Jan. 28, 1999, reports:

> The pope continued the theme of unity at his final ceremony Wednesday evening at the Cathedral Basilica of St. Louis, where representatives of many faiths - Judaism, Hinduism, Seventh-day Adventists - joined him in prayer.

> A Catholic spokesperson addressed the congregation and the attending media, saying:

> For many people outside the Catholic community with willingness and graciousness, our brothers and sisters of the ecumenical and inter-religious community, have accepted the invitation to come together this evening with Your Holiness.

> Pastor Booker. T. Rice of the Northside Seventh-day Adventist Church made a welcoming address and presentation to the pope:

> Pope, **Your Holiness**, your historic visit to St. Louis, Missouri, has served as a "catalyst" in the creation of this [ecumenical] program and it transforms your presence into a lasting legacy for our region. Today, we present to you this proclamation, announcing the creation of "Faith beyond Walls". Your commitment to improving interfaith relations has fostered an environment wherein **the spirit of collective faith**, positively actioned, can thrive. In addition, we also present you with this banner, the emblem of "Faith beyond Walls". We hope and pray that it will inspire interfaith communities around the world to focus their efforts on improving health and the quality of life for all humanity. Again, we welcome you to our region.

It cannot be said that this extended hand of welcome and fellowship was the work of a lone radical pastor. There was no ensuing publication in the church papers or in the secular papers to disavow this action. We cannot but conclude therefore that the conference was reaching out to the papacy, even to join as brothers in faith.

The video of this event can be found online. I am reminded of the words from the pen of inspiration:

> Shall the Ark of the Covenant be removed from this people? Shall idols be smuggled in? Shall false principles and false precepts be brought into the sanctuary? **Shall antichrist be respected?** Shall the true doctrines and principles given us by God, which have made us what we are, be ignored? ... This is directly where the enemy, through blinded, unconsecrated men, is leading us. (Ms. 29, 1890, in *Manuscript Releases*, vol. 21, p. 448)

Incidentally, at this same time and event, Danny Vierra's "Modern Manna" ministries hit the streets in a campaign to raise awareness of the three angels' messages, by handing out a booklet, *Is the Virgin Mary Dead or Alive?* Utilizing a band of forty "non-invasive foot-soldiers" they distributed from their stock of 100,000 booklets. In a video coverage of this project entitled "Victory in St. Louis," it is stated:

> And soon, after the Holy Spirit had been poured out and their mission completed, an apology would be offered by the General Conference of Seventh-day Adventists to the Pope of Rome, "... begging pardon for their [Modern Manna's] bigotry."

Again, we are reminded of the prophetic lines:

> As the Protestant churches have been seeking the favor of the world, false charity has blinded their eyes. They do not see but that it is right to believe good of all evil, and as the inevitable result they will finally believe evil of all good. Instead of standing in defense of the faith once delivered to the saints, they are now, as it were, apologizing to Rome for their uncharitable opinion of her, **begging pardon for their bigotry.** (*The Great Controversy*, pp. 571, 572, emphasis added)

There has been some confusion over whether Pastor Rice was a representative of the Seventh-day Adventist Church or not. He has pastored for 14 years at this time of writing, the *New Horizon Seventh-day Christian Church*, which is said to be outside of the "sisterhood of Seventh-day Adventist churches." A graduate of Oakwood College in theology and biblical languages, holding a Certificate of Divinity from Andrews University, he has pastored at least eight churches, including the *Northside Seventh-day Adventist Church*. One of the items on his list of credentials and accomplishments is title of President of the St. Louis Clergy Coalition and is currently First Vice President and Chairman of Police Affairs in St. Louis County Branch, NAACP. A St. Louis television broadcast screen shot carries the caption: "Pastor B. T. Rice: Northside Seventh Day Adventist Church & President of the St. Louis Clergy Coalition" (http://1ref.us/in).

An extinct online obituary entry created in 2008, by the New Horizon 7th Day Christian Church, stated:

> Orchestrated by the rearing of a righteous mother, D__ accepted Christ at a young age at Newstead Avenue Missionary Church under the pastorate of The Late Rev. Roy Harris. Through the ministerial influence of her brother, E__, she and A__ united with **Northside Seventh-day Adventist Church under the leadership of Pastor G. D. Penick and Pastor B. T. Rice.** Ultimately, alongside her husband, D__ culminated her walk with the Lord as a charter member of **New Horizon Seventh-day Christian Church, also led by Pastor B. T. Rice** ... (http://1ref.us/io, names redacted, emphasis added)

9. *Joint statement issued by Seventh-day Adventist Church and Roman Catholic Church in Poland*

After fifteen years of dialogue, a pact was signed with the Catholic Church, aimed at "improving relations without compromising each other's identity." The actual document itself speaks of the "members from the Adventist side" as "*the priests*," while naming Jan Krysta as the "president of the *South Diocese* of the Seventh-day Adventist Church." The agreement signed by both parties believes that the Seventh-day Adventist Church "in its teaching and service ... cultivates the most important principles of Catholic faith...."

Ray Dabrowski, for "The Adventist News Network" [ANN] stated:

> The Seventh-day Adventist Church cannot be treated either as a 'new religious movement,' or as a sect," declares a joint statement drawn by the Roman Catholic Church and the Adventist Church in Poland.
>
> The statement was signed by representatives of the Churches, including Pastor Wladyslaw Polok, president of the [Seventh-day] Adventist Church in Poland, and Archbishop Alfons Nossol, chairman of the Polish Episcopate's Commission for Ecumenical Affairs. (Ray Dabrowski, " 'Adventist Church Cannot be Treated as a Sect,' Say Adventists and Catholics in Poland," available at http://1ref.us/ip, accessed 12/18/16)

The document purposed to declare mutual recognition as full ecclesiastical bodies and to uphold religious liberty, "conducted on the basis of partnership," in a spirit of respect and Christian love. Professor Zachariasz Lyko, who was for many years the leader for the Polish Adventist Church's public affairs, stated: "As Seventh-day Adventists we seek to take a positive approach to other faiths." "It is always better to engage in a respectful conversation than in a confrontation that often prevents achieving desired changes."

It is interesting to note that the church thinks that we might bring about changes through "conversations" and joint-declarations with that woman who sits on many waters with her daughters. We are told that Babylon would never get better but only worse. She is on a collision course with God's people and will never abide by any agreement to respect religious freedom. We are given a distinctive and unpopular message to preach—obviously a task considered most unpleasant. The church should be about that business, proclaiming angels one, two, and three, but what is it that is done instead? Seeking partnership? What else could we possibly think to achieve by this, and where is the divine mandate for it?

"This document affirms religious liberty," said Poland's Pastor Polok. Again, since when did the papacy care about religious liberty? "Have these persons forgotten the claim of infallibility put forth for eight hundred years by this haughty power?" asked Ellen White. "How can she renounce the principles which governed her course in past ages?" (*The Great Controversy*, p. 564). Would the Seventh-day Adventist churchman be completely oblivious of the chapter in *The Great Controversy*, "Liberty of Conscience Threatened," with its explicit exposition of the purposes of the papacy and her ways of covering them over with a "conciliatory" and Christ-like veneer? Beneath the "variable appearance of the chameleon," states the Lord's messenger, "she conceals the invariable venom of the serpent" (*The Great Controversy*, p. 571). The document cites the fact that "relations between Catholics and Adventists have not been the best in the past." I should suppose not, those relations historically rooted in the Protestant Reformation as they are!

So here we have an agreement entered into which surely reflects a new Seventh-day Adventist position on the papacy. Furthermore, it is done without the knowledge of the laity and reported after the fact. Arthur Maxwell, beaming about his 1962 audience with Pope John XXIII and his great expression of love and of the new attitude of the Catholic Church, had said, "It's a new day, friends! It's a new day." Indeed, it is.

Ellen White warned: "The papacy is just what prophecy declared that she would be, the apostasy of the latter times. 2 Thessalonians 2:3, 4.... Shall this power, whose record for a thousand years is written in the blood of the saints, be now acknowledged as a part of the church of Christ?" (*The Great Controversy*, p. 571).

Dabrowski continued, reporting on the document content, which says:

> With regret we recognize cases when the different religious and civic circles have denied the ecclesiastical status of the Seventh-day Adventist Church, even referring to it as a 'sect.' Such an approach is unacceptable and, we believe, it is highly detrimental for the mutual relations.

Why should we be concerned about what the papacy, the world, or any other churches of Babylon think of us? Does Adventist leadership still believe that the papacy is the great Antichrist power? Apparently not! The signed ecumenical statement says that "it is highly detrimental for the mutual relations." What mutual relations? What kind of "relations" was enjoyed when thousands were coming out of the fallen churches, under the preaching of the second angel? Would they not have been a little "strained"? Are we to now have "relations" with the great Antichrist of Revelation 13? The Lord asks, through Paul, "What concord hath Christ with Belial?" (2 Cor. 6:15).

Dabrowski closed his report, citing Professor Zachariasz Lyko:

> Over the years, however, as the exchange of information between us took place, **we noted many confessional similarities** but also differences. The Catholic side recognizes in the document the Christocentric character of our beliefs, and especially our belief in the Trinity, **as well as ecclesiological identity of the Church**, a status affirmed by an act of the Polish Parliament. **On our part, we spoke of a need to change attitudes toward our denomination and recognized the openness of the Catholic Church, especially in recent times, toward the Bible.** (emphasis added)

"The Catholic side recognizes in the document ... our belief in the ... ecclesiological identity of the Church." What Church is he talking about? The Roman Catholic Church, or the Seventh-day Adventist Church? Perhaps it does not really matter? Both Catholic and Adventist Churches now wield "ecclesiological authority" over their members. Both systems excommunicate (disfellowship) members for the crime of "insubordination," of not recognizing the ecclesiastical authority of the Church.

"We noted many confessional similarities...." Should this not make us uneasy? "There is as great a difference in our faith and that of nominal professors, as the heavens are higher than the earth," Ellen White observed (*Spiritual Gifts*, vol. 2, p. 300). This statement would be applicable with even greater force to the Roman Catholic Church, one would think. "The people need to be aroused to resist the advances of this most dangerous foe to civil and religious liberty" (*The Great Controversy*, p. 566), not be soothed with signing statements of friendship and mutual respect and noting all the wonderful commonalities.

10. *The Lima Document*

The first major step toward the realization of the WCC's Faith and Order Commission's stated ecumenical goal came in 1982 in the transmission of the "Lima text" (on Baptism, Eucharist, and Ministry [BEM]) to the churches, a document by which the denominations are to recognize each other's baptism, communion service, and ordained clergy, requesting their response as a vital step in the ecumenical process. On the back cover of the document is found the following statement:

> Over one hundred theologians met in Lima, Peru, in January 1982, and recommended unanimously to transmit this agreed statement—the Lima text—for the common study and official response of the churches. They represented virtually all the major church traditions: Eastern Orthodox, Oriental Orthodox, Roman Catholic, Old Catholic, Lutheran, Anglican, Reformed, Methodist, United, Disciples, Baptists, **Adventist** and Pentecostal. (quoted in Watchman, What of the Night?" 1995 Jan – Mar, p. 6, available at http://1ref.us/iq, accessed 12/18/16, emphasis added)

Let the reader take heed as a corrective to a story that is spread far and wide that the vote was *not* an acceptance of the statement itself but a positive response (it was a unanimous vote) to transmit the document to the churches. Dr. Raoul Dederen of Andrews University, who was one of two Adventist representatives who took part in this vote, confirmed to William Grotheer that they abstained from voting approval of the document (Grotheer, "Rome's Vision for Church Unity," p. 6).

Even so, this high-level involvement with the Lima text (which the Adventist Church recognizes as one of the WCC's most significant publications) is not innocent. *The church is obviously playing a facilitative part in the affairs of high-powered ecumenist agenda* in its approval of sending out an instrument of the ecumenical machinery.

The Church's response to the text itself, thankfully, was to outline some areas of concern and disagreement because it was "too influenced by the Orthodox, Anglican, and Roman Catholic members of the Faith and Order Commission" (Grotheer, "Rome's Vision for Church Unity," p. 6).

The Standishes have provided a cursory review of the points in the document of interest to Seventh-day Adventists:

(a) *Baptism.* To encourage all churches to make no issue of the mode of or baptism practiced or the age at which a person is baptized as long as an adult consents in the decision. If baptism is by immersion, that is acceptable, as equally as is infant sprinkling.

(b) *Eucharist.* To encourage all churches to accept equally the various concepts regarding the communion service, whether trans-substantiation, con-substantiation, or the understanding that the bread and wine are symbols of the broken body and spilled blood of Jesus Christ.

(c) *Ministry.* To encourage all churches to work for the unchurched but never to proselytize from other churches. (adapted from Colin and Russell Standish, *Spiritism in the Adventist Church*, p. 87, wording not from B.E.M.)

So, these have been some selections of reports on Adventist ecumenism, which were in some cases localized or specific events, and, in some cases, national and international, selected at random from the large amount of available material in books and articles and online research. The ecumenical inroads are so commonplace that it would be rare, at least in western Adventism, to find an Adventist who has not seen an example of it at the local level.

We have left out many significant examples to avoid giving an inordinate amount of space to this large subject. Not mentioning the joining of conferences to national Councils of Churches in a number of instances, we did give one example of the North German Union joining the ACK as a "guest member," which is a "side door" entrance. Oftentimes, these memberships are spoken of as "personal" memberships on the part of the church representative. Even the Catholic Church had taken this approach to being a part of the WCC. Both churches have an interest in not raising the consternation of their laity, as both view themselves as the one true church, and it would be deemed a compromise to have anything to do with such liaisons of other churches. Even today, there are elements within Catholicism that view their church as going down a heretical road in its post-Vatican II friendliness and open arms to the churches of the world.

The ACK sets forth its objective clearly:

Promoting unity among Christians—this is the goal of the ecumenical movement. This unity is expressed in worldwide as well as national, regional and local alliances. (ACK—info, p. 2, cited in Colin and Russell Standish, *Tithes and Offerings: Trampling the Conscience*, p. 105)

Article 14 of the constitution of the ACK states that "The means necessary for the duties of the ACK are raised by both members and GUEST MEMBERS, according to their size and financial ability" ... [emphasis added by Standish]. Thus if the S.D.A. Church becomes a guest member it would be obliged to donate some of God's means for the promotion of the satanic ecumenical movement. (*Tithes and Offerings*, p. 105)

We could also speak more about the various alliances with Protestants and their programs, such as Bill Hybels' "Willow Creek," where Adventists have hoped to learn from them how to grow their churches. Why would we consult Babylon? That is like asking Satan how to win souls to Jesus. Yes, the devil is full of advice, if we will only lend him an ear. He will help us to bring people to a false Christ. So our churches sent their pastors to receive training, and they came back to their churches, hoping to increase the size of their congregation and plant new congregations through entertaining services and community programs, instead of the undiluted message. We have fallen prey to worldly philosophy, measuring success by amassing institutions, member count and the size of offerings.

When Protestantism shall stretch her hand across the gulf to grasp the hand of the Roman power, when she shall reach over the abyss to clasp hands with spiritualism, when, under the influence of this threefold union, our country shall repudiate every principle of its Constitution as a Protestant and republican government, and shall make provision for the propagation of papal falsehoods and delusions, then we may know that the time has come for the marvelous working of Satan and that the end is near. (*Testimonies for the Church*, vol. 5, p. 451)

Are Seventh-day Adventists reaching across the gulf and clasping hands with the papacy and the evangelicals? Let the reader decide.

As the storm approaches, a large class who have professed faith in the third angel's message, but have not been sanctified through obedience to the truth, abandon their position and join the ranks of the opposition. By uniting with the world and partaking of its spirit, they have come to view matters in nearly the same light; and when the test is brought, they are prepared to choose the easy, popular side. Men of talent and pleasing address, who once rejoiced in the truth, employ their powers to deceive and mislead souls. They become the most bitter enemies of their former brethren. When Sabbathkeepers are brought before the courts to answer for their faith, these apostates are the most efficient agents of Satan to misrepresent and accuse them, and by false reports and insinuations to stir up the rulers against them. (*The Great Controversy*, p. 608)

Unsanctified ministers are arraying themselves against God. They are praising Christ and the god of this world in the same breath. While professedly they receive Christ, they embrace Barabbas, and by their actions say, "Not this Man, but Barabbas." Let all who read these lines, take heed. Satan has made his boast of what he can do. He thinks to dissolve the unity which Christ prayed might exist in His church. He says, "I will go forth and be a lying spirit to deceive those that I can, to criticize, and condemn, and falsify." **Let the son of deceit and false witness** [*the ecumenists preaching a false gospel*] **be entertained by a church that has had great light, great evidence, and that church will discard the message the Lord has sent**, and receive the most unreasonable assertions and false suppositions and false theories. **Satan laughs at their folly, for he knows what truth is.**

Many will stand in our pulpits with the torch of false prophecy in their hands, kindled from the hellish torch of Satan. If doubts and unbelief are cherished, **the faithful ministers will be removed** from the people who think they know so much [*while the pulpit is occupied with Satan's agents, the faithful ministers will no more be found—where are they?*]. "If thou hadst known," said Christ, "even thou, at least in this thy day, the things which belong unto thy peace! but now they are hid from thine eyes." [Luke 19:42.] (Ms. 92, 1897, in *Testimonies to Ministers*, pp. 409, 410, emphasis added)

Awful is the outcome of the rebellion of the apostate leaders who have preached smooth things and taken their followers down into union with the end-time persecutor:

The people turned upon their ministers with bitter hate and reproached them, saying, "You have not warned us. You told us that all the world was to be converted [*could this be by presenting a "united Christian witness"?*], and cried, Peace, peace, to quiet every fear that was aroused. You have not told us of this hour; and **those who warned us of it you declared to be fanatics and evil men**, who would ruin us." But I saw that the ministers did not escape the wrath of God. Their suffering was tenfold greater than that of their people. (*Early Writings*, p. 282, emphasis added)

This writer is not a complete stranger to charges of like nature as we read in the above statement. Being a watchman has its consequences, while honesty and integrity require being willing to deliver a straight message and die to the desire to enjoy the pleasures of popularity.

It appears that Adventists really did once believe that there was a great danger coming from the ecumenical movement. Leadership still says so to the general lay population, more or less, but we go right on ahead and play footsie with apostate Christendom, despite the constraints it puts upon us in fulfilling our mandate and giving a distinctive call:

On the basis of Bible prophecy and the writings of Ellen G. White, SDA's anticipate the eventual success of the ecumenical movement, both in eliminating the divisions of Protestantism and in reuniting Christendom by bridging the gulf that separates non-Catholic communions from Rome. **The ecumenical movement will then become a concerted effort to unite the world and to secure universal peace and security by enlisting the power of the civil government in a universal religio-political crusade to eliminate all dissent.** SDA's envision this crusade as **the great apostasy** to which John the revelator refers **as "Babylon the great."** They understand, also, that **God's last message of mercy to the world** prior to the return of Christ in power and glory **will consist of a warning against this great apostate movement, and a call to all who choose to remain loyal to Him to leave the churches connected with it**.... (*Seventh-day Adventist Encyclopedia*, pp. 410, 411, emphasis added)

It is impossible for you to unite with those who are corrupt, and still remain pure. "What fellowship hath righteousness with unrighteousness? and what communion hath light with darkness? and what concord hath Christ with Belial?" [2 Cor. 6:14, 15.] **God and Christ and the heavenly host would have man know that if he unites with the corrupt, he will become corrupt**. (*Review and Herald*, Jan. 2, 1900, adapted from Ms. 1, 1869, emphasis added)

Let Ezra speak:

Now when the adversaries of Judah and Benjamin heard that the children of the captivity builded the temple unto the LORD God of Israel; then they came to Zerubbabel, and to the chief of the fathers, and said unto them, **Let us build with you: for we seek your God, as ye do**; and we do sacrifice unto him since the days of Esarhaddon king of Assur, which brought us up hither. But Zerubbabel, and Jeshua, and the rest of the chief of the fathers of Israel, said unto them, **Ye have nothing to do with us to build an house unto our God; but we ourselves together will build unto the LORD God of Israel**, as king Cyrus the king of Persia hath commanded us. (Ezra 4:1–3)

No further comment is required.

The Apostate Bloom

Conformity to worldly customs converts the church to the world; it never converts the world to Christ. (*The Great Controversy*, p. 509)

Do we really believe that God by some celestial oversight failed to furnish His church with the secrets of genuine evangelistic success? Do we dare to suggest by our actions that He hid these secrets in the bosom of the churches of Babylon? Over and over again we hear that there is much to learn from the Charismatic Movement. But we avow that we have absolutely nothing to learn from that apostate source. Can a poisoned fountain send forth pure water? (Russell and Colin Standish, *The Road to Rome* [1992], p. 28)

Over the generations, *apostasy*—rooted in rejection of the latter rain message, disobedience to the Spirit of Prophecy, and alliances with the world—*has crept in*, curling its tendrils about the latticework of Adventism. Then, like a noxious vine bearing black flowers on a moonless night, it has bloomed and released its intoxicating fragrance.

With all our eagerness to be accepted by the mainstream Christian world has come the marginalization of the advancing light of the gospel as it came in two calls to the Advent people. As we have sought acceptance through ecumenical "conversations," "making ourselves known," and "learning from others," the denomination has let its banner drag in the mud and lost our biblical identity. It was in this environment in the late 1980s that this writer began to notice that, when subjects like the nature of Christ were brought up in Sabbath School, class members would say, "Not this again," as eyes would roll.

We need to explore a number of areas in what we will call the "the apostate bloom." These items will be discussed not so much as isolated historical elements but as cause-and-effect manifestations within the meta-narrative of the devoured generations. It is the woeful blossoming of an invasive species, and its fruit is now setting in readiness for the final ripening of the grape harvest of the "vine of the earth" (Rev. 14:18, 19).

Species: The bloom of worldly entertainment methodologies in celebrationism, music, theatrics

> And he put forth the form of an hand, and took me by a lock of mine head; and the spirit lifted me up between the earth and the heaven, and brought me in the visions of God to Jerusalem, to the door of the inner gate that looketh toward the north; where *was* the seat of **the image of jealousy**, which provoketh to jealousy.
>
> And, behold, the glory of the God of Israel *was* there, according to the vision that I saw in the plain.
>
> Then said he unto me, Son of man, lift up thine eyes now the way toward the north. So I lifted up mine eyes the way toward the north, and behold northward at the gate of the altar this **image of jealousy** in the entry. (Ezek. 8:3–5, emphasis added)

> We are eagerly looking toward the churches of Babylon and envying their success. (*The Road to Rome*, p. 31)

As we set out to study "Celebrationism," let us keep in mind the linkage of the concept of "celebration" with religious practice.

Let us bear in mind that celebrating is a pagan custom. Those of us who labor for God in Asia see the raising of the arms, the eyes tilted heavenward, the swaying of the bodies, the beating of the drums, the activation of the tambourines and other "ecstatic" behavior on a regular basis. Those who do not travel to the Orient may observe the same behavior in the Hare Krishnas locally. They learned it from Babylon and they, too, are on the road to that acme of Babylonian religion, Rome. (*The Road to Rome*, p. 30)

At the urging of the General Conference, the late 1970s saw the beginning of the introduction of "celebration churches."

Celebrationism is generally a subdued form of the charismatic worship style. Not always content to remain docile, it has even broken out in such manifestations as "holy laughter," "slain in the spirit" and "tongues speaking." The "Milwaukie New Life Church" in the Oregon Conference, 1997, was one such church, which ended up splitting over the issue. That particular church had become a training center for Seventh-day Adventist pastors to learn how to implement celebration-style worship programs into their churches.

This writer has spoken with members of a large city celebration-style church who were involved in tongues-speaking. Yet, more generally, it does not go that far, being confined to live band rock-style music in "praise" performances, theatrics, and generally entertainment-oriented services. It has been documented that celebration-style church often break away from the Seventh-day Adventist Church and sometimes even go over to Sunday worship, as in the case of Pastor David Snyder of the Milwaukie New Life Church who, in the late 1980s, quit the church, joined a Sunday service church and took many Seventh-day Adventist members with him.

That we should bring nothing of a theatrical nature—of show and display—into worship services or religious instruction is well established by our Lord as a principle of conduct. The introduction of hilarity, clapping, levity and laughter is not appropriate for the conveyance of eternal truth. Christ used simple illustrations from nature and human experience to get His message across, but He did not use comedic monologue, commission mimes or theatre troupes to illustrate His lessons, arouse curiosity, create a sensation or foster a carnival atmosphere that would invite applause and cheers. In His life and ministry, He showed us how to work and, through the Spirit of Prophecy writings, gave us instructions applicable to our generation as well. The counsel given is not to shape our teaching to the tastes of the prevailing culture. We need only show a few passages from inspiration to establish clearly what is good and correct:

> It is not for the workers to seek for methods **by which they can make a show**, consuming time in **theatrical performances and musical display**, for this benefits

no one. It does no good to train the children to make speeches for special occasions. They should be won to Christ, and instead of expending time, money, and effort to **make a display**, let the whole effort be made to gather sheaves for the harvest. (*Christian Education* [1894], p. 134, emphasis added)

The presentation before me was that if Elder [Franke] would heed the counsel of his brethren, and not rush on in the way he does in making a great **effort to secure large congregations**, he would have more influence for good, and his work would have a more telling effect. He should **cut off from his meetings everything that has a semblance of theatrical display**; for such outward appearances give no strength to the message that he bears ... He will not place so much **dependence on the musical program**. This part of his services is conducted **more after the order of a concert in a theater**, than a song service in a religious meeting. (Lt. 49, 1902, in *Evangelism*, p. 501, emphasis added)

When professing Christians reach the high standard which it is their privilege to reach, the simplicity of Christ will be maintained in all their worship. **Forms and ceremonies and musical accomplishments are not the strength of the church**. Yet these things have taken the place that God should have, even as they did in the worship of the Jews. (Ms. 157, 1899, in *Evangelism*, p. 512, emphasis added)

We are handling subjects which involve eternal interests, and we are not to ape the world in any respect.... (Ms. 96, 1898, in *Evangelism*, p. 139)

Ministers should not make a practice of **relating anecdotes** in the desk; it **detracts from the force and solemnity of the truth presented**. The relation of anecdotes or incidents which **create a laugh or a light thought** in the minds of the hearers is **severely censurable**. The truths should be clothed in **chaste and dignified language**; and the illustrations should be of a like character. (*Review and Herald*, Aug. 8, 1878, art. A, in *Evangelism*, p. 640, emphasis added)

There is much counsel in these lines, in fact, too much to miss. All of the methods we see utilized in the celebration-style of "doing church" are described by the testimony of the Spirit as "fanciful representations" (Ms. 59, 1900, in *Evangelism*, p. 182), "common fire," "expensive display," "spirit of enthusiasm," "theatrical performances," "excitement," "strange things" "entertainments," and "fanaticism." Against all of these things we are to "close and bolt the doors firmly" (*Gospel Workers*, p. 383; Ms. 19, 1910; Lt. 17, 1902, in *Evangelism*, p. 138). It is said to bring zeal only for a while, but this soon dissipates and leaves the soul discouraged and depressed. This methodology to stimulate worship and spirituality could be described metaphorically as "spiritual caffeine." The desires for them are a "temptation and a snare to God's people" (*Counsels to Teachers*, p. 325).

However, the leadership sweeps all of this away. For example, former NAD President Alfred C. McClure stated: "[While] ... our theology is uncompromisingly biblical, our methodology needs to be predominantly cultural." Then too, Bert Jackson, Berwick Adventist Community Fellowship publicity officer, said:

Part of our task as Adventists is to translate—to convert eternal principles of the Adventist message into people's immediate context. That means leading into our message through their culture, through their interests ... beginning with a contemporary worship and witnessing program contoured to the needs and expectations of unchurched people. (in Gary Krause, "Our Western Global Mission," *Adventist Review*, March 6, 1997, p. 17)

From the North American Division Evangelism Institute (NADEI) we are told:

At SEEDS '97 you will explore the practice of: ... Taking God's church to the people through marketplace evangelism, lifestyle evangelism, ministering with compassion, using culturally relevant methods. (Reported on www.tagnet.org site, link no longer available, cited by video documentary "Are You Ready For Church," 1:04.20, by AdventHerald, available at http://1ref.us/ir, accessed 11/10/16)

The message from heaven to the church is:

What was the origin of the great apostasy? How did the church first depart from the simplicity of the gospel? By conforming to the practices of paganism, to facilitate the acceptance of Christianity by the heathen. The apostle Paul declared, even in his day, "The mystery of iniquity doth already work." 2

Thessalonians 2:7. During the lives of the apostles the church remained comparatively pure. But "toward the latter end of the second century most of the churches assumed a new form; the first simplicity disappeared, and insensibly, as the old disciples retired to their graves, their children, along with new converts, ... came forward and **new-modeled** the cause." —Robert Robinson, *Ecclesiastical Researches*, ch. 6, par. 17, p. 51. To secure converts, the exalted standard of the Christian faith was lowered, and as the result "a pagan flood, flowing into the church, carried with it its customs, practices, and idols." —Gavazzi, Lectures, page 278. As the Christian religion secured the favor and support of secular rulers, it was nominally accepted by multitudes; but **while in appearance Christians, many "remained in substance pagans, especially worshiping in secret their idols."** —*Ibid.*, page 278. (*The Great Controversy*, p. 384, emphasis added)

Are the various forms of rock music and the appetite for theatrical entertainments part of those "customs, practices, and idols"? Undoubtedly so. Adventist News Network reports:

The Church's strategy is to present the Bible and salvation in terms that people will understand. This may mean that 'traditional' methods will need to be adapted to fit the cultural perspectives of those being addressed ... ("Adventists Want to 'Make Gospel Relevant'," Jan. 20, 1998)

There is a principle in operation in the fallen human experience that is easier to slide into wrong habits than to develop the right ones and that, once a wrong course has been pursued, it is difficult to change back. It is better to never start compromising these principles in our worship settings because of the difficulty of reversing our course later.

When there has been a departure from the right path, it is difficult to return.... It takes less time and labor to corrupt our ways before God than to engraft upon the character habits of righteousness and truth. Whatever a man becomes accustomed to, be its influence good or evil, he finds it difficult to abandon. (*Testimonies for the Church*, vol. 4 [1879], p. 578)

Fanaticism, once started and left unchecked, is as hard to quench as a fire which has obtained hold of a building. Those who have entered into and sustained this fanaticism, might far better be engaged in secular labor; for by their inconsistent course of action they are dishonoring the Lord and imperiling his people.... (Ms. 76a, 1901, in *General Conference Bulletin*, April 23, 1901)

The roots of Celebrationism are ecumenical. Rome's path to unity is not based in truth as found in the Word of God but in a common liturgy.

The liturgical emphasis of Vatican II can be summarized in a single word—*Celebrate*. No less than 536 times in 150 pages is this word or those derived from it (such as celebration, celebrating, etc.) used in the liturgical document produced by Vatican II. (Bob Trefz, *Freedom's Ring*, vol. 2, no. 1, p. 1)

It is significant that Rome encourages the use of "popular religious songs" among psalms and sacred music as being suitable musical Celebrations. *Vatican II Documents*, p. 91. Rome also dictates the physical methods associated with Celebration. While it claims that we must celebrate internally, it stipulates that on the other hand, [it must be] external also, that is, such as to show the internal participation by gestures and bodily attitudes, by the acclamations, responses and singing. *Vatican II Documents*, p. 84. (*The Road to Rome*, p. 50)

Unfortunately, there is no warning being given by the church regarding the agenda at work. "On the contrary, much support is given [*in mainstream church periodicals*]. In a church which a few short years ago publicly declared that the charismatic movement demonstrated the appearance of the false latter rain (see the Statement of the 1973 Annual Council, among others), this is a startling development" (*The Road to Rome*, p. 50).

What is the philosophy and purpose of Celebrationism and how is it to be achieved?

The purpose of the "celebration" format, started about 1987, was to unite both conservatives and liberals into celebration worship services with that "wide variety" of activities and music, from hymns to ultra band music. The "church-planting" method, started about 1995 and now in progress, is to raise up new celebration churches. In this way, the conservatives will not be disturbed and will continue supporting the denomination. (Vance Ferrell, "A Celebration Training Manual," part one of two, p. 2, available at http://1ref.us/is, accessed 12/18/16)

The music in celebration-style worship utilizes forms of rock, with the rhythmic accents on beats 2 and 4, which is syncopation, also known as the "back-beat." The purpose of syncopation is sensual, to appeal to the body and to promote dance movement. It has simply been called "dancy" music. One only need to watch children in front of the loudspeakers when syncopated music plays. Parents love to think that their toddler children are particularly musically inclined when they bounce and dance to the music. It is cute, but it merely demonstrates how the music overrides frontal lobe processing, stimulating the part of the brain that moves the body. There is no talent involved in it, any more than a pond would be talented for producing ripples when a pebble is cast upon its surface. Add whatever message to this for lodgment in the mind—the body does not care. Ask people what they like about this or that popular band and most often you will hear the answer, "*the beat.*" The Beatles and the hip-gyrating "Elvis-the-Pelvis" Presley popularized rock music. What more evidence is needed?

All historians of contemporary music know that Rock 'n Roll developed in the 1950's and had its roots in black and Pentecostal gospel music. Indeed, in the NBC television production of the early career of Elvis Presley, one complete episode portrayed how Elvis developed his music from the Pentecostal church services he attended with his mother and father as a young lad. In this episode, Elvis was appearing on his first Grand Ole' Opry country music show. The crowd was not responding to his rendition of a beautiful ballad. Elvis was "bombing" as the entertainment industry would describe the incident. In his mind's eye, Elvis was taken back to the Pentecostal church he attended as a lad and was impressed by the audience's response to the wild gyrations of the minister at the service. He could clearly see the reaction of the people to the minister's loud preaching and crowd-control methods. Presley immediately broke into a black Rhythm and Blues tune and began to imitate the gyrations of the Pentecostal minister he had observed. At that precise moment the legend of Elvis Presley was born. The cameras focused in on his mother and girl friend standing at the side of the auditorium. The camera neatly captured the expression of astonishment on their faces. Their stunned expression revealed that they too realized there was a power, a supernatural force at work that neither they nor Elvis could ever reverse. This supernatural demonic musical influence eventually killed Elvis Presley, *and it will destroy an individual or group, denomination or church, who dare to embrace this dangerous last-day delusion* of Satan! (Neil C. Livingston, *The Greatest Conspiracy*, p. 17, available at http://1ref.us/it, accessed 12/15/16)

The combination of body swaying and dancing, hands in the air, high volume, low lighting, with the singing of repetitive words and phrases in crooning styles, seen also at modern secular rock concerts, is often little more than sweet sentimentalism in contrast to the more substantial and Scriptural foundation of hymns. This all readily lends to more of a *self-centered enjoyment* than a *God-centered contemplation* of truth.

The Spirit of God has revealed that this would come into the Adventist movement.

In 1898, Satan, through a false teaching known as the "Holy Flesh Movement" in Indiana, made an unsuccessful attempt to introduce a false Christ and a "Pentecostal" or "Celebration" type of worship into the Seventh-day Adventist Church. Elder S. S. Davis, Indiana Conference evangelist, developed these strange new teachings never before known among Seventh-day Adventists. Elder R. S. Donnell, President of the Indiana Conference, along with a majority of the ministry of the Conference was swept away by the erroneous teachings. The advocates of this strange new phenomena believed the movement was the outpouring of the "Latter Rain," and the teachings swept through the Indiana Conference with the speed of a prairie fire. (*The Greatest Conspiracy*, p. 14)

This phenomenon, using long prayers, extended "hysterical preaching," and strange, "loud instrumental music" with bass drums and tambourines, rose up just ahead of the "Pentecostal tongues-speaking movement" which developed "in the clapboard store-front, skid-row churches of Los Angeles" (*The Greatest Conspiracy*, p. 16). Anyone who is even remotely familiar with the discussion of this subject has read or heard the following statement:

The things you have described as taking place in Indiana, the Lord has shown me would take place just before the close of probation. **Every uncouth**

thing will be demonstrated. There will be **shouting**, with **drums**, and **dancing**. The senses of rational beings will become so confused that they cannot be trusted to make right decisions. And **this is called the moving of the Holy Spirit.**

The Holy Spirit never reveals itself in such methods, in such a bedlam of noise. This is an invention of Satan to cover up his ingenious methods for making of none effect the pure, sincere, elevating, ennobling, sanctifying truth for this time.... A bedlam of noise shocks the senses and perverts that which if conducted aright might be a blessing. **The powers of satanic agencies blend with the din and noise to have a carnival, and this is termed the Holy Spirit's working.**...

Those participating in the supposed revival receive impressions which lead them adrift. They cannot tell what they formerly knew regarding Bible principles. (Lt. 132, 1900, in *Manuscript Releases*, vol. 21, p. 128)

To put it simply, they "lose it." The letter goes on to tell how it would come into the camp-meetings. This author has witnessed it personally at a Canadian camp-meeting, and one can find video documented evidence freely available on the Internet showing all kinds of mayhem and irreverence.

Better never have the worship of God blended with music than to use musical instruments to do the work which last January **was represented to me would be brought into our camp meetings.** The truth for this time needs nothing of this kind in its work of converting souls.... (Lt. 132, 1900, in *Manuscript Releases*, vol. 21, pp. 128, 129, emphasis added)

Of course, what we are looking at today is not the full-blown manifestations such as rose up in Indiana, or what we see in many of the charismatic churches today. Satan knows he cannot get this past Adventists, at least *at this time*. He will work it in by a more subtle form, while emphasizing gospel teaching that is quite compatible with mainstream Protestant Christianity (identified by the second angel).

Ellen White was in Australia, at the time, and received the first-hand reports of it from Elder Stephen Haskell, whom the General Conference sent in to investigate. It is interesting to read what he said:

There is a **great power** that goes with the movement that is on foot there. It would almost bring anybody within its scope, if they are at all conscientious, and sit and listen with the least degree of favor; **because of the music that is brought to play in the ceremony.** They have an organ, one bass viol, three fiddles, two flutes, three tambourines, three horns, and a big bass drum, and perhaps other instruments which I have not mentioned. They are as much trained in their musical line as any Salvation Army choir that you ever heard. In fact, their revival effort is simply a **complete copy of the Salvation Army method,** and when they get on a high key, **you cannot hear a word from the congregation in their singing, nor hear anything**, unless it be shrieks of those who are half insane. I do not think I overdraw it at all. (Letter #1, S. N. Haskell to Ellen G. White, Sept. 25, 1900, in *Ellen G. White: The Early Elmshaven Years: 1900–1905*, p. 102, emphasis supplied)

This level of loud music and even "extended hysterical preaching" is not uncommon in celebration style churches of today. I have heard it on occasion. Once, around the year 2010, while attending a Seventh-day Adventist church in the city of New Orleans—*a conference church*—my family was treated to an astonishing spectacle. While on extended travels, we enjoyed checking in on some of these city churches to observe the proceedings. Here, we had the unforgettable experience of being subjected to an entire service set to ear-splitting hard rock, including the "greet each other" exercise and the "welcome the visitors" exercise. It was pure pandemonium. Then the preacher, a highly educated man with a long and distinguished service record in the church, delivered a "message" that had three delivery levels: excited shouting, agitated bellowing, and super-charged screaming. All I remember about the content of that message is that it was nonsense. In the words of Elder Haskell, I do not "overdraw it at all." It was nothing less than *obscene*. My two then pre-teen children, who had been earlier exposed to grandma's charismatic "rock and roll church," were rather perplexed by what we had just witnessed in an Adventist church. I left the "church service" that Sabbath day, visibly trembling, and it took a full hour for my nerves to return to a normal state. I wrote to that conference to inquire what that was all about, but received no response whatsoever.

Ellen White, in response to Haskell's description, stated:

Those things which have been in the past will be in the future. Satan will make music a snare by the way

in which it is conducted. God calls upon His people, who have the light before them in the Word and in the Testimonies, to read and consider, and to take heed. Clear and definite instruction has been given in order that all may understand. (Lt. 132, 1900, in *Selected Messages*, bk. 2, p. 38, emphasis added)

How and why did all of this come into the Seventh-day Adventist church? In a January 2001 tract publication, author and researcher Pastor Vance Ferrell tells how Celebration churches came into Adventism:

During the 1980s, many faithful believers appealed to conference presidents because their local pastor was leading the members into compromising our historic beliefs and standards. Unless those appealing for help were wealthy, their pleas were generally ignored. They were rewarded for their concerns by being stripped of their church offices and gradually edged out. As a result, many of our most faithful members left the denomination in that decade.

Desperate to find sources of income which would replace the donations that the faithful took with them in the late 1980s, General Conference leaders looked to current trends among Sundaykeepers for solutions. As a result, Celebration churches were initiated, in which bands, loud music, and theatrical skits were used to bring more worldlings into the church. Entertainment became the key to action. ("A Powerful New Way to Change the Church—Life's Answer Church," Waymarks 1059, p. 1)

Evangelism in the church used to be with a view to bringing souls to a genuine intelligent conversion to Christ and a desire to follow Him in all things. The inculcation of specific distinctive doctrinal beliefs, standards for Christian intellectual development and practical living of the faith, along with the truth that conversion produces an active Christian witness and service of the believer, were an inherent part of the acknowledged agreement of candidates to be fulfilled by choice according to the power of the Holy Spirit. However, the celebration movement was to operate on entirely different principles, based upon a Pentecostal type of appeal.

"Celebrationism" has gradually been going out of vogue, as many members voted with their feet or starting sending tithes and offerings to independent ministries who did not succumb to the new methods. So the idea of converting the traditional churches to celebration churches has somewhat faded away, although most churches today retain some of the elements. Again, money support became an issue. Older members got tired of the theatrical Pentecostalism. Also the loss of entire churches that would break away from the denomination and take the tithe and offerings with them became a serious concern.

Pastors from all over the continent were sent to David Snyder's Milwaukie, Oregon, celebration church for training. Snyder, who in earlier years had studied acting and theatrical work, was ideally suited for the task. However, within a very few years both he and other celebration pastors began leaving the denomination, and sometimes taking members and even whole church companies with them. (Vance Ferrell, "A Second Seventh-day Adventist Denomination is Starting! Ron Gladden's New Church," Waymarks 1234, p. 1, available online at http://1ref.us/iu, accessed 12/18/16)

So the answer to this was to revamp the program. In the mid–1990s a new method was acquired from the Sunday-keepers, called seeker-sensitive "church planting." Adventists eagerly enlisted in the programs of the mega-churches of Bill Hybels' "Willow Creek" in northern Illinois and of Rick Warren's "Saddleback Church" in southern California. In this way, Adventists acquired the knowledge and skill to build up "anything goes" churches that would pull the "seeker" off the street, get him or her quickly into membership and hopefully take in the tithes and offerings to keep the church program running.

Who else do we know that engaged in all manner of compromise to assimilate the pagan hordes? Whatever happened to "be ye separate"?

The methodology in "church planting" is essentially the same kind of approach to worship as Celebrationism, while retaining the same gospel message akin to the "perseverance of the saints" (once-saved-always-saved) while avoiding any real dealing with the three angel's messages and the sanctuary teaching. The theological thrust is based upon a continual mantra of "the gospel," "grace," and "by faith alone." While these concepts are proper so long as they are in the context of the true advancing light of the ongoing Reformation, as exemplified by the teachings of "the Advent message," "the third angel's message," "the sanctuary message," and "the truth," we find this is not at all the context. These Adventist phrases are generally not part of what one might hear in the gospel teaching of churches with celebration or church plant strategies. The new "church plants" studiously avoid all of that, avoiding as well anything that would readily identify the center as a "Seventh-day Adventist" church, favoring instead names that reflect general Christian fellowship. In the church plant program, what is thought to be "perfectionism" continues to be denigrated in favor of an "it's-all-been-done-at-the-cross" Protestant Reformationism.

God does not require us to cloak our faith to secure patronage, and He takes a rather dim view of it.

Men will employ every means to make less prominent the difference between Seventh-day Adventists and observers of the first day of the week. A company was presented before me under the name of Seventh-day Adventists, who were advising that the banner, or sign, which makes us a distinct people should not be held out so strikingly; for they claimed that this was not the best policy in order to secure success to our institutions. But this is not a time to haul down our colors, to be ashamed of our faith. This distinctive banner, described in the words, "Here is the patience of the saints: here are they that keep the commandments of God, and the faith of Jesus," is to be borne through the world to the close of probation. While efforts should be increased to advance in different localities, there must be no cloaking of our faith to secure patronage. Truth must come to souls ready to perish; and if it is in any way hidden, God is dishonored, and the blood of souls will be upon our garments. (*Testimonies for the Church*, vol. 6, p. 144)

Ferrell went on to say:

Under the former celebration plan, when a regular Adventist church was switched over to the celebration pattern by its pastor, faithful believers became upset and tended to leave. The new people coming in believed and practiced no standards; they gave little in tithes and offerings. The older ones who were leaving were taking their donations with them. Church leaders discovered that they were losing rather than gaining.

The church planting plan was different in just one key aspect: Instead of changing an established Adventist church into a celebration church, an entirely new church was raised up in a separate building in a different location. In this way, a new celebration church could be started—without disturbing historic believers in their established churches.

Church planting became the big push in the mid- and late-1990s, as efforts were made to start brand-new celebration churches.

In 1996, the SEEDS conferences began, which trained Adventist pastors and promoted the new-style planting of celebration churches, hopefully at an even faster rate. ("Ron Gladden's New Church," Waymarks 1234, p. 1, available at http://1ref.us/iu, accessed 11/10/16)

Of course, the church would never agree with Ferrell's explanation for its strange activity. However, one cannot but see that there is a concern about money support. The church's promotion of this new style of worship, which has been encouraged to exist as 'Adventism in a parallel universe,' is dealing with the issue of tithes and offerings in a manner contrary to established church practice. The payment of tithes has never been tied to membership, but in the church plant operation, it is suggested that it be made a rule. In a 27-page, 8½ x 11 document, labeled, "Life's Answer Church ... *Approved by: The Seventh-day Adventist Church*" (emphasis added), outlining the "church planting" plan, stipulates:

Membership will be renewed annually and those who do not routinely attend, do not support the body with tithe and offerings, and who are not involved with missionary service will be dropped from membership. (p. 9)

This same document outlines how this program is to "meet the needs of first generation unchurched people—not the needs and worship preferences of current Seventh-day Adventists (p. 1) and how the numbers of experienced Seventh-day Adventists are to be kept to a minimum, that they are to serve as facilitators of the process or attend only if they bring "explorers" (code for non-Seventh-day Adventists) with them. "As such, the congregations will be characterized as intra-denominational" (p. 6).

Such "converts" would not be very pleased to know that they have been so baited, in order to fund the 'mother ship.' What happens if they come to a traditional service? What will they think is going on? This writer has seen how the "two churches" in Adventism operate in the reverse situation. A local Canadian church, at an expense of over seventy thousand dollars, conducted an evangelistic campaign by bringing in an "Amazing Facts" evangelist from the United States. This campaign resulted in over twenty new members. The pastor, operating a celebration-style church, then sequestered the new converts into a backroom study for Sabbath School, as most of the teachers in the mainstream church classes were much more traditional in style and theology. It was only a matter of weeks before virtually all of those new members were lost. What they had heard at the Amazing Facts evangelistic meetings, which had so fired them up, was not being taught in this church. Some said that this Seventh-day Adventist Church was what they had just come out of and, in confusion, they left and never came back.

There is a mantra of "cultural relevancy" promoted among the membership as a means of selling the celebration worship style. The demand for "relevancy" produces a claim that by the use of entertaining styles, the church will supposedly attract the "unchurched" and the "backslidden." At the same time, it allegedly makes church more attractive to our own youth so they will not be so tempted to leave for the worldly attractions—because we have brought those same attractions into the church. What a thought!

> In their efforts to reach the people, the Lord's messengers are not to follow the ways of the world.... (*Testimonies for the Church*, vol. 9, p. 143)

We are wondering if perhaps the altars to Ba'al in the apostate Israelite church wasn't a "culturally relevant" style of worship? Were they doing any differently than their modern counterpart, in all their dancing around the altar, praying for fire (the Holy Spirit), to show that the Lord accepted their worship?

> Elijah, early in the morning, stands upon Mount Carmel, **surrounded by apostate Israel** and the **prophets of Baal**....
>
> With stern and commanding voice Elijah cries: "How long halt ye between two opinions? if the Lord be God, follow Him: but if Baal, then follow him. **And the people answered him not a word.**" Not one in that vast assembly dared utter one word for God and show his loyalty to Jehovah.
>
> What astonishing deception and fearful blindness had, like a dark cloud, covered Israel! This blindness and apostasy had not closed about them suddenly; it had come upon them gradually as they had not heeded the word of reproof and warning which the Lord had sent to them because of their pride and their sins. And now, in this fearful crisis, in the presence of the idolatrous priests and the apostate king, **they remained neutral**. If God abhors one sin above another, of which His people are guilty, it is doing nothing in case of an emergency. Indifference and neutrality in a religious crisis is regarded of God as a grievous crime and equal to the very **worst type of hostility against God**. (*Testimonies for the Church*, vol. 3, pp. 280, 281, emphasis added)

Why have the people stood by with a careless attitude, neutral in their stance, allowing the leaders to sell out the church? Did they forget they had a prophet? Or did the television, movies, sports, comedy and worldly music make them forget how to read? Certainly there has developed a lack of taste or inclination for serious reading.

How has leadership so convinced the laity to accept all of this deviation? Part of it is in the expression of a great concern for the decline of values, spirituality, knowledge, and missionary zeal as found in the church. This has been the basis for desiring something—anything—to kick-start the church again. It is not a dead philosophy even today that the Celebration forms will achieve the fix that is needed, not only in spirituality, but in numbers of converts. Rome feels the same way, that "**liturgical forms** offer the basis for the return of the 'separated brethren' and the conversion of non-Christians" (*The Road to Rome*, p. 52, emphasis added).

> The Spirit of the Lord is at work in the present-day ecumenical movement in order that, when the obstacles hindering perfect ecclesiastical communion have been surmounted, the unity of all Christians may at last be restored and shine forth, for all peoples are called to be a single new people, confessing one Jesus, Saviour, Lord, professing one faith, celebrating one eucharistic mystery. (Secretariat for the Promotion of the Unity of Christians, *Spiritus Domini*, April 16, 1970, cited in *The Road to Rome*, p. 52)

The Seventh-day Adventist Church states:

We are deeply concerned about local churches across North America. Most are not growing. There is a lack of warmth and inclusiveness. Large numbers of youth and adults in their thirties are inactive. Outreach and service to the community is in danger of being lost in comfortable rituals. Needs are not being met. Families are at risk. Giving and volunteering are down. Local leadership often places a higher priority on maintenance than mission, and pastors become discouraged or exhausted. **There is a grave danger that the precious Adventist message will not be passed on to the next generation.** ("The San Diego Covenant," prepared by the North American Division and quoted in *The Adventist Review*, March 7, 1991, p. 23, emphasis added)

So, the church turned to "creative methods of evangelism" as the answer. In the "Proposal of the North American Division of Youth Evangelism Taskforce subcommittee on Seeker Sensitivity" by Stefan Brugman, A. Allan Martin, Deirdre Martin, and Pastor Randal Wisbey, which was created to "formulate plans that would enable churches throughout the North American Division to develop ministries and worship services in which youth and young adults would be more specifically ministered to," we find the overall rationale for the program to "intentionally create a community of believers in which the spiritual journey of the seeker is communicated, allowed for, and legitimized; to empower this, seeker sensitive churches will be developed in every union of the North American Division." Part of this plan of "creative methods of evangelism" to "meet the needs of the young adults" would be, of course, to "update the music." It was recommended under implementation and budget strategies to subsidize the operation by sending local church leaders to Willow Creek conferences to learn "culturally relevant methods."

Yet, is a shallow form of religion the answer? Celebration services do not generally focus on deep calls for confession and repentance, for reformation and the claiming of the Holy Spirit to receive power to obey God and forsake sin. There is a general fear of "legalism," so that such calls would be deemed "old covenant" in this day of "grace" and "freedom in Christ." While we are living in the antitypical day of atonement and called to a solemn assembly, the celebration church does not want to hear about afflicting the soul (Lev. 16:31). Rather, it wants the assurance of a "completed work at the cross." It wants a "safe place" for seekers, for the unchurched. Discussion of sin and obedience is not politically correct, nor does it attract the mainstream willingly unregenerate. These are not the kind of seekers who are burdened with sin. Rather, they prefer to keep their sin while celebrating the unburdening of their guilt. The good news they want is that Jesus has obeyed *for* me. It is not so serious that they are living a weak and flesh-directed life while they are celebrating "in the Spirit." Doing church like this is not a training to overcome by the blood of the Lamb but celebration for not being "under the law." Thus, it is an antinomian avoidance of the gospel that brings obedience into one's life through the merits of Christ.

Yet, in spite of all the warnings, those who love the celebration style of worship will praise it and let nothing stand in their way, claiming that it has great effect, brings God near, and appeals to those who would otherwise never set foot in a church. Nonetheless, the reality is that the entertaining appeal of dramatic presentations, repetitive lyrics, "dancy" rhythms and "blue notes" have a hypnotic effect and set a higher value on emotion than intellect. It is a species of mind control. That is why Vatican II promoted it. Yet, this is what Heaven says:

> And while those who are devoted to these sciences **laud them to the heavens because of the great and good works which they affirm are wrought by them**, they little know what a power for evil they are cherishing; but it is **a power which will yet work with all signs and lying wonders,**—with all deceivableness of unrighteousness. Mark the influence of these sciences, dear reader, for the conflict between Christ and Satan is not yet ended. (*Signs of the Times*, Nov. 6, 1884, emphasis added)

Signs and wonders are how Babylon "does church." What has Seventh-day Adventism to do with that kind of "church," when we are to follow Christ into the most holy place in the antitypical day of atonement? True Adventism will shun what an offshoot imposter will embrace, for it denigrates the fundamentals of our faith, such as the entrance of Christ into the most holy place of the heavenly sanctuary in 1844 and all the biblical exposition that goes with it. (Desmond Ford, you will remember, was the creator of the new theology that became so popular in Adventist academia.)

The typical day of atonement was not a day of festivities. It was the most solemn Sabbath of the year. Each individual had a work to do in examining his soul in the light of God's holy law. It was a day when sins were confessed and forsaken. Those who neglected this work were put out of the congregation.

In the vastly more significant antitypical day of atonement, we dare not do less. This is the day for the straight testimony of the True Witness to the church of Laodicea, rather than a day of following worship practices which are specifically designed to dull the senses to the awesome times in which we live. (*The Road to Rome*, p. 41)

Further doctrinal ramifications

Earlier we referred to a letter written by Stephen Haskell, reporting on the Indiana "Holy Flesh" movement. There was a second letter, in which Haskell described the strange doctrine taught by these people in the Indiana conference, claiming to be Seventh-day Adventist. It is most interesting to compare how their Christology lined up with that of modern Celebrationism.

> When we stated that **we believed that Christ was born in fallen humanity**, they would represent us as believing that Christ sinned, notwithstanding the fact that we would state our position so clearly that it would seem as though no one could misunderstand us. Their point of theology in this particular respect seems to be this: **They believe that Christ took Adam's nature before he fell**; so He [Christ] took humanity as it was in the garden of Eden, and thus humanity was holy, and this is the humanity which Christ had; and now, they say, the particular time has come for us to become holy in that sense, and then we will have "translation faith" and never die." (Stephen Haskell, Letter #2, to Ellen G. White, Battle Creek, Michigan, Sept. 25, 1900, in Herbert Douglass, *Messenger of the Lord*, p. 199, emphasis supplied)

Ellen White rebuked the men who led out in this teaching and stated: "There is not a thread of truth in the whole fabric" (quoted by G. A. Roberts, "The Holy Flesh Fanaticism," June 11, 1923, Ellen G. White Estate, DF 190, p. 2, available at drc.whiteestate.org/read.php?id=53032, accessed 10/25/16). There is not a thread of truth in any point of the Holy Flesh teaching, nor in the agitated music that goes with it, nor in the doctrine of the pre-fall nature of Christ attached to it. Today, this doctrine is inextricably associated with celebrationism, for it embraces a Christ who is dissociated from our nature, and, therefore, is no example for us on how to keep the law. We cannot be expected to keep it as He did. Obedience is not a general theme in the teaching of the entertainment churches. The doctrinal foundation for the entertainment church's view of Christ, which entered the church in the third generation through the Evangelical Conferences, provided a tidy framework for the development of celebrationism. Celebrationism is a de facto "Holy Flesh" revival, as judged by its musical philosophy and view of the nature of Christ,* yet it does not making any claims to having a sinless nature. Sanctification is fulfilled in another way, through the declaration of sanctification in the "cheap grace" gospel.

*In *Selected Messages*, bk. 2, p. 31, there is a compiler's note written by Arthur White that erroneously states that the Indiana movement Holy Flesh position was that Christ acquired prelapsarian status (the pre-fall sinless nature) in Gethsemane. The historical reality is that the participants in the Holy Flesh movement believed that this was His state from birth. A discussion of this matter can be found in Neil C. Livingston's *The Greatest Conspiracy*, pp. 22–28. It is well worth reading for its astonishing content relative to the new theology position on the nature of Christ, showing the entrenchment in this theology at high levels of church administration and the apparent willingness to use highly manipulative tactics to maintain the status quo of error.

Species: the bloom of Babylonian church-growth paradigms—CGM, Purpose-Driven Church, and the felt-needs focus

> Take heed to yourself that you are not ensnared to follow them, after they are destroyed from before you, and that you do not inquire after their gods, saying, "How did these nations serve their gods? I also will do likewise." You shall not worship the LORD your God in that way; for every abomination to the LORD which He hates they have done to their gods; for they burn even their sons and daughters in the fire to their gods. (Deut. 12:30, 31, NKJV)

> We cannot be complete in Christ and yet be ready to grasp those things that come from the so-called great men of the earth, and place their wisdom before the wisdom of the greatest Teacher the world has ever known. To seek knowledge from such sources is represented in the word as seeking to drink from broken cisterns that can hold no water. (*Testimonies for the Church*, vol. 7, p. 204)

> A new order of things has come into the ministry. There is a desire to pattern after other churches, and simplicity and humility are almost unknown. Young

ministers who desire to be original introduce new ideas and new plans for labor. They open revival meetings and call large numbers into the church. But when the excitement is over, where are the converted ones? Repentance for sin is not felt. The sinner is entreated to believe in Christ and accept Him, without any regard for his past life of sin and rebellion, and the heart is not broken. There is no contrition of soul. The professedly converted ones have not fallen upon the Rock Christ Jesus. (*Signs of the Times*, Dec. 27, 1899)

We need to spend a little time here on the modern philosophies of evangelism, or "church growth," that have been eagerly consumed by Adventists as one would a cool, fresh glass of Florida orange juice. This new model has been imbibed in the belief that high numbers of attendees, though initially rather worldly-minded, would become settled converts in time. It became popular to hear the metaphor of the church as a "hospital for sinners."

If you lower the standard in order to secure popularity and an increase of numbers, and then make this increase a cause of rejoicing, you show great blindness. If numbers were an evidence of success, Satan might claim the pre-eminence; for in this world his followers are largely in the majority.... It is the virtue, intelligence, and piety of the people composing our churches, not their numbers, that should be a source of joy and thankfulness. (*Testimonies for the Church*, vol. 5, p. 31)

The effect of the new outreach model on spirituality and Bible knowledge for the "unchurched" is not left to speculation. The experiment has run for some time, and the outcome is observable. We can now overlay the use of the celebration model with actual developments that came about under it. A long time ago, Elder Waggoner observed:

There is a widespread conviction or sentiment that nothing more is needed for the redemption of society than a rearrangement of social conditions; salvation will be wrought by science and sanitation; the heart will be cleansed by an external application; lusts and envies, and hatreds, will cease when the body's cravings are satisfied. On the top of these vain dreams there comes the clamour for a social gospel ... The preacher is to put into the background the eternal truths that he may cater for temporal wants. (E. J. Waggoner, *The Present Truth*, vol. 11, May 9, 1895, p. 292)

These words ring with the sound of prophecy, for this is exactly what was to take place on a large scale in the mainstream Christian world almost a hundred years later. Unfortunately, Adventists seem to ever demonstrate a "me too" attitude and follow the crowd wherever it goes.

We make no distinction between celebrationism and church growth movement principles because the two are linked—part of the church growth strategies in the new paradigm is cultural relevancy through entertainment. This ties into the "felt needs" aspect of church growth. Christian A. Schwarz, church growth expert on the importance of enthusiastic worship services says:

Is the worship service an inspiring experience for those who attend it? It is this area that clearly separates growing from non-growing churches. People who attend inspiring worship services unanimously declare that the church service is—and for some Christians this is almost a heretical word—"fun." (*The ABC's of Natural Church Development*, p. 14)

Yet, is "fun" the purpose of the church?

Growing churches are creating an atmosphere, an environment of fun. So fun has replaced holiness as the church's goal. Having a good time has become the criterion of an excellent, growing church, since fun and entertainment is what consumers want. Yet Bible references encouraging churches to become havens of fun are, as one may suspect, lacking. John MacArthur observes, "Many Christians have the misconception that to win the world to Christ we must first win the world's favor. If we can get the world to like us, they will embrace our Savior. That is the philosophy behind the user-friendly church movement." (Gary Gilley, *This Little Church Went to Market*, p. 19, citing John A. MacArthur, Jr., *Reckless Faith*, p. 52)

John MacArthur, as a Sunday-keeping, immortality of the soul, eternally-conscious torment preacher, is but one Babylonian calling out other Babylonians, yet his words are helpful to us in describing this new paradigm model for church:

"User-friendly" was first used to describe software and hardware that is easy for the novice to operate. Applied to the church, it describes churches that offer a decidedly benign and non-challenging ministry model. In practice, it has become an excuse for importing worldly amusements into the church in an attempt to attract non-Christian "seekers" or the "unchurched" by appealing to their fleshly interests. The obvious fallout of this preoccupation with the unbelievers is a corresponding neglect of true believers and their spiritual needs.

If you want to know how user-friendly a church has become, the emphasis, or de-emphasis, on biblical preaching is the yardstick. A church that buys into the new paradigm sidelines provocative and convicting sermons for music, skits, or videos—less confrontational mediums for conveying the message. Even when there is a sermon, it is frequently psychological and motivational rather than biblical. Above all, entertainment value and user-friendliness are paramount. (John MacArthur, "What's Wrong with 'User-Friendly'?" June 11, 2009, available at http://1ref.us/iv, accessed 1/27/16)

The church plant/church growth movement (CGM) paradigm plays into the ecumenical goals of the 1982 Lima Document (BEM, see above #10 under "Ecumenism Ascending") in its thrust to minister to the "Fringe and Former Church members" and "the Secular and Unchurched," while leaving out Babylon (no proselytizing allowed) as stated in a 1996 conference endorsement of one of these church plants in the South Australian Conference, aptly named "The Grove Adventist Church" (*Half a Century of Apostasy*, p. 59).

The Lord says to us, Seventh-day Adventists are not to place themselves under the counsel and instruction of teachers who know not the truth for this time. The molding and fashioning of minds should not be left to men who have not comprehended the importance of a preparation for that life which measures with the life of God. (*Review and Herald*, March 12, 1908, in *Counsels to Parents, Teachers, and Students*, p. 401)

Many urge that by uniting with worldlings and conforming to their customs they might exert a stronger influence over the ungodly. But all who pursue this course thereby separate from the Source of their strength. Becoming the friends of the world, they are the enemies of God. For the sake of earthly distinction they sacrifice the unspeakable honor to which God has called them, of showing forth the praises of Him who hath called us out of darkness into His marvelous light. 1 Peter 2:9. (*Patriarchs and Prophets*, p. 607)

Bill Hybels' "Willow Creek," a market-driven, new-paradigm church model

In 1975, a young minister named Bill Hybels started an inter-denominational Pentecostal style worship center near Chicago. Its focus was on church growth, and it grew into a "mega-church," which became a new term in Christendom, denoting a church with membership of 2,000 or more. The term was later found to be inadequate to describe the immensity of some of the churches, so the term "giga-church" was coined for mega-churches with over 10,000 members. Not all big churches use the new paradigm church growth strategies, but the two that we are going to focus on here because of their impact on Adventism *do*.

A market-driven church is shaped by an approach to ministry that is focused on large numbers. How appealing to Adventists! This writer has a close associate who, having worked in a local conference office for many years, related how, when a discussion arose amongst the leading men, regarding the pros and cons of an issue or plan of action and it was realized that it really wasn't an important issue relative to church mission, it would be quipped, tongue-in-cheek, "Well, it won't mean any more baptisms!" The new paradigm church stratagem is fueled by an industry of church growth and marketing experts such as Rick Warren and his *Purpose Driven Church*; George Barna and his *Step by Step Guide to Marketing the Church*; Lee Strobel's *Inside the Mind of Unchurched Harry and Mary*; and Director Christian A. Schwartz' "Institute for Natural Church Development." In these books and programs, "you will find a plethora of marketing techniques and only passing references to the book of Acts" (*This Little Church Went to Market*, p. 17).

The philosophy of bigger is better has sounded good to Adventists, even though the testimony of the Lord warned that in "large churches ... there is a special danger of lowering the standard" and it would be better to be broken up into more isolated groups and "made to stand alone" ("A Promise of Life Eternal," *North Pacific Union Gleaner*, March 9, 1910). In other places, the testimony of the Lord has emphasized their inactivity, low interest in imparting light and great interest in worldly pursuits. Repeatedly, she admonished churches to break up and get out into the field to do the work. The model of congregating with a pastor to hover over the people was never the right model, and yet it is the model the church has adopted, and we have reaped the results that were predicted to come—that the church would become feckless and inefficient for their work. Pastors were to be itinerate and raise up churches while elders were to be appointed for the work of tending to small local congregations.

By human standards in terms of numbers, the Willow Creek model of Bill Hybels became a huge success—in thirty years it achieved an attendance of 17,000 in the Sunday seeker services and 6,000 in the mid-week believer services. The church formed the Willow Creek Association (WCA), which garnered a membership of 2,200 churches. The Standish brothers reported in 2006: "At least 56 of those are Seventh-day Adventist churches and 3 are Seventh-day Adventist Conference organizations" (*Half a Century of Apostasy*, p. 62). Seventh-day Adventists became quite caught up in the philosophies and methods of the church-growth movement and began sending pastors to Willow Creek to receive training that would supposedly result in increased membership. However, what frequently has occurred is that these churches become worldly and entertainment-driven, and they start pulling in attendees from the surrounding churches for their updated and culturally relevant and exciting programs and services. Take notice of what Mrs. White had to say about shifting of membership in growing a large church:

> **The church in Fresno is composed of fragments of other churches**. They are not ignorant of the Scriptures and the power of God; and if they are what God would have them be, they will be light-bearers to the world. **This church is too large**. Many ought to be out carrying the light of truth to those who are in darkness. If they neglect this the woe of God will be upon them. Let them not carry there, but go out as workers together with God. **We are not here in this world to please and glorify ourselves**, but to be co-laborers with God. Probationary time is about to close. Now is the time to work, and that without delay. ("A Consecrated Ministry," Ms. 1a, 1890, in *Manuscript Releases*, vol. 6, p. 153, emphasis added)

It is only a backslidden church that can think to send its ministers into the precincts of Babylon to eat the delectable dainties of the king's table. What are they thinking? The Standish brothers inform us:

> The Willow Creek Association is an organization of a fallen church of Babylon. It is a Charismatic, Sunday-keeping church. These Conferences and Churches have now gone to a fallen church of Babylon in order to improve Seventh-day Adventist Churches. Just as well may they go to the witch of Endor!

> Lest it be thought that those Conferences and Churches have incurred the displeasure of the Church organisation, ... we direct the readers' attention to the documented evidence to the contrary. An article in the *Adventist Review*, 18 December, 1997 made three headlined points:

1. "Adventists should give Willow Creek a fair shake."

2. "Adventists should continue gleaning from Willow Creek."

3. "Gleaning from Willow Creek's message does not mean forfeiting our message."

These sub-headings contain two disgraceful admonitions and one absolute falsehood. [See *Patriarchs and Prophets*, p. 607, cited above.] How can we be so blind?

The *Review* article cited above stated:

> Fact: Adventists, both pastors and lay people, consistently make up one of the largest groups at Willow Creek's half-dozen annual seminars....

> Already the fruitage of this union with Babylon is well known to Church administrators. Again quoting from the same *Adventist Review* article, we find it admitted:

> Fact: The three latest Adventist churches to divide or depart [from the organisation]—Oregon's Sunnyside, Maryland's Damascus and Colorado's Christ Adventist Fellowship—were clearly influenced by Willow Grove [Creek] (*Half a Century of Apostasy*, pp. 62, 63).

Thomas Mostert, president of the Pacific Union Conference in 1995, wrote a book *Hidden Heresy: Is Spiritualism Invading Adventist Churches Today?* (2005), pointing to Bill Hybels' "Willow Creek," Rick Warren's "Saddleback," and even Robert Schuller's "Crystal Cathedral" as primary exhibits of the manner in which spiritualism is invading the Adventist church through absorption of worship and church-growth styles that bring with them the acceptance of unbiblical Babylonian theology.

Sidebar discussion: What is spiritualism?

We may very well ask how these things constitute spiritualism? The new paradigm church is certainly worldliness, even apostasy from the truth in many respects, considering the weak gospel that undergirds it. All of this we can readily understand as apostasy, but how is it *spiritualism*? When we speak about spiritualism, as it now manifests here on earth, we are simply hearkening back to the sophistry of Satan from the beginning, to the lies he told through the "old serpent" at the tree:

> Satan has long been preparing for his final effort to deceive the world. **The foundation of his work** was laid by the assurance given to Eve in Eden: **"Ye shall not surely die." "In the day ye eat thereof, then your eyes shall be opened, and ye shall be as gods, knowing good and evil."** Genesis 3:4, 5. Little by little he has prepared the way for **his masterpiece of deception in the development of spiritualism**. He has not yet reached the full accomplishment of his designs; but it will be reached in the last remnant of time. Says the prophet: "I saw three unclean spirits like frogs; … they are the spirits of devils, working miracles, which go forth unto the kings of the earth and of the whole world, to gather them to the battle of that great day of God Almighty." Revelation 16:13, 14. Except those who are kept by the power of God, through faith in His word, the whole world will be swept into the ranks of this delusion. The people are fast being lulled to a fatal security, to be awakened only by the outpouring of the wrath of God. (*The Great Controversy*, pp. 561, 562, emphasis added)

The basic idea that many people have when we refer to spiritualism is that of gross occultic activity, necromancy, séances, ouija boards and all manner of divination. Pagan and earth religions of animism and shamanism with their spirit guides, pantheism, and panentheism are all certainly spiritualism. Yet, the basic idea underpinning all of these is the philosophy surrounding belief in the immortal soul and the antinomian and rebellious, "Do as thou wilt, this is the whole of the law." Satan told the angels that they had the law built in. There was within them a guiding inner light that would always and only direct their ways in righteousness. What need did they have of God or His law telling them what to do? Frequently we hear today the philosophy of "follow your heart." We see it on the packaging of food products; we hear it in kid's movies, pop songs, advertising, and of course, in pop psychology. What is so sinister about following your heart? The answer is that it denies that following one's own way leads to death, that there is such a thing as sin. The devil's twin lies at the tree are: "You will be as gods, knowing good and evil" and "you shall not surely die" as a result of disbelieving God and doing your own thing. These are the basic stuff of spiritualism, which says that the spirit goes on after the body dies. It says that you can be "spiritual" all on your own—all you need is "love." Yet, this is a false version of love. It is a selfish love, and it does not consider God's righteous agape love as the love that has life in it.

In the context of the discussion of celebrationist felt-needs, church-growth, and new-paradigm Evangelicalism, we see spiritualism in the appeal to what the carnal heart wants and thinks it needs, as well as in the evangelical gospel of antinomianism, where we are "not under the law." It is in the once-saved-always-saved denial of needing to go beyond forgiveness and rise above sin in its prelapsarian teaching that the Saviour was not touched with our infirmities; and its papering the window to the heavenly sanctuary where the work of cleansing sinners and preparing a final generation translation-ready purified church that shines as the stars. It is in these that we find the foundation of all that is called spiritualism. Any such teachings are incompatible with the true gospel experience that prepares souls to stand in the presence of Almighty God as probation closes shortly before God's children are glorified at His appearing (Dan. 12:1–3; Rev. 6:17; 7:14; 14:5; 19:7).

> Even in its present form, so far from being more worthy of toleration than formerly, it is really a more dangerous, because a more subtle, deception. While it formerly denounced Christ and the Bible, it now professes to accept both. But the Bible is interpreted in a manner that is pleasing to the unrenewed heart, while its solemn and vital truths are made of no effect. Love is dwelt upon as the chief attribute of God, but it is degraded to a weak sentimentalism, making little distinction between good and evil. God's justice, His denunciations of sin, the requirements of His holy law, are all kept out of sight. The people are taught to regard the Decalogue as a dead letter. Pleasing, bewitching fables captivate the senses and lead men to reject the Bible as the foundation of their faith. Christ is as verily denied as before; but Satan has so blinded the eyes of the people that the deception is not discerned. (*The Great Controversy*, p. 558).

In short, virtually every falsity and error one can examine will go into the same trash can of "spiritualism."

If we were to construct a flow chart—a very large flow chart—with all the known errors on it, we could represent this visually. The new age teaching that "all paths lead home" is true, if the "paths" are Satan's errors and "home" is perdition. "But the path of the just is as the shining light, that shineth more and more unto the perfect day" (Prov. 4:18). In contrast to Satan's pluralism and rebellious philosophies, there is only one true Light and that is the Light of Truth, the One who said, "I am the Way, the Truth, and the Life" (John 14:6), and no person will see the Father but he that goes through Christ. "But he that doeth truth cometh to the light, that his deeds may be made manifest, that they are wrought in God" (John 3:21), and further, this is why Christ came, as John wrote: "This then is the message which we have heard of him, and declare unto you, that God is light, and in him is no darkness at all" (1 John 1:5).

Pagan New Age spiritualism, while tending more heavily toward the less subtle occult philosophies of Eastern mysticism, has its Christianized counterpart, and we know that the big names of Bill Hybels and Rick Warren have links to others who are more involved with the more Christianized form. Thomas Mostert described Hybels' associations with Robert Schuller, mentioning that "Hybels often works with Rick Warren and Robert Schuller in conducting training programs." It is well known that Schuller and his *The Hour of Power* at the "Crystal Cathedral" was a big player in mystic Christianity and was a pop psychology motivational powerhouse. Rick Warren, whom we shall discuss shortly, was not so much in league with the New Age Christian mystics, according to Douglass, but certainly has used much of their literature. Douglass says, "*Association* and *affiliation*—two words that trouble many regarding Warren's connections to many New Agers or to those in the new spiritualism movement" (*Truth Matters*, p. 91). I believe that this is much more troubling today than it was at the time Douglass penned these words. In any case, one can openly deny *affiliation* yet at the same time their *association* through use of the books and teachings of those whom they deny, as well as their use of buzz words that overlap with the New Age mystic community, weaken any claim they may have against affiliation. As one of many examples:

Warren: "What is the driving force in your life?" Twenty-four years earlier, Schuller wrote, "The Eternal Creative Force of the universe we call God can surge within your being to give you self-belief, self-esteem, self-love, self-confidence! Without it—you're sunk, with it—you're invincible" ["Discover Your Possibility," 1978]

The significance of these connections is recognized by anyone who is acquainted with New Age terminology—"force" is a key New Age concept. Confusion arises when Christians accept language without any warning about New Age implications leading swiftly into the new spirituality. This is called overlapping terminology. (*Truth Matters*, p. 94)

A leader can easily say, "Well, that's not how it is meant to be taken," but when the books he is reading from and citing to his audience are picked up and read by them, they are being indoctrinated in a way in which the preacher said he didn't mean. Also, when that leader is taking teaching from those books, he is reading them himself and imbibing the ideas contained in them. How can he not be teaching them? It is confusion and tends to make that leader's sincerity suspect. These links make it unsafe for us to read material written by unbelievers in the truths of the third angel's message for spiritual gain and instruction.

There is another source of danger against which we should constantly be on our guard, and that is the works of infidel authors. Such works are inspired by Satan, and no one can read them without loss to the soul. Some who are affected by them may finally recover; but all who tamper in the least with their foul influence place themselves on Satan's ground, and he makes the most of his advantage. They invite his temptations, and they have neither wisdom to discern nor strength to resist them. With a fascinating, bewitching power, unbelief and infidelity fasten themselves upon the mind. To harbor them is like taking to your bosom a serpent, whose sting is always poisonous and often fatal. (*Signs of the Times*, May 19, 1887)

Having looked at the broad meaning of spiritualism, then, we find that Thomas Mostert is on target in associating the new paradigm church, the Church Growth Movement, Purpose-Driven phenomenon with spiritualism. In chapter four of his book ("Dangers in Mixing Truth and Error"), he reproduces the statements of faith of various new paradigm churches, including Saddleback (Rick Warren), Willow Creek (Bill Hybels), Crystal Cathedral (Robert Schuller), and Lakewood (Joel

Osteen), noting that there is "no mention made of the law of God or obedience," which is of course a telltale marker of Satan's spiritualism. (See *Hidden Heresy*, pp. 55–63.) Ellen White wrote:

> There is a **spurious experience** prevailing everywhere. Many are continually saying, "All that we have to do is to believe in Christ." They claim that faith is all we need. In its fullest sense, this is true; but they do not take it in the fullest sense. To believe in Jesus is to take him as our redeemer **and our pattern**. If we abide in him and he abides in us, we are partakers of his divine nature, and are **doers of his word. The love of Jesus in the heart will lead to obedience to all his commandments. But the love that goes no farther than the lips, is a delusion**; it will not save any soul. Many reject the truths of the Bible, while they profess great love for Jesus; but the apostle John declares, "He that saith, I know him, and keepeth not his commandments, is a liar, and the truth is not in him." [1 John 2:4.] While Jesus has done all in the way of merit, we ourselves have something to do in the way of complying with the conditions. "If ye love me," said our Saviour, "keep my commandments." [John 14:15.] (*Historical Sketches of the Foreign Missions of the Seventh-day Adventists*, pp. 188, 189, emphasis added)

The condition of the religious world at the end is characterized in the third angel's message, which shall be given under the power of the fourth angel of Revelation 18. Verse 2 says that it has become the habitation of devils. The rejection of the Sabbath is also connected to spiritualism, along with spiritual "manifestations," which prime the people to accept spurious religious teachings:

> With every rejection of truth the minds of the people will become darker, their hearts more stubborn, until they are entrenched in an infidel hardihood. In defiance of the warnings which God has given, **they will continue to trample upon one of the precepts of the Decalogue**, until they are led to persecute those who hold it sacred. Christ is set at nought in the contempt placed upon His word and His people. As **the teachings of spiritualism are accepted by the churches**, the restraint imposed upon the carnal heart is removed, and the profession of religion will become a cloak to conceal the basest iniquity. A **belief in spiritual manifestations opens the door to seducing spirits and doctrines of devils**, and thus the influence of evil angels will be felt in the churches. (*The Great Controversy*, p. 603, emphasis added)

It is not only dangerous but it is forbidden to attempt to give our distinct final-call message from any kind of "confederation," which is "from the standpoint of the professed Christian churches" (see below). They are not teaching a message of being separate from the world but are, in so many ways, blurring the lines between the world and the church while at the same time keeping the law of God out of view. In disobeying this principle, we stand to *gain* nothing except the spirit of the world and, at the same time, we will *lose* our discernment.

> While this message is sounding, while the proclamation of truth is doing its separating work, we as faithful sentinels of God are to discern what our real position is. We are **not to confederate with worldlings**, lest we become imbued with their spirit, lest our spiritual discernment become confused, and we view those who have the truth and bear the message of the Lord **from the standpoint of the professed Christian churches**.... (Lt. 86a, 1893, in *The Ellen G. White 1888 Materials*, p. 1161, emphasis added)

Mainstream Christianity preaches a gospel that is devoid of the law of God. Therefore, the entire approach to evangelizing the masses by mainstream Christianity's methods—whether "churched" or "unchurched"—will be under the influence of teachers who do not have the third angel's message. The power for adding to the church "such as should be saved" will be derived by the use of methods other than the presentation of the third angel's message. The final message of present truth given to the world by God's people will emphasize the relation of the gospel to the law of God. It will be seen as a message in diametric opposition to the evangelical gospel that does away with the law. It will proclaim the power of God to live in harmony with all points of the law, through faith in the merits of Jesus Christ.

> If we would have the spirit and power of the third angel's message, we must present the law and the gospel together, for they go hand in hand. (*Review and Herald*, Sept. 3, 1889)

To do other than this is to be in league with spiritualism.

"America's Pastor," Rick Warren, Saddleback, and the Purpose-Driven movement

Rick Warren has been called "America's Pastor," and his "Purpose-Driven" movement, founded in 1980, has significantly shaped the programs of churches and the thinking of individuals. Over the years, numerous books have been written on Warren and his influences. If your church has not been influenced by Pastor Warren and his philosophies, then likely you are part of a home church or you are an independent! Thomas Mostert described the "Purpose-Driven" movement in his book:

> Saddleback Church in Lake Forest, California, has 22,000 members with a mailing list of over 80,000 names. Rick Warren is one of the leaders [as of 2005; in 2016, its membership was over 30,000]. Rick Warren is one of the leaders many are following. Pastors are paying to download his sermons from his pastors.com Web site [http://1ref.us/iw]. His book *The Purpose Driven Church* has sold more than a million copies. In 2003 he followed it with the best-selling nonfiction hardcover book of all time, *The Purpose Driven Life*. It has now sold more than twenty-two million copies.... Hundreds of Adventist churches are studying this book—or have been. This one pastor is a force to be reckoned with! (*Hidden Heresy*, pp. 33, 34)

"Already," wrote Mostert, "we are seeing the fruitage of Warren's influence in Adventist churches. Pastors in several conferences have announced that they are no longer going to preach controversial doctrines from the pulpit. They indicate their plan is to become 'seeker sensitive' on Sabbath morning" (*Hidden Heresy*, p. 43).

This "seeker-sensitive"—or "seeker friendly"—approach to church growth is a philosophy built upon the concept of appealing to the "felt needs" of the "unchurched." Herb Douglass talked about this in his book, *Truth Matters*, bringing a definition of "felt needs" for us to consider:

> "Felt" needs in the twenty-first century usually include loneliness, sense of failure, low self-esteem, anger, and resentment. These character problems are behind virtually all addictions, whether drug, alcohol, sex, or tobacco. (*Truth Matters*, p. 45)

The problem comes in when these are addressed with a false approach, using non-biblical methods with a secular humanist approach to self-esteem psychology rather than addressing the sin problem directly through preaching and teaching. It has become taboo to address seekers as having a sin problem. It is not seen as "seeker friendly." Douglass goes on:

> But lying further behind these problems is the pervasive sin problem that all men and women must face up to. Treating these commonly described "felt" needs without dealing with the sin problem only postpones genuine, long-lasting relief and recovery. (*Truth Matters*, p. 45)

Gary Gilley, a non-Adventist minister who has written well on the "new paradigm" church in *This Little Church Went to Market*, addressed the "gospel of felt need," pointing to the problems created by modern psychology, which has created a generation of entitlement. Today's "seeker" has come to expect that "their needs should be met, jobs would be provided, money would be available, and problems would be solved," (and all in an entertaining style to fulfill the need for amusement), resulting in a "generation of young adults who want and expect everything right away" (p. 70). This does not bode well for any religion that talks about dying to self, sacrificing to the point of death, and living for God and others. Biblical preachers cannot reach the Willow Creekers' "unchurched Harry and Mary" because they would have to say:

> "Look Harry, ... your selfish, proud heart reveals just how sinful and rebellious you really are." They would have called Harry to repentance from such a lifestyle, and to faith in Christ for forgiveness of these very sins. Then they would have challenged new-believer Larry to abandon his self-centeredness, call for a life of self-sacrifice, humbly allowing the Spirit of God to transform him into Christ-likeness. (*This Little Church Went to Market*, pp. 70, 71)

Douglass asked, "What kind of a seeker-friendly approach did Jonah make as he sought to satisfy the Ninevites' 'felt' needs" (*Truth Matters*, p. 46). Or, do we think that Jeremiah would have met with better success had he consulted George Barna and attended a church-growth seminar?

Then there's Jesus! Warren notes that Jesus "began with people's needs, hurts and interests." He refers to our Lord's first sermon in Nazareth, where Jesus announced His preaching agenda by quoting from

Isaiah 61, closing with His application to His listening audience.

But Warren does not read on! What kind of reception did Jesus get? Luke wrote, "Then all those in the synagogue, when they heard these things, were filled with wrath, and rose up and thrust Him out of the city; and they led Him to the brow of the hill on which their city was built, that they might throw him down over the cliff" (Luke 4:28, 29).

Did Jesus give His hometown a smooth message? He gave them what they needed to hear, but not what *they* "felt" to be important. If He had stressed only the love and mercy of God and avoided sin and judgment, He would not have turned off the home crowd. But Jesus was forthright and straightforward about what it took to follow Him. Unlike the seeker-friendly approach, Jesus was not afraid of turning off people. (*Truth Matters*, p. 47)

When asked about his muting of sin and judgment, Warren replies that rather than threaten sinners, "we believe in attraction evangelism. We believe in loving people into the kingdom." Warren sees worldly, weary people in need of self-esteem, interpersonal relationships, mood enhancement, and motivation for success—not more judgment and guilt. In other words, Saddleback Sam (a researched composite of people in Southern California) is offended by "outmoded" forms of evangelism. (*Truth Matters*, p. 18)

Evangelical great, A. W. Tozer (1897–1963), warned of a new thing in the church of Christ:

If I see aright, the cross of popular evangelicalism is not the cross of the New Testament. It is, rather, a new bright ornament upon the bosom of a self-assured and carnal Christianity whose hands are indeed the hands of Abel, but whose voice is the voice of Cain. The old cross slew men; the new cross entertains them. The old cross condemned; the new cross amuses. The old cross destroyed confidence in the flesh; the new cross encourages it. The old cross brought tears and blood; the new cross brings laughter. The flesh, smiling and confident, preaches and sings about the cross; before the cross it bows and toward the cross it points with carefully staged histrionics—but upon that cross it will not die, and the reproach of that cross it stubbornly refuses to bear. (*Joy Unspeakable*, p. 128)

What he saw in his time would only intensify as this way of "doing church" became mainstream in evangelical Christianity. With its petting of felt needs and its attraction of crowds through pleasant sound-bites of feel-good, self-help, self-loving, ego-boosting pop psychology, by virtue of its emotional and entertainment appeal, this format has served to self-legitimize the popular cross in the minds of church leaders. All the while, the laity, of course, love to have it so. Those who do not buy into the standard wisdom of self-esteem gurus are viewed as cranky, crusty, crackpots with barren souls—haters of puppies and kittens, happy endings, mom-and-apple-pie, *and* little children!

Did Jesus heal the sick and raise the dead as Warren claims? He certainly did. Did he do so because he understood Maslow's 'Hierarchy of Needs', which teaches that more important needs (such as the spiritual) will not be of concern until more basic needs (such as physical comfort) are met? Not at all. By studying too much psychology and not enough Scripture Warren misses the whole point of Jesus' miracles—to serve as a sign of his divinity and messiahship (Luke 11:2–6). A closer look at Jesus' evangelism shows that he always quickly got to the heart of the real need of his audience—their sin which separated them from God (e. g. John 3; 4; Mark 10:17–31)—in contrast to loneliness, poor self-esteem, lack of fulfilment, etc.... (*This Little Church Went to Market*, p. 48)

Likewise, the prophet Haggai sweeps aside the concerns of the felt-needs and gets to the heart of the issue:

Now therefore thus saith the LORD of hosts; Consider your ways. Ye have sown much, and bring in little; ye eat, but ye have not enough; ye drink, but ye are not filled with drink; ye clothe you, but there is none warm; and he that earneth wages earneth wages *to put it* into a bag with holes. Thus saith the LORD of hosts; Consider your ways. Go up to the mountain, and bring wood, and build the house; and I will take pleasure in it, and I will be glorified, saith the LORD. Ye looked for much, and, lo, *it came* to little; and when ye brought *it* home, I did blow upon it. Why? saith the LORD of hosts. Because of mine house that *is* waste, and ye run every man unto his own house. (Hag. 1:5–9)

Gilley went on to contend that the gospel message has not been repackaged into a new format to better reach people but has been altered in that "the means for progressive sanctification and biblical living have been shifted from the biblical to the therapeutic" (*This Little Church Went to Market*, p. 49). To adequately and aptly flesh this out before moving on, we turn again to a longer passage in Gilley's text:

> Psychology, which follows the medical model, wants us to believe that a great number of our emotional and mental problems are really illnesses (we must distinguish here between true physical injuries and diseases of the brain from sinful choices and actions that have caused emotional or mental discomfort and distress). These problems have come upon a person, just as the flu might, and therefore are not the individual's fault. Since the person cannot help himself he need take no responsibility for his actions and can look for someone or something else to blame. For example, a man with a bad temper may blame his anger on his abusive father. Rooted deep in his "subconscious", he has been told, is a resentment and bitterness toward this father (which he may not even recognize) that is now being "acted out" in his own temper tantrums. Unfortunately, the man does not know this. So, he attempts to curb his anger through prayer and Bible reading, but it does no good. What he needs is a psychological expert to uncover the root forces behind his behaviour. When he discovers that he is an angry man because of his father, he can blame his problems on dad and feel better about himself. Once all of this happens (which could take years) he will begin behaving better, or so the theory goes.
>
> The biblical approach, however, is that our man is responsible for his own actions. While it is true that he may have copied or learned bad behaviour from his father, and while it is true that his past will affect his present, nevertheless, this is no excuse for sinful actions. It is not necessary for this man to understand all that has happened in his past, nor is it helpful for him to shift blame. He must take responsibility for his own actions, confess his sins and seek to change according to biblical principles. (*This Little Church Went to Market*, p. 50)

In the March 2005 issue of *Ladies Home Journal*, Warren wrote in his monthly column "five truths" to get self-esteem:

- *Accept Yourself.* God accepts you unconditionally, and in his view we are all precious and priceless....

- *Love Yourself.* "God really does love me without strings attached."

- *Be True to Yourself.* Discover, accept and enjoy your unique "shape" [*which refers to Warren's S.H.A.P.E. program*].... Be content with them [your weaknesses].

- *Forgive Yourself.* God doesn't expect perfection but He does insist on honesty. When I honestly admit my errors and ask forgiveness in faith, He doesn't hold a grudge, doesn't get even, and doesn't bring it up again....

- *Believe Yourself.* Start affirming the truth about yourself! The truth is that God has created you with talents, abilities, personality and background in a combination that is uniquely you. It's your choice. You can believe what others say about you, or you can believe in yourself as God does, who says you are truly acceptable, lovable, valuable and capable.

If the reader is going through these and not catching the subtle errors involved, then it could very well be because there has been too much of this philosophy absorbed from popular books, sermons, and churches. Elder Herbert Douglass breaks it down:

> Does any of this sound like the gospel? Or is it pop-psychology? Let's look at his first affirmation. Where in the Bible do we find that God "accepts" us unconditionally? It's true that He *loves* us unconditionally, but we are unacceptable to God in our natural state. However, we are *made* acceptable "in Christ," with all that Paul means by that phrase.
>
> Where in the Bible are we told to "love ourselves"? We are told to love God with all our heart, soul, and mind and to love others, as we already do ourselves (see Matthew 22:37–40; Ephesians 5:28, 29). In fact, the only Bible text that speaks of "self-love" connects it with the evil of the last days (see 2 Timothy 3:2).
>
> Where in the Bible do we find that we should tell unbelievers that it is OK to accept themselves when they may be dead in their sins (see Eph. 2:1)? Such counsel may be soothing, but does it point them to Jesus, who will indeed make them "true" to themselves?
>
> Where in the Bible do we find a hint about forgiving ourselves? We are called to "repent" and "confess"

our sins to Him, and *He will surely forgive.* But we don't have the ability or authority to "forgive" ourselves. God invites us to *accept* forgiveness, to believe that our guilt is removed and that the future is brighter than the past.

Where in the Bible are we to believe in ourselves? Yes, we are to believe—but *on the Lord Jesus* (see Acts 16:31). (*Truth Matters*, pp. 89, 90)

Warren said God does not expect perfection. Yet, we know that God does. We have been commanded directly: "Be ye therefore perfect, even as your Father which is in heaven is perfect" (Matt. 5:48). Jesus' emphasis was on loving others—not on loving ourselves. Ellen White also stated very clearly: "God expects of us perfect obedience to his law" (*Review and Herald,* January 28, 1904) and "righteousness without a flaw, without shortcoming in His sight" (Lt. 55 [Dec. 8] 1886). Though, of course, He does not expect this of our own selves.

Gilley concurred with Douglass's appraisal:

> ... there is very little understanding or desire for biblical truth and theology even among Christians. The Bible is not being expounded in many pulpits today. Christian radio saturates the airwaves with talk shows and psychology experts. Christian magazines aimed at the laymen are full of testimonies but devoid of solid spiritual food, and so few believers study the Word for themselves. As a result, we are a spiritually starved people who are no longer able to discern truth from error. So, when an appealing error such as psychology rears its head, we are all too ready to accept it as being from God. (*This Little Church Went to Market*, p. 53)

We could continue discussing Rick Warren and his purpose-driven church regarding the philosophies and programs he promotes in relation to his involvement in the ecumenical agenda and his involvement with figures in the world such as rock star Bono of the band U2 and even the pope, but this is not so much a study on Warren as it is on the involvement of Adventism in Babylon's altars and the idolatry of the world. We have needed to give enough of what the world is doing in order to get the picture of what it is that the Seventh-day Adventist Church is seeking to emulate.

We have covered the basic ideas of the CGM movement and how it has purported to build up the church. Yet, in the end, those involved in it decided that something was not right about it. They believed that the time had come to take the movement to the next level. At the time, I was watching and waiting for this settling further into the black night of the darkness of spiritualism. Seeing the rise of "emerging church" (EC) spirituality, it was becoming obvious that there was a shifting of the new paradigm on the horizon to yet another, *newer* paradigm—that of Jesuitism, with the Ignatian "disciplines" of the new "emerging" spirituality or "Christian" mysticism. What a perfect fit for the consumers of "seeker" religion, for these would be folks who consider themselves "spiritual, but not religious," a natural fit for people who claim they are "into spirituality, not religion ..." (Richard Cimino and Don Lattin, "Choosing My Religion," *American Demographics,* April 1999, pp. 60–65).

> Into spirituality, not religion ... Behind this shift is the search for an experiential faith, a religion of the heart, not the head. It's a religious expression that downplays doctrine and dogma, and revels in direct experience of the divine—whether it's called the "Holy Spirit" or "cosmic consciousness" or the "true self." It is practical and personal, more about stress reduction than salvation, more therapeutic than theological. It's about feeling good, not being good. It's as much about the body as the soul ... Some marketing gurus have begun calling it "the experience industry." (Cimino and Lattin, p. 62, quoted in *This Little Church Went to Market*, pp. 17, 18)

We noted in Gilley's statement above how that "biblical truth and theology" has suffered under the new-modeled Christian church, creating a famine for the Word of God even as the Bible is quoted in pulpits and books and even though worshippers have Bibles at home along with Bible apps installed on their hand-held devices.

Species: The bloom of spiritualism—the train to perdition has a station in Adventism: The spiritual formation, contemplative spirituality, and the emerging church (EC) phenomenon

> Further, how is it that Protestants in general, but Seventh-day Adventists in particular, have been missing out on these great spiritual truths? The underlying idea is that these beneficial practices were lost in the Reformation. And now we are told that fortunately for all of us, the Catholic monastic system had them all along, particularly the Jesuits. This is not just

an idea about how to enhance your devotional life. Neither is it a way for seminaries to teach spiritual maturity to young pastors. It is the engine on the ecumenical freight train and it is headed right for us. Indeed, it is halfway through town. (Greg Lundquist, "Spiritual Formation," p. 8, available at http://1ref.us/iw, accessed 2/3/16)

It is true that spiritualism is now changing its form and, veiling some of its more objectionable features, is assuming a Christian guise.…

Even in its present form, so far from being more worthy of toleration than formerly, it is really a more dangerous, because a more subtle, deception. While it formerly denounced Christ and the Bible, it now professes to accept both.… Pleasing, bewitching fables captivate the senses and lead men to reject the Bible as the foundation of their faith. Christ is as verily denied as before; but Satan has so blinded the eyes of the people that the deception is not discerned. (*The Great Controversy*, pp. 557, 558)

Looking ahead for a moment, in October 2007, the online version of *Christianity Today* ran a story about a study done at Willow Creek that caused them to backpedal and "rethink" what to do about church. This "rethinking" was not new at that time, for it had been well underway for a number of years, in the "emerging church" paradigm. The article was called "Willow Creek Repents?" and had the subtitle, "Why the most influential church in America now says 'We made a mistake' " (available at http://1ref.us/iy, accessed 12/18/16). The study revealed that there was an assumption that participation in church programs equated to spiritual maturity. Unfortunately, that is all it was—an assumption. The people were not learning the Bible nor growing as Christians. The executive pastor of Willow Creek, Greg Hawkins, summed up the article saying:

Our dream is that we fundamentally **change the way we do church**. That we take out a clean sheet of paper and we **rethink** all of our old assumptions. Replace it with new insights. Insights that are informed by research and rooted in Scripture. Our dream is really to discover what God is doing and how he's asking us to transform this planet.

The phrase "rooted in Scripture" is misleading. What it is describing is not any such thing. In the postmodern emerging church environment, Scripture is not the ultimate authority. Rather, it is a source of repetitive "breath prayers" for mystic encounters with "God," twisted away into ethereal philosophical meanderings that pose as enlightenment, relying heavily on new and exotic Bible "translations" such as *The Message.*

"ReThink" and "ReChurch" were to become some of the buzz words of the next cutting edge paradigm, the "emerging church." In fact, Robert Schuller held a "Rethink Conference" at his Crystal Cathedral January 2008, the general philosophy of which was that Christianity, as we have known it, has run its course and must be replaced. Roger Oakland, a watchman on the walls from the Sunday-keeping world, who was at this conference as an observer and reporter, wrote:

The conference opened with an on-stage dialogue between Schuller and McManus. [*Irwin McManus is another leader of the new spirituality movement.*] Schuller gave a brief overview of his accomplishments through his many years of ministry. He explained how pleased he was to be able to look back at **the tremendous leaders he had mentored over the years**, which include Willow Creek's seeker-friendly pioneer pastor **Bill Hybels**, the six million member Church of God in Christ's Bishop Charles Blake, and **Rick Warren** who has pioneered the purpose driven church and the purpose driven life. (Roger Oakland, "Rethinking Revised," available at http://1ref.us/iz, accessed 12/18/16)

When Willow Creek was in the process of "Rethinking," I shared the article, "Willow Creek Repents," in an email newsletter that I was publishing for Seventh-day Adventists. With it, I included the following introductory comment:

The cat is definitely out of the bag—and has been prowling about for some time already—on the wrong-headedness of the Church-Growth paradigm, with its "seeker-sensitive," "felt needs" programming. Not to mention all the entertaining of itching ears.… What I am starting to suspect, as this CGM paradigm becomes passé, the tactic will change. Enter the "Emergent Church," with its Christian Mysticism as depicted in practices that come under the category of "Spiritual Formation," such as Spiritual Directorships, Contemplative Prayer, Labyrinths, etc. New, but old. The same old Babylonian, New-Age Occultism, repackaged. (Kevin Straub, email newsletter, Nov. 3, 2007)

Again, the following year, I was reporting on Rick Warren's bringing in the New Age sympathizer Leonard Sweet as one of the trainers in his 2008 "Saddleback Small Groups Conference." Sweet, an "emerging church" leader, had been affiliated with Warren since at least 1994 when they did an audio series together. Introducing that report, I stated:

> A while back, I learned of Willow Creek's study on the spiritual status of their members as it related to their programming. It was discovered that the satisfaction levels of members with the church's paradigm negatively correlated with their spiritual maturity. Therefore, it was suggested, there was a need to rethink the way they "do church," to take out a clean sheet of paper and start afresh. I understood right then, as a flash of insight, that the seeds of spiritualism which had been quietly sown within the church growth movement (CGM) and which had been putting out its leaves in the form of "contemplative spirituality/spiritual formation," was about to flower. The busy bee pollinators such as Leonard Sweet, Brian McClaren, Irwin McManus and others have been faithfully doing their work. At the present time, the fruit is setting. (Kevin Straub, email newsletter, April 7, 2008)

In fact, it had already been underway for some time:

> Bill Hybels and the Willow Creek Community Church have jumped onboard the mystical bandwagon, and Willow Creek is not only one megachurch that is located west of Chicago; it is also a network of more than 12,000 churches that hold the same philosophy. The fall 2007 issue of Willow magazine featured "Rediscovering Spiritual Formation" by Keri Wyatt Kent. It is a glowing recommendation for mystical practices, including monastic communities. She cites Richard Foster and other contemplative mystics. While noting that some conservatives are suspect of the new mysticism, she says that the practices have largely become mainstream. (David Cloud, "Evangelicals Turning to Roman Catholic Contemplative Spirituality," April 15, 2013, available at http://1ref.us/6v, accessed 12/18/16)

Although Willow Creek's admission of failure in the pragmatic CGM/felt needs paradigm came after the close of the fourth generation, taking us into Chapter 9 of this book (post–2004), we find that the "emerging church" paradigm was already making its way into Adventism in the latter part of the fourth generation. Let us wind back a bit and start to examine some of these developments, with the caveat that we shall make further comment in the epilogue, as this species of spiritualism continued to bloom within her borders after 2004, especially in that new Youth Movement called the "One Project."

What do we mean by "mysticism"? Ellen White used the word broadly, linking it to—

- theosophy and other Eastern religions; to spiritism in the health and healing realm, as connected to mind cures, magnetic and electric forces in the body;

- spiritual darkness that undermines the inspiration of the Bible while presenting as lofty truth but which comes from human imagination and reasoning posing as wise decoding of mysteries;

- the false religion of Egypt;

- delusions of Satan that cloud the spiritual vision;

- day-dreaming and reverie, superfluous, fanciful, imaginary doctrines;

- the antithesis of the Bible, which the true study of the Bible would cure, as its living principles would be practiced in obedience;

- the Alpha of apostasy as was seen in J. H. Kellogg's pantheistic ideas which were promoted in his book, *The Living Temple*.

It is this last point that is especially relevant to us as we look at contemplative spirituality:

> We need not the **mysticism** that is in this book. **Those who entertain these sophistries will soon find themselves in a position where the enemy can talk with them**, and lead them away from God. It is represented to me that the writer of this book is on a false track. He has lost sight of the distinguishing truths for this time. He knows not whither his steps are tending. The track of truth lies close beside the track of error, and both tracks may seem to be one to minds which are not worked by the Holy Spirit, and which, therefore, are not quick to discern the difference between truth and error. (Lt. 211, 1903, in *Review and Herald*, Oct. 22, 1903, emphasis added)

John Markovic, professor of history at Andrews University, identified mysticism as "a spiritual-intellectual notion that truth proceeds 'from certain inner lights'" ("Lover or Seducer? Does 'Spirituality' Mean More Than One Thing?" *Adventist Review*, June 27, 2013, p. 18). In the study of contemplative spirituality, one will become aware that emergent teachers sometimes allude to or have connection with the Quaker "inner light" teaching. George Fox, the main founder of the Quaker "Religious Society of Friends," espoused direct experience with God through following a voice within. By *being silent, waiting on God*, and *going within*, the Light would teach them all things and would also destroy sin and establish the kingdom of Christ within their hearts. This is contemplative teaching. It is reminiscent of the lines that Lucifer used when he convinced a third of the angels to follow in his claim that "angels needed no law; but should be left free to follow their own will, which would ever guide them right" (*Signs of the Times*, Jan. 9, 1879, in *Spirit of Prophecy*, vol. 1, p. 22). This is the very origin of the "inner light" teaching!

Mysticism's purpose is to escape the material world in the achievement of a union between the divine within and the divine without through methodologies that pierce the veil between physical reality and the world of the unseen. Barbara Bradley Hagerty, in *Fingerprints of God: The Search for the Science of Spirituality*, explained that mystic experiences transcend the ability of language to convey them. They often appear as an epiphany that is of a higher reality than the physical world and are transient, quickly fading. When they come, they do so suddenly and forcefully, pushing the practitioner aside as if to possess him or her (p. 25). William James, in *The Varieties of Religious Experience: A Study in Human Nature*, declared ominously, "the mystic feels as if his own will were in abeyance, and indeed sometimes as if he were grasped and held by a superior power" (p. 3). What power is that? Let the reader discern.

Mysticism can be fuzzy and hard to define for those who are unacquainted with the fusion of Eastern Mysticism, or the "New Age Movement," with fallen Christianity's mystic traditions that derive from teachings of the Dark Ages past, especially of Jesuit founder Ignatius Loyola, producing a new spiritual experience called "contemplative" spirituality. Remember that the purpose of Jesuitism has always been to derail Protestantism and to regain for Rome that which the Reformation took from the Roman Catholic Church. *What evil genius it is to instill a new Reformation for a decadent church that is simply the undoing of the first, genuine Reformation.* The people have forgotten the past and do not study the past, and they are an easy target for the designs of the beast. How time works to heal all wounds!

I will let Roger Oakland further introduce our discussion of the "emerging church" with a helpful summary of the subject, noting that he is not a Seventh-day Adventist:

> I am reminded of the ecumenical nature of the emerging church, which is driven by contemplative spirituality that traces back to ancient Roman Catholic mystical practices. Contemplative spirituality provides a mystical formula also known as "spiritual formation" in order to get closer to Jesus. The problem is that this state of silence achieved is similar to that which is reached through eastern meditation, and the realm reached is not the presence of God but the possible presence of demons. The Bible is very clear in its warning against practicing divination, which uses mystical methods to conjure up the spirit world. Yet, a growing number of evangelical churches are incorporating contemplative into their church body. (Roger Oakland, "Rethinking Revised," available at http://1ref.us/iz, accessed 1/28/16)

This "state of silence" is a key element that drives the emerging church paradigm. It is introduced to the seeker after a spiritual connection to God as a means of clearing the mind of all conscious thought to "experience God." Within the emerging church paradigm, there are various means to enter this altered state of consciousness, such as focusing on the breath, repeating Christian words or snippets of Scripture as a mantra, and visualization. These parallel the auto-hypnotic methods of Transcendental Meditation in Eastern occultic religion and the hallucinogenic concoctions and driving rhythms of shamanistic religions.

More detailed information about these means for altering consciousness is widely available for those who desire further study. In this segment, I will take descriptive material from my paper, "*Rethink* and *Break Forth*: Shall Seventh-day Adventists Send Their Leaders to Drink From Cisterns Such as These?" written for a local Canadian Seventh-day Adventist church board the beginning of 2008 as they were preparing to send worship leaders to an evangelical conference of Sunday-keeping leaders in the city of Edmonton, Alberta, for training by various emerging church leaders on methods of conducting corporate worship. Some of these very same leaders had just come to the Edmonton conference, "Break Forth" from Robert Schuller's "Rethink" conference. Here are some opening remarks that I presented to the church board:

> We are now told by the Super-Size-Me church leaders that the Megachurch, Purpose-Driven, Church Growth Movement paradigm does not work. It has not been attracting the "unchurched" so much as the bored "other-churched" and furthermore, it has not been producing spiritual "grown-ups." In fact, it has been determined through in-house research that the more spiritually grown up the congregant, the less attractive they find these environments. *These are their own published conclusions.*
>
> They say that now it is time to "take out a clean sheet of paper." When I read about this great Willow Creek realization and confession, I was thinking, "Here we go. What are they going to bring on, now? This will be the time to really rev up the deceptions. We can expect it to get a whole lot darker, almost guaranteed."
>
> I see it happening. It is not new, but has been developing all the while the CGM paradigm was failing. Now, we are to morph into whatever higher spiritual plane in which we are supposed to be dwelling through the birthing process implied in the term "Emerging Church." (Kevin Straub, "*Rethink* and *Break Forth*: Shall Seventh-day Adventists Send Their Leaders to Drink From Cisterns Such as These," Jan. 1, 2008.)

Some of the key facilitators in bringing the new contemplative paradigm forward are Warren, Hybels, and Schuller, even though they are not categorized as "contemplatives" themselves. This form of mysticism has been a fantastically successful plan for the prince of darkness in furthering the reach of spiritualism into the churches.

"Lighthouse Trails Research Project" is probably the foremost voice exposing the inroads of the "emerging church" phenomenon today within the greater context of mainstream Christianity, a voice arising from within the precincts of evangelical Sunday-keeping, immortality-of-the-soul Christianity itself. Such a voice is an example of the rocks crying out. The February 13, 2007 edition of their online "Coming from the Lighthouse Newsletter" states that "Mysticism, New Age ideology and a *return to Rome*, are the building blocks of the emerging church" (available at http://1ref.us/j0, accessed 1/29/16).

Later we will shine more light from "Lighthouse Trails" on the destroying rocks that are threatening the safe passage of segments of the Adventist ship. However, first we will return to the 2008 paper, "*Rethink* and *Break Forth*," as we gain more understanding of what the "emerging church" paradigm is all about.

It is yet more capitulating to surrounding culture, only this time not in the accommodation of worldly tastes in entertainment but in the philosophical accommodation to postmodern thinking.

The Devil is playing on many peoples' understanding that Christianity today is thoroughly corrupt and introducing the EC as the solution; a return to true spirituality. Out with the contemporary big-production style worship and in with the experiential and the mysterious.

"People increasingly long for the mystical and the spiritual rather than the evidential and facts-based faith of the modern soil.["] Dan Kimball, *The Emerging Church*, (Grand Rapids: Zondervan, 2003), p. 60

"The things that seeker-sensitive church[es] removed from their churches are the very things [*postmodern*] nonbelievers want to experience if they attend a worship service." [Kimball, p. 115]

The postmodern wants to reconnect to the past. They want traditions and religious symbols rather than slick excellence, polished performance and state-of-the-art structures found in modernity.… The emerging church appears to be the latest flavor of the day in a church age which allows itself to be defined by its culture rather than by Scripture. Gary Gilley, *The Emerging Church - Part 1*, p. 1 [available at http://1ref.us/j1, accessed 3/29/17]

"… the emergent church is a movement chasing a culture." [Gilley, p. 1]

I dare say, isn't that what Rome did?

Those in the EC paradigm are sometimes referred to as "contemplatives." The "Spiritual Formation" movement is just another way of saying "Contemplative Spirituality." This depicts the mystic elements of the new spirituality, with its New Age practices of meditative/contemplative/breath prayers, candles, labyrinth exercises, yoga, lectio divina, etc. The contemplatives

"… are interested in religious experiences and feelings. They want a sense of the supernatural. They are not interested in systematic theology, tightly woven apologetic arguments or logical reasoning. But they are attracted to spiritual mystery" [Gilley, p. 2]

One can certainly sympathize with this, as many of us are weary of

> " 'church-lite,' consumer spirituality, church buildings that look like warehouses or malls, CEO pastors, educational programs structured like community colleges and church services that are reminiscent of a Broadway musical." [Gilley, p. 2]

So what believers are made to think is that they are making a return to "vintage church" but this is a deception, for this does not refer to a return to the primitive church of the apostolic faith, but to a vintage church that has been derailed by medieval Catholicism. The sensory experiences of the latter has been foisted on contemplatives as spiritual experience.

> … just as the seeker-sensitive church saw felt-needs as the means of linking with unbelievers, so the emerging church sees spiritual experience as that means. The philosophy is basically the same, just the methods have changed. [Gilley, p. 2]

We've touched a little on *methods*, now let's look quickly at the *message*. Adventism's *Ministry* magazine has this to say about it:

> Thus, from the very start, the Emerging church has been ecumenical, with an emphasis on global awareness as well as local involvement. Second, the Emergent church is also a historical grass-roots development. Since the 1960s, the population has been gradually moving away from organized religion and toward personalized spirituality. We are only now seeing the results of the influence TV celebrities, spiritual Internet sites, and postmodern academia have had on the masses. In other words, Emergent theology reflects what has been happening in family rooms across the country for several generations. Spiritual gurus on various TV shows have replaced the local priest and the pastor. While watching TV, people have been formulating their own spirituality. Unaware of the subtle changes in its thinking, the populace has become what is usually referred to as a postmodern generation—post-world wars, postcolonial, post-Western and, notably, post-Protestant, even post-Christian. This sociohistorical aspect is usually taken for granted by Christians as something they can do nothing about; therefore, why bother with it?
>
> The spine of the Emergent paradigm of thinking, or the Emergent matrix of reality, is "both/and" rather than the traditional Western "either/or." The Emergents refuse to separate reality. The very notion of emerging is to accept the idea that all voices need to be heard, that all narratives (stories) need to be told, and that whatever emerges out of it all is the Emergent metanarrative—if there is such a thing. No individual and no group can have a metanarrative that dominates all the others. According to this thinking, the biblical great conflict narrative between Christ and Satan, between good and evil, is pushed to the side, ignored, or downplayed. It is misinterpreted as intolerant, judgmental, divisive, repulsive, and nonapplicable to contemporary social needs. It should be of no surprise that the Emergents have a difficult time dealing with the subjects of atonement and the destruction of sinners. (John Jovan Markovic, "The Emerging Church: A Call to Action and Authenticity," *Ministry*, March 2010, p. 19, available at http://1ref.us/j2, accessed 02/09/17)

Returning once again to the 2008 paper, *"Rethink and Break Forth"*:

> The church of today is said to be emerging from a traditional understanding of the church into a "postmodern expression." Post- as a prefix is difficult to use as a definition of anything, because it only defines what you are not. However, defining postmodernism need not be impossible, for one need only look around to find: a plethora of philosophies in every sphere; blowing winds of doctrine from every direction; many living in their own idea of reality; and the ability of the contemporary mind to hold many of the conflicting simultaneous ideas in an Orwellian mode called "doublethink," (that apparatus which is very useful to the globalist elite, New World Order folks—I heard a lady in London say, "we have to sacrifice our freedoms for liberty"), and one has a fix on our world of no boundaries, no truth, if a fix can be had on something so slippery!
>
> "Attempting to combine postmodern philosophy with biblical theology is a tricky business, as one might imagine; we should not be surprised that

unanimity in the understanding of this attempted merger will not be found.... Truth claims are held with suspicion within postmodernism.... Since the very heart of postmodernity is rejection of absolute authoritative truth, yet Christianity claims to be the proclamation of absolute authoritative truth, a head-on collision is almost unavoidable. What is to be done? Something has to give and that something seems to be truth." [Gilley, p. 3]

"Experience, not Scripture, becomes the basis for truth. [*Albeit a malleable truth, for the people are taught that their reality is just a model and it must remain subject to revision and revolution, upon the basis of new experience.*] 'People today,' Leonard Sweet writes, 'are starved not for doctrines but for images and relationships and stories.' [Leonard Sweet, Andy Crouch, et al., *The Church in Emerging Culture: Five Perspectives*, Leonard Sweet, ed., (Grand Rapids: Zondervan, 2004), p. 35]. There is no absolute truth or ultimate reality in the emergent agenda. Even Scripture is appreciated for its mystery, not its presentation of truth. [Gilley, p. 4]

This synopsis must be kept concise, I know, but before we leave it, I have to make mention of three more defining *-isms* that relate to the EC philosophy.

Deconstructionism—is a literary approach that seeks out apparent contradictions in a text in order to come up with new ideas that may even be out of harmony with the original text. Humpty Dumpty says, "When I use a word, it means what I choose it to mean—neither more nor less." That's deconstruction. It "guts words of their meaning and redefines them according to one's own preference" (Gilley, p. 4). [*Sadly, we know what happened to Humpty.*]

Pluralistic Relativism—The outcome of EC philosophy is that all paths lead home. Nobody is right and everybody is right. After deconstruction, this is all that is left. We may not like this very much, but we should get used to it for now, because it is a good treatment for the cancer of *final orthodoxy* as found in absolutist/colonial/totalitarian modernity, say EC leaders, such as Brian McLaren in *A Generous Orthodoxy*, pp. 286-7.

Ecumenism—The EC is ecumenism on steroids. In fact, why call it Christian, at all? The new missiology says that God doesn't care what religion you are, just add Jesus to what you already have:

1. **You can keep your own religion**—Buddhism, Islam, Hinduism, Mormonism—you just need to add Jesus to the equation. Then you become complete. You become a Buddhist with Jesus, a Hindu with Jesus, a Muslim with Jesus and so on.

2. **You can throw out the term Christianity** and still be a follower of Jesus.

3. **In fact, you can throw out the term Christian too.** In some countries you could be persecuted for calling yourself a Christian, and there is no need for that. Just ask Jesus into your heart, you don't have to identify yourself as a Christian. ["The New Missiology—Keep Your Own Religion, Just Add Jesus," available at] http://1ref.us/j3, accessed 1/30/16]

Here is what is said by some popular postmodernists:

"For me, the beginning of sharing my faith with people began by throwing out Christianity and embracing Christian spirituality, a nonpolitical mysterious system that can be experienced but not explained." —Donald Miller, *Blue Like Jazz*, p. 115.

"I must add, though, that I don't believe making disciples must equal making adherents to the Christian religion. It may be advisable in many (not all!) circumstances to help people become followers of Jesus and remain within their Buddhist, Hindu, or Jewish contexts."—Brian McLaren (leader of the Emerging Church movement), author of *A Generous Orthodoxy*.

"I'm not talking about a religion this morning. You may be Catholic or Protestant or Buddhist or Baptist or Muslim or Mormon or Jewish or you may have no religion at all. I'm not interested in your religious background. Because God did not create the universe for us to have religion."—Rick Warren, September 2005, *United Nations, Interfaith Prayer Breakfast to 100 World Delegates.*

"Does a little dose of Buddhism thrown into a belief system somehow kill off the Christian part? My Buddhist cousin ... is a better 'Christian' ... than almost every Christian I know." Dan Kimball, *The Emerging Church*, (Grand Rapids: Zondervan, 2003), p. 53. (Kevin Straub, "*Rethink* and *Break Forth*: Shall

Seventh-day Adventists Send Their Leaders to Drink from Cisterns Such as These?" Jan. 8, 2008, available at http://1ref.us/j4, accessed 12/18/16)

Emerging Adventism

The foregoing has been presented as background for observations about mysticism that is coming into Adventism during the fourth generation.

> Spiritual darkness has covered the earth and gross darkness the people. There are in many churches skepticism and infidelity in the interpretation of the Scriptures. Many, very many, are questioning the verity and truth of the Scriptures. Human reasoning and the imaginings of the human heart are undermining the inspiration of the Word of God, and that which should be received as granted, is surrounded with a **cloud of mysticism**. Nothing stands out in clear and distinct lines, upon rock bottom. This is one of the marked signs of the last days. (Ms. 16, 1888, in *Selected Messages*, bk. 1, p. 15, emphasis added)

Here Ellen White was describing the skeptical "higher criticism" of the educated elites' approach to the Bible, but the words are an apt description of the contemplative spirituality of today. There is a "cloud of mysticism" that has surrounded the introduction of the curricula of "Spiritual Formation" into the ranks of denominational Adventism. While voices of concern have been raised, institutional officials have downplayed any perception that there could be an association between the general trend in pop Christianity and its shift into the contemplative emerging church paradigm. It is rather promoted as simple training in the principles of discipleship. But if that is true, then why adopt confusing language?

Believers should have no part in employing the loaded terminology of new age spiritualism. Conveying the gospel message to the present generation does not require such language for any reason. Using this kind of language in our preaching and teaching does not make us relevant. It only makes us vulnerable to the infiltration of powerful occult and new age dogma, as undiscerning readers and listeners are desensitized to the vocabulary and are introduced to books written by spiritualists. Through even an "innocent" use of language, the bridge is easily crossed from the *possibly innocuous* to the *decidedly insidious* and finally, through its literature, to the *openly apostate*. The church has its own vocabulary that comes from the Bible and the Spirit of Prophecy. Let us use it, be known for it, and be identified by it. Let us become once more the "people of the Book" who are untainted by the seductive verbiage of worldly philosophies, which have pulled at us to incorporate the spiritualism of the new age movement and the emergent church apostasy.

In all fairness, some may inadvertently or ignorantly use the vocabulary of spiritual formation, only to discover that its use has created a problem. This is what Adventist leader Derek Morris came to acknowledge.*

> **More than 25 years ago**, I embraced the "spiritual formation" movement. In retrospect, I must confess that I was somewhat careless and naïve. I had good intentions but lacked wisdom.
>
> **I soon realized** that not everything promoted under the umbrella of spiritual formation was Christian or in harmony with the Scriptures. I regret any confusion that I caused during those early years of ministry. I would have saved myself and others much heartache if I had heeded the inspired counsel of Paul to "Examine everything carefully."
>
> I had started teaching a class called "Spiritual Formation." As I came to a clearer realization that some were advocating nonbiblical teachings under the umbrella of spiritual formation, I made every effort to base all of my instruction on the Bible. Over time, I realized that even the use of the term spiritual formation created confusion. I finally changed the name of the class to "Christian Spirituality," which more accurately described its contents. (Derek Morris, "Editorial: Examine Everything Carefully," *Ministry*, Aug. 2012, p. 5, emphasis added)

[*The case of Morris' quarter-century naiveté is curious. How can a Seventh-day Adventist leader study and promote mystic authors such as he did as adjunct professor teaching Spiritual Formation at Andrews University in 2010 and not know that he is promoting Jesuit spirituality? While declaring that he abandoned mystical spiritual formation in the early to mid-1980s, he wrote up his 1987 dissertation on "spiritual direction" discussing his year-long experiment in submission to mystic experiences (to be examined further below). He then went on to write a paper entitled, "Spiritual Formation in Ministry," to be presented before the Evangelical Theological Society Meeting slated to be held at Southern College in the early 1990s, making positive use of *The Practice of Spiritual Direction*, a book authored by Jesuits. In that book, there is no question about the mystical nature of spiritual formation. We may also note his continuing use of contemplative teachers in his pastoral work at Calimesa Seventh-day Adventist Church from 2001–2004. The assistant pastor at that time was Ken Curtis, and part of his responsibilities was to teach spiritual formation. Curtis has testified that there was no indication that Pastor Morris had abandoned spiritual formation. The materials used in their small group program included materials by non-Seventh-day Adventist authors—including Catholic authors—that are clearly promoting mystical spiritual formation (available at http://1ref.us/j5, slides 70–84, published 2014, accessed 2/7/16).]

So it was at the very end of the fourth generation that we see the first bold waves of the emerging church tide washing over Adventism. Moving forward into the next generation, it would break upon the shores of the church and bring with it an increasing involvement with Babylonian teachers in seminars and retreats, recommended books and university programs, and a highly visible apostasy present in the denomination at the time of this writing.

The Seventh-day Adventist Worldwide "Spiritual Formation" was initiated in 2001, as can be seen in a February 3, 2004 article of the Adventist News Network.

> The Adventist world church created the International Board of Ministerial and Theological Education (IBMTE) in September 2001, designed to provide overall guidance and standards to the professional training of pastors, evangelists, theologians, teachers, chaplains and other denominational employees involved in ministerial and religious formation, or spiritual formation, in each of the church's 13 regions around the world. (Wendi Rogers/ANN, "ANN Feature: Church, Congregations Increase Focus on "Spiritual Formation," Feb. 2, 2004, available at http://1ref.us/j6, accessed 2/2/16)

It is said that the current president of the General Conference, Ted Wilson, was on the IBMTE in 2001 when it was resolved to implement spiritual formation in the world church. An Adventist couple wrote an excited letter and publicly posted it, asking Elder Wilson about this matter:

> It is reported that you were the "vice chair" of that committee; is that true? Did you not know that it was RC Spiritual Formation that was being taught and instituted into the SDA Church? How could you not know? The above article in ANN clearly identifies it as RC Spiritual Formation! [implied by the article: "a lot of Protestants are in the same boat—we are rediscovering it"] …
>
> You gave warning at the GC Session in 2010, but just a few months later, Andrews University officially made it part of the required classes for all ministerial students! (Rich and Joyce Weber, "Saying and Doing," Jan. 2012, available at http://1ref.us/j7, accessed 12/18/16)

To our knowledge, no attempt has been made to answer their query.

Even the Sunday-keeping watchdogs of contemporary Christianity, the folks at "Lighthouse Trails Research," have picked up on this on their blog, "From the Lighthouse," and reported to their concerned readership:

> How far will the emerging mystical church move into Seventh Day Adventism? A [Feb. 3] 2004 article in the Adventist News Network, "Church, Congregations Increase Focus on 'Spiritual Formation[']," gives more than a glimpse to the answer to this question. "Spiritual formation is a topic being raised by many pastors and church leaders in a growing number of Christian denominations," the article states. It adds:
>
> For the Seventh-day Adventist Church, a "wake-up call" was sounded after a 2002 survey showed that though doctrinal understanding was high, there were several "areas of concern." [Adventist News Network, Oct. 9, 2002]
>
> The article says that "concerns can be linked to how the church rates in the area of spiritual formation, which has been defined by one Adventist Church pastor as 'the process of becoming a mature Christian disciple of God.[']" Spiritual formation, another term for contemplative spirituality, eventually leads into the arena of the emerging church (both are based in mysticism). The article goes on: "Today this subject is receiving serious emphasis in Adventist institutions, as well as in local congregations." ("New Age Sympathizer Leonard Sweet to Speak at Seventh Day Adventist Conference," Sept. 5th, 2008, available at http://1ref.us/j8, accessed 12/18/16)

How far will the emerging church move into Adventism? This is the question that they ask, and we only need spend a little time in research to find that it has covered a lot of ground, spurring on a number of expositional projects by Adventist leaders such as Steve Wohlberg, Stephen Bohr, Herbert Douglass, Hal Mayer, and others. Elder Rick Howard, author of *The Omega Rebellion*, wrote:

> In spiritual formation seminars, students are taught to use contemplative prayer as the tool to gain entry into this silence, whose realms can only be reached by the total *absence* of thought, consideration, and reflection, the exact opposite of what contemplation and meditation really mean. *This is the distorted and deceptive use of these words by those involved with spiritual formation.…* It has always been essential knowledge among the initiated that this slowing down of the thoughts is the mechanism that enables contact with the "supernatural realms." (Rick Howard, *The Omega Rebellion*, p. 137)

Thoughts on the Omega

Much has been made of the concept that the "Omega of Apostasy" is the latter end of the spiritualism arising from Kellogg's pantheism, which is known in Adventist history as the "Alpha of Apostasy." However, there is much more to the concept than this. Even Rick Howard has recognized the possibility, ending his book with the open-ended question, "IS THIS THE OMEGA, OR AN ELEMENT OF IT?" (Howard, p. 205). It is the position of this author that it is an element, or a fruition, of the Omega. The Omega would have to have its roots in the departure from the faith resulting from the rejection of the 1888 message as the cure to Laodiceanism. This departure did not begin to show distinctly until the middle of the 20th century, even as mystic elements were coming into the seminary at Washington through Elder Vandeman's promotion of the teachings of E. Stanley Jones (as reported in the Wieland and Short history of the third generation). In our post–2004 comments, we will show again a connection to E. Stanley Jones in the emerging church infiltrations. Yet, the Omega is more than all of this. It also has to do with the entire fruitage of departing from the God-given message, ignoring the counsels of Ellen White in so many areas, capitulating to Babylon in the Evangelical Conferences, and forging ecumenical alliances with Babylon.

It should be noted that Ellen White said there was an aspect of the Omega that would take us by surprise:

> Be not deceived; many will depart from the faith, giving heed to seducing spirits and doctrines of devils. We have now before us the alpha of this danger. **The omega will be of a most startling nature**. (Lt. 263, 1904, p. 4, "To Our Leading Physicians," in *Manuscript Releases*, vol. 7, p 188, emphasis added)

After many years of studying the "devouring," or apostasy, of the Seventh-day Adventist movement and church, it suddenly occurred to me that the startling nature of the omega is not so much any of its *substance* but the *nature* of it, just as stated by the pen of inspiration. Others have now written on this subject. However, at the time, it was to me as a fresh thought. If we were simply looking for a certain species of doctrinal aberration and find that it is spiritualism in another guise, where would the element of shock in that be? The alpha was already a species of spiritualism (even though, it too was more, in that it was the rejection of the counsel of God given through the prophetic ministry of Ellen White). It would not be any surprise to see it merely come back in another form. No, there is more to it than simply a species of error. The departure of spiritual formation is only one in a long line of apostasies that have been introduced into the denomination.

Again, the element of surprise is the *nature* of the apostasy. The first entry in my dictionary for "nature" states: "The essential qualities or characteristics by which something is recognized." In the case of the omega, it is not recognized by any particular species of error. Rather, it is identified by the way it has been introduced and the stand towards it taken by the faithful.

What do we mean by all this?

In the alpha of apostasy, the leadership retained its integrity, and the apostate element found itself *outside* the denomination. Such is not the case in the omega. As the latter end of the apostasy has worked itself out, a reversal becomes apparent to the student of history and true Seventh-day Adventism. As the end nears, we will find that the apostates are not ejected from the denomination but have rather become its leaders! Look at this item from the pen of Ellen White as one of the clues:

> In the future, deception of every kind is to arise, and we want solid ground for our feet. We want solid pillars for the building. Not one pin is to be removed from that which the Lord has established. **The enemy will bring in false theories, such as the doctrine that there is no sanctuary. This is one of the points on which there will be a departing from the faith.** Where shall we find safety unless it be in the truths that the Lord has been giving for the last fifty years? (*Review and Herald*, May 25, 1905, emphasis added)

This example of "one of the points" of departing from the faith does not come largely from outside elements that have been relieved of their credentials or their invitation to teach and preach or their membership. This is very much an "inside job" as there has been a gradual repudiation of the historic three angel's messages in the denominational educational institutions. The theological training of this generation of church officers and ministerial leaders and teachers echoes the evangelical world, and the distinctive message regarding the cleansing of the sanctuary is but faintly heard in mainstream Adventist pulpits today if at all. In other words, we may hear lip-service to the most holy place ministry of Christ, but the teaching has been stripped of its efficacy, at best, in a general avoidance or, worse, in a derision of the truth of the character perfection of the final generation of faithful, who are to stand without sin after the close of probation and before the second coming (also known as "Last Generation Theology" or LGT). The fundamental of the sanctuary doctrine is pejoratively referred to as "perfectionism," which is to imply "legalism" or a works-based salvation for the final generation.

In a document of unknown origin, this concept is perfectly expressed, as follows:

> Say I was in the days of The Alpha AFTER THE SEPARATION TOOK PLACE—after Ellen White and others expelled the detractors from the organized body. If I was to say to myself, "I want to hear this false doctrine I am being told about so often. I want to hear it for myself! I want to seek those who preach it and have a talk with them!" Where would I go to talk with those who teach the heresies? Hey, the organization kicked them out. It therefore stands for reason that in order to hear what I want to hear, I would have to go out of the domain and jurisdiction of the organized body to seek out the men who are teaching heresy, because they were expelled.
>
> We now have a very STARTLING difference when we consider doing the same with The Omega. Remember Ellen White declared to us that men would come among us stating that there was no sanctuary. This is a part of The Omega Apostasy, and the separation between the two groups of actors had already taken place. The "detractors" are disfellowshipped and banned from church owned property. If I was therefore to say to myself today, "I want to hear the false doctrine preached by the apostates. I want to seek those who teach that there is no heavenly sanctuary," and then ask myself, "Where would I go to find these men?" Right away I would run into a very STARTLING problem after attempting to seek these men out. The problem? If I venture to investigate the "detractors" in order to locate this heresy, I would find out that I would be wasting my time. I WOULDN'T FIND ANY OF THE "DETRACTORS" WHO WERE EXPELLED FROM THE CHURCH ORGANIZATION TEACHING IT. UNPRECEDENTED!
>
> If you want to find men teaching that there is no heavenly sanctuary among many other heresies, you would have to visit and check our seminary, colleges, and maybe even some of our very pulpits. This has often been cited even by able leaders of the denomination who still occupy position, as the cause of the commotion today between the denominational organization and the private self-supporting ministries. You can see that people among us are bringing what they claim is the new "Gospel" that forbids discussion on the special revelations of prophecy given to the Adventist Church. You can see all over the denomination that ministers refuse to teach these things as the Papacy gets ready to strike, saying that neither Christ nor salvation are in them, even though Christ Himself gave these revelations and commanded them to be preached. ("The Secret of the Omega!" pp. 3, 4, available at http://1ref.us/j9, accessed 12/18/16)

Regarding the statement, "I wouldn't find any of the "detractors" who were expelled from the church organization teaching [*that there is no sanctuary*]," the truth is, there are "detractors" outside the denomination who make this assertion, citing their disbelief of the sanctuary message as one reason they left the church. It is also true that there remains a conservative element within the church, albeit a minority, who still teach the reality of the sanctuary, even with its Last Generation Theology implications. Where the author of the article is likely coming from is that many have been marginalized or even disfellowshipped for teaching the historic belief regarding the sanctuary message. Many have simply left to form independent bodies or home churches, and the mainstream point to these as "detractors," or "offshoots." This situation is likely to get much worse as we head into the final crisis.

Returning to the article, we note that the author summed up the matter this way:

> This is confusing to most Adventists, for they were always taught to consider the leadership who maintain control of the denominational organization to be

true leaders and to have the blessing of God. **To most of our people, the definition of an apostate is not one who opposes the mission or message, but one who opposes those who maintain control over the denominational system.** Here is where the Omega apostasy will catch them completely by surprise. ("The Secret of the Omega!" p. 13, emphasis added)

Here is the crux of what Elder Douglass admitted to this writer in private conversation: " 'churchianity' is the bane of the church." The institutional mindset is blind to the true nature of the apostasy and it is looking for some great departure from the *church* rather than a departure from the *faith once delivered to this movement.* Those with the institutional mindset are looking for a situation to arise in which all the dross is purged from the church and all that remains is pure gold. The pure gold, they believe, will carry the church through to a final victorious finalization of the work.

I would assert that the surprise of the church's true state occurs under different situations. For some readers, it may be at the present time. For others, it could have occurred many years ago. I can still remember when it struck me and how I pondered how telling my church brethren that the church had apostatized would come across as almost blasphemous to their ears, even as it sounded to mine. Even more, the startling nature of the situation is ever present, even to this day, as one continues to examine what has happened, what is happening and what will continue to happen right on through the little time of trouble and the great time of trouble to come. For those who have believed in their church, the shock never wears off.

Spiritual Formation officially set loose on Adventism in the latter part of the Fourth Generation

As we reported above, church leaders officially decided in September 2001 to take Spiritual Formation to the world field. It was really something that was only being formed as a "movement" in the 1990s, so for Adventism to follow this trend so closely is somewhat alarming since the norm for "me too" Adventism has been to accept innovations from other churches as more of a latecomer. That it came so quickly in this case only serves to show how normative it had become in the denomination to see things in nearly the same light as other churches.

What are some examples we can point to in the fourth generation that demonstrate that Spiritual Formation was alive and well in the denomination?

The September 1988 *Ministry* magazine published "Spiritual Directors: Companions on the Way," by Kristen Ingram, giving to the Seventh-day Adventist ministerial force positive encouragement to take a new direction in spirituality by its recommendation of spiritual formation authors and practices. Buzz words such as "silence" and using the name of Jesus as a "centering device" began to be thrown about. Mystics like Morton Kelsey (embraced by the Alpha Course) and Henri Nouwen have been promoted.

An article entitled, "Stillness is Golden," in the November 2004 *Signs of the Times* Australia/New Zealand edition, promoted "centering prayer."

> Contemplation is essentially wordless, but its core cry is "I consent to Your presence and Your action within." (See Psalm 139:1–4; Romans 8:26, 27.) Feel your hunger for connection with the Divine and express your adoration. God is waiting to connect with you (Revelation 3:20), but it may take some time for you to focus. If you are distracted by thoughts, let them float past you without following. One method, called "centering" prayer, encourages you to refocus on God by internally saying one of the names of God that you relate to. This can help you to be present to God again ("Stillness Is Golden," *Signs of the Times*—Australia/New Zealand, Nov. 2004, quoted by John Witcombe, "Summer 2009: Critique of the book *Hunger*," available at http://1ref.us/ja, accessed 12/18/16)

What about Spiritual Directorship?

In the same way that the New Age movement made Transcendental Meditation and Cosmic Consciousness acceptable to the general public, Spiritual Formation has made Eastern-style meditation, the divine inside you (cosmic Christ) and some Catholic practices like solitude (monasticism) and confession to people (spiritual directors) palatable to Protestant Christians. (Greg Lundquist, *Spiritual Formation*, p. 5)

Spiritual direction is to come from a qualified "Spiritual Director" who mentors the supplicant in the process of Spiritual Formation. In practice, the director becomes a de facto confessional. Seventh-day Adventist pastor and professor Derek Morris, who began his journey into spiritual formation in 1973, wrote:

For much of the Christian era the practice of spiritual direction was confined to Catholicism, particularly monasticism and the Society of Jesus. In recent years there has been a revival of interest in spiritual direction as a resource for personal spiritual formation among both Catholics and Protestants. A leading Protestant advocate of spiritual direction is Tilden Edward, director of the Shalem Institute for Spiritual Formation in Washington, D.C. As I began my own prayerful search for a spiritual friend, I came across the significant work by Tilden Edwards, Spiritual Friend: Reclaiming the Gift of Spiritual Direction. I strongly recommend this book as a valuable resource. There, for the first time, I caught a glimpse of the real value of spiritual direction as a means of nurturing spiritual life. ("Spiritual Formation in Ministry," pp. 6, 7, quoted in Ludquist, p. 8)

The program of Spiritual Direction enlists trained Spiritual Directors who are seeded throughout mainstream Christendom as human guides in the process of one's desire to come into a greater knowledge or experience of God. In reality, these comprise a network of priests of the new confessional who are little more than agents to feed souls into the machinery of the coming great apostasy in the mark of the beast crisis. Such a statement may seem somewhat conspiratorial or far-fetched, yet, if we understand prophecy correctly, we will see that this is the only result that can come of not trusting in God alone.

Everyone needs a practical experience in trusting God for himself. Let no man become your confessor; open the heart to God; tell Him every secret of the soul. Bring to Him your difficulties, small and great, and He will show you a way out of them all. He alone can know how to give the very help you need. (*Gospel Workers* [1915], pp. 418, in *Mind, Character and Personality*, vol. 2, p. 777)

Spiritual Directors International (SDI) defines it as follows:

Spiritual direction: an encounter that explores a deeper relationship with the spiritual aspect of being human. Spiritual direction helps people tell their sacred stories every day. Spiritual direction describes the ancient process of accompanying people in their spiritual journey toward freedom and peace. Meeting regularly in spiritual direction supports spiritual formation. Spiritual direction is available to people of all faiths and people who are spiritual but have no religion, commonly known as "none." (available at http://1ref.us/jb, accessed 2/3/16)

The "Spiritual direction dictionary" at SDI clearly ties "spiritual direction" into contemplative spiritual formation. The entire "spiritual direction" world is a bubbling cauldron—a witch's brew—that goes beyond the simple Christian counseling of an experienced elder and takes the participant into another realm of interspiritual disciplines for people who are on a "journey" to find their spiritual center and connect with "God," which would include whatever a person conceives Him to be.

A major advocate of Spiritual Formation, Dallas Willard wrote:

Most of the activities commonly identified as "religious" activities can be a part of the process of spiritual formation, and should be. Public and private worship, study of scripture, nature, and God's acts in human history, prayer, giving to godly causes, and service to others, can all be highly effective elements in spiritual formation. But they must be thoughtfully and resolutely approached for that purpose, or they will have little or no effect in promoting it.

Other less commonly practiced activities such as fasting, solitude, silence, listening prayer, scripture memorization, frugal living, confession, journaling, **submission to the will of others as appropriate, and well-used spiritual direction** are in fact **more foundational** for spiritual formation in Christlikeness than the more well known religious practices, and are essential for their profitable use. (Dallas Willard, "Idaho Springs Inquiries Concerning Spiritual Formation," available at http://1ref.us/jc, accessed 2/3/16)

Seventh-day Adventist Pastor Hal Mayer defined the "spiritual director":

When a person finds a human "spiritual director" who guides him in his spiritual life, it is called spiritual direction. This takes the place of the Bible as the guide of life. The new focus is placed on a human being who guides the "cohort," as the person being directed is called. The superior is known as the spiritual director, who is trained to do this sort of thing. He himself is a cohort under a spiritual director of his own, and so the hierarchy goes.

Seeking advice and counsel from godly men and women is important and can be helpful in dealing with difficulties and problems of life, but obedience to a spiritual director is quite another matter. Now even in seminaries, young pastors are taking courses in spiritual direction, and they learn how to relate to a spiritual director. (Hal Mayer, "Summer 2011: The Emergent Church and Spiritual Formation" Oct. 27, 2011, available at http://1ref.us/jd, accessed 2/3/16)

Is Spiritual Directorship a functioning element of Adventist leadership? The Seventh-day Adventist chaplaincy program has embraced it. The Adventist Chaplaincy Ministries Department offers "Ecclesiastical Endorsements" for the specialized ministerial disciplines of pastoral counselor and spiritual director. In the case of the latter, "The applicant must qualify as a practicing spiritual director, which requires training and certification from a recognized spiritual formation training program." Of course, Adventist universities have these programs, so endorsement is not hard to obtain for a minister that seeks this career path in his/her ministry. These programs may claim not to be "that kind" of spiritual formation, but their recommended reading material says otherwise. It always comes back to this. How can we say that we are not serving alcohol at our table if we are filling the glasses from vats of vintage at the winery over in the valley?

What other training programs might be acceptable? We will let the chaplaincy department answer that themselves. The July-September 2003 edition of *The Adventist Chaplain* included information on "spiritual direction" by the editor, Martin Feldbush. He revealed that, while serving as a chaplain near Chicago, he took a class in Spiritual Direction at DeAndreis Theological Seminary, a Roman Catholic seminary. He explained that it was his "introduction to the classic ministry form refined through the centuries by Catholic religious and clergy and in recent decades discovered by many Protestants as well." He also asked two Seventh-day Adventist women, Delcy Kuhlman and Diane Forsythe, who were trained as spiritual directors, to give an overview of their ministry. The article states that "several spiritual direction training programs are available for chaplains and pastors" and that more information is available by visiting http://1ref.us/je and taking the navigation bar to "Training Programs and Retreats." The article ends by suggesting that "some of the better-known programs are The Shalem Institute and The Upper Room," though there are others as well. Information about the Shalem Institute for Spiritual Formation is found at their website, http://1ref.us/jf, and for The Upper Room, also known as The Academy for Spiritual Formation is found at http://1ref.us/jg.

Many have observed that spiritual directorship is a means to implement the new Protestant confessional. As confession is one of the spiritual disciplines, it is more than a foot in the door for one human to make confession of sin to another. Again, *it is intended to function as a full confessional, with power to forgive sins.* An example of this new thinking on confession is found in the words of Peter Amsterdam of "The Family International," a generic Christian organization founded in 1968, who wrote:

Besides confessing our sins to God, Scripture also speaks of confessing our sins to others.

Therefore, confess your sins to one another, and pray for one another so that you may be healed. The effective prayer of a righteous man can accomplish much. If you forgive the sins of any, they are forgiven them....

Martin Luther said that "secret confession" to another Christian, although not required by Scripture, was "useful and even necessary." John Calvin also commended private confession for any believer who is "troubled and afflicted with a sense of sins, so that without outside help he is unable to free himself from them."

There are times when individuals confess their sins to the Lord, but don't feel it is enough; they don't have peace that their confession has restored their fellowship with God. In times like these, it can be beneficial to confess the sin to a trusted brother or sister in the Lord. *In such instances God has given us our brothers and sisters to stand in Christ's stead and make God's presence and forgiveness real to us.* Making a verbal confession of sin to a trusted fellow Christian, along with the effective prayers prayed by that Christian, is sometimes needed to bring the realization of forgiveness, resulting in peace of heart, mind, and spirit.

Of course, such a confession wouldn't be made to just any Christian, as not all of our brothers and sisters have the necessary empathy or understanding to receive a confession, neither can every Christian be counted on to keep the information in absolute confidence. Richard Foster gives some further qualifications for a person who will be receiving a confession:...

- When one is opening their griefs to you, discipline yourself to be quiet. Don't try to relieve the tension by making an offhanded comment, as it's distracting and even destructive to the sacredness of the moment.

- Don't try to pry out more details than necessary. If you feel they are holding something back due to fear or embarrassment, it's best to wait silently and prayerfully.

- Pray for them inwardly and imperceptibly, send prayers of love and forgiveness toward them. Pray that they will share the "key" that will reveal any area needing the healing touch of Christ.

- Once they have confessed, pray for them out loud, and in the prayer, state that the forgiveness that is in Jesus is now real and effective for them. **You can say this in a tone of genuine authority because** *If you forgive the sins of any, they are forgiven them*.

- Ask God to heal their heart and mind from any wounds the sin has caused (Peter Amsterdam, "The Spiritual Disciplines: Confession," July 15, 2014, available at http://1ref.us/jh, accessed 2/4/16, emphasis added).

More about Derek Morris

In his paper "Spiritual Formation in Ministry," Seventh-day Adventist professor and president of HOPE channel, Derek Morris, described Spiritual Directorship by citing another author who said, "It is an open relationship where your fear, feelings of rebellion, critical attitudes, misgivings, etc., are confessed ... Your Spiritual director is one to whom you want to reveal your hidden self" (Elizabeth O'Conner, *Call to Commitment*, p. 201). In a later paper, "Nurturing the Pastor's Spiritual Discipline of Prayer through the Dynamic of Spiritual Direction," his 1987 Abstract of Graduate Student Research is listed on the SDI website among their collection of theses and dissertations, we find:

Problem. Current research demonstrates that we cannot assume that seminarians have received sufficient guidance in spiritual formation prior to the completion of their Seminary training. Therefore, there is a great need to explore ways of nurturing spiritual formation for those involved in pastoral ministry. It was the purpose of this present study to explore the potential of spiritual direction as a dynamic for nurturing the pastor's spiritual discipline of prayer.

Method. A spiritual friend, who had received training in spiritual direction, was selected with guidance from Shalem Institute for Spiritual Formation. A twelve-month case study was established with the author of the present study as the directee. The experience was recorded in a spiritual journal.

Results. The process of spiritual direction proved to be a powerful dynamic in nurturing the spiritual discipline of prayer in the directee. The spiritual journal records a process of significant spiritual formation.

Conclusions. While no normative conclusions can be drawn, the recorded experience of the author is a testimony to the potential of spiritual direction as a dynamic for nurturing spiritual life in ministry. (Derek John Morris, "Nurturing the Pastor's Spiritual Discipline of Prayer through the Dynamic of Spiritual Direction," Andrews University, 1987, pp. 2, 3)

Morris submitted himself to a Jesuit Spiritual Director who was approved by the Shalem Institute, and he concluded after a year that he had experienced something powerful as he was formed spiritually through the process of "Developing a Contemplative Attitude, Sensing My Spiritual Poverty, Moving in Solitude and Silence, Healing of the Imagination," and "Contemplative Reading of Scripture" as described in section IV of his dissertation, where he cited various sources such as noted Ignatian spiritualists William J. Connolly, Henri Nouwen, Richard Foster, and Armaud M. Nigro's *Prayer: A Personal Response to God's Presence* from the "Jesuit Center for Spiritual Growth." Nigro is professor emeritus at the Jesuit school, Gonzaga University. Johannes Metz is another Catholic theologian who was recommended to Morris by his director as part of his spiritual formation program. The reader must compare the writings of these writers to the writings of Ellen White to discern the spirit of the counsels.

Let us consider now Morris' experiment with "focused meditation" (imagination or visualization). For the exercise, Morris meditated on Revelation 3:20 and responded to Jesus' call. He recorded in his prayer journal his "deep spiritual experience":

When I invited Jesus into my house, I could find no words to say. My head was spinning. Finally I blurted out, "I love you," and fell into His arms. (Morris, p. 124)

Richard Foster, whom Morris cited in his dissertation, teaches that such experiences are not imagination, but that they are actual encounters with the living Christ who speaks in His own voice. The next day, Morris led a group of about forty people in this method of encountering Jesus. When he shared his experience regarding Revelation 3:20 with his "spiritual friend," Barry, his director, cautioned that a demon is always nearby in such exercises, so one must always test one's experiences by asking if they lead to freedom and if they produce virtues such as love, peace and self-control.

The following day, Morris did a focused meditation on Matthew 11:28. He described Jesus coming to him again.

> "Do you see," Jesus said, "how easily you accept your own burdens and try to carry them yourself? Come to me. Let me carry your burdens and give you rest." I began to cry. "Yes, Lord, that is what I want. I surrender to you." Then, in my focused meditation, the Lord laid His hand upon my head and said, "Receive the power of the Holy Spirit." I could actually sense a surge of power in my body. It lasted for several seconds. This is a new experience, where physical sensation is involved. (Morris, p. 126)

From that time on, focused meditation became a significant element of his spiritual life. "During those times of communion, the Lord and I engage in powerful dialogue, a dialogue not only of words but of lives.... One morning He invited me to spend time in focused meditation on the attempted seduction of Joseph by Potiphar's wife. I made this entry in my journal just a few minutes after the meditation was over":

> The scene came vividly before me, and the seduction was very strong. For a moment I hesitated, and I **sensed that I was in great danger**. Then I remembered Joseph, and I said quickly, "How can I do this wickedness, and sin against God?" And I fled. Once I was out of the room, **the intensity of the temptation** left me. I saw the Lord standing by my side and encouraging me. **I sensed freedom and peace**. The Lord affirmed my response, and told me that in this way victory would always be mine as I trusted in Him. I praise the Lord for ministering to me in this regard. (Morris, pp. 126, 127, emphasis added)

See how this sense of freedom and peace meets with his spiritual director's two tests of authenticity. Yet, are these the tests to which we must subject our experiences or is there not a higher standard—going by every word of God? Morris claimed victory in the meditation through the words of Scripture, which those who have seen his televised Sabbath School classes know he regularly promotes through the use of Scripture songs. However, the methodology of the meditation contradicts the Lord's teaching on how to pray, for the Lord does not suggest that we place ourselves in the way of temptation (Matt. 6:13). The "testimony of Jesus" tells us:

> Temptation is enticement to sin, and this does not proceed from God, but from Satan and from the evil of our own hearts. "God cannot be tempted with evil, and He Himself tempteth no man." James 1:13, R.V.
>
> Satan seeks to bring us into temptation, that the evil of our characters may be revealed before men and angels, that he may claim us as his own.... (*Thoughts from the Mount of Blessing*, p. 115)

Our meditations on the Word should not encourage us to approach danger. Rather, it should in itself be a guard against temptation.

> There should be **no approach to danger**. If the thoughts were where they should be, if they were stayed upon God, and the **meditations of the soul** were upon the truth and the precious promises of God and the heavenly reward that awaits the faithful, they would be **guarded against Satan's temptations**. But, by many, vile thoughts are entertained almost constantly...." (Lt. 51, 1886, in *Manuscript Releases*, vol. 21, p. 385, emphasis added)

I want to append this recounting of Morris' experiences by saying that the various discussions of individuals in this book are not to focus on personalities but rather to shed light on greater issues. Having scanned through several years of *Ministry* magazine online, it appears, in all fairness, that Elder Morris has not promoted the teaching of emergent spirituality in his work as editor of the periodical. Our purpose here has been to point to the baleful influence that personality has had upon the denomination, in particular, in the willingness of the denomination to promote this kind of work in the fourth generation. Having been involved as heavily in spiritualism as we have demonstrated, the man himself should probably have been dealt with according to the principles taught in *Early Writings*, p. 101. That he is in a high position in the church today, along with others who are active in spiritual formation, shows that there is little regard for the dangers of contemplative spirituality and such a dearth of truth at all levels that it cannot be effectively met and overcome.

Therefore, as we have taken some time to analyze it, this modern "spiritual direction" is not what the average church member might think it is. Some in leadership, in education, and in church literature might spin "spiritual direction" as a spiritually mature listening ear with a mouth occasionally speaking a word of advice to help the person to know God in a deeper way. Pastor John Witcombe wrote:

> The practice of training disciples and apprentices was common in Jewish culture even before the time of Christ. When Jesus walked the earth, He gave us an example of servant leadership and discipleship. Spiritual direction has some commonalities with Biblical spiritual apprenticeship, **but focuses on the development of mystical practices that Christ never supported**. ("Spiritual Direction," March 17, 2010, available at http://1ref.us/ji, accessed 12/19/16, emphasis added)

So here again, when we are looking at the promotion of a good thing, like "discipleship," then let us call it that, rather than confusing it with a terminology that leads readily into spiritualism by virtue of the words themselves bringing the seeker into contact with teaching materials and teachers that are coming from a place of occult mysticism.

Do not be fooled by this philosophizing. Much of it can sound like good solid approaches to a stronger spiritual life. Yet, we must not marvel when Satan shows himself to be a crafty devil, appearing as an angel of light. Of such, we are told to beware. Smooth tones, pleasing speeches, plausible suggestions for getting closer to God, and smiling, handsome faces are all means of catching the soul that lets down its defenses. The philosophy we are dealing with is Jesuitism, rooted in the very principles and practices of Ignatius Loyola's *Spiritual Exercises*.

> There is no denying that Ignatius Loyola was very spiritual. A contemporary of Martin Luther, he could pray his mystical prayer for five hours in the morning, with tears, in what he called "the presence of God". And then go to work planning the murder of tens of thousands of Protestant Christians. To recommend this man as someone who could teach others how to discern between good and evil is a travesty. It is an insult to thousands of Protestant Christian martyrs.... (Lundquist, p. 9)

There is no good reason whatever for Adventists to be seeking through Babylon ways to teach members to improve their spiritual lives. It is preposterous to the extreme. Lundquist concluded his paper with the statement:

> The idea that we should accept as our teachers the Roman system that rejected the Reformation, and the Protestants who have rejected the Ten Commandments and the Seventh-day Sabbath at their core, is not sustainable. The idea that the Protestant world has lost sight of the true path leading to devotional life with God—but that the Catholics and their most zealous defenders the Jesuits, have kept it safe for us all these centuries, so we could "rediscover" it at the close of earth's history is untenable. (Lundquist, p. 14)

To say the least!

Finally, before moving to the next species of spiritualism's "blossoms" in Adventism, let us be clear that we are dealing with "deep ecumenism" in this great union of mystic spirituality and the Babylonian churches:

> The Protestants of the United States will be foremost in stretching their hands across the gulf to grasp the hand of spiritualism; they will reach over the abyss to clasp hands with the Roman power; and under the influence of this threefold union, this country will follow in the steps of Rome in trampling on the rights of conscience.
>
> As spiritualism more closely imitates the nominal Christianity of the day, it has greater power to deceive and ensnare. Satan himself is converted, after the modern order of things. He will appear in the character of an angel of light. Through the agency of spiritualism, miracles will be wrought, the sick will be healed, and many undeniable wonders will be performed. And as the spirits will profess faith in the Bible, and manifest respect for the institutions of the church, their work will be accepted as a manifestation of divine power. (*The Great Controversy*, p. 588)

According to New Age leader Matthew Fox, spiritualism is a key element to the final coming together of all religions. In his 1988 book, Fox wrote:

> Without mysticism there will be no "deep ecumenism," no unleashing of the power of wisdom from **all** the world's religious traditions. Without this

I am convinced there will never be global peace or justice since the human race needs spiritual depths and disciplines, celebrations and rituals, to awaken its better selves. The promise of ecumenism, the coming together of religions, has been thwarted because world religions have not been relating at the level of mysticism. (*The Coming of the Cosmic Christ: The Healing of Mother Earth and the Birth of a Global Renaissance*, p. 65, quoted in "Is God in Graffiti?" available at http://1ref.us/jj, emphasis in original)

Species: The bloom of Neuro-Linguistic Programming and Seventh-day Adventism

Cut away from yourselves everything that savors of hypnotism, the science by which satanic agencies work. (Lt. 20, 1902, in *Selected Messages*, bk. 2, p. 350)

While it is believed that one human mind so wonderfully affects another, Satan, who is ready to press every advantage, insinuates himself and works on the right hand and on the left. And while those who are devoted to these sciences laud them to the heavens because of the great and good works which they affirm are wrought by them, they little know what a power for evil they are cherishing; but it is a power which will yet work with all signs and lying wonders—with all deceivableness of unrighteousness. Mark the influence of these sciences, dear reader, for the conflict between Christ and Satan is not yet ended. (*Spiritual Gifts*, vol. 4b [1864], p. 81, adapted in *Signs of the Times*, Nov. 6, 1884)

False theories, clothed with garments of light, will be presented to God's people. Thus Satan will try to deceive, if possible, the very elect. Most seducing influences will be exerted; minds will be hypnotized.

Corruptions of every type, similar to those existing among the antediluvians, will be brought in to take minds captive.... He will employ the power of mind over mind to carry out his designs. The most sorrowful thought of all is that under his deceptive influence men will have a form of godliness, without having a real connection with God....

Satanic agencies are clothing false theories in an attractive garb, even as Satan in the Garden of Eden concealed his identity from our first parents by speaking through the serpent. These agencies are instilling into human minds that which in reality is deadly error. The hypnotic influence of Satan will rest upon those who turn from the plain word of God to pleasing fables.

It is those who have had the most light that Satan most assiduously seeks to ensnare. He knows that if he can deceive them, they will, under his control, clothe sin with garments of righteousness, and lead many astray.

I say to all: Be on your guard; for as an angel of light Satan is walking in every assembly of Christian workers, and in every church, trying to win the members to his side. I am bidden to give to the people of God the warning: "Be not deceived; God is not mocked." Galatians 6:7. (*Testimonies for the Church*, vol. 8, pp. 293, 294)

You will also discover that most of the techniques in different types of psychotherapy are nothing more than hypnotic phenomena. (John Grinder and Richard Bandler, *Frogs into Princes*, p. 100)

In this segment, we are going to wind back a few years and show the introduction of Neuro-Linguistic Programming (NLP), which would have done nothing but grease the wheels of further incoming spiritualism and afterwards develop fully into the Spiritual Formation movement.

Dr. John S. Savage was a United Methodist minister who received advanced university training in various branches of psychology and counseling. After earning four degrees from East Coast universities and becoming certified in NLP, he founded LEAD Consultants, Inc., of which he is president. A certified psychotherapist, he is hired by churches, organizations, and corporations to work with educational design, problem solving, conflict management, team-teaching, and research. He is also a visiting professor at Princeton Theological Seminary and several other educational institutions.

His methods are not only used in industry and schools, but Protestant and Catholic churches are in keen demand of his services as well. He presents his educational materials in training classes which he calls LAB I (The Calling and Caring Ministries) and LAB II (Training to be a LAB I Leader). This training is to teach pastors and church members new methods of working with people, in order to call them back into active church attendance. The trainees are taught how to be "callers"—this is the word given to those trained in NLP techniques.

LAB I uses Neuro-Linguistic techniques to train

students in better listening skills for visitation and reclaiming of non-attending former members. LAB II equips the student to teach others the same techniques. The concern is that the training also teaches a subtle method of hypnosis known as "Ericksonian Hypnosis," based on the work of Dr. Milton H. Erikson, an expert in advanced methods of hypnotism. Erikson specialized in hypnotizing individuals without their being aware of it. It was believed that surreptitious hypnotism would be far more successful than traditional methods in patient manipulation and mind conditioning. This is because it overcomes client resistance by embedding "therapeutic" interventions in seemingly casual conversation. (There is an overlap of techniques between this and memory implantations, which we discussed earlier in this book.)

Milton Erickson's work was later enlarged by Richard Sandler and John Grinder. They took his findings and combined them with discoveries made by others and then endeavored to make Ericksonian hypnosis even less obtrusive in order to increase its effectiveness. Hypnotism involves communicating what you want another to perform and getting him/her to perform it. This is something that we ordinarily do all the time, but hypnotism is getting the other to act upon your desires in spite of whether or not he had intended to do it, whether or not he knew why. Hypnotic mind control is used to change actions and beliefs instead of force or coercion, but it is a fine line of difference.

Is such influence moral? No, it is completely outside the realm of righteousness! When a person works any system of mind over mind with intent to effect thought manipulation apart from a fully aware "reasoning together," he does it apart from moral considerations. He does it to serve an agenda apart from another's desire, consent and cooperation. Nowhere in the hypnotic changeover does the manipulator ever concern himself with convincing the subject of a new belief pattern. He just feeds it subconsciously, as a person would upload a file to a computer system, outside of and away from any conscientious judgment.

> The major positive attribute of an altered state of consciousness is that you don't have to fight with a person's belief system. The unconscious mind is willing to try anything, as far as I can tell, if it is organized and instructed in an appropriate way. (John Grinder and Richard Bandler, *Trance-formations: Neuro-Linguistic Programming and the Structure of Hypnosis*, p. 99)

On December 3-7, 1990, at Takoma Park, Maryland, by special arrangement with LEAD Consultants and Dr. Savage, under the auspices of the Potomac Conference of Seventh-day Adventists, our leaders took a follow-up course in "Conflict Management and Corporate Pain." Yet, on May 5-10, 1991, at Takoma Park, they were to take the most advanced course that Dr. Savage offers to the churches: LAB II. (See brief description above.) An August 1991 list of names can be found online showing about 200 Seventh-day Adventists who were trained by Dr. Savage in Lab II.

Russell and Colin Standish have a recording of a leading Seventh-day Adventist pastor on file recommending hypnotism as good for Adventists:

> We need to teach our people how to do what I am doing with you now in church. If I can do it in the University Church with 3,500 sitting there joined elbow to elbow, you can do it in your church—regularly. Tape recording of a Seminar presented to American Seventh-day Adventist Pastors by the Senior Pastor of the Loma Linda University Church. (*The Road to Rome*, p. 116)

What is the speaker in the above passage doing, to which he makes reference?

> The only time we have them [*God's people*] at our—at our command in a sense—we're going to hypnotize them—they're suggestible people. The only time we can do that is on Sabbath. (*The Road to Rome*, p. 117)

The Standish brothers have related that some Seventh-day Adventist pastors have denied that Neuro-Linguistic Programming is used in the Lab I and Lab II courses. Yet, here is the Standishes' statement:

> We possess the official LEAD Consultants Lab I Work Book. We obtained it from the South Pacific Division. On pages 15–16 are listed skills for Effective Listening. One of those cited is Neuro-Linguistics. On page 44 there is an entire page devoted to Neuro-Linguistic Programming. Page 5 lists Neuro-Linguistics among the goals of Lab School and the final page lists the book, *Frogs into Princes: Neuro-Linguistic Programming* (Bandler and Grinder) as the first book on its reading list. (*The Road to Rome*, p. 117)

The page devoted to neuro-linguistic programming says that effective communicators listen for the learning dominance of the one they are addressing and respond in the dominant mode of the speaker's language—whether that person is visual, auditory, or kinesthetic. It may be that Lab I and Lab II instructors do not require the additional reading of the recommended book *Frogs into Princes*. We have not surveyed all known instructors of Seventh-day Adventist leaders to see whether they have read the book or required it for class participants. Nor have we surveyed our leaders who have taken the courses to find out if they have read the book.

The manual of a pastor in the Carolina Conference contains a handwritten note from the class lecture that says: "<u>Frogs</u> <u>into</u> <u>Princes</u>, Bandler & Grinder, WARNING, goes into hypnotism." We are thankful for some who see the dangers and make a note about it. However, a handwritten note in a manual out of a local conference is hardly sufficient warning of the hidden dangers. How lax can we be? So, here again we have another example of diving into the dumpsters behind Babylon's buildings to scrounge about for anything that might be helpful to God. How eager we are to attempt to "Christianize" the methods of Satan.

Adventist missionary and Director of Laymen Ministries and LM Productions, Jeff Reich, researched NLP and drew out its New Age, pagan, and psychic connections. He interviewed NEINLP and LEAD hypnotists to get information on Adventist involvement with these mind control techniques. He spoke with Dr. Savage personally and asked him if he used NLP in the training seminars. He confirmed that the forty-hour LAB I contained about five hours of training in NLP hypnotic techniques and LAB II contained more, verifying that NLP is based on Ericksonian hypnosis and that Christian leaders regularly use hypnosis. Some might think that Reich's report about hypnosis was a misunderstanding because Savage wrote a letter to Lab II graduates answering the concern: "I do not teach hypnosis nor any form of it. I am not trained to do so, so that even if I wanted to I could not." (Letter, March 10, 1992, in *Issues: The Seventh-day Adventist Church and Certain Private Ministries*, p. 429). We each have to make up our own minds when it comes to conflicting reports. The question I would ask is whether a teacher who chose to include the devil's course materials as background reading in his program of instruction should be trusted when he insists that he does not teach hypnosis. That is doublespeak.

The Standish's report that Lab II was presented in Perth, Melbourne, and Sydney in September and October of 1990, to Adventist pastors, under the full approval of conference Union and Division officials. Why would any of our leaders want to use mind-control on people? Satan is good at getting us to do his things if we can plausibly have a good motive, it seems.

The "good" reason to learn these hypnotic technique [*sic*] is so that you can influence individuals for their "good." Thus if you desire to win back backslidden members, this program teaches you how to achieve "success" by controlling the mind of the one you have called upon.

On a wider scale, pastors can use these mind control methods for "good" purposes in the church. (*The Road to Rome*, pp. 117, 118)

One of the practical approaches taken in NLP is to induce the subject to bring childhood experiences to the surface and then, while these memories are being accessed, introduce changes to the subject in order to effect healings. The authors of *Frogs into Princes* claim that they took an asthmatic person and gave her an altered memory of growing up without asthma, and "not only did she lose her allergic response to animals [for which she tested negative], but also to the things she had been found to be allergic to by the skin-patch testing" (Bandler and Grinder, p. 100).

In the Perth, Australia sessions, Adventist pastors were subjected to suggestions to take their minds back to childhood events. The techniques of bringing up the "inner child," to use a New Age term, are for purposes of manipulation called *reimprinting* and *reframing*, and it can be utilized to effect a change of beliefs. The Standish brothers related how the brochure for the "New England Institute of Neuro-Linguistic Programming" claims to have "over 24 'sleight of mouth' patterns for reframing and belief change." And they explained:

Just as a magician uses sleight of hand to alter the usual perceptions of the eye, the NLP practitioner uses "sleight of mouth" to alter the mental perception of beliefs. The implications of this technique are alarming. God has *never* given to man the right to control the mind of another person. Only Satan grants such a "privilege." God presents to us the duty to take His Word to mankind, believing that the Holy Spirit will change the hearts and minds of men. The methods of Lab I and II are false in that they seek to act even on unwilling participants. Thus techniques are taught to overcome the resistance of people, a form of coercion the Holy Spirit never uses. He enters the hearts only of the willing. It is true that he Holy Spirit tenderly woos the unwilling, but He never seeks to overcome their wills.

A related technique that is used is that of *embedding*. This technique introduces new "facts" into the consciousness of people, "facts" drawn up by the practitioner of NLP. It is also frequently used by professional counsellors. Invariably the new "facts" embedded go back to the person's childhood and focus on parental sexual or physical abuse. Yet such abuse may never have occurred. However, so powerful are these hypnotically-induced suggestions that they become "reality" to the one counselled... These techniques are devilish. (*The Road to Rome*, pp. 119, 120)

Jan Marcussen gave an example of NLP used in Adventism, as follows:

On June 15, 1996, at the Rocky Mountain camp meeting, [Rocky Mountain Conference] President Jim Bauer [James Brauer] ... came out on the platform to speak at that meeting, he was dressed as a Catholic monk, with the scull cap, the crucifix, the rosary beads, and the whole Catholic regalia.... The broken, fragmented thoughts throughout much of the talk is one element of NLP. It is calculated to cause mild confusion to the listeners—but within those fragments are statements which the speaker (A) knows are against the beliefs of the listeners, (B) wants the listeners to start getting acquainted with, and start unconsciously accepting, so he states them in broken, fragmented thoughts, which cannot be easily connected—which bypass the logical reasoning of the human mind, and lodge in the subconscious to be more easily accepted later. An example of this were his words, "Have you ever heard on the radio people praying the rosary?" Then disconnected thoughts, then, "there is so much merit attached to it. And so by going all the way around here [*while fingering the rosary*] I receive some extra merit. Somehow I overcome what I know I'm doing wrong. And so I pray." He also used fogging, and pacing, [*NLP techniques*] ... to break down any barriers, and win the confidence of the audience.... Some direct quotes from his talk are: "there is a sect within the Adventist church." After using the word "logical" in a good way, then more disconnected thoughts, he said, "Now, see, Roman Catholicism is logical." (Aug. 1996 Newsletter, quoted in "SDA Apostasy Information – Seventh-day," available at http://1ref.us/jk, accessed 12/19/16)

This technique of confusing the mind is a fundamental of NLP practice. It is a method used to get past the frontal lobe gatekeeper and program the subconscious.

When you were with Erickson, did you have the experience of being slightly disoriented, fascinated and entranced by the man's language?

Man: I was bored.

Milton uses boredom as one of his major weapons." (*Frogs into Princes*, p. 135)

Using vocabulary and sentence structure in vague and confused patterns will mystify the listeners. They might imagine the speaker is very intelligent because he or she is going right over their head, so to speak. So they accept the teaching without proper research and verification or comparison with what they already know from inspiration. They are being switched to an alpha state of brain waves so that the more alert beta state will not interfere with the practitioner's intent to program the mind.

There are other interesting methods brought into play, such as story-telling, where the teller will keep branching, embedding story within story within story in such a way as to confuse the mind, or in such a way as to implant teaching through metaphor, which will be processed at the subconscious level and work itself out in behavior change in the future without the subject knowing even how this change came about. All of this is referred to as "secret therapy." "Pacing" is a building of rapport through mirroring, where the behaviors of the subject are matched by the practitioner, such as posture, respiratory rate, tempo and tone of voice, etc. This goes beyond merely seeking to connect with the subject's learning styles. "Anchoring" establishes sensory triggers for desired responses. This kind of practice goes beyond Pavlovian behavioral conditioning, as claims are that it can effect immediate change, rather than a laborious and repetitive process over time. An interesting point to note on anchoring is that it can be done by mime artists. Mime has become popular in recent decades:

Anchoring is an amazing thing. You can anchor air and people will respond to it. Any good mime anchors air by his movements, defining objects and concepts in empty space. Recently I was teaching a sales course and somebody said, "You always tell us to be flexible. What happens if you try a whole bunch of stuff, and someone responds to you really negatively?" I said, "Well, the first thing to do is move, and then point to where you were, and talk about how terrible that is. That's called dissociation." (*Frogs into Princes*, pp. 90, 91)

We are only skimming the surface here and could spend a lot of time looking at the mechanics of this style of hypnotism. We would caution that hypnosis is not something to delve into for the merely curious. It is occult knowledge, and, with it, Satan uses curiosity to gain a foothold in the psyche. We were not meant to have power over other minds in these ways. Herein is the grave danger posed to those who might receive the instruction found in Lab I or Lab II—even if they do so to be helpful out of good intentions in perfect innocence. The student will be subjected to lessons in NLP whether they want them or not, and, in taking up further reading and research, they will be subject to esoteric knowledge and methodologies that are of demonic origin.

Relation of NLP to Spiritual Formation

Mysticism is the foundation of the Spiritual Formation program in the emerging church movement. In *The Road to Rome*, we find a correlating of NLP to mysticism.

> Neuro-Linguistic Programming is based upon Eastern mysticism, as is hypnosis. Seventh-day Adventists are now seeking to equate Sister White's writings with those of mystics. After quoting from the book, *Thoughts from the Mount of Blessing* in which Sister White invites,
>
> Let us in imagination go back to that scene, and, as we sit with the disciples on the mountainside, enter into the thoughts and feelings that filled their hearts. (*Thoughts from the Mount of Blessing*, p. 1)
>
> A most improper question is posed:
>
> I mean, that sounds like a Buddhist talking, doesn't it? Tape Recording of seminar presented to American Seventh-day Adventist Pastors by the Senior Pastor of Loma Linda University Church.
>
> Speaking of Sister White, the presenter later asserted:

That's Adventism's best known mystic in action....

[The speaker] then declared:

I believe that your imagination—in conjuring up images—is dealing with equal truth as in Scripture, because the Scriptures say that the same spirit that inspired it, inspires us to understand it. (*The Road to Rome*, pp. 120, 121)

Visualization techniques are used in contemplative prayer, "centering" exercises, and Bible meditation. There is a not-so-coincidental similarity between what we are looking at in the foundations of NLP and in the mind sciences employed in Spiritual Formation, which originated in Jesuit Ignatius Loyola's *Spiritual Exercises*. Should it be any surprise that Seventh-day Adventist pastors and conferences could be later led down off the garden path into the weeds of contemplative spirituality?

> I saw that Satan was working through agents **in a number of ways** [*as in the many "species" of spiritualism we have explored*]. He was at work **through ministers who have rejected the truth** [*perhaps from attending classes taught by professors who obtained their credentials from Babylon*] and are given over to strong delusions to believe a lie that they might be damned. While they were preaching or praying, **some would fall prostrate and helpless**, not by the power of the Holy Ghost, but by the power of Satan breathed upon these agents [*from the spiritual feebleness that results from the false gospel, which takes people back to the first apartment, or possibly through charismatic manifestations that we have yet to see develop in the churches*], and through them to the people. **While preaching, praying, or conversing, some professed Adventists who had rejected present truth used mesmerism** [*perhaps NLP techniques, Spiritual Direction, Spiritual Formation techniques*] to gain adherents, and the people would rejoice in this influence, for they thought it was the Holy Ghost. Some even that used it were so far in the darkness and deception of the devil that they thought it was the power of God, given them to exercise. They had made God altogether such a one as themselves and had valued His power as a thing of nought.
>
> Some of these agents of Satan were **affecting the bodies of some of the saints** [*touch, magnetic/electric current, new age healing therapies*]—those whom they could not deceive and draw away from the truth by a

Satanic influence. Oh, that all could get a view of it as God revealed it to me, that they might know more of the wiles of Satan and be on their guard! I saw that Satan was at work in these ways to distract, deceive, and draw away God's people, **just now** in this sealing time. I saw some who were not standing stiffly for present truth. Their knees were trembling, and their feet sliding, because they were not firmly planted on the truth, and the covering of Almighty God could not be drawn over them while they were thus trembling.

Satan was trying his every art to hold them where they were, until the sealing was past, until the covering was drawn over God's people, and they left without a shelter from the burning wrath of God, in the seven last plagues. God has begun to draw this covering over His people, and it will soon be drawn over all who are to have a shelter in the day of slaughter. God will work in power for His people; and Satan will be permitted to work also.

I saw that the mysterious signs and wonders and false reformations would increase and spread. **The reformations that were shown me were not reformations from error to truth.** [*This is the startling nature of the Omega of apostasy.*] My accompanying angel bade me look for the travail of soul for sinners as used to be. I looked, but could not see it; for the time for their salvation is past. (*Early Writings*, pp. 43–45, emphasis added)

Concluding Thoughts Regarding the Fourth Generation

We have come to the end of our coverage of the fourth generation, which completes a cycle of time in the course of modern spiritual Israel. The sowing of early Laodiceanism eventually worked itself out in the alpha of apostasy as the cure for the Laodicean condition was spurned and history revealed an ongoing program of propaganda to make the truth into a lie. It is the common belief today that the 1888 message was ultimately accepted and that it is the 1888 message that is being taught today. In actuality, what is being taught is a gospel that is more allied with the fallen churches than with the sanctuary message and the judgment hour message of present truth. So, the deception is twofold: the Seventh-day Adventist Church did *not* accept the message and, therefore, she is not now teaching that message.

It should be obvious by now that we cannot have men and women getting degrees in theology and ministry from Babylonian institutions and then teaching in Seventh-day Adventist institutions and have only the truth to teach to the next generation of pastors, teachers and church administrators. To do so would mean that, after studying with Sunday-keeping evangelical and Catholic professors, they would be combating the very error they were taught, standing alone with the three angel's messages on the Babylonian plains of Dura. Yet, this is not what they were doing there. They were writing exams, reading books, taking notes, producing papers, theses, and dissertations for the approval of Babylonian educators. Becoming learned in the things of Babylon, these students have come back to God's people, not with fresh insights and advanced light in the Word of God, but with teachings that take us back into Babylon, Egypt, and Rome.

As we have looked over the entire scope of the four generations, it has been interesting to see how that, in every generation, there was a special working in the first watch to bring back the light and bring in everlasting righteousness.

In the first generation, we had the Millerite movement and the establishment of the three angels' messages. The messages deteriorated and the movement became lukewarm and Laodicean, and God could not close up the work in that generation.

In the second generation, the call of God's messengers, Jones and Waggoner, brought the true gospel emphasis in the 1888 message. The message was rejected; the alpha of apostasy was launched; Battle Creek fell, and God could not close up the work in that generation.

In the third generation, A. G. Daniells wrote *Christ our Righteousness*, and Taylor G. Bunch pointed out the parallels between modern Adventism and ancient Israel. Neither was allowed to have its proper effect. The leadership fought against the idea that the true gospel message was rejected and the way into the most holy place in heaven was again lost to the people, and the way was paved for the introduction of the omega of apostasy. Spiritualism entered the church through the ideas of non-Seventh-day Adventist ministers and authors, and God could not close up the work in that generation.

Then, in the fourth generation, the second call messengers, Wieland and Short, reintroduced the 1888 message, making it widely available for those interested in the debate. At the same time, Adventist doctrine became muddied through the wrangling of the Evangelical Conferences and the publication of *Questions on Doctrine* and the changes in denominational books. In the fourth generation, heresies developed, worldliness increased, ecumenism was encouraged, and spiritualism, corruption and different schisms arose within the denomination. In response, splinter groups left the church, some coming out of the weeds and others who were completely aberrant. However, in the pendulum swing to "historic Adventism," many have not been able to avoid legalistic tendencies. Additionally, many have not been able to avoid the desire for kingly rule in setting up copycat hierarchical structures of their own. The revival of the great truths opened up in 1888 was a reality, and the advancing light of God's character was brought forth. Yet, it was too little, too late, to have its proper effect, and God could not get His people ready to finish the work in that generation.

Out of the ashes of conflict would arise the return of the latter rain in the true message of righteousness in a people who would follow on to know the Lord, forming up the foundation for the generation of the restoration.

CHAPTER 9.

Adventism Today

2004 and Beyond

Now, what do we do with the ongoing story in Adventism in this second watch (the midnight watch) of the first generation of a new time cycle in Adventism, which we believe is the "Generation of the Restoration" of Joel 2:25? Do we issue a report of another one hundred pages? We will not do this. The fourth generation was difficult enough to stomach without going through reams of documentation to prove that things have only gotten worse. We will not even touch the Sunday worshipping services conducted by some Seventh-day Adventist churches. We will not get into the inroads of the LGBTQ community into Adventism. Yet, we will explore the continuance of the emerging church paradigm, specifically for the purpose of recognizing an intriguing linkage back to the third generation, which we will highlight at the end of this short discussion.

The Explosion of Contemplative and Mystic Spirituality in Adventism

We could especially detail the further development of contemplative spirituality. In this latter time period, we have far more expansive programs growing up in many places, such as teaching in the schools based upon not only the works of non-Seventh-day Adventist authors steeped in spiritualism, but even Seventh-day Adventist professors. A look at former Walla Walla College president, Jon Dybdahl's book, *Hunger: Satisfying the Longing of Your Soul* reveals serious issues concerning the recommended path to relationship with God.

The invitations to non-Seventh-day Adventist ministers who teach contemplative spirituality to instruct Adventists have proliferated like dandelions. Tony Campolo, for instance has been brought in to address Adventist congregations in many locations, such as Union College, Walla Walla College, and Oakwood University.

We find that nothing has halted the progress of mysticism in the Seventh-day Adventist Church—despite President Ted Wilson's opening admonitions at the beginning of his presidency—considering programs such as the 2010 discipleship program for Seventh-day Adventists, called *iFollow*, or the youth movement called "The One Project."

There is little point in discussing these programs here, when many ministries and individuals within mainstream, independent and supporting-independent Adventism have covered this ground extensively. These would include John Witcombe, Ron Duffield, Steve Wohlberg, Hal Mayer, Herbert Douglass, Stephen Bohr, and others. One can view the "Omega Emerging" series of videos on YouTube, produced by the self-supporting ministry "Operation Iceberg" (see http://1ref.us/jl). Even non-Seventh-day Adventist researchers have shone a spotlight on Adventism for bringing in such Satanic teachings, as we find in *Lighthouse Trails'* "Seventh-day Adventist Theological Seminary Integrating Contemplative/Emerging Spirituality Into Degree Program" (available at http://1ref.us/jm, accessed 2/22/16).

One thing that should be pointed out, however, is that one of the favorite non-Seventh-day Adventist ministers brought in to lead Adventists in the new spirituality is none other than Prof. Leonard Sweet who is a key leader in the "Emerging Church" movement.

The following information is based upon the expositional work of Ron Duffield:

Leonard Sweet is currently the E. Stanley Jones Professor of Evangelism at Drew University, Madison, NJ, and a Visiting Distinguished Professor at George Fox University in Portland, OR, a Quaker institution.

The One Project is the brain-child of five youth leaders in the United States and was organized in 2010: Japhet De Oliveira, director of the Center for Youth Evangelism and chaplain for missions at Andrews University; Alex Bryan, senior pastor at the Walla Walla University Church; Sam Leonor, pastor for La Sierra University; Tim Gillespie, pastor for young adult ministries at Loma Linda University Church of Seventh-day Adventists; and Terry Swenson, campus chaplain for Loma Linda University.

4 of the 5 key leaders of the One Project graduated with DMin degrees from George Fox University, with direct mentorship from Leonard Sweet. Sweet's philosophy, language, theology, and organizational planning can be easily seen and recognized in One Project leader's home churches, such as Tim Gillespie's "Re-Live" (now under Roy Ice leadership), Sam Leonor at La Sierra, and Alex Bryan at Walla Walla University Church (now moving to Kettering).

Upon examining some videos and information of the seminars and speakers at a One Project gathering in Seattle, 2012, the following becomes apparent:

- The One Project format is designed after Emerging Church styles. Much Emerging Church language is used: "conversations," "facilitators," "recalibrate." There is promotion of Emerging Church books. Many of their Adventist "partners" appear "progressive/liberal" in nature.

- Adventist history appeared to be redefined and rewritten by One Project speakers.

- There seemed to be an implication that Adventist lifestyle has been a hindrance in reaching others.

- Concepts of Adventism's unique calling and the "remnant" idea were belittled and disparaged.

- Biblical "doctrine" seems to be presented as somehow separate from the "gospel" message.

- The book of Revelation was not mentioned except in a negative way or with negative connotations.

- The Adventist Church was knocked continually for its stance on ordination and homosexuality.

- There is a great desire to bring about "change" to Adventism in every regard. The use of "conversations" to bring about these changes was indicated.

- There seems to be a lot more to the One Project agenda than what first meets the eye, what is published about the Project, and what is stated in their goals—"Jesus All."

("The Emerging Church and The One Project Summary Paper," on "The Emerging Church and The One Project" resource disk)

No documented exposition of the One Project or the Emerging Church and Spiritual Formation infiltration into Adventism will be done, here, as such information is widely and readily available. Yet, before we leave this subject, it is important to notice the linkage between Leonard Sweet, E. Stanley Jones and Adventism. Remember that it was Methodist E. Stanley Jones who worked along interreligious lines to connect the Christian faith with non-Christian traditions, particularly in his creation of "Christian" ashrams in India. E. Stanley Jones was promoted by George Vandeman at the Adventist Theological Seminary on the campus of Washington Missionary College in Takoma Park in the late 1940s, arousing the consternation of Elders Wieland and Short who were there in attendance in 1949. Wieland voiced his concern to the seminary president Denton E. Rebok and was summarily ejected from the institution, escorted by the latter to his apartment to clear out his belongings that very day. Currently, Leonard Sweet is an E. Stanley Jones Professor of Evangelism, preparing students for ministry in local churches and working at various institutions to provide courses in Masters and Doctor of Divinity programs.

Again, just to connect the dots, the reader should recognize that four of the five founders of the One Project were under the direct mentorship of Leonard Sweet, E. Stanley Jones Chair, at George Fox University. E. Stanley Jones spiritualism is back with a vengeance, even seven times stronger. We would also emphasize that just as the third generation of institutional Adventism answered "we will not" to the second call messengers, Wieland and Short, who called for a halt to the false gospel being brought to the church at that time through the work of E. Stanley Jones, so today, in this first generation of a new cycle, do we find an affirmation of that decision in the influence of Jones upon Adventism via the leaders of "The One Project." Consequently, the restoration is not coming to an institution but to a people who are following on to know the Lord.

The "Protestantization" of Adventism Nurtured by Questions on Doctrine

It is appropriate in bringing this book to a close that we review a pithy article by Fernando Canale, entitled, "A Close Look at the Adventist Mind" (available at http://1ref.us/ik, accessed 2/22/16). I recognized in his writing a highly pertinent coverage of Adventism's legacy of the "drift" of earlier generations. It is a tidy summation of the machinery of the Omega of apostasy that got underway in the late 1940s.

His thesis is that Adventism has all but abandoned the principle of *sola scriptura*, which is a shocking thing to say, until one takes a really honest look at what has happened. I had not realized that, in the capitulation to mainstream Evangelicalism, this is exactly what has happened, for, actually, evangelicalism is *not* rooted in Scripture alone like fundamental Protestantism from which it springs. Rather, it is also rooted in "the multiplicity of theological sources used by evangelical and Roman Catholic theologians." Canale asserted that, given the current conditions and paradigm, "the way back to Rome is only a matter of time." O, praise the Lord! Here is an Adventist theologian who sees what is going on. Ellen White warned: "It is a backsliding church that lessens the distance between itself and the Papacy" (*Signs of the Times*, Feb. 19, 1894). I spoke with Herbert Douglass about Canale's article, and he responded by saying,

> [*Regarding the sanctuary as the key to interpret Scripture*] Canale is the only seminary teacher who truly understands this meta-hermeneutical principle. For 70 years now, I have tried to express all this in unfolding the Great Controversy Theme—and have found the breath of "good" Adventist colleagues to be very hot and resentful. Trying to remain pedestrian in my teaching, writing, preaching, I have simply tried to show the great overview of the sanctuary doctrine by emphasizing the core connection between the right understanding of sin, humanity of Christ, JXF [Justification by Faith], character growth, overcoming sin, and why Jesus waits. All this I find rooted in the sanctuary model.
>
> Canale is the clearest interpreter of Scripture since Andreasen—although Andreasen may not have the experience of C, especially since he did not live long enough to see the disintegration of the Adventist purpose and message. (Herbert E. Douglass to Kevin Straub, email, Dec. 19, 2013)

An enduring legacy of all of the drift that we have covered in this book is something referred to by Fernando Canale as "The Protestantization" of Adventism.

> Early in the 21st century, Adventism faces deep and entrenched doctrinal divisions. Gradually, scholars, theologians, religious leaders, and believers have come to experience Adventism as a cultural/religious rather than a theological phenomenon. Imperceptibly, church leaders accommodate Adventist life and mission to the evolving theologies, liturgies, and ministerial paradigms of American evangelical culture. Consequently, evangelical theologies and practices are increasingly shaping Adventist thinking. (Fernando Canale, PhD, "A Close Look at the Adventist Mind," *Perspective Digest*, vol. 17, Issue 4)

Our readers may have come to recognize this state of affairs, or perhaps are just now learning about it. Yet, the majority of Adventists have not seen it. Canale acknowledged that there has come to be a radical departure "from the experience of early Adventist pioneers who, dissatisfied with traditional Protestant theologies, decided to follow their own understanding of scriptural truth and abandoned their evangelical denominations to become the remnant church," which would continue to advance the Reformation until the end (Canale). With this abandonment came a return to the *sola scriptura* principle. This principle is not actually descriptive of "Protestant and American evangelical theological methodology," which is "the principle of multiple revealed sources that they received uncritically from the Roman Catholic theological system" (Canale). Evangelicals "have implicitly assumed the philosophical principles of Plato and Aristotle as retrieved by Augustine and Aquinas"—principles which shape the Protestant-evangelical theological paradigm.

Since early Adventism used Scripture alone to construct its theology, the next step forward in the Reformation naturally brought to light the distinctive teachings of "the sanctuary, the law of God with the Sabbath, the non-immortality of the soul, and the three angels' messages." These fundamental "pillars" of Adventism were established to function as the foundation of Adventism's theology.

> The subject of the sanctuary was the key which unlocked the mystery of the disappointment of 1844. It opened to view a complete system of truth, connected and harmonious, showing that God's hand had directed the great advent movement and revealing present duty as it brought to light the position and work of His people. (*The Great Controversy*, p. 423)

> The correct understanding of the ministration in the heavenly sanctuary is the foundation of our faith. (Lt. 208, 1906, in *Evangelism*, p. 221)

It was Bible study that informed the Adventist pioneers that made the sanctuary the key macro-hermeneutical principle in Adventism's systematic theology. Protestantism, on the other hand, left *sola scriptura* behind, for in actual practice, Luther, Calvin, Arminius, and Wesley gained many insights on the "basis of Roman Catholic interpretation of the material and hermeneutical conditions of theological methodology" (Fernando Canale, PhD, "A Close Look at the Adventist Mind," "*Perspective Digest*," vol. 17, no. 4). By this he means that the revelation that guided their theology is not the Bible alone, but the Bible plus tradition.

The Protestantization of the Adventist mind was given great impetus by the answer to *Questions on Doctrine*'s first question: "What doctrines do Seventh-day Adventists hold in common with Christians in general, and in what aspects of Christian thought do they differ?" (p. 21). The book's answer is that, with the exception of a few points (as if "the existence of the heavenly sanctuary, the investigative judgment, the Spirit of Prophecy, the three angels' messages, and the seal of God and mark of the beast" are only minor teachings), Adventists hold, in common with major Christendom, the "eternal verities," i.e., evangelical doctrines on the Trinity and salvation. There is a problem here in that the distinctive doctrines of Adventism are not perceived as having any bearing upon Froom's "eternal verities," which are in fact, "most of the content of evangelical systematic theology" (Canale).

From this simple answer to a complex question, an increasing number of Adventists today assume their beliefs are evangelical, notably, the central doctrines of Christianity. One can see why they feel free to use evangelical books to learn their theology and ministerial paradigm. (Canale)

Froom carried forward his campaign in *Movement of Destiny*, teaching that the distinctive doctrines handicapped early Adventists, with the teaching of the sanctuary doing the most damage in that it distanced Adventists from the evangelicals. Yet, Froom never went so far as to suggest that we discard the teaching. He did uphold it as important, even while pointing out that neither the early church nor the reformers taught it. Froom, as the principal actor in this story, sought to "soften its divisiveness by ignoring its hermeneutical role" and by downgrading it from "hermeneutical key" to "distinctive doctrine," which would serve to reshape the Adventist norms in theological methodology, teaching and ministerial practice in the overall inculcation of the "Protestantization of Adventism" (Canale).

> Thus, in many ways, Froom articulated **the gospel** as the new hermeneutical principle in Adventism. As we have seen above, the sanctuary doctrine continued to be an important distinctive eschatological emphasis, but leaders no longer conceived or used it as the hermeneutical key to understand all Christian doctrines, including the gospel. At least after QOD the gospel **as understood by the evangelical theological tradition** became the hermeneutical key to interpret all doctrines, including eschatology and the sanctuary. (Canale, emphasis added)

The floodgates have therefore been opened in Adventism for pluralism. Once we admitted a theological method that supersedes *sola scriptura*, we abandoned the sanctuary model as our overall hermeneutic and left Adventists no longer deriving "their theological understanding from Scripture alone but also from the multiplicity of theological sources used by evangelical and Roman Catholic theologians" (Canale).

When, during the 1960s, more Adventists ventured into the halls of secular universities and evangelical seminaries, their Adventist experience and self-understanding became strongly influenced by the emerging Protestantization of Adventism nurtured by QOD. As they faced millennia of unfamiliar theological thinking, a sense of bewilderment overcame many young Adventists....

Desmond Ford revealed the consequences of this methodological combination. According to him, justification by faith and historical-critical methodology leave the sanctuary doctrine groundless. Moreover, the traditional Adventist interpretation of the sanctuary doctrine contradicts the view of a complete atonement in Christ. On this basis, Ford and many after him believe Adventists should recognize their error and reject the sanctuary doctrine and the historical interpretation of apocalyptic prophecies in Daniel and Revelation. (Canale)

Because of this change, a large segment of contemporary Adventism rejects and even scorns the notion that Adventism is *the continuation of the Reformation with a calling from God to proclaim the last message of mercy to the world in contradistinction to the mainstream Evangelical gospel of Babylon*. Contemporary, progressive Adventism sees itself as one among many churches that make up the visible body of Christ. This is *ecumenism*, which paves the way for an Adventist mindset that will accept the threefold union of the beast, the false prophet, and the dragon. This new mindset is why leadership feels at liberty to utilize the teaching of evangelical and even Catholic sources of theology, doctrine, and ministerial methodologies.

At the beginning of the 21st century, the supernatural power/praise paradigm of ministry of evangelicalism is replacing the Bible study/theological understanding paradigm of ministry of earlier Adventists. As a result of this mostly unrecognized phenomenon, the Protestantization of Adventism is reaching the pews around the world. According to the Protestant ministerial paradigm, God grants salvation by His supernatural decision and power. Consequently, the ministerial method becomes the proclamation of the Cross as complete atonement, justification, and the assurance of salvation. As a result, those Adventist ministers who follow the Protestant paradigm no longer see the need for Bible studies as a condition for baptism, spirituality, or salvation. (Canale)

Is this a reality in your church? Who has escaped it? The "Protestantization of the Adventist mind and lifestyle" is progressing in scope and intensity, causing a severance from Bible doctrine through transformation of the thoughts, feelings and actions at the experiential level. This has caused a gradual drift as the "hermeneutical role of the doctrine of the sanctuary in its theological methodology" has been replaced by "the evangelical hermeneutical principle of justification by faith" (Canale). This course of action has served to pave the road back to Rome instead of fulfilling our calling to advance the Reformation. Canale concluded:

> Yet the further theological discovery of the Adventist pioneers is not complete. To overcome the Protestantization of Adventism, **contemporary Adventists must complete the restoration of truth left incomplete by the Protestant Reformers and early Adventist pioneers**. Adventists must develop the sola scriptura systematic theology project at the scholarly level. This requires a shared understanding of the conditions of theological methodology and a solid commitment to scholarly research that challenges the strong houses of Christian theology to establish Christianity upon an eternal basis. This project should include the development of Adventist theology in neglected scholarly disciplines, such as fundamental, biblical, systematic, and ministerial theologies.
>
> In a time when Protestant leaders are going back to Rome, Adventist leaders, administrators, pastors, and scholars should be going back to Scripture and using the sanctuary doctrine as the hermeneutical key to understand the complete and harmonious system of biblical truth. When the inner logic of God's Word, through the educational ministry of the Holy Spirit, penetrates our hearts and we treasure it in the inner recesses of our spirits, we will no longer experience doctrine as "brain" knowledge but as the transforming and saving power of God through the Holy Spirit. Then the church will be of one mind, and Adventism will fulfill its God-given final mission. (Canale, emphasis added)

This is what I talk about all the time. The Reformation was to advance! Adventists today have before them the task of completing the restoration of truth. Only in its final advance will true Christianity be established "upon an eternal basis." That is to say, it will be efficacious to the bringing in of "everlasting righteousness" (Dan. 9:24). This development will take place when Jesus, the fourth angel, unites His voice with the third. Dear reader, today this is being fulfilled in your ears. The developments of the glory of the angel of Revelation 18 focus on "the character of God, the nature of sin and the real issues at stake in the great controversy" (*The Great Controversy*, p. 569). None of this can happen unplugged from the sanctuary doctrine as our overarching hermeneutic and raison d'être. When we go into this continuation of advancing light, we find a radical challenge to one of the major "strong houses of Christian theology"—the evangelical teaching regarding God's wrath and the nature of divine punishment.

Adventism has embraced a duality with regard to the justice of God as a flip-flopping, by some unknown mechanism for which there has been provided no hermeneutic, between "active" and "passive" wrath (i.e., proactive punishment and destruction by fiat power vs. the hiding of His face, or the "giving over" principle). It has been discovered that God is unchanging in His dealings, and He is all light, *all life*. There is no death or violence in God at all. (See 1 John 1:5; cf. John 1:4, 9.) Neither is in Him to give. Both are always the natural consequence of taking sin to its ultimate conclusion, when grace no longer stays the execution of the result of free will, exercised in the wrong direction and making self one's god. "Like Israel of old the wicked destroy themselves; they fall by their iniquity. By a life of sin, they have placed themselves so out of harmony with God, their natures have become so debased with evil, that the manifestation of His glory is to them a consuming fire" (*The Great Controversy*, p. 37).

Another major strong house has to do with issues in ecclesiology, i.e., hierarchical vs. theocratic governance of the church and the ending of the great controversy. Church organization by tiers of human authority, committees, conferences, votes, rule books, etc., is all under a form of wrath that we may refer to as God's "permissive will," which is simply the divine accommodation of faulty human paradigms. Yet, all that is of man has to be broken up entirely in the generation of the 144,000 as they accomplish the final work. In the end, God must be allowed, at last, to fully take the reins of control into His own hands.

It is a fundamental of last generation theology that ultimately there must be a completion of "the restoration of truth left incomplete by the Protestant Reformers and early Adventist pioneers" (Canale). Adventism has not accomplished it, and, unless Adventists get out of the rut they are in, they will never accomplish it. This writer does not hold out hope that they will escape. The drift has been too far, the house has been left unto them desolate, and the structure will be blown away in the coming storm and tempest (see *Battle Creek Letters*, p. 81). It is far past the day of playing church. Churchianity is dead, though it has a name of being alive, as was the case with Sardis (Rev. 3:1), the church that became fallen Babylon at the rejection of the first angel's message in the mid-19th century. Modern Laodicea is Sardis revived. Yet, there is a living church, and it is carrying the advancing light of the loud cry of the third angel. In it there is no central organization by any earthly administration but only a heavenly one. It is described in Malachi 3:16–18 and maintained on an individual basis, under the True Vine. Those who are part of it are entering into the Philadelphian experience at this very time.

Where is This All Going, and Where Has the True Church Gone?

Finally, then, what is our individual responsibility in these matters? Where is the true church and church militant when the mainstream organized religious body—the denomination—is apostate? Will the denomination finally repent and be "fixed"? Does this fix lie in the two main points suggested by David Dennis, former denominational watchdog at headquarters?

> I am convinced change within the church can only come from two sources: (1) **lay people, through voice and financial boycott** making their concerns heard and demanding a greater level of accountability; and (2) the political timidity, which currently frightens **church employees** away from speaking out, **will have to give way to an internal revolt**, demanding change. (David Dennis to Jan Paulsen, "An Open Letter," Oct. 30, 2001, emphasis added)

Are *laity vocal protest and monetary boycott* along with *employee revolution* even remotely likely? Today, most of those who care about these issues are in independent movements or home churches. These would certainly not be denominational employees. There are members in the mainstream who are semi-aware and concerned, but they are tied to the denomination by the *purification myth* and its attending notions of unconditional election for the denomination, that the church institution directed by the General Conference is the "ship that will go through."

Surely one must realize, having studied the four generations of the devouring pests, that the restoration promised will be *to the people of God* as *individuals who have remained steadfast in the faith* once delivered to the saints and not to an organization of conference committees. The restoration is of those who embrace the three angel's messages in the context of the gospel light of 1888. These will live in the advancing light of present truth which develops further out of the "truth as it is in Jesus," bringing us to deeper understanding of the glory of God, which is His character.

To expect an organizational cleansing would require such a revamping of the structure and its institutions that the church would be virtually unrecognizable from what it is today. Obedience to all that God has instructed in the areas of health care and education alone would mean an entire repudiation of those systems as they currently exist and function. The only plausible plan for returning to the blueprint would be a total abandonment of these worldly enterprises through sell-off to the world, which values them for what they are. The proceeds could then be put into carrying out the work that should have been done from the start. Further, the organization itself, as it is, would have to disband, repudiating all that tends to the exercise of "kingly power."

One could continue to list all the changes that would come, but the bottom line is really this: When the final crisis begins to unfold, there will be increasing pressures upon the organization for its stance regarding the seventh day being the Sabbath of the Lord God and against its mission to proclaim the gospel, which includes repentance for sin and claiming the power of the Holy Spirit to keep all of the commandments of God. The world will not tolerate this. It will at first look the other way, as Sunday laws will only demand business closures. Such closures will bring the inconvenience of not being able to go shopping and not being able to operate our private businesses on Sunday. However, the Sunday-closure laws will harden into penalties for doing any kind of work on Sunday, and then they will turn decidedly anti-Sabbatarian and anti-proselytizing. As a result, there could be only two possible outcomes for the General Conference church organization:

1. Disband the organization and go underground as a completely de-centralized people with no layers of human governance to preside over the leaders and people.

2. Capitulate to the New World Order and openly become one with Babylon.

In the case of the first option, there would be no more denominational enterprise in the earth, no more public media channels broadcasting and publishing any Sabbath message, nor any conference directives or programs for the "closing of the work." There would be no more institutions operating as Sabbatarian institutions. All of this would be outlawed.

> At present Sunday-keeping is not the test. The time will come when men will not only forbid Sunday work, but they will try to force men to labor on the Sabbath, and to subscribe to Sunday observance or forfeit their freedom and their lives. But the time for this has not yet come, for the truth must be presented more fully before the people as a witness. (Ms. 22c, 1895, in *Review and Herald*, April 6, 1911)

> In the last conflict the Sabbath will be the special point of controversy throughout all Christendom. Secular rulers and religious leaders will unite to enforce the observance of the Sunday; and as milder measures fail, the most oppressive laws will be enacted. It will be urged that the few who stand in opposition to an institution of the church and a law of the land ought not to be tolerated, and a decree will finally be issued denouncing them as deserving of the severest punishment, and giving the people liberty, after a certain time, to put them to death. Romanism in the Old World, and apostate Protestantism in the New, will pursue a similar course toward those who honor the divine precepts. (*The Spirit of Prophecy*, vol. 4, pp. 444, 445)

If the reader is tracking closely with what is being said here, he or she will realize that, with current events unfolding as they are and the actual state of the denomination in the world as it is, there is no time left for the expected *denominational* purification, or shaking. Purification will indeed take place, but it will be at the level of individuals and not institutions.

This purification would be the shaking of God's people. Yet, there are two shakings. In the purification of the church, we would be looking at the second and final shaking. The first shaking has to do with the matter that we have discussed at length in this book, the reception of the Laodicean message. We will come back later to a more thorough discussion of the first shaking as it fits better within our discussion of the distinctions and relationships between the apostate, militant, and true churches.

The first shaking, which we could call the "Counsel of the True Witness to the Laodiceans" makes a distinction between *the apostate* and *the church militant* (the church militant is the wheat and tares church), while the second shaking, which we could call "the great final test," separates the wheat from the tares through the pressures of the final crisis of the Sunday legislation. This is the "mark of the beast" crisis period in which it is said that the church will appear as about to fall but does not fall.

The people of the world will point to the extremity of the Sabbath-keepers as evidence of their having lost all favor with God.

> Yet to human sight it will appear that the people of God must soon seal their testimony with their blood as did the martyrs before them. **They themselves begin to fear that the Lord has left them to fall by the hand of their enemies**. It is a time of fearful agony. Day and night they cry unto God for deliverance. **The wicked exult, and the jeering cry is heard: "Where now is your faith? Why does not God deliver you out of our hands if you are indeed His people?"** … Like Jacob, all are wrestling with God. Their countenances express their internal struggle. Paleness sits upon every face. Yet they cease not their earnest intercession. (*The Great Controversy*, p. 630, emphasis added)

At this time and in the lead-up to it, even prior to the death decree, it will certainly appear as though the church, God's faithful remnant who give the loud cry, is about to fall. How? *Not by internal apostasy causing great numbers of Adventists to quit membership, but by external sanctions threatening the faithful with extinction.*

> In this time of persecution the faith of the Lord's servants will be tried. They have faithfully given the warning, looking to God and to His word alone. God's Spirit, moving upon their hearts, has constrained them to speak. Stimulated with holy zeal, and with the divine impulse strong upon them, they entered upon the performance of their duties without coldly calculating the consequences of speaking to the people the word which the Lord had given them. They have not consulted their temporal interests, nor sought to preserve their reputation or their lives. Yet when the storm of opposition and reproach bursts upon them, some, overwhelmed with consternation, will be ready to exclaim: "Had we foreseen the consequences of our words, we would have held our peace." They are hedged in with difficulties. Satan assails them with fierce temptations. The work which they have undertaken seems far beyond their ability to accomplish. **They are threatened with destruction.** The enthusiasm which animated them is gone; yet they cannot turn back. (*The Great Controversy*, pp. 608, 609, emphasis added)

The church we are speaking about is the church militant.

> It remains, while the sinners in Zion will be sifted out—the chaff separated from the precious wheat. (Lt. 55, 1886, in *Manuscript Releases*, vol. 12, p. 324)

> When the law of God is made void, **the church will be sifted by fiery trials**, and a larger proportion than we now anticipate, will give heed to seducing spirits and doctrines of devils. **Instead of being strengthened when brought into strait places**, many **prove** that they are not living branches of the True Vine; they bore no fruit, and the husbandman taketh them away. (Ms. 48, 1891, in *The Ellen G. White 1888 Materials*, p. 901, emphasis added)

The second shaking

This *proving*, or shaking, of the church, like the first shaking, has nothing to do with the notion that the unfaithful will leave the organization. *It cannot be* because, as already pointed out, there can be no organizational structure giving the true loud cry in operation at this time. Such a structure would be illegal under the new laws. Initially it would come under penalties of fines and the revocation of its corporate registrations. The General Conference of Seventh-day Adventists, *if it were actually proclaiming the third angel's message*, would automatically lose its 501(c)3 tax exempt status. This is because, if upholding her historic teachings, she would come against the very system that created and is now enforcing the Sunday laws. To proclaim the teachings as we find them in the Bible and in the Spirit of Prophecy, such as in *The Great Controversy*, would immediately entangle her with the law because, under the new world order, the revelations in this book would be deemed hate speech, political involvement, and terrorism. To be true to her prophetic calling she would be working against the papal system, against the Protestant world, against the Spiritualists, against the environmentalists (backing the Sunday law), and against the secular government. As the Bible says, "all the world wondered after the beast," and this would mean that they would be against "all the world."

[*As this book is being prepared for publication, the Trump administration in the United States is looking at eliminating the Johnson Amendment, which prohibits political lobbying by religious organizations. This would allow churches to politicize and not only influence voters, but it would also open the door for tax-deductible donations to political candidates. All of this is in keeping with giving the church power over the state, as we know will happen. However, the other two issues, regarding hate speech and terrorism, would still present a problem.]

Students of prophecy and current events are well aware that the groundwork for New World Order unity began years ago and that it is advancing at the present time. The rules may change, but they will always fit the agenda of the Luciferian plan. All registered churches have had to play by the rules, and it will continue to be so. *If* the organization had somehow become purified at an earlier time, returning to her true foundation and *if* she had risen up "terrible as an army with banners" to truly be the church militant at the time of crisis and *if* she would have survived the earlier, milder sanctions, she would absolutely not find it possible to hold up under the imposition of increasingly severe penalties. Loss of tax-exempt status would seriously threaten, if not entirely wipe out, her ability to function financially. On top of this would come the further burden of fines. She would be ordered to retract statements made in publications. Many of Ellen White's books would be outlawed as hate literature. Her leaders would come under the same financial punishments and eventually face prison sentences. Her properties would be confiscated. Vigilantism and vandalism would wreak havoc. Then would come the imposition of the embargo on buying and selling. Any kind of license to practice as a religious organization would by this time be entirely out of the question.

Can you see it? Such an organization must fall and would fall. "Storm and tempest would sweep away the structure" (Lt. 242, 1903, in *Battle Creek Letters*, p. 81).

Then what is this shaking if it is not a picture of the separation of "tares" or "bad fish" from *the General Conference organization*, in keeping with the picture in the *parable of the tares* and the *parable of the net* in Matthew 13, which portray the separation of the good from the bad. The fact is that, as the *church militant* of the unseparated "wheat and tares," or "good fish and bad fish," is doing its Spirit-directed work in giving the loud cry, the gospel net is bringing in more of the good and the bad (Matt. 22:10). (This gathering should not be confused with the evangelistic programs of the General Conference corporate structure.) While this is happening, there is also an ongoing shaking of God's professed remnant during the length of the crisis of the Sunday laws from its inception until the close of probation. The final separation of the good and bad does not come until the judgment of the living and the close of probation.

> When the mission of the gospel is completed, the judgment will accomplish the work of separation....
>
> When the work of the gospel is completed, there immediately follows the separation between the good and the evil, and the destiny of each class is forever fixed. (*Christ's Object Lessons*, pp. 122, 123)

The establishment of the death decree, fixing the date and time for the midnight hour genocide, takes place *just prior to* the judgment of the living and the close of human probation, which then begins the time of Jacob's trouble.

> When Christ shall cease His work as mediator in man's behalf, then this time of trouble will begin. (*Patriarchs and Prophets*, p. 201)

> It is in a crisis that character is revealed. When the earnest voice proclaimed at midnight, "Behold, the bridegroom cometh; go ye out to meet him," and the sleeping virgins were roused from their slumbers, it was seen who had made preparation for the event. Both parties were taken unawares; but one was prepared for the emergency, and the other was found without preparation. So now, **a sudden and unlooked-for calamity, something that brings the soul face to face with death**, will show whether there is any real faith in the promises of God. It will show whether the soul is sustained by grace. **The great final test comes at the close of human probation**, when it will be too late for the soul's need to be supplied. (*Christ's Object Lessons*, p. 412, emphasis added)

> "And at that time shall Michael stand up, the great prince which standeth for the children of thy people: and there shall be a time of trouble, such as never was since there was a nation even to that same time: and at that time thy people shall be delivered, everyone that shall be found written in the book." [Dan. 12:1.] **When this time of trouble comes, every case is decided; there is no longer probation**, no longer mercy for the impenitent. The seal of the living God is upon His people. This small remnant, unable to defend themselves in the deadly conflict with the powers of earth that are marshaled by the dragon host, make God their defense. **The decree has been**

passed by the highest earthly authority that they shall worship the beast and receive his mark under pain of persecution and death.... (*Testimonies for the Church*, vol. 5, pp. 212, 213, emphasis added)

It is in the imposition of the threat of death upon the church militant, whose gospel work in giving the loud cry under latter rain power has come to its end, that the great final test comes upon God's people. Satan understands what the truth is. The Lord allowed Ellen White to hear him in his war room laying down his strategy.

We led the Romish Church to inflict imprisonment, torture, and death upon those who refused to yield to her decrees, and now that we are bringing the Protestant churches and the world into harmony with this right arm of our strength, we will finally have a law to exterminate all who will not submit to our authority. **When death shall be made the penalty of violating our Sabbath, then many who are now ranked with commandment-keepers will come over to our side**. (*The Spirit of Prophecy*, vol. 4, p. 338, emphasis added)

Once probation closes, there is no more changing of position. Therefore, Satan's bid to secure commandment keepers to his side must take place before the close of probation. Some might think that, because Satan has openly revealed it, it must not be valid or reliable information. Yet, God gave Ellen White a view of Satan's game plan, and she recorded it. She is also clear by other revelation about what is to happen:

As the storm approaches, a large class who have professed faith in the third angel's message, but have not been sanctified through obedience to the truth, abandon their position and join the ranks of the opposition. By uniting with the world and partaking of its spirit, they have come to view matters in nearly the same light; and **when the test is brought**, they are prepared to choose the easy, popular side. Men of talent and pleasing address, who once rejoiced in the truth, employ their powers to deceive and mislead souls. They become the most bitter enemies of their former brethren. When Sabbathkeepers are brought before the courts to answer for their faith, these apostates are the most efficient agents of Satan to misrepresent and accuse them, and by false reports and insinuations to stir up the rulers against them. (*The Great Controversy*, p. 608, emphasis added)

Understand that all through the period of the setting up of the image to the beast and the mark of the beast, "as the storm approaches," many of those who are in the message will fall out—they will be sifted out. It is not only at the final point of the establishment of the death decree that the shaking takes place, but it is shortly after the death decree that the process is finalized and probation is closed.

Said the angel: "God will bring His work closer and closer to test and prove every one of His people." Some are willing to receive one point; but when God brings them to another testing point, they shrink from it and stand back, because they find that it strikes directly at some cherished idol.... If any will not be purified through obeying the truth, and overcome their selfishness, their pride, and evil passions, the angels of God have the charge: "They are joined to their idols, let them alone," and they pass on to their work, leaving these with their sinful traits unsubdued, to the control of evil angels. Those who come up to every point, and stand every test, and overcome, be the price what it may, have heeded the counsel of the True Witness, and they will receive the latter rain, and thus be fitted for translation. (*Testimonies For the Church*, vol. 1, p. 187)

When the testing time shall come, those who have made God's word their rule of life will be revealed. In summer there is no noticeable difference between evergreens and other trees; but when the blasts of winter come, the evergreens remain unchanged, while other trees are stripped of their foliage. So the falsehearted professor may not now be distinguished from the real Christian, but the time is just upon us when the difference will be apparent. Let opposition arise, let bigotry and intolerance again bear sway, let persecution be kindled, and the halfhearted and hypocritical will waver and yield the faith; but the true Christian will stand firm as a rock, his faith stronger, his hope brighter, than in days of prosperity. (*The Great Controversy*, p. 602)

At the time of crisis, God's people will be found scattered throughout the world in various situations. They will be found in every domain:

- *the mainstream* has its five "wise virgins" who arise and trim their lamps and follow on when "the voice of the bridegroom and the voice of the bride" calls out to them, "Behold, the Bridegroom cometh, go ye out to meet Him" (*Christ's Object Lessons*, p. 406). This call begins even now as we realize that the voice is not from official Seventh-day Adventist controlled conference bodies;

- *the "supporting ministries"* not directly controlled by the denomination but working, nevertheless, to bring members into the denomination and channeling tithes into the denomination also have their own contingent of wise virgins;

- *the truly independent* Seventh-day Adventist organizations, including home churches not tied to the denomination, do not send members to the denomination for baptism and registration, nor do they turn over tithes and offerings to the denomination, are labeled "offshoots" by the mainstream, employing various tactics to keep the membership from hearing them out; these organizations are not "purified," for they also have their wise and foolish virgins; yet, some of these will be more than wise virgins—they will be part of "the voice of the bride" giving the final call;

- *"other,"*—individuals that do not fit into any of these categories due to circumstantial isolation for a variety of reasons (such as sickness, incarcerations, family bindings or other persecutions, geographical isolation, or shunning by the denomination, etc.), though possessing the light of the third angel's message, will also rise up in heeding or giving the call as individual situations would vary.

In order to more clearly understand how the second shaking "out of the church"—the crisis shaking—will occur, we must have a well-defined concept of what the church is in its various spheres of existence. Study carefully, as we discuss the terms and concepts of the various churches and how they relate to one another—

the professed church;
the true church;
the apostate church (two kinds—wicked Israel and fallen Babylon);
the church militant—the "wheat and tares" church;
and the church triumphant—the purified church.

We will unpack the distinctions further as we go, but here are the main talking points with regard to these various entities:

1. All the churches listed above are "the *professed* people of God." With the exception of fallen Babylon, all claim Adventism as their religion. Within those laying claim to hold to the third angel's message are three: apostate Israel, the wheat, and the tares.

2. *The church militant, which encompasses the true church, is a servant to the true third angel's message.* It is not apostate.

3. The true church is the wheat part of the church militant. By the time probation is closed, there will be no more church militant. The true church will be sealed and purified, and the tares will have left them.

4. The church militant will have tares in it, mixed up with the wheat, but it is not an apostate church.

5. The purified church contains no tares. It is pure wheat. It is the true church that has emerged from the church militant. Every member of the purified church, though it is not yet manifest immediately at the close of probation, is united to the church in heaven. The purified church has no earthly registry.

6. The church triumphant is the true "emerging church," for the people of the purified, true church light up with glory as they come out on the other side of the time of Jacob's trouble at the time of the fifth plague when it is said that "their captivity is turned" and the wicked experience the darkness and "terrible awakening" in realizing that they have been fighting God.

7. There are two apostates: Babylon and wicked Israel. We are not discussing Babylon here; our view is only of those professing to be Seventh-day Adventists.

8. Tares are not open sinners or apostates. They have their place with the wheat and purport to be of the true church, upholding the third angel's message. They are not accurately distinguished by the church members and there should be no attempts to remove them.

9. An entity that refuses to give the truths of the third angel's message cannot be the church militant, or the true church. It is a mere profession of the faith, not a reality.

10. An entity that refuses to give the truths of the third angel's message is not composed of wheat or tares; it is an apostate and therefore an open sinner.

The following diagram graphically illustrates these points:

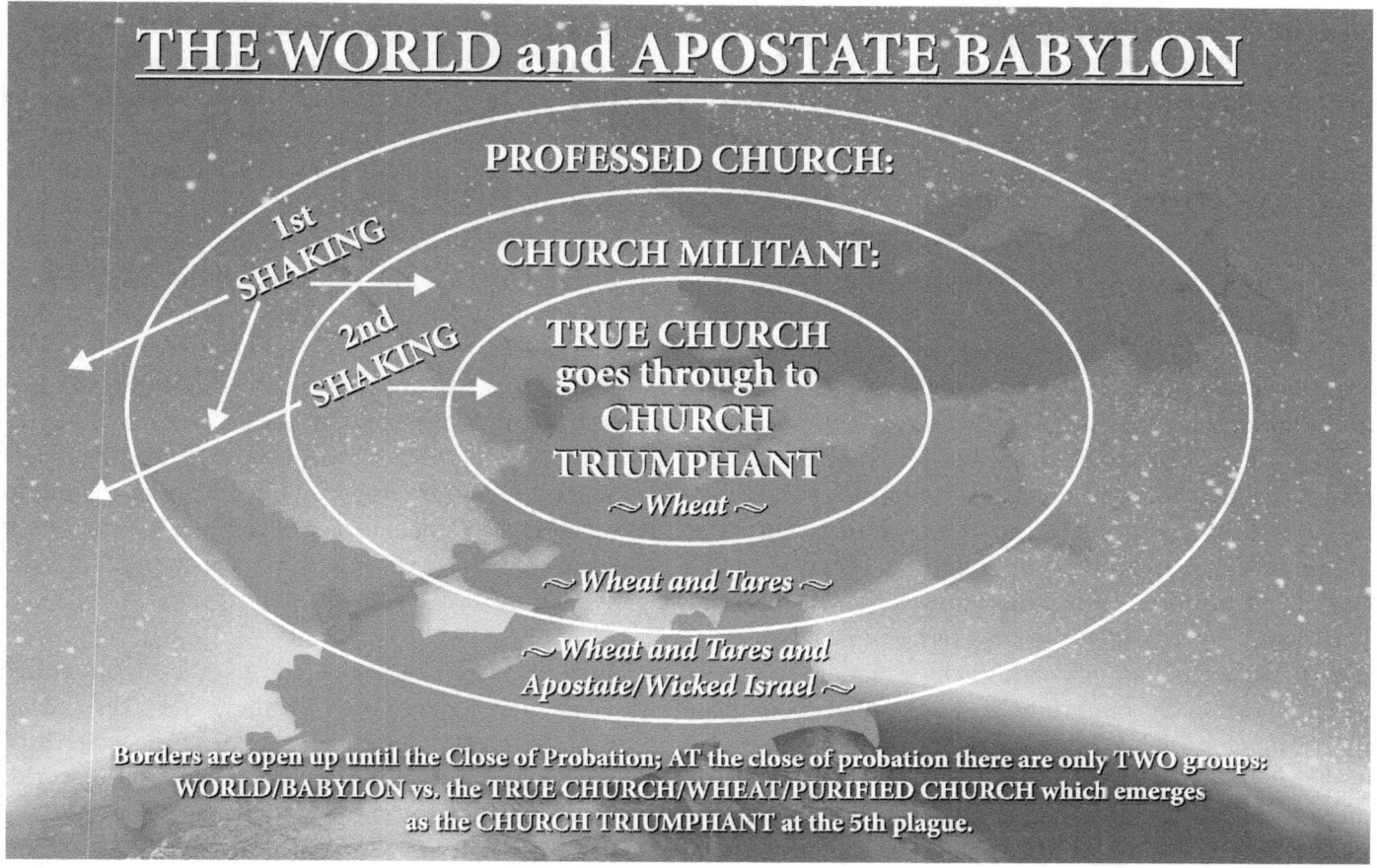

These groups are in flux up until the close of probation, with individuals moving in and out as depicted by the two shakings and the arrows. When the process is all settled and every soul is fixed with the seal of God or the mark of the beast, there is no more church militant or professed church but only the true church and the apostate world.

Together with the truth as it is in Jesus, these several points are what we need to understand to make the shift from "churchianity" to the final generation remnant church of God. This is the church that will deliver the loud cry of the third angel's message to the world with clarity, in its purity, and by the unction of the Holy Spirit alone. It will be completely devoid of error and will deliver the message entirely outside of all that would previously have been known as "the common order" (church machinery, human organization). This is a paradigm shift for most Adventists, who have been taught to believe teach, and act as though the conference-controlled entity, *as it is today,* is the church militant with its embedded true church (wheat), and this is the entity that will deliver the loud cry of the third angel. However, the conference-controlled entity is not an exclusive vessel of the church militant. *It is by definition the mainstream body, the largest visible contingent of the **professed** remnant church only.* There are other legitimate professors! The members of the mainstream General Conference professors of the third angel are not the only ones who have a claim on "remnant church" status, even though they have legally obtained ownership of the name "Seventh-day Adventist."

The point is that membership in the organizational Seventh-day Adventist Church is not a prerequisite for coming into the church militant. Today many people from Babylon and the world will join to one of the other of groupings within professed Adventism. People within Adventism already may migrate to another group within Adventism. Under the loud cry of the third angel many more people will come into the church militant who do not presently have the truths of the third angel's message. This will include souls in the mainstream denominational church! Many from the world, Babylon, and the professed church who have come in under the loud cry will enter into the church militant only to prove themselves tares in the end, leaving the church. They will not be able to endure the pressures brought to bear upon them. They become apostates under the second shaking. They will not shake down into a professed church of apostate Sabbatarians, for there will be no such thing. Such exists today, but under the crisis of the second shaking, this group will break up. There will be only two groups in the end.

Often we hear the conference leaders, teachers and ministers calling itself "The Remnant Church" while using the following statement of Mrs. White to prove it will never fall: "The church may appear as about to fall, but it does not fall. It remains, while the sinners in Zion are sifted out …" (Lt. 55, 1886, in *Manuscript Releases*, vol. 12, p. 324). In that statement, she was referring to the church militant being purified and leaving only the faithful souls. If we compare the conference church entity to the professed church, the church militant, and the true church, we can determine which church the conference is assisting. The Spirit of Prophecy has given us descriptions of each church to make this determination.

It is extremely important that we understand the time frame for Ellen White's statement about the church not falling. It is simple to determine, as the immediately preceding sentence reveals it: "Satan will work his miracles to deceive; he will set up his power as supreme" (Lt. 55, 1886). When will Satan go forth with miracle-working deceptions in the context of supreme power in the earth? It is none other than during the time of enforced Sunday observance, for Sunday observance is the vehicle Satan uses to establish this supremacy:

> In the counsels of the synagogue of Satan it was determined to obliterate the sign of allegiance to God in the world. Antichrist, the man of sin, exalted himself as supreme in the earth, and through him Satan has worked in a masterly way to create rebellion against the law of God and against the memorial of his created works.… **The false sabbath has been upheld through superhuman agency** in order that God might be dishonored. **It is a sign of Satan's supremacy in the earth**, for men are worshiping the God of this world. (*Signs of the Times*, March 12, 1894, emphasis added)

Returning to the context of Ellen White's statement in Letter 55, 1886, we read in the immediately preceding paragraph:

> **We are to be ready and waiting for the orders of God**. Nations will be stirred to their very center. **Support will be withdrawn** from those who proclaim God's only standard of righteousness, the only sure test of character. And all who will not bow to **the decrees of the national councils** and obey the **national laws to exalt the sabbath instituted by the man of sin** to the disregard of God's holy day, will feel, not the oppressive power of popery alone, but of the Protestant world, **the image of the beast**. (Lt. 55, 1886, emphasis added)

Notice that we "are to be ready and waiting for the orders of God." It does not say, "the orders of the church," nor "the orders of the conference leaders," nor "the orders of the pastors and elders." The leaders are not going to be directing this. The message is going out, but it is not going out from the churches. In fact, the question is asked by inspiration:

> **Will the churches heed the Laodicean message?** Will they repent, or will they, notwithstanding that **the most solemn message of truth—the third angel's message—is being proclaimed to the world**, go on in sin? This is the last message of mercy, the last warning to a fallen world. If the church of God becomes lukewarm, it does not stand in favor with God any more than do the churches that are represented as having fallen and become the habitation of devils, and the hold of every foul spirit, and the cage of every unclean and hateful bird. Those who have had opportunities to hear and receive the truth and who have united with the Seventh-day Adventist church, calling themselves the commandment-keeping people of God, and yet possess no more vitality and consecration to God than do the nominal churches, will receive of the plagues of God just as verily as the churches who oppose the law of God. Only those that are sanctified through the truth will compose the royal family in the heavenly mansions Christ has gone to prepare for those that love Him and keep His commandments. (Letter 35, 1898, in *Manuscript Releases*, vol. 19, p. 176, emphasis added)

This is a stunning statement. In it, we can see that the question is whether *the churches*—those professing to be the Seventh-day Adventist church of God, as is obvious in the entire context—will heed the message *at the very time that the "last message of mercy,"* which is the fourth angel proclamation of the loud cry of the third angel, *is going forth*! The message is being sounded, but the churches are not sounding it! The denomination is not involved in it. Rather, here is the stance taken by leadership (please bear with the inserted notes—these are important highlights):

There is to be in the churches a wonderful manifestation of the power of God [*not coming down from the voice of the conference and the voice of the ministers, as seen above, but from the voice of the bride and the voice of the Bridegroom*], but it will not move upon those who have not humbled themselves before the Lord, and opened the door of the heart by confession and repentance. **In the manifestation of that power which lightens the earth with the glory of God** [*the fourth angel loud cry*], **they will see only something which in their blindness they think dangerous, something which will arouse their fears, and they will brace themselves to resist it. Because the Lord does not work according to their ideas and expectations, they will oppose the work.** "Why," they say, "should not we know the Spirit of God, when we have been in the work so many years?"—Because **they did not respond to the warnings, the entreaties of the messages of God**, but persistently said, "I am rich, and increased with goods, and have need of nothing." [*This is the message to the Laodiceans.*] **Talent, long experience, will not make men channels of light**, unless they place themselves under the bright beams of the Sun of Righteousness, and are called, and chosen, and **prepared by the endowment of the Holy Spirit**. When **men who handle sacred things** will humble themselves under the mighty hand of God, the Lord will lift them up. He will make them men of discernment—men rich in the grace of his Spirit. Their strong, selfish traits of character, their stubbornness, will be seen in the light shining from the Light of the world. "I will come unto thee quickly, and will **remove thy candlestick** out of his place, except thou repent." If you seek the Lord with all your heart, he will be found of you. (*Review and Herald*, Dec. 23, 1890, art. B, emphasis added)

The leaders will all fall into the same category as the people, yet Mrs. White is especially focusing here upon the leaders, warning that their position and experience have no relevance in making them channels of light. Only the endowment of the Holy Spirit, in confession and repentance, will confer upon them a place in the closing work. We can see that a candlestick can be removed. God has not made men the light of the church!

This figure illustrates the eternal vigilance of our Saviour. Christ is in the midst of the seven golden candlesticks, walking from church to church, from congregation to congregation, from heart to heart. He who keeps Israel neither slumbers nor sleeps. If the candlesticks were left to the care of human beings, how often they would flicker and go out. But **God has not given His church into the hands of men. Christ, One who gave His life for the life of the world, is the Watchman of the house. He is the Warder, faithful and true, of the temple courts of the Lord. We are not dependent on the presence of priest or minister** [*or conferences and committees*]. We are kept by the power of God. The presence of Christ is the secret of our life and light. (*Signs of the Times*, Feb. 12, 1902, emphasis added)

This statement shows us that the watchman of *this church* is already in the house. This is not a church given into the hands of men. The force of logic tells us that this is the true church and that a church keeping Christ outside knocking at suppertime is a different church. A church barring the door to Christ would be a church controlled by men.

Coming back to the theme of this segment, then, we must sort out the terms of the "professed church," the "church militant," the "true church," and the "church triumphant." It is important to define these terms clearly so that we know which church it is that is "going through." We must avoid becoming confused or deceived into looking to an earthly organization with its human leadership structure legally registered in corporate law, owning institutional buildings through its layers of franchises (divisions, unions, local conferences, and individual church institutions) *as somehow having come into possession of an unconditional promise*. No entity in earth's history has ever received such a carte blanche—not even the ancient Israelite nation-church itself, *through and to which* the Almighty Himself personally came.

The oft-quoted passage brought forward above, which promises that *the church may appear as about to fall but does not*, is usually quoted out of context, and most people do not put forth much effort to research and read for themselves, so they are subject to having their minds conditioned to false beliefs that are very hard to overcome later. It is to be noted that, in its original form

(Letter 55, 1886, to Haskell and Butler, published in *Manuscript Releases*, volume 12, as MR No. 994, "An Appeal to Live the Truth and Share It," pp. 319–328), we find a general theme of warning that, if the church does not live up to her privileges, she *can* and *will* fall. This goes entirely against the way that this statement is used in the church today to train the members into a mindset of unconditional promise. Therefore, we know that *there is a church that can fall*, which is the denominational enterprise, and *there is a church that will not fall*. It is important for us to be able to distinguish between these so that we are clear on the matter of which church it is that we must strive to hold fast.

Let us go on in our analysis of Ellen White's 1886 letter:

I think of His great sorrow as He wept over Jerusalem, exclaiming, "O Jerusalem, Jerusalem, which killest the prophets, and stonest them that are sent unto thee; how often would I have gathered thy children together, as a hen doth gather her brood under her wings, and ye would not" [Luke 13:34]! **God forbid that these words shall apply to those who have great light and blessings.** In the rejecting of Jerusalem it was because great privileges were abused, which brought the denunciation upon all who lightly regarded the great opportunities and precious light that were entrusted to their keeping. **Privileges do not commend us to God**, but they commend God to us. **No people are saved because they have great light and special advantages, for these high and heavenly favors only increase their responsibility.** (Lt. 55, 1886, *Manuscript Releases*, vol. 12, p. 319, emphasis added)

When Jerusalem was divorced from God it was because of her sins. She fell from an exalted height that Tyre and Sidon had never reached. And **when an angel falls he becomes a fiend.** The depth of our ruin is measured by the exalted light to which God has raised us in His great goodness and unspeakable mercy. **Oh, what privileges are granted to us as a people! And if God spared not His people that He loved, because they refused to walk in the light, how can He spare the people whom He has blessed with the light of heaven in having opened to them the most exalted truth ever entrusted to mortal man to give to the world?** (Lt. 55, 1886, emphasis added)

Internal corruption will bring the denunciations of God upon this people as it did upon Jerusalem. Oh, let pleading voices, let earnest prayer be heard, that those who preach to others shall not themselves be castaways. My brethren, we know not what is before us, and our only safety is in following the Light of the world. **God will work with us and for us if the sins which brought His wrath upon the old world, upon Sodom and Gomorrah and upon ancient Jerusalem, do not become our crime.** (Lt. 55, 1886, in *Manuscript Releases*, vol. 12, pp. 319, 320, emphasis added)

Conditionality permeates this entire letter. So, when we read the letter in its entirety, we must realize that there are two churches brought to view: There is an organization that can fall, and there is a remnant church comprised of individuals that will not fall. The latter church is the true and purified church, which is the true body of Christ, *the church we read about in this oft-repeated statement.* Yet, this statement is proclaimed in Adventist pulpits as assurance that the organized professing church, the conference church, is the biblical remnant—or at least that the remnant members are found solely within her borders and that the organized church will lose the insincere sinners, and then what will be left is the purified remnant General Conference-directed church! Yet, we cannot read it this way. *The church that appears as about to fall but that does not fall consists of the overcomers who are in perfect obedience to all of God's commands through the power of true Righteousness by faith!* The church in view is the one in existence at the time that its earthly support is withdrawn, under the oppression of the crisis of the image of the beast and Sunday laws, when the embargo against Sabbath-keepers being able to buy and sell will be enacted. This church cannot be *conference-directed* because the conference, as a Sabbath-keeping organization, could, under the new legislation, only operate as a criminal enterprise. It could not continue to operate openly. Neither could it legally own anything. This church that "may appear as about to fall, but ... does not fall" is, therefore, people only, not a corporation with holdings. The repetition of thought on this point is necessary because we are into the shifting of paradigm for most members of the Seventh-day Adventist Church. The thought must "sink in." The direction of the threatened church cannot be under a hierarchy of men. It can be only *God-directed*. He has the horses' reins in His own hands. He is not directing through intermediate human agents.

The loud cry church under duress is the church militant coming to the very end of its purification process as it prepares to enter the time of Jacob's trouble under the falling of the seven last plagues, as a purified church. When Satan's power is supreme, it will be all over for the world, and probation will have closed. It is *this* church which appears as about to fall but does not fall. It is the character-perfected church that has come to fully reflect Christ's image and the glory of God. Read the statement again in context:

> We are to be ready and waiting for the orders of God. Nations will be stirred to their very center. **Support will be withdrawn from those who proclaim God's only standard of righteousness,** the only sure test of character. And **all who will not bow to the decrees of the national councils and obey the national laws to exalt the sabbath instituted by the man of sin** to the disregard of God's holy day, **will feel, not the oppressive power of popery alone, but of the Protestant world, the image of the beast.**
>
> Satan will work his miracles to deceive; he will set up his power as supreme. **The church may appear as about to fall, but it does not fall.** It remains, while the sinners in Zion will be sifted out—the chaff separated from the precious wheat. This is a terrible ordeal, but nevertheless it must take place. None but **those who have been overcoming** by the blood of the Lamb and the word of their testimony will be found with the loyal and true, without spot or stain of sin, without guile in their mouths. We must be divested of our self-righteousness and arrayed in the righteousness of Christ.
>
> The **remnant** that purify their souls by obeying the truth gather strength from the trying process, **exhibiting the beauty of holiness amid the surrounding apostasy....** Many of the ministers are half paralyzed by their own defects of character. They need the converting power of God.
>
> **That which God required of Adam before his fall was perfect obedience to His law. God requires now what He required of Adam, perfect obedience, righteousness without a flaw, without shortcoming in His sight. God help us to render to Him all His law requires. We cannot do this without that faith that brings Christ's righteousness into daily practice.** (Lt. 55, 1886, to G. I. Butler and S. N. Haskell, *Manuscript Releases*, vol. 12, pp. 324, 325)

We can see then, that there are different conditions to being part of the professed church and the church militant. The professor has a name and a claim. The member of the church militant has the true third angel's message and not a Babylonian substitute. Further, if the members are to emerge on the right side of the shaking and become, at the very last, the purified true church and the church triumphant, they will need to meet the appropriate conditions. For this statement to apply to the conference-directed church, all its members will have to meet the criteria of obedience. Yet, in the "church-that-does-not-fall" statement, we have a view of a church that *has met the criteria of the true church*, having *emerged triumphant on the other side of the shaking as an obedient and pure church. To assist the church militant and become part of the true and ultimately triumphant church, individuals and ministries must meet the inspired criteria.*

The True Church in the Bible and the Spirit of Prophecy

Individuals must meet each of the criteria mentioned below to be a part of the true church. Human organizations and ministries must meet the same criteria to be assisting this church.

> The church is God's fortress, His city of refuge, which He holds in a revolted world. Any betrayal of the church is treachery to Him who has bought mankind with the blood of His only-begotten Son. From the beginning, faithful souls have constituted the church on earth. In every age the Lord has had His watchmen, who have borne a faithful testimony to the generation in which they lived. (*Acts of the Apostles*, p. 11)

> God has a church. It is not the great cathedral, neither is it the national establishment, neither is it the various denominations; it is the people who love God and keep His commandments. "Where two or three are gathered together in My name, there am I in the midst of them." [Matt. 18:20.] Where Christ is, even among the humble few, this is Christ's church, for the presence of the High and Holy One who inhabiteth eternity can alone constitute a church. (Lt. 108, 1886, in *Manuscript Releases*, vol. 17, pp. 81, 82)

> Those who keep God's Commandments, those who live not by bread alone, but by every word that proceedeth out of the mouth of God, compose the church of the living God. (Ms. 24, 1891, in *Manuscript Releases*, vol. 19, p. 242)

> God calls the church His body. The church is the bride, the Lamb's wife. God is the Father of the

family, the Shepherd of the flock. But a mere outward connection with any church will not save a man. It is personal faith in a personal Saviour which brings the soul into spiritual union with Christ. (Ms. 121, 1899, in *Manuscript Releases*, vol. 16, p. 277)

And the dragon was enraged with the woman, and he went to make war with the rest of her offspring, who keep the commandments of God and have the testimony of Jesus Christ. (Rev. 12:17, NKJV)

And He put all things under His feet, and gave Him to be head over all things to the church which is His body, the fullness of Him who fills all in all. (Eph. 1:22, 23, ESV)

Paul wrote, in 1 Corinthians 12:13, that we become part of the body of Christ (the true church) when we are baptized with the Holy Spirit. God's true church is made up of faithful individuals who have the spiritual qualifications. An organization or ministry must also be faithful if it is to be considered an instrument used by the true church.

The Church Militant

Individuals, organizations or ministries must meet certain criteria to be legitimate supporters of the church militant. Members of this church—the "wheat and tares" church—both appear to be good on the surface. Blatant sinners are not part of this church, as they are obviously disobedient to God and the truth and, therefore, must be considered separate from the church militant. They may profess to be giving the true message. However, if what they are giving is not the true message, then they are not doing the work of the church militant. The church militant only gives the true message.

Notice in the following statement how the true message that proceeds from the oracles of God—the law with the Sabbath, the Sanctuary, and the Spirit of Prophecy—will be given to the world through this church:

The work is soon to close. **The members of the church militant who have proved faithful will become the church triumphant** [144,000]. In reviewing our past history, having traveled over every step of advance to our present standing, I can say, Praise God! As I see what God has wrought, I am filled with astonishment and with confidence in Christ our Leader. We have nothing to fear for the future, except as we shall forget the way the Lord has led us, and his teaching in our past history.... If we **walk in the light as it shines upon us from the living oracles of God**, we shall have large responsibilities, corresponding to the great light given us of God. We have many duties to perform, because we have been made **the depositories of sacred truth to be given to the world** in all its beauty and glory. We are debtors to God to use every advantage he has entrusted to us to beautify the truth of holiness of character, and **to send the message** of warning, and of comfort, of hope and love, to those who are in the darkness of error and sin. (Lt. 32, 1892, to "Brethren of the General Conference," in the *General Conference Daily Bulletin*, Jan. 29, 1893, p. 24, emphasis added)

God leads a commandment-keeping people who embrace the truth and obey Him. Offshoots teach error, for they have "shot off" from *the truth*, and they ignore the commandments. They are not led by God. Notice:

God has a church upon the earth, who are his chosen people, who keep his commandments. He is leading, not stray off-shoots, not one here and one there, but a people. The truth is a sanctifying power; but the church militant is not the church triumphant. There are tares among the wheat. "Wilt thou then that we gather them up?" was the question of the servant; but the master answered, "Nay; lest while ye gather up the tares, ye root up also the wheat with them." The gospel net draws not only good fish, but bad ones as well, and the Lord only knows who are his. (Lt. 57, 1893, in *Review and Herald*, Sept. 12, 1893)

The church militant and the true church promote the pure truth—

The house of God, which is the church of the living God, the pillar and ground of the truth. (1 Tim. 3:15)

If we are not promoting the truth, nor doing the Lord's work, then we are not assisting the church of God and do not distinguish ourselves as wheat.

Personal faults are found among some of the individuals in the church militant:

Let every one who is seeking to live a Christian life, remember that the church militant is not the church triumphant. Those who are carnally minded will be found in the church. They are to be pitied more than blamed. The church is not to be judged as sustaining these characters, though they are found within her borders. Should the church expel them, the very ones who found fault with their presence there, would blame the church for sending them adrift in the world; they would claim that they were treated unmercifully. It may be that in the church there are those who are cold, proud, haughty, and un-Christian, but you need not associate with this class. (*Review and Herald*, Jan. 16, 1894)

There is a difference between one who is a tare and an "open sinner." Open sinners are not a part of the church militant, and should either be removed or we should remove from them. However, tares should remain and not to be judged.

Christ has plainly taught that **those who persist in open sin must be separated from the church, but He has not committed to us the work of judging character and motive**. He knows our nature too well to entrust this work to us. Should we try to uproot from the church those whom we suppose to be spurious Christians, we should be sure to make mistakes.... The tares and the wheat are to grow together until the harvest; and **the harvest is the end of probationary time**. (*Christ's Object Lessons*, pp. 71, 72, emphasis added)

So, if an organization or an individual is participating in open sin, it is not part of God's church. This is a key point. An additional key point, which produces the paradigm shift that we are seeking to foster, is that we must make a distinction between the professed church and the church militant. *When we realize that a class of professed people of God and even the church's leadership are not giving the third angel's message in verity, though it has been sent them from heaven, they are classed as though in open rebellion. They are the same as open sinners.* If they are preaching another gospel—the gospel of Protestant Reformationism—and calling it the heaven-sent light, they are not preaching the "third angel's message in verity," no matter what they call it. It is a *mere profession*. More than this, it is apostasy. Organizations and individuals must see that they are guilty of lending their influence to the side of Satan if they are failing or refusing to give the third angel's message.

If they do not pass this test, they are not part of the church militant.

And **through lack of zeal for the promulgation of the third angel's message, many others, while not apparently living in transgression, are nevertheless as verily lending their influence on the side of Satan as are those who openly sin against God**. Multitudes are perishing; but how few are burdened for these souls! There is a stupor, a paralysis, upon many of the people of God, which prevents them from understanding the duty of the hour. (*Testimonies for the Church*, vol. 8, p. 119, emphasis added)

The first shaking

Those who are shaken out at the first shaking are those who have rejected and lost the third angel's message. These are the ones upon whom has come the "stupor" and "paralysis" depicted in the above testimony. However, before we go on, we must exercise caution with this. There are many in the church who are ignorant of the difference between the true gospel and the one they have been taught by their teachers and leaders. It is not for us to judge any individual, for we do not know their circumstances. Yet, we may discern whether their belief or teaching is either true or counterfeit. The point that we would emphasize here is that the first shaking has to do with decisions made by professed people of God regarding the Laodicean message. To reject that message is to be shaken out of the church and into Babylon or the world. Their rejection of the message precludes their having any involvement in the activity of the church militant. This does not mean that one would see such an one leaving the church structure. Not at all! Oftentimes those who refuse to be shaken out of the true gospel, having accepted the counsel of Jesus to the Laodiceans, will find themselves having to seek another class for fellowship as they are rejected by their congregations through marginalization, being placed under censure, or being disfellowshipped for their stand upon the message. It is far easier for those who are shaken out of the message to stay in "the church" as members in good standing in the denominational structure. More often than not, one will find the typical conference church tolerating members of the true church, though it is not uncommon to find outright intolerance.

The pen of inspiration makes it easy to understand that the Lord was not trifling with the church when He sent his men to bring His people forward:

The church of God is to shine as a light to the world, but Jesus is the illuminator, and He is represented as moving among His people. No one shines by his own light. The Lord God almighty and the Lamb are the lights thereof. The message given us by A. T. Jones, and E. J. Waggoner is the message of God to the Laodicean church, and woe be unto anyone who professes to believe the truth and yet does not reflect to others the God-given rays.... (Lt. 24, 1892, in *The Ellen G. White 1888 Materials*, p. 1052)

We have shown elsewhere that, if the message had been accepted, the work would have closed. Yet, Christ was rejected in the Holy Spirit, and the truth was kept from the people and from the world by our own brethren. It was a striking success for the enemy of souls (*The Ellen G. White 1888 Materials*, p. 1575). The facts we here desire to underscore and prove are that *the 1888 message of true gospel light is the loud cry of the third angel for the closing of the gospel call in the world, and it is the message that causes a shaking amongst God's people.*

If God's people do not first accept this message, then how can they give it? If they remain seated in their churches but are not moving upon the heaven sent light, then *what are they but shaken* out of their true faith and calling? It matters not that they are sitting in "Moses' seat" (Matt. 23:2) as professors of the true faith.

We can know by the inspired page that the message of the *loud cry of the third angel*, which is the fourth angel's closing call of Revelation 18:1, is *the 1888 message*, which is the everlasting gospel. A careful cross-referencing of *Testimonies to Ministers*, p. 299, with *The Ellen G. White 1888 Materials*, p. 1575, proves it conclusively. The first passage identifies "the loud cry of the third angel" as that message which "goes forth to lighten the earth ... under the direction of the angel who joins the third angel," while the second passage identifies it as the "Lord's message through Brethren Waggoner and Jones," which was the "light that is to lighten the whole earth with its glory" that was resisted by the brethren and kept away from the world.

Inspiration also declares:

Several have written to me, inquiring if the message of justification by faith [*the 1888 message of Jones and Waggoner*] is the third angel's message, and I have answered, "It is the third angel's message in verity." The prophet declares, "And after these things I saw another angel come down from heaven, having great power; and the earth was lightened with his glory." ... How will any of our brethren know when this light shall come to the people of God? **As yet, we certainly have not seen the light that answers to this description**. God has light for his people, and all who will accept it will see the sinfulness of remaining in a lukewarm condition; they will heed **the counsel of the True Witness** when he says, "Be zealous therefore, and repent. Behold, I stand at the door, and knock: if any man hear my voice, and open the door, I will come in to him, and will sup with him, and he with me." [Rev. 3:19, 20.] (*Review and Herald*, April 1, 1890, emphasis added)

This light came in 1888, but she wrote two years later that it had not come. How so? "*As yet*," we have not seen this light raised up *by* the denomination. We have seen it raised up *in* the denomination—messengers come here and there, as they did in Jones and Waggoner—but always with the same results. As often as the attempt has been made to bring the light, the prophesied results have consistently taken place, for God does not lie (Jer. 5:1, 2, 20, 21, 23, 24; Matt. 22:3, 4, 6, 8). The highlighted point is that the preaching of this message produces a shaking. What this means is that the rejection of the message causes the rejecter to be shaken out. Here again is the startling reality that most denominational members have not thought about or understood correctly: *The shaking does not have relevance with respect to location in a building or membership on a corporate registry. It is not a **physical** or **administrative** shaking. It is a **spiritual** shaking.* It has to do with one's relation to *the truth,* not his or her relation to *a common-order organization!*

Therefore, whenever this message is preached, it will have its effect. *It will produce a shaking.* Let us connect the following passage with the previous passage, noting that, if A = B and B = C, then A = C when these variables are representative of:

A = The 1888 Message, or fourth angel, which is the loud cry of the third angel (Rev. 18:1) that lightens the earth with His glory (*Testimonies to Ministers*, p. 299; *The Ellen G. White 1888 Materials*, p. 1575).
B = The counsel of the True Witness, which is the message to the Laodiceans; and
C = The cause of the shaking.

Therefore, *the 1888 message is what causes the shaking* (A = C). That A = B is seen in *Review and Herald*, April 1, 1890 (shown above). That B = C is established by the following statement:

I asked the meaning of the shaking I had seen. I was shown that it would be caused by the straight testimony called forth by **the counsel of the True Witness** to the Laodiceans. It will have its effect upon the heart of the receiver of the testimony, and it will lead him to exalt the standard and pour forth the straight truth. This straight testimony, some will not bear. They will rise up against it, and this will **cause a shaking** among God's people. (*Review and Herald*, Dec. 31, 1857, emphasis added)

This means that the message that is to lighten the world and close the work of the great controversy in its pre-millennial phase must first move God's people. It must produce a remnant who understand it, live it, and move with it. The enemy of souls does not want Seventh-day Adventists to understand these "blockbuster" truths!

It behooves every reader who has not been impressed with what has been said in this segment to go back again and understand the claims and see the evidence brought in from inspiration to support those claims.

The members of the church militant are not shaken by the first shaking. Even the tares have withstood that shaking! That there are tares in this church is a fact irrelevant to the first shaking. The church militant is made up of individuals and groups who appear to do good things for the Lord. They embrace the third angel's message, they labor for the cause, they sigh and cry for what they see in the professed church, and they even participate in *reform* as "historic Adventists" or as those who are yet further along in the advancing light of the fourth angel glory of the message of God's character. Superficially, the wheat and the tares both appear to be genuine concerning their service to the truths of the third angel's message. They have the right message. Those who are not cooperating with God in giving the last message of mercy cannot be a part of this church. If they participate in the world's trends, their profession is only *a claim*—a claim that, in reality, has no substance in actual teaching, ministry, or life. These trends may include the emerging church with its spiritualistic practices and doctrine, the evangelical "gospel" with its doctrinal errors, the ecumenical movement that, in failing to identify Romanism for what it is, has forgotten its Protestant status. In disobedience to the counsels and commands of God, they make the testimonies of none effect, while claiming to be the remnant people of God with the Spirit of Prophecy.

The pure truth, the true message, will be given to the world by the church militant. The question then arises: Is the conference part of the church militant? Does it appear as wheat or as open sinners, failing to give the third angel's message, the final message of mercy, the truth as it is in Jesus, thereby excluding itself from the church militant? After all that we have studied in **Section II** of this book, the answer should be obvious.

The Professed Church

The general conference structure is an organization, or ministry, that professes to be an assistant to God's Seventh-day Adventist movement on earth (which carries the three angels' messages). In fact, the belief is that the General Conference organization *is* the very embodiment of that movement, not merely an assistant to it. In other words, there is an assumed proprietorship of the third angel's message, denoting not only legal but divinely bestowed ownership of the message of present truth. The reader must decide if they should agree with this attitude or position, for it is the exact paradigm under which the structure conducts its operations and to which the faithful church member directs his or her tithes, offerings and evangelistic support.

It is also under this paradigm that, on the one hand, the organization teaches its members that they alone are the true "body of Christ" in the world. Though this teaching does appear in church literature and the pulpit, it is not so much an overt teaching as an inference that members note in choosing to remove themselves from the church register. Those who leave the church are considered to be outside the body of Christ. It is this writer's opinion that this inference employs coercion through fear to prevent the loss of membership and financial support. Then, on the other hand, there is an opposing view arising out of the ecumenical trend in the denomination, which holds that all the Christian religions, even Catholic, are ministering Christ to the world. These others are missing some of our distinctive doctrines, but the basic gospel message is said to be the same. This would make all of them part of the body of Christ. It is very hard to strike a balance when juggling mutually incompatible theories. The church has a tremendous challenge on its hands to hold two types of believers together in tension—the "liberals" and the "conservatives."

Coming back to our discussion of the "professed" church, we include the "independent" Adventist organizations and ministries. Whether these are "supporting ministry" or truly independent, they profess to be assistants to God's Adventist movement. Such organizations and ministries are less likely to assume the exclusive and proprietary attitude in relation to other Adventist bodies.

They will not be as prone to say they are the only ones who may have the third angel's message in their organization. At the same time, they will not view any non-Adventist as part of the *remnant* "body of Christ" *at an organizational level*, though recognizing that any *individuals* living up to all the light they have are in Christ.

Any individual who claims to be Adventists is part of the professed Adventist Movement and Church (the spiritual church, not the General Conference church). However, organizations and individuals must experience what they profess in order to be genuine. To be members of the true church, professed Adventists must be obedient to the *message* and true to the *message*. When professed Adventists are true to the message and obedient to it, they are part of the true church. We understand that there are tares in the church militant, and, while these do not actually have the experience of the message, they have the understanding of the message and teach it with their lips. The presence of tares in the church militant does not negate the fact that those who have the profession of the message along with the experience of the message are members of the church militant as well as of the true church. However, the tares are not part of the true church. Tares are not united to heaven but only moving along with the church militant and members of the true church.

When the mere professors of Adventism *become* true to the message and obedient to it, they then *become* members of the true church that resides within the church militant. *Being baptized into a denomination or organization is not what makes it so.* The human record-keeping of baptisms and the issuing of certificates are merely administrative processes. These do not necessarily reflect the spiritual reality. Baptism into a denomination with earthly books of record is an extraneous attachment of man's devising. So also is the notion that only duly ordained clergymen with denominational credentials are qualified to baptize. Is this a new thought? It may be. Yet, that does not mean it is not true. Inspiration declares it:

> Another thing I want to tell you that I know from the light as given me: it has been a great mistake that men go out, knowing they are children of God, like Brother Tay, [who] went to Pitcairn as a missionary to do work, [but] that man did not feel at liberty to baptize because he had not been ordained. That is not any of God's arrangements; it is man's fixing. **When men go out with the burden of the work and to bring souls into the truth, those men are ordained of God, [even] if [they] never have a touch of ceremony of ordination. To say [they] shall not baptize when there is nobody else, [is wrong].** If there is a minister in reach, all right, then they should seek for the ordained minister to do the baptizing, but when the Lord works with a man to bring out a soul here and there, and they know not when the opportunity will come that these precious souls can be baptized, why he should not question about the matter, **he should baptize these souls**....
>
> We must not put men into straight jackets that are going out to proclaim the gospel of peace among those that are in midnight darkness and idolatry and all these things. And we must lead these men with our prayers, earnest prayers, and our hearts to go with them, and bid them Godspeed, and for the Lord to prosper them. That is what we must do. ("Remarks Concerning Foreign Mission Work," Ms. 75, 1896, emphasis added)

We need to know these things in order to be prepared for the work that we have ahead of us in giving the last message of mercy to a world reeling under the coming tempest. We are to baptize into Christ, under the final gospel call of the fourth angel repetition of the third angel's message. An elder should do the work if available, but this should not be taken to mean that he must be ordained under the authority of mainstream Adventism. Not in today's environment. Such an elder is likely working on another plan, baptizing into Christ and into a denominational enterprise requiring vows of allegiance to itself. These things should be self-evident, yet confusion reigns.

We have been emphatic on this matter to the saturation point because it is a culturally and theologically reinforced paradigm of many generations that the denominational enterprise of Seventh-day Adventism is the true church and the body of Christ. Ministers and teachers condition the minds of the people to believe this while even articulating the mutually exclusive concept of salvation not being in groups but on an individual basis. In other words, many will nod their heads and say, "Amen" even when one preaches, "A church cannot save you," or "The church is not the building," yet they go right on believing and acting as though one must be in the church denomination to be saved and that being outside of it means being lost. A denominational church elder once told this writer—*in writing*—that he was outside of "the body of Christ" for his stance. Herein lies a most glaring break with logic and truth, for, if we equate the true body of Christ with anything less than the wheat, we have a body of Christ that admits sin. The body of Christ is the true church in which there is neither spot nor blemish. The body of Christ is within the church militant, but it is not ultimately the church militant, comprised of wheat and tares, and it is certainly not the professing church containing open sinners or those who neglect or deny the true third angel's message.

The body of Christ cannot be visibly demonstrated in any kind of registry of human organizations. It is only known to heaven. It is the invisible and true church.

Most Adventists have the misconception that the professed Adventist church denomination and its supporting ministries can never fall. They believe that they will "go through safely into port" no matter what apostasy the professed church or ministry embraces today, for, in the end, the church will be purified of such things. Only those who comprise God's spiritual true church will go "safely" into port out of the church militant. The Advent movement is going through to the end, but only those who love and obey the truth will be part of that movement. Only such will comprise the true church that will enter port.

The professed church of God may be possessed of wealth, education, and knowledge of doctrine, and may say by her attitude, "I am rich and increased with goods, and have need of nothing;" [Rev. 3:17] but **if its members are devoid of inward holiness, they cannot be the light of the world**.... (*Signs of the Times*, Sept. 11, 1893, emphasis added)

Not by its name, but by its fruit, is the value of a tree determined. If the fruit is worthless, the name [*be it Jew, Christian, or Seventh-day Adventist*] **cannot save the tree from destruction.** John declared to the Jews that their standing before God was to be decided by their character and life. **Profession was worthless.** If their life and character were not in harmony with God's law, **they were not His people**. (*Desire of Ages*, p. 107, emphasis added)

After the professed church has begun following Satan by practicing disobedience, the Lord sends messengers to turn them from disobedience and back into harmony with the law of God and the testimony of Jesus. If people listen to God's reproofs and rebukes, a revival and reformation can occur, and the lost sheep of the house of Israel will be reclaimed. If nobody will listen to messages of warning, then mercy makes its last plea prior to the falling of God's judgments (*The Desire of Ages*, p. 587).

It is clear that this church can fall! Though she may make the profession that she is the church that is going through, this does not make it so. There is a principle of sowing and reaping that God does not and cannot alter. We see it in Isaiah 57:

> For the iniquity of his covetousness was I wroth, and smote him: I hid me, and was wroth, and he went on frowardly in the way of his heart. (Isa. 57:17)

Read also:

> **Unless the church, which is now being leavened with her own backsliding, shall repent and be converted, she will eat of the fruit of her own doing, until she shall abhor herself.** When she resists the evil and chooses the good, when she seeks God with all humility and reaches her high calling in Christ, standing on the platform of eternal truth and by faith laying hold upon the attainments prepared for her, she will be healed. She will appear in her God-given simplicity and purity, **separate from earthly entanglements**, showing that the truth has made her free indeed. **Then her members will indeed be the chosen of God, His representatives**. (*Testimonies for the Church*, vol. 8, pp. 250, 251, from Ms. 32, 1903, emphasis added)

Take heed to the obvious conditionality in the above statement: "Unless the church ... she will," and "When she ... she will." *When she is converted she will be God's church*!

The statement continues, as follows:

> The time has come for a thorough reformation to take place. When this reformation begins, the spirit of prayer will actuate **every believer and will banish from the church the spirit of discord and strife.** Those who have not been living in Christian fellowship will draw close to one another. One member working in right lines will lead other members to unite with him in making intercession for the revelation of the Holy Spirit. There will be **no confusion**, because all **will be in harmony** with the mind of the Spirit. The barriers separating believer from believer will be broken down, and **God's servants will speak the same things**.... (*Testimonies for the Church*, vol. 8, p. 251, emphasis added)

What church is the servant of the Lord talking about here? Notice in another place she wrote:

> **Are we hoping to see the whole church revived? That time will never come.** There are persons in the church who are not converted, and who will not unite in earnest, prevailing prayer. We must enter upon the work individually. We must pray more, and talk less.... (*Review and Herald*, March 22, 1887, emphasis added)

Isn't that interesting? In one place she said that, when a thorough reformation has begun, "the spirit of prayer will actuate *every believer*," eliminating all discord from the church. Yet, in another place, she said that the "time will never come" when the whole church will be revived. Clearly, we must do some interpreting regarding which church she is talking about because obviously they cannot be the same one.

Let us continue to examine what the professed church looks like. The professed church can follow the same trajectory as ancient Israel:

> The sin of ancient Israel was in disregarding the expressed will of God and following their own way according to the leadings of unsanctified hearts. Modern Israel are fast following in their footsteps, and the displeasure of the Lord is as surely resting upon them. (*Testimonies for the Church*, vol. 5, p. 94)

The professed church may change leaders (from Christ to Satan) while embracing apostasy:

> If when the Lord reveals your errors you do not repent or make confession, His providence will bring you over the ground **again and again**. You will be left to make mistakes of a similar character, you will continue to lack wisdom, and will call sin righteousness, and righteousness sin. **The multitude of deceptions that will prevail in these last days will encircle you, and you will change leaders, and not know that you have done so.** (*Review and Herald*, Dec. 6, 1890, emphasis added)

This warning has sadly proved true. The error of rejecting the righteousness of Christ in 1888 has led to two more specific rejections of the messages in the 1950s and *again* in the 1990s. The "third angel's message in verity," the gospel as it is in Jesus, and the nature of His ministry in the second apartment in this sealing time had been replaced by the false gospel of the fallen churches as the *proposed* message of present truth—the *purported* message of Seventh-day Adventism. Sin has been called righteousness when the popular gospel of the Babylonian church dresses up cheap grace for the unregenerated heart. A multitude of deceptions has come into Adventism, swirling about with every wind of doctrine in the mainstream and independent churches alike. Ecumenism, worldliness, and spiritualism have been making major inroads. The leaders have changed while leaders and laity alike are unaware of what has happened. Ellen White saw in an early vision how that the people of God who went into the most holy place would later leave it and join those who were still praying in the holy place, not knowing that Satan appeared to have taken up the throne there in an attempt to carry on the work of God (*The Day-Star*, March 14, 1846).

Notice that a large class in Adventism will abandon the message. They have for so long enjoyed "pleasant truth" that it has robbed them of all desire for "present truth":

> As the storm approaches, a large class who have professed faith in the third angel's message, but have not been sanctified through obedience to the truth, abandon their position and join the ranks of the opposition. By uniting with the world and partaking of its spirit, they have come to view matters in nearly the same light; and when the test is brought, they are prepared to choose the easy, popular side. Men of talent and pleasing address, who once rejoiced in the truth, employ their powers to deceive and mislead souls.... (*The Great Controversy*, p. 608)

And when that storm comes, what is the result? Ellen White listed several goals she was shown that Satan designed to achieve that he might establish "New Movement" Adventism. These have all been fulfilled except for the final outcome:

> ... storm and tempest would sweep away the structure. (Letter 242, 1903, in *Selected Messages*, bk. 1, p. 204)

She answered the potential outcomes of rejecting the "pillars of our faith," saying:

> Who has authority to begin such a movement? We have our Bibles. We have our experience, attested to by the miraculous working of the Holy Spirit. We have a truth that admits of no compromise. Shall we

not repudiate everything that is not in harmony with this truth? (Lt. 242, 1903, in *Selected Messages*, vol. 1, p. 205)

A professed church is comprised of individuals or organizations that say they are part of God's church. However, anyone can make a profession. Yet, to become part of the church militant and, more importantly, the true church, one must strive. If we are only a member of the professed church, we may be lost.

Profession alone is nothing. Names are registered upon the church books upon earth, but not in the book of life. (*Testimonies for the Church*, vol. 1, p. 504)

Having looked at a number of statements about the church, it becomes apparent that we cannot take every church statement to mean the conference-controlled entity. We must read with principles in mind and carefully consider the context at all times. Also, we must bear in mind that a person or entity may have been, at one time, in obedience and been a servant to the true remnant church, yet may fall from such a standing to become merely a professor. Utmost caution is warranted in our thinking that we not fall prey to denominational pride and the notion of unconditional election in that which we call "churchianity."

True Organization

The Conference church would establish firmly in the minds of its members that it is the true organization. Yet, we find by careful study of the question of what the church is, in its various distinctions, that only God's organization made up of those who are obedient to the message can be the true organization. Therefore, God's organization is any ministry which is spreading the pure truth.

- God accepts all those ministries that do a faithful work, but an organization, no matter how large it is, is not the all-encompassing church. It can assist the true church, or church militant, *if it is faithful*.

- Is a corporation God's church? Are buildings God's church? Does God's church have a street address or post office box number? No. *People who are faithful to God comprise His church*.

- Organizations, corporations, institutions and buildings are simply tools used to assist those who are doing the work. *Organization of the right type is very necessary in conducting the Lord's work*. By coming together and joining forces, we can be a ministry with checks and balances, accountability and strength, united to follow through in conducting the Lord's work.

- The purpose of the church organization is never to create a hierarchy or set up rulers over the people to tell the laborer where to go and how to work for God. This is hard for the people of the churches to understand. Unbelief has created a situation in which members lack sufficient faith to let God direct each believer in a harmonious organization without the interference of human machinery. So, God allowed a substitute, letting humans look to other humans to guide and direct in the accomplishing of His work.

- The purpose of true organization—God's organization—is to be only a facilitator, as a servant; organization is simply a vehicle to carry out a purpose higher than making a name for itself. It is to carry a message of truth and of the advancing light of the Reformation. It will not be static in this regard. It is an assistant to the true church in heaven. Whether a given organization is the church militant or not will depend on its faithfulness to heaven's purpose.

- An organization that loses its heavenly credentials, in that it carries heaven's message no longer, loses its status as the church militant and becomes merely the professed church. However, for a certain amount of time, there would yet remain within its precincts individuals of the church militant. The second shaking which comes under the period of crisis will sort these out.

Do not put your trust in organizations! Notice that Isaiah tells us that the time comes when all of the churches are in trouble:

And in *that day seven women* shall take hold of *one man*, saying, We will eat our *own bread*, and wear our *own apparel*: only let us be *called by thy name*, to *take away our reproach*. (Isa. 4:1)

"That day" is the last days (Isa. 2:2, 11, 17). "Seven" signifies totality. "Women" are churches. *The Seventh-day*

Adventist organization does not escape this prophecy. Who is the one man if not Christ? They say, "We will eat our own bread." What is the true bread? It is the Word of God. It is the doctrine and teachings. So, they want their own teachings. What is apparel? It is righteousness! They want their own righteousness. According to Paul in Romans 10:1-3, Israel sought to establish her own righteousness, a righteousness that is not of God. Like them, all Christendom wishes to go their own way while still claiming Christ Jesus and calling themselves Christians, that they may escape condemnation.

Where Then Shall We Go?

Many readers will by this time be "shaken" to their core, understanding many things in light of the evidence and history they have not seen before. If they persevered to read this far, many will feel anger and indignation or fear and uncertainty. Many will be wondering what the next step should be. We listen to "the testimony of Jesus":

> Every one will reveal the character of the bundle with which he is binding himself. The wheat is being bound up for the heavenly garner. The true people of God are now bound up for the heavenly garner. The true people of God are now pulling apart, and the tares are being bound in bundles ready to burn. Decided positions will be taken.… The Lord in great mercy has sent messages of warning to them [*self-indulgent and controlling leaders*], but they would not listen to reproof. Like the enemy who rebelled in heaven, they do not like to hear, do not correct the wrong they have done but become accusers, declaring themselves misused and unappreciated. (Lt. 13, 1892, in *The Ellen G. White 1888 Materials*, p. 995)

> Dark hours of trial are before the church because they have not obeyed the warnings and reproofs and counsel of God. What a bewitching power comes upon human minds to do contrary to the oft repeated will of God, and close the eyes and stop the ears, when Jesus is calling to them to hear His voice. He says, "My sheep hear My voice." …
>
> Before the great trouble shall come upon the world such as has never been since there was a nation, those who have faltered and who would ignorantly lead in unsafe paths will reveal this before the real vital test, the last proving, comes, so that whatsoever they may say will not be regarded as voicing the True Shepherd. The time of our educating will soon be over. We have no time to lose in walking through clouds of doubt and uncertainty because of uncertain voices. (Lt. 13, 1892, in *The Ellen G. White 1888 Materials*, p. 1002)

We must study and know the third angel's message for ourselves; we must pray and receive the Holy Spirit and challenge church leadership to give the message to the people, and we must talk to the people where we can. Moreover, we must each work in our designated sphere, helping our brethren and sisters to better understand the faith of Seventh-day Adventism. Even though we will not fix the church denomination, these are things we must still do. Even though most will not pay heed to anything we have to say, we must say it anyway:

> Declare this in the house of Jacob, and publish it in Judah, saying, Hear now this, O foolish people, and without understanding; which have eyes, and see not; which have ears, and hear not: Fear ye not me? saith the LORD … But this people hath a revolting and a rebellious heart; they are revolted and gone. Neither say they in their heart, Let us now fear the LORD our God, that giveth rain, both the former and the latter, in his season: he reserveth unto us the appointed weeks of the harvest. (Jer. 5:20-24)

In verse 24, the *New Living Translation* has: "… assuring us of a harvest when the time is right." Here is the false teaching that we must just keep sitting in church and wait for the latter rain, for we are promised to receive it in God's good time—not a moment too soon, not a moment too late.

> Your iniquities have turned away these *things*, and your sins have withholden good *things* from you. For among my people are found wicked *men*: they lay wait, as he that setteth snares; they set a trap, they catch men. As a cage is full of birds, so *are* their houses full of deceit: therefore they are become great, and waxen rich. They are waxen fat, they shine: yea, they overpass the deeds of the wicked: they judge not the cause, the cause of the fatherless, yet they prosper; and the right of the needy do they not judge. Shall I not visit for these *things*? saith the LORD: shall not my soul be avenged on such a nation as this? A wonderful and horrible thing is committed in the land; the prophets prophesy falsely, and the priests bear rule by their means; and my people love *to have it* so: and what will ye do in the end thereof? (Jer. 5:25-31)

These words are more for the professed Israel of God today than they were for the people living at the time of Jeremiah. "Said the angel, 'Ye have done worse than they'" (*Review and Herald*, Jan. 6, 1863).

It is time to break loose from the stranglehold of "churchianity." The inner workings of the church's machinery are clogged and jammed with all manner of debris and dry of the lubricating oil of the Holy Spirit. The maintenance men have all been fired or have left, leaving the machinery in this pitiful state of disrepair. Yet, we should not give up hope. We still have a work to do, and we will not need the human machinery of the organization to accomplish it.

> Let me tell you, if your heart is in the work, and you have faith in God, you need not depend upon the sanction of any minister or any people; if you go right to work in the name of the Lord, in a humble way doing what you can to teach the truth, God will vindicate you.... (*The General Conference Bulletin*, April 3, 1901, in *The Ellen G. White 1888 Materials*, p. 1746)

> Unless those who can help in _____ are aroused to a sense of their duty, they will not recognize the work of God when the loud cry of the third angel shall be heard. When light goes forth to lighten the earth, instead of coming up to the help of the Lord, they will want to bind about His work to meet their narrow ideas. Let me tell you that the Lord will work in this last work in a manner very much out of the common order of things, and in a way that will be contrary to any human planning. There will be those among us who will always want to control the work of God, to dictate even what movements shall be made when the work goes forward under the direction of the angel who joins the third angel in the message to be given to the world. **God will use ways and means by which it will be seen that He is taking the reins in His own hands.** The workers will be surprised by the simple means that He will use to bring about and perfect His work of righteousness.... (*Testimonies to Ministers*, p. 299)

Let us drive this point solidly home—*it will not be the organization, under the auspices of conference leadership, that closes the work.* There is a direct word of the Lord on this, underscoring clearly the direct parallel between ancient Israel and the modern Israel of the Seventh-day Adventist organization:

> In His Word the Lord declared what He would do for Israel if they would obey His voice. But **the leaders of the people** yielded to the temptations of Satan, and God could not give them the blessings He designed them to have, because **they did not obey His voice but listened to the voice and policy of Lucifer. This experience will be repeated in the last years of the history of the people of God**, who have been established by His grace and power. **Men whom He has greatly honored will in the closing scenes of this earth's history pattern after ancient Israel.** (Ms. 5, 1904, in *Manuscript Releases*, vol. 13, p. 379)

The individual children of God who will ultimately comprise His true church will be called to do the work of the Lord in the closing scenes of this earth's history. Every gift, under the guidance of the Holy Spirit, will be exercised to preach and teach the third angel's message in verity under the power of the present truth. Pastors and evangelists will preach; teachers will teach; writers will write; each one will contribute their part, and God will use each laborer to do that which they have been given. We must understand that, when we do this, it will shake things up. The truth will not go forward without consequences. Many messengers will be poorly received and even thrust out of fellowship. We will be called upon to "gather warmth from the coldness of others, courage from their cowardice, and loyalty from their treason" (*Testimonies for the Church*, vol. 5, p. 136). Jesus knows all about it.

Some will be asking the question, "Then where do we take the people who shall receive the third angel's message?" It will be a time when things will return to the conditions of the early church. We will have to gather in small groups, in homes, and in rented rooms and buildings. The time will surely come when gathering in this way will be absolutely necessary because of persecution. We should be working now to establish centers of assembly that are safe havens for continued studies, free from the interference of those who would control what the people should have and what they should not.

This is an age of signal rejection of the grace God has purposed to bestow upon His people, that in the perils of the last days they may not be overcome by the prevailing iniquity, and unite with the hostility of the world against God's remnant people. Under the cloak of Christianity and sanctification, far-spreading and manifest ungodliness will prevail to a terrible degree and will continue until Christ comes to be glorified in all them that believe. In the very courts of the temple scenes will be enacted that few realize. God's people will be proved and tested, that He may discern "between him that serveth God, and him that serveth Him not."

Vengeance will be executed against those who sit in the gate, deciding what the people should have, and what they should not have. These take away the key of knowledge. They refuse to enter in themselves, and those that would enter, they hinder. These bear not the seal of the living God. All who now occupy responsible positions should be solemnly and terribly afraid lest in this time they shall be found as unfaithful stewards. (Ms. 15, 1886, in *Manuscript Releases*, vol. 11, pp. 85, 86)

In every reform, there is opposition from the establishment. All reformers have had to bear stripes on their back. This means that we must be willing to receive persecution. The prophets who came to ancient Israel were rejected, tortured, and killed. Yet, in the days of Christ, the leaders could say, "If we were in those days we would not have done to our prophets the way that they did." Nonetheless, Jesus said to them, "You are indeed doing the same thing to Me, so all of the guilt which comes upon the fathers also rests upon you." This is what is happening also in Adventism, and, although some think that a great repentance is coming to the denomination, we would want to carefully examine that claim for truthfulness.

There has therefore been progressive "shaking" in the Adventist world. It is not because of the message, per se, but is, rather, because the giving of the "straight testimony" excites the ire of ecclesiastical authority, and their attempt to stand in the way of the message causes a shaking among God's people. The leaders are shaken out, and those who follow them without studying for themselves are also shaken out, though they all together may continue on as faithful members, leading out in church and attending church and contributing to the financial support of the institution and her programs. We know the familiar testimony from *Early Writings*, p. 270, and have discussed it in this book. The shaking therein described has been underway since the time of the alpha of apostasy and has only intensified during the time of the omega, which got underway in earnest in the mid-twentieth century.

In the environment of the modern shaking time, we will hear a lot about "off-shoots," and those who stand for the truth would be labeled as "off-shoots." What is the definition of an "off-shoot?" Is it not self-evident? An "off-shoot" is that which veers away from the trunk or main stem of the plant. The church, we are told, is the "pillar and ground of the truth" (1 Tim. 3:15). Therefore, any time anyone "shoots off" of *the truth—and not off of an organization*—he or she is an "off-shoot." Stand firm on the truth—the truth as it is in Jesus—without regard for what people say about you or do to you. Stand firm for the truth, and you cannot be an "off-shoot." Just walk straight in the consecrated path of Jesus.

Ever since 1964 and even earlier, more and more Adventists have been exposed to the message of Jones and Waggoner, and many have accepted the wonderful light. It may be that some readers are now understanding these things for the first time. It may be that your mind is being significantly agitated. You are finding out that God sent your church a message and that it was not heeded. Do not wait for your church to tell you about it. It is your responsibility to go and find out what that message has for you, what it means to you, and how you can be part of the people God is raising up to proclaim the last message of mercy to the world.

Some of those who have picked up the message have continued to walk in the advancing light of God's glory according to Hosea.

> Come, and let us return unto the LORD: for he hath torn, and he will heal us; he hath smitten, and he will bind us up. After two days will he revive us: in the third day he will raise us up, and we shall live in his sight. Then shall we know, *if* we follow on to know the LORD: his going forth is prepared as the morning; and he shall come unto us as the rain, as the latter *and* former rain unto the earth. (Hosea 6:1–3)

The glorious messages of the *righteousness of Christ* and of the knowledge of the *character of our God* are doing a great work of preparing the people who are following on to know the Lord. This is evidence enough that we are now advancing even beyond the third day of Hosea 6:1–3, which ended in 2004, and that we are, in fact, moving into the very time of the latter rain baptismal outpouring of the Holy Spirit, the generation of the restoration. Let us determine, each one, by the grace of God and in the power of the risen Christ through the Holy Ghost, to rise up to the occasion and strive to be among the 144,000.

We are here on the verge of eternity. We are surely the final generation. We have come to the kingdom for such a time as this.

We invite you to view the complete
selection of titles we publish at:
www.ASPECTBooks.com

We encourage you to write us
with your thoughts about this,
or any other book we publish at:
info@ASPECTBooks.com

ASPECT Books' titles may be purchased in
bulk quantities for educational, fund-raising,
business, or promotional use.
bulksales@ASPECTBooks.com

Finally, if you are interested in seeing
your own book in print, please contact us at:
publishing@ASPECTBooks.com

We are happy to review your manuscript at no charge.

www.ingramcontent.com/pod-product-compliance
Lightning Source LLC
Chambersburg PA
CBHW081757300426
44116CB00014B/2147